THE MASTER'S PLAN

MY GUIDE TO A
SUCCESSFUL LIFE AND CAREER

BILL BATTLE

Whitman Publishing, LLC
PUBLISHING SINCE 1934
Whitman.com

The Master's Plan
My Guide To A Successful Life and Career

© 2021 Whitman Publishing, LLC
1974 Chandalar Drive • Suite D • Pelham, AL 35124
ISBN: 0794848834
Printed in China

Correspondence concerning this book may be directed to
Whitman Publishing, Attn: The Master's Plan, at the address above.

The full catalog of Whitman Publishing books is online at www.Whitman.com.

CONTENTS

INTRODUCTION

This is the story about my life. It is amazing how the twists and turns, the places you go, the people you meet, and the experiences you encounter shape and impact your life. My story is a living example of a circuitous path that enjoyed many ups and downs, many life-changing experiences, and many people who had a positive impact on my life. The "ups" were more enjoyable than the "downs," but in the end, the lessons and strengths brought about by the "downs" probably were more valuable. Hopefully this book will share life lessons learned along the way that some may find beneficial, while others may just enjoy the ride.

Sports were very important to me. I was exposed to many sports at an early age and fell in love with their competitive nature. Having gone to a high school that won six football games in four years, it was pretty amazing to be offered scholarships to several universities. I accepted an offer from The University of Alabama. I thought if you could play four years under Coach Paul "Bear" Bryant, you would really be something. I was not disappointed. After college, some interesting opportunities led me to the University of Oklahoma, The U.S. Military Academy and the University of Tennessee, all as an assistant coach. Another interesting opportunity led me to become the head football coach at Tennessee — at the ripe old age of 28.

After coaching, I decided to see if I could make it in the business world. A very strange set of opportunities led me to Selma, Alabama, to work for my first little league football coach at a construction materials company. That opportunity led to the formation of a trademark licensing company in 1981 that started with the representation of Coach Bryant, and then The University of Alabama. From there The Collegiate Licensing Company (CLC) grew to become one of the largest trademark licensing companies in the country, and the guiding force in collegiate licensing. With an excellent staff, a lot of cooperating universities, and a little luck, we accomplished our goal of helping create a major new revenue stream for colleges and universities.

The company was sold in 2007 to media conglomerate IMG, but they decided to leave everything in place. It continued to run smoothly for four years as the fastest growing and most profitable division of IMG. As big companies do, IMG decided to make some changes in 2011 that caused several of our top executives to leave for different opportunities. I stayed with the company until 2013 as a consultant and enjoyed a semi-retired life. The company continued to flourish.

They kept the CLC name until 2017 when the brand was changed to IMG College. Interestingly, in 2019, IMG College merged with Learfield, the

largest remaining competitor in the collegiate "media rights" business. Greg Brown, CEO of Learfield, was named CEO of the new conglomerate. Learfield had bought a licensing company, although most of its clients were non-Power 5 universities. With the merger, Brown had two licensing companies that he quickly decided needed to be merged for many different reasons. In May 2019, Brown announced they were bringing back the CLC brand as the name of their two licensing companies that were merging. Those combined companies are being run, at the time of this writing, by one of our best at CLC, Cory Moss.

On May 21, 2019, Brown wrote an email to my son Pat and me that read:

"In case you don't happen to follow this daily, today was a celebration of sorts for what you all built. It was a retro day on the name front that was unanimously embraced by all of the College Sports industry. Sometimes this business of college sports loses its way by trying to be cool and in so doing throws out some of the parts of it that made it great.

"Kudos to you for your vision so many years ago. I just have the privilege of sharing the news and have had little to do with building an iconic brand synonymous with college sports like you two men did. Congratulations and thanks for creating CLC!"

Michael Smith, longtime writer with the *Sports Business Journal* wrote:

"Welcome Back CLC.

"When I started covering college sports for SJB, I spent a day in Collegiate Licensing Co.'s Atlanta office with Bill Battle, his son Pat, and then-COO Derek Eiler. They gave me a tutorial on the collegiate licensing business that I still remember well. Ever since IMG acquired CLC in 2007, however, the company looked less and less like the one Bill Battle founded four decades ago. IMG eventually did away with the CLC brand in favor of the much more corporate-sounding IMG College Licensing in 2017.

"Today, Learfield IMG College said it is bringing back the CLC name. The company's two licensing businesses, Learfield Licensing Partners and IMG College Licensing, are merging into a single division known as CLC. Count me as someone who loves the move. No three letters are more synonymous with the business of college sports than CLC. The name still carries plenty of juice on campuses across the country, which is why Learfield IMG College President and CEO Greg Brown brought it back.

"Longtime CLC and IMG exec Cory Moss will oversee the combined licensing business, which owns the rights to nearly every school in D-1. Moss knows the CLC approach better than anyone at the company — he was hired in 1995 and learned licensing from the Battles. Representing the CLC name will mean something to Moss, who, like me, grew up in Greensboro and graduated from Page High School. OK maybe not at the same time; Moss is a lot younger than me."

In 2013 I was called to come back to The University of Alabama as athletics director to follow Mal Moore, my former teammate and longtime friend, as his health declined rapidly. It was not something I ever aspired to do, but it was the single most flattering opportunity I ever had.

I signed up for four years as AD. Those four years were incredibly interesting. After three years and some health issues along the way, I decided I would stay through the fourth year, but told the president that he needed to find the next person who could come in and hopefully lead the program for many years. I think he hired the best available athletics director in the country, and I know Greg Byrne will be successful at Alabama. He has been successful and has earned a "10" rating in my judgment.

The last chapter in this book is about dealing with cancer, heart disease, back surgery and COVID-19. I am very fortunate to have some of the best health care available in Tuscaloosa at the Manderson Cancer Center, UAB Cardiology, UAB Hospital, Andrews Sports Medicine, St. Vincent's in Birmingham, Emory in Atlanta and the Multiple Myeloma Clinic at New York University. I am also fortunate to have the opportunity at present to continue to be involved with the university, and can hopefully help the athletics director, the president and the chancellor, as well as the Athletics Department and university development teams.

I still enjoy Tuscaloosa and being involved in the athletic and cultural activities around the university. My life has been richly blessed, and I am most appreciative of all the people and programs with which I have had the pleasure of being associated.

I have had the pleasure of being married to two exceptional women. My first wife, Eugenia Stubbs Battle, and I were married in the summer before my senior year at Alabama. We grew up in the same neighborhood, schools and church. She was a year older than me and had nothing to do with me until after her senior year in high school. That summer we started dating. When fall came, she enrolled at Alabama. We continued to date that year on and off, but when I enrolled at Alabama, we dated exclusively until we got married in 1962.

Eugenia was a very talented young lady. As a child she played the piano and sang in the church choir. She actually played the piano in my Mother's Sunday school class. She was an outstanding student and graduated in elementary education. She taught for a year in Tuscaloosa during our first year of marriage. We had three children together: Pat, Mike and Shannon. Eugenia was a great mother, and did a great job of being both mom and dad to our kids while I was coaching.

After Alabama, we moved to Norman, Oklahoma, with a new baby. I got a Master's Degree and served as a graduate assistant coach under Coach Bud Wilkinson. Nine months later, we moved to Fort Sill, Oklahoma, for six weeks for my Officer's Basic Course as an Army Second Lieutenant in Field Artillery. From there we went to West Point, New York, for two years. I was a defensive coordinator on the Plebe (freshman) football team, then a varsity receivers coach under Coach Paul Dietzel.

Our next move to Knoxville, Tennessee, was as a varsity receivers coach under Coach Doug Dickey for four years. When Coach Dickey left Tennessee to coach at the University of Florida, his alma mater, I was named head football coach at age 28. I spent the next seven years in that capacity. My record there was 59-22-2 and we won four of five bowl games. Three of our teams finished in the Top 10 and two more in the Top 20. We lived in Knoxville for 11 years, and two of our children, Mike and Shannon, were born there. Being a coach's wife is a very difficult job, and Eugenia was exceptional.

After the Tennessee experience, we moved to Selma, Alabama, to start a new career. Changing careers is difficult, whoever you are, and it was definitely challenging to me and to us. As we started our new licensing company four years later, Eugenia got involved and was extremely helpful in getting the business up and running. Then we made another move, this time to Atlanta, which was a far better place to build a business. Pat, Mike and Shannon all worked in the business, as did Pat's wife, Alice Ann, and Mike's wife, Mary Fleeta. This was a great time for me, as all contributed in different sections of our business.

Starting in Selma and continuing after our move to Atlanta, Eugenia and I began to have problems that we thought we could solve, but were never able to do so. We separated for a year in 1996, and in 1997 we decided that we should get divorced. It was a very difficult experience for both of us, but if one can have a friendly divorce, we had one. We continued to be friends, and shared children and grandchildren until her death in 2016.

A few months after our divorce, I was traveling on business to Shreveport, Louisiana. After a bad experience with a client with whom I was working, I decided to leave a day early. I almost missed the flight and had to return my rental car from Avis (whose office was off-campus) into the Hertz office and asked if they would return it. They said they would be delighted. I got on board just as the door was closing and sat next to a very attractive woman. I slept most of the way to Atlanta, but had some brief conversation before we took off and again after they woke me up for the landing. Her name was Mary, and we found we had some mutual acquaintances, and exchanged business cards before we parted company. She was from Birmingham.

A few months later I was in Montgomery winding up our business there, but planned to go to my place on Lake Weiss. I had to go through Birmingham to get there. It was Friday and I knew she would probably have a date and really wasn't sure if she would even recall who I was. I called her that morning before my meetings. Mary did remember who I was and didn't have a date. We agreed to meet for a drink. That led to dinner, and afterward, she took me home to meet her 12-year-old daughter, Kayla. I decided not to go to the lake. I left her house about midnight and planned to take them out to brunch the next morning. There was a huge softball tournament in town and it took me a few hours to find a hotel.

That was the start of a romance that lasted for six years of dating, until Kayla graduated from high school and enrolled at The University of Alabama. Mary and I married in November 2003 and Mary moved to Atlanta. Ten years later, in 2013, we moved to Tuscaloosa, as I accepted an offer to become the Alabama AD. Isn't it amazing that before we met on the plane that day that neither of us had ever been to Shreveport, I almost missed the flight, and ended up sitting next to Mary. We bonded, fell in love, and became partners in life.

Mary is very athletic, loves to ride horses, water ski, snow ski, snorkel and scuba dive, and has turned into a very proficient fly-fisher. She is also a Summa cum Laude graduate of the University of Texas School of Nursing. After being an oncology nurse for several years, Mary went back to college at UAB and got her Master's Degree in healthcare administration. She then went to work for Med Partners, and later, two different startup companies. When we met, she was putting doctor's groups together with insurance companies in one of the startups. She lived in Birmingham, but was traveling four days a week for her job. Neither of us had ever been to Shreveport before or since then, but I'm sure glad we did that day.

But what is really amazing to me is that in 2014, when I was diagnosed with cancer, I was married to an oncology nurse, and even though Mary had not practiced actively in years, she kept her license active. She knows the ins and outs of health care, which has been extremely valuable to me as I have dealt with my diseases. Health care in this country is very complex and difficult. If one does not have an advocate, he or she is in serious trouble.

At the time of this writing, we are again enjoying semi-retirement, and especially enjoying our four children and eight grandchildren: Pat and Alice Ann Battle, and children Will, Mary Raines and Annie; Mike and Mary Fleeta Battle, and child Mary Catherine; Shannon and Chad Tanner, and children Denver and Mary Scott; and Mary's daughter, Kayla, who is married to Frankie Smeraglia, and their two young boys, Hudson and Reynolds. Thanks to grandson Will Battle and his wife Danielle, we were blessed with our first great-granddaughter, Miss Allie Battle.

I love to study leaders and their quotes and stories. One of my favorite stories takes place in the olden days. There was a wise old man in the village who all the young people went to see for advice before they left to seek their fame and fortune. This one impatient young man approached him and said, "please give me the most important piece of advice you have." The old man thought awhile and said, "If you only want one piece of advice I will tell you that when your opportunity comes, jump at it." The young man said thank you and started to walk away. After a few steps he turned around and said, "How will I know when my opportunity comes?" The old man replied, "Just keep jumping."

There is much wisdom in that story. I am blessed that many opportunities have come my way over my lifetime. I have been fortunate to jump on some of them, and with many other people in support, turn them into positive experiences.

The name of this book, *The Master's Plan*, I believe had a lot to do with my journey and the opportunities presented and taken. I never wanted to be an athletics director, even when I was a coach and even when I got the call to come to Alabama. After I had accepted the job, I moved into one of the two executive suites in Bryant Hall and lived there for three months until we found a house. Mary went back to Atlanta to prepare to move and figure out all the things that needed to be done in leaving our comfort zone.

On a trip from Atlanta back to Tuscaloosa, I received a call from my former assistant trainer at Tennessee, Leroy Mullins. He did a great job for us at Tennessee, and I think the world of him. I don't believe I had seen or spoken to Leroy since he left UT to be the head trainer at the University of Mississippi, but my phone rang that day and Leroy was on the other end. He said, "I'm so glad to see you back working with young people." I said, "Leroy, that wasn't in my master plan." Leroy responded, "Well, it was in *The Master's* Plan."

As I have thought about that since he told me, I have come to the realization that all the things that happened could not have come by accident. I surely didn't have any plan except to become a college coach, and I didn't make that one until my junior year at Alabama. I truly believe there was divine intervention in my getting offered and taking the Alabama AD job, and I know there was in several specific incidents after I took the job. Looking back, I believe it has been there all my life.

So, this is the "Cliffs Notes" version of my life. Hopefully, the rest of the book will shed some light on adventures in each of these areas, people who had an impact on my life, lessons learned that I believe led to success, and how important it is in life to recognize opportunities and take a leap of faith to capture them.

—*Bill Battle*

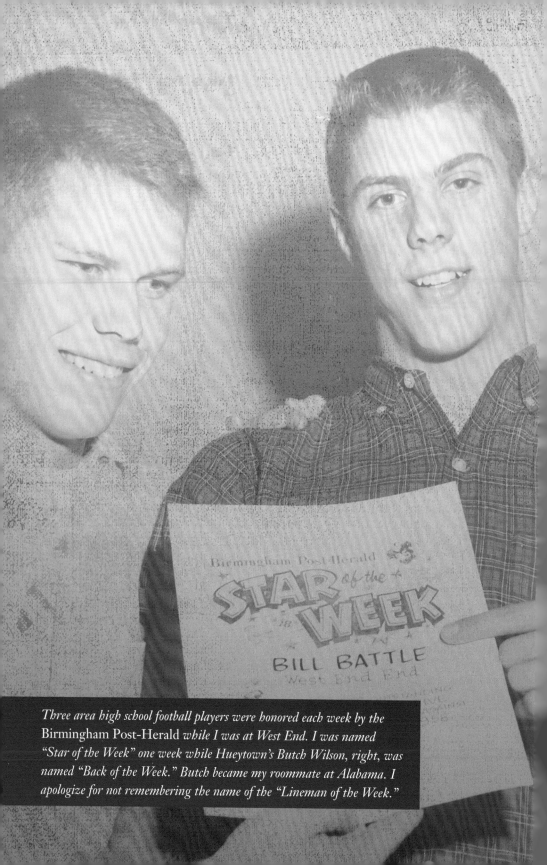

Birmingham Post-Herald
★ STAR of the ★
WEEK
BILL BATTLE
West End End

Three area high school football players were honored each week by the
Birmingham Post-Herald *while I was at West End. I was named*
"Star of the Week" one week while Hueytown's Butch Wilson, right, was
named "Back of the Week." Butch became my roommate at Alabama. I
apologize for not remembering the name of the "Lineman of the Week."

CHAPTER 1

GROWING UP IN BIRMINGHAM, ALABAMA

It was Dec. 8, 1941, the day after Pearl Harbor was bombed and war on Japan was declared, that my mother gave birth to me in the West End Baptist Hospital. I can't imagine how frightened my parents must have been as our country entered the war against Japan. My life has been popping and cracking ever since.

THE FAMILY

I grew up in a typical middle-class family. My dad, William Raines Battle Jr., was a professor at Birmingham-Southern College. He and my mom both graduated there. Dad was an outstanding athlete during his time there and excelled in football, basketball and baseball. He was captain of the baseball team, all-conference in 1928 and 1929 in football, and honorable mention all-conference in basketball. He won the Robinson Silver Loving Cup given to the "Best All-Around Athlete" at the college in 1930. During those years, Birmingham-Southern vs. Howard College was the "big game" in Birmingham.

After graduation from Birmingham-Southern, he coached football and basketball at Snead Seminary in Boaz, Alabama, from 1930 to 1935. He also taught history and civics, and established physical education and intramural programs for men and women. During that time, he earned his Master's Degree at Peabody College in Nashville. From 1935 to 1940 he served as Director of Intramural and Physical Education, and Instructor in Education at Florida Southern College in Lakeland. He started the physical education and intramural programs there and designed a building to house those programs.

In 1940, he returned to Birmingham-Southern as Professor of Physical Education and Intramural Director. He took two years (1944-1946) to serve as Lieutenant in the U.S. Navy, including eight months as Gunnery Officer, an armed guard aboard the S.S. William Hunt. He returned to Birmingham-Southern from 1946-1949 and then 1952-1974, when he passed away.

The two-year sabbatical he took in 1950-1951 was very interesting. His roommate in college moved back to his hometown, Gadsden, Alabama, after graduation and entered the business world as a Dr. Pepper bottler. In a few years he had done very well financially in that business, had a beautiful house and even had a nice lake house. My mom and dad visited him and his family, and got to thinking maybe teaching would never get them those niceties in life.

My dad put together a group (I think it was two of his brothers) and bought the Dr. Pepper franchise in Birmingham in 1951. I was 10 years old at the time. He would go to work before my sister, Jean LeMerle, and I got up and came home after we went to bed. He was accustomed to dealing with university professors and students, and found dealing with truck drivers, who might go home after work on Friday and not come back until Tuesday or Wednesday, not to his liking. He also had to deal with complaints from customers when they did not get what they wanted, and some were pretty slow to pay.

During that time, we didn't spend much time together, but I did get my first lesson in economics and brand management. One night when we did get together my dad asked me what I did that day. I told him after school I went to Hobbs Drug Store and read comic books and drank a Coke float. That may have been the maddest he ever got at me. He shouted, "A Coke float, why didn't you get a Dr. Pepper float?" I responded, "I can get all I want of those at home!" I quickly learned that was not a good answer and also learned in very frank and concise language why! He endured that opportunity for two years and had had enough. Fortunately, Birmingham-Southern had not replaced him and he returned to his old job and lived happily there ever after. We were able to spend a lot more time together after that than we had before his business venture. He loved to fish, and some of our best times together were on lakes and rivers in Alabama.

My Mother also graduated from Birmingham-Southern in education. She didn't work when my sister, Jean LeMerle, and I were pre-schoolers. LeMerle was four years older than me. When I started school, Mom went to work teaching English at Pleasant Grove Junior High School outside of Birmingham.

LeMerle, being the older sister, had a lot to do with me learning to read before I got to school. I had some great teachers in Elyton Grammar School and actually learned to read and write pretty well growing up. But southern diction is slow and somewhat lazy. Some of my buddies didn't speak with great English, and I drifted into speaking the same way. My mom and I had serious discussions about that growing up. I remember one summer she frustratingly said, "If you will just speak with better grammar, I'll give you 10 dollars at Christmas." Man, 10 dollars was a lot of money to me at the time and that definitely got my attention. I don't think I probably deserved it, but I did try and she did give me the 10 dollars. As with many lessons from parents, that one in later years became very important to me and I was proud of her insistence in improving my communication skills. I have always tried to impress upon everyone who has ever reported to me the importance of being able to communicate effectively.

My grandfather on my Mother's side, Charles H. Scruggs, was a general contractor who built houses. He actually built his house on the corner of 6th Street and Cotton Avenue in Birmingham, and our house next door. I never knew him as he passed away before I was born.

The only grandparent I knew was Ida Jean Scruggs, my Mother's mother. She was one of the neatest people I ever met. She was an angel, and her pep, energy and positive attitude made up for me not knowing the other three grandparents. In her later years, she was stricken with arthritis and evolved from a tall straight woman into a small, bent-over body as she aged. But until her death, she was full of energy and always the life of the party. Her two sons, Charles and Billy, went into the plumbing supply business right after World War II. They were very successful and the only members of our family who ever made any money. They lived in Tampa, Florida.

They bought the Rainbow Cottages in Indian Rocks Beach, Florida, and moved my grandmother and her sister Pinkie down to manage them. The sunshine and warm weather agreed with them. My mom and dad were both school teachers and didn't make a lot of money, but did have long summer vacations. We spent about two or so weeks a year down there and those were some of the greatest times of my childhood.

My cousins Dennis, Charles and Janice were children of my uncle Charles and aunt Sarah. Dennis was closer to my age than the other two. He was a couple of years older than me, but we spent a lot of time together during our visits. We fished from the Rainbow Cottages pier and the beach. From there we caught catfish, pinfish, sheepshead, pompano, flounder and other species. We often saw stingrays and big manta rays. We also did a little spearfishing. We could take a small motorboat a few hundred yards offshore, locate coral reefs below, and catch some grouper, blackfish, redmouth grunts and an occasional shark.

We swam, and when the ocean got rough, we rode the waves in big truck inner tubes my uncles got for us. Jumping off the pier was against the rules of the cottages, but, as mischievous boys will do, we drove my grandmother and her sister Pinky bananas by doing all kinds of dives off the pier. Another mischievous thing we did was a result of us buying great tasting clear-seed peaches when we passed through Chilton County, Alabama, on our way to Florida. We would search the house, find where they were hidden, take a few and leave an IOU behind! Dennis was a little older and far more wise in the ways of the world than I, but I tagged along to some sorority beach parties and learned a lot!

My grandfather on my dad's side, William Raines Battle, was a Methodist preacher. He was educated at Young Harris College in Georgia and graduated from Vanderbilt University. He loved baseball, and some say if he didn't go into the ministry, he could have been a professional baseball pitcher. He also loved to hunt and fish. He worked as a logger and evolved into a bank president. When he felt the call to ministry, he dove in with both feet. He was a circuit rider at several churches when he proposed to my grandmother, Annie LeMerle Allen. He promised her $17 a month and all the fried chicken they could eat. She had planned to be a missionary, but decided to be a preacher's wife.

As Methodist ministers change about every four years, he moved his family all over the state during his career. He built churches in Tuscumbia, Piedmont and Talladega. He and Annie LeMerle had four sons, Bill, Laurie, Jean and David before she died during an influenza epidemic on Dec. 5, 1918. My dad was their oldest son. Reverend Battle then married Ms. Inez Massengale and together they had three daughters and a son, Blanche, Mary Virginia, Martha and Tommy.

I had seven sets of aunts and uncles on my dad's side and two on my Mother's side. They must have listened to the Good Lord's words to "go forth and multiply," and as a result, I have 28 first cousins.

My aunts and uncles on my dad's side were all college educated, with dad, uncle Laurie and uncle Jean all getting post-graduate degrees. They were all good members of the Methodist Church, except aunt Mary Virginia, who adopted uncle Chuck's Catholicism. They were all active community leaders and great believers in the importance of family.

We had family reunions quite often. At the time I was growing up, those didn't mean much to me. I enjoyed them OK but never was too excited about going. Uncle Dave always said, "Cousins need to meet cousins to keep this family together." As I grew older, I grew to believe what uncle Dave said, and have hosted several reunions at our Selma home, at our cabin on Lake Weiss, and the latest with 64 attendees in 2018 at our farm in Ellijay, Georgia. Cousins are important, but to attain the title of "Uncle" or "Aunt" in our family comes with serious respect and responsibility attached.

My uncle Jean was the family historian. He was a longtime Dean of Education at the University of South Florida in Tampa. He spent several summers teaching at Cambridge and Oxford in England. He sent postcards on occasion from Battle, England. That city was named after The Battle of Hastings, which was fought in 1066 when William the Conqueror from Normandy captured England by conquering King Harold's Saxon army. Battle, England, was just a hillside but he vowed that he would build a monastery there if God gave him the victory. He did just that. The monastery, known as Battle Abbey, became the center of a devout, religious force, which accompanied a dominating military that shared the power over England for nearly 500 years.

The name "Battle" and its derivations evolved from that event. The people of Normandy had come from the Scandinavian countries, France, and Western Europe to form their own culture. Our ancestors lived in England for years before Matthew Battle, one of three brothers, and his wife Anne, ventured across the Atlantic Ocean in 1647 and settled in Surrey County, Virginia.

Research in the *Battle Book* published in 1992 says that my generation is the 11th generation from when Matthew came over from England. Mary and I went to Battle, England, a few years ago. It is about an hour drive from London. The ruins of Battle Abbey remain and are a central piece of the town. There is a museum that illustrates the details of the Battle. The ruins of the Abbey are still in great shape. The architecture and building materials are mindboggling when thinking that it was built back in the 11th century.

The name "Raines" (my grandfather's, my dad's, and my middle name) came from a sixth-generation Calvin William Battle who married Sarah "Mary" Ann Raines, born July 17, 1819, and died July 1, 1894. Calvin William was a member of the Georgia Legislature, a Methodist and a farmer. They settled in Warren County, Georgia. My son Pat carried on that name with his oldest daughter, Mary Raines, as did my daughter Shannon with her son, Denver Raines.

Being raised in a middle-class family with parents who were both school teachers, my value system was pretty much set by the time I finished my senior year in high school. We lived in a three bedroom, one bath home, with the third bedroom (my room) being an add-on with no connection to our coal furnace heating system. I had a lot of quilts and blankets during the winter months. When I was about 12, we shut down the furnace and installed gas heaters in each bedroom.

We only had one phone, and that was a four-party line for a while, and then graduated to a two-party line. Jerry Elliott and his family lived a few houses down the block and we found out they were the other party on our two-party line. (You will read more about Jerry later in the book). For those who never enjoyed those thrills in life, there were two different ring tones to determine which party would pick up each incoming call. Jerry and his sister, Ann-Marie, were teenagers. Jean LeMerle was also a teenager, so you can imagine how little available time was left. As a 4-year younger brother, I liked to sneak around trying to listen whenever LeMerle brought over a boyfriend. Occasionally I could pick up the phone when the Elliot tone rang and listen in to their conservations. That wasn't very nice and I later regretted it, but what the heck, I was just a kid!

The single bathroom was a much bigger issue. There was a lot of fussing going on when one of us occupied the bathroom too long while others were waiting. Speaking of fussing, in our small house, one could hear voices raised throughout the house. I never remember Mom and Dad ever being in an argument. They were living examples of opposites attracting. Mom loved bridge parties, tea parties and social circles, while Dad loved sports, fishing and hunting. They also really enjoyed their jobs. While teaching junior high school

English, I'm sure my Mom put just as much pressure on them to improve their conversation skills as she did me. Dad enjoyed teaching students to swim, dive and play tennis or softball. He believed that participation in intramural sports taught students not only how to improve their skills, but also to improve their levels of physical fitness.

Mom always told us that "Anything worth doing is worth doing well." Dad taught, "Nothing good comes after midnight," and "If you can't pay cash, don't buy it." They obviously taught us a lot more, but those three are hard to top.

School, Church and Community

Much of my life growing up in Birmingham revolved around Elyton Grammar School, West End High School, Walker Memorial Methodist Church, West End Theatre and Hobbs Drug Store. Of course, when I turned 16, my horizons expanded around town and to some extent around the state.

Elyton Grammar School, still in existence today, was within easy walking distance from home. Somewhere around the fourth grade, we all took an exam in which the top students would go into an enriched curriculum. I must have been the last selected, but looking back, it was another in many blessings in my life.

Our homeroom teacher, Miss McInnis, was a great teacher. Between Miss McInnis and my Mother, I developed good English and writing skills, and that class gave me a solid base in pretty much all subjects to go on to high school.

As a grade school kid, I played and practiced a lot of sports, but many days some of my buddies and I would spend a fun afternoon at Hobbs Drugstore. It had a state-of-the-art — at least to me — soda fountain, and we consumed our share of milkshakes, malted milkshakes, ice cream sodas, and Dr. Pepper, Coke and root beer floats. Hobbs also had two big rotating racks that held comic books. We became educated pretty well on all the current comic book characters.

A typical Saturday, when not playing sports, was to walk or ride bikes to the West End Theatre, about a mile or so from the house. For 25 cents one could get a ticket to the theatre, a bag of popcorn and a soft drink. Roy Rogers, Gene Autry, Hopalong Cassidy, Lash LaRue and The Lone Ranger were featured stars. Many a day when I got home from the theatre I spent hours thinking about and play-acting being the hero and fighting the bad guys. In those days, the good guys always won, so in my experience between good and evil, good always prevailed. I know that's not reality, but to me it was a pretty good foundational value to have.

On Sundays we always went to Sunday school and church. Mom and Dad both taught Sunday school classes, and we always stayed for church services. Every so often, we would have "Dinner on the Grounds." Ladies in the church would cook their favorite dishes, and after church we would go to a vacant lot next door and eat some of the finest food one could imagine. Educational and recreational activities in the church had a great deal to do with my expanding value system.

On most Sundays after church, we would go home and eat Mother's finest fried chicken, rice, gravy and homemade biscuits. Strawberry shortcake and coconut cake were my two favorite desserts. Occasionally we would go out to eat and that would always be at Britling Cafeteria in downtown Birmingham. My favorite there was chicken and dressing with cranberry sauce, and green beans or another vegetable. Yeast rolls or corn bread was available and I loved both, and still do.

After lunch on a pretty regular basis we would drive out to Battle Hill in Graysville, Alabama. It wasn't all that far a drive, but it was definitely out in the country. My uncle Dave and uncle Laurie built homes up on a ridge pretty much surrounded by trees. Uncle Laurie, during those years, spent most of his time in Washington, D.C., as a congressman from the 9th District, so he wasn't home much.

Uncle Dave was one of the coolest uncles one could have. He was definitely a pragmatist. He and aunt Jo had four children: Rose, Joe Laurie, Bill and Ginny. Rose was almost exactly my age and the others were younger. Uncle Dave decided that since the children were at the age that they might draw crayons all over the walls, he just wouldn't finish the walls until they got of age to know better. Concrete block walls seemed fine to me.

One Christmas, uncle Dave bought his kids a horse. The fact that uncle Laurie was staying most of the year in Washington made it an easy decision to make "Big Red's" stable in uncle Laurie's garage. We took turns riding Big Red much of Christmas afternoon. None of us knew anything about horses. After a few hours with each of us kids riding Big Red, it was again my turn. He had done pretty well up to this point, but he was pretty much ready to go back to his stable. Timing is the key to everything, and unfortunately for me, Big Red decided the right time was now. He took off on a dead run heading back to his stable. I was holding on for dear life when I saw a clothesline coming at me fast. It was high enough not to catch Big Red, but it was coming at me about chest high. My reaction was to lean to the left to get my body profile lower. Unbeknownst to me, all the riding we had done had loosened the cinch that kept the saddle on tightly. As I leaned, the saddle slid with me and I fell off, tumbled a few times and fortunately with nothing hurt but my feelings.

Another Christmas, uncle Dave bought his kids a monkey. That may have been the most unique of all gifts, as the monkey was quite a character. He would get into the sugar canister and eat all the sugar. He would steal pies that were cooling in the windowsill. I'm not sure what happened to the monkey or Big Red, but neither stayed around too long after Christmas.

We enjoyed great times on Battle Hill.

SPORTS

I grew up around the Birmingham-Southern campus playing every kind of sport available. I was exposed to football, softball, baseball, tennis, basketball, swimming, horseshoes and ping-pong. There were even two seasons in those days that my kids never experienced — marble season and yo-yo season. I'm not sure where they were on the calendar, but they seemed to arrive every year at my grammar school.

In marble season, a contest consisted of a ring (any size was OK) drawn in the dirt. Contestants would agree on how many marbles each would put in the ring. They were tightly pushed into a circle at the center of the ring. The object was for the shooter to put his knuckles on the ground outside the ring. He held his favorite "shooting marble" (taw) between his thumb and middle finger with his forefinger lightly holding the taw in place. With his thumb as the force, he would shoot his marble into the pile and break them up, like in pool. If he knocked one out of the circle, he picked it up and it was his. If he didn't, the next shooter was up. He could move around the circle to get a favorable position for one or more marbles. The key was to knock a marble out, but keep your taw inside the circle. If you did, you continued to shoot until you missed. An excellent shot occurred when the taw solidly hit a marble in the ring, knocking it out, and the taw stayed in the ring spinning in the dirt, and well positioned for the next shot. The game actually was a lot like pool, except it was played on the ground with no cues. Good marble players would come to school with a pocket full of marbles and go home with all four pockets full. A bad player might see the reverse results.

There was one other interesting rule that made for lively reaction skills. When the school bell rang ending the period, everyone around could yell "Gray Horse" and grab for the marbles in the ring. I have no idea where that move came from, but a video of a group hanging around watching contestants all diving into the ring to get what they could, would have been awfully fun to watch. By the end of the season, the regular players seemed to all have faded jean pockets, which I guess was caused from stretching from the marbles. It was also characteristic to see holes in the knees of the side the shooter used, as that knee, and sometimes both, were on the ground when shots were made.

Yo-yo season started when representatives from Duncan Yo-Yo Company came around, accompanied by professional yo-yo experts. Not only could they perform every trick in the book with a yo-yo, they could also carve your name and a palm tree or some other neat design on the side of the wooden yo-yo. We would all get a few quick lessons and spend weeks trying to do more tricks and get better doing them. Some tricks that I recall were Walking the Dog, Around the World, Man on the Flying Trapeze, and Spaghetti. We all pretty much mastered those, but there were others that were beyond our skill level. I don't recall any particular contests we participated in other than challenges from our classmates and those above and below us.

There wasn't any damage to clothes in yo-yo season, but there were a few casualties. The wooden yo-yos were pretty solid. When working on yo-yos inside the house, if the string broke at the wrong time, windows, mirrors and other breakables were at risk! And if a person was in front of the yo-yoer, his or her head or upper body was at risk on certain throws.

Before high school, I played organized YMCA baseball. They had 11-, 13-, and 15-year-old leagues. I played on 11- and 13-year-old teams before going to high school. There were no uniforms or rules about what kind of shoes we wore. Shorts and jeans were the typical dress, and shoes ranged from barefoot to real baseball shoes with spikes. Most wore tennis shoes.

The neatest thing to me was the coaches. They were football players at West End High School. They were all 16 or older so they could drive us around to play at different elementary schools around the city. The elementary school baseball fields were not very good. The coaches would cut grass and drag the infield, trying to get rocks, glass and other things that might be there out of the way. The players would pitch in and help.

We developed great relationships with the coaches. We admired them from the start because of who they were. They all captured our beliefs in them because they were knowledgeable about baseball. They had a pleasant personality that made playing fun. It wasn't long before we would tackle them and jump on them for fun. They were also high-character, strongly religious individuals who didn't allow swearing or any kind of obnoxious behavior.

I did play one year of organized Little League ball. It was coached by parents, had uniforms and names of professional teams, and had stands where parents and other spectators could watch. It was fun, but not nearly as fun to me as being taught by the high school football players.

I also played one year of organized football before high school. Larry Striplin was a basketball player at Birmingham-Southern. He would hustle down to Woodward Park a few afternoons a week to coach our 110-pound football team to supplement his scholarship at BSC. Unfortunately, for me, I was young and slow. Most of the team were one or two years older, which at that age made a big difference in development. I didn't play much, but the team did win the City Championship. Larry was an excellent coach and we had some very good players. As you will read later, Larry was a great mentor to me several years later and had a tremendous impact on my career.

When I was 11 or 12, a bunch of my friends and I went over to West End High School one August day. The football team was working out, but they were on their own getting in shape before the coaches were allowed to participate. It was fun watching them, and even more fun having gotten to know some of them through their baseball coaching. The captain of the team was Keith Wilson. He was one of the YMCA baseball coaches and a terrific human being. We enjoyed watching them work in groups and go through all the routines that each position group was using to get ready for the season.

Then it came time to work on conditioning and run sprints. Keith called them up and said "OK we're going to run X number of 100's." One of the players in the background said, "Aw come on Keith, we'll get enough of this when the coaches come out." Keith walked back to where the voice came from and got up face to face and said, "There is no shortcut to success, get on the goal line and let's run." The team immediately went back to the goal line and ran the sprints. That message from peer to peer had a great impact on me. "There is no shortcut to success" became a principle that I tried to adopt and live.

Keith and the 1953 West End Lions went on to win the State Championship. He was a small, quick running back and defensive back. Keith wanted to go to Alabama or Auburn in the worst way, but they deemed him too little. He went on to a successful career at Kansas State University.

Keith came back into my life during my first year as head coach at the University of Tennessee. He was coaching Condredge Holloway, a great quarterback and three-sport star. I do not know how much Keith helped, but he certainly didn't hurt, as we were able to attract Condredge to UT where he became a great two-sport star in football and baseball, breaking records in both sports.

I think I had a football in my cradle when I was a baby. Sports were very important to me. I loved them all, and many hours of my life were spent shooting basketballs at a goal on the garage, playing catch with Dad or friends, and playing ball at parks or on vacant lots in the neighborhood. In those days we could walk or ride bikes all around the neighborhood and even the community with no fear of danger.

I loved competition. When taught a certain skill, I was driven to work on that skill until I mastered it, or at least improved. It was fun playing with neighborhood friends.

We created a lot of games in unique places. Of course we played on regular fields and courts, but we also played touch football, two on a side, in a dead end street on which one of my buddies lived. The offense consisted of a center/receiver and a quarterback, the defense was a rusher and a defensive back. The center would snap the ball back to the quarterback and take off running a route. The rusher had to count to three or five before coming after the quarterback. The curbs were the sideline boundaries. Playing this for hours really taught us skills of passing, catching, guarding receivers and running routes.

Another interesting game was played in baseball season down at Woodward Park. It allowed us to work on certain skills, while not running or using much energy. We played on tennis courts at the park that had a wire net, and tall wire fencing on each end of the court. We used regular baseballs and bats. Two on a side would either be batters or fielders. The pitcher stood behind the net, the fielder stood wherever he wanted in the back of the court. The pitcher pitched to the batters, located on the others court's back line, one at a time until he got three outs. The batter only got one strike.

If he swung and missed, fouled it off, hit the ball on the ground before it got to the net, hit to the pitcher or fielder on the fly, or hit it over the back fence — he was out. And if the latter happened, he had to run around and get the ball hit over the fence. If he hit the net on a fly, it was a single. If he hit the ball over the net and it hit the ground before it got to the back fence, it was a double. If he hit the back fence on a fly, it was a triple, and if he hit one of the vertical poles, or the horizontal poles at the top of the fence (and it stayed in the court) it was a home run. That game taught us how to swing and place the ball on offense, and how to react and catch on defense. It was a great game to play before or after real baseball games or practice over on the field that used more energy.

In basketball season, we either played in someone's backyard or at Harrison Park, which had an indoor basketball court. If you came to Harrison Park on Saturdays during basketball season, you'd better bring your A-game. If your team won, you stayed and played the next challenger. If you lost, you went to the back of the line. We usually played two or three men teams of half-court basketball. Games were to 8 or 15 baskets, depending on the number waiting to play.

This was before the 3-point shot, and there were no free throws. If there was a serious foul, the team that got fouled kept the ball. If there was a dispute, the guys watching made the call. If you scored, your team kept the ball and started the next play from around mid-court. So, a good team could score and win out, if they could score on every possession. That didn't happen very often. It was very competitive and a lot of fun.

WORK EXPERIENCE

I was expected to do certain chores around the house that included cutting the grass in summer and putting coal in the furnace in winter — until we converted to gas heaters in each room. During the summer, I tried to earn spending money by cutting neighbors' grass. That required knocking on doors and getting work, then doing it well enough to keep the business.

My dad told me, "If you cut Mrs. Jones' grass for a dollar and she feels she got two dollars' worth of work, you will keep her as a customer. If she feels she only got 50 cents worth, you won't be invited back." That message resonated with me back then, and has stayed with me through the years. You know, service seems to be hard to find these days. Whenever you do find it, it is special.

One of my greatest experiences, from a work perspective, was getting a paper route in the seventh and eighth grade prior to high school. *The Birmingham News* branch office was a rectangular concrete building filled with tables for "paper boys" to work, rolling their papers and loading them up to deliver around the community. At one end was an opening to the outside that enabled delivery trucks to unload papers in bundles of 25 to 50, and wired together with bailing wire, through the opening and on to a long roller belt into the building.

Boys would get their allotment and take them to their respective work station. Two boys facing each other on opposite sides of the table would begin to roll papers in preparation for delivery. The technique was interesting. We could buy rolls of string from the branch. With a piece of string in your mouth, connected with the roll of string to your left (if you were right-handed), you would then take a paper from the stack on your left, place it on the table in front of you, and using both hands, begin to roll it as tightly as possible. When the paper was rolled, you would take the rolled paper in your right hand, take the string from your mouth with your left hand, and slap the wet end onto the paper. In a circular motion, using both hands, you would wrap the string around the middle of the paper six to eight revolutions. At that point, your left hand would encircle the rolled paper and briskly slide it down over the string two or three times, thus sealing the string to the paper. Then in one motion with your right hand, you would move the paper briskly to the right, breaking the string held by the left hand, which would go to the mouth, while the right hand moved the paper to a stack on the right and then grabbing another paper to be rolled. All this could be done in a matter of a few seconds once the skill was learned, and boys often competed on how fast they could get theirs done.

I had 85 customers, and on days other than Thursdays and Sundays, could roll 85 papers in about an hour. On Thursdays and Sundays, the advertising section made the papers a lot bigger and they took more time to roll. Having 85 papers to deliver was not a huge amount, but it was very comfortable to me. During delivery, about the worst thing that could happen was to miss a house — or a block! I did miss an entire block one Sunday morning, about four or five houses on each side of the street. If complaints came in about not receiving a paper, a "complaint boy" would drive out and deliver the paper with a charge to the paper boy of a dollar per replaced paper. Getting an $8 to $10 hit was a big deal. It didn't take long to learn to never get complaints.

Papers cost a nickel to consumers on Monday through Saturday, and the Sunday paper cost a quarter. So the responsibility of collecting 55 cents from 85 subscribers determined profits. We got 3 cents of every daily and 15 cents for every Sunday paper, so about 33 cents per paper delivered per week. *The Birmingham News* got about 22 cents.

> This first job was a great business experience for a young pre-teen. It taught all of the characteristics of a successful business:
>
> • Marketing and Sales — It was my responsibility to acquire customers, keep them satisfied, and try to add new customers;
>
> • Accounting — It was my responsibility to collect on a regular basis as well as keeping up with customers who were either slow-pay or no-pay. I had to pay my "bill" each week to *The Birmingham News* whether I collected enough or not;
>
> • Running the business — Rain, snow, sleet or ice, the paper had to be delivered every day, and placed in a yard or porch to suit the customer. Relationships needed to be made over time to keep customers more satisfied and to make collecting much easier.

This was an everyday business, and in the two years I delivered papers, I always had a little money in my pockets. My bicycle had a big basket that would hold 85 papers on most normal days. The basket was standard issue for all at the branch. We also were able to buy big canvas bags that could be packed to carry another 40 to 50 papers. On big advertising days, we would fill the basket, then fill the bag, and carefully stack the bag on top of the full basket and attach it with bailing wire. The larger papers would make the bicycle top heavy.

I remember my first Sunday delivery. On Sundays, the papers were huge, and I was still learning how to roll, so my papers were not rolled all that tightly. The road on the block of the branch was pretty well full of potholes, with a hill from right to left as we left the branch. Sunday papers came to the branch about 2 a.m. Sunday morning. Most everyone wanted to come on in and get the work done early.

As I was leaving the branch with a very top-heavy bike on my first Sunday, I got about 50 yards downhill to the left and hit a pothole. It was pitch-black dark! The front went down, and the rest of the bike and I flew over the handlebars. Of course, all the papers in the bag spilled all over the street, and others exiting the branch saw me and laughed or called me "Rookie" — or worse names — in jest.

Actually when the canvas bag was filled, one pretty much couldn't see anything over the top, but could see the curb and the middle line in the streets. Many times we would exit right out of the branch, climb the hill and get on Tuscaloosa Avenue, which was well lit, and at 3 a.m. in the morning, had very little traffic. We would ride in the middle of the road, which we could navigate successfully, and we would hear oncoming traffic and move over.

As I said earlier, delivering papers was my first real job, but I would be remiss if I didn't tell you that I sold peanuts at a few Birmingham-Southern basketball games, too. The gymnasium at the time was nice, but never anticipated large crowds. There may have been pullout bleacher seats on one side. The other side had a few rows of folding chairs, which were also set up at each end. Having a place for the media was no problem as they rarely covered Birmingham-Southern games. Maximum attendance was about 250. I was pretty shy, and at 10-11 years old, walked around very quietly with my strap-on tray that held bags of peanuts. My Mother saved my first quarter earned, and to this day, my safety deposit box at Bryant Bank holds a very small envelope that reads in my Mother's handwriting, "First Quarter Billy Battle earned." Now isn't that a sweet Mother?

After delivering papers, my next real job took place in the summer before my senior year at West End High School. Two young Birmingham-Southern grads, Dave Upton and Fletcher Yielding, bought out a hardware store and started a new company named Southeastern Bolt and Screw Company. It was just a few miles from my house and I often walked/ran to or from work. I had turned 16 that past December, so I sometimes took a car, if both family cars weren't being used.

The first order was to go over to the acquired hardware store and pack up all nuts, bolts, screws, long steel rods and whatever else was bought and move it to the new company. That took a few weeks to get the new warehouse organized. They bought a new "threading machine" that applied threads to long steel rods that were used in construction.

My salary was $1 an hour, six days a week, $48 cash on Fridays. It was a great job as it involved a lot of lifting and handling heavy items. It was a good job to stay in shape for the upcoming football season, my senior season at West End. The office and warehouse were located on 2nd Avenue North between the West End Community and downtown Birmingham. Niki's, a still famous restaurant in the Birmingham area, had a great meat-and-three restaurant a block or so away. Early on in my time there, Dave and Fletcher invited me to go eat lunch with them. I did, and the food was great. When the bill came, mine was about $3.50. I gladly paid the bill, but as I thought about it walking back to the office, it dawned on me that that took 3 1/2 hours of work. I decided then and there, that cash flow model didn't work for me and I was a bologna sandwich man thereafter.

Dave and Fletcher hired a very nice man, Mr. Goss, to run the threading machine. On a break one day, Mr. Goss told me that I should ask the boss to let me learn how to operate the threader, as that would be a very marketable skill later on in life. When I approached Dave and Fletcher, they laughed and said, "We've got other plans to keep you busy all summer."

I was only there in June and July, as football started in early August. The company became very successful, and Fletcher and Dave became extremely successful entrepreneurs in the Birmingham area.

WEST END HIGH SCHOOL

When I started at West End, I was so excited to play all sports there. Unfortunately for me, I was young, fat and slow. My birthday was Dec. 8 and I started school in January as part of the first grade class that had been there since September. I was one of the youngest in my class, which lasted all the way through school. I had heard that if you were "warm and breathing" that you could make the "B" team football squad.

I was actually one of the two slowest players on the team. There were not many avenues of success for me, but when wind sprint time came, it was a fight to see if I could beat the other guy more times than he beat me! Success is a moving target in life, and if I beat ole Clyde in wind sprints, I considered that a successful day.

I had been practicing in the line at guard, center or tackle — wherever there was an opening. But then the first game rolled around. The dress-out squad was posted on the wall in the locker room. I anxiously went over to check the list and was devastated to see my name missing. All the other players soon filed out of the locker room, I sat there, head in hands, tears flowing down my face and trying to figure out what to do.

A varsity manager wandered through the locker room and saw me over in the corner. His name was Pat Dougherty and his brother Bill was in my freshman class. He asked what was wrong and I told him. He thought a minute and said, "Let me go check on something." In a few minutes, he came back with a game jersey that was a little more faded than the rest, but was the same color. The helmet was a different color, but I didn't care — I had a uniform and was going to dress out. That was a very big deal to me. I've often wondered what I would have done if I had not felt a part of the team. Would I have given up football? I don't know, but if I had, my whole life would have turned out much differently. My freshman year in football was a real struggle.

I played "B" team basketball as a freshman and actually did pretty well. After basketball season, I went to my "B" team football coach, Cotton Roy, and told him I was excited about playing baseball. He said, "Boy, you're not playing baseball, you're running track. You need to learn how to run."

I went out for track and they put me to running the 440-yard dash. After I learned what that was about, I thought that was about the cruelest thing someone could do to a young boy. But that turned out to be great advice. The 440 is really a sprint around the entire track. As time went on, I actually got pretty good in the event. It helped that I grew about 6 inches between my sophomore and junior years. Going from a short, fat, slow guy to a tall, skinny, faster guy was a nice metamorphosis.

I was always hungry to win a medal, a ribbon or a trophy. We never got trophies for participation and I really don't believe in them today. Running the 440 in practice didn't take all that long, so in order to win more ribbons, etc., I tried to do a lot of events in track. I threw the shot put and discus, ran the 440-yard dash, and the mile relay. I also worked hard at and enjoyed pole vaulting. I did get to 10 feet, which won a few dual meet points, but the good vaulters in the city were up to 13 or 14 feet. In those days, the poles were stiff with little or no bend. It is fascinating to me today to watch the flexible poles that shoot vaulters up in the 16- to 17-foot range.

My sophomore year in football was not much better than my freshman year. I was still in the short, fat, slow range and didn't get to play enough to even letter, but did get to dress out every game and played in a few. Coach Ward Proctor, who had a great record at West End over the years, was retiring after the year. A young 22-year-old coach named Sam Short replaced him.

I started on the basketball team in my sophomore year, and played pretty well. We had two big guys that year, Clyde Frederick and Bud Moore, who were seniors. Clyde got a basketball scholarship to Alabama and Bud got a football scholarship. Clyde scored 60 points in one game. We had a really good team.

My best buddy at West End High was a young man named George Payne. George was an amazing athlete and an even better human being. He was 5-foot-1, weighed about 150 pounds, and played fullback and middle linebacker. He had a hairy chest and was shaving at about 12 years old. At 150 pounds he could military press over 200. He was quick as a cat, could get to full speed in two or three steps, and would knock your block off on defense.

Going back to "B" team days, the varsity got preference on the field, so many days we ran wind sprints after dark. Coach Roy would send managers up to the parking area in a lot above the field and have all available cars turn on their lights toward the field. There was a big seven-man blocking sled over close to the field near one end zone. In reminiscing years later with Coach Roy, he said George would often sneak over and hide behind the blocking sled. If he wasn't missed after a few sprints, he would take off to his house, which was just a few blocks from the school. Coach Roy said, "Many days George was home eating supper by the time the rest of the team had showered and headed for home."

George was that kind of guy, full of life all the time. The girls all loved "Georgie," as they called him. One year we shared a tall locker together in the hall. In those days, parking, speeding or other tickets were given in a small yellow envelope that had carbon copy printing on the outside. A parking ticket was a couple of dollars but a speeding ticket was a $35 fine. When in need of cash, George would get a parking ticket, smudge out the carbon and write in speeding $35. He would then go around between classes and ask the girls for a little help. One day, in the middle of George's scam, I went to the locker to change books and the bottom of the locker was covered in about three inches of coins. He was definitely a smooth operator.

My junior year in football was much better for me. I had played every position in the line. We had an outstanding quarterback named Carson Southard with a very good arm. The problem was, we didn't have any receivers who could catch the ball. By this time I was taller and faster, and because I had played baseball and basketball growing up, I had good hand-to-eye coordination. I could catch passes!

The first few games continued to see me playing in the line. Finally, about mid-season, they let me try out at end. Coach Short had brought in the "FLY-T offense" featuring wideouts, players in motion and airing the football out. The last few games I caught enough passes, and played well enough on defense, to attract the interest of a few college scouts.

As I went into my senior year, 1958-59, Coach Paul W. Bryant had come back to Alabama. In 1957, Auburn went 10-0, beating Alabama 40-0, and winning the National Championship. Alabama went 2-7-1. When Coach Bryant was hired at Alabama, Auburn was the "King of the Hill" at the time, but I was really fascinated about what I saw and heard about Coach Bryant. Bud Moore, a teammate at West End, was at Alabama and I talked to him a lot about what was going on.

Our senior year, George was moved from fullback to guard as Coach Short had continued to refine his new offense. It was ahead of its time in those days with a lot of formations and motion. It was a passing offense to take advantage of Carson Southard's passing ability. It also featured pulling guards, and

George was a great one, although he was broken hearted about not getting to carry the ball from the fullback position.

I had been the primary receiver to Carson's passes, and because of the system, caught a lot of them and scored a lot of touchdowns. We had some tough battles with Gadsden High is the past, but this particular year they were not as good. We scored early and had the game pretty much out of reach. I caught a pass on a crossing pattern and had to run laterally to find a seam to turn up toward the goal line. As I turned up, there was one man between me and scoring. My peripheral vision let me see George close behind. I turned around and lateraled the ball to George, blocked the one remaining defender, and George scored the touchdown. He was so excited and had a big grin on his face. That was worth a million dollars to me. All of a sudden the smile turned upside down and his body language slumped with frustration. He saw a flag thrown on the play and the officials were taking it back. It seems our quarterback had gotten full of himself in the pursuit of the play and clipped a guy about 25 yards behind the ball. We were all buddies on the team, but I don't know if George ever forgave Carson for taking away his touchdown.

I was recruited by Auburn, Alabama and Georgia Tech, and heard from Tennessee and Florida. Auburn continued to win but Coach Bryant turned Alabama around his first year by going 5-4-1. His worst loss was in the opening game against LSU, which won the National Championship in 1958. Alabama was within striking distance late in the fourth quarter but LSU scored late to win 13-3. They lost to Auburn by less than a touchdown when an Alabama receiver dropped a scoring pass in the end zone late in the game that, if caught, would have won it.

Georgia Tech actually was the first to offer me a scholarship. I had all the respect in the world for Coach Bobby Dodd at Tech and Coach Shug Jordan at Auburn. At the end of the day, I thought, man if you could play for Coach Bryant for four years, you would really be something. I did, and I definitely wasn't disappointed.

Florida invited me to a game that fall. I knew I was going to Alabama, but wanted to take the trip primarily because my cousin, Dennis Scruggs, was a freshman scholarship player there. I talked to Coach Bryant and told him what I wanted to do. He told me that he didn't want me to take the trip. He said, "I'll take you to Florida sometime." I didn't take the trip and didn't know what to think about his offer. I never thought about it again, but after our Orange Bowl victory after the 1962 season, he approached me in the locker room and said, "I told you I would take you to Florida!" I can't believe he remembered, but we both enjoyed a big laugh.

George got a scholarship at Auburn to be a football manager. He could have done the same at Alabama, but his brother, an Auburn fan, talked him out of it by saying Coach Bryant would run him off. That pretty much ended one of the best friendships of my life. We reconnected years later in Atlanta, and I actually hired his daughter to be my secretary at The Collegiate Licensing Company. She was amazing and worked a couple of years, but wanted to start a family and I encouraged her to follow her dreams. George and I got together occasionally in Atlanta, but our worlds at that stage were too far apart to continue our close relationship.

My senior year, the *Welion*, West End's student newspaper, headlines read, "West End Ends Successful Grid Season 4-4-1." Now winning four games in a season does not stand for success many places, but at West End, those four games brought our total wins in four years to six! The 4-4-1 record was a success.

We actually had a much better team than our record indicated. Two of our players received scholarships to Auburn, I went to Alabama, and three others went to junior colleges and played there.

One of the athletic accomplishments of which I am most proud was in the state championship track meet in 1959. I made it to the finals in the 440-yard dash. To me, coming from where I was as a freshman, to making the final eight runners in the state championship race, was monumental. I came in last of eight runners, but ran my best time all year of 51.8 seconds.

Going to high school at West End was a great experience. The academics were good and provided a solid foundation for moving on to college. I'm very glad I played three sports, and believe that basketball and track (as well as baseball before high school) all contributed to my ability in football. Honors at West End included: Started and lettered three years in basketball; Lettered three years in track; Started and lettered two years in football; All-City as an end on both offensive and defensive teams; Offensive lineman of the year in City, All State, All Southern, All American; Played in the Wigwam Wisemen All-American Game in Baton Rouge, Louisiana; Played in Alabama All-Star game; Mr. West End; Most Likely to Succeed – Senior Class.

LESSONS LEARNED

- "Anything worth doing is worth doing well" — Kathleen Battle
- "Nothing good happens after midnight" — Bill Battle Jr.
- "If you can't pay cash for it, don't buy it" — Bill Battle Jr.
- If your dad is a Dr. Pepper bottler, don't buy Coke floats. Be loyal to protect your brand.

- "There is no shortcut to success" — Keith Wilson
- Cousins need to get to know cousins; family reunions and family history are important to future generations.
- If you give your customer more value than the dollars you receive, you will keep the business.
- Sports can teach life lessons far beyond the physical aspects; team dynamics enable the group to be far stronger than the sum of its individual parts.
- Making a dollar an hour and eating a $3.50 lunch doesn't make economic sense; cash flow is probably the most important part in every small business.
- While your goal may be to be a star on a championship team, it may take being a poor player on a losing team to work your way up.
- Success is a moving target, once you reach your goal you either get better or you get worse.
- Having a job as a youngster, like a paper route, can teach valuable life lessons; deliver papers every day, rain or shine, collect from customers at least enough to pay your bills, develop efficiency in rolling and delivering papers, build relationships with your customers, your boss and your peers.
- Communication skills are important in every job; the hand-written note is becoming a lost art.
- It's great to have mentors throughout your journey — as a sounding board, a role model, and to pick you up when you are starting to feel defeat.

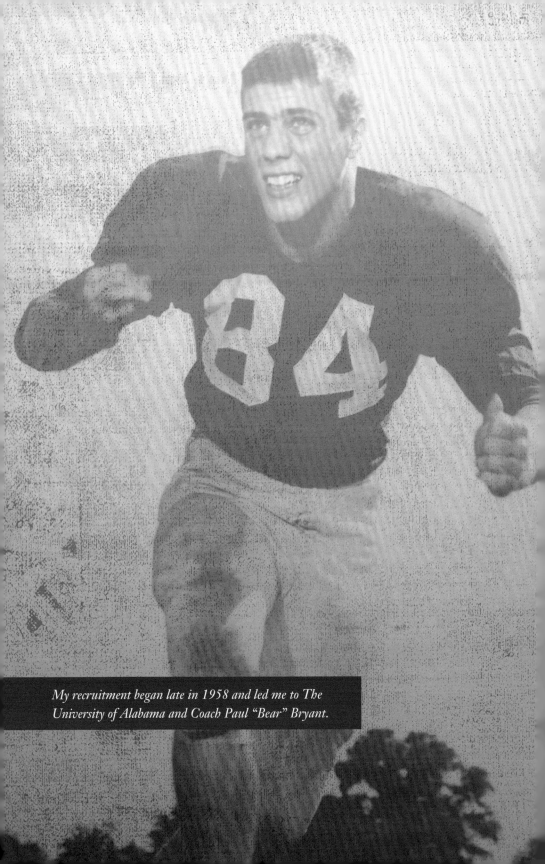

My recruitment began late in 1958 and led me to The University of Alabama and Coach Paul "Bear" Bryant.

CHAPTER 2

PLAYING AT THE UNIVERSITY OF ALABAMA

In 1957, my junior year in high school, Alabama was coached by J.B. "Ears" Whitworth. He had a 2-7-1 season and lost to Auburn by 40-0. The Tigers, coached by Coach Ralph "Shug" Jordan, went 10-0 and won the mythical national championship. Auburn was on probation that year due to a recruiting rules violation. They were not allowed to go to a bowl game, but in those days, they were allowed to win the national title.

When Coach Whitworth was fired after the 1957 season, Paul William "Bear" Bryant was named Alabama's new head football coach and director of athletics. When he took over, Alabama was at the very bottom of the college football world and Auburn was at the top. The Crimson Tide had lost four straight years to Auburn by a combined score of 128-7, three years under Whitworth and one in Coach Harold "Red" Drew's last season.

Coach Bryant accepted the Alabama job, but agreed to coach his Texas A&M team in the Gator Bowl. John David Crow was an All-American running back and Heisman Trophy winner that year for the Aggies. They played Tennessee in the Gator Bowl and lost 3-0. Before Coach Bryant took his team to the Gator Bowl, he did not renew most of Coach Whitworth's staff and made Hayden Riley, who was an assistant basketball coach, the head football recruiter. He hired one of his favorite players from his time at Kentucky, Jerry Claiborne, and sent him to Tuscaloosa to join Coach Riley in recruiting.

In those days, most high school seniors in the South signed around the first week or two in December. Several players had already signed at Alabama before Coach Bryant got to the campus. His first class turned out to be exceptional, including Billy Neighbors, Pat Trammell, Billy Richardson, Tommy Brooker, Mal Moore, Bill Oliver, Jimmy Sharpe and others.

Coach Bryant had coached at Maryland in 1945, taking over a team that had gone 1-7-1 in 1944 and improving it to 6-2-1. He left after one year in a disagreement with the president. His eight-year record at Kentucky was 60-23-5, beating Oklahoma in the Sugar Bowl, Villanova in the Great Lakes Bowl and losing to Santa Clara in the Orange Bowl. In four years at Texas A&M, his record was 25-14-2 after going 1-9 in his first year in 1954.

Losing to Tennessee in the Gator Bowl before coming to Alabama after the 1957 season brings up an interesting side note. Coach Bryant's biggest nemesis at this point in his career was Tennessee. He coached eight years at Kentucky from 1946-1953. During his first seven years there, General Robert Neyland was the coach at Tennessee — one of the all-time greats. Coach Bryant's eight-year record against UT was 1-6-1, and his victory came his last year at Kentucky after Coach Neyland had retired. Coach Bryant had the great quarterback Babe Parilli at Kentucky, and during Babe's four years there, they didn't score a point against Tennessee. As a matter of fact, in Coach Bryant's seven years against General Neyland, Kentucky only scored a total of 20 points and was shut out in five of the seven.

Although his success against the General was not good, in 1950, Coach Bryant led his team to an 11-1-0 season (loss was to Tennessee), an SEC Championship (Kentucky's first ever) and a Sugar Bowl victory over Oklahoma. The Sooners, coached by Bud Wilkinson, were the power of the Midwest and went into the game heavily favored with a mighty team loaded with offensive talent. A lightning-quick split-T offense had carried Oklahoma to 31 straight wins.

Coach Bryant designed a multi-look defense that often ballooned to a nine-man front. To beat a juggernaut like Oklahoma, he deemed it necessary to do something radical. He put four tackles in the defensive line, including moving an offensive player, Walt Yowarsky, to defensive end. Walt had played on defense only once in his life, but Coach Bryant wanted his biggest men on defense to shoot gaps in the Oklahoma line. Walt was 6-foot-2, 208 pounds! The thought was that Oklahoma would move the ball some in the middle of the field, but when they got close to the goal line, Oklahoma wasn't strong enough to move them out.

The strategy worked to perfection. OU led in first downs 18-7, rushing yards 189-84, and total offense 227-189, but Kentucky went into halftime ahead 13-0, thanks to good defense and Parilli's 7 of 9 passing. On the first possession of the second half, Oklahoma drove to the Wildcat 4-yard line with a first down and goal to go. On third down from the 2, Yowarsky shot into the line and threw Oklahoma quarterback Billy Vessels for a 5-yard loss. An incomplete fourth-down pass ended the Sooner drive. Maybe the two most important stats of the game were Coach Bryant's gap-shooting defensive strategy causing five fumbles, with Kentucky recovering all five. The other was an unprotected punter strategy that allowed only a half-yard return on Kentucky's eight punts.

Following Kentucky's 13-7 win, Earl Roby, the sports editor of the *The Louisville Courier-Journal* wrote, "The University of Kentucky earned its greatest football triumph since it took up football in 1881. In a game that was a reversal of the Kentucky-Tennessee tussle, the Wildcats crashed Oklahoma's National Champions to earth so forceful that the Sooners fumbled repeatedly. They ended the 31 game winning streak at 31, and richly deserve all the honor that goes with such a single achievement."

Yowarsky won the Sugar Bowl MVP award. Bob Gain won the Outland Trophy. Parilli, William Jameson and Charlie McClendon, the future longtime LSU head coach, were also stars. Oklahoma finished the regular season No. 1 in both the AP and Sagarin polls, as they averaged 34.5 points a game. Coach

Bryant left Kentucky after the 1953 season with an impressive 60-23-5 record, and the victory over Oklahoma remains to this day the greatest victory in Kentucky history. In the 1990s, Jeff Sagarin, who compiled the Sagarin computer rating for *USA Today*, deemed the 1950 University of Kentucky Wildcats the National Champions for the 1950 season. Up to the time of this writing, Kentucky had won only two SEC championships — one in 1950 under Coach Bryant, and the other in 1976 under Fran Curci.

Fran's team went 8-3, but secured the SEC Championship on a 62-yard touchdown pass from Derrick Ramsey to Greg Wood to beat our 1976 Tennessee team 7-0. I announced my resignation the next day. The following year, Kentucky went on probation but went 10-1. Fran was a good coach and we are still good friends. We coached in all-star games and took family trips together over the years.

I believe Coach Bryant patterned his basic football philosophy after General Neyland. He believed in playing great defense, having a strong running game, and having an effective kicking game. Field-position football is still important today, but probably more important when scoring wasn't so prolific. During my time working with Coach Bryant in his business activities, we talked a bit about General Neyland and those days. Their teams were well conditioned, disciplined to the point of minimizing mistakes, but forcing opponents to make mistakes, and when they did, capitalizing on them. We'll talk more about Tennessee later.

I never met Coach Vince Lombardi of Green Bay Packers, but from what I have read about him, I do believe he and Coach Bryant were very much alike in football philosophy. In a book written by All-Pro offensive guard Fuzzy Thurston, he said of Coach Lombardi, "He would push a team to the brink of mutiny, but he always knew when to pull back."

There were many times when you feared Coach Bryant, and many others when you hated him; but he could always say or do something, often very small, that made you change your mind and believe in him and his philosophy. Many of his former coaches and players went into coaching at other universities. Some tried to be like Coach Bryant. Some pushed teams to the brink of mutiny, but did not know when to pull back and, as a result, their careers were short-lived. Others went on to coach to their own personalities and were successful.

Years later when I was the head coach at Tennessee, former LSU Coach Charlie McClendon and I spent a lot of time talking at SEC meetings. "Cholly Mac" had played for Coach Bryant at Kentucky. After reading an article listing 42 coaches who played or coached for Coach Bryant, Cholly Mac said, "They write about how many coaches Coach Bryant has put into coaching. They never write about those he has put out." Unfortunately, a few years later, Cholly Mac and I both were added to the latter list!

Our 1959 class was the first "full" class that signed under Coach Bryant. That class consisted of another strong group of mostly state of Alabama players, i.e., Lee Roy Jordan (from Excel), Butch Wilson (Hueytown), Cotton Clark (Kansas, Alabama), Gary Martin (Dothan), Richard Williamson (Fort Deposit), Benny Nelson (Huntsville), Jimmy Wilson (Haleyville), Charley Pell (Albertville) and others. Cotton lived in Kansas, Alabama, but went to school at Carbon Hill. Richard lived in Sandy Ridge, went to school at Fort Deposit, and got his mail in Letohatchee.

My recruitment began late in 1958 after I moved to split end on offense and defensive end. It picked up in 1959 as my senior year unfolded. Bud Moore was a senior at West End High School when I was a sophomore. He signed with Alabama in 1957 under Coach Whitworth, but went through the grinding first year of Coach Bryant's tenure in 1958. I communicated regularly with Bud during my junior and senior years. We still communicate today.

Recruiting in 1959 was much different than that of today. I was invited to several Alabama games in Birmingham and Tuscaloosa. In one particular game at Legion Field, the recruits and the freshmen were seated on the sidelines with the team. Freshmen were not eligible in those days. I do not recall who Alabama was playing, but I was sitting with Billy Neighbors and Pat Trammell, who were freshmen at the time. Pat had a flask of Jack Daniel's in his coat pocket and would take a nip or two every now and then to stay warm. I got into an interesting conversation with Billy when I asked, "Is Coach Bryant really as tough as it appears?" Billy broke out in a speech that went on for about five minutes. It basically consisted of his opinion that the state university was the place to be, and ended with "and I don't care how tough the coach is, I don't even care if the coach is Hitler, you need to come to the state university!"

I was very impressed with watching Alabama practices. Coach Bryant brought in "quickness drills" and did a series of calisthenics, not in the rhythmic way that normal calisthenics are done, but movement done on sound. Players were lined up in a group in normal fashion. The leader would say, "Side Straddle Hop" then "Ready." All players would simultaneously break down in a "football position," feet shoulders width, knees bent, eyes straight ahead and arms bent. The leader would say "Hike" and everyone as quickly as they could would move their hands to their helmet and slide their feet out a few inches. The next "Hike" would bring feet quickly back in and hands slapping on hip or thigh pads. That would repeat five or six times, and then move on to the next exercise. That was only one of the many changes Coach Bryant and his staff implemented. He emphasized quickness over size. His teams featured re-action, toughness and aggressive play.

His practices were extremely well organized. The schedule was broken up into periods. At the end of a period, the head manager blew a whistle and ev-eryone — players and coaches alike — would sprint toward the place on the field for the next period. His games were also different from the rest of the league. In his first year, he was not blessed with a lot of talent from the Whit-worth era. His plan was to be as good as possible on defense. The substitution rules required players to play both ways. If a player came out twice in a quarter, they couldn't re-enter in that quarter. He put his best players there, but if you couldn't play defense, you didn't make the first team. The offense, with less talent, was designed not to lose the game with turnovers and big losses of yard-age. Field-position football was the way the game was played. Much time was spent on the kicking game.

The defense was aggressive and often caused fumbles or intercepted passes. If they occurred on the opponent's side of the field, the offense could some-times score touchdowns, but at least they needed to kick field goals. Not many teams scored much in those days. A 21-14 game was a high-scoring game.

One of Coach Bryant's favorite plays when he had a defensive team much better than an offense was the "quick kick." The offense lined up in a typical T-formation with the quarterback under center, the fullback behind the quar-terback, the tailback usually to the left or right of the fullback, and the wing-back lined up in one of several places on the opposite side of the tailback. He might be in the backfield in a true T-formation, or he could line up in a slot between tackle and end, a wing outside the tight end, or flanker as a wideout. The center snapped the ball through the quarterback's legs to the fullback, who caught the ball, took one step to the right and kicked the ball end-over-end over the defensive safety's head. Because of the relatively low angle, the ball usually hit and rolled a long way. It was not uncommon for a quick kick to go 50-60 yards.

In his first season at Alabama, Coach Bryant used that play a lot. If Alabama was backed up deep in its own territory he would often kick on first or second down to catch the opponent off-guard and to gain valuable field position for his team.

One of Coach Bryant's close friends was successful businessman Julian Lack-ey. I was talking to him one day and asked what he thought about how Coach Bryant was doing in his first year. He said, "He's my man, he's turning Alabama football around, I don't understand what he's doing, but I think he's doing a great job!"

There was no doubt that there was a new sheriff in town and good things were about to happen with Alabama football. As the season progressed, it became clear to me that I wanted to be a part of Coach Bryant's program. I thought I could get a good education at any of the schools under consideration, but at the end of the day, I believed if a boy could make it through Coach Bryant's program for four years, he would become a real man.

Coach Bryant came to my house when I signed. My dad had invited our preacher to attend the signing. Coach Bryant got there early and had great conversation with my mom, dad and me. Before too long, Coach Bryant said laughingly, "I've never had to wait on a preacher before in signing a player." Fortunately, Dr. Harold Martin showed up pretty soon thereafter and all ended very well.

At the time, I weighed 178 pounds. In those days, the better players on our high school team played the whole 48 minutes. I was rather emaciated, but Coach Bryant told me, "Don't gain any weight." He believed in being lean, mean and quick.

After I signed, I was told they would help me get a job during the Christmas holidays, and summer if I wanted one. The job I got that Christmas was with EBSCO Industries, a Birmingham firm that began as a magazine subscription company, but today is one of the largest private companies in Alabama and one of the top 200 in the nation. My job was selling magazine subscriptions. I made 50 percent of all the money I collected on sales. Coach Bryant gave me the names of a few people to call on.

The job introduced me to some neat people, who sent me to other people, and I very much enjoyed getting to know them. In addition, I made a couple of hundred bucks, which in 1959 was a lot of money to me.

That summer I worked at a subsidiary of Baggett Transportation. North American Tractor and Trailer had offices in Birmingham. It was hot, tough work all summer, but helped get me in good shape for the fall. We primarily worked on over-the-road trailers. The worst two jobs there involved working inside trailers in 95-degree weather: replacing the insulation in the sides and tops; and following the welder to grind the welds under the bottom of the trailers. The insulation was made of fiberglass, so particles would get all over you, make you itch and scratch, far beyond when you completed the job. To grind the welds, you laid on your back on the ground under the trailer and held the grinder up to "neaten up" the welding materials. Sparks flew everywhere, many hitting your face, arms and body. In Birmingham summer heat, those were two tough jobs! But it paid $1.65 an hour, and those were pretty good wages in 1959.

When August 1959 rolled around, I was invited to play in the Alabama All-Star Game in Tuscaloosa and the Wigwam-Wiseman All-American Game in Baton Rouge, Louisiana. In the Alabama All-Star Game, we got to meet all the players from around the state. Most were going to Alabama, Auburn or Mississippi State. One of my most vivid recollections about that experience was early in practice, when I kept hearing loud collisions going on in different drills around the practice field. It didn't take long to figure out that Lee Roy Jordan was involved in most of them. Lee Roy came from Excel, Alabama, with a population of 500. Being from Birmingham, I had not heard of him before, but surely was glad he was on my team that game and at Alabama the next four years.

We rode the train, which was a very interesting experience for me, to the All-American Game in Baton Rouge. Buster Frank from Huntsville was on the train when we started. Buster's brother Butch was a senior player on Alabama's 1959 team. It seemed like at every of the many stops we made, other players in the game boarded the train.

Billy Jackson was a Georgia signee I met on the train. Billy was an outstanding running back from Florida. We got to be friends during our stay that week. Billy was very confident and explained that his family and friends expected him to be the MVP in the game. I thought at first that was arrogance, and those that could do it didn't need to talk about it. But he was very good in practice and did end up winning the MVP award. I discovered that what Billy had was confidence and not arrogance, and if you can back up what you say, it's not bragging.

One of the funny things that happened was we all received watches with the Wigwam-Wiseman logo on the face, except I didn't get one in my packet. When I went over to check on it, the person I talked to said they were out. Then he said, "Oh, wait a minute." He went in the back and brought one out and gave it to me. When I got back to my room, I found it didn't work, but I had the souvenir anyway!

REPORTING TO ALABAMA IN 1959

The 1959 class was the first "full class" that Coach Bryant and his staff signed. About half of the 1958 class was signed by Coach Whitworth's staff. We had all heard stories about how tough the first year was and how many players quit. Some left in the middle of practice. Others left after everyone had gone to bed, as footlockers being dragged downstairs were heard many times.

I think in some ways Coach Bryant protected us as we were "his players." We signed up after his first year and understood what was expected of us — at least we thought we did. There was a drastic change in most every respect from high school.

We were assigned to live in Friedman Hall, formerly known as the "Ape Dorm" in reference to the undisciplined players that occupied the building in the previous few years. Coach Bryant changed that image and the culture of the team right off the bat. His first meeting with the 1958 team was scheduled right after lunch at 1:00. The team meeting room was right across the hall from the dining hall. Promptly at 1:00, the meeting room door was closed, with an assistant coach positioned outside. I am told that those who came late were not allowed to enter, and told to pack their bags and get out of the dorm.

I wasn't there so I can't confirm whether or not that happened, but I do know that in the four years of my tenure we held regular team meetings in that room and usually right after lunch. Coach Bryant and a blackboard were positioned in the front of the room, just to the left of where the players entered. The team was seated in chairs facing the front. Those who came in late were usually confronted and embarrassed by Coach Bryant with the whole team watching. Our motto for meetings became "Better Never Than Late." It was almost better to skip the meeting and hope roll call wasn't taken or you were otherwise not missed. But it did ingrain in us to get there early.

The dining room was a cafeteria-style room with four-top tables throughout. Players entered the room, moved to the left and walked down to the front where they picked up a tray and moved it along a rail to the right. First up were salads and/or fruit and dessert. Then the steam table carried the meats and vegetables. Then came the milk or iced tea. We were allowed only one serving, and one pint of milk. Heck, when I was in high school after a practice I'd come home and drink a quart of milk before ever starting to eat! Coach Bryant wanted his players lean, mean, quick and agile.

There was one phone in the dorm, which was positioned just outside a small lobby that might seat eight to 10 people. As you might imagine, long lines appeared outside the phone booth, and players in line were pretty aggressive about making the conversations of the occupants short and sweet.

Coach Bryant told me when I signed that I was going to be the next "swing end." I wasn't exactly sure what that meant, but because I was a pass-catching end my junior and seniors year in high school, I assumed it meant a lot of passes would be coming my way. When I got the playbook, I thought they had left out the section on passes. Coach Bob Ford, our freshman coach, told me, "Oh no, the playbook is complete. Coach Bryant believes in that old saying that when you pass, three things happen, and two of them are bad." I quickly decided I had better learn to block and play defense.

When we reported to the equipment room to draw our uniforms, I was shocked. It was the worst I had ever seen. The shoes were old high-top shoes and very stiff. They appeared to be worn by players for many years previously.

Pants, jerseys, shoulder pads and gear were all hand-me-downs. The jerseys had a flap that came from the rear end through the crotch and attached to buttons on the front. Our equipment at West End, at least on the varsity, was far superior to what they gave us at Alabama. I know money was a problem in those early days, but as time and winning football games progressed, equipment and facilities improved dramatically.

The equipment manager at the time was another freshman named Sang Lyda. Sang was passing out the old worn-out gear and took a lot of flack from the players. It bounced off him like water off a duck, and a big smile and quick wit made a very positive impression. We all became good friends and teammates. Sang loved Alabama so much, he never left until he retired.

Gary White, the head manager, said of Sang, "He never met a stranger. He could be around someone for a minute, and when he left, they would be friends. Sang served as a manger in his early career and a trainer under the legendary Coach Jim Goostree for most of his years. Sang retired in 1995 and was inducted into the Alabama Athletic Trainers Association Hall of Fame in 1998. Sang passed away in 2016 at age 75. Wimp Sanderson, longtime assistant and head basketball coach, said of Sang, "He was a friend to all the players. He decided whether they could play or not and wouldn't allow the coach to play them unless they were well enough to play. He set a great example for the players and is truly missed."

Coach Bryant and his staff heavily emphasized that winning was expected. A sign in his office read, "Winning isn't everything but it sure beats anything that comes in second." He also had a sign that read, "When the going gets tough the tough get going."

One of the first examples of teaching players the importance of winning took place in 1958 after the first A-Day spring game. The staff divided and drafted players for their respective teams. They were told that after the game, the losing team would have to serve the winning team dinner. The winning team feasted on a steak with a nice salad, baked potato, green beans and apple pie a la mode for dessert. When they finished dinner and exited the dining hall, the losing team went through the cafeteria line. They were served a bowl of soup and an apple! Do you think they got the message?

Coach Bryant believed that steak was the best of all dinner options. As a result, players on the training table ate steak every night during the season. We still went through the cafeteria line and only had one serving, but football training table food for the travel team was far better than what the rest of the team and other student-athletes were served.

He also believed that if football didn't make it, no sports would make it at Alabama. As athletics director and head football coach, he had a lot of power.

He made Hayden Riley, an assistant basketball coach, his head football recruiter. He also took scholarships from other sports to bring in football players. It seemed like we had 100 players report for duty my freshman year, including 200-pound swimmers and track athletes.

When other conference universities complained about these tactics, the Southeastern Conference passed a rule saying that if a player wasn't on a football scholarship, he could not compete in a varsity game. So Coach Bryant then offered one-year Olympic sport scholarships to football players. If they proved to be good in their first year, he would put them on football scholarship the next three years. That led to the rule that if a player did not sign a football or basketball scholarship, they could never play either sport.

In those days, football rules provided for limited substitutions. Players could only enter a quarter twice. There was one exception on offense and defense for a "wildcard player" who could enter as much as needed. That required every player to be able to play both offense, defense, and all plays in the kicking game. As such, practices were organized accordingly; defensive coaches would occupy one end of the field and offensive coaches on the other during team drills.

Paul Dietzel, a young coach at LSU, started a trend of having three squads: the "First Team," the "Chinese Bandits" and the "Go Team." The "First Team" practiced about 50 percent of team drills on offense and a like amount on defense. The "Chinese Bandits" practiced about 60 percent on defense and 40 percent on offense. Their name suggested they were as tough on defense as a gang of Chinese bandits. The "Go Team" practiced 60 percent on offense and 40 percent on defense. The "Third Team," if you will, didn't get to play much. That was how our team practices were set up. Everyone participated in the kicking game practices. Coach Dietzel figured out how to motivate all those teams receiving recognition, which worked better than calling them the first, second and third teams. That experiment strongly suggests there is value in titles.

The limited substitution rule made it difficult for players above 225 pounds or so to play. Weight training was pretty much non-existent during my time at Alabama. There were individuals who believed in lifting weights, and did so on their own, but there was very little emphasis on lifting for the team. Heavy emphasis was placed on quickness, speed, agility and toughness.

That is why Coach Bryant limited the amount of food we ate in the cafeteria. He talked about those "big, fat boys at Auburn" and how we would "out-quick them." Auburn's training table provided family-style servings of meat, vegetables, etc., placed on tables for players to eat as much as they wanted. It was actually pretty nice for the players and may have helped in recruiting as well.

He often talked about Auburn in a negative light. Some of his choice comments were, "I'd rather beat that cow college across the state than all the rest of the teams on our combined schedule." One day he called Auburn's office about 7 a.m. and asked to speak to Coach Jordan. The receptionist said, "Our coaches don't come in until 8:00." Coach Bryant said, "What's the matter honey, don't y'all take your football seriously!" There was no doubt heavy emphasis was placed on preparing for and beating Auburn.

So understanding that Auburn had massacred Alabama from 1954 to 1957 and Coach Bryant returning to Alabama in 1958, how many points do you think Auburn scored on Alabama during my four years there from 1959 to 1962? Would you believe none? If so, you'd be right — zero, zippo, nada! Scores were 10-0 (1959), 3-0 (1960), 34-0 (1961) and 38-0 (1962).

Years later when Coach Bryant was our first client in our sports management and licensing division, I got a chance to see all the contracts he signed with Alabama. I had taken him some licensing contracts to review and approve. They were in a manila envelope. When I handed them to him, he turned around and put them in the credenza behind him. The next week I called and told him I would be there Thursday and I needed those contracts. He said he would have to get them as they were in his vault at the bank. I couldn't imagine why he would have put those contracts in his vault, but told him again I was coming Thursday and needed to pick them up.

When I came to see him he handed me a manila envelope, which I stuck in my briefcase. When I got home and opened it, there were all of his employment agreements with the University of Alabama. I couldn't believe it. His first contract paid him $17,500. He didn't want to make more than the Deans. But, the university did furnish him with a house in Indian Hills and a $10,000 a year expense account, which he did not need to report to the school.

The most remarkable document was a letter from President Rose after Coach Bryant had led Alabama to its first "real" National Championship in 1961, i.e., by the Associated Press and United Press International. The letter read partially like this:

Dear Paul,

Congratulations on winning your first National Championship. You have brought honor and fame back to the University of Alabama in the few short years you have been here. You are gracious to turn down our offer to reward you for the championship, but we are sending you a check for $5,000 anyway.

Coach Bryant coached from 1958 to 1982 and never let the university pay him $100,000 until about 1978 or '79 when he learned his retirement was based on the last three years of employment. He never made a lot of money, but people did give him a lot of stuff. At Texas A&M, I think a wealthy oil man gave him an oil well that produced some annual income. Only when Jimmy Hinton gave him some stock in Zeigler Meats did he ever make any serious money. It wasn't long after that that the Pope rescinded the requirement that Catholics couldn't eat meat on Fridays. Of course, ardent Alabama fans said it happened because of Coach Bryant's ownership in a meat company!

Coach Bryant really didn't need money. He lived for doing what he loved to do, which was to coach football and mold boys into men. He was the best ever at that in his time.

Freshmen were not eligible to play on the varsity during my time at Alabama. In 1959 we played three freshman games under Coach Bob Ford. Most of our time at practice was spent helping put on the offenses and defenses of the varsity opponents each week. We did go through individual drills working on fundamentals, but did not have time for a lot of preparation against our three opponents.

Our first freshman game was against Mississippi State in Denny Stadium (before it became Bryant-Denny Stadium). When we arrived, the stadium seated 32,000. There were bleachers in the north end zone and nothing in the south end zone. In a few years Coach Bryant built a nice little house on the grounds outside the south end zone as a recruiting hospitality center where coaches entertained prospects and their parents before and after games. It was a first-class facility, as were all things built by Coach Bryant — people and buildings.

About the only thing I remember about that game (or any of the three freshman games for that matter) was that we were three points ahead with the ball on our own 5-yard line and about a minute to play. Coach Bryant came down from the press box or stands, or wherever he was sitting, and signaled for us to call time out. He told us to give them a safety. On the fourth down, he told us to get in punt formation, for the line to hold out their rushers as long as we could, and for the punter to secure the ball tightly, move around along the back boundary line as long as he could, and step out of the end zone before anyone got close to hitting him.

We had never practiced that, and honestly, I had never heard of doing that, but we executed the safety. That gave Mississippi State two points. After the safety, we were still ahead and were able to kick the ball to them from the 20-yard line. We had played good defense throughout the game, and were able to hold them for the remaining seconds on the clock. I thought that was a brilliant strategy!

Our second game was against Tulane in New Orleans. We flew out of Tuscaloosa in two old planes, Martin 4-0-4s. For most of us, it was our first flight ever. We stayed in the Jung Hotel, which to us was the height of luxury. One of our players, Tom Bible, we were told, came from a home with no electricity or running water. He was an outstanding player who lived outside of Piedmont,

Alabama. He was "Mister Inside" and high school teammate Carlton Rankin, who also signed at Alabama, was "Mister Outside." They won a state championship at Piedmont High School. As a side note, my grandfather, a Methodist preacher, built a church in Piedmont when he was assigned to that district.

Coach Ford called a team meeting in the hotel soon after our arrival. When the roll was called, Tom Bible was missing. Carlton said when he last saw him, he was outside the hotel watching the automatic doors open without anyone touching them. Sure enough, Tom was still outside watching people go through those doors, each time saying, "Amazing!"

I can't leave this place without telling a few more Bible stories. Tom's roommate was Marlin "Frog" Mooneyham. Most everyone on the team had a nickname, which were mostly given by upperclassmen. The second- and third-floor rooms in Friedman Hall were configured in four-bedroom wells. There was a common bathroom to accommodate occupants of those four bedrooms. One day soon after we arrived at Alabama, Tom went out to take a shower. When he came back in he said, "Man that water is cold!" Marlin said, "Isn't there any hot water?" He looked funny at Marlin and said "Hot water? There were three knobs and the first one turned on the water in the shower, the second one made the water come out at the bottom faucet, and I didn't see any need to turn on the third one!"

Tom was an accomplished hunter, fisherman and overall outdoorsman. Many days in the off-season, he would come in with a cooler of fish and it wasn't uncommon for the occupants of Tom and Marlin's four-bedroom to find live crappie swimming around in three of the four lavatories in the common bathroom, until he found time to clean them.

Being resourceful from his upbringing outside of Piedmont, Tom got tired of buying minnows to catch fish. His solution was to remove the screens from the outside dorm windows and make minnow traps.

Tom was also somewhat skilled as a taxidermist. The first dead animal that I recall him bringing to the dorm was a beaver that he had killed and stuffed. He used the stuffing from an upholstered chair in his room. He placed it just inside his closet, facing outward. His room was one that attracted other players for "bull sessions." When they came in one by one after hearing conversation and laughter, Marlin would announce that his mom had sent a pack of her famous chocolate chip cookies, and ask the guest to fetch them from the closet. When they opened the door and saw that beaver staring at them, the reactions ranged from screaming and jumping half way across the room, to slamming the door shut and cursing up a storm.

Tom was deaf in one ear with a busted eardrum. The word was he could inhale a cigarette, hold his nose and blow smoke out his ear. I never saw that but I did know he had an alarm clock with a bell on each side and a hammer in the middle. If Tom was sleeping with his good ear down and the alarm went off, it would not only wake everyone in that four-bedroom well, but the vibrations from the hammer swinging back and forth against the bells would walk the clock off the table and add a crash on the floor as the grand finale.

Unfortunately, Tom met with an untimely death a few weeks after we left for summer vacation before our senior year. On the last day of finals, Tom and I went over to a small lake in Northport where earlier I had caught a 5 ½-pound bass, the biggest I had ever caught. The next day he left for his new home in Mobile where his family had moved.

The story I heard was that Tom took his 10-year-old nephew fishing with him in a creek that must have been pretty cold. It was deep in the woods and probably a few miles from the main road. Tom's fishing lure got hung up in the middle of the creek on a sunken log. After trying several ways to shake it loose, he decided to swim out and get it. A short while later he surfaced and was thrashing around. His nephew said, "Uncle Tom are you playing with me?" Tom said, "Go get help." The young man couldn't drive and had to run back to the highway, flag down a car, and get someone to come out with him. By that time, Tom had drowned. We heard that most every muscle in his body had cramped. Of all the ways for Tom Bible to die, drowning would have been at the bottom of the list. Our team was devastated.

Now, back to our freshman year. Unfortunately, we lost to Tulane, and Coach Ford was pretty harsh with words toward us. We did go on to beat Auburn in Auburn. Again, no one really got too excited about freshman games, but it was important for us to improve after the Tulane loss, and especially to beat Auburn.

After the season I went to see Coach Sam Bailey, Coach Bryant's righthand man, and actually the person who did most of the "athletic directing" for him. The positions of head coach and athletics director are way too much for one man to handle without incredible staff support. Coach Bailey was all of that and more for Coach Bryant.

I asked Coach Bailey if I could sign up for that magazine-selling job again over the Christmas holidays. He said, "No, we've offered that job to a good junior-college running back who has signed with us." Reality had set in.

In those days we were given $15 a month laundry money. Every two weeks we would go into Coach Carney Laslie's office and get $7.50 whether we needed it or not. We would walk in one at a time. Coach Laslie had a big stack of bills with $5's on one side and $1's on the other. He had a big pile of quarters spread out around his desk. We would walk in and sign our names on a pad. Coach Laslie would pick up the stack of bills, lick his fingers and peel off a five and lay it down, turn the stack over in his hands, lick his finger again and peel off two ones, lay them down and push two quarters and the bills across the desk to us. I swear, I went through four years at Alabama, came in twice a month and Coach Laslie went through exactly that same routine every time. Fifteen dollars a month was not very much money, but I promise you there was no one on the team that missed picking up that $7.50 every two weeks.

The Athletics Department was located in the building that is Moore Hall today. Coach Bryant's office was on the ground floor, on northeast corner of the building facing the Quadrangle in front and Foster Auditorium on the east side. The freshmen dressed and showered upstairs, the varsity downstairs.

Foster Auditorium housed the varsity basketball practices and games. The main football practice field was out the back door of the Athletics Department heading south. Players crossed the street and walked between two women's dorms to get to a big field with Coach Bryant's tower in the middle. The fields were surrounded by women's dorms.

We occasionally practiced on Thomas Field, where the Alabama football team practices today. The only difference is that in 1959, I don't believe there was a single brick on what today is the Mal Moore Athletics Facility, the weight room/indoor practice field, the Sewell-Thomas Baseball Stadium and Coleman Coliseum. The only similarity between then and now are the green curtains surrounding the field Coach Bryant erected to prevent outsiders from watching practice.

When we went to Thomas Field to practice, we walked. We came out the back door of the Athletics Department, walked by the women's dorms and practice fields, and the few blocks heading east to Thomas Field at the intersection of what is now Paul Bryant Drive and Hackberry Lane. There was a bank on the northeast corner and a drive-in restaurant on the southwest corner called the Dog House. I vividly remember many times in the spring and fall seeing 100 degrees on the bank sign. On many occasions when we walked past the Dog House, the owner would come out with a big box of chewing gum and hand out sticks of gum to passing players.

My room in Friedman Hall was on the first floor and the southwest corner, which was in the back of the building with fraternity houses across the alley. There were four bedrooms in our little section, but they were configured differently from the upstairs wells. Butch Wilson, a big, fast running back from Hueytown, Alabama, was my roommate. Butch was a nice, quiet, personable young man off the field, but he would knock your block off on the field. He was a talented runner, but being such a good blocker, he didn't get to carry the ball as much as he probably deserved. Butch won the Jacobs Blocking Trophy his senior year, which went to the best blocker in the SEC. To me, that is the most prestigious award presented. He played five years with the Baltimore Colts and two with the New York Giants.

I would be remiss if I didn't tell some stories about Butch. He was one of the all-time great people, but did have a mischievous streak in him. He loved to lurk behind furniture indoors, or trees and bushes outside, then jump out and scare someone out of their wits when they walked by. After a couple of those, coming out of our bathroom at night after lights were out, nearly gave me heart attacks, I tried to always be alert when doing so in the future.

Two quick stories. Butch was bad to snore, and his bed and mine were end to end against one wall. I was a light sleeper and I don't remember him waking me up with snoring, but if he went to sleep before I did, it was hard for me to go to sleep. Finally I figured out how to solve the problem. I would turn out the lights, pull up the covers like I was asleep, and whistle as loud as I could. Because we were all conditioned to react to sound under Coach Bryant drills, Butch would pop up in the bed like a jack-in-the-box and look around for what caused that sound. It took months before he figured out that trick. I could lay down and hope to get to sleep before he started "sawing logs" again.

The other story involved Butch's goldfish. He was too cheap to buy a real goldfish bowl with pebbles and greenery, etc. for the fish to feed and get oxygen. He got a gallon mayonnaise jar out of the dining hall and put his three or four goldfish in the jar. If he didn't change the water regularly, the fish would come up to the top and gurgle for oxygen. As I said earlier, I was a light sleeper and couldn't go to sleep with noise in the room. The gurgling fish annoyed me and kept me from going to sleep. It sounded like water dripping to me. Between Butch's snoring and his fish gurgling, I had to really get creative. I gathered up several pairs of socks, each of which were rolled up into a ball. When I turned out the lights and the fish were gurgling, I would toss a pair of socks up on the dresser, hit the jar, causing the goldfish to scurry to the bottom. I would try to get to sleep before they came back to the top. Some nights it took several bombings before I went to sleep.

Butch and I were both pretty quiet and maybe even a little shy. Buddy Wesley, a small senior linebacker, and one of Coach Bryant's favorites due to his toughness and all-out effort, said about Butch and me, "I bet there aren't five words a semester uttered to each other by those guys!" We actually talked a lot, but we both believed "actions speak louder than words."

Butch dated and later married Susie Vines, one of my fellow schoolmates at West End High School. After his professional career, they settled on a beautiful farm just off I-20/59 in McCalla, Alabama. While Butch successfully ran a family-owned and operated sporting goods store for years, he was able, for the most part, to live his dream, which was, "to sit on his porch and watch his cows grow."

Back in the dorm, Darwin Holt and JoJo Sisia were in the adjoining rooms connected by a common toilet and shower. On the other side of the hall were Mike Fracchia and Cotton Clark, and Buford Shirley and Hugh Ogle were also in the adjoining room. Darwin was a small linebacker at Texas A&M and the only Aggie player to follow Coach Bryant to Alabama. He may have been small but he sure played big in games. Cotton was a good running back and a great free safety. More about him later. Fracchia was a great running back who was the MVP in the Sugar Bowl in our National Championship Game against Arkansas on Jan. 1, 1962.

Coach Bobby Drake Keith, a young A&M graduate and end coach, lived in the dorm at that time with his wife. He and Gene "Bebes" Stallings were the ends on Coach Bryant's first team at Texas A&M that experienced firsthand the infamous pre-season camp in Junction, Texas. A book and movie were written about "The Junction Boys."

Mike Fracchia came into our room at the end of our first semester and sat down to talk to Butch and me. He told about how he was signed up for four courses, and when he went to the first class, his name wasn't called during roll call. He said he never went back. He was definitely at practice every day and was the best running back on the field — freshman or varsity. Butch and I were both dumbfounded. One of us stammered out, "Well what did you do with your time?" He said, "I just went to the Supe Store, drank coffee and visited with the coeds." He asked me, "What would you do?" I said, "I think I would go home!" We finally came to our senses and told him to go see Coach Keith. In a few minutes we heard the door to our suite open, and as they were opening the door to Mike's room, we heard Coach Keith say, "Now what do you mean you haven't gone to class all year?" Whatever they did, Mike made up his classes in the spring and summer semesters and was eligible to play our sophomore season. Thank goodness he did, as he became one of Alabama's all-time best running backs. Unfortunately, a knee injury cut short his professional career, but we would not have won the national title in 1961 without him.

After the 1959 football season, we had a few weeks off in January since in our semester system, finals were not taken until the second week after we came back to school. Soon after that we began "Winter Workouts." We had heard they were pretty bad, and they lived up to expectations. They were held up-stairs in a gymnasium in the Athletics Department. It was not well ventilated and had a musty smell. There were garbage cans positioned at several places around the gym that were there as we "worked out the impurities" from Christmas holidays.

There were four stations, with the first being agility drills on a mat, and wrestling on the second mat. At the third station, we worked on blocking and tackling drills against dummies, and the fourth was a weight-training session. The first three were so taxing, that the weight station was more of a catch-your-breath time. Light weights were used and we weren't pushed too hard there.

The garbage cans drew considerable attention and use, especially during the first couple of weeks. Coach Bryant believed that there was more carryover from spring training to fall camp if spring training was pushed back as late as possible in the spring semester. That meant the "Winter Workouts" lasted longer. We were definitely in good shape when spring practice began.

Our first spring was not nearly as difficult physically as expected. There was no immediate pressure to get players ready to play games. The coaches were trying to look at all players to determine who to play at what position in fall camp. Coach Bryant recruited athletes. Many fullbacks became guards. There was at least one quarterback in high school that played tackle at Alabama.

We worked a lot on fundamentals, as you might imagine, and had some tough drills. Coach Bryant spent a lot of time on his tower where he could see all drills. The original tower was made of wood and was primitive compared to his later ones made of metal. He did have a metal railing at the top to keep him from falling, and there was a chain that latched over the opening he used to enter and exit.

Because most of his coaches either played for him or coached for him at early ages, we found that they were maybe more scared of him than we were. There could be groups on both fields scattered all around the tower. When the chain clanked against the vertical rail, eyes from all over the field switched to the tower to see him coming down. When he hit the ground, activity in all groups picked up considerably, especially in those areas to which he was heading. It was not unusual for him to single out a player and show him how to block or tackle, often knocking them to the ground. He was still a big, strong guy.

When team drills came, there were so many players they wanted to look at that most positions had alternates. Obviously, with no alternate you participated in every play your team ran. If you had an alternate, you only participated in half of the plays. We would check out the practice list beforehand to not only see where we were listed, but to see if we had alternates.

Tommy Brooker, Bill Rice, Jap Patton, Mike Hopper, Jimmy Box and I were all ends. Six ends meant that all three teams had an alternate. Bill Rice, who was a real character, walked in the dressing room one day and said, "Where the *%#! is Brooker?" Someone said, "He has gone to his grandmother's funeral." Bill said, "That lucky S.O.B., I don't even have a grandmother!" Bill ended up having a successful business career and spent his last few years teaching in his hometown at Troy University. I know he was a great teacher, because he had so many stories to tell about his very exciting and energetic upbringing. I would have loved to have attended one of his classes.

When spring practice ended, I was listed on the first team. We had time to prepare for final exams and I did pretty well in my first year of academics at Alabama. On advice from my dad, I enrolled in the College of Arts and Sciences, and took English, history, Spanish and biology. My biology teachers were the most interesting, and those courses were the most enjoyable to me. I couldn't wait for fall practice to come around, but I was soon to learn, my education in big-time college football was just about to begin.

THE SOPHOMORE YEAR

In the summer of 1960 I again worked at North American Tractor and Trailer sweating, replacing insulation in tractor walls, grinding welds on the under trailer, and many more jobs that tended to keep me in pretty good shape. In addition, the coaches sent us workout programs that started fairly mildly in July but increased in intensity in August. Those who went by those instructions came back in pretty good shape.

The big test when we returned to school was running a mile. I think backs and ends had to run a mile in 6 minutes and linemen in 6:30. I cannot recall exactly which, but those were close. Not many missed their required times. Those who did had to work out after practice, which was difficult to ever get back in shape and still learn the lessons taught in fall camp.

The atmosphere in the fall was much more intense than in the spring. The first weeks were designed to determine who had improved from spring to fall, and get the right players in the right positions. As I said, I had a chance to be a starter. I was in good physical shape, but I soon found out I did not have a clue about what it takes to win at the college level. I had never been through the mental toughness required to live through constant practices and game film sessions. Coaches ran plays back and forth on 16-millimeter projectors showing either lack of effort or poor technique. It took a while to be able to take hard criticism in front of the whole team and have the mental discipline to make that a learning experience. To me, at first, it was a teardown of confidence.

The week before our first game we found out six players were ruled academically ineligible and could not play in 1960. We opened with Georgia in Birmingham. I had been injured and did not get to play much in our 21-6 victory over the Bulldogs. What I recall about that game was a good Georgia running back named "Flying Fred" Brown. He was the only player on the field who was not wearing a facemask. I guess the rules didn't make facemasks mandatory at that time. Most of the backs and ends had a one-bar facemask that offered some protection, but frequently allowed elbows above and below the bar.

Our defense chased Georgia quarterback Fran Tarkenton all over Legion Field, keeping him in check. Pat Trammell and Bobby Skelton played quarterback for Alabama. Bobby was a free spirit and an asset to the team as a passer and keeping us loose with his antics. Pat was a great leader and an outstanding all-around quarterback. He was All-State in football and basketball, and a pre-med student from Scottsboro, Alabama.

We scored all three touchdowns in the second quarter and played dominant defense throughout the game. Billy Richardson ran for 105 yards and was named SEC Back of the Week. Following Coach Bryant's philosophy of "Three things happen when you pass and two of them are bad," Alabama threw eight passes and completed three for 29 yards. Billy Jackson, my buddy from the Wigwam-Wiseman game in the summer, returned a fourth-quarter punt for 78 yards to set up Georgia's only score.

"Not since Red Drew's 1954 eleven slammed Tennessee 27-0 has the Tide exhibited a more devastating punch against a SEC rival," reported one newspaper.

The next week we played Tulane to an ugly 6-6 tie in New Orleans. Tulane scored toward the end of the first half but missed the point-after attempt to take a 6-0 lead into halftime. The Tulane line outweighed the Crimson Tide line, and offensive output was limited by both teams.

We failed on three chances in the red zone, with one missed field goal and two on downs. Pat Trammell led a last-minute 55-yard drive for the tying touchdown. On fourth down at the Tulane 25 Trammell hit Butch Wilson (my roommate for three years) for 19 yards to the Tulane 6. Two plays later Trammell scored on a 4-yard keeper. A bad snap from center kept us from attempting the winning point-after. Alabama fumbled eight times and lost three. An onside kick was successful, recovering the ball at the Tulane 46. A 36-yard pass from Trammell to Tommy White made it to the Tulane 12 as time expired.

The press was complimentary: "As fine a fourth quarter as any Alabama team has played. They took control of the game on offense and defense." As was Coach Bryant: "We didn't hit anybody in the first half, but the boys acted like they wanted to play in the second half."

On Sunday when I went over to watch the film with the coaches, Bud Moore had already had his session with them. I said, "How did it go?" He said, "Rough, and you had a bad game." I replied incredulously, "I did?" I didn't remember doing anything bad. When we went through the film, I didn't really do anything too bad. I just didn't do much of anything! That film session was not much fun to watch. Coaches were yelling and it was not a pretty scene. I was just beginning to learn "The Big Eye Don't Lie" — as the film sessions were called.

Alabama and Vanderbilt games over the previous three years ended in ties. Before the 1960 game, Coach Bryant said, "If we tie this one, we ought to quit playing."

We beat Vanderbilt 21-0 in Birmingham the following week under what was billed as "A major nighttime football debut." On Tuesday of that week we had a full scrimmage. Coach Bryant said afterward, "We went about it more like menfolk than what we've been doing. It was just the kind of thing this team needed."

After a scoreless first half, we scored three touchdowns and a safety. After a Vandy fumble on the first play of the second half at their 28, we ground out an eight-play drive with Billy Richardson scoring from the 1-yard line. On the next Vandy series, a snap over the punter's head resulted in a safety and a 9-0 lead. Bama took the ensuing free kick and marched 49 yards with a perfect 36-yard Skelton to Norbie Ronsonet touchdown pass. Bud Moore, a tackle, and my former teammate from West End, intercepted a late fourth-quarter pass and took it 32 yards for the final touchdown.

"Vandy got the best of the Tide in the first half as they made six first downs to Alabama's one, but those gallant Bama forwards simply knocked the fight out of Vandy with terrific tackling," said one press report. "Vandy crumbled before the hard knocking of the Crimson Tide in the second half. Alabama's kicking game was great."

During fall camp and the first few games of the season, Coach Bryant put me on either the first team or the third team. I would have probably been satisfied with being on the second team as a sophomore, but I sure wasn't happy being on the third team. I believe he was sending me a message to either be good or be gone. Whether he was or wasn't, I busted my tail trying to move up, and I did!

On the third Saturday in October, we played Tennessee in Knoxville. As discussed earlier, Coach Bryant's record in eight games at Kentucky, one at Texas A&M and two at Alabama was 1-8-2. He seemed much more tense and nervous about this game than any others thus far in the season.

Tennessee featured a single-wing attack and was coached by a General Neyland disciple named Bowden Wyatt. The backfield formation consisted of a tailback who stood about 4 or 5 yards behind the center, a fullback who normally lined up behind either guard and about 3 or 4 yards deep, and a wingback who lined up usually right behind a guard or an end. The tailback was a good all-around athlete who could run, pass and kick. The fullback was a good blocker and ball carrier. The wingback was a blocker first and ball carrier second. The wingback in 1960 was Jim Cartwright, a three-time Jacobs Trophy winner awarded to the best blocker in the SEC.

We had an open date before Tennessee, which gave us two weeks to prepare. I made it back into the starting lineup for the UT game, but was a little wary of our defensive game plan — at least as it pertained to my position at end. In the single-wing attack on sweeps around end, the wingback teamed up with either a pulling guard or the fullback to attack the end. We were taught to take on the top blocker with shoulder and forearm, as we typically did with all blockers. However, we were taught to take on the lower blocker with our hip, which didn't make much sense to me, and it didn't work as Tennessee won 20-7.

Pat Trammell didn't play against the Vols due to injury. The game got off to an awful start for us on the opening kickoff with a big collision and a lot of bodies flying around. Laying on the ground, I saw Buddy Wesley lying face down with arms extended in front of him. His hands were quivering. He was unconscious, probably a concussion. The helmets we wore in those days were called "suspension helmets." The plastic shell was very visible inside. Connected to a band fastened to the inside circumference of the helmet were bands that met in the top of the helmet. They were all tied together with a small piece of rope in a knot. A rubber connector fit through the rope circle to hold it in place with a larger piece that covered the outside of the rope, protecting the head from the rope. For whatever reason, on purpose or not, Buddy had not put that rubber piece in his helmet.

On the first play from scrimmage, we fumbled and Tennessee recovered. Five plays later Billy Majors flipped an 8-yard pass for a touchdown. We received the kickoff and did not make a first down. On the punt, the ball hit our punter in the hands, bounced to the ground, and Mike Lasorsa caught the ball on one bounce and took it 41 yards untouched into the end zone to take a 14-0 lead with only three minutes gone from the clock.

We played the rest of the game 7-6 but dug too deep a hole to get out of in the first five minutes. We led UT 11-5 on first downs, 185-30 rushing, and 67-8 passing. We also fumbled five times, lost two and lost the game 20-7. After getting ahead 14-0, Tennessee went very conservative on offense and protected its lead. Neither team scored in the second half.

From a team perspective, it actually wasn't as bad as it sounded, at least to me. Individually, however, I knew I had a bad day on defense. Jim Cartwright and a good single-wing attack made it tough on our defensive ends, and especially for me.

Coach Bryant didn't fly back on the plane with us. Coach Pat James, our defensive line coach, was the assistant in charge of that game. Coach Bryant assigned an assistant coach to take one team and study that team all year. He would assist heavily in the game plan and give the weekly scouting report to our team.

On the plane ride back to Birmingham, we didn't have anything to eat. Normally we would have a box lunch of sandwiches, fried chicken, or something. We landed in Birmingham, and before getting on the bus back to Tuscaloosa, most tried to stop at a concession stand and get something to eat or drink on the ride home.

When we got back to the dorm, Coach James blasted us. He fumed, "I saw you *%#!ers buying candy and stuff at the airport. Bed check tonight is 11:00, and if you aren't here, you might as well not come back. And besides that, you'll have a 'gut check' every day next week."

We got that message loud and clear, but to get the real message we all found a place to watch Coach Bryant's TV show that came on at 1:00 every Sunday afternoon. He wanted the show to be in the afternoon to give people around the state a chance to go to church in the morning. The "Bear Bryant Show" was probably the most watched program in Alabama. Coach Bryant was a great communicator, and he used this forum to recruit, raise money, and schmooze people at the university and around the state to make them feel good, and make Alabama football relevant.

Coca-Cola and Golden Flake sponsored his show. There was always a cold Coke and bowl of Golden Flake potato chips on the set. Since we didn't have a television set in the dorm, we typically went to various homes, fraternity or sorority houses to watch the show to gauge Coach Bryant's mood. Maury Farrell was the moderator and opened with "Well Coach, it was a tough day in Knoxville yesterday but we still have a cold Coca-Cola and some good Golden Flake potato chips to ease the pain a little." Coach Bryant shoved the bottle and bowl to the side, looked directly into the camera with a scowl and said, "I don't know about that Maury, but I do know our players have been sitting in meetings looking at their watches and wearing that sweet-smelling aftershave lotion eager to get over to Sorority Row. I'll tell you one thing, this week we're going to run off the riff-raff!" He went on to say, "We beat ourselves before the game got started. The first thing we need to do is get fundamentally sound and start fighting for our lives."

If you don't think that scared the daylights out of all of our team, you must be from a different planet. That week may have been the worst week of my life. Coach Bryant put different colors on each team in practice. The first team wore crimson, the second team wore white, the third team wore blue, and the fourth team wore green. When I went to get my basket, I had an orange jersey! It was terrible, but I did manage to play my way back up to the first team.

A week later, Lee Roy Jordan recovered a Houston fumble on the 31-yard line, then eight plays later quarterback Goobie Stapp, playing for the injured Trammell, scored on a 1-yard end run. On the next series, Billy Richardson intercepted a pass and returned it 12 yards to the Houston 18-yard line, then Richardson dove in for the score with 1:50 remaining in the first period.

Houston's ball-control offense pushed for a 17-play, 73-yard drive to the Alabama 9 in the second quarter and a 16-play, 54-yard drive to the Tide 12 in the third, but both threats were stymied by the Tide defense.

Butch Wilson's interception in the fourth quarter gave Alabama its only taste of Houston territory in the second half. Moving from our own 48 to the Cougar 16, we turned the ball over on downs as the clock wound down in the 14-0 win. We outgained Houston on the ground 185-118 but the Cougars had an 118-3 passing yardage advantage. Stapp's punting was a big factor, booting six for a 45.2 average, including one for 62 yards that got the Tide out of trouble after a third-quarter Houston drive. And Richardson got off a 64-yard quick kick in the second quarter.

"If they were the New York Giants I couldn't be prouder of them," Coach Bryant told Frank Clayton of *The Tuscaloosa News* about his team during a lull in the singing and laughing by the Crimson Tide in the dressing room. "I thought our linemen held them off pretty well, although Houston gained a lot of yards on hook passes." He went on to say, "Our line was outweighed but I was proud of the way they contained the Houston attack." We had planned to pass against them quite a bit, but after we got those two quick scores, we played it pretty close to the vest.

Charlie Land of *The Tuscaloosa News* wrote: "Alert Alabama cashed in on early Houston mistakes for a pair of first-quarter touchdowns and then outlasted the heavyweight Cougars for a 14-0 homecoming victory before 30,000 fans at Denny Stadium."

That week the University of Alabama Board of Trustees announced the approval of a 12,000-seat addition to Denny Stadium, which would take capacity from 30,000 to 42,000. They also approved the construction of a long-awaited field house. About the same time, Birmingham, billing itself as the "Football Capital of the South," committed to adding upper decks on both sides to increase Legion Field capacity to 50,000.

After Houston, we played Mississippi State in Starkville. We were ahead 7-0 at halftime and went in the locker room feeling pretty good. We were sitting around in chairs and some were in those desk-chairs like in grade school. Pat Trammell, our quarterback, and probably one of Coach Bryant's favorite players ever, was sitting in one of those desk-chairs with his helmet off and a Coke bottle on the desktop. Coach Bryant walked in, went over, grabbed Pat, and shook him. The Coke bottle went flying, and Coach Bryant told us how bad we were playing and how ashamed he was about how we were representing our university and our "mommas and papas"! We went out the second half and didn't play much better as the score ended 7-0.

The following week we played Furman and beat them 51-0 in Denny Stadium. This was our first game in Tuscaloosa. Coach Bryant wanted to get us out of the dorm, as parents and friends would hang out around Friedman Hall the night before and the day of the game. We spent Friday nights before home games in an old Army barracks at Northington campus. The campus had a very interesting history, and was later demolished. The old hospital building we stayed in was not in great shape, but was probably available to Coach Bryant at a very low cost. We slept on metal cots, which were not very comfortable. I would call the whole experience as "Spartan-like," being very generous. We had meetings, a pre-game meal, and got taped up before going to Denny Stadium to play the game. I don't think I remember this experience as something really cool, but it was cool to be a part of Coach Bryant's team wherever he took us, and it was nice to get away from the hustle and bustle of game day around the dorm.

As a side note about the Northington campus, Scott Parrott, *Tuscaloosa News* staff writer, wrote on July 23, 2003: "To some it was an eyesore. To others it was a historical treasure. Either way, very little remains of the Northington campus, once home to American GI's and hospital patients, movie sets and young married couples. Soon it will be all gone. Workers began tearing down the final eight buildings of the former military barracks and hospital last week, and by Tuesday afternoon, only one remained. Alan Scott of Virginia Wrecking Company said everything should be cleaned out in a month."

The University of Alabama, the landowner, wanted to sell the 5.05 acres between Northington Elementary School and University Mall for $1.3 million. That meant razing the old buildings to make the property more attractive.

The old red barracks tucked away behind McFarland Mall was once a part of Northington General Army Hospital. During World War II, the property held German prisoners. At one time, the property was bigger, but it was destroyed to build McFarland Mall. After World War II, the then-president of the University of Alabama, Raymond Paty, acquired Northington from the federal government and turned it into supplemental housing for veterans.

The land also became the property of the State Mental Health Department. The University and State Mental Health Department swapped, with UA taking the peach orchard near Bryce and the Mental Health Department taking Northington.

In the 1970s before the mall went up, change did not come easily. As many as 300 Northington area residents appeared for hearings for the rezoning of the property from institutional to business.

And then Burt Reynolds came along. Northington literally went up in smoke on the big screen for the 1979 stunt extravaganza film, "Hooper," starring Reynolds and Sally Field, and directed by Hal Needham. The movie contained stunt sequences shot in Tuscaloosa and Birmingham, some of which featured Northington's smoke stacks blowing up and falling down.

Mark Hughes Cobb, staff writer for *The Tuscaloosa News*, wrote on Sept. 6, 2018:

In February 1978, Burt Reynolds, who died Thursday at the age of 82, and the crew of "Hooper" shook up Tuscaloosa. Reynolds, along with co-star Sally Field, his then-girlfriend, Robert Klein and Jan-Michael Vincent flew in from Hollywood to shoot stunt scenes in and around the demolition of the old Northington hospital complex, making way for what is now University Mall.

Director Hal Needham had Reynolds and Field in the 1977 film "Smokey and the Bandit," a $300 million worldwide hit that helped the former stuntman find his dream project, "Hooper," about an aging performer (Reynolds) being chased by a young punk upstart (Vincent).

For a couple of weeks, Reynolds, Vincent, and stunt performers drove hot cars through, around and under falling smoke stacks, walls of fire, and gusts of debris expelled from collapsing buildings. The film crew nicknamed the perilous Northington shoot "Damnation Alley."

Warner Brothers had brought in about 150 cast and crew in late January, and hired hundreds of locals as extras and in various support services. The city of Tuscaloosa earned about $2,900 for eight firefighters on standby, and $1,000 for a licensing fee. Another $10,000 was paid to 47 off-duty policemen who provided crowd control for fans turning out to get a glimpse of the stars. Shooting began in Tuscaloosa on February 1, 1978; Needham estimated they spent about $1.2 million on the film, nearly one-sixth of the film's budget, on the 14 Northington stunts.

Crowds watched a Volkswagen shoot about 50 feet in the air, saw Klein, playing the director in the film-within-a-film, yelling at Reynolds and Vincent from a helicopter, and endured seemingly slow-motion chases and stunts that took the better part of the cold February day.

Footage shot in and around Tuscaloosa appears during several action-filled minutes near the closing of "Hooper,, followed by a bridge jump shot along Highway 78, near Sumiton. Reynolds, coming off "Smokey and the Bandit," "Deliverance," "The Longest Yard" and "Semi-Tough", was the biggest movie star in the world at the time, having topped the list of box-office leaders five years in a row, a feat equaled by only Tom Cruise and Bing Crosby.

While the experience staying there before home games in 1960 wasn't all that great, following the history of the Northington complex has been a lot of fun.

Against Furman, we rushed for 195 yards and completed 16 of 27 passes for 268 yards. Touchdowns came in droves: a Bobby Skelton 8-yard pass to Butch Wilson and a 3-yard pass to Digger O'Dell; a Pat Trammell 1-yard sneak; a Cotton Clark 1-yard rush; a Walter Cureton 62-yard run; and a Goobie Stapp 52-yard pass to Jerry Spruiell, who also blocked a punt for a safety.

Coach Bryant had praise for backs Billy Piper, Buddy Wesley and Cornell Johnson, end Bill Rice, and for me. "Battle's resurgence toward the high peak set for him in September is particularly gratifying to his coaches. Bama's hurting at ends. Battle is needed badly. Battle played his best game of the year. Tackles Charley Pell, Joe Sisia, Bobby Boylston and Tom Coon graded well, as did Billy Neighbors and Roy Holsomback at guard."

Next came Georgia Tech, coached by Bobby Dodd. The big games for us every year were Tennessee, Georgia Tech and Auburn. "Big games" were gauged not only by the coaches' energy in preparing us for those games, but also by the demand for tickets.

We were given four tickets to every game and were allowed to buy four for our families. In film grading sessions after games, they were not all bad as I might have implied earlier. When we were playing well and winning, the sessions were pretty good. We were given "RBI's" when we made really good plays. As you probably know, an RBI is a baseball term meaning "Runs Batted In." Coach Bryant was a huge baseball fan, but why he picked that term for a big play in football, I do not know, but we all were highly motivated to get them. Getting RBI's allowed you to buy another pair of tickets. Since demand was so high for those three games, we used the RBI's we earned to buy tickets to whichever of those games were next. We obviously used tickets for family and friends, but sales of those tickets helped provide spending money for our needs above and beyond what our scholarship offered. I'm not sure if "scalping" tickets was against the law or NCAA rules, but if so, I feel certain the statute of limitations has expired by now.

By this time in the season, Trammell was our first-team quarterback, Bobby Skelton was the backup and Stapp contributed, in addition to punting. Bobby was a free spirit, funny guy, always laughing, joking and having fun. Bobby loved to pass. This was "BN" — Before Namath — and Coach Bryant still believed that when you pass, three things can happen, and two of them were bad. Bobby played a lot, as the first and second teams each played about 7 1/2 minutes a quarter. As a "wild card," Pat (and one defensive player) could also play with the second team as well as the first, and often did.

The first half against Georgia Tech went very badly. Tech scored on an 8-yard first-quarter touchdown by Jimmy Nail after recovering a fumble at the Alabama 9. Billy Richardson blocked the point-after try. Another fumble in the second quarter led to a 47-yard field goal and a 9-0 Tech lead.

On a second quarter series with Skelton at quarterback, Coach Bryant called for a running play on a crucial third down. Bobby checked to a pass that went incomplete. As Bobby came off the field, a very upset Coach Bryant went to meet him. Among other things, Coach Bryant said, "You'll never play another down!"

Tech drove for another touchdown with 13 seconds before the half. They missed the point after, but a 15-0 lead seemed insurmountable at the time. We had gained only 34 yards, and our only first down came on a 12-yard Stapp run. Tech had 107 yards on the ground, 70 in the air, and was supremely in command.

The Tech visiting locker room had risers and theater-style seats. At the half, we all hustled into the locker room fighting for seats in the back. No one wanted to be on the front row where they might get grabbed like Trammell had been in Starkville.

For several minutes, Coach Bryant did not come in the room. We got to thinking maybe he was so embarrassed that he went home. Pretty soon he came strolling in. He was a big man with baggy pants, hands in pockets, jingling change or keys, and whistling. He walked up to the chalkboard, turned to us and said, "We've got 'em right where we want 'em. They are not as good as I thought they were. We are going to embarrass them in front of their fans. All we need to do is change a few little things." He turned and started drawing plays on the board.

We were all in shock. Looking back, if he had come in and fussed at us, we would have lost confidence even more than we already had, and we would probably have lost 30-0. He lifted us up, gave us hope, and we responded.

The second half looked like a different team had emerged from the locker room. After two stops, a 14-yard Tech punt set us up in good field position. Fracchia, Trammell and Leon Fuller scored touchdowns in the third quarter, but a pass attempt for the two-point conversion failed. We started the fourth quarter down 15-6 on our own 18. Trammell went down with an injury. Coach Bryant, who had told Skelton earlier in the game he would never play again, called him up to the sideline. He put his arm around him and said, "I'm going to give you one more chance!"

Skelton led an 82-yard drive that ended with an 8-yard pass to Herbie Ronsonet. O'Dell converted and it was 15-13 with 8 minutes to play. Gambling all the way, we lost the ball on downs on our 40 with 5:17 left to play. We forced a punt and set out again from the 20. Three minutes 21 seconds were left to cover the 80 yards. Skelton passed to White for 10, Fuller for 9, and a first down by inches by Fuller to the 40. A pass to me took it to the Tech 42, and we took a timeout with 34 seconds to play. Three plays later, a pass to Ronsonet gave us a first down at the 32. Skelton scrambled and almost got to the line of scrimmage as he shot a pass to Butch Wilson at the Tech 6. Somehow, with the clock running out, Skelton got the tee on the ground and called for the snap from center. O'Dell kicked a wobbly, wounded-duck-looking field goal that seemed like it took five minutes to get there, but it finally did, and we had snatched victory from the jaws of defeat, 16-15. Tech didn't really lose, as much as we won a classic game for the ages.

A dogpile ensued and a happy bunch of Crimson Tide players laughed, hugged, cried and celebrated. It was certainly the biggest moment in my athletic career. I felt like I had finally contributed to help our team to a great comeback victory over a top SEC opponent. Our outnumbered fans inspired us in the second half, outshouting the Tech faithful, and staying around for the postgame celebration. Alabama fans have always been the best.

We were sluggish in a 34-6 win over Tampa. We had three passes intercepted — the number we had in the previous eight games — but we rushed for 229 yards, and had 201 passing yards on 10 of 28 attempts. Our defense limited Tampa to 34 yards rushing and 7 of 19 passing for 116 yards.

Then came the Auburn game.

Coach Bryant said before the game, "Auburn is the best team we've played without a doubt and I doubt seriously if we'll have a chance to beat them. We'll be after 'em though."

We took advantage of a Tommy Brooker field goal and a bone-crunching defense to beat Auburn 3-0 in Birmingham. Alabama completely dominated play in the first half, rolling up 10 first downs to Auburn's one, and gaining 120 yards to Auburn's 23.

Then we couldn't get our running game going while Auburn tried desperately to mount an aerial attack. Tide defenders effectively stymied the Tiger attack by intercepting three passes. Lee Roy Jordan picked one off in the second quarter, while Leon Fuller and Bobby Skelton had interceptions in the waning minutes of the game.

The Tigers moved the ball mostly in their own territory in the second half and never got in position to go for a tying field goal. Both teams' punting games were excellent. Billy Richardson quick-kicked 70 yards in the fourth quarter, with an earlier quick-kick for 46 yards. The Tide held Auburn to 63 yards on the ground and 71 in the air. Bama finished with 149 rushing and 30 passing. It was a classic defensive field-position football game.

"The performance of this Alabama team was the best by a team of mine in all my years of coaching," Coach Bryant told the media. "We felt all along that we would have to match their kicking game if we hoped to win. Auburn had the best kicking game in the conference. Saturday we had our best day of punting, kicking off and covering kicks. That's why we won. We quick-kicked some because we wanted to keep the ball away from Jimmy Burson, their punt returner. Our boys played pretty good defense, but if our kicking game hadn't been so good, we wouldn't have won."

The victory over Auburn wrapped up an 8-1-1 season, bringing Coach Bryant's three-year total to 20-7-4, with four of those losses coming in his first year. Before Coach Bryant, the three previous years were 4-24-2.

Coach Bryant then accepted a bid to the second-annual Bluebonnet Bowl in Houston against the University of Texas. One pre-bowl media release painted the picture this way:

"Alabama's line boasts neither great heft nor speed but when the Crimson Tide goes against Texas in the Bluebonnet Bowl on December 17, it will carry one of the proudest defensive records in the nation. "We haven't outweighed anybody up front all year and I don't expect we will against Texas," said Coach Bryant. As for size, only one regular forward, Billy Neighbors, weighs more than 200 pounds. The Tide overall defense yielded an average of 157 yards per game, which is tops in the SEC and one of the best in the nation. This is a football team without a star. With an 8-1-1 record, not a single player made the first or second team All-SEC. A different star emerged each week.

Bluebonnet Bowl starters' weights

End:	*Bill Battle (188), Norbie Ronsonet (190)*
Tackle:	*Bobby Boylston (192), Charley Pell (189)*
Guard:	*Billy Neighbors (215), Jack Rutledge (188)*
Center:	*Lee Roy Jordan (198)*
Quarterback:	*Pat Trammell (190), Bobby Skelton (175)*
LHB:	*Leon Fuller (160)*
RHB:	*Butch Wilson (195)*
FB:	*Mike Fracchia (185)*

We stayed at the Shamrock Hilton, which was probably the nicest hotel any of us had ever seen. We all got 10-gallon cowboy hats, and most of us bought cowboy boots while we were out there. It was a great trip for us, and we were very proud of our record and our invitation to a good post-season bowl game.

The Texas team we played was built the same as us. They had a great defense and kicking game team, too. The fact that we played to a 3-3 tie pretty much says it all.

A national television audience and 68,000 fans watched a defensive duel as Alabama and Texas put on an interesting but touchdown-less game. We missed an excellent opportunity when Skelton completed a 49-yard pass to Bill Rice in the first quarter down to the Texas 7. Then Skelton got a yard on his first try, passed to halfback Ray Abruzzese for 3, then lunged over the goal — only to see the ball spotted at the 1. Skelton swears he scored! On fourth down, Billy Richardson was stopped for no gain.

The third quarter saw an Alabama drive bog down at the Texas 13 where Tommy Brooker kicked a field goal to take a 3-0 lead. A fourth-quarter Longhorn drive was stopped at our 3-yard line and Texas kicked the tying field goal. On the last play of the game, Texas threw a pass to the Alabama 18. Interference was called on us, and Texas got an opportunity to win with a field goal with no time on the clock. Justice was done as the 35-yard attempt was off the mark and the game ended in a 3-3 tie.

THE JUNIOR YEAR IN 1961

Before the 1960 fall semester ended, many of us were told we needed to sign up for a 1961 spring semester class in the College of Education called "Advanced Sports Techniques." Alabama had recently signed Joe Namath and hired Howard Schnellenberger. Coach Bryant introduced Howard as one of the most knowledgeable coaches of the passing game in the country. He said Kentucky couldn't beat many teams, but they seemed to always beat Tennessee, and Howard was always in charge of that game for the Wildcats.

I was in the College of Arts and Sciences at the time as a biology major and psychology minor. Arts and Sciences students did not receive credit for taking College of Education courses. The above-mentioned class met NCAA rules in that it was offered to all students. There were five or six regular students in the class, which was taught by Alabama football coaches and met three times a week — one-hour classes on Mondays and Wednesdays, and a two-hour lab on Fridays — in pads! I had to audit the class, with no credit.

The first class came on a cold, rainy day in January. We all met in a classroom over in Dressler Hall, the physical education building. The coaches called roll, introduced themselves, and one began to draw on the chalkboard. He talked about football philosophy, certain formations, strategies and techniques. I thought to myself, "Man this is going to be a great course. We're going to learn a lot about football philosophy and history."

The next class came on a cold but sunshiny day and we found ourselves outside — in pads, and running plays. The passing game I was so worried about as a freshman was showing up now. All it took was the successful recruiting of Namath and the hiring of Schnellenberger to make it happen. Joe was a freshman in 1961 and couldn't play on the varsity, but the philosophy that "when you pass three things happen and two of them are bad" was forever in the past — at least until the arrival of the Wishbone offense in 1971.

As usual, Coach Bryant postponed spring practice as late as possible. After three months of "Advanced Sports Techniques" classes, we were locked and loaded for spring practice. Our passing game was installed, and we were in good football shape. Spring practice went very well and we all believed the 1961 season would be a great one for Alabama.

But first, let me tell you about the ROTC.

In 1961, the military draft was still in place, and although the Vietnam War had not yet begun, young men of age were still being drafted for service. I decided if I was going to serve, it would be better to serve as an officer, as opposed to an enlisted man. All males at Alabama had to go through two years of ROTC classes, either Air Force or Army. I chose the Army, and then chose to continue into the advanced ROTC program through my junior and senior years. After completion of those two years, and a summer camp in Fort Benning, Georgia, each member of the class would get their Commission as a Second Lieutenant in the U.S. Army.

One of the nice things about this advanced ROTC course was payment of $47.50 a month. With that check, the $15 a month laundry money, and what was earned in a summer job and selling tickets, my life was pretty good.

Late in the spring of our sophomore year, we attended presentations of the different branches of the Army we might choose to enter. We saw presentations from: the Infantry — ground troops who went into battle on the front lines wherever the fighting was done; the Artillery — the presentation we saw was "Air Defense" artillery, and films showing rockets and high-tech weaponry that looked cool and exciting; and the Quartermaster Corp — the units who purchased, accounted for, and provided supplies to the various branches of the Army.

I chose the Artillery, thinking it was about supporting the Infantry in wartime, way behind enemy lines through rockets, missiles, and such. What I found out in our first class during my junior year was that at Alabama, "Field" Artillery was taught, not "Air Defense." Field Artillery at that time featured primarily 105 and 155 howitzers (cannons). The guns were indeed behind the infantry troops, although not very far. Second Lieutenants were primarily assigned as "Forward Observers" who were located in front of the infantry with the responsibility of finding the enemy, figuring out the proper coordinates, and calling in fire from the howitzers. That was a shock! The average lifespan of a Forward Observer in combat was about 45 minutes.

But getting back to the 1961 season, that summer, Coach Bryant asked the backs and ends to go to summer school. The plan was to spend a fair amount of time throwing and catching, but for some reason, he may have found out that may be an NCAA violation, so we never did it. I enjoyed going to summer school, with no football practice and just going to school and doing whatever you wanted to do afterward. The classes met every day, so it was pretty easy to remember the coursework when finals came around. I took some real courses, but I also took golf. Where I grew up, we didn't have access to country clubs, so I never had a golf club in my hand except for putt-putt courses. There wasn't much teaching, so whatever I was supposed to learn in the class didn't take. The University Golf Course was adjacent to the V.A. Hospital grounds. The first tee was positioned with a fence about 25 yards to the right and the V.A. grounds on the other side. Most of my shots from the first tee ended up for the V.A. to use later! Slice!

Staying for summer school was great in that I had time to work out and stay in shape. The extra hours taken would have let me graduate in 3 1/2 years. The only reason it didn't was that before my senior year I switched to the College of Education and had to take an additional 18 hours to get a Teacher's Certificate. That allowed me to get a minor in physical education along with my biology major and psychology minor, which would in turn enable me to get a Master's degree in physical education.

I had decided I wanted to be a college football coach. Lessons taught by Coach Bryant, Coach Stallings, Coach Schnellenberger and others made me want to do the same for others. My dad, a proponent of the liberal arts education, convinced me to do undergrad work in Arts and Sciences to get a broad-based education and then get more focused in graduate school.

My two-year ROTC program mandated that I serve for two years after graduation. Fortunately, I was able to be deferred from active duty immediately after graduation in spring 1963 to go to graduate school. I spent the next year trying to figure out where I wanted to go that would enable me to learn football from another outstanding coaching staff, and get a Master's degree that should help with future employment. I actually hit the jackpot, which I will explain going into my senior year.

My second varsity season was much better than my first. I knew what to expect and had learned a great deal from the previous year. Our coaches had done a fabulous job of preparing us for every game. But in most every game our opponents would come up with blocking schemes on offense and stunts on defense designed to confuse us. Having seen so much from staff over the course of a season allowed quicker recognition and knowledge of technique to cope. Of course, there were still the challenges, but there was no substitute for experience. The detailed preparation at every position was amazing. When you have position coaches like Gene Stallings and Howard Schnellenberger, you are a pretty lucky guy.

Our team was very close. We had personalities that were hard driven that made us stay in line. We also had personalities that kept us loose and laughing. I didn't think about it at the time, but in hindsight, we had everything we needed to win a championship — experience, great team dynamics, character, drive, humor, preparation, and a head coach who was the best I ever saw at getting the most out of everyone around him. That talent went beyond players and coaches. It permeated the entire Athletics Department staff, and went through faculty, the president, the trustees, the fans, and even the media.

"If this year's team can remember how last year's aggregation won the games it did, a successful season lies ahead," Coach Bryant said to the media before the 1961 season. "Last year's team did it by fighting, battling, bleeding, and beating people physically. If we go out waltzing around and wondering when we are going to get good, we will never be good.

"If we were playing Georgia tomorrow, we would probably start Bill Battle and Tommy Brooker at ends," he continued. "All our ends played so poorly starting last season, but I think too many of them were going steady. They picked up later in the season and Battle is a sound football player."

It is amazing how much confidence one can gain over two years' experience, playing at the elite level in college football with and against the best in the game. To have the kind of coaching we had gave us knowledge, technique, a winning system, and confidence in ourselves to do our job. It also gave us confidence in everyone around us.

Coach Bryant's greatest strength was in making average players feel like they were good, and good players feel like they were great. He was exceptionally good at building true team dynamics — 11 players with one heartbeat, all pulling in the same direction in relentless pursuit of a common goal. With that kind of focus, good teams could beat great teams.

The 1961 season started very well with a 32-6 victory over Georgia in Athens. The Bulldogs' Wally Butts had retired from coaching after the 1960 season but continued on as athletics director, while Johnny Griffith took over as head football coach. Unfortunately for Coach Griffith, he underwent an emergency appendectomy on Friday night. He missed the game and a pundit wrote, "Johnny Griffith, Georgia football coach, had to surrender his seat on the bulldog bench Saturday afternoon when he gave up his appendix to a surgeon's knife in an emergency appendectomy. He must have had his surgery set back two months as he listened to Alabama's lopsided victory over his Dawgs."

The Tide defeated Georgia with a field goal, a pile-driving touchdown, a pass for a touchdown, and, most of all, a defense that appeared to grow more resolute by the season. Georgia avoided getting skunked when in the last two seconds Dale Williams ripped a pass to Carlton Guthrie, who wrestled it away from two Tide defenders in the end zone.

Next came Tulane at Ladd Stadium in Mobile. A crowd of 33,000 was treated to some old-fashioned Alabama defense. A first-quarter 22-yard Trammell-to-Brooker touchdown pass got us off to a great start. Tim Davis missed the point-after attempt, one of the few he ever missed, but he kicked a field goal later in the third quarter to make the score 9-0. Alabama came up short on several scoring opportunities when the Green Wave, which always played the Tide tough, made clutch defensive plays. Tulane's only drive in field-goal range ended in a missed try. Alabama played savage defense and limited the Green Wave to 84 yards rushing, 27 yards passing, and their first shutout in 21 games. Billy Richardson averaged 48.5 yards on two quick kicks, with the second going 50 yards and leading to a fumble that Davis cashed in on with the field goal.

Coach Bryant was asked after the game by a scribe, "Have you used the quick kick before?" Coach Bryant replied, "It was our offense three years ago!"

Despite the win, the Tide dropped from No. 3 to No. 4 in the polls. Iowa, Ole Miss and Georgia Tech were ranked 1, 2 and 3, respectively.

We traveled to Nashville to play Vanderbilt before 32,000 at Dudley Stadium. Coach Bryant went to a platoon system, with the first team practicing 50 percent on offense and 50 percent defense; the second team practicing 60 percent on defense and 40 percent on offense; and the third team practicing 60 percent on offense and 40 percent on defense. He tried to do that in 1960 but we had so many injuries, he couldn't make it work. This idea was developed by a young Paul Dietzel in 1958 when he had a "White Team," two-way "Chinese Bandit Team" (defense), and "Go Team" (offense). With All-American running back Billy Cannon, and the Chinese Bandits, who were fierce on defense, Coach Dietzel and the LSU Tigers won the National Championship in 1958.

Pat Trammell, Mike Fracchia and Larry "Dink" Wall scored touchdowns in the 35-6 victory. Vandy scored a touchdown in the second quarter, but Billy Richardson blocked the point-after try. Our defense again smothered the Vandy attack. Coach Bryant in his post-game wrapup said that I had played my best game.

"The Noblest Roman of them all" is how the media described North Carolina State All-American quarterback Roman Gabriel. Standing at 6-foot-4, 218 pounds, he was probably the highest-rated collegiate quarterback by NFL scouts and brought an outstanding passing attack to Tuscaloosa. After a 1-yard sneak in the second quarter, the Crimson Tide responded with 26 unanswered points and won the game 26-7. Trammell threw touchdown passes to Richard Williamson and me in the second quarter, and he added a 5-yard TD run in the fourth, as did Eddie Versprille from 45 yards out. A crowd of 30,000 watched Trammell complete 10 of 14 passes for 155 yards and two touchdowns, while Gabriel completed 16 of 23 for 123 yards. The Alabama defense held North Carolina State to 5 yards rushing and intercepted two of Gabriel's passes.

Before the game began, there was a ceremony dedicating a Denny Stadium addition of 12,000 seats, which brought capacity to 44,000. Denny Stadium was built in 1929, and the 1925 Rose Bowl and National Championship team was honored during the weekend. Wallace Wade was hired in 1923 by President Mike Denny to build Alabama football into a national power. In 1925, Coach Wade took the first Southern football team to play in the Rose Bowl. A five-day train ride transported the team and fans to Pasadena, California. The train stopped along the route to practice. Coach Wade, being paranoid like most coaches are, brought several 50-gallon drums of water on the trip, because he didn't trust what the train or the Rose Bowl Committee might serve to his team. The Tide upset a mighty Washington team 20-19 and Alabama football was indeed put on the map. Alabama presidents succeeding Dr. Denny have pretty much all embraced football as being part of the University of Alabama's DNA.

Coach Wade won two more national titles, his last in 1930. He took three teams to Pasadena, beating Washington and Washington State, and tying Stanford. He was replaced by Coach Frank Thomas in 1931, and Thomas' teams won National Championships in 1934 and 1941. (In 1943, there was no team as a result of World War II). Coach Thomas made three appearances in the Rose Bowl, beating Stanford and Southern Cal, and losing to California.

Coach Bryant played on the 1934 team. During my time working in Selma from 1977-1983, I attended a reunion of that 1934 team in the home of one of the players, Bob Ed Morrow, who also lived in Selma. They had a great time visiting and telling stories. The coolest part to me was watching that old black-and-white 16-millimeter film and listening to the comments. They could anticipate plays that happened about 50 years ago. My favorite was Coach Bryant saying, "Uh-oh, don't watch this next play, I'm about to get knocked on my back!" I guess the football version of "war stories" comes about as close as any to the real thing. We can all recall special football games and special plays from 50 years ago, but sometimes have trouble remembering what we ate for breakfast!

Next came Tennessee at Legion Field in Birmingham, where the capacity was 48,000, but the east side upper deck wasn't completed, so it was declared unsafe and 8,632 seats were left vacant. Fans were offered seats in unsold and hastily constructed end zone seats with folding chairs, or the option of getting their money back.

Coach Schnellenberger had indeed scouted Tennessee down to the most minute detail, and he told us that we could win big against the Vols. Tennessee scored first on a 53-yard first-quarter field goal, a UT record. Also during the first period, one of the strangest plays I ever saw happened on a Tennessee pass. There was a scramble for the catch by a Tennessee player and an Alabama player. The ball popped up in the air, Tommy Brooker had fallen and was on all fours getting up. The ball landed squarely on his back and stayed there. Everyone standing around, including me, was dumbfounded and stood there a few seconds. Finally, a Tennessee player picked up the ball from Tommy's back and started running. We all looked like "Keystone Kops" scrambling to make the tackle.

Fortunately, from there we scored two touchdowns in the first quarter and 34 unanswered points in the 34-3 win. Trammell, Fracchia, Butch Wilson and Billy Richardson scored touchdowns. Tim Davis kicked two second-quarter field goals and four point-after attempts. We had 16 first downs to Tennessee's five; 186 yards rushing to their 38; and 12 of 19 passes for 156 yards to UT's 2 of 10 for 23 yards.

Mel Allen did the telecast on ABC Television, saying Coach Bryant overcame his Tennessee jinx, as Alabama beat Tennessee for the first time since Red Drew's team beat them in 1954. Coach Bryant praised Coach Schnellenberger's preparation for the game and later admitted, "this might be the greatest game a team of mine ever played." Alabama moved up in the polls from No. 5 to No. 4.

In our first night game of the year, we shut out a tough Houston squad 17-0 at Rice Stadium in Houston. After a scoreless first quarter, we took a 10-0 lead into halftime on a 33-yard Davis field goal and a 5-yard Trammell pass to Bill Oliver. Trammell scored on a 5-yard run to make it 17-0. On Houston's only drive in the first half, Billy Richardson blocked their field-goal attempt.

We held Houston to 55 yards rushing and 11 of 28 passing for 140 yards, with five of those completions coming on a 71-yard third-quarter drive to the Tide 7. Alf Van Hoose wrote in *The Birmingham News*, "Battle broke up the party and saved the Tide whitewashing by stealing a Houston pass at the goal line and rambling 34 yards." Actually, if I could have beaten the one man that tackled me, I could have taken it back 100 yards, as everyone else was way back around the end zone.

At the half, three of us were diagnosed with a "hip pointer," a bruise on the iliac crest. They are quite painful, and Coach Goostree, our trainer, had us lined up for a team doctor to give us a Novocain shot to cover up the pain and sensitivity for the second half. Lee Roy Jordan was first in line. The doctor would jab the needle in and Lee Roy would flinch in pain. He jabbed and Lee Roy flinched and groaned about three more times. I was third in line and said, "I'm feeling pretty good right now, I don't need this shot" and started to walk off. Coach Goostree grabbed me and shoved me back in line saying, "Get your butt back over here." Fortunately, the doctor finally found the right spot and technique on Lee Roy, and then I got a shot with without pain.

We were a bruised team heading into the Mississippi State game but played well enough to get our third shutout of the year, 24-0 on homecoming. We held the Bulldog offense to 107 yards rushing and 69 passing, while intercepting two passes and recovering two fumbles. Trammel, Richardson and Wall scored touchdowns, and Davis kicked a 26-yard field goal. It was a rain-soaked victory, as the field got very wet in the second half, and every trip to the ground led to some serious sliding. It was a fun time, especially since we were ahead, but I had never experienced a game in those conditions.

There was one play in the game that I still hold over my roommate Butch Wilson's head. What might look like a serious scoring drive for State ended on a second-quarter field-goal attempt. Tommy Brooker took the ball off the kicker's toe and returned it to the MSU 17. A 15-yard penalty took us back to the 32. Ed Miles of the *Atlanta Journal-Constitution* reported, "But then came another unscheduled play of the sort that the Tide does so infamously well. Trammell's third-down pass was tipped fully 15 feet in the air through Butch Wilson's hands and caught on its wobbly descent by Bill Battle for a 20-yard gain to the MSU 10. But it was not enough for a first down and Tim Davis made the 3-point kick." I have that play on You Tube and show it to Butch every now and then.

Interestingly enough, 1961 was a year the Tournament of Roses and the Pac-10 had not come to terms with the Big Ten contractually. Since Alabama had gone to Rose Bowls in the 1920s and '30s, we thought we may have a real shot at going to Pasadena if we took care of business. That was a very exciting feeling. We knew if we played well the rest of the way, we would get a bid to a New Year's Day bowl, and if it could be the Rose, that would be wonderful! We had moved up to No. 2 behind No. 1 Texas after beating State.

Against the Richmond Spiders, we took a 34-0 lead by halftime and added five touchdowns in the second half. Everyone got to play. Our starters scored on their first three possessions and retreated to the sidelines to rest for the next week's game against Georgia Tech in Birmingham.

The east upper deck at Legion Field was still considered unsafe, and the 8,632 seats sold to fans would be offered end zone seats, or get their money back. Coach Bryant, who held dual positions of head football coach and athletics director said, "In making our budget for this season we were counting on the revenue from those upper deck seats. After the season we will ask for an adjustment, but I can assure you it will be handled in a professional manner."

In mid-November the Southern California Chapter of the Football Writers Association gave 13 votes to Alabama, six to Minnesota, and one each to Ohio State and Purdue. No other teams received votes. Either Southern Cal or UCLA would represent the Pac-10 in the New Year's Day game in Pasadena. They would meet on Saturday, Nov. 28 to decide the Big Five (West) title. The Big Five had no current contract with the Big Ten, but undoubtedly the Football Writers Association would approve a game with a Big Ten foe if Southern Cal or UCLA preferred to invite one. Later that week, *The Birmingham News* reported that a source close to the powers-that-be at Alabama said there would be no Rose Bowl trip unless present plans were changed. Powerful racial groups had extracted from Rose Bowl officials promises that no school that practiced segregation would be invited.

An Alabama football team that was probably the nation's finest college grid machine met its sternest test of the season in a convincing manner, wrapping up a powerful Georgia Tech team with a rock-ribbed defense and a steady offense for a solid 10-0 victory before 53,000 fans at Legion Field.

Tech's only scoring opportunity came after a Trammell fumble in the first quarter that gave them the ball at the Tide 42. Three plays later, Tech had to punt, and that ended their scoring chances for the day.

Trammell broke up a defensive struggle with two long scoring drives, with Fracchia scoring from 17 yards out in the second quarter and Davis kicking a 32-yard field goal in the third. Alabama's defense earned its fourth straight and fifth total shutout of the year.

"I think our team's got class," said Coach Bryant. "They convinced me today that this is a great team."

The Monday following the Alabama-Georgia Tech game, Furman Bisher of the *Atlanta Journal Constitution* wrote an article calling on Alabama to take steps toward eliminating what he called "unnecessary football violence." He criticized the action of Alabama linebacker Darwin Holt, who came together with halfback Chick Graning of Georgia Tech in a vicious hit in the fourth quarter. Bisher's article included a statement that, "It's virtually a requirement that a young man who plays football for a Bryant team behave in a most violent manner during the course of a battle."

In Tuscaloosa, Coach Bryant said, "Holt came to me after the game and was all torn up. He said he hit the Tech boy." He quoted Holt as saying he didn't know why he did it. Soon after, Coach Tonto Coleman, a Tech administrator, came to the Alabama dressing room. Coach Bryant said, "I told him Darwin wanted to apologize, but felt this was too close to the heat of the battle, so he will write a letter when he gets home." Bryant said he planned no disciplinary action.

Coach Bryant asked the SEC for an official and public review of the charge of excessive roughness in the Alabama-Tech game. Bryant asked that Commissioner Bernie Moore and a committee of officials review the game films and make a public report. In Atlanta, Tech Coach Bobby Dodd declined comment beyond repeating that he planned to write a letter of protest to Bryant about the flying elbow that injured Graning.

Then Coach Bryant agreed to show Alabama's game film to a group of sports writers. *Birmingham News* sports editor Benny Marshall, who was among the viewers, wrote, "Alabama was more sinned against than the sinner. In the matter of elbows, Darwin Holt was easily outdone 10-1 by Georgia Tech elbows. Does that excuse Holt? Certainly not. But if I were Coach Dodd, I'd look again before protesting."

Marshall further wrote that Larry Stallings was perhaps the most active engineer in the elbow department and he's an ingenious chap. Four times on one play he popped Curtis Crenshaw. Moments later he was snapping Billy Neighbors' head back twice. He quoted Trammell as saying a Tech player came to him after the game and apologized for tackling him long after he had handed off the ball. Trammell said, "That's what they told him to do."

Football is a tough, physical game that teaches blocking and tackling according to rules set by administrators and governed on the field by officials. Coach Bryant definitely coached his players to be physical, but he never even thought about crossing from the "physical" to the "dirty." As a matter of fact, he would chew out players who got 15-yard penalties for holding, hitting late or unsportsmanlike conduct. I heard him say to many a player coming off the field after one of those penalties, "You haven't made us 15 yards all year!"

Alabama and the Sugar Bowl made their romance a reality shortly after the Crimson Tide smashed Auburn 34-0 before 54,000 fans at Legion Field. We beat the Tigers with four second-half goal-line stands, preserving one of the most remarkable defensive records in southern football history: 26 quarters without giving up a touchdown, and 23 quarters without an opponent scoring (George Shuford kicked a 53-yard field goal in the first quarter of the Tennessee game).

Auburn moved the ball pretty well from the shotgun but never got close to scoring as we took a 24-0 lead into halftime. In the third quarter, the Tigers got to the 14 and 26, only to have Lee Roy Jordan and me intercept passes. In the fourth, Auburn's Don Machen raced 45 yards with a lateral from Bobby Hunt to move to the 2. Our first team re-entered the game, and three running plays yielded a half yard. On fourth down, Butch Wilson broke up a pass to secure our sixth shutout of the year.

"I'm so proud of this team," said Coach Bryant in the locker room. "They proved they were good when they asked to go back in when Auburn got to the two. Normally I wouldn't have let them go back in but they were proud of their record against scoring and went in and stopped them. This is the greatest bunch of kids and the greatest football team I've ever been associated with." And with that, the seniors grabbed Coach Bryant and dunked him unceremoniously in the shower. A good time was had by all those wearing crimson!

Coach Bryant, Pat Trammell and Dr. Rose accepted The MacArthur Bowl Trophy in New York at the annual National Football Foundation Hall of Fame presentation in December. Alabama finished No. 1 in the final AP and UPI polls. At that time, the National Champion was decided before the bowls were played.

There is an interesting side note regarding the timing of voting on National Champions in college football, and Alabama was right in the middle. In 1964, Joe Namath's senior year, Alabama was declared both AP and Coaches' Poll national champs prior to playing Texas in the Orange Bowl, but the Tide lost to the Longhorns (although Joe still swears he scored on a fourth-quarter sneak that would have won the game!) In 1965, it was decided the national championship vote would take place after the bowl games. Alabama lost its opening game 18-17 to Georgia on a disputed call in which a Bulldog player caught a pass with his knees on the ground and pitched a lateral to a player who then scored. The Tide stumbled again when young quarterback Kenny Stabler lost track of downs with time running out at the 1-yard line against Tennessee with the score tied 7-7. On fourth down, he thought it was third, and threw the ball out of bounds to stop the clock. Alabama went on to finish strong but still carried an 8-1-1 record and No. 4 ranking into the Orange Bowl against No. 3 Nebraska. Coach Bryant's thinking was if No. 1 Michigan State lost to UCLA in the Rose Bowl and No. 2 Arkansas lost to LSU in the Sugar Bowl, the Orange Bowl would decide the National Champions. That is exactly what happened. Despite being outsized, Alabama outgained Nebraska 518-377 and completed a masterful 39-28 victory and Coach Bryant's third national title in five years.

They call the 1966 season "The Missing Ring." Alabama went 11-0 and beat Nebraska 34-7 in the Sugar Bowl, but finished just No. 3 in the final AP Poll behind No. 1 Notre Dame and No. 2 Michigan State. Even though the Notre Dame-Michigan State game ended in a tie, voters appeared to be bound and determined that the undefeated, untied Alabama team was not going to win three in a row!

But getting back to Sugar Bowl after the 1961 season, 82,910 fans packed Tulane Stadium to watch a battle to the end. Arkansas fought furiously for an upset, making it suspenseful right down to a frenzied last minute, which found us running the clock out no more than 6 inches from our goal line.

In the first quarter, after the first eight minutes, the first team came out to rest. Brooker, the other end, came over to me and said, "They ain't so tough." I replied, "Man, when they run that sweep, they come at you with a lot of bodies." Then after our second-quarter rest, Brooker came over, his nose was bleeding and he said, "I see what you mean!"

We marched 79 yards on our first possession, led by a 43-yard run by Fracchia and a 12-yard touchdown run by Trammell. Davis made it 10-0 with a 23-yard field goal late in the third quarter. Except for a 23-yard field goal by the Razorbacks, we had all the defensive answers to protect the victory.

With three minutes left in the game, we punted and Arkansas took over on their own 20. Quarterback Billy Moore kept for 3 to the 23. George McKinney, also a quarterback, came in and heaved a long pass downfield intended for Jimmy Collier, who was swept off his feet by defensive halfback Butch Wilson. Pass interference gave the Razorbacks the ball on our 37-yard line. McKinney barely missed on two long throws to halfbacks Lance Alworth and Paul Dudley, then Butch intercepted his third pass at the goal line, and as he did, his foot brushed the sidelines at the 1-foot line. Ninety seconds remained on the clock. Trammell kept twice on sneaks for no gain. On third down, we were offsides. Trammell then made it to the 1-yard line over Lee Roy Jordan's back and stayed in the huddle as the last 10 seconds ran off the clock.

The Hogs played us closer than anyone else, and they were one of the toughest teams we played all year. They scored on a field goal, the first since the Tennessee game, but we refused to allow a touchdown for the sixth straight game, and never let Arkansas cross midfield but once in each half.

It was a cold and windy day in New Orleans, but winning a National Championship warmed all Alabama fans. As a player on this great team, I was grateful for the opportunity to be a small part. How many people can wear a National Championship ring? It was a very special accomplishment by a group of coaches and players who worked all year to go undefeated, untied, and gave up only 25 points in 11 games.

MY SENIOR YEAR IN 1962

After winning the National Championship in 1961, and having another stellar recruiting class, we were picked to be among the top teams in 1962. Our alumni base and fans certainly expected us to be very good again, as did our returning players. One of the most heralded players from the 1961 freshman class was quarterback Joe Namath. It didn't take many practices for coaches and players alike to realize that Joe was a special player.

We went through another "Winter Workout" program in the upper gym in the Athletics Department and it was obvious there was a lot of talent on the '61 freshman class other than Joe. Spring practice went smoothly for those who returned as starters, as we knew what to expect. It was our class' time to assert the leadership that the previous senior classes gave to us. We were ready, willing, and able. We were deep, talented, experienced and highly motivated to win back-to-back national titles. Upper classmen took pride in helping the freshmen and sophomores learn the system, as well as expectations from coaches. But I can tell you, film sessions after winning games were a lot more fun than after losses.

Coach Bryant told everyone that when things went well, he gave the credit to players and assistant coaches. When things went badly, he took the blame. And he did — to the media. But after losses, the blame got passed to where it belonged: those of us in the film-grading sessions! Fortunately, there weren't many losses over the last four years.

Eugenia and I got married in June 1962. We had dated for four years. She had graduated and had gotten a job teaching at Verner Elementary School. I knew Coach Bryant wanted all his players under one roof, but this was a life decision that I was ready to take on. I told my dad we were getting married in June, so we would be "adjusted to marriage" by the start of football season. He thought that was the funniest thing he had ever heard, and kidded me about it for years.

I knew I could stay on at Alabama after my senior season and be a graduate assistant coach, but I wanted to go somewhere else and learn from a different coach. Coach Bud Wilkinson at the University of Oklahoma was where I wanted to go. Coach Wilkinson was legendary like Coach Bryant, and had an incredible record. He was also the chairman of President Kennedy's Council on Youth Physical Fitness. I was also interested in that program and thought if I could get that opportunity, it would help me develop a reputation with another coaching staff. I wrote Coach Wilkinson a letter asking if I could come out for the 1963-64 year. Unfortunately, that was the only letter I wrote and I didn't hear back from him. As the '62 season neared, my full focus went to getting in great physical shape for my senior year.

We stayed in Tuscaloosa the summer before my senior year and I worked at Baggett Transportation, located on Highway 11. Eugenia drove me to work every morning. In the afternoons I would run home the few miles to our apartment.

When we arrived at work each day there were five or six of us who unloaded an 18-wheeler onto cargo vans, which we each loaded and delivered around Tuscaloosa. One day, early in my work there, I had to make a delivery to Bryce Hospital, the state insane asylum. I don't recall if my delivery was to the dining hall or not, but either way, I got there about noon and the smell of fresh bread drew me inside the kitchen. I inquired about the bread and was told they bake it fresh every day and was asked if I wanted some. I said, "Most definitely" and saw they were baked in small loaves. My new friend gave me a piping hot loaf, broke it apart in the middle and stuck about a half a stick of butter in there. The butter melted quickly. To complete the package, a cup of cold milk was also added. Needless to say, I visited around lunchtime all summer if my route took me anywhere nearby.

With my lifting and delivering on the job, and my runs home after work, I reported back to fall camp in the best shape of my life. Fall practice went very well and as usual Coach Bryant and his staff had us more than well prepared to face the University of Georgia in our home opener in Birmingham.

When Wally Butts stepped down as Georgia's head football coach after the 1961 season and became their athletics director, one of his early recommendations was to move this game from Tuscaloosa to Birmingham. It was a wise financial move, as the new Birmingham stadium addition provided 54,000 seats to Tuscaloosa's 42,000. The record crowd of 54,000 allowed Georgia to receive its largest payday ever in the state of Alabama, $97,000.

Joe Namath made his debut in fine style as he hit Richard Williamson with a 52-yard touchdown pass four minutes into the first quarter. Before the game ended in a 35-0 Tide victory, he had completed two more touchdown passes to Cotton Clark, while completing 10 of 14 for 179 yards, but two of the incompletions were actually dropped by receivers. Namath added 36 yards rushing. We dominated the stats with 23 first downs to Georgia's seven, 273 yards rushing to 37, and 191 passing to 79. Clark scored another touchdown rushing, giving him 18 points for the day, putting him in the lead in SEC scoring. Hudson Harris scored the last touchdown on a 25-yard run. Lee Roy Jordan and Namath earned SEC and national honors for their play.

The bad news for me about this game was that in the second quarter, I got clipped from the backside and tore a medial collateral ligament in my knee. I was playing defensive end. The flanker lined up to my outside came in motion back toward the ball. I had never seen that type motion before. When the ball was snapped Georgia ran a sweep to my side. On my way up field and outside, the flanker was going full speed and hit me low. I immediately felt my knee loosely holding together the femur to the lower tibia and fibula. I was sick. Surgery was not usually done on that injury. I missed the next game against Tulane and wore a big brace in the next few games after that. Speed for me was not a great asset, and playing in a knee brace was an additional handicap.

The Tide rolled from the start against Tulane in New Orleans, with Namath passing, Eddie Versprille running, and Butch Wilson scoring two first-quarter touchdowns on runs of 7 and 1 yards. Then Tulane, under new head coach Tommy O'Boyle, surprised the Tide with a new formation they had not used previously — the shotgun. They completed a 6-yard pass to a Tulane receiver who caught the pass close enough to the back end zone line to be debatable. It was the first touchdown scored against us in 36 quarters dating back to the first quarter of the North Carolina State game in 1961. It must have made our players mad though, as they scored 22 more points in the second quarter and eight more in the second half for a 44-6 final. Cotton Clark added three touchdowns and a two-point conversion on the night. It was an awful feeling for me to miss playing because of the knee injury, but it was wonderful to win big against a team that usually played us very tough.

Despite the convincing win over Tulane, we fell to No. 2 in the AP Poll prior to a victory over Vandy in Birmingham. Coach Bryant was relieved, but not happy, about the win. It was 7-7 at the half. Vandy scored its first touchdown of the season when Terrell Dye recovered a Cotton Clark fumbled punt in the end zone to take a 7-0 lead. We responded on the ensuing drive with a 19-yard touchdown pass from Namath to Butch Henry to tie the game. We took a 14-7 lead early in the third when Namath threw a 34-yard touchdown pass to Richard Williamson. With 13 minutes left in the game, Vandy made two drives deep in Alabama territory. The first ended with me sacking the Vandy quarterback and causing a fumble recovered by tackle Dan Kearley. The second ended with a pass intercepted by Benny Nelson. Tim Davis kicked a field goal in the fourth quarter to make the final score 17-7.

"Football is just four things — seeing, hearing, movement and contact," Coach Bryant said. "Now we had seeing and hearing against Vandy, but not much movement and contact. This can be corrected with good old-fashioned sacrifice. You may get tired of hearing me talk about sacrifice, hard work and desire — but you don't win many games by the Fancy Dan style."

With the victory over Vanderbilt, coupled with an Ohio State loss to UCLA, we moved back into the top position in the polls prior to the game against Houston. Our defense was dominant against the Cougars in the 14-3 win, allowing minus-49 yards rushing and 6 of 13 passes for 45 yards.

Namath had his worst game of the season, completing 4 of 10 passes for 56 yards. On his one interception, Gene Ritch picked it off for the Cougars and was led on a 69-yard return with a big end running interference. Namath, the last player to have a shot at tackling him, maneuvered around the blocker to make the tackle at the 11-yard line. The Bama defense held and Houston kicked a field goal for its only score, putting the Cougars up 3-0. We took a 7-3 lead in the second quarter when Lee Roy Jordan recovered a Houston fumble in the end zone. Cotton Clark scored the final touchdown in the third quarter on a 3-yard run. I did make it back to earn some playing time. The knee brace I was wearing was awkward but worked OK as time went on.

We dropped back to the No. 2 spot in the week leading up to playing Tennessee in Knoxville. Going into this game, the all-time record between Alabama and Tennessee was 19-19-6. UT chose the Alabama game to dedicate an addition to Neyland Stadium and a $100,000 contribution to the Robert R. Neyland Academic Scholarship Fund. It was in old Denny Stadium on Oct. 20, 1928, that General Neyland made his most profound debut. On the opening kickoff, Gene McEver, a sophomore tailback, swept through the Alabama team for 98 yards. It was the match that lit a startling 15-13 upset of Alabama. "Of all the games, I'll take that victory over Alabama as my greatest thrill," said General Neyland on his last visit to Birmingham.

The 1962 Alabama team carried a 22-game unbeaten streak into the Tennessee game. We had 15 victories in a row, and one of the best records in the country for holding the opponents in check. In the last 18 games, no opponent had scored more than one touchdown, and only three teams had been able to do that in the last four years, which covers 38 games. It was a beautiful fall day with bright colors of yellow, orange and red on trees in the hills framing the stadium.

A rugged Alabama team softened the Vols with two first-quarter field goals and then added touchdowns on long air strikes to a smashing 27-7 victory. The triumph cracked a long-standing jinx for Coach Bryant, who in eight years at Kentucky and four at Alabama had never beaten the Vols on their home field.

Early in the second quarter Namath completed a 10-yard touchdown pass to Benny Nelson. The two-point pass was batted down, making the score 12-0 going into the half. Defensively it was a war up front with both teams playing typical Alabama-Tennessee smashmouth football. A Vol 56-yard drive for a touchdown from Bobby Morton to wingback Jerry Ensley made the score 12-7 with less than a minute to go in the third quarter. It began to appear that an upset was in the works, but it wasn't to be.

Namath took control after the UT touchdown. First he completed a pass to Benny Nelson to the Tennessee 47. After a running play lost a yard, Joe fired a long pass to Richard Williamson for a 45-yard gain to the UT 3. From there Cotton Clark took it in over left tackle and Tim Davis kicked the extra point, making the score 19-7.

A promising Tennessee drive on the next possession was slowed by a 15-yard penalty, and on the next play I recovered a fumble on the Tennessee 39 to set up the final touchdown drive. Billy Piper caught an 11-yard pass from Namath, then ran 5 more for a first down at the Tennessee 25. Jack Hurlbut replaced Namath at quarterback. Carlton Rankin drove to the 20, then Hurlbut hit Benny Nelson for a 20-yard touchdown. Hurlbut ran for the two-point conversion, making the score 27-7 with 8:30 left on the clock.

Early in the fourth quarter Coach Bryant called me over and asked if I could take Charley Pell's place at defensive tackle. I had never practiced a down at that position but I lined up next to him most of the time and pretty much knew what he did, so I said, "Yes sir, I can do that."

Coach Bryant said after the game, "Battle made some of the greatest plays I've seen an end make. He played both ends, and toward the end of the game, when Charley Pell got hurt, he had to play tackle on defense." I appreciated him saying that. And I actually enjoyed playing tackle, because in some ways it was easier. Playing end and having to defend off-tackle plays, as well as those that go outside, makes for a much greater area to defend.

The stats in the Tennessee game seemed to go in UT's favor, as they made 14 first downs to our nine and had 187 yards rushing to our 76, but we completed 10 of 14 passes for 168 yards to their 67. We intercepted four of their passes to their none, and they recovered two fumbles to our one. Our passing game and pass defense won the game. It was a huge win for Coach Bryant and for our team. It was definitely a much better feeling for me, even in the knee brace, than the game two years earlier that we lost 20-7.

About this time of year, every team starts to feel the grind of three weeks of fall practice and now five straight games. Even when you are 5-0 and ranked No. 1 or 2 all season, the drudgery of practice and the bumps and bruises of a contact sport begin to accumulate. It starts to wear you down, both physically and mentally. The solution to that feeling comes from coaches picking you, yet still demanding excellence at practice. "Variety is the spice of life." So mixing practice routines up and allowing some levity to creep in can provide relief to get through late-season drudgery.

It also helps to have certain personalities in players to bring laughter into tense situations. Bobby Skelton brought that to our team in 1960 and 1961. In 1962, the character was Cotton Clark. Cotton started the season with three touchdowns in each of the first two games and added more every week. We kidded Cotton about having more total points than rushing yards gained. Cotton also was a great free safety on defense. He also had a great knack of making short-yardage first downs and touchdowns. He could find cracks to shoot through when they didn't seem to be there. He was also one to "shoot the bull," bragging about being the No. 1 scorer in the SEC, with all his buddies taking it with a grain of salt, and coming back with the "more points than yards gained" argument.

One week Cotton said, "Man I'm really concerned about this team we're playing," and someone replied, "Why, is Tulsa's defense really good?" Cotton said, "No, they aren't that great, but I'm afraid there will be someone in the stands to assassinate me. That's about the only way I can be stopped!" Now most people couldn't say something like that and get away with it, but from Cotton, we knew he was just "jiving" us and we all laughed, and threw back an insult or two his way.

Tuesday and Wednesday were the two hardest days of practice during game week, in pads and concentrating on offense and defensive game plans. On this particular Tuesday, the first team was in a defensive period. Coach Gene Stallings was the defensive backs coach and defensive coordinator. Cotton, as told earlier, was our free safety, and his "Cardinal Rule" was to always stay as deep as the deepest receiver on the field. As luck would have it, the blue (scout) team ran a pass play, a wide receiver ran past Cotton and the quarterback hit him for a touchdown.Coach Stallings took off on a dead run and got in Cotton's face, chewing him up one side and down the other as they walked back to the defensive huddle. When Coach Stallings turned and walked away, Cotton looked over at his defensive halfback and said loud enough for everyone to hear, "You know, when you're on top, everybody is out to get you!"

That broke up the team in laughter and even Coach Stallings joined in. It's really important that every team and every organization, when times get tough and work becomes drudgery, to have leaders who can take the work seriously, but not themselves. It is amazing the role that laughter plays in the success of organizations everywhere.

The headline read: "*Tide Power Routs State 20-0 with Namath and Battle Leading the Way*" followed by this paragraph:

"Anyone who doubted Joe Namath, a cocky 195-pound quarterback from Beaver Falls, Pennsylvania is as good as advertised should have seen "Old Joe" in action in Starkville, Mississippi here Saturday. The brilliant sophomore, showing all the poise of a senior in his third year as a starter, connected on 12 of 19 passes for 150 yards and two touchdowns, both going to senior end Bill Battle. On the ground, the swarthy Alabama Yankee was just as brilliant, rushing for 69 yards on 12 carries. With the Crimson Tide defense putting on the stops, there was never any doubt as to the outcome of this SEC battle before 26,000 fans at Scott Field."

After Mississippi State received the opening kickoff and punted four plays later, Namath led a 64-yard drive. Cotton Clark, Butch Wilson and Eddie Versprille did the running, with Richard Williamson and Wilson catching passes, down to the State 4-yard line. Cotton scored the first touchdown and finished with 52 yards on 11 carries, despite being doubtful while recovering from a bout with tonsillitis earlier in the week. This touchdown pushed his points to 68 and kept his lead in SEC scoring. His 11 touchdowns were one shy of the Alabama school record for a season held by Bobby Marlow of the early 1950s vintage.

The second touchdown came early in the second quarter when Wilson intercepted a Sonny Fisher pass on the Tide 31, one of four intercepted by Bama players.

Alf Van Hoose wrote, *"Battle Set-Up Big Play with Little-Bitty Play"* — "Little things add up to big things we are taught from the cradle up. End Bill Battle scored two touchdowns Saturday in a 20-0 conquest of Mississippi State. One of those, the first, was strictly due to a bit of quick thinking and reaction, both virtuous and both by Battle. The play turned into an oddity because Alabama had the ball and Namath fired a pass, and Battle ended up playing pass defense — pass defense being one of several jobs that Mr. Battle does so quietly and competently it escapes general attention.

"On first and 10 from the State 27, in the second quarter, Bama on top 7-0, Namath rolled right to throw," Van Hoose continued. "State's Gene Gibbs and Howard Benton rushed Joe to do him bodily harm. Namath stopped and launched the ball. Whether it was intended for Battle or not, the pass was tipped and suddenly there was a knuckle ball sort of popup coming down just beyond the line of scrimmage with two Bulldogs posting themselves to do some intercepting. They didn't though because Battle, who had been ready to catch a pass, ungentlemanly dived into the State reception committee of two and knocked the ball down. It happened so smoothly that I don't think many people appreciated the action, but everybody caught the next play; the one which Namath called another pass, executed it, and Battle caught it on the 27-yard line and took it home in Jim Taylor of the Packer's Style. He was going to score a touchdown as a couple of starters challenged him inside the 5-yard line, but they didn't stand a chance for a second — and so the scoreboard was flashing six. Battle must have enjoyed the cheers immensely. He deserved them."

The third touchdown came when Billy Piper returned a Bulldog punt midway in the third quarter and returned it 46 yards to the State 17. After a few runs to the State 8, Namath hit me in the back of the end zone for our second touchdown connection that day.

State moved inside our 50-yard line five times, but each time, led by Lee Roy Jordan, our defense put out the fire. The defense was stifling, limiting the Bulldogs to 13 first downs, 88 yards rushing and 89 yards passing. We had 20 first downs, 234 yards rushing and 150 yards passing.

Miami then came to Denny Stadium for homecoming, and almost spoiled the celebration, as the Hurricanes led 3-0 at halftime.

George Mira, known as El Matador, lived up to his billing, as our defense chased him all over the field and never caught him. He was known for scrambling from one side to the other, and the staff at Miami did something I had never seen before or since. With a quarterback that scrambles as part of the planned offense, on many occasions he would lose his bearings as to where exactly the line of scrimmage was. Throwing the ball after passing the line of scrimmage results in a penalty. But a Miami assistant coach was placed at the line of scrimmage on a knee, and on such plays as Mira was scrambling, the coach would twirl a towel in the air entering his peripheral vision and helping prevent him from crossing the line.

The exciting pass-oriented offense brought by Miami moved the ball up and down the field as El Matador picked our defense apart. We also helped them out with an interception and a fumble that set them up with four scoring threats deep in our territory in the first half. But when push came to shove, our defense rose to the occasion, allowing only a field goal from the four drives. Billy Piper and Cotton Clark interceptions stopped two drives. A third was stopped on downs by a fourth-and-1 tackle by Dan Kearley. The fourth drive produced the field goal.

Leaving the field at halftime down 3-0 left a bad taste in our mouths. We were confident we would beat them in front of our home crowd. Coaches and players remained very positive that we would emerge victorious. The second half was a different story. Coaches made adjustments to go over the areas in their passing game that surprised us, and we went back out with fire in our eyes and the realization that our quest to repeat as National Champions rested on this game.

Namath was brilliant in the second half, and on our second possession, he orchestrated a 79-yard drive behind his 38-yard run and a 36-yard pass to Cotton Clark. Clark, who broke Alabama's scoring and touchdown records for a single season during this game, scored on a 1-yard plunge to put us ahead for good 7-3. Defensive halfback Jack Hurlbut recovered a fumble at the Miami 27, which set up another touchdown. Namath ran for 15 yards and Clark took it into the end zone from the 7 yard line. Ingram Culwell completed a fake extra-point pass to me for a two-point conversion, making the score 15-3.

We scored on our next three possessions. A 51-yard drive culminated with a 12-yard touchdown pass from Namath to me. The same combination was good for a two-point conversion, putting the game comfortably out of reach at 23-3. The next drive went for 79 yards, mostly behind Namath passing, and he took a 1-yard sneak in for the next touchdown. Hurlbut took over at quarterback at that point, and after setting it up with a 21 yard run to the Miami 1, scored from the 1.

Clark's two touchdowns gave him 13 touchdowns, best ever for an Alabama back, and the 12 points boosted his scoring total to 80 for another record. The previous record was 72 points. Cotton's head swelled, but his teammates were very capable of bringing him back to earth.

Namath moved to within 6 yards of the season passing record set by All-American Pat Trammel in 1961. We finally caught Mira on a scramble for a loss late in the game that brought his total yards rushing to minus-13. Miami netted only 83 yards rushing and 185 passing. The Hurricanes picked up 197 of their 268 total yards in the first half. Alabama gained 293 of its 392 total yards and scored 35 unanswered points in the second half.

After the game, we were voted No. 1 in the nation, but then came a stunning 7-6 loss to Georgia Tech in Atlanta.

"We saw one of the greatest games I have ever seen," Coach Bryant said. "Everyone on our team today played as hard as they could. I'm just as proud of our team today as for any game they have played. It was certainly a great victory for Tech. They were well prepared for us, both mentally and physically. I handicapped our team with some of the calls I made from the sidelines. In the first quarter when we went for it on fourth down we made a mistake. I called the last play of the game that was intercepted. We were close enough to kick. If I had it to do over I would run two plays into the line and kick the field goal on fourth down."

The loss ended a long string of victories that few teams in the country can ever boast of attaining. And to top it off, Alabama had just moved up to the top ranking in college football. Bama had won 19 straight and gone 26 games without a loss. It had been two years since Coach Bryant had to address the media after a losing game.

Coach Bryant praised the work of the Tech linemen. "We knew they would be good and that's why we passed more than normal. The passing game probably kept us in the game and probably got us out of the game, too."

Coach Bobby Dodd also witnessed one of the greatest games ever. "Today was the greatest victory ever won by a Georgia Tech football team, bowl games or regular season," he said. "I don't have to say we played our best game ever against a superior Alabama team that deserved the No. 1 ranking that it had prior to today. I have so many things to be proud of that it is difficult to sort them out. I am proud of the way our team came up with big play after big play in the closing minutes when Alabama had several opportunities to win. Our pass defense had one of its best days against one of the best throwers we have faced. It was a great win and I know that I have never been happier."

The game itself was physical SEC football, played before a record Grant Field crowd of 52,971. Both teams surprised their fan base by deserting their T-formation offense and going to the shotgun. Alabama, on its first series, had Namath lined up at tailback and Hurlbut at quarterback. Bama went to the passing game to offset the 27 pounds per man advantage the Tech line had over the Tide's offensive line.

Alabama had 13 first downs to Tech's 9, 78 yards rushing to Tech's 77, and 161 yards passing to Tech's 49, but the tale-telling stat was Alabama's four interceptions and one fumble lost, to Tech's one interception and one fumble lost. Namath's poor percentage of passes completed for 161 yards with three interceptions was due primarily to tremendous pressure from the Georgia Tech front line. I caught five passes for 66 yards, while fellow ends Clark Boler had four for 47 and Richard Williamson four for 43.

Mike McNames, a fullback/linebacker, intercepted a Namath pass in the second quarter after defensive end Billy Martin hit Namath as he was throwing. It resulted in a floater, short of its target, and McNames returned it to the Alabama 14. Two plays later McNames blasted over from the 9-yard line. The extra point by Billy Lothridge made it 7-0.

We had only three first downs netting 28 yards rushing and 47 yards passing in the first half. The only penetration in the half was to the Tech 49, which resulted in a turnover on downs.

Tech came up empty on two first-half drives, but the 7-0 score was enough for the win. One drive was stopped by a Butch Wilson interception and the other with a missed field goal. The Yellow Jackets were dominant in the first two quarters with their huge defensive line that outweighed Alabama by 27 pounds per man. They were solidly in control in the third, but desperately defensive in the fourth quarter when the Tide launched an effort reminiscent of the storybook 16-15 victory there in 1961.

We finally caught a break in the fourth quarter when a 63-yard quick kick left Tech on its own 15. Lee Roy Jordan made a big stop on third and 1 to force a Tech punt. Lothridge fumbled the snap from center and evaded Alabama rushers for long enough to kick, but during the play it was ruled that his knee touched the ground on the Tech 9.

After a first down offsides penalty and an incomplete pass, Hurlbut came in and completed a 5-yard tackle-eligible pass to Clark Boler. Namath returned and fired down the middle to me at the Tech 2 despite the presence of two eager defenders. With the game hanging in the balance, Clark crashed over right tackle for the touchdown with 5:32 remaining. Hurlbut rolled out to his right on a two-point conversion attempt, and just when it looked like he would score, McNames and tackle Ed Griffin knocked him down inches from the goal line.

Alabama successfully executed an onside kick, with Benny Nelson recovering the ball at the Tech 33. On first down Frank Sexton intercepted a Namath pass, but on the 28-yard runback, Sexton was stripped of the ball and Richard O'Dell recovered the fumble. Namath, Hurlbut and Clark moved the ball to the Tech 16 with a little over a minute to go. I was playing tight end on the left side with a flanker to my outside. I ran a flat route while the flanker ran a curl. Hurlbut threw to me going outside, the pass was high and I barely touched it with the tip of my middle finger — and it landed right in Don Toner's hands to end the game and push us out of our No. 1 ranking.

In the aftermath of the upset, a tall man from Alabama pushed his way through the crowd to the Georgia Tech dressing room. He knocked on the door and was met by tackle Larry Stallings and halfback Tom Winingder. They both had changed into street clothes when they stepped forward to meet Coach Bryant. "It was a great victory and one I know you are proud of. I want to congratulate you and your teammates." Coach Dodd entered the room about that time and Bryant turned and said, "If a coach can survive a game like that, he can survive anything."

The Iron Bowl game was on national TV, and from that perspective, the fans viewed a perfectly green field with precise stripes, with "Alabama" in block letters in one end zone and "Auburn" in the other. In reality, the field was painted green over ground with virtually no grass, and a surface that felt extra hard. On Friday we came out to practice and the hard rubber cleats on our shoes sounded like we were running on concrete.

You see, Legion Field hosted a tremendous amount of football games every year, including all Big Five high school home games, the three or four Alabama and Auburn games, and the annual Thanksgiving Day Crippled Children's Clinic game featuring the two top high school teams in the county. It seems the man (or crew) designated to putting fertilizer on the field got mixed up and applied a triple dose. The result was it burned up the grass just a few weeks before the first game of the season. Sod was brought in, but it couldn't withstand the pressure from every Friday and Saturday all season long.

Reaching back in time for the moment, on many days when our team gathered on benches behind the Athletics Department waiting for the time to go to practice, players would occasionally tape stripes, lightning bolts and other designs on their black leather shoes and prance around. These antics drew laughter from the audience, knowing that Coach Bryant wouldn't stand for that kind of monkey business, and sure enough, they were all removed before we hit the practice field.

So back to Auburn game day. When we went down Saturday morning for the pre-game meal, there were boxes of shoes lining two walls in the room. They were filled with soccer shoes, lightweight Puma and Adidas shoes with small molded-sole cleats, and complete with white stripes. We were like kids at Christmas finding our sizes, and everyone was exclaiming "Lightning Shoes!" We ran out on the field later that day and were zooming around the field in much more comfortable shoes than the previous day, and much more comfortable than the Auburn team's shoes on game day. It was definitely a brilliant tactical move by Coach Bryant on a Friday afternoon.

The story was that Fred Sington, a former All-American tackle at Alabama, was at our Friday practice. He owned several sporting goods stores around the state and knew that soccer shoes would be much more appropriate on the Legion Field surface than what we were wearing on Friday. Coach Bryant made the decision to see what they could round up. Chief Joe Smelley, one of the State Troopers who guarded Coach Bryant on game day, was in charge of State Troopers statewide. Soccer was a pretty obscure sport in Alabama in the early '60s, and no store had enough to supply the needs of a college football team. But Sington got on the phone and told all of his store managers to hold their stores open and to call other sporting goods storeowners they knew to buy all the soccer shoes they could buy. State Troopers all over the state picked up shoes and drove them to Birmingham, with carloads coming in all night.

The shoes were much more than a mental lift. Those shoes on the Legion Field surface created a strategic advantage. It was also a boost for the soccer shoe industry. High schools and colleges all over the country began to stock those shoes for conditions like we faced, or for practice shoes, or on artificial turf, which was a coming phenomenon that by the 1970s was on college football fields all over the country.

I would be remiss if I didn't give you some history on the Iron Bowl before talking about the 1962 game.

The "Iron Bowl" name was applied to the Alabama vs. Auburn rivalry game played in Birmingham, the Pittsburgh of the South. Iron ore was mined in nearby Red Mountain and turned into "pig iron" in the Sloss Furnace beneath a 1st Avenue North overpass in the city. The first Alabama vs. Auburn game was played in Lakeview Park on Feb. 22, 1893. Auburn won 32-22 before an estimated crowd of 5,000.

In 1906, Alabama hired Doc Pollard, a coach from Dartmouth, to improve its football program. In the Alabama-Auburn game that year he brought with him an unconventional, but legal, shift on offense that confused the Auburn team. Alabama won 10-0. The Auburn coach was so infuriated with the shift that he said he never wanted to play Alabama again. There was also an economic dispute that added to the tension. Alabama, as the host team, was obligated to pay per-diem expenses to Auburn. Alabama paid $3.00 per player and Auburn wanted $3.50. There was also a dispute over the number of players who received the money.

As a result, the two teams did not play each other from 1907 to 1947, when the legislature threatened to withdraw money from the schools if they didn't play. Student body presidents from each university met in a Birmingham park and literally "buried a hatchet" to commemorate the start of a new era in the Alabama-Auburn rivalry.

It has been said that everyone in Alabama, regardless of the college or university they might have attended, was forced to pull for either Alabama or Auburn in their annual football game. These are two great universities with outstanding academic and athletic programs. Their alumni and fans are very passionate about their respective institutions. Bragging rights to the victors last for 365 days. Two quotes I read recently sum up the importance of the Iron Bowl to its respective fan bases.

"If people in the state didn't have Alabama vs. Auburn football to talk about, there wouldn't be much conversation throughout the year." This is a phenomenon that doesn't just exist in the communities of the two universities; it permeates in every city and county in the state.

"In Alabama we don't let something as silly as education get in the way of who we pull for when it comes to something really important like the Alabama vs Auburn football game." There are diehard fans who were born into families that taught them to be loyal to one university, even though they may have gone to the other university due to the curriculum.

When the game was played in Birmingham, the atmosphere was unbelievable. Regardless of records, the stands were full. One side of the stadium was filled with crimson and white attire and the other half, orange and blue — hopefully all licensed products, of course. Much of the time, one, if not both, were highly ranked in the SEC and in national polls. It was and still is one of the most passionate rivalries in the nation.

The game was played in Birmingham every year from 1948 to 1988 and intermittently until 1998, when both universities decided to switch the game's location annually between campuses for economic reasons, but the "Iron Bowl" tag stayed in place. To this day, the game still evokes tremendous passion on both sides, but the home team has over 90 percent of the seats. That has resulted in a much different game atmosphere than the 50-50 split in Birmingham. The coaches and players still play with extra special intensity, as bragging rights for the next year is very meaningful. In recent years, the winner of the Iron Bowl on many occasions has moved on to the SEC Championship Game in Atlanta.

There are many storied rivalry games around the country, but in Alabama, the Iron Bowl is not just a rivalry game, it's a way of life.

In the week leading up to the 1962 Iron Bowl, Clyde Bolton wrote, "The Alabama Crimson Tide will be back where it started the year, personnel wise, Saturday against Auburn. For the first time since the opening victory over Georgia, Paul Bryant will have the 11 starters who opened the year. They played the first quarter dominating the Bulldogs, then Bill Battle pulled up lame and Charley Pell followed. It was a sign of things to come and Coach Bryant never got that team reassembled. Now bidding for a fourth straight victory and shut out over the Tigers, the Tide is favored by 17 points."

Bolton continued, "The subject of today's dissertation are two men who will no doubt catch their share of passes. They are Richard Williamson and Bill Battle. Paul Bryant, who measures his adjectives thoughtfully, called Williamson and Battle the best pair of ends in the SEC. Battle spent most of the year when all-star teams were being picked, slowed by a knee injury that occurred in the opening game. He missed the Tulane game and played in a cumbersome brace the next few games. He is healthy now and has played extremely well in our last few games."

We dropped from No. 1 the week before the Georgia Tech game to No. 5 after an open week before the Auburn game. We also accepted a bid to the Orange Bowl that week to play the top team in the Big Eight Conference. Coach Bryant was a master at controlling the bowl in which he wanted to play. After he and the UA president made their choices, the bowls all fell into place very quickly. In those days, bowls were not supposed to make deals before a deadline, usually the week before the last games were played. As one can imagine, there was a lot of back room negotiating much earlier than that. It caused successful young Nebraska coach Tom Osborne to comment, "Somebody needs to stop that ole son-of-a-buck from manipulating where all the bowls are choosing teams."

The 1962 Iron Bowl started with a crimson bang as my roommate Butch Wilson took the opening kickoff and returned it 92 yards to silence the Auburn crowd. For all practical purposes, the game was over, because Auburn went on to turn the ball over on four fumbles and three interceptions. Two of the Tide interceptions by Butch and me stopped budding Tiger drives in the second half.

We rolled to two quick touchdowns within a 90-second span early in the second quarter to take a 21-0 lead going into halftime. A 75-yard drive, which ended with a 15-yard run by Namath, made it 14-0. The third touchdown came on a blocked punt that we had practiced for all four years I was in school. At that time, the rule was that the team that blocked a punt could not advance the ball past the point at which they recovered. The rule didn't cover clumsy efforts to recover the ball that advanced it toward the goal line. Chink Wilson blocked the punt and a swarm of crimson clad players stumbled and fumbled, batting and slapping and couldn't pick it up. It started at the 20-yard line and it rolled into the end zone. I beat tackle Dan Kearley to recover the ball for a touchdown. It was phenomenal play, and to this day, fun to watch on YouTube.

The third quarter saw a 15-yard Namath to Cotton Clark touchdown and a 39-yard field goal by Tim Davis, who earlier had missed one from 52 yards out. Early in the fourth quarter, Namath hit Richard Williamson for the final Tide touchdown.

With seven minutes to go in the third quarter, Jimmy Sidle led an Auburn drive to the Alabama 39. The first team for Alabama returned to action, and shortly thereafter, Butch Wilson intercepted a Sidle pass to end the threat.

We punted on the next series of downs and again the kick proved to be a great offensive weapon. Ace Auburn defender Billy Edge tried to field the punt, but in the process, I nailed him, causing a fumble, and Jimmy Wilson recovered at the Tiger 16.

Early in the fourth quarter, Jack Hurlbut stopped another Auburn drive to the Alabama 34 with another interception. The next Auburn drive went to the Alabama 21 on completions of 33 yards to end Don Downs and 22 yard to Ronny Baynes. The Tide regulars returned again to foil the Auburn offense. This time, I intercepted a Sidle pass at the Bama 24 to end the Tigers' scoring opportunities.

Coach Bryant said to us after the game, "You did a wonderful job out there today and we're just as proud of you as your parents. Now drive carefully, behave yourselves, and don't stay out too late."

Coach Bryant went on to say to reporters, "I guess it sounds like the same old record, but I'm mighty proud of this victory and I'm particularly proud of our seniors. I'm grateful to have been associated with them. The game was much closer than the score. Auburn had some bad breaks, but on the other hand we got more than our share of the breaks."

The seniors, other than me, in alphabetical order, were: Cotton Clark, Elbert Cook, Ingram Culwell, Lee Roy Jordan, Mal Moore, Richard O'Dell, Charley Pell, Bob Pettee, Jimmy Sharpe, Gerald Stephens, Richard Willliamson, Butch Wilson and Jimmy Wilson. This was as fine a group of young men as could be found on one team anywhere.

So the regular season had ended and we were one play away from winning another National Championship. We were proud of our 9-1 season to date and looked forward to playing Oklahoma in the Orange Bowl. A few weeks after the Iron Bowl and Orange Bowl, I ran into a friend who played on the Auburn team. He said, "When you guys came out on the field with those soccer shoes, the game was over!"

From a personal perspective, I hated I was injured in the first game, but was blessed to be able to recover and play well toward the end of the season. I am particularly proud that in the four years that I played at Alabama, Auburn did not score a single point. Blanking Auburn from 1959-1962 I think more than made up for the 40-0 shellacking they put on us in 1957.

I am also proud I played on the Alabama team that not only helped Coach Bryant win his first national title, but also helped bring Alabama football back to its proper place at the top of the college football world.

Then came my last game as a player on the Crimson Tide.

Playing No. 8 Oklahoma in the Orange Bowl was a serious challenge. The Sooners wrapped up an 8-2 regular season and Big Eight Championship by winning their last seven games, putting up 247 points to opponents' 19. Their losses came in their second game of the year, 13-7 to Notre Dame, and second game, 9-6 to Texas.

President John F. Kennedy flipped the coin for the opening kickoff, which allowed Alabama to receive. Kennedy sat on the Oklahoma side, as Coach Bud Wilkinson was the chairman of Kennedy's Council on Youth Physical Fitness. While Kennedy did not visit the Alabama side of the field, he did meet with an Alabama cheerleader and an Oklahoma cheerleader at halftime. "The Crimson Tide whipped Oklahoma 17-0 to win the 29th playing of the Orange Bowl before a sun-splashed crowd of 73,390 that included President John Kennedy and a national television audience," wrote Charlie Land of *The Tuscaloosa News.* "About all that Oklahoma fans and players got to enjoy was the 70 degree weather and an agreeable touch of breeze."

The game and the statistics were about even, the difference being that when Alabama had scoring opportunities, it made them count and Oklahoma failed to convert on theirs. It was a clean, hard-fought game almost devoid of penalties. We had one delay of game 5-yard penalty in the second quarter. Oklahoma had a 12-yard penalty on the kickoff following Alabama's first touchdown.

On our second possession Cotton Clark returned a 48-yard Joe Don Looney punt for 20 yards to the Alabama 30. Namath needed only nine plays to get the ball into the end zone. Versprille ran for 3, then Namath passed to me for 7. Versprille got 4, Clark ran for 5 and Namath for 5 for another first down at the Oklahoma 37. Three plays later Namath fired one to Richard Williamson for a 25-yard touchdown. A Tim Davis extra point made it 7-0 with 7:35 left in the first period.

Oklahoma roared back with a 23-yard run by Jim Grisham and a 56-yard pass from quarterback Ron Fletcher to end Allen Baumgardner, who was caught from behind by halfback Benny Nelson at the Bama 6-yard line. On the next play Grisham fumbled and end Mike Hopper recovered for the Tide. The Sooners had another chance when Versprille fumbled and the ball was recovered by John Porterfield on the Tide 31. Grisham carried on consecutive plays to the Alabama 16, and on his next 10-yard run, he fumbled again and Don Kearley recovered at the Alabama 8.

Clark punted out of bounds at the Oklahoma 8 and the Tide defense pressured the Sooners with a sack back to the 4. Looney punted to Piper, who returned the ball 14 yards to the Sooner 34. Three plays later Namath executed the option perfectly, at the last second pitching it to Clark, who ran 15 yards for the touchdown. Davis made the extra point with 6:43 left in the half.

Toward the end of the third quarter, Frankie McClendon rushed Looney's punt, almost blocking it, and to get it off, kicked it straight up in the air. The punt only went 5 yards and out of bounds at the Oklahoma 32. We pushed to the OU 2 before Namath lost a yard on a third-down play and elected to go for an easy field goal rather than try for the touchdown. Davis kicked it through, with Ingram Culwell holding, and we had the game under control at 17-0 with 2 minutes left in the third quarter.

In the middle of the fourth quarter, the Sooners drove from their 35 to the Alabama 18. The next four plays lost 2 yards and Oklahoma turned the ball over on downs. Later, a run and lateral play with Monte Deer and halfback Paul Lea teaming up for a 36-yard gain took the ball to the Alabama 18. Grisham ran for 7 to the 11, but two Looney runs netted nothing. Alabama took over on downs and ran out the clock for the 17-0 victory.

During the game, Namath made a major statement about his ability and the fact he had two more years to play for Alabama. During the press conference,

Coach Bryant said, "N-A-M-A-T-H, you'll learn how to spell it pretty soon." Lee Roy Jordan made 31 tackles during the game.

Coach Wilkinson was very complimentary of our team, saying, "They were a much better prepared team for the game and did a superior job of coaching. Their timing was excellent. Their line was quicker offensively and defensively than ours. Our line didn't give us enough time to fake or pass and theirs did."

Coach Bryant also praised the blocking of the Tide line, and said this was Namath's best big game. "I thought our line blocking was the best since our first game against Georgia when our players started getting hurt."

Alabama used 42 players to Oklahoma's 24. If the 70 degree weather was a factor, it favored Alabama after the Tide took an early lead.

Charlie Land wrote, "Paul William Bryant is not supposed to be a sentimental man. His popular public image would have you believe he is a football coach who has no time for such. Saturday night though a mellow Bryant could contemplate with considerable pleasure the achievements of another of his football teams. And you can safely bet that he doesn't think of it as his 1962 team, but as Charley Pell and Jimmy Wilson, Jimmy Sharpe and Joe Namath, Lee Roy Jordan and Cotton Clark, Butch Wilson and Tim Davis, Ingram Culwell and Bill Battle, and Richard Williamson and Eddie Versprille and all the rest.

"They won 10 football games this season," Land continued. "They lost one 7-6 to Georgia Tech. On New Year's Day, 1963 the evidence would have you believe that Alabama again was the best in the nation. Oklahoma, a fine football team, was demolished 17-0. The Sooners had some heavy guns and they never quit trying. Alabama was simply too much for the Big Eight Conference Champion.

"The seniors in particular could look back with pride. Most of them helped Alabama win 29 games in their three varsity years. During that span they lost only twice and tied twice. All three years ended in bowl games and they didn't fail there either. Texas was tied 3-3 in the 1960 Bluebonnet Bowl, Arkansas was beaten 10-3 in the 1962 Sugar Bowl, and Oklahoma conquered 17-0 in the 1963 Orange.

"This is practically the last of our national championship team. A lot of these seniors were the guts of that team too. When I went around the dressing room shaking hands with the players, it was all I could do to keep from choking up. They are like thoroughbreds in everything they do. They out-do what I think they can't do. They have been that way all along, even in the game we lost this season. And that was no ordinary team we beat this afternoon either. They just don't' know anything about losing. I thought if the game was close we would probably win because of them. But I was real worried they would beat us good. I was just underestimating those little fellows again," Land concluded.

After the game, there was an Orange Bowl party at the prestigious Indian River Country Club hosting both teams. A few years later, bowls did away with post-game parties hosting both teams, as the losing teams quit coming. Both teams did show up, and it was a great event that we could mix and mingle. Coach Bryant took me over to meet Coach Wilkinson after dinner. As I mentioned earlier, I had written him a letter before the season asking if I could come to Oklahoma as a graduate assistant and get my Master's degree, coach football, and work with him if appropriate in his off-season work as chairman of President Kennedy's Youth Physical Fitness program. Since he never replied to my letter back in August, I figured he had trashed it and probably didn't even remember. To my surprise, the first thing he said to me when we met was, "I got your letter back in August and we would be most happy to bring you on as a graduate assistant to help coach our freshman team and work on your Master's degree." We had a very pleasant conversation and I left there "on top of the world."

After the 1961 National Championship, Alabama alumni were so excited about the team moving so quickly from the bottom of the college football world in 1957 to the top, alumni associations around the state started to have special days in graduating seniors' hometowns, honoring them for their success. Most pitched in and bought cars, or other significant gifts to give to the players as they started out their careers. That tradition carried over to the 1962 season as well, and the Birmingham Alumni Association gave me a new 1963 Chevrolet Impala. That was legal back in those days, as our NCAA eligibility was over after our last game.

Well, Lee Roy Jordan was from Excel, Alabama, population 500. They asked Lee Roy what kind of car he wanted. He was pretty sure he would sign a professional football contract, and with that would come a new car. So he told them he didn't want a car, he wanted a registered Black Angus bull. It must have been tough to raise that kind of money in Excel, so at most every game there would be people in the street like Shriners, with signs saying, "Help buy Lee Roy a Black Angus Bull." That struck everyone as so cute, and Lee Roy played so well that alumni associations across the state thought Lee Roy's bull needed some female companionship. By the end of the season, Excel gave Lee Roy the registered bull, and six or seven different alumni groups presented Lee Roy with registered Black Angus heifers all bred to championship stock.

So Lee Roy outsmarted all of us as he started out after college with a soon-to-be herd of 13 to 15 registered Black Angus stock. If anyone deserved accolades, Lee Roy Jordan did. He was probably the best football player with whom I was ever associated.

Lee Roy, Butch Wilson and I were selected to play in the Senior Bowl at Ladd Stadium in Mobile, Alabama, right after the Orange Bowl. Tom Landry from the Dallas Cowboys coached the North team and Weeb Eubank from the New York Jets coached the South team. Most of the players had reported a few days earlier and gotten in a few practices. Those of us who had played in New Year's Day bowls were behind in the game plan "learning curve" with not many days to catch up. I never saw such big guys in my life at Alabama! Most of us were about 200 pounds, plus or minus, but there were many 250- to 275-pound players who would be viewed as small now, but to me they were giants.

I was assigned to play end in a 4-3 aligned defense, which at Alabama would have been a defensive tackle. I was lined up in a four-point stance on the outside shoulder of 270-pound Penn State tackle Charlie Sieminski, a second-team All-American. I weighed maybe 205 and the only time I ever played this position was in the fourth quarter of the Tennessee game when Charley Pell got hurt.

The North had a typical Ohio State-style battering ram of a fullback who was about 5-foot-11 and 230 pounds. Their plan was to run at me, which we expected anyway. I decided I wasn't going to get knocked back, so I played very low to the ground while protecting my turf, and making them go inside or outside of my skinny body. I figured if I could occupy my man and my patch of turf, Lee Roy would get them — and he did!

I tried to rush on dropback passes and that was such a mismatch. After trying to go inside or outside, I finally gave up and tried to get in the passing lane to knock the ball down. I actually tipped a pass up in the air and intercepted it to stop a fourth-quarter drive.

We jumped out to a big lead and were ahead 33-6 after three quarters. The rule in many All-Star games like this is set to help avoid blowouts. When a team is behind two touchdowns or more, they get to receive kickoffs regardless of who scores the touchdown or field goal. So in the fourth quarter the North started an incredible comeback. They would score and we would kick it back to them. They would score again and we would kick it back to them. With limited numbers of players on the team, our defense got pretty tired as we never got off the field in the fourth except for a few snaps.

With the score at 33-27 the North was on another drive and near our 30-yard line. A big collision occurred around a broken-up pass in our secondary. Lee Roy was laying on the ground, his mouth bleeding, and a couple of teeth were laying there beside him. He came to Alabama with a front tooth missing, but now he was missing two or three!

Jim Goostree, our trainer at Alabama, participated in the Senior Bowl every year and alternated teams. This year he was the trainer for the North squad, but he was the first on the field to look after Lee Roy. Finally, Lee Roy stood up, and the trainers collected his missing teeth. Coach Goostree had a handful of gauze and had started to lead Lee Roy off the field. Lee Roy grabbed the gauze out of Coach Goostree's hands, stuffed it in his mouth and said, "Let's play!" I knew how tough he was, but I guarantee you that the hair on every teammates' neck was standing up with this show of courage.

The drive continued with the big fullback grinding 4 or 5 yards at a clip. With a little over a minute to play the North had a first and goal from the South's 3-yard line. They handed the ball off to the fullback three straight times and Lee Roy and crew stuffed him. On fourth and 2, the quarterback kept it and was thrown for a 2-yard loss. We ran out the clock and won 33-27.

This was the first "professional" game for the players, as the winning team received $800 per player and the losing team $600 per player. Now, the $200 difference meant a lot to me at the time, but Lee Roy had received a herd of registered Black Angus stock and signed a lucrative contract to play for the Dallas Cowboys. That came with a nice signing bonus and a new Buick Riviera. So why would Lee Roy risk staying in the game in the fourth quarter, with a significant injury, and a game that was not all that important to anyone other than those playing it? It certainly wasn't for an extra $200. It was the competitive fire that drove him to be the best linebacker in college football, and that helped carry Alabama to a 29-2-2 record with an SEC and National championships on its resume.

Probably 95 percent of the players in this game signed National Football League or Canadian Football League contracts. I had a chance to sign with the Hamilton Tiger Cats but decided I was not big enough to be a professional tight end and not fast enough to be a split end. I was ready to get out to Oklahoma and figure out how to become a college football coach.

The spring semester at Alabama with no football practice or Winter Workout program was a pretty cool time for me. At the time, the A-Club was an active organization on campus and consisted of letter winners from the major sports and conference champions for the Olympic sports. I was elected president of the A-Club my senior year. The A-Club initiation was pretty brutal from a "hazing" perspective, but it was a tradition that Coach Bryant probably went through, and strongly supported.

In the by-laws, A-Club members had the right to keep any other letter jackets or sweaters from high school or colleges off campus. We never enforced that, as it wasn't that prevalent, but it was interesting to see the power that had been in place for many years. Joe Namath was raised in Beaver Falls, Pennsylvania. He didn't know a lot about Alabama traditions. He decided he didn't need to go through the initiation that involved shaving heads, and a lot of things worse than that. Coach Bryant called Joe into his office. When Joe emerged from the meeting, he decided he really did want to go through the initiation. As president of the A-Club, I decided to take him through. He went through the initiation with class and humility, and earned even greater respect than ever. Later Joe told me the "whole story" and I'll leave it to him if he ever wants to tell you.

Joe has always been a great teammate wherever he has been. The 1962 team was primarily a senior team. As a sophomore, Joe played like a senior in every game except the Tech game, and their two monster defensive ends, Martin and Davis, had a lot to do with that one. Joe earned the respect of everyone for his demeanor during practice and games, his leadership skills, and his talent. He is known as a great passer, but he was a great option quarterback until he suffered the first of several knee injuries.

As president of the A-Club, I was responsible for organizing a spring party. Jimmy "Chink" Wilson was the secretary-treasurer. When we got the job, we also got a checkbook. We assumed there was money in the account and started spending money to hire a band, pick the menu, and all things necessary to make for a successful party. Chink got an emergency call from Coach Carney Laslie, Coach Bryant's CFO, in addition to many other duties. When we got there, he jumped on us, asking, "Why are you spending all this money — checks are bouncing at the bank right and left." Obviously, that was a real-life learning experience, as neither of us knew much about finance. We didn't even have personal checking accounts. So after that I figured I had better go see Coach Bryant and make sure what we were thinking would be acceptable. I asked him if we could have shrimp cocktails for appetizers. He said, "If you win, you can have anything you want." I guess we had won enough, because we had a great party that to us was extravagant.

Coach Bryant was in a talkative mood at the party and asked me what I wanted to do after graduation. I told him I wanted to be a college coach. He said, "Don't do it if you can't live without it." But he went on to say, "But I'll tell you this, 'Bebes' Stallings and Bobby Drake Keith are making $10,000 a year and there aren't many people in any profession making $10,000 a year."

I'm not sure my dad at Birmingham-Southern College was making that much. My goal in life at that moment became to make $10,000 a year. I thought if I could make that much, I could live a great life. Now, you have to understand, in 1963, gas was about 25 cents a gallon, a new car was $2,000, and a nice home was $20,000. My other goals, other than becoming a college coach, were to live in an air-conditioned house, eat real butter at meals, have a player piano, and a polar bear skin rug!

Over the years, I acquired all but the polar bear skin rug! Bob Frazier, executive vice president at the University of Montana, who managed their licensing program, made Montana the first client to sign a 10-year agency agreement with The Collegiate Licensing Company. Later on, he gave us a beautiful white mountain goat skin rug. It occupies a prime spot today in our mountain house in Ellijay, Georgia. I call it our "Polar Goat" rug!

Words cannot express how much I learned during my four years at Alabama. Lessons learned in the classroom were great and very necessary to my preparation for life after college. However, lessons learned on the practice and playing fields under Coach Bryant and his staff had a far greater impact on me as to what it takes to be successful in life. Self-discipline, preparation, mental toughness, time management, leadership and team dynamics were just a few. I will be forever grateful for my time spent at The University of Alabama.

Honors at Alabama included:
- Three-year starter;
- All-SEC Scholastic Team;
- Third-leading scorer on 1962 team, with 28 points behind Tim Davis and Cotton Clark;
- Frank Thomas Award — Outstanding member of the football team who has excelled in scholarship, sportsmanship, team spirit and leadership;
- Jimmy Moore Award — A-Club Member with highest scholastic average;
- ODK Honorary Leadership Organization;
- Jasons Senior Men's Honorary leadership organization;
- Scabbard & Blade — ROTC leadership organization;
- President of the A-Club

LESSONS LEARNED

- Winning isn't everything, but it sure beats anything that comes in second.
- Better never than late. Being punctual is a trait everyone should adopt; arriving late to a meeting is rude to others in the meeting. A leader should not tolerate tardiness in staff members.

- If you push your team to the brink of mutiny, you'd better know when to pull back and get them on your side again!

- Football (and maybe other experiences) teaches self-discipline, preparation, mental toughness, time management, leadership, sacrifice, work ethic, competitiveness, teamwork, to learn to take your licks and fight back, to be so tired you think you're going to die, but instead of quitting, you learn to somehow fight a little harder. You learn to believe in yourself because you know how to rise to the occasion. Those lessons carry over to the rest of your life.

- It is important to improve in all three areas of your life — physical, mental and spiritual. If you don't learn anything else, learn to discipline yourself and be prepared when game time comes. Proper preparation prevents poor performance.

- Humility is a great trait. Be gracious in defeat, and humble in victory.

- Variety is the spice of life. Organizations need to be focused on the mission and intense in its pursuit, but it is helpful to have staff members who can inject humor into tense situations.

- In sports you are taught to "fight." Not to fist-fight, but to take your licks, get back up and come back again after you've been knocked down. That can happen to you in life, several times.

- There is no substitute for experience, and it can oftentimes beat talent. Combining talent and experience usually adds up to success. Unfortunately, much of the time getting to be experienced comes from going through some bad experiences!

- To really grow, it takes stepping out of your comfort zone and making sacrifices. Sometimes you get beaten up, but that's what it takes to expand your horizons.

Great mentors to me, other than Coach Bryant, were
(clockwise from left): Bud Wilkinson, Oklahoma;
Doug Dickey, Tennessee; Bob Woodruff, my athletics
director at Tennessee; and Paul Dietzel, West Point.

CHAPTER 3

THE ASSISTANT
COACHING
EXPERIENCE

Our 1963 graduating class left Tuscaloosa at just about the same time Bryant Hall, the new Taj Mahal of athletic dorms, was being finished. The 1963 freshman class and all underclassmen moved in that August. I'm told that Coach Bryant put the individual names of his 1958-'62 teams up in various rooms as being a principal part of building that fine residence. Because of my career path after I graduated, it was many years before I saw the dorm at all, and it had been renovated by then.

There were two executive suites that Coach Bryant put in the dorm to house visiting dignitaries. They were "Hyatt Regency nice." I am proud to say that when I came back in 2013 as Director of Athletics, I moved into one of those suites for three months until we bought a home in Tuscaloosa. So, I finally did get to live in Bryant Hall.

The summer of 1963 was interesting in that before I departed for Oklahoma as a graduate assistant coach under Coach Bud Wilkinson, I had two major projects to complete. First, I had to go to a six-week summer camp at Fort Benning, Georgia, to complete my ROTC obligations at Alabama. Second, I had to oversee the birth of our first baby. Patrick was due on Sept. 15, the same day I was to report to Oklahoma. The heat, humidity and training at Fort Benning made for a challenging summer. It was basic training at its finest. I had heat rash on top of poison ivy from crawling around in the woods playing soldier in 95 degree heat and about equal humidity. Looking back on it, though, it was a good exercise to go through. I did very well in the final standings, but going through it was miserable at times.

When I finished I returned home to get ready to go out to Oklahoma. Patrick waited until Aug. 24 to "discover America." Eugenia stayed in the hospital for three days after delivery. When she came home the next day, I left Birmingham with all of our worldly belongings in a 4x6 trailer, but I was driving the new 1963 Chevrolet Impala that the Birmingham Alumni Association had given me. In 1963, there were few, if any, interstate highways between Birmingham and Norman, Oklahoma.

Coach Wilkinson understood my reason for being late. I had rented a two-bedroom furnished apartment that I had ready when Eugenia and Patrick flew in six weeks later.

Here are some economics for you. My senior year at Alabama, Eugenia and I had a two-bedroom furnished apartment in Tuscaloosa's Northington Campus. It cost $45 a month with all utilities paid. I will have to say that when we moved in, Eugenia, who had lived in the palatial Alpha Chi Omega house on campus, sat down and cried! I had lived in Friedman Hall, the athletic dorm, and thought our apartment was a pretty cool place. It's all a matter of perspective. But I was appalled when I found out the two-bedroom furnished apartment we rented in Oklahoma cost $65 a month, and we had to pay the utility bills.

As mentioned earlier, Eugenia taught at Verner Elementary School in Tuscaloosa and made $250 a month. I never will forget, with her first paycheck, we went to the Sears store and bought a television set with remote controls. There were only three channels at the time. There was a big round knob on the TV set that would allow manual changing of stations that went "click, click, click" as the knob turned. With the remote control we could sit across the room, press the remote button, and get the same "click, click, click" from the knob. What a great invention!

We had saved much of her $250 a month salary. That, plus the $800 Lee Roy Jordan helped each member of our Senior Bowl team get. I also got money from selling tickets, which gave us a few thousand dollars in savings. At the first of each month, we would take a hundred out of savings to go with the $103 I got from Oklahoma. With that we would buy a month's supply of baby formula, because the last week of the month usually got a little thin grocery-wise.

When I arrived at Oklahoma, Coach Wilkinson was very nice to me. Bobby Drake Keith, who was one of our end coaches at Alabama, had joined the OU staff a year or two earlier and was a friendly face out there. The Oklahoma varsity staff and freshman staff were all very welcoming. John Tatum, John Markas and Leon Cross, also grad assistants, were friendships that have lasted throughout the years. Leon was an All-American guard on the Sooners' 1962 team, John Tatum was an outstanding center/linebacker on that team, and John Markas was the captain of the 1962 Duke team and was also president of the Duke student body. Each became very successful in their chosen careers.

Oklahoma was ranked No. 4 in the nation going into the 1963 season. A very young team finished the 1962 season ranked No. 8 in the AP Poll, winning the Big Eight Conference championship and losing only to Notre Dame 13-7 and Texas 9-6 in the second and third weeks of the season. They won seven straight Big Eight games before losing to our Alabama team 17-0 in the Orange Bowl. It was a very optimistic team going into the 1963 season.

Having played against them in the Orange Bowl, I was very knowledgeable about their personnel. The OU athletic facilities were very comparable to ours at Alabama. One thing that was different was their cafeteria served meals that allowed players to get as much as they wanted. I thought the food was excellent.

I knew Joe Don Looney was a special talent, a running back who was 6-foot-2 and weighed about 225 pounds. He was a Big Eight 60-yard dash indoor track champion. He was legendary as a very talented player, but he was also quite eccentric. I was told that in the 1962 season, twice in games when OU was trailing, he went up to Coach Wilkinson and said, "Put me in coach, I'm ready!" Both times he broke long touchdown runs to put the Sooners ahead.

So, I was eating lunch in the cafeteria on Wednesday before the varsity was to open up against the Clemson Tigers. I was sitting alone at a table and Joe Don sat down with me. He spoke, introduced himself and then took the first bite of his lunch. He threw his fork down on his plate and exclaimed, "I wouldn't feed this crap to my dog!" I actually thought it was pretty good chow, but didn't say anything. He continued, "But I'm ready for ole Clemson!" I thought, man if he did what I was told he did last year, and he's ready for this one three days before the game, he may put on a show this Saturday.

Clemson was coached by Frank Howard, another eccentric personality. One of Coach Bryant's favorite stories about Coach Howard materialized when they were opposing head coaches in an All-Star Game. Coach Howard was an Alabama graduate and a friend of Coach Bryant's. They got together before the game and Coach Howard said to Coach Bryant, "Now look here Paul, it wouldn't look good to our alumni if one of us was to beat the other badly. If either of us get two touchdowns ahead let's agree to 'call off the dogs.'"

The fourth quarter arrived in the game and Coach Bryant's team was leading by a touchdown. Not too long after that they scored another touchdown. Coach Howard's team received the kickoff and had to punt. When Coach Howard saw Coach Bryant's first team come back on the field, he started waving a towel at Coach Bryant across the field. Coach Bryant didn't look his way and his team made a first down. Coach Howard started yelling from across the way, "Beah, Beah," and waving his towel much more aggressively. When they made another first down, Coach Howard came out in the middle of the field, waving his towel and shouting, "Beah, Beah — you S.O.B., I surrender!" Coach Bryant cracked up.

Game day finally got here and I was really excited to watch this team play, and especially to watch Joe Don splinter the Tigers. On the first series, Joe Don carried the ball twice for maybe 2 or 3 yards each. He was also the punter. OU didn't make a first down on its first possession and everyone lined up to punt, except Joe Don, who was walking off the field. Coach Wilkinson was blown away, had to call time out, and ran over to Joe Don and said, "What the heck are you doing?" Joe Don calmly replied, "My legs are tightening up and I can't play anymore."

Oklahoma was behind Clemson at the half, but its talent and depth wore down the Tigers in the second half for a 31-14 win with 62,034 fans watching.

OU had to travel to Los Angeles the following week to face the No. 1 USC Trojans. The Sooners won 17-12, and that victory on the road set their fan base on fire. The OU coaching staff was happy with the win, but was a bit uncomfortable with the play of Mr. Looney. He did score a touchdown on a wingback reverse, but played very poorly in the game, getting a kick blocked and making other errors that looked like lack of effort. He indicated he had a stone bruise on his heel and had a hard time running full speed.

On the practice field from the start of the season, when the team broke up into position drills, Coach Wilkinson always coached the backfield. The varsity and freshmen worked on different fields, except when the freshmen were working against the varsity putting on scout team looks for the opponent of the week. Coach Wilkinson knew that having played offensive and defensive end at Alabama for three years, I knew how to play defensive end against the option. So every time Coach Wilkinson worked with the backs, I was assigned to that station to help the quarterbacks make decisions on their option reads; and holding a dummy, when I was also assigned to make the running backs make decisions on their cuts after getting handoffs on the belly play.

Oklahoma had an open date between the Southern Cal game and the Red River Shootout against Texas in Dallas. Darrell Royal, an Oklahoma graduate, was the Texas coach and had won a few straight games against his alma mater.

Joe Don was interviewed during the open date week and was quoted as saying, "We're never going to beat Texas until we get rid of this open-date week." I was pretty shocked at that, but watching him in backfield drills that week was even more shocking. Most of open date week, the team was allowed to dress in shorts, shoulder pads and helmets. Open dates that I remember at Alabama were more like spring practice than fall, and I never recall going out dressed in anything but full pads.

On this particular day during Coach Wilkinson's backfield drills, he let them take off their helmets. Joe Don would line up and run the plays at about half speed, which really screwed up the timing of the play. The other players started to get on Joe Don. Finally Coach Wilkinson said, "Joe Don, either get with it or go in." With a sour look on his face, he walked over, got his helmet and started to go in. Coach Wilkinson said, "What are you doing?" Joe Don said, "You told me to go in." Coach Wilkinson responded, "I said to get with it." With that, Looney threw his helmet across the field to where the other helmets were laying and got back in the backfield. He maybe ran 3/4 speed after that, but nothing else was said to him.

Joe Don carried the ball against Texas the next week about five or six times, gaining about 5 or 6 yards in our 28-7 loss. It is my understanding that on Sunday following the Texas defeat, the captains came in to see Coach

Wilkinson and told him they didn't want Joe Don on the team the rest of the way. He was dismissed from the team that day. Joe Don's father was quoted as saying that his son was being used as a scapegoat over OU's inability to beat Texas.

In the June 21, 2017, edition of *Sports Illustrated*, Andy Benoit wrote "The Greatest Player Who Never Was":

"If you want a messenger boy, call Western Union," Joe Don Looney remarked to Head Coach Harry Gilmer after Gilmer asked him to send in a play from the sidelines during what would be among Looney's final moments as a Detroit Lion.

He turned pro under comparison to Jim Brown and nearly 30 years later, was invoked by Coach Don Shula as an early era form of Herschel Walker. But Looney's professional career lasted just 5 years for that many teams, driving all of his coaches crazy. He was a fascination of the media. He did a stint in Vietnam. Six years after his final game, he was travelling the world, having discovered Siddha Yoga.

You might expect Joe Don Looney's story to be that of brazen, perhaps even heroic individualism. A counter culture icon stuck in an era of conformity. A different cat who walked away from the glories of pro football in search of deeper meaning.

Twenty-five percent of NFL teams dumped him and after that, none of the other 12 showed any interest. About this time, his army reserve unit was called up to Vietnam. Looney contested this. He was part of a group that sued on the grounds the Commander-in-Chief was not authorized to order a reserve unit to fight in an undeclared war. The lawsuit failed and Looney was shipped to Phu Bai South Vietnam."

If interested, read *Sports Illustrated*'s feature story on Looney's return from Vietnam in the Aug. 4, 1969 issue, *Sports Illustrated Vault*.

The rest of the season played out with wins over Kansas, Kansas State, Colorado, Iowa State and Missouri, before the big game for the conference championship. The Oklahoma-Nebraska game for the title was scheduled to be played Nov. 23, 1963. Unfortunately, this was a devastating time in history. On the day before the game, President John F. Kennedy was assassinated. I remember that Friday like it was yesterday. I had gone back to the apartment after class for lunch and saw the developing scene in Dallas on TV. It was hard to believe, and the word "shock" seemed like an understatement.

That night in Lincoln, Nebraska, university officers and officials had lengthy conversations. They were counseled by the NCAA and Big Eight officials. Neither state nor school wanted to play the game because of the national tragedy, but Oklahoma had a game the following week against Oklahoma State. Orange Bowl officials were on hand and needed to know about a representative. The championship game was a sellout, thousands had traveled to Lincoln and TV staffs were on hand. Finally, late Friday night, it was the decision of all the officials involved that the game be played. However, all pre-planned festivities were cancelled and the huge crowd stood in silent tribute to President Kennedy prior to the kickoff. Flags were at half-staff.

Nebraska kicked a first-quarter field goal to give the underdog Cornhuskers a 3-0 lead. They took that lead into halftime. In the third quarter, Lance Rentzel fumbled a punt return at the OU 15-yard line. The ensuing touchdown gave the Huskers a 10-0 lead. Another OU fumble recovery at its own 32-yard line set up another Husker touchdown to make the score 17-0. Oklahoma scored on a Ronnie Fletcher to John Flynn touchdown pass, but a Sooner pass was later intercepted at the OU 36 and run to the 15. Four plays later, the Huskers scored a touchdown and it was 23-7 with 7:15 left. On the first play after the kickoff, Nebraska intercepted another pass, returning it to the OU 1. Another TD made it 29-7 with 5:43 remaining.

Oklahoma refused to quit, and after recovering a Huskers' fumble, scored with 1:59 left to play. Another Huskers' fumble set up the final touchdown for the Sooners for a final of 29-20. As the nation was in shock, I can't imagine what Coach Wilkinson was going through, as he worked with President Kennedy on the Council on Youth Physical Fitness.

The Sooners beat Oklahoma State 34-10 the following weekend to end the season 8-2-0 with a No. 9 ranking by the AP Poll. There was great disappointment in the season that started so well, but losing the Big Eight Championship and Orange Bowl berth to Nebraska was devastating to the Sooners. It was probably an unfair setting for Coach Wilkinson and the Oklahoma team with President Kennedy's assassination the previous day. There was no bowl for the Sooners after the Nebraska loss, and my plans to work with Coach Wilkinson in the Physical Fitness Program were not to be. Soon after that game, Coach Wilkinson announced he was retiring to run for Oklahoma Senate. Unbelievably to me, he lost the race, as he went under with the Barry Goldwater reverse landslide.

My off-season was spent studying. As a grad assistant, I was only supposed to take 12 hours a semester. I needed to take 15 a semester to get out in one year, as that's all I thought I could stand. I got permission to take 15 and did pretty well in my course work, getting my Master's degree at the end of the spring semester.

I also hustled around refereeing church league basketball games at $5 each whenever I could. Another way I earned a little extra cash during the season was watching high school games every Friday night and grading potential recruits. I got with the head recruiter and told him I wanted to cover the game the greatest distance away from Norman. At that time in my life, I didn't understand depreciation, but I had a good grip on cash flow, and that 12 cents a mile I got in cash more than paid my gas and oil expenses in my new Chevy.

One of my supposed cost-saving transportation measures was buying a used bike for $5 to get to class and leave the car at home. It may have been worth more than $5, but definitely not much. The chain slipped, and my mechanical aptitude being pretty near zero, I didn't know how to fix it. I learned to live with it without getting hurt too badly. Two things I didn't anticipate in my bike-riding adventures were, if the wind was blowing against me (and it was always blowing out there in some direction), I had to stand up and pedal or just get off and push the bike. The other thing I never saw before or after was "goat heads." On my first attempt to go to class, I was dealing OK with the wind and cut across a vacant lot to save time. By the time I got across the lot I noticed my tires were losing air. When I inspected the tires, there were several little sandspur-looking things all over my tires. I guess they are a sort of sandspur, but have two sharp spurs sticking out of a round body that actually did resemble a goat's head. There were too many punctures to fix, so I ended up buying new tires, which cost almost as much as my bike!

The most valuable information I learned while at OU was that some former players had been assigned to the Army Athletic Association at West Point to coach football as part of their Army service commitment. I didn't know where West Point was, but I knew that its coach, Paul Dietzel, with All-American running back Billy Cannon, had won the National Championship at LSU after the 1958 season. I went home that night and looked at my set of encyclopedias a salesman sold me while at Alabama. I was surprised to learn it was in New York, just about 60 miles north of New York City.

I wrote Coach Dietzel a letter explaining my two-year military commitment and my having played for Coach Bryant at Alabama, and coaching for Coach Wilkinson at Oklahoma. Coach Dietzel had coached under Coach Bryant at Kentucky in 1951-52 and I'm certain they talked. Some two weeks later, Coach George Terry called and said they had checked me out and thought they could get my orders changed. I was so excited I couldn't stand it. Here was a chance to learn under another great coach and expand my horizon with another set of coaches and leaders at the U.S. Military Academy. I had been scheduled to report to an artillery unit in Jasper, Alabama, so indeed getting my orders changed to the Army Athletic Association at West Point was one of the best moves of my career.

After graduation from Oklahoma, I reported to my first U.S. Army Training at Fort Sill, Oklahoma. When I signed in there for six weeks of artillery training, as the song goes, "I was in the Army now!"

July and August at Fort Sill was as hot as Alabama, but not nearly as humid. As a second lieutenant, my base salary was $222.22 per month, but I think we got $110 for temporary duty and $47.50 for subsistence. I can't remember if we had to pay rent or not, but if we did, it wasn't much, and $379.50 was better than $103 a month.

I went to class every day, although some days were spent in the field. We were taught the specifics of the 105-millimeter howitzers (cannons) and the art of being a forward observer. The latter entailed getting in position to observe the enemy on the battlefield and communicating with the guns to "call in fire" on the targets.

The targets in this case were old automobile and tank bodies strewn around the valley in various positions. We were positioned on a hill overlooking these targets. We were given a set of coordinates at our location, and from there we estimated the coordinates of the targets we were trying to take out. We would send the gunner, via radio, a set of coordinates using the bracket system to try to destroy the target with the fewest number of attempts. Hopefully the first call for fire would land close to the target. From there we would calculate coordinates on the opposite side of the target but closer. Then we would come back to the original side but closer. When we were confident of the coordinates of the target, we would call to the guns, "fire for effect." With that, the howitzers would pound the target into oblivion.

That part of the drill was very interesting and actually a lot of fun. It was fun because this was a training exercise. Putting this knowledge to use in combat would be an entirely different situation. The forward observer in combat was to get in position to see the enemy in order to call in fire from the howitzers. If the forward observer could see the enemy, it was highly likely the enemy could figure out the location of the forward observer.

Fort Sill was actually an enjoyable experience. It was like going to work every day, and coming home in the afternoon to family. We had weekends off, and with a little extra spending money, we lived pretty well.

With the course at Fort Sill behind me, we loaded up and took off to West Point. The Army sprang for the cost of moving our belongings, which were relatively small. We had never driven on interstate highways before, but we got a serious education as we drove to our new home. Dealing with interstate highways for the first time was confusing. I remember we got off at three or four different exits that said "Baltimore." It would have been funny if it wasn't so difficult to get back on the right road. Thanks to the future inventors of the GPS!

When we finally arrived at West Point, we were excited to check in and see what kind of quarters might be available. We went to the Army Athletic Association and met the coaches that were there that day. Ms. Harriet DeMarest was Coach Dietzel's assistant, and what a remarkable presence she was. She introduced us around and made us feel welcome.

We then went to the office where we were to officially sign in. To our dismay, we didn't find a two-bedroom furnished apartment for $45 a month, or for $65 a month. There was absolutely nothing on the post available to a second lieutenant except the Bachelor Officer Quarters.

In the fall of 1964, the Vietnam War had not yet escalated to the point that it would in future years. Housing on post was available by rank, and there were only a handful of second lieutenants there. West Point was a highly desired assignment, so all of the housing on the post was taken.

We were told to look for apartments in the town of Highland Falls, which was adjacent to the Academy. There were no vacancies there. The next closest town was Newburgh, which was about 30 miles to the north, over Storm King Mountain. There were no available apartments there either. Tad Schroder, who was single at the time, invited us to stay with him while we looked. We couldn't believe the spot we were in.

A few days later, we met a realtor in Newburgh who was married to a captain in the Army. He taught at West Point. She told us there was a new apartment complex that would be open in about six weeks. She offered to let us camp out with her until the apartments opened. So Eugenia, 1-year-old Patrick and I moved into one bedroom in a large old house with our realtor, her husband and another boarder.

I went to work every day in the car, so it was tough on Eugenia and the baby to live like that for six weeks. When the apartments finally opened, the two-bedroom apartments rented for about $400 a month, and were unfurnished. I was making about $450 a month, but buying furniture for the apartment and the cost of living took all the rest of our savings. One day, Eugenia was excited to tell me when I got home that her mom had sent her a check for $35 and told her to go buy a new dress. She took me to work that day and planned to go shopping in Newburgh. We had lived pretty sparsely those days and new clothes weren't at the top of the list. When I got home that night Eugenia was crying. I asked what the problem was and she said, "On the way to Newburgh I got stopped by a policeman and got a $30 speeding ticket. I just turned around and came back home." That broke my heart and I vowed if we ever made enough money, she could go spend whatever she wanted.

Coaching at West Point was a great experience for me. It was worth the personal sacrifice we made, just as it was at Oklahoma. I would have paid to serve under Coach Bud Wilkinson and Coach Paul Dietzel. My assignment was to serve as defensive coordinator of the Army Plebe (freshman) team under the leadership of Coach Tom Cahill in the fall of 1964.

All of the military academies are very special places. They each have their own form of beauty. The graduates they turn out are well-educated men and women, who are taught current events, social manners and etiquette, as well as a top-rated academic curriculum. Most who get out of the service at some point become very successful leaders in whatever their chosen profession.

The Plebes at Army arrive on campus around the first day of July. They go through what is termed at Army, "Beast Barracks." I don't know what goes on there, but I'm told they strip you down to the basics of your being, and then build you back up in the Army way. The Plebes got mentally browbeaten, physically challenged, sleep deprived, and sometimes food deprived. When they get through, they welcome two-a-day football practices and anything other than what they are doing. Now, this was my impression back in 1964-65. Things may be totally different now, but the veterans look back and say how many wannabe cadets during or after "Beast Barracks" felt the call to practice law or the ministry or many other occupations, just to get out of there.

I remember our first practice well. Early in the team period, one of our defensive linemen made a mistake. I was fired up just to be on the field coaching, and went over to him and called out his name as he was getting off the ground. When he saw and heard me, he popped to attention, threw his head and shoulders back, and said, "Yes sir!" I never had a player respond like that and I saw he was terrified, thinking he might be in trouble. I put my arm around him and said, "Hey Johnny, relax man, this is just a game!" As he relaxed a little, I told him what I thought he did wrong and what to do differently the next time. I learned early in my tenure that at West Point, discipline was not a problem with the Cadets.

I also remember our first Plebe game. We were at home in Michie Stadium and playing the University of Massachusetts. I was so fired up I couldn't sleep the night before. We had practiced hard and I thought we would kill anybody named UMass. As I mentioned earlier, the Cadets went from dawn to well after dark, and in addition to the upperclassmen harassing them, they also now had to study. The curriculum was not easy. Unbeknownst to me, they were definitely sleep deprived.

At the time, Plebes dressed in the huge gym building a few blocks from the stadium. On the short bus ride to the stadium, about half the players on the team were asleep. They obviously had a lot more on their plates than this football game. Unfortunately, we played that way and UMass kicked our butts. I was discouraged, but went back to work learning the nuances of our defense when I could get time with our varsity coaches.

All of the Plebe coaches and a few of the varsity coaches spent pretty much every weekend scouting upcoming opponents. Army played a pretty healthy schedule. We opened up with The Citadel and Boston College at home, then to No. 1 Texas in Austin, Penn State at home, Virginia in Charlottesville, Duke and Iowa State at home, Syracuse in Yankee Stadium, Pitt at home and Navy at JFK Stadium in Philadelphia. We beat The Citadel, Boston College and Iowa State and were 3-6 going into the Navy game. The Army team played very well against a tough schedule, losing 17-6 to Texas, 6-2 to Penn State, 35-14 to UVA, 6-0 to Duke, 27-15 to Syracuse, and 24-8 to Pitt.

If you have never seen an Army-Navy game in person, put it on your bucket list. If you are a football fan, I promise you will be very impressed with the entire event. Having the entire Corp of Cadets from Army and the Brigade of Midshipmen from Navy in the same stadium is spectacular. There are generals and admirals everywhere you look.

Speaking of generals, I learned that there was no direct correlation between class rank and making general officer. As many in the bottom half of the class made general as those in the upper half. Leadership is not always shown in grade-point average.

The Cadets and Midshipmen, when they are Plebes, are taught about traditions at the Academies, and somewhere along the line they are taught very sophisticated cheers. When they spout those cheers in unison, it is quite different than any other team's cheers that I've heard. It is quite thought provoking to realize that the First Classmen (Seniors) are playing their last game for their schools, and within a few short months may be shipping out to countries where they are apt to be in harm's way.

In 1964, quarterback Roger Staubach's senior year at Navy, Army beat the Midshipmen 11-8. It was a huge win for Army. That game is looked at as half the season by the coaches, players and fans, so our 4-6 record was considered a winning season.

ARMY VS. NAVY — 1964

The 1963 Army-Navy game, the year before I got there, was a hard-fought game that ended 21-15 in favor of Navy. Staubach, a junior, had broken free on several runs that contributed to the Navy victory. Army had really concentrated on containing him after his outstanding performance, including running, in the 1962 debacle. Rollie Stichweh greatly outplayed him in 1963, as Navy's three TDs were on runs by fullback Pat Donnelly. It was unbearable to the Army team, as that victory marked Navy's fifth win in a row. It was made even more unbearable as Army was on the Navy 2-yard line when time expired. The win sent the No. 2 Midshipmen and Staubach, the Heisman Trophy winner, to the Cotton Bowl.

It was a gut-wrenching loss, and the Army team got together after that game and vowed that they would beat Navy in 1964. Navy thought otherwise. A victory for Navy in 1964 would give them six straight, never before achieved in the series. It would also tie the annual rivalry at 30 victories each. The Navy lead cheer at the game in Philadelphia's John F. Kennedy Stadium was "Six and Even." Army's battle cry was "Nix on Six."

Both teams had struggled during the 1964 season with injuries and lack of depth. Navy was 3-5-1 and Army was 3-6. Records didn't matter when those teams met. Navy coach Wayne Hardin said before the game, "We've lost some battles, but we don't intend to lose the war."

Army scored quickly. On the third play a fierce blitz led by linebacker Sonny Stowers tackled Staubach in the end zone for a safety. That play sparked the Army team. In a second quarter rally, Stichweh, who had played brilliantly in the '63 game, hit tight end Sam Champi with a touchdown pass to cap a 54-yard drive. A missed extra point resulted in only an 8-0 lead. Navy roared back by driving 64 yards, with sophomore fullback Tom Leiser's 1- yard plunge before halftime. A two-point conversion tied the score. On the two-point play, an all-out Army rush swarmed Staubach, but somehow, while being dragged down, he got the pass away to flanker Phil Norton. Navy wouldn't score again.

Army mounted a drive that stalled at the Navy 10-yard line with 9 1/2 minutes on the clock. Barry Nickerson entered to kick the field goal. Barry had been recruited by Navy, but wound up at Army when his application got hung up at Navy. Asked if he felt pressure, he said, "I've already missed an extra point, there were 100,000 plus people in the stands, and if I miss this thing I'm running out of here." He nailed the kick center of the uprights.

On the final play, Staubach completed a pass deep in Army territory and the tackle was made by Stichweh, one of a small group who had played 60 minutes. When the final horn sounded, a sea of gray uniforms poured out of the stands engulfing the players and reveling in the victory earned by these outstanding players who each gave their all to make amends for the previous year's loss.

Most of the seniors on both teams had tours of duty in Vietnam after that game. In a get-together years later, many spoke about how football had prepared them for conflict overseas, and how this game in particular was strength they drew from during tough times. It was very fitting to learn that in 2012, when Rollie Stichweh was enshrined in the Army Sports Hall of Fame, Roger Staubach was a speaker at his induction ceremony.

Working with the varsity coaches with scouting reports and every film session I could get into, I busted my tail to learn as much to help the varsity coaches as much as I could. I found out that Frank Gibson, the varsity receivers coach and a captain in the Army, was changing tours of duty in the spring of 1965. "Gibby" was a great guy and I had gotten to know him very well. Fortunately for me, Coach Dietzel promoted me from Plebe defensive coordinator to varsity receivers coach for the spring and all of 1965. Man, what a great opportunity. Not only did I get Gibby's position as varsity receivers coach, but I got an even greater blessing from him when I moved into his vacated apartment in Highland Falls.

As mentioned earlier, Highland Falls was adjacent to the Academy. Not only did I not have to drive over Storm King Mountain every day, but my rent in Highland Falls was $150 a month. That was like a $300 a month raise. Highlands Falls was not the nicest community in the world, but it was convenient to the Academy and the price was definitely right. We sent out Christmas cards when we were there. Our address was 13 Mountain Avenue, Highland Falls, New York. We got back a response that said, "Oh, 13 Mountain Avenue, Highland Falls, NY, sounds like such a beautiful, peaceful place!" It was far from it, but it was home for a year, and we enjoyed our time there.

Our apartment was over a beauty shop and a storage facility. Our entrance was up the outside back stairs, leading to a flat roof, which was our "back yard," and led to the only entrance/exit at our place. The roof covered the storage facility below. It had rails around it, so 2-year old Pat could ride his tricycle out there, play games and build snowmen in the winter. It was actually pretty cool.

One story about my travel over the Storm King Highway took place before our move to Highland Falls in early spring 1965. Tad Schroeder, our head recruiter, and I were taking an early flight out of New York City to attend a few days of Baylor's spring practice. I had to get up and at 'em pretty early, and there was snow and ice all over the roads. Up there, they had the equipment to plow snow and put down salt to keep traffic flowing. I wasn't too worried until I was going downhill on the mountain and my car started sliding. I did what I was supposed to do, but my car ended up sideways in the median, sliding downhill, knocking down those little aluminum stakes that marked the roads when snow was high. I finally came to a stop no worse for the wear, but I realized I had gotten out before the snow plows and salt trucks. I sat in my car, heart pounding, until the plows and salt trucks came. I did meet up with Tad and we made it to New York in time to catch our plane out to Waco, Texas.

By 1965, the rules had changed from limited to unlimited substitutions. That meant that players could go in and out as needed, and they no longer had to learn to play both ways. Practices changed dramatically as coaches could now select players best suited for either offense or defense, and work with them 100 percent on whichever side of the ball they were suited. With double the time, they could come up with more sophisticated schemes, which made the overall game better. As life in the 1950s and '60s advanced more technologically and in most all areas, it was evident that the game of football should follow.

Because of the rule change, Coach Dietzel decided to move more to a passing offense than the run-oriented option offense he had employed in the past. Army had a strong-armed quarterback more suited to that type offense. The primary mission of Tad's and my trip to Baylor was to learn all we could about their passing-game philosophy, strategy, problems and opportunities.

John Bridgers was the head coach at Baylor, where he had a very successful tenure and was well known for his passing-game acumen. In addition to Coach Bridgers and staff, famous Baltimore Colts wide receiver Raymond Berry was there working out and helping the staff. I had heard about Raymond Berry from Coach Howard Schnellenberger, our offensive coordinator for two years at Alabama. Raymond had a reputation for having an incredible work ethic. They said with the Colts he would bring a chaise lounge into the film room, as he might spend eight hours there on many days. Raymond kept a chart of every game, every opponent, and every defensive back he went up against. On the practice field, they say when running plays were called in team drills, Raymond would have a backup quarterback throw to him as he ran a certain route. After the catch he would run back to the line of scrimmage and the quarterback would throw him another pass, making him reach right, left, high or low to get the ball on a comeback.

Coach Bridgers, his staff and Raymond Berry were extremely accommodating to us during our visit. I learned a ton on that trip and it broadened my horizons tremendously as a receivers coach. I'm sure glad I didn't slide off the mountain and miss that learning opportunity!

Schroeder assigned recruiting territories to assistant coaches. We had to identify prospects there, and had regular recruiting meetings to put our prospects on a board by position as "black" (elite), "gold" (could play as a sophomore), or "white" (could play his last two years).

Before my time at Army, a recruiting incident occurred that created some negative publicity for the Army football program under Coach Dietzel. Appointments to West Point were not usually given until late spring in the calendar year. Most of the rest of Division I schools signed in December, or at least by National Signing Day in February. Coach Dietzel's reputation at LSU was able to get his coaches into the houses of athletes who might never have considered West Point. The Army coaches told the players it was acceptable to sign with another university, but the player should advise that university's coach that if he were to receive an appointment to the Academy, the player planned to accept.

Soon after Coach Dietzel's arrival at Army in January 1962, a student-athlete was being recruited by both Army and Clemson. He told Coach Dietzel about his family's request that he go ahead and sign with Clemson, but he wanted to attend the Academy. He did, and when his appointment came through a few months later, he told Coach Frank Howard at Clemson he intended to accept the appointment.

Coach Howard, as mentioned earlier as a unique character, blasted Coach Dietzel and the Academy, saying it wasn't proper to make a young man headed for our armed forces break a commitment and change schools.

Due to the incident with Clemson, we had to physically record in writing every phone call and every contact we made with prospective student-athletes. In our overall recruiting program, we were able to have admitted to West Point a certain number of "qualified alternates," e.g., those who didn't receive one of many appointments granted every year, but qualified academically. At the beginning we had to ask all prospects to write their congressmen and senators requesting an appointment to the Academy. In addition, those who finally said they wanted to come to the Academy, we asked them to sign a "Superintendent's Statement." This was a one or two paragraph mimeographed sheet saying that, if they chose to sign earlier in the year with another university, they could, but they would tell that university if they got an appointment to the Academy they would take it.

I had the state of Florida to recruit. Three times a year I would go check out a "bare bones" car from the motor pool, load up Eugenia and Pat, drop them off in Birmingham, and head down to Florida. I would either start on the Gulf Coast or Atlantic Coast, depending on appointments I had made. The first week I was running, the second week I was trotting, by the third week, man, I was dragging.

I was recruiting a player from South Florida. He was a pretty good player and a pretty good student. I thought with a year in prep school he would develop in both areas, and be a really good candidate for West Point. He signed with Florida, and even though he had signed the Superintendent's Statement with us, I don't think he told them of his desire to go to West Point. When the time came and he told them he was accepting West Point's offer, Coach Ray Graves went ballistic. He had finished spring practice and was on either a recruiting trip or vacation, but traveled to a different city every day for a week. Each day he would talk to reporters in that city and blast Coach Dietzel and West Point.

After about the third day I got the word the superintendent wanted to meet with me. I was scared to death, but I had all the files of my recruitment of this young man and the all-important Superintendent's Statement with his signature. Coach Dietzel drove me over and obviously sensed my nervousness. In a calming voice, he said to me, "Don't worry Bill, if someone's not suing or complaining about you, you probably aren't making much progress." That made me feel a little better and the meeting with the "Supe" went well, too. It all soon died down and we all went on about our business.

The business of coaching at West Point, and I assume all the Academies, is quite unlike coaching at state universities. The recruiting process is much more complex and difficult, especially with the four-year obligation following graduation. It is a five-year obligation today, but there are exceptions made if a player can sign with an NFL team.

So now, I was a varsity coach, which was much different than coaching Plebes. It was getting to work early and staying late at night — Sunday through Thursday — watching films of the upcoming opponent, preparing the game plan, installing the game plan to the team, and then playing the game on Saturday. Sunday was spent grading Saturday's film. It was 16-millimeter film in those days. If the cadets had time, we would review the film with them.

Time was a rare and valuable commodity at the Academy. If you were able to get them for three hours a day, that was incredible. During that time they had to get taped and dressed for practice on the front end, and of course, showered and dressed after practice, which counted in the three hours. If you chose to watch film, that cut into our actual practice time. And if they needed training room time to treat an injury or illness, that also took away from field practice time. The players had to be in dinner formation with their respective companies around 6:15 and march into the mess hall, except the week before the Navy game; then they could come on their own a few minutes after dinner began.

We had to be as creative as we could. Before practice we would try to get them together by position to talk to them as they dressed. We would often walk with them in groups to practice, getting as much meeting time as possible, taking advantage of every minute of those three hours.

The players were a genuine pleasure to coach. They were thirsty for knowledge and very disciplined in their approach to most everything they did. They were overachievers, and leadership was something they were taught every day as they prepared to graduate and go out into their chosen U.S. Army branches as second lieutenants to lead other men.

There was one tradition at West Point that was my favorite of all the great traditions there. Every afternoon at about 5 p.m., "Retreat" was sounded, followed by the cannon firing and the "To the Colors" was sounded by bugle. At the sound of "Retreat," everyone on the football field, which was relatively close to the flagpole, would stop what they were doing, face the flag, and remove their head gear with their right hand. When the cannon fired, they would put their right hand over their heart, while putting their headgear on their left shoulder. When the American flag had been lowered, and the music stopped, the right hand was dropped, and they replaced their headgear.

That took maybe two minutes, but the scenery from that place on the post was spectacular for 360 degrees. To our left over the Parade Field called the Plain, were the gray stone buildings, which housed academic and administration operations. Behind us, and all along to our right, was the Hudson River flowing between the Academy on one side and beautiful tree-covered mountains on the other.

Nowadays, coaches on any practice field in a two-hour practice are focused on getting as many repetitions as possible for the players, whether in individual drills or team drills. They are evaluating techniques, assignments, proper meshes, proper blocks, tackles, positioning, etc., ad infinitum! They are focused and intense as they try to take advantage of every minute. They are typically totally unaware of anything in their surroundings beyond the field.

I fit into that category as well, but every day when the cannon fired, we removed our hats, stood at attention, and for a minute or two, we turned football off. It was a near-spiritual experience. Autumn up there is beautiful. Since it happened every day, I almost felt I could see the leaves changing from green to yellow, red and orange before my eyes. It was magical to me, very inspiring, and maybe even life changing to the extent that I was able to enjoy that small amount of seconds and appreciate God's beauty in a way I never would have without the bugle and cannon stopping the merry-go-round throughout the fall.

The 1965 season as a varsity coach was an incredible learning experience for me. I had learned a lot during my year at Oklahoma and a lot more in my Plebe defensive coordinator role at West Point. But there is a huge difference from being a Plebe team coach and a varsity coach. The complexity of the schemes, the intensity of the practice sessions, and the teaching situations were all new and exciting to me.

The fact that the football rules changed in 1964 from limited substitutions (as explained in my playing time at Alabama) to an unlimited substitution was also helpful to me. We all spent the off-season between 1964 and 1965 plotting strategy to take advantage of the relatively new rules. I was on the front end of the rules change, which I thought put me on an even keel to a certain extent with more experienced offensive coaches.

The fact that players could enter and exit the game with no restrictions changed entirely the way practices were constructed. Previously, all three teams had to learn how to play all phases of the offense, defense and kicking game.

Unlimited substitutions encouraged coaches to select players to spend all of their time on offense, and a different set of players selected to focus all of their time on defense. The kicking game was split. Offenses would focus on punt coverage, field goals, extra points and kickoff returns. Defenses would focus on punt returns, field goal and extra point rushes, and kickoff coverage.

Army opened the season in 1965 with Tennessee. Larry Jones, defensive line coach, and I went to Knoxville to cover their spring game. I was now 23 years old. We were in the Knoxville airport and a young 6-foot-4, 230-pound guy walked up to me and said, "Hi, I'm Bob Johnson, a player at the University of Tennessee, and I'm here to pick up a prospect. Are you a prospect?" I was flattered and very impressed with this guy's looks. We didn't have anyone on our team that looked like him. I said, "Sorry, I'm not a prospect," and then introduced Larry and myself and told him who we were and what we were doing.

Bob became an All-American center at Tennessee and had a great pro career with the Cincinnati Bengals. Bob had two younger brothers, Tom and Paul, who would both later be outstanding players at UT during my coaching tenure there.

After Army opened at Tennessee in 1965 and lost 21-0, it beat VMI 21-7 at home, beat Boston College 10-0 at home, lost 17-0 to Notre Dame at Shea Stadium in New York, beat Rutgers 23-6 at home, lost 31-14 at Stanford, lost 29-28 to Colgate at home, lost 14-3 to Air Force at Soldier Field in Chicago, beat Wyoming 13-0, and tied Navy 7-7 at JFK Stadium in Philadelphia. A 4-5-1 record was not what we had hoped for.

The 1965 Army-Navy game could only be described as a defensive struggle. It was a dark, dreary day in Philadelphia. Coach Wayne Elias, former head coach at the University of Virginia, was in his first Army-Navy game, as he succeeded Wayne Hardin, who had resigned after the 1964 season.

In the second series of plays, Army defensive end Tom Schwartz crashed into Navy quarterback Johnny Cartwright as he was attempting a short pass to his halfback. The ball went flying backward and was ruled a fumble that came to a halt at the Navy 31-yard line. Sam Champi, Army's other end, recovered the ball. Shortly thereafter, halfback Sonny Stowers bolted for a 25-yard touchdown to give the Cadets a 7-0 lead.

Navy rallied late in the second quarter when Cartwright hit his receiver Murray on a perfect touchdown pass with 63 seconds left in the first half. The rest of the game was a defensive struggle as Army continuously rushed Navy's quarterback and covered their receivers. They held Navy to 16 yards rushing. The 7-7 tie left neither side happy, but both teams were proud of their defensive efforts.

A fortuitous thing happened the weekend I was scouting the Air Force Academy that fall when they were playing UCLA in Colorado Springs. Earlier in the fall, Tennessee had tied Alabama in Birmingham, a major victory for the underdog Vols, led by second-year head coach Doug Dickey. It was the highest of highs for the Vols. Unfortunately, the lowest of lows hit two days later when three UT coaches were riding to work together early Monday morning and where struck by a train when crossing a railroad track. Ultimately all three died. Coach Dickey did an incredible job keeping the team together and finishing the season 8-1-2 with a makeshift staff.

Bob Woodruff, a Tennessee graduate and former head coach and athletics director at the University of Florida, was the current athletics director at Tennessee. Coach Woodruff was scouting UCLA for Tennessee that weekend as an example of the "all hands on deck" attitude with everyone pitching in to help replace the three coaches. He knew the AD at the Air Force Academy and flew out a couple of days before the game to visit with an old friend.

Early in the game, Coach Woodruff came up and introduced himself to me. He asked if we were driving back to Denver to the airport after the game to fly back home, and if so, could he ride there with us. Of course we welcomed him to join us on the ride to the airport. As you will read later, that ride had life-changing implications for me. We had a great conversation during the ride about his playing time at Tennessee, his coaching and athletics director career at Florida, and his short tenure as AD back at Tennessee where he hired Coach Dickey. Of course, we also talked about my playing time at Alabama, my graduate assistant experience at Oklahoma, and my current responsibility at Army.

After the season, I was thinking about interviewing for a job. I didn't get out of the Army until mid-June, but I had saved two years' worth of personal leave — 30 days a year — so that, in the event I was offered a job, I could take 60 days to go to that university's spring practice. Some of the "young coaches" on the Plebe staff and I would talk about interviews from time to time. The conversation most always included the question, "How much should I ask in salary if I get an offer?" I remembered my conversation with Coach Bryant in 1963 when he told me that Coach Stallings and Coach Keith were making $10,000 a year and not many people in any profession were making that much. This uncertainty about salary was in 1966, so some of us boldly decided the value of living on post, shopping at the PX, enjoying the perks around the Academy, was worth $9,500.

One night toward the end of the 1965 season, we worked late and I was staying that night with Tad. Afterward, Coach Dietzel drove me to Tad's house. As he pulled up to the house, he said, "Bill, we've enjoyed having you on our staff this fall and I'd like to offer you a full-time position when your

Army tour ends this summer." I was so stunned, I didn't say anything. My mind was churning, thinking about all the conversations the young West Point coaches had had about this moment. So at the end of what must have been an awkward time for Coach Dietzel, he said, "Well, good night, hope you get a good night's sleep."

I got out of the car saying, "Good night" and fussing at myself for not responding at least in some way to Coach Dietzel's generous offer. Without much sleep that night I decided to respond to him with the idea that if I could get housing on the post, I would take the job. We never discussed money or anything else. Fortunately for me, and probably for him, he came back in a day or two and told me that at that time there was no room for him to secure an additional house on post for a civilian coach.

I didn't believe that a man should ask his secretary to write letters to other employers about getting a job, so Eugenia, Pat and I went over to the offices about 10:00 one evening to write application letters. I wasn't going to write Coach Bryant, as I thought he knew where I was and if he was interested he would contact me. So I decided to write to coaches John McKay at Southern Cal, Darrell Royal at Texas, Ara Parseghian at Notre Dame, Bobby Dodd at Georgia Tech and Doug Dickey at Tennessee. At least I was aiming high!

Our offices were equipped with those high-tech electric typewriters at the time. Eugenia was a good typist, but had only used manual typewriters. After an hour, she had only gotten two letters written, to Coach Dodd and Coach Dickey. Every time she would put her fingers on the keyboard, it would quickly type all eight keys. With no way to correct mistakes, she went through dozens of pages and started again. Finally I said, "To heck with this, it's late, let's go home."

The American Football Coaches Convention that year was in January in Washington, D.C., at the Shoreham Hotel. Since I didn't get out of the service until June, I was assigned to make a three-week recruiting trip to Florida. On the way down, Coach Dietzel allowed me to spend a couple of days at the convention.

In the meantime, Coach Gomer Jones, who succeeded Coach Wilkinson at Oklahoma, had been fired after two years and was replaced by Coach Jim McKenzie, who had played for Coach Bryant at Kentucky. When he got the job, he hired one of his Kentucky teammates, Pat James. Coach James was our defensive line coach at Alabama and had been promoted to defensive coordinator by the time I was a senior. Coach McKenzie lured Coach James away from Alabama to join him at Oklahoma. Before I left West Point for the convention, Coach James called me and said they wanted to hire me to come back to

Oklahoma. That was very encouraging, but I didn't want to go back to Oklahoma. I wanted to go south!

When I left to go to the convention, I had learned that Coach Jerry Claiborne, who had left Alabama while I was there, was the head coach at Virginia Polytechnic Institute (VPI), and he had an opening for a receivers coach. Somehow I made contact and arranged an interview shortly after I arrived in D.C. The interview was going very well as we traded stories about where we each had been since he left Alabama. Then he asked, "How much money are you expecting?" I stumbled around, as that was an uncomfortable subject for me at the time and finally said, "Well, what I think I have at West Point is worth $9,500." Now remember that after my conversation with Coach Bryant in 1962, my goal in life was to make $10,000 a year, and it still was. Coach Claiborne leaped forward in his chair and blurted out, "$9,500! I was assistant head coach at the University of Alabama and only made $8,500." At that point, I determined that the interview wasn't going as well as I had thought, and also that Coach Bryant must have started paying his coaches better after Coach Claiborne left!

Later that day I was standing in the lobby of the Shoreham Hotel talking with friends when I saw Coach Dickey heading our way. I recognized him from his pictures. About the time he was walking by our group, someone in our group introduced me to another person who had just walked up. When Coach Dickey heard my name, he turned around and looked but kept on walking.

After a while, Coach Dickey circled back, introduced himself and told me he had received my letter. He said, "I have offered the job, but if he doesn't take it, I'd like to talk to you." I later found out that he had offered the job to Jerry Elliott, who had played on Auburn's 1957 National Championship team and was currently coaching on the Auburn staff. Jerry was a few years older than I was, but we had lived on the same block in West End in Birmingham. He was a hero of mine growing up. As a side note, we were on the same two-party telephone line for a few years.

Fortunately, Jerry turned down the job and Coach Dickey called me to his room. "I'd like to have you and your family come down to Knoxville for a visit," he said. I said, "I've been to Knoxville, coach, I don't need to come visit." He said, "How much money do you want?" After my experience with Coach Claiborne, I didn't know what to say, but finally said, "I don't know coach, maybe eighty…." He said, "Eighty-five hundred?" I said, "Sounds good to me." So we shook hands and I had a job at the University of Tennessee, which to me, ranked at the top of the SEC with Alabama.

After that meeting, I was very excited and happy. I had time to get to the AFCA luncheon and looked forward to telling my Army buddies the good news. The convention was my first, and seeing all the great coaches like Bryant, Royal, Parseghian, Hayes and others and hearing them speak was like a dream. As I was sitting at my table before my buddies arrived, I felt someone sit down beside me and put his arm around my shoulder. It was Coach McKenzie from Oklahoma. He said, "Are you ready to come to Oklahoma?" I said, "No sir, coach, I've decided to go to Tennessee with Coach Dickey." He said, "Does money make a difference?" I said, "No sir." He said, "I'll offer you $9,600." I about fainted, but said, "No sir, I told Coach Dickey I was coming to Tennessee and that's where I'm going." He wished me luck and said if I changed my mind to give him a call.

I was still ultra-excited about going to Tennessee. Later that day I ran into Coach Dickey, told him about the offer at Oklahoma, and told him I was excited about coming to Tennessee at $8,500, but was there any room? He said, "How about $9,500." Man! I was going to Tennessee making only $500 less than my goal in life. How could life be any better than that!

I counted back 60 days from the end of Tennessee's spring practice, and using my leave time, I reported to UT in the spring. Our staff met for a few days when the players left on spring break and the coaches left to go recruiting. I had gotten to my first high school and was meeting with two bright young coaches, Rex Dockery and John Paty. They both became very successful coaches, Rex at the college level and John in high school. We were drawing X's and O's on the blackboard and getting down in stances talking techniques and doing things that coaches do. Then an assistant came in and told me I was wanted on the phone. I was told that all coaches were to come back to the offices. A serious automobile accident had occurred and at least three players had been killed. After losing the three coaches back in the fall and now this, one wondered how much tragedy this program could stand.

With sadness, we started spring practice when the players returned the following week. When I saw the level of talent on the Tennessee team, I knew I was back in the SEC. As receivers coach, I was extremely blessed to work with Austin Denney, a 6-foot-2, 220-pound senior tight end who signed with the Chicago Bears after the 1966 season. He played three years with the Bears and one with the Buffalo Bills. The split end was Johnny Mills, a senior who had had a phenomenal junior year, but broke his arm in the final regular-season game in Memphis against UCLA. More about this later. The flanker was sophomore Richmond Flowers, a world-class high hurdler from Montgomery. In addition, we had good depth behind them. I was in heaven!

After spring practice, I returned to West Point as persona non grata since Army again played Tennessee, this time in October in Memphis. Tad gave me a cubicle somewhere down in the basement that smelled like a dungeon. He gave me a recruiting research project to work on to list cities and states that Army football players had come from over the past 20 years — or something like that.

Interestingly enough, upon my return, I found that Coach Dietzel and his entire staff had taken jobs at the University of South Carolina. As I learned later, after the 1965 season, Coach Dietzel came to the realization that West Point had changed so much since he was there in the 1950s that it was very difficult to get enough blue-chip players to compete with the schedule Army was playing. He had offers from several schools but turned them down.

Dietzel wrote a document that spelled out what he believed he needed to win at the Academy and gave it to his superiors. A month went by with no response. Three weeks before spring practice he received an offer of a 10-year contract from South Carolina to become both head football coach and athletics director. He went to the Superintendent General Don Bennett and discussed the situation. Bennett told him that leaving at this late date would be very difficult for the Academy, but to do what he needed to do. Coach Dietzel and his staff believed their chances to win were much better at South Carolina than at Army, and a week later, he was released from his contract at Army. He took with him his varsity staff of George Terry, Jim Valek, Bill Rowe, Bill Shalosky and Larry Jones. There were only six coaches on his varsity staff in 1965 and I was the sixth. Had I accepted Coach Dietzel's offer a few months earlier, I guess I would have gone to South Carolina instead of Tennessee.

Tom Cahill had been named head coach at Army. It was definitely a different atmosphere there as Coach Cahill was building his staff and getting his program organized to face the upcoming schedule. I was glad that Tom got the job and felt like his love for the Academy would help him do well.

Also on the Athletics Department staff at the time was head basketball Coach Bob Knight. Bob had come to the Academy as a private first class and was an assistant coach for two years before succeeding Coach Tates Locke for the 1965-1966 season. I struck up a friendship with Bob during the May-June time I spent working on projects until my two-year commitment to the Army was up. I would work a half day on Tad's recruiting project, and play golf with Bob on many days in the afternoon. As a new head coach, he was on one of the major sporting goods manufacturer's honorary staffs and was equipped with clubs and a huge supply of golf balls — enough for both of us. The golf course at the Academy was immaculate. I wasn't a good golfer, but enjoyed the social side of playing with Bob.

Bob was also a huge baseball fan. When Roger Maris and Mickey Mantle were playing for the Yankees, we went several times into the city, which was only about an hour's drive from West Point. One of my most memorable nights ever came when the Yankees were playing the Los Angeles Angels. Bob knew Dean Chance, a pitcher for the Angels who was the youngest ever to win the Cy Young Award in 1964. I think maybe they went to high school together. Anyway, he wasn't pitching on this night and came over and visited with us before the game in the primo seats he had provided us. There was a huge Velva Sheen sign in right field with actress Mamie Van Doren prominently featured on the ad. Dean pointed up to the sign and boastfully said, "I'm dating her!"

After the game, we went to dinner together. I wish I had brought a recorder to capture some of the most entertaining stories between Bob Knight and Dean Chance. He brought us autographed baseballs for our sons, both named Patrick, and about the same age. It was definitely a night to remember.

There were many perks to those associated with the U.S. Military Academy other than getting to work with some of America's finest young men. We could shop at the PX, which offered a wide variety of groceries and merchandise at reasonable prices. I mentioned the excellent golf course. There was also a very nice ski slope that cost $12 a year to join. Our athletics director, Colonel Murphy, was a West Point graduate and was on the ski team when he attended the Academy. He had a collection of skis and boots, and since we wore the same size shoe, he loaned me a pair of boots and skis. Back then, men used skis that were about a foot taller than their height. It was definitely a challenge to learn how to ski there, but over two winters I learned at about a low C grade. There were lots of bumps and bruises along the way, but I grew to love skiing and introduced my kids to the sport.

Another perk was the ability to attend plays in New York City courtesy of the USO. Friends tried to get us to go to plays over our stay there and I always declined. My reasoning was that the only plays I had ever seen were high school plays and I thought they were awful. Finally, I reluctantly agreed and was mentally prepared not to like what I was about to see. That night we saw "Cactus Flower" starring Lauren Bacall. I was hooked. Soon after that we attended a musical, which I was also mentally prepared not to like. It was "Superman," which was a high-energy singing, dancing, flying across the stage on wires extravaganza. The USO provided free tickets to active Army officers, and we always had orchestra seats. I have enjoyed Broadway plays ever since as the most entertaining performances possible.

An additional treat was available to West Point staff, cadets and graduates. Mama Leone's was a great Italian restaurant in the city that provided extra special seating and dining experiences to West Pointers. The family had two sons who were West Point grads. We always tried to get to the city early enough to enjoy a feast at Mama Leone's before the plays.

THE UNITED STATES MILITARY ACADEMY AT WEST POINT

Mission: To educate, train, and inspire the Corps of Cadets so that each graduate is a commissioned leader of character committed to the values of "Duty, Honor and Country" and prepared for a career of professional excellence and service to the nation as an officer in the United States Army.

I would be remiss if I didn't mention some of the history of the Academy and its influence on American life. It was a genuine honor and stroke of luck — or part of the Master's Plan — that I was able to spend my two-year military obligation coaching football there. The Academy's impact has gone far beyond its role in preparing officers for a career in the Army.

Graduates who have gone into public life after service in the Army have had an impact on virtually every sector of our lives, including business, law, medicine and many other fields. It is a little known fact today how much impact the Academy has had in collegiate football, basketball and the formation of the NCAA.

Dennis Mahan Michie was Army football's founding father. His dad, Peter Michie, was an 1863 graduate and Civil War veteran who was present at Robert E. Lee's surrender at Appomattox. The older Michie returned to West Point after the war and served as a permanent professor for more than 30 years.

In that time, Dennis Michie was born April 10, 1870, raised on West Point and entered the Academy in 1888. As a cadet, Dennis Michie organized and led the first Army football team. As team captain, he then enticed the Naval Academy to challenge West Point in a game, which the Naval Academy accepted. The challenge led to the first Army-Navy football game in 1890, which was held on the Plain at West Point and ended in a 24-0 Navy victory. Unbeknownst to both opponents, this game gave birth to one of the greatest rivalries in all sports. Following his graduation in 1892, Michie remained at West Point for a year and was the first coach of the Army football team, finishing with a record of 3-1-1.

Promoted to captain, Michie fought in Cuba during the 1898 Spanish-American War. In the battle for Santiago, Michie was leading his men on a patrol along the San Juan River. He was shot and killed in action on July 1, 1898. Michie's body was returned to West Point, where he is buried in the West Point Cemetery. His father passed away three years later in 1901 and is also buried at West Point. A short distance up the hill from the cemetery, Michie's memory is immortalized by the West Point football stadium dedicated and named in 1924.

In 1999, *Sports Illustrated* ranked its worldwide "Top 20 Sports Venues of the 20th Century" and Michie Stadium was ranked third, preceded by Yankee

Stadium and Augusta National. *SI* eloquently described the Army football experience as, "Game day at West Point begins three hours before kickoff with the Cadet parade on the Plain. It's a scene straight from 'The Long Gray Line,' surpassed only by the view of the Hudson River from the west stands at Michie Stadium. The Corps of Cadets seated together and dressed in gray and black evoked memories of when Army was one of the most formidable of college football powers, and cannon blasts shake the stadium to its foundation every time the Black Knights score. It doesn't matter in the least that national champions are no longer decided here."

Since its initial construction in 1924, Michie Stadium has undergone several expansions, and currently seats 40,000 spectators. The stadium offers spectacular views of the Academy and its surroundings. If you have not visited the campus and seen a football game there, put it on your bucket list. It's only 60 miles from New York City.

BRIGADIER GENERAL PALMER PIERCE, USMA 1891

According to a *New York Times* article on Jan. 1, 1908, "Had it not been for Captain Pierce, it is doubtful if football would have recovered yet from the blows struck at it during the agitation for its abolition, when educational forces seemed to be arranged against it. The debt of gratitude that the lovers of the great gridiron sport owe to the former director of athletics at West Point is far greater than any, save a few, recognize."

Such was the praise given to then Captain Palmer E. Pierce, an 1891 graduate of West Point and unlikely savior of college football, as the sport teetered on the brink of extinction. In hindsight, Pierce, who once served as West Point's athletics director, clearly is one of the unsung heroes of college sports in general. Remarkably, this unlikely sports hero served the nation simultaneously as both a distinguished Army officer and a fierce advocate of intercollegiate athletics as the National Collegiate Athletic Association's (NCAA) first president for 21 of its first 24 years of existence.

By 1905, college football had proven to be a popular but dangerous sport with few rules, minimal equipment, and no standardization across institutions. In that year alone, 18 football players died on college football fields. Moreover, colleges and universities struggled with fully embracing such an enormously popular sport that provided entertainment, but had little academic purpose and seemed to undermine the true nature of American higher education. In light of this struggle, many institutions largely favored abolishing football, while President Theodore Roosevelt, an ardent fan of the game, also warned academia to reform or abolish football.

While teaching at West Point, Captain Pierce attended a December 1905 conference of America's 13 football-playing institutions convened to reform the sport. His significant influence at that conference convinced the other members of the need to regulate, not only football, but college athletics in general, and encouraged the formation of the Intercollegiate Athletic Association of the United States (IAAUS), the precursor to the NCAA. Pierce's leadership not only helped save football through greater regulation, standardization and with a drastic decline in fatalities, but he also was an outspoken advocate of the inherent educational value of sports and for integrating college athletics into the academic structure of member institutions. At the 1907 NCAA convention, he prophetically declared, "I firmly believe the Association will finally dominate the college athletic world." Indeed, more than a century later, the NCAA is still the governing body regulating the entire college athletic world.

From 1906 through 1930, Pierce's NCAA presidential span was interrupted twice for his combat service to the nation. In 1916, he was a member of the Punitive Expedition in Mexico against Pancho Villa, then during World War I, where he served in France as commander of the 54th Infantry Regiment and Assistant Chief of Staff of the American Expeditionary Force. Earlier in his career he had also seen combat during the Spanish American War.

Pierce retired from the military as a Brigadier General in 1930 after 39 years of service, but he continued to serve his alma mater as president of the Association of Graduates from 1931-1934. He also ended his tenure as NCAA president, but not before institutionalizing and validating the NCAA's role as a legitimate organization within American higher education. Pierce died on Jan. 17, 1940, and is buried in the West Point Cemetery. One of the largest rooms at the NCAA headquarters in Indianapolis, Indiana, the Palmer E. Pierce Ballroom, honors his legacy and contribution to the world of college athletics.

COLONEL EARL "RED" BLAIK

In honor of its legendary football mentor, Army christened the Michie Stadium playing surface as Blaik Field in 1999. A gridiron innovator, Blaik compiled an 18-year Army record of 121-33 and brought the Academy its only National Championships in 1944 and 1945. The Army team went undefeated from 1944 through 1946, with 27 wins and one tie. In the 1946 season, both Army and Notre Dame went undefeated, but the Irish were awarded the mythical national title.

Blaik coached three Heisman Trophy winners: Doc Blanchard, Glenn Davis and Pete Dawkins. Nineteen of his players and coaches went on to become head coaches in college or professional football. The most noteworthy of that group was Vince Lombardi. Coach Paul Dietzel, under whom I served, had also coached at Army in 1953-54 under Colonel Blaik before winning a national championship at LSU in 1958. He came back as head coach at Army from 1962-1965, and then on to South Carolina from 1966-1975, where he served as both head football coach and athletics director. He finished his career as the AD at LSU.

In its 1944 undefeated season, Army's final game was against its perennial nemesis, Navy, a powerhouse team that had run off six straight wins. With war raging on, Blaik believed at the time there was more interest in that game than "any other ever played." After a fourth-quarter Navy score, Army's lead was cut to 9-7. At that point Army's two star running backs Blanchard and Davis took over with outstanding performances that turned a close contest into a 23-7 Army victory.

To underscore the importance of that win, General Douglas MacArthur sent the following wire upon the game's conclusion: "The greatest of all Army Teams. We have stopped the war to celebrate your success."

GENERAL ROBERT R. NEYLAND

General Robert Neyland led Tennessee to four National Championships in football, and served in both World Wars. But before that, he was an Army football player on the undefeated 1914 team.

Neyland became one of Army's all-time greatest athletes, lettering as a football lineman and a baseball pitcher, and was three-time brigade heavyweight boxing champion. He won 20 straight games as an Army pitcher, including all four victories over Navy. He played football with other legendary cadets, including Dwight D. Eisenhower, Omar Bradley and James Van Fleet. During his junior year, the 1914 Army team went 9-0, winning the National Championship. He turned down a lucrative $3,500 contract with the New York Giants in order to serve in World War I.

He served as head coach of Tennessee football three separate times (1926-34, 1936-40, 1946-52), achieving an overall record of 173 wins, 31 losses and 12 ties, with four national titles (1936, 1940, 1950, 1951). The victories included 112 shutouts, with six shutout seasons. During his first seven seasons as UT's coach, he posted an incredible record of 61-2-5.

He left Tennessee in 1935, recalled to active duty in the Army to serve in the Panama Canal Zone, but he returned to Tennessee the following year. His 1938 National Championship was won, remarkably, without giving up a single point. It helped secure his position as one of the greatest defensive coaches in history.

He returned to the Army in 1941 after the bombing of Pearl Harbor and served as chief supply officer in the incredibly challenging theater of China-Burma-India in World War II, where he served under General "Vinegar Joe" Stillwell (USMA 1904). Given the nearly impossible task of supplying Stillwell's Army over the Himalayas, Neyland stepped up and helped win the war. Brigadier General Neyland received the Distinguished Service Medal and Legion of Merit, and was made an honorary member of the British Empire.

He returned to Tennessee in 1946 and resumed his career as head coach of Tennessee football. The first few years back were challenging, but he managed to cast aside any doubts of his outstanding leadership abilities when Tennessee won National Championships in both 1950 and 1951. He retired after the 1952 season, but remained in the role of athletics director from 1952 until his death in 1962. In 1956 he was enshrined in the College Football Hall of Fame.

The University of Tennessee football venue bears the name Neyland Stadium, not only because of his legacy, but because he personally designed the stadium and planned expansions that took place after his death.

Early in his career, Neyland developed seven maxims that he made all his players and coaches memorize. They are still in place today at Tennessee: 1) The team that makes the fewest mistakes will usually win; 2) Play for and make the breaks and when one comes, score; 3) If at first the game or the breaks go against you, don't let up, put on more steam; 4) Protect our kickers, our quarterback, our lead, and our ballgame; 5) Ball (fumble), oskie (interception), cover (kicks), block (self-explanatory), cut and slice (more blocks), pursue and gang tackle (all 11 defensive players get to the ball carrier) — for this is the winning edge; 6) Press the kicking game. Here is where the breaks are made; 7) Carry the fight to our opponent and keep it there for 60 minutes.

GENERAL DOUGLAS MACARTHUR

General Douglas MacArthur, one of the most revered graduates of the Academy, served as superintendent of the Academy from 1919-1922. The Academy has 26 different sports, and every cadet is expected to participate in at least one. One of General MacArthur's most famous quotes while the superintendent there is boldly displayed in the Athletics Department, "Upon the fields of friendly strife are sown the seeds that, upon other fields, on other days will bear the fruits of victory." Athletics is firmly integrated into academia at West Point.

Army also had a significant impact on basketball. Bob Knight coached at Army, Indiana and Texas Tech. Coach Knight broke Dean Smith's record of all-time NCAA basketball wins. Bob also coached Mike Krzyzewski, a 1969 USMA graduate, who broke Coach Knight's record, and at the time of this writing is still the winningest college basketball coach in the history of the sport. One of Coach Krzyzewski's memorable quotes, "I don't look at myself as a basketball coach, I look at myself as a leader who coaches basketball."

In June 1966 when my Army tour ended, I left West Point with very fond memories. My two-year association with the Academy and with Coach Cahill, Coach Dietzel and his staff provided me with a great education in what college coaching was really about. I made friends for life there, and developed great respect and love for the U.S. Military Academy. Most importantly, I believed that my experience at Alabama, Oklahoma and now West Point had prepared me to make a contribution at my next assignment at the University of Tennessee.

When we were in Knoxville for spring practice in 1966, we decided we would rent an apartment for a few months until we decided which section of town we wanted to live and to be able to take our time waiting for the best opportunity to buy a house. The rule in buying houses in those days was 2½ times your annual salary. We looked and found a few subdivisions in West Knoxville that we liked. The formula said we could spend up to about $24,000. We found a house bigger than we needed for $28,000. I was too nervous about money to pull the trigger on that one. We found a house that we liked in Walker Springs subdivision that was just being finished. They were asking $21,500. It was a three-bedroom, two-and-a-half bath ranch-style house on about an acre of land. There were woods in the back of the house that extended way beyond the property line. My realtor was talking honestly with me and one day told me, "If I were you, I don't know if I would buy now, interest is sky high." Interest at the time was 5 ¾ percent! I decided that we needed to buy a house before the season started, as I wouldn't be able to think about it after we got busy.

I asked the contractor how much it would cost to add central air conditioning. He told me $2,000. That put the house at $23,500 and right at my limit, so we said OK. It was a great deal, and made even greater that there were three other assistant coaches in that same subdivision.

In spring practice I had gotten to know Austin Denney, Richmond Flowers, Terry Dalton, Mike Price and the other receivers. Johnny Mills, our split end, had broken his arm pretty badly in the last game of the season against UCLA. I had watched film of him and he was an outstanding split end. He didn't have great speed, but he could accelerate off the breaking point as well as anyone I ever coached. That ability enabled him to distance himself from the defensive backs enough to be open on a well-timed pass, and he had great hands.

I invited Johnny over to our apartment for dinner early in the summer after I got back from West Point. I had heard that he was an eccentric personality.

In spring practice, he had a full arm cast and couldn't participate at all. We had a great visit that day at our apartment and we learned a lot about our respective philosophies of life. He had a great year, caught a lot of key passes, and definitely kept everybody loose whenever he did come to practice.

Johnny loved to play in games but he didn't care much for practice. He was from Elizabethton, Tennessee, and was a small-town boy. One of his hobbies in Knoxville was hopping on a southbound train as it slowed down coming through town. His particular train had a regular route hauling coal from Corbin, Kentucky, to Etowah, Tennessee, and back. The train would stop in Etowah so it was easy for him to get off. He walked into town, had a favorite sub sandwich place he liked, and enjoyed going to the jail and visiting with the sheriff and his deputies. When the time came, he got back on the train headed for Corbin. The problem on that leg of the trip was that the train didn't slow down when it got to the place Johnny wanted to get off. He would jump, hit, and roll. The trainer told me he broke about four casts and they couldn't figure out how he did it.

His train-riding hobby wasn't really discovered until one day in the spring when he took one of our better track athletes with him on his hobo expedition to Etowah. There was a big track meet that weekend and his buddy that night was expected to score a lot of points in the events in which he excelled. All went well until the return to Knoxville and the time came to hop off the train. Evidently, his buddy hadn't learned the "hit and roll" technique as well as Johnny and he banged himself up pretty badly. He missed the meet that weekend and Johnny was scolded for his part in the situation.

He knew all the trains that passed through Knoxville and even knew the engineers' names. One day later in the fall when he was at practice, we (or at least I) were deeply involved in drills and focused on improving technique. I felt an arm wrap around my shoulder and it was Johnny. He pointed down toward the railroad track below the practice field and said, "That's the 4 o'clock train headed for Etowah and the engineer's name is Mr. Johnson." I laughed and said, "Get your butt back over in line and think about what we're doing."

In our first game of the 1966 season against Auburn in Birmingham, it was terribly hot. Johnny had caught six or eight passes in the first half. At halftime after everyone had settled down and the position groups started meeting, I asked, "Where was Mills?" I found out he was in the training room and they had him packed with ice. He didn't practice much in fall practice due to his healing arm. He did come back and play in the second half and was a factor in our victory over Auburn. The 11 passes he caught in that game was a Tennessee record. The previous record was 10, set by Jim Powell in 1948 and matched by Mills in the 1965 UCLA thriller in Memphis. Austin Denny caught two touchdown passes in the 28-0 victory over Auburn, and Terry Dalton another.

Later in the year, Johnny was diagnosed with a mild case of mono. That allowed him to check into the hospital on Sunday, get out on Thursday in time to go through practice Thursday and Friday in shorts or sweats, play the game on Saturday, and check back into the hospital on Sunday. He got away with that for a few weeks, as he was an expert at missing practice.

Although I only worked with him one year, he was the one player who called me regularly through the years. When I was head coach at Tennessee and when I was in business at CLC, I had my calls screened carefully by our receptionist. Whenever she would ring my office and say, "He wouldn't tell me his name but said to tell him I'm the man that made him who he is today." I said, "I know who it is, put him through." We remain friends today and try to get together a time or two every year. I have remained close to several of our former players, and it is amazing how much I learned from them about things that happened during the years that I never knew about when I was coaching!

Having gone through spring practice with the Vols put me light years ahead of where I would have been had I come in after I finished my tour of duty in June. It was a great decision to save up 60 days of personal leave to be able to do that. When I did return in June I had some time to get better acquainted with the University of Tennessee. Coach Dickey, Ray Trail and George McKinney were part of the Arkansas team we played for the National Championship in the Sugar Bowl my senior year at Alabama. Ray was an outstanding interior lineman for the Razorbacks, and George was a quarterback and a team captain.

Our offices at the time were in Neyland Stadium. We were in pretty close quarters in cubicles. My cubicle mate was McKinney, our defensive secondary coach. At the time our facilities were pretty Spartan-like. We were eagerly awaiting the completion of the new Stokely Athletic Center, which would have the basketball arena, football offices, team dressing room, training room and equipment room. All sports coaches offices were housed there, along with the AD and administrative staff offices. The ticket office was also located there, along with Air Force ROTC offices. It was a glorious new building that was finished in time for the 1967 season. The entire southwest part of the campus was expanding into property recently cleared in an urban renewal project. Fraternity houses, the Tom Black Track, and the Natatorium were all built in this 1966-67 timeframe.

Dr. Andy Holt was president, and with Bob Woodruff leading athletics, Doug Dickey coaching football and Ray Mears coaching basketball, Tennessee was poised for great things. I remember going into the season being very excited to be back as a part of the Southeastern Conference. Being at Tennessee was special to me. I vividly remember playing in Knoxville as a sophomore and again as a senior. The sophomore experience was pretty bad; the senior experience was much better. As one of the few people who have been in both the Alabama and the Tennessee dressing rooms in big games during the 1960s and '70s, the respect that each team had for the other was powerful.

Many times I was asked by Tennessee fans if I had mixed emotions about playing against Alabama. I thought that was a dumb question. My loyalty was 100 percent with the team with which I was associated. Of course, I will always have strong feelings for Alabama and Coach Bryant, but I wanted to help prepare our team the very best I could to earn his respect as an opponent.

The 1966 Tennessee football team was a good one, finishing 8-3 overall and No. 14 in the Coaches' Poll. We defeated Auburn 28-0 at Legion Field in Birmingham and Rice 23-3 at home. We went to Grant Field in Atlanta with a No. 8 ranking to face Georgia Tech, which had a secondary comprised of players small in stature, but quick, fast, agile and tough. Bud Carson had joined Coach Bobby Dodd's staff and put in a pro defense that was a lot different from what we had been seeing. We played about as well as we could play on defense, but our offense was baffled by the defensive scheme. Tech intercepted three passes, with two of them stopping UT drives and the third setting up their winning field goal in a 6-3 victory.

The next week Tennessee faced No. 3 and undefeated Alabama in Knoxville, and it was another classic defensive struggle. The Vols jumped out to a 10-0 lead, as Dewey Warren completed a 6-yard touchdown pass to tight end Austin Denney, and Gary Wright, from Bear Creek, Alabama, kicked a 40-yard field goal. That remained the score at the half and continued through the third quarter.

The Crimson Tide fourth-quarter comeback drive was capped by a 1-yard Kenny Stabler touchdown run. Coach Bryant decided to go for two and Stabler completed the two-point conversion to Wayne Cook to make the score 10-8. With 3:23 to go in the game, Alabama's Steve Davis kicked a 17-yard field goal to go ahead 11-10.

Tennessee received the kickoff and began a drive of its own. A halfback pass fooled the Tide secondary and got the ball over midfield. With a first down on the Tide 11-yard line and under a minute to play, the Tennessee staff had a decision to make. The decision was made to run the ball a couple of times to get the clock down to a few seconds and kick the winning field goal. As fate would have it, the Tennessee fullback ran the ball to the 1-yard line and on the right hash. That's probably the hardest place on the field to kick a field goal. The kicking team went in and the ball was kicked. The Tennessee holder raised his arms signaling that the kick was good, and Coach Bryant threw his hat down in disgust on the sideline. But then the referee signaled no good. Evidently, the ball sailed over the right goal post or just barely outside. The game was over and Alabama kept its unbeaten streak alive and went on to an undefeated season. In the dressing room after the game Coach Bryant was asked, "What if that kick had been a foot to the left?" Coach Bryant calmly replied, "We'd have blocked it!"

Undefeated Alabama ultimately lost the national title when Notre Dame and Michigan State tied late in the season and were named Co-National Champions, with Alabama ranked third.

Tennessee went on to defeat South Carolina 29-17, Army in Memphis 38-7, and Chattanooga 28-10 at home before losing to Ole Miss the next week at home 14-7. In the Ole Miss game, Johnny Mills caught passes for an SEC-record 235 yards, and Austin Denny caught the Vols' only touchdown. Tennessee defeated Kentucky and Vanderbilt at home 28-19 and 28-0, respectively, to wrap up a 7-3 record (4-2 in SEC) and land a berth in the Gator Bowl against Syracuse.

Syracuse was coached by legendary coach Ben Schwartzwalder and featured a strong running game behind All-American backs Larry Csonka and Floyd Little. Tennessee kicker Gary Wright kicked two first-quarter 38-yard field goals to give the Vols a 6-0 lead. Dewey Warren threw a second quarter touchdown pass to Richmond Flowers to make the score 12-0. Right before the half, Tennessee lined up to kick a field goal but a fake fooled the Syracuse defense as Warren completed a touchdown pass to Denney to take an 18-0 lead into halftime. Two-point conversions were missed on both Vol touchdowns.

As we were running off the field and into the locker room, I'll never forget hearing our defensive coordinator shout, "Hot dog boys, they have to come out passing in the second half and we're going to kick their butts!" Well, they came out passing in the second half alright. They would throw it back to big Csonka one time and let him run inside, then the next time they would throw it back to Little and let him run outside.

Little ended up with 216 yards on 29 carries while Csonka had 114 yards on 19 carries, but Tennessee ended up winning the game 18-12. Probably the biggest play of the game came on a fourth-down attempt from the 1-yard line. A hole opened up and Csonka drove into the hole full speed. He was met head on, one on one, by linebacker Paul Naumoff. In a perfect form tackle, Naumoff hit Csonka hard under the chin and drove him back, saving the touchdown. It was one of the hardest hits I've ever seen. The victory wrapped up an 8-3 season, with losses only to No. 3 Alabama 11-10, Georgia Tech 6-3 and Ole Miss 14-7.

After the 1966 season, I spent most of the off-season, when I wasn't recruiting, in the film room. I broke down every offensive play and compiled a huge three-ring binder notebook with information by game. I wanted to know the offensive play against the defense called, whether or not the play was good, and if not, why not. A good play on normal yardage was 4 yards (4 yards x 3 downs = first down). On short yardage, it was a good play if it made a first down or touchdown. On long yardage, it was a good play if it made a first down or touchdown.

As an assistant coach, whenever I was in town I tried to spend many noon hours playing handball at the YMCA. I grew up playing handball at the Birmingham YMCA and continued to play when time and place was convenient at Alabama, Oklahoma, West Point and now Tennessee. I developed a great friendship with George Mooney, the longtime voice of Vols radio. I was 24 when I got to Knoxville and George was 48. He was in amazing shape, as he was an elite water skier in summer and snow skier in winter. We had very competitive lunchtime matches, with one of us winning about 21-18 in two out of three games. We came out of those matches soaking wet with perspiration. That kept me in pretty good shape. As we were getting dressed before the matches, the final thing George did was hang his toupee on a hook in his locker. He got some kidding about that.

During those first few years at Tennessee, I would often run wind sprints or stadium steps with the team. That obviously didn't last after my assistant coaching days, but it was fun while it lasted.

Sometime in the spring of 1967, I heard that West Point had developed a computer scouting program. I called my best friend at Army, Cammie Lewis, and asked him about it. He said it was great and he would send me all their info. Cam was a former quarterback at Army and one of Coach Dietzel's finest. He was the son of Pappy Lewis, the famous West Virginia coach. Cam and I became best friends and would discuss football or recruiting philosophies for hours on end over our two years together as coaches at West Point. We remained good friends until he passed away in 2018.

I didn't know much about computers, but I knew that all the film room time I had spent over the winter had interfered with my handball time. I got with our defensive coordinator and we figured out what reports he needed, and I knew what reports we needed on offense. With that information I blindly stumbled in over at the University Computer Center. I met with the dean and we had a very pleasant conversation. At the end of the meeting, he said he would be pleased if his department could help the football team.

He assigned me two young ladies who knew nothing about football, just like I knew nothing about computers. I learned enough to be dangerous. In 1967, the computers were huge and occupied most of a good-sized room. The language was "Fortran" and the printouts came on green and white paper, about 10 inches by 20 inches. The pages were attached, so a report might be 2 to 3 inches thick.

We worked together all summer. Through trial and error, we came up with reports that were very meaningful in scouting our opponents, and scouting ourselves. We would spend about the same amount of time breaking down film Sundays and Mondays, but we could do so in a form that could be programmed by our new friends in the computer department. I would take over info on Sundays as we developed it. Later that night, or the next day, I would go over and get boxes full of those big green and white paper reports. The computer enabled us to get more and better reports, which then we had time to compile manually. It also allowed us to scout ourselves, which was hard to find time to do manually.

So actually, I guess I was ahead of my time as a "nerd" in 1967. Years later at CLC, my staff found that hard to believe, as for years I refused to get a computer to use email. I didn't see the point when I had a great secretary, Linda Jordan, who could effectively handle all my correspondence. When email became used by many of our clients, I finally broke down and learned. At that time, emails were also very popular with my grandchildren.

During the 1966-1969 years in the off-season, we tried to visit other schools to study what they were doing and to keep up with the trends. One of our most memorable trips saw our offensive staff of Jimmy Dunn, Ray Trail and me making a trip out to the University of Southern California to study their offense. Coach John McKay welcomed us and spent an inordinate amount of time going over philosophy and strategy of their offensive system. We spent hours watching film. USC probably ran the power sweep as well as anybody in the country. It was very helpful to us to get a personal tutorial from this Hall of Fame coach.

We were very impressed with the philosophy, but even more with the talent that made those plays work. What we saw both on offense and defense were players that "rose above coaching" in making plays. We were not as impressed with their individual techniques as we were their athletic ability. We discussed their recruiting and found them to be in a pretty special place. They said they rarely spent a night away from home as there were 10 million people in Los Angeles County, and high school football was excellent there. They also had about a thousand junior colleges in the state, which was like being able to redshirt dozens, if not hundreds, of players. Coach McKay really had a good thing going and owned the city during his tenure there.

One of the most enjoyable parts of the trip was when Coach McKay took us to lunch at Julie's, a famous campus restaurant. I had heard of three-martini lunches but never witnessed one until this trip. Coach McKay enjoyed his martinis, along with a long cigar. He told great stories, many about his friendship with Coach Bryant. The one that was most memorable was that after a big Southern Cal victory, Julie's was packed with fans when suddenly someone brought Traveler, the beautiful Southern Cal Trojan horse, into the restaurant. A fan strapped a martini bucket to the horse's mouth. The horse promptly crapped on the floor, which caused the chef to throw down his chef's hat and walk out of the restaurant.

I told Coach McKay that the lifestyle of a Southern Cal coach is quite different from that of a Tennessee coach. When you come to Knoxville, we'll take you to lunch on the strip, feed you metworst, white beans and cornbread, and if you don't like buttermilk, maybe you can get a cold beer!

We also took a trip to visit the Dallas Cowboys. Gil Brandt showed us around. Gil was famous for scouting and bringing little-known players from obscure universities to become great players for the Cowboys. He opened up their film room to us and we spent hours watching film, and seeing how the Cowboys under Tom Landry operated. Coach Gene Stallings, who coached for Coach Bryant and Landry, made a comment something like, "Coach Landry would research every particular situation, every play. I didn't think we ever made a call that wasn't a perfect call offensively or defensively. On the other hand, Coach Bryant was a little bit more of a people person. Our X's and O's weren't any better than anybody else's, but the players thought that they were." Gil treated us like royalty and our trip was very educational.

We also spent a few days at Purdue. They had a very effective passing game back in those days and always seemed to give in-state Notre Dame fits. They really had a history of good tight ends and used very imaginative ways to get the ball to that position group. Everywhere we went, the coaches were so nice about sharing information. I don't think coaches were as paranoid about sharing back then, as long as we weren't playing each other.

Our staff also did a good job of receiving visiting college coaches, and we did a great job every year of working with high school coaches. We held an annual coaching clinic for high school coaches and brought in outstanding speakers at the college and high school levels. We continued working hard to do that through my head coaching tenure as well.

The 1967 season at Tennessee was a great one. We went 9-2 overall and were crowned SEC Champions after going 6-0 against conference opponents.

We ended up with a No. 2 ranking in both AP and Coaches' polls. We lost our opening game 20-16 against UCLA under the lights in the L.A. Coliseum, and our final game 26-24 against Oklahoma in the Orange Bowl at night. We won all games in between those two.

Also in 1967, another monumental change was made. As an assistant coach, I wasn't privy to the politics of such decisions, but it was decided to allow our staff to sign African American players. We knew that whoever we signed, we must be successful in making the right choices, preparing them for what was to come, and being beside them if they ever encountered struggles along the way. Our two choices were Albert Davis of nearby Alcoa, Tennessee, and Lester McClain from Nashville. Albert was a star all four years of his high school career. He was big, strong, fast and tough — the ideal running back. Lester was tall, rangy and fast with good hands and good speed.

Tennessee was more ready for integrated athletics than the Deep South states, in my opinion. I remember well our recruitment of Albert. In those years we were able to do some things in recruiting that are not allowed today. At a Vols basketball game in winter 1967, at halftime, we could lower the lights and shine a spotlight on our recruits as we introduced them to our crowd. Albert was very well known to our fans, as he had made headlines throughout his career at Alcoa. When he was introduced, everyone in the stands stood and gave him a thunderous ovation, then broke out in a loud chant of "Albert, Albert, Albert!" Tennessee was ready. Unfortunately, we lost out on Albert, but we did get Lester, who became UT's first African American player.

As receivers coach during Lester's freshman, sophomore and junior years, I got to know him very well. He was solid in every sense of the word, as a player, a teammate and a student, and he had a great sense of humor. I do not know the pressure he must have felt, but he never let it show. He was the perfect fit to break the color barrier at Tennessee. He had an excellent season as a sophomore in 1968, catching 29 passes for 329 yards and six touchdowns. Lester became the first African American player in the SEC to score a touchdown, and was the third-leading scorer on the team with 36 points behind placekicker Karl Kremser's 46 and tailback Richard Flowers' 42. His junior season was not as good statistically, but the most memorable play of his career may have been the 82-yard touchdown pass he caught against Memphis State for a new school record. He was definitely a solid leader and receiver on our 1970 team, my first year as head coach of the Volunteers.

The '67 opener with UCLA was a nail biter. UT led for the entire game until All-American and Heisman Trophy winner Gary Beban made one of his classic rollouts on a fourth down and 2 yards to go late in the fourth quarter. Not only did he make the first down, but he pulled it down and ran for the go-ahead touchdown. An interesting stat was that UCLA did not punt the entire game, but they had seven fumbles and two interceptions that the we capitalized on to almost win the game.

From there, the Vols won nine straight. With Dewey Warren emerging as the starting quarterback, Coach Dickey moved Charlie Fulton from quarterback to tailback to take advantage of his running and athletic ability. In the second game of the season against Auburn in Knoxville, Warren was injured in the third quarter, leaving the game with a 14-13 Tennessee lead. Fulton led a strong running and passing attack that extended that lead to a 28-13 victory. He netted 103 yards rushing and 48 passing, and as a result, was named Back of the Week in the South.

The following week against Georgia Tech, Fulton went out with a rib injury late in the first quarter. Bubba Wyche, a highly recruited quarterback out of Atlanta, was next in line and came through like the champion he is. Bubba guided us to a 24-13 victory over the previously undefeated Yellow Jackets, completing 8 of 16 passes, and became the second substitute quarterback to win Back of the Week in the South.

The 1967 version of Alabama vs. Tennessee was a typical, hard-fought game and was won at the wire. Bubba answered any questions about his preparedness right off the bat as Tennessee took the opening kickoff and drove 75 yards for a touchdown and a 7-0 lead. Alabama responded on its third possession with a drive, capped by a Kenny Stabler option run for a touchdown to tie the game at 7-7. UT drove to the Alabama 15 in the second quarter but fumbled. The Tide drove deep into Vols territory but had a field goal blocked. Tennessee cornerback Jimmy Weatherford stopped another second-quarter Bama drive with an interception.

In the third quarter, we capped a long drive with a halfback pass from Walter Chadwick to tight end Ken DeLong to go ahead 14-7. Later in the quarter, safety Mike Jones intercepted a Stabler pass to set up a 47-yard field goal by Karl Kremser, making the score 17-7.

In the fourth, the Tide intercepted a pass that led to an Alabama touchdown, making it 17-13. Later in the fourth quarter, Albert Dorsey intercepted three Stabler passes, with the last one being returned for a 31-yard touchdown, sealing the 24-13 UT win. Dorsey was named National Defensive Player of the Week for his performance. The victory by Tennessee stopped Alabama's undefeated streak at 23 games. Coach Dickey had brought Tennessee back from the bottom of the SEC in four years to successfully compete with Alabama and Ole Miss.

We beat LSU 17-14 the next week, as Dewey Warren returned to his quarterback position. Kremser kicked a 43-yard field goal with a minute left, but

LSU drove it right down the field, only to miss a game-tying field goal from the 26 at the end.

The Vols traveled to Tampa the next week to help dedicate the new Tampa Stadium. More than 50 Vols, everyone who made the trip, got to play in the 38-0 victory over the Spartans.

After a 35-14 victory over Tulane, we faced Ole Miss in Memphis. Tennessee had lost to the Rebels for eight straight years, but we beat them 20-7 behind the running of Walter Chadwick, who ran for 115 yards and was named Back of the Week in the South. Fulton returned to work after a month layoff and gave the Vol offense a noticeable lift. The Vol defense, led by All-American linebackers Jack Reynolds and Steve Kiner, limited the Rebel defense to 52 yards. The Vols closed the regular season beating Kentucky 17-7 in Lexington and Vanderbilt 47-14 at home.

With a bid to the Orange Bowl to play Oklahoma, we went to Miami on Dec. 24. Taking families away from home for Christmas could have been difficult, but spending a week on Miami Beach in late December was a pretty special treat. The hospitality of the Orange Bowl Committee made it a great experience. And we probably made all the kids back in Knoxville mad, as we all had young children and told them Santa Claus was coming early, because he knew we would be in Miami.

The Big Eight champion Sooners jumped out to a 19-0 halftime lead. We couldn't move the ball on them on offense and couldn't stop their offense. But we made some adjustments at halftime and turned the game around in the second half.

In the third quarter Jimmy Glover intercepted a Sooner pass and returned it 36 yards to get the Vols on the scoreboard at 19-7. A few minutes later, Jimmy Weatherford intercepted another Oklahoma pass and returned it to the Sooner 17-yard line. After a few tough yards got the ball to the 5, Fulton took a pitchout in for a touchdown, making the score 19-14. Another long Vol drive stalled deep in OU territory, so Karl Kremser kicked a 26-yard field goal to get to 19-17.

A fourth-quarter "pick six" from the Tennessee 18 gave Oklahoma a 26-17 lead with 9:35 remaining. But an unruffled Warren led us on a 77-yard drive, with key runs from Chadwick and Fulton, and receptions from Flowers and DeLong. Warren sneaked across from the 1 and with a successful Kremser kick, the score was 26-24 with 4:05 left to play.

OU Coach Chuck Fairbanks elected to go for the first down on fourth and 2 from his own 43-yard line with 1:54 left in the game. All-American running back Steve Owens was given the ball, but was stopped dead in his tracks by linebacker Jack Reynolds. With seven seconds remaining, Coach Dickey sent in Kremser to kick a 43-yard field goal.

Karl was Tennessee's first-ever soccer-style kicker. He was recruited by UT's head track coach, Chuck Rohe, who was also our head football recruiter. Chuck recruited some great players to Tennessee who were outstanding in both football and track. Karl was a great athlete who could high jump several inches higher than his own height (I never could figure how anyone should be able to do that). A 43-yard field goal was a chip shot for Karl, so we were all confident he would make it to complete a great 27-26 comeback and Orange Bowl victory. The protection was good, the snap and hold were good, and Karl made great contact with the ball. It was sailing about 3 feet outside the right upright. On nine out of 10 of Karl's kicks, they would hook about 5 or 6 feet to the left. This one didn't hook at all and sailed straight outside the goal post.

The game was played as close as close could be. We each had 18 first downs. Oklahoma had more rushing yards and Tennessee had more passing yards. Total offense was Tennessee 332, Oklahoma 310. We each had three turnovers.

Despite the bowl loss, we did win the SEC Championship for the first time since 1956. It was really cool to get SEC Championship rings as a reward for an outstanding season.

Between the 1967 and 1968 seasons, Coach Woodruff, with Coach Dickey's involvement, decided to install artificial turf in Neyland Stadium. It would be the first outdoor collegiate stadium to have artificial turf, and the coaches at Auburn and Georgia were very much against this move. The growing seasons in Auburn/Opelika and Athens, Georgia, are much more favorable to year-round grass surfaces than Knoxville. If teams practiced in the stadium very much, as we liked to do for filming purposes, by mid-October there was no grass remaining between the hash marks. Film taken in the stadium, due to the increased height and location of the cameras, was much better than from the tower on the practice field. Coach Woodruff was ahead of his time in many of the things he initiated, and this was his boldest move up to this point. It worked out very well for the Tennessee program. We could practice as much as we wanted, let the band practice, and the turf was consistent throughout the year.

In order to facilitate draining during rain, an 18-inch crown was built in the middle of the field. That didn't seem like much, nor did it look like much, but it did have a significant effect on the drainage. It also had a pretty consistent effect on opposing passers. They were able to adjust for the most part during pre-game warmups, but their first several out-routes thrown from the middle of the field ended up in the first or second row of the stands.

The other effect on opponents was a fear of falling on the turf. It did cause "rug burns," so players protected themselves by wearing sleeves on their elbows, and some wore long socks to protect their lower legs. However, it was a very fast track when dry, and it was very playable during a rain. Players enjoyed that attribute, and in spite of the Georgia coach's aversion to artificial turf in general, I bet the UGA fullback named Kemp, who broke for an 80-yard touchdown in our opening game, felt pretty good about playing on the surface.

Wet weather was a different deal. We experimented with all kinds of shoes and cleats, probably more than anyone in the country. In dry weather, we practiced in the molded-sole soccer shoes our Alabama teams wore against Auburn in 1962. Some players elected to play in those shoes, but the bulk of our team wore regular cleated shoes with short, wide cleats. In wet weather, we installed longer cleats that worked very well.

Chuck Rohe was a great track coach at Tennessee, and as head football recruiter, every good football player that he recruited was a free scholarship for his track program. Richmond Flowers was probably his greatest accomplishment, primarily because he got him out of Montgomery, and Richmond's father was an Alabama graduate. Richmond was a highly recruited athlete, and Coach Bryant hated to lose him. The winning edge for Tennessee was the combination track-and-football opportunity for Richmond.

Richmond was a great story. As a youngster, he had to wear braces to straighten his feet. He may well have been the character that Winston Groom wrote about in *Forrest Gump*. Richmond entered Tennessee in 1965. When I got there in 1966, his freshman coach told me the year before that he was a great potential receiver because of his speed, but he couldn't catch the ball. I took that as a challenge to help him improve in that area.

Richmond was a great high hurdler, and ended up being the best in the country before he was done. The plan was for Richmond to play football and run track in 1965, 1966 and 1967, then redshirt him to run in the 1968 Olympics, and then return in 1969 for his senior year in football and track. It was a great plan.

Richmond didn't grow up playing baseball and basketball, which is when most kids learn the hand-to-eye coordination required for catching a football. He ran track instead. He was a great competitor and was eager to learn anything that would help him accomplish his goals. If he didn't think it helpful, he was pretty vocal about why he didn't want to do it. One thing that comes to mind was our test to the team returning for fall camp. We made everyone run the mile to see what kind of shape they were in. Backs and ends had to run a faster time than that required of linemen. Richmond didn't have a problem making his required time, but he was quite vocal about how ridiculous it was as a test when it did nothing to help with football skills. He was probably right about that, but it was a pretty good test of whether one was in good enough physical condition to go through the fall camp practice in the August heat in pads. He didn't have a problem with the extra hours we spent throwing and catching the football in every possible angle that might occur in a game. He was a great competitor and contributed greatly to the success of our 1966 and 1967 seasons.

In the summer of 1968, Richmond was the fastest high hurdler in the country. That spring Coach Rohe held his annual Dogwood Relays and invited the top high hurdlers in the world to come. Willie Davenport, Irv Hall and Richmond were the top three, and Richmond beat them both going away.

A month or so later, Richmond pulled a hamstring pretty badly. It was discolored something awful in purple, red and yellow while healing. The Olympic trials were held in August. Nothing heals a torn hamstring better than rest. He went through every treatment our doctors and trainers could think of, but the healing process was slow. He made it back to compete in the trials, but he ended up being the first man out. Evidently, the rules in qualifying are pretty rigid. If I were running things, I would have brought him along, hoping that the few weeks between the trials and the games would allow more healing, and perhaps he would improve enough to contribute. But I don't know anything about that and obviously they didn't see things that way. As it turned out, Davenport won the gold medal and Hall won the silver. A healthy Richmond Flowers would have brought home the gold.

Richmond returned to Knoxville very depressed and weighing about 165 pounds compared to his 185 playing weight. He came back the week we opened the season against Georgia. We had converted a free safety to running back because our starter in 1967 had graduated and we needed more competition at that position. In the Georgia game, we were down 17-9 with time running out. We drove the ball down around the Georgia 20-yard line with time for one play. I never saw Coach Dickey do this before or after, but during the timeout, he made up a play we hadn't run in practice. I could have said he drew it up in the dirt, but we had just installed tartan turf, so that wouldn't work. Coach Dickey called for a twin wideout formation to our left. The slot receiver ran a slant across the middle and our split end ran a post deep behind him. Georgia's Jake Scott was an All-American free safety and a great player. As the play unfolded, Scott held his position watching the slant, and our split end Gary Kreis ran behind him to catch a 20-yard touchdown pass to make the score 17-15 as time expired. We still had to make a two-point conversion to tie the game.

The summer before the season, I was recruiting in Louisville, Kentucky. At that time of year, coaches from several universities were in town. Word got around on the practice fields that some were meeting at a certain hotel bar for a beer that evening. I went over and we had fun talking about prospects and drawing X's and O's on napkins. I got a great goal-line run play from a coach at Murray State University who had a very sophisticated passing game (I wish I could recall his name). I brought it home, sold it to our staff, and that was the two-point play that was called to go for the tie.

We lined up in a pro right formation, tight ends and flankers to the right, split end to the left, and split backfield, i.e. fullback and tailback lined up behind the guards on each side. Georgia was in man coverage and with Scott lined up over the tight end, our primary receiver on the play. When the ball was snapped, the backs flared wide to each side. The tight end stayed in and blocked for three counts, and the wideouts stayed wide. As the tight end blocked, Scott drifted outside with the flaring fullback. The tight end blocked three counts, released inside and was wide open. The pass was completed and we had scored a touchdown and two-point conversion to tie the game with no time left on the clock. Obviously our crowd went wild, and we celebrated accordingly.

Some of the Georgia fans complained that we were happy about a tied football game. Bob Woodruff, our AD, came up with what I thought was a great response. He said, simply, "Well, Georgia lost the win and Tennessee won the tie!" How about that one!

After the game, the offensive coaches got together and decided the moving of the safety to running back wasn't working and we needed speed at tailback to run our offense. We quickly got dressed and hauled over to the dorm to meet with Richmond. We told him we needed speed and we would put him at tailback. He didn't need to redshirt, he needed to be back on the team. He was intrigued with that idea and his competitive spirit quickly kicked in. He was excited to see what he could do at tailback. That definitely wasn't his best position for the pros, but the experience would probably help him in many ways, and it would definitely help our team.

After Coach Rohe recruited Richmond from Alabama, Coach Bryant decided he wasn't going to lose any more track/football players. DeLoss Dodds was the AD at Texas who I met when we were trying to get them to join CLC. He was definitely one of the best in the business. DeLoss and I had several conversations about many things. This one day he told me before he came to Texas he was the track coach at Kansas. He was very successful there and he told me that Coach Bryant tried to hire him to head up the track program at Alabama. This happened in the late 1960s or early '70s about the time Coach

Bryant committed to building a track program. He said they were going to put enough money in it to compete at high levels. DeLoss didn't come to Alabama, but Coach Bryant built a great track facility, the "Sam Bailey Track and Field Stadium," named for one of Coach Bryant's best and brightest assistants. The Tennessee people called it "the track that Richmond Flowers built!"

With Richmond at tailback, we could pretty much run our offense, and he was obviously a good receiver out of the backfield. While Richmond got the bulk of the carries at tailback, we had four other tailbacks that had from 19 to 35 carries during the 1968 season.

Our fullback for the 1966, '67 and '68 seasons was Richard Pickens. He had a short, stocky frame, but could get to full speed by step number two or three. Richard was a major force in our offense, not only as a good blocker, but as a ball carrier as well. He was our second-leading rusher in 1966 and 1967, and our leading rusher in 1968. I believe Richard could make 4 yards on the quick handoff or trap up the middle against any defense in his sleep. He was a really good one.

Dewey Warren and Charlie Fulton had graduated, and Bubba Wyche and Bobby Scott were our quarterbacks. Bubba was a seasoned veteran by this time and we were comfortable with his play. Bobby Scott was a highly recruited quarterback out of Rossville, Georgia, who served as a solid backup, and it was an excellent grooming ground for him to be a starter in the future.

We had a pretty salty defense led by linebackers Steve Kiner and Jack Reynolds, defensive backs Jimmy Weatherford and Bill Young, and linemen Vic Dingus, Neal McMeans and Dick Williams.

After Georgia, we defeated Memphis State at home by building a big lead early and ruining a 17-point MSU comeback bid.

We beat Rice 52-0 in Houston. Bill Baker returned a punt 51 yards on the second possession to set up the first Vol touchdown, a Bubba 15-yard keeper. The reserves played a lot, and Scott made his debut at quarterback by completing 12 of 22 passes for 170 yards and two touchdowns. Karl Kremser kicked a record-tying seven extra points.

The next week in Atlanta saw Georgia Tech complete 25 out of 63 pass attempts. Lester McClain emerged as a Vol star in his fourth game as a sophomore. He scored twice on sensational receptions, and for his efforts, he was awarded the UPI Southern Offensive Player of the Week. Richmond Flowers carried 20 times for 101 yards, and his outside pressure on the Tech defense enabled Richard Pickens to gain 81 yards inside on 12 carries, as Tennessee prevailed 24-7.

Alabama had lost a close game to Ole Miss in Jackson, but we were prepared for a typical defensive struggle against the Tide, and we got one. ABC televised the game, and Keith Jackson, the best collegiate announcer ever in my opinion, called the game.

Tennessee drove for a score on its first drive when Pickens took a screen pass about 30 yards to the 5, and Flowers dove across the goal line on fourth and 1 for a 7-0 lead. Alabama forced a short punt later in the first quarter that led to a field goal, making it 7-3. The hitting was vicious. Neither passer had much time to throw and there were several sacks on both sides.

Kremser kicked a 54-yard field goal in the third quarter to give Tennessee a 10-3 lead. He missed subsequent field-goal attempts of 55 and 53 yards. Alabama quarterback Scott Hunter led a fourth-quarter drive that scored a touchdown with 17 seconds left. Coach Bryant elected to go for two but UT broke up a pass at the goal line to keep the score at 10-9.

Alabama recovered its onside kick on the Tennessee side of midfield. Hunter completed two passes to get Alabama to the Tennessee 20. A hurry-up field-goal attempt from the 20 was blocked by Jimmy Weatherford, who had intercepted an earlier pass and played a tremendous game to lead a tough Tennessee defense.

It was a great game between two longtime opponents. Tennessee earned the close win, but the Alabama comeback at the end had to make Tide fans proud of their team's great effort.

After we defeated Tommy Prothro's UCLA Bruins 42-18 in Neyland Stadium, we lost 28-14 to Auburn in Birmingham, which eliminated us from the SEC title contention. This was the first loss to Auburn I had ever experienced. We finished the season strong with victories over Ole Miss 31-0 and Kentucky 24-7 at home, and 10-7 over Vanderbilt in Nashville.

We were pleased to get a bid to play in the Cotton Bowl on New Year's Day. We were not so pleased to play Texas, who had tied Houston 20-20 at home in their opener and then lost 31-21 to Texas Tech in Lubbock. At that point, they changed quarterbacks and made a total commitment to the Wishbone offense coached by recently hired stellar high school coach Emory Bellard. The Longhorns demolished Oklahoma State 31-3 the next week, then beat Oklahoma 26-20 in Dallas. Texas scored at least 35 points in every one of their next six victories while averaging 40 points a game.

The Wishbone offense featured riding the fullback on its basic plays and reading the tackle. If he stayed wide, they handed the ball to the fullback who often ran untouched to the safety. If the tackle came inside, the quarterback pulled the ball out and optioned the end, deciding to keep or pitch to the tailback, depending on the end's play. Their personnel was perfect to run that offense with a bruising but athletic fullback, an exceptional tailback, and a wily quarterback who could make quick reads and proper decisions in the preciseness required in that attack. They also had a stellar split end that could embarrass defensive backs trying to cover one-on-one when other defensive backs committed to stop the run.

To make things more difficult, it appeared the burnt orange jerseys got a little darker and pretty much the color of the pigskin with which we were playing. That made defending against the quarterback-fullback exchange a lot harder trying to see if the quarterback was handing to the fullback or pulling out to go to his next option. Trying to get scout team personnel to duplicate the speed and precision of Texas was near impossible.

It was a cold, windy, miserable day in Dallas. The Cotton Bowl Committee was extremely hospitable, but the Longhorns weren't. They beat us soundly 36-13. The game wasn't much fun, but to get to play in another New Year's Day Bowl was exciting.

I can guarantee you that Richmond Flowers was the difference in Tennessee's 8-2-1 overall record, 4-1-1 in the SEC, a No. 7 Coaches' Poll ranking and No. 13 in the AP Poll.

The 1969 team was built to win a championship. The defense featured senior linebackers Jack Reynolds and Steve Kiner, and sophomore Jackie Walker, while defensive backs Mike Jones, Tim Priest and captain Bill Young were experienced. The offense featured Bobby Scott and Phil Pierce at quarterback, tight ends Ken DeLong and Gary Theiler, wide receivers Lester McClain, Gary Kreis and Joe Thompson, offensive linemen Chip Kell, Phillip Fulmer, Don Denbo, Mike Bevans and David Browne, and fullbacks Curt Watson and Steve Wold. We also had two great kickers in Herman "Thunderfoot" Weaver at punter, and George Hunt on field goals, extra points and kickoffs.

Tennessee opened against Chattanooga, led by very successful Coach Scrappy Moore. Bobby Scott started his first game and successfully defeated the outmanned Moccasins 31-0.

The next week found Auburn coming to Knoxville. The Vols were still licking their wounds from the previous year's defeat, which had knocked Tennessee out of the SEC Championship race. It was a 45-19 victory, although the game was in real doubt, as Auburn fought fiercely and closed the gap to eight points in the fourth quarter, with momentum on their side. Benny Dalton, in his first start at "Monster Man" (a defensive position that was the forerunner to the strong safety), turned back a key Auburn third-down play with a crushing tackle that forced the Tigers to attempt a field goal. As Auburn desperately tried to add another score, Tennessee, in less than two minutes, turned two fumble recoveries and an interception into three more touchdowns.

Then we defeated Memphis State 55-16 in Memphis. Scott threw a touchdown pass to McClain for a school-record 82 yards, and tailbacks Don

McLeary and Bobby Patterson scored touchdowns on the ground. The defense played very well, grabbing three fumbles, and Priest had two interceptions.

The next week brought Georgia Tech to Knoxville. The Vols scored in all four quarters and the defense stymied the Tech offense, which scored late and went for two to make the final score 26-8. The AP departed from its Southeastern Lineman of the Week honor going to a single player, as it was awarded to both Reynolds and Kiner.

The next week was the "Third Saturday in October" and the Vols traveled to Birmingham to face Alabama. It was an incredible day for Tennessee as the Vols won 41-14. There were spectacular plays all over, as Scott won the UPI Southeastern Offensive Player of the Week and Kiner was named National Player of the Week by the AP and *Sports Illustrated*. Kiner threw Tide quarterbacks for losses on five plays, intercepted a pass, caused a fumble, made 11 tackles and three assists, and forced hurried throws four other times. Linebacker Jackie Walker scored a touchdown by scooping and scoring on a fumble recovery, and Bobby Majors crossed the goal line twice on punt returns, although one was called back for a clipping penalty.

We traveled to Athens the following week to meet the Georgia Bulldogs. In the first quarter, everything that could go wrong did go wrong. We were lucky and very good defensively to get through the first quarter only down 3-0. Curt Watson, from Crossville, Tennessee, took over in the second quarter. He and Don McLeary each scored touchdowns in lightning fashion to take a commanding 14-3 lead. Hunt kicked a fourth-quarter 38-yard field goal to seal the Bulldogs' fate, 17-3. The defense played magnificently, but the afternoon belonged to Watson, the powerful sophomore who broke at least 15 tackles and galloped for 197 yards to break Tom Tracy's single-game rushing record from 1934 against North Carolina.

South Carolina came to Knoxville an inspired team, and brought a running back, Warren Muir, who rushed for 159 yards against a good Vol defense. Overall, USC rushed for 204 yards and gained 142 through the air. Three interceptions by the Vols, two by Priest, played a big part in UT's 29-14 victory. South Carolina pulled within 16-14 with 5:40 left to play, but the Vols drove 76 yards for the clinching touchdown on a 40-yard Scott to end Gary Kreis pass. Moments later, Priest's second interception set up a 7-yard touchdown pass from Scott to DeLong.

At this point in the season, if we could win two of our three remaining games against Ole Miss in Jackson, Kentucky in Lexington and Vanderbilt at home, we would lock up the SEC Championship. Ole Miss was next on our schedule, and the Orange Bowl told us we had their bid if we won or even played close.

We were badly nicked up with the accumulation of bruises, bumps and tears that go along with football after seven games. Bill Young, our safety, couldn't play. Steve Kiner, who had a partial shoulder tear, probably shouldn't have played, but he did, with a chain holding his arm about 5 to 6 inches from his side to keep the arm from going above 90 degrees.

But Steve had to play. In fall camp, a group of SEC area writers formed "the skywriter's tour" and traveled via bus to all SEC schools to watch practices and talk to the coaches and players. I was in the audience as the writers were interviewing coaches and players. The session was just about over, and one writer in closing asked Kiner, "Who do you think will win the conference?" Kiner replied, "I think Tennessee will win the conference title." The writer said, "I've heard Ole Miss has all the horses." Kiner responded in a very kidding way, with no sign of cockiness or slander, "The trouble with you newspaper guys is you don't know horses from mules."

As you can imagine, that got the headlines all over the conference for the next week, and surfaced again the week of the Ole Miss game. I'm told Johnny Vaught, the famous Hall of Fame coach at Ole Miss, obtained a mule and draped a cloth over the animal's back with "MISTER KINER" in large letters on both sides. The mule was paraded around the Ole Miss campus all week.

The Ole Miss crowd was as fired up as any I ever witnessed. After we arrived in Jackson and were walking through the airport to our buses, various airport attendants screamed, "Hee-Haw, Kiner, Hee Haw!" That yell followed us throughout the airport. The next day when we rode buses into the stadium two hours before kickoff, the Ole Miss student section was full and was yelling, "Go to hell Tennessee, go to hell!" That kept up until the game was almost ready to start.

It was one of those days where all the good things happened to the bad guys and the bad things happened to the good guys. The Rebels took the opening kickoff and drove 82 yards for a touchdown. Tennessee established a drive that was stopped in relatively easy field-goal range, but it hit the crossbar and bounced out.

On the next Ole Miss possession, quarterback Archie Manning carried the ball on a fourth-down attempt from around the 3-yard line. Our defense had him stopped cold at the 2, but Archie purposefully fumbled into the end zone and a Rebel recovered for a touchdown. A subsequent Ole Miss field-goal attempt hit the crossbar and bounced through the upright.

The Rebels, behind a brilliant performance by Manning, knocked off the undefeated Vols 38-0, their third victory that season against undefeated teams at Mississippi Memorial Stadium. The other two victims were Georgia and LSU. Jack Reynolds performed nobly in a losing effort, making 14 tackles and seven assists. Our Orange Bowl bid was lost, but our chances of winning the SEC Championship were still alive if we could beat Kentucky and Vanderbilt in the next two weeks.

Our offensive line coach, Ray Trail, said after the loss, "I believe if we hadn't showed up, they'd have chosen up sides and fought each other!" That's about the way the whole game went.

Much later in time, I crossed paths with Archie Manning and we discussed our games together. Archie is one of the classiest people I have ever met and as humble as can be. His family is All-American in every way. We talked about Ole Miss whipping us so badly in 1969, but I reminded him that two years earlier when Ole Miss came to Knoxville, we intercepted five of his passes. He vehemently responded, "I didn't throw five interceptions that day…I threw six!"

The next week the Vols traveled to Lexington to play Kentucky. By that time of year, the bluegrass had turned brown, and the visiting dressing room was the worst in the conference. The team dressed in several different small rooms. The Wildcats always played Tennessee hard, as I believe UT was their biggest rival.

The Kentucky team surprised us with an all-out air attack, completing 28 passes for 440 yards, but we escaped with a 31-26 victory. Leaders in the victory were Bobby Majors with a 72-yard punt return for a touchdown, and Jackie Walker's interception and 54-yard return that set up another touchdown. Punter Herman Weaver had a punt that died on the 1, and on the next play, Reynolds recovered a fumble for a touchdown. Gary Kreis caught 11 passes to tie Johnny Mills' record from 1966. Reynolds and Kiner led the team in tackles with 12 each.

The next week Vanderbilt came to Knoxville for the last regular-season game. Our offense that didn't play well in the previous two games came to life and rolled for 450 yards, with 302 on the ground. Curt Watson, who was injured early in the Ole Miss game, came back for 115 yards rushing. We broke open a 7-7 game with two touchdowns, a field goal and a safety to go into halftime with a comfortable 26-7 lead. The final score was 40-27. The 20 points Vandy scored in the fourth quarter were mostly against reserves.

The win over the Commodores gave Tennessee its second SEC Championship in three years. We lost the Orange Bowl bid with our bad loss to Ole Miss, but received a Gator Bowl bid, which was also a great bowl with excellent hospitality. I can say that our drop in performance against Ole Miss and Kentucky was largely due to injuries to key players on both offense and defense. That's not an excuse, but it is a fact.

The Gator Bowl trip became interesting as we were matched up against the Florida Gators. A few days before the game, the story broke that Coach Dickey was returning to his alma mater, the University of Florida.

One day during Gator Bowl practice in Jacksonville, Coach Woodruff came up to me and invited me to lunch. After practice I met him and we went to Ponte Vedra for lunch. During the conversation, he said, "If Doug leaves, I think we have three coaches on our staff that would make good head coaches and you are one of them. Where will you be a few days after the game?" Obviously, that was before cell phones. I told him I would be at my parent's house in Birmingham and gave him the number. But I really didn't think Coach Dickey would leave.

Game day came and the atmosphere around both teams was strained about the coaching upheaval. Florida had a very good team with quarterback John Reaves and wide receiver Carlos Alvarez, both having a great year. We outgained the Gators 214-90 on the ground and had numerous occasions to win the game, but the Gator defense rose to the occasion in the red zone and held on to the 14-13 victory. We ended the season with a 9-2 overall record.

The 1969 season was still a great one for Tennessee in winning its second SEC Championship in three years, but the luster was diminished by the fact that Coach Dickey did decide to leave for the University of Florida.

LESSONS LEARNED

- Depreciation is important, but cash flow is king. I asked the head recruiter to send me to the farthest high school to watch prospects because the 12 cents a mile I got in cash more than paid for the gas and oil expenses in my new Chevy.

- Pay attention in your job and learn everything you can about the organization. One of the most valuable things I learned while a graduate assistant coach at Oklahoma was that some former Oklahoma players with a military commitment had gotten assigned to the U.S. Military Academy to coach football.

- There is more than one way to skin a cat. Coach Wilkinson's personality was in many ways 180 degrees different than Coach Bryant's, but his goals and his ability to reach those goals were very much the same.

- Be focused and intense in pursuit of the mission, but take time to watch the leaves change in the fall and the dogwood and azaleas bloom in the spring. Take time to think and be creative in solving problems.

- Are General Neyland's seven axioms applicable to your business? I think so. They are: 1) The team that makes the fewest mistakes usually wins; 2) Play for and make the breaks, and when one comes your way — score; 3) If at first the breaks go against you, don't let up, put on more steam; 4) Protect our kickers, our quarterbacks, our lead, and our ball game; 5) All members of the team zeroed in on fundamentals that win the game makes for the "winning edge"; 6) Press the kicking game (or whatever is your key component) for here the breaks are made; 7) Carry the fight to our opponent and keep it there for 60 minutes.

• Life is too short not to enjoy every moment. If you can't afford major vacations or other pleasures, be creative and find little things that make you happy. The best things in life are free. How you perceive them makes the difference.

• We all have 24 hours in a day. What we do with them determines our success in ventures and in life.

• There are opportunities in America scattered around everywhere. Good ideas are a dime-a-dozen. Those who can take an idea and turn it into something positive can enjoy success.

• It is a good idea to keep a diary or catalog of activities and accomplishments in written form. It is great reference material to retrieve for future needs.

• Be loyal to the organization with which you work. If that is a problem, go to work elsewhere.

• If you are in the mix in an interview for a major promotion, don't assume that you either will or won't get the job before it is offered. Keep your head down and be your best during the interview.

Coach Bryant was known to say something funny when it was least expected, like before this game in Birmingham.

CHAPTER 4

MY HEAD
COACHING YEARS

I celebrated my 28th birthday on Dec. 8, 1969. A few days after the Gator Bowl, Tennessee Coach Doug Dickey accepted the Florida job while I was in Birmingham visiting my parents and enjoying a few days off before returning to Knoxville. I got the call from Bob Woodruff that Coach Dickey had accepted the UF job, and for me to come on back to Knoxville to talk about the head coaching position.

Prior to that call, when we were back in Jacksonville and the speculation was high that Coach Dickey was leaving, both offensive coordinator Jimmy Dunn and defensive coordinator Doug Knotts came to me and said if they were named head coach, they wanted me to be the offensive coordinator. I was very flattered and thought at that point that if Jimmy got the head job, I had the OC job at Tennessee, and might get an offer from Coach Dickey to be the OC at Florida. I really thought Coach Woodruff would hire Jimmy, as he was the offensive coordinator at UT and played quarterback for Coach Woodruff when they were both at Florida.

In our first meeting back in Knoxville, Coach Woodruff met with Jimmy, Doug and me. Coach Woodruff said he thought we had a good staff and wanted to see if we could keep it together. He said that he was going to leave the room for a few minutes and for us to talk among ourselves and see if we could all work for each other if one of us were named head coach.

When he left the room I told Jimmy and Doug I would be pleased to work for either of them, and I was certain Coach Woodruff didn't have enough guts to hire a 28-year-old head coach at Tennessee. Jimmy said he could work for either of us. Doug said he loved us both but we were both offensive coaches, and if he got the job he needed a defensive guy as one of his two top assistants. When Coach Woodruff came back in the room, we told him of our conversation. He said, "OK, I'll meet with you individually. Bill you come at 7:30, Jimmy you at 8:00, and Doug you come at 8:30."

I was definitely the most relaxed candidate in the room because as I had told Jimmy and Doug, I didn't think I really had a chance at the job due to my age. I did strongly believe I could do the job, as I knew our players very well, knew our program that had won two championships in the four years I was there, and knew our staff and university leaders. I also had staff members in mind if current staff members went with Coach Dickey to Florida.

When I met with Coach Woodruff the next morning he told me he thought my ideas on discipline were timely, and how well he thought I had fit in and grown since my first year. We talked about several other things and after a while, he said, "I think you know who I'm going to name as head coach." As the relaxed candidate I was, I replied, "Yes I know who you are going to name." He said, "I'm not sure you do, the way you said that." I thought to myself,

"Holy Moly, he's talking about naming me!" From that point on, I assure you I was not the most relaxed candidate.

When I left the room, I met Jimmy coming in. We spoke, and being good friends, I told him I thought I had a chance. He responded that Coach Woodruff had gotten pressure from somewhere and he (Jimmy) was announcing that day that he was going with Coach Dickey to UF. Then it took about three days for Coach Woodruff to do whatever he needed to do to make the announcement between Doug and me.

I had approached Doug earlier and told him if I got the job I'd like for him to stay to be our defensive coordinator. He declined to say that he had been passed over at Duke, and if he were passed over for a 28-year-old at UT, he would never get a head coaching job. It had been a nerve-wracking three days, but finally I got the call from Coach Woodruff to put on my TV clothes and meet him at the President's Mansion at 10 a.m.

University President Dr. Andy Holt had been in that role for many years. He was a tall man who had become almost legendary as a beloved Tennessean in the twilight of his career at UT. When I got to his residence, he and I met alone for a few minutes. He started by saying that my name was a surprise when Coach Woodruff recommended me for the job, "but when we looked at your background and your influence in your four years as an assistant here, it made all the sense in the world." Then he asked me if I drank and if I went to church. I responded that I drank socially and was on the board of the Bearden Methodist Church. He told me that he attended many university alumni gatherings and other meetings and found that drinking ginger ale had worked well for him over the years. That was pretty much all that Dr. Holt and I talked about before the official announcement that day in January 1970 that changed my life forever.

It didn't take long to find out there was so much more to deal with sitting in the head coach's chair than sitting in an assistant's chair. The media was a huge difference. The media in those years primarily consisted of newspapers. We had two papers in Knoxville, the *Knoxville Journal*, a morning paper, and the *Knoxville News Sentinel*, an afternoon paper. One was very aggressive, and both were "ticked off" if the university or our department gave a release to the other one.

In addition to media, I had never had anyone work for me, nor had the responsibility to hire and fire. I was now responsible for about 10 coaches, two secretaries and a few graduate assistants, as well as about 100 football players.

Coach Woodruff was helpful as a mentor, but it sure would have been nice if I had taken a course on management, media and budgets. I guess I stumbled through that eventually, but would have appreciated help. When the governor was running for office a few years later, I saw that he had hired a public relations firm to come in to advise on many difficult issues. They were involved in planning for all public statements and building a strategy to release those statements in a timely manner that would show progress in the program being built. They would also be helpful in crisis management situations. I think today's coaches do have more help in not only dealing with the media and the public, but also in helping develop motivational themes for the season, as well as on a weekly basis in dealing with the team. With the dollars involved in today's game, I think that is money well spent.

As it turned out, the 1969 season completed my education as an assistant coach. Playing four years under Coach Bryant, and learning under assistant coaches Gene Stallings, Howard Schnellenberger, Dude Hennessey, Pat James, Jerry Claiborne and others, provided a solid background in how to build a championship team. The opportunity to work under Bud Wilkinson his last year in coaching at Oklahoma was a marvelous experience for me. Then getting a chance to coach two years at West Point under Paul Dietzel, and at the same time fulfilling my two-year military commitment, was another great experience. Getting back to the SEC as a varsity coach for four years under Doug Dickey was a dream come true. We went to four bowl games and won two SEC Championships during those four years.

All four coaches — Bryant, Wilkinson, Dietzel and Dickey — were trying to get to the same end result: To make men out of boys by teaching them discipline, time management, respect for rules; channeling their energy into learning the importance of team dynamics; learning complex offensive and defensive schemes in preparation for competition at the highest level of intercollegiate athletics; learning the sacrifices necessary for becoming a champion on and off the field; and, to win championships.

One of the most valuable lessons learned for me during those 11 years was that to be effective as a leader, you had to be yourself. I couldn't be Coach Bryant. All four coaches had different personalities. None were like Coach Bryant. Coach Wilkinson was an English major. They all had mental toughness and the ability to teach and manage assistant coaches and teams within the greater university guidelines and principles. And they all had to manage, one way or another, the press. I thought I was pretty well prepared to be a head coach at the highest level, even though I knew I had a lot more to learn about football and the overall responsibility that came with being a head coach.

I inherited a very good Tennessee team in 1970, but since I lost both coordinators, I needed to find good replacements for those positions. I had been with Larry Jones for two years at Army and knew he was a good defensive coach. He had stayed on Coach Dietzel's staff when he moved from West Point to the University of South Carolina in 1966, the same year I came to Tennessee. Larry was a great hire as defensive coordinator.

Jim Wright was my selection as offensive coordinator. Jim played for Coach Bryant at Texas A&M and was highly thought of as OC at Mississippi State. He was really ahead of his time in offensive thinking, and I prevailed on him to join our staff.

We implemented winter workouts exactly as we had been running them, and things went very well. We were getting ready for spring practice, getting our offensive and defensive schemes ironed out, and getting new coaches acquainted with players they would be coaching.

One day I got a call from Mickey O'Brien, our great trainer who was close to retirement, and had actually groomed Jim Goostree. Coach Goostree was our trainer at Alabama and went on to a long and successful career. Unfortunately for me, I only got to spend a couple of years with Mickey as our trainer before he retired. Anyway, Mickey asked me if I knew that Tim Townes, who had both bones in his forearm broken in fall practice 1969, had not properly healed but didn't want me to know.

Tim was a small walk-on defensive back, about 5-foot-10 and 160 pounds, who had played linebacker at Bearden High School in Knoxville and entered UT in fall 1969. Early in fall practice we had the freshmen rushing our punt team on the goal line coming out. Tim rushed in to block the punt, but in the process, Herman "Thunderfoot" Weaver's leg broke Tim's arm.

I knew Tim was a great young man, smart and tough, but really didn't think he would be a player that could help our team. I went down on the field where our team was going through winter workouts and called him over. I said, "How are you doing Tim?" He said, "Great." I said, "How's your arm?" He said, "Great." I said, "That's not what Mickey told me." With that, big tears formed in his eyes, and he said, "Coach, I missed all of fall practice, I can't miss spring practice." I said, "Tim, you don't want to risk permanent injury to your arm, you can't go through spring practice." Tim, with tears rolling down his face, said, "Well coach, they are going to break it and re-set it, and if I'm going to get it broken, I'd rather do it in spring practice!" About that time, tears formed in my eyes and I began to think this was a special young man. A lot more on his story to follow.

When it came time to play our spring game, I thought that as the head coach, I should probably make some sort of impactful statement to the press. My statement was, "Tennessee is going to win today!"

As the game was played, with me watching from the press box, our assistant coaches "chose up sides" and proceeded as we had done in the past. It turned out to be a pretty good game except for the fact that Jamie Rotella and James Woody, two of our three projected starting linebackers in the fall, went down with knee injuries. They were taken to the hospital and operated on that night. That was the medical policy in those days. The operation took place as soon after the injury as possible. I thought to myself and told others, "I'm not sure Tennessee won today!"

With those knee injuries, Jamie and James were put in full leg casts for about six weeks. The cure was almost worse than the injury. When their legs came out of the casts, the atrophy that occurred was ridiculous. The thigh was about half the size of the non-injured leg. The rehab to get the muscle size and strength back up to normal was several weeks. Today's treatment is far different and superior, and in some cases, if it's only torn cartilage, players are back playing in three or so weeks.

I felt like we had gotten overweight as a team after the '69 season, because it was important to me to be quick and agile. Even though substitution rules favored "beefing up" at least in the offensive and defensive lines, I guess my experience as a player under Coach Bryant influenced that thinking. Before our team left for the summer, I encouraged them to come back to camp lean and mean.

I called Chip Kell, our All-American center/guard into my office and told him to lose 20 pounds or he wasn't getting a uniform. Now, Chip was a great player. He was one of only two on our team to bench press 400 pounds. Don Denbo, also a guard, was the other. Neither had ever made the prescribed time in our fall camp test running a mile.

Chip couldn't believe his ears. He was an All-American who had outstanding seasons the previous two years. He tried to explain that it was hard for him to lose weight. I stuck to my guns. He left unhappy, but said he would try. He did lose the weight and made his time in his fall camp mile run, although Coach Trail, who was holding the watch, helped him several seconds. That was a great morale boost to our team, and many others had also dropped some pounds. Our team returned in excellent condition.

As Jamie and James were healing in the summer, I guess our third projected starting linebacker Ray Nettles must have felt he wasn't getting enough attention because he tore his knee up working out on his own July 4. Thankfully, all three were healed and ready for action when fall practice rolled around. We had great doctors and medical staff, as well as trainers, at Tennessee.

I decided in my first fall camp as head coach to take time to give the entire team a course in speed reading. If one can't read, how can he be expected to graduate from college? It was a brief course that just covered the basics, but measured reading and comprehension. I hope it helped, but if nothing else, it showed our team I was committed to trying to emphasize the importance of reading and getting a degree. One of our upcoming seniors, Don Denbo, broke all the records in the course, and while I can't recall his scores, I remember he read at a level like President Kennedy, with very high comprehension.

Don was a 5-foot-11, 220-pound offensive guard. He started for Tennessee his three varsity years. As mentioned earlier, Don and Chip Kell were the only two on our team who could bench press 400 pounds. Don was quick as a cat in a 5-yard box, but beyond that, he was pretty slow. Every year in the off-season the coaches would go over personnel and almost always determine that we needed to find someone to beat Don out. But his strength, quickness and intelligence never let anyone beat him out. Line coach Ray Trail would get mad at him from time to time and say to him, "Denbo, go read the library!"

In 1969 we were playing Georgia in Athens. The Bulldogs played an even-front defense, with two of the quickest guards in the SEC. We were worried that they were so quick, when we pulled our guards to lead our sweeps, their guards would be right behind them and throw our backs for a loss. We put in a counter play where the guard on the side of the sweep would pull like he was leading the sweep, and our other guard would pull and trap the defensive guard who was chasing the pulling guard to keep him from staying at home and tackling our tailback, who got the ball over the center/guard gap. The combination of the two plays were working beautifully and allowed Curt Watson and Don McLeary to gain a total of 386 yards rushing in the game. When we reviewed the film, we saw that Denbo, who was supposed to trap the defensive guard, never touched him. We asked him why, and without blinking he said, "serendipity." We had to go to a dictionary to see what he was talking about. The definition of "serendipity" is the faculty of making valuable discoveries by accident. How about that for an answer! How frustrated the Georgia guards must have been while watching the films as we left the onside guard unblocked on both the sweep and the counter, and gained nearly 400 yards rushing.

Another good Denbo story involved Lester McClain, our first African American football player. The late 1960s and '70s showed a great deal of change in American youth, and some of it obviously involved dress and appearance. Don came in a team meeting one day with a freshly done "curly perm." His hair was all curly and kinky and actually looked pretty weird to most. As expected, the team broke out in laughter and started jawing with Don about his new hairdo. As things quieted down a little, Lester stood up and said, "That's OK, Don, we can't all have straight hair!" That brought the house down and was a great example of why we could never have found a better man to break the color barrier at Tennessee than Lester.

1970

Our first game in 1970 was against SMU, coached by Hayden Fry, who had an All-American quarterback named Chuck Hixon. Hayden was an offensive genius. His philosophy was to have multiple formations, shifts and motions, and did everything possible to confuse the defense before the ball was snapped. It was a very difficult job to prepare for all of their offensive packages, but having done so helped a great deal as the season progressed.

Larry Jones, our defensive coordinator, brought a slightly unorthodox defensive scheme that probably gave SMU some pre-snap problems. Buddy Bennett, our secondary coach who was hired from East Tennessee State University, brought an aggressive approach to pass defense, with an emphasis on intercepting passes. He employed some drills in practice that were new to both Larry and me, but he made believers of our defensive backs and of our staff.

We had lost eight of 11 starters on defense, and the only back with even one defensive play of experience was our captain and strong safety Tim Priest. We were picked about sixth by the pre-season pundits. Bobby Majors played his sophomore year as a receiver but was moved to free safety. Bobby had great vision for seeing everything on the field, and free safety was his best position. Two upcoming sophomores, David Allen and Conrad Graham, were our two corners. We were confident that our three untested starters would be good in time, but didn't know how much time it might take.

Our depth was not very good. But now back to Tim Townes. Tim had reported for fall practice in excellent shape, and had run a very good time in our mile test for conditioning. You recall from previous writing that he had missed all of fall practice as a freshman with a broken arm, and all of spring practice with the arm that hadn't healed. A few days after our players reported, I saw Tim walking around on crutches. I called down to Mickey, our trainer, and asked what was wrong with Tim. Mickey said he had a stress fracture in his foot caused from running too much during the summer.

The week before the game the young man who was our first backup at strong safety and free safety had a summer school incomplete in a course that determined his eligibility, and he turned up ineligible. Miraculously, Tim Townes' stress fracture got better. He had been in every meeting from fall '69 to fall '70. Coach Bennett and Coach Jones convinced me he was our best bet to go into the season as first backup at both strong and free safety.

So, I go into my first game as a head coach with three untested defensive backs, pretty much an untested front, and if either safety goes down, an undersized walk-on with almost no practice time replacing an injured strong or free safety.

We did have several starters returning on offense and believed it would need to carry the load until our defense matured. We didn't have to wait long. The defensive front, led by tackles Bill Emendorfer and Frank Howell, stopped the SMU running game cold, winding up with minus-12 yards rushing. The secondary, sparked by Priest and Majors, choked off the SMU passing game, holding Hixon, a senior, without a touchdown for the first time since early in his sophomore year. Bobby Scott's passing and Curt Watson's running kicked in 358 yards of offense, 140 through the air and 218 on the ground.

The 28-3 victory was very sweet to the Vol Nation and couldn't have been a better start to the new era in Tennessee football. And, by the way, Tim Townes played some at strong safety, but he played a lot on special teams. One of our prestige awards every week was the "Hardest Hit of the Game Award." Tim won that for a tackle he made in kickoff coverage. He probably weighed only 165 pounds, but would hit you with all 165 of those pounds if he had a chance. Every week we would take the play that won the award, cut it out of the 16mm film that we used back then, splice it into a loop, and put it in the locker room on Monday for the team to see over and over and over again.

The following week we traveled to Birmingham to face Auburn, led by All-American quarterback Pat Sullivan. We led 10-7 at the end of the first quarter, but four interceptions and a fumble gave the Tigers a 29-10 lead going into the fourth. We regained our composure, made a run in the fourth quarter and had a chance at the end, but Sullivan, who had riddled our defense all afternoon, came up with a 33-yard run that settled the issue and gave Auburn a 36-23 victory.

I had told the players if they were injured, if they could manage to get off the field, it would save us a timeout. As mentioned earlier, all three linebackers had invasive knee surgery prior to the season, but all came back. Unfortunately, early in the Auburn game, co-captain James Woody got hit low and tore his knee up again. He went down at about the hashmark on our side of the field. It was obviously a serious injury, but before our trainers could get out to see him, he courageously dragged himself off the field. That was not the intention of my message to the team about saving timeouts, but Woody definitely sent his own message to the team that he was a team player and he was "all in for Tennessee." It was one of many examples of his leadership and why the team elected him co-captain before the season started.

It was good to come back home the next week as we licked our wounds and tried to correct our mistakes in time to face Army. Tom Cahill was the head coach succeeding Paul Dietzel, and was enjoying success as leader of the Cadets. Tom was the Plebe head coach my first year at West Point — a great man and an outstanding coach. Our team responded extremely well after the

Auburn loss, and we pushed out to a 28-3 halftime lead. We were able to play reserves most of the second half. Dennis Chadwick, 6-foot-3 sophomore from Atlanta, took over a 21-3 lead and directed the attack with three more touchdowns, including a perfectly timed pass to Merlyn Hood for a 19-yard touchdown. Linebacker Bill McGlothlin added a 31-yard interception return for a touchdown.

The next week we traveled to Atlanta to play 4-0 Georgia Tech. It was a frustrating first half as we drove inside Tech's 25 five times and came away with only 10 points. Bobby Scott hit Joe Thompson for a 14-yard score and George Hunt kicked a 30-yard field goal. The three other drives ended with a fumble, an interception and a missed field goal. The defense played extremely well and we took a 10-0 lead into halftime. Scott hit Stan Trott for a 10-yard touchdown in the third quarter. The defense held the Tech attack to a paltry 54 yards in the 17-6 win, as the Yellow Jackets scored late.

The third week in October brought Alabama to Knoxville. On Friday evening before the game, we hosted the Alabama official party at the University Club. Coach Bryant came in smiling and walked over to me, put his arm around my shoulder and said, "I know you're going to sleep real well tonight." As might be expected, I didn't sleep well, if at all, that night, but the Good Lord seemed to smile on our team the next day.

Now, as you recall, Tennessee had beaten Alabama three years in a row, and our team had great respect for the Tide, but did not fear them. Scott Hunter and Neb Hayden, in a pro-style offense, combined to throw 51 passes for 271 yards, and our secondary and linebackers intercepted eight passes. A relentless rush by our front led to three interceptions by Priest, and linebacker Jackie Walker returned an interception 22 yards for a touchdown. Priest was named UPI Defensive Player of the Week as we won 24-0, Alabama's first shutout since 1959.

I always tried to be cool, calm and collected during games, and be thoughtful about everything I said before, during and after games. That came from Coach Bryant's teachings "to be prepared for everything that might happen." That day, about 30 seconds before the end of the game, and before I had even thought about a post-game comment, my players lifted me up on their shoulders and ran me out to midfield. I was face to face with Coach Bryant after a 24-0 victory and my mind went completely blank. To this day I can't remember what was said, but Coach Bryant was complimentary, and I was probably babbling some kind of coach speak.

Coach Dickey's return to Knoxville with the Florida Gators was met with mixed emotions from Vol fans. Some were mad he left, though most were glad for the time he spent in Knoxville. Florida came in prepared to stop the UT running game. Their defensive schemes enabled Bobby Scott to pass for 385 yards in 21 completions, breaking Bubba Wyche's single-game passing record of 338 yards in 1968. Joe Thompson caught two touchdown passes and Curt Watson ran one in from the 3-yard line. On the defensive side of the ball against Florida, Conrad Graham returned an interception 36 yards for a touchdown and Jackie Walker returned one 19 yards for a score.

After a 38-7 shellacking by the Vols, Coach Dickey, in a very classy move, with his team running off the field toward the visitors dressing room, stopped and tipped his cap to Tennessee fans. He got a well-deserved standing ovation.

The following week we made our annual trek to Memphis. There were 400 miles between Memphis and Knoxville, and Coach Woodruff believed it was a good PR move for our fans, and for recruiting, to play a game there every year. This year's opponent in Memphis was Wake Forest. Cal Stoll, in his second season as head coach of the Demon Deacons, had led his team to an ACC Championship.

Our Vol team put on a show for our Memphis audience, beating Wake 41-7. Our defense surrendered only one touchdown on a 61-yard sprint by speedster Junior Moore. On offense, backs Watson and McLeary were both injured, so we turned, predictably, to backup fullback Steve Wold, who ran for 92 yards and two touchdowns on 15 carries, and, less predictably, to Bobby Scott, who chalked up runs of 52 and 47 yards, with two touchdowns.

The next week we traveled to Columbia to play South Carolina, coached by Dietzel, which put me against my fourth mentor in six weeks. We led 10-3 on a 32-yard Scott to Stan Trott pass and a George Hunt field goal, which carried over to the fourth quarter. Then things really got wild.

Hunt missed a field goal, a rare occurrence that injected life into the Gamecocks. Carolina quarterback Tommy Suggs completed a 48-yard pass that, along with a two-point conversion, put South Carolina ahead for the first time 11-10. The Vols responded with a 44-yard drive, capped by a 20-yard Scott to Watson touchdown pass to go ahead 17-11. Then a really weird thing happened. Suggs threw a long, high pass to Jimmy Mitchell. Bobby Majors, a great safety, was in position to intercept. Bobby got tripped up and fell, allowing Mitchell to go 61 yards to take an 18-17 lead.

At that point, there was only a minute or two left on the clock. The South Carolina fans were jubilant. I think a good many left the stadium to start their victory party. We received the kickoff and started a drive against the clock. About the time we crossed midfield, Watson, our best running back, came to the sideline with an injury. With seconds on the clock and a third down with 7 or 8 to go, Wold ran a 17-yard draw to get us into field-goal range. Hunt calmly stepped in and kicked the game-winning field goal as we escaped with a heart-throbbing (for us) and heart-breaking (for them) 20-18 victory. Walker, who intercepted two passes and recovered a fumble, was named AP Southeastern Lineman of the Week. It was a gritty victory in a hostile environment.

After an open date, we clobbered Kentucky 45-0 in Knoxville. Our secondary intercepted four passes, with Majors getting two, and Priest and David Allen one each. On offense, behind All-American guard Chip Kell, our backs rushed for 360 yards, Watson scored two touchdowns and Stan Trott caught a 13-yard touchdown pass from Scott. Reserve running backs George Silvey and Roger McKinney led a fourth-quarter assault that accounted for 192 yards.

A record-breaking defensive performance ensued the following week in Nashville against the Commodores. Majors got his ninth and 10th interceptions and Priest his ninth, moving the team total to 34. In the last few minutes of the game, Danny Jefferies intercepted a Vandy pass, giving UT its 35th of the year, a new SEC record. Majors was named UPI Defensive Player of the Week. McLeary ran in from the 4-yard line and Gary Theiler caught a 4-yard touchdown pass to give us a 14-0 first-quarter lead, which carried to halftime. Vandy scored in the third quarter to make it 14-6 and a nail-biter going into the fourth. A classic demonstration of ball control in which we maintained possession for 33 plays to four thwarted a Vandy comeback. A pass from Dennis Chadwick to Trott sealed the 24-6 victory.

We hosted UCLA in Knoxville the next week. A Tennessee drive in the second quarter ended with a McLeary touchdown from the 1-yard line to take a 7-0 lead into halftime. Lester McClain caught a 13-yard touchdown pass from Scott to match an 18-yard Bruins touchdown and take a 14-7 lead into the final quarter. A UCLA field goal made it 14-10, but then we launched a long, ball-control, clock-eating drive. We were inside their 20 with about two minutes left, and I felt very confident we had the game won. About that time, our veteran quarterback, Bobby Scott, floated a pass out in the flat. The UCLA defensive back broke on the ball, picked it off at their 15-yard line and took off running up our sideline, with no orange jersey within 20 yards of him. To this day, I have this mental picture of that UCLA player running up our sideline in slow motion as we fell behind 17-14 with very little time on the clock. We went into our two-minute offense, 67 yards from paydirt. There were two incredibly big plays in that drive. Early on our side of the 50, we had a third down and 7 or 8. Scott threw a pass to Lester McClain coming across the middle 10 to 12 yards deep. The pass was a little high but I remember seeing Lester's hands emerging from the crowd and grabbing the ball for a critical first down. The other big play came on fourth and 4 at the UCLA 29. McCleary caught a pass from Scott for the first down, and two plays later, Watson broke through the line, almost fell down, recovered and scored the winning touchdown. We kicked off, UCLA ran three plays, went for it on fourth down and we stopped them deep in their territory. We scored a final touchdown on a 1-yard McCleary plunge for a hard-fought 28-17 victory, which gave us a 10-1 record and a bid to the Sugar Bowl.

It had been a long time since Tennessee had made it to the Sugar Bowl and our fans were excited to get back to New Orleans. We were paired up against an outstanding 9-2 Air Force Academy team, coached by Ben Martin. Although UT had suffered consecutive defeats in the Orange, Cotton and Gator bowls over the previous three years, this would not be the fourth straight bowl loss. We scored the first four times we had the ball and mounted a 24-0 first-quarter lead. McLeary scored twice, Scott threw a touchdown pass to Gary Theiler, and Hunt kicked a field goal and three extra points.

Then we endured an all-time bowl experience never witnessed before or since — at least by me. Somehow, by somebody, a dog got loose on the field. This was Tulane Stadium and not the Super Dome, but the dog ran out in the middle of the field and the officials stopped play. Our team was playing very well and I was frustrated that this was breaking our momentum, while the officials were trying to catch the dog. When chased, the dog would run down to the end of the field, eluding the officials. Fans at that end of the field would stand up and cheer, causing the dog to take off running to the other end. Then that would be repeated — over and over. Smokey, our Blue Tick Hound mascot, was straining at his leash, eager to go out and take care of this interloping dog. I shouted to let Smokey loose, but nobody heard nor cared. This went on for what seemed to me to be 10 to 15 minutes. Finally, someone caught and removed the dog. In watching the replay that day, ABC had their regular yardage charts posted something like this:

Rushing Yards

Tennessee	250
Air Force	150

Maybe to keep viewers interested and staying tuned in a 24-0 start to the game, they began posting something like the following:

Rushing Yards

Tennessee	250
Air Force	150
Dog	640

Whether it was the break or not, both teams played a little sloppy over the remaining three quarters. Be that as it may, our defense, led by linebackers Ray Nettles, Jamie Rotella and Priest, held the Falcons' offense to minus-12 yards rushing. We intercepted four more passes, taking the season total to 40, an NCAA record. Majors returned a punt 57 yards for a third-quarter touchdown and Hunt kicked another field goal in the fourth for a resounding 34-13 Volunteer victory.

The entire Sugar Bowl experience was fantastic. The Sugar Bowl Committee did a great job with our players, coaches and the Tennessee official party.

So, in my first year as head coach of the Tennessee Volunteers, I had the opportunity to coach against four of my mentors: Coach Tom Cahill at Army, Coach Paul Bryant at Alabama, Coach Doug Dickey at Florida, and Coach Paul Dietzel at South Carolina. By the grace of the Good Lord, and the ability of our players and coaches, we were able to defeat all four on our way to an 11-1 season.

After each game, I taped an hour-long television show that played on Sundays at different times in the five major Tennessee markets. John Ward, who gained fame as play-by-play announcer in UT basketball and football broadcasts, organized and moderated the show. He was one of the most organized and smartest people I've ever worked with.

The show was taped in a TV studio across town from where I lived, at midnight after every Tennessee game. We could make it back to do the show at midnight even after away games, for the most part. When we played on the West Coast or other faraway places, we had to adjust, but that was a rare occurrence.

In every case over the seven years I was there, when I walked in the studio at 11:30 or 11:50, a script was on the set that highlighted what we were going to talk about. We never really went by the script per se, but it gave me an idea of what we were doing, and it was pretty easy to follow John's lead.

Because we worked with 16-millimeter film that was converted to tape during our session, time was a precious commodity. John didn't trust planes that might not be able to deliver due to weather, so he had automobiles and drivers who drove the finished tapes to Bristol, Chattanooga, Nashville and Memphis — 400 miles away — to ensure the show would always go on.

Rumor was the reason we taped at midnight was that Coach Woodruff got the best rental rates for the studio at that time. I didn't care. The TV show was a valuable promotional piece for Tennessee football, and with Ernie Robertson doing the film production and John Ward doing the organization and execution, a professional piece always went out. It did make for short nights though.

I didn't realize the personal effect the TV show would have on my life. As an assistant coach, I was recognized by many at the university and those fans closest to the program. But, after one season of television, I could hardly go anywhere in the state without being recognized. As you can imagine, that had both good and bad implications. But whether good or bad, being head coach at the University of Tennessee put my and my family's lives squarely in the middle of "the fish bowl" — and was both exciting and a little scary.

The captain of the 1970 team was Tim Priest, with co-captains Chip Kell and James Woody. In the NFL Draft after the season, Lester McClain was selected by the Bears, Bobby Scott by the Saints and Kell by the Chargers.

1971

As we approached the 1971 season, we knew we should be stronger on defense since we played so many young players who got better as the 1970 season progressed. We lost our outstanding quarterback, Scott, and the anchor of our offensive line, Kell, to graduation, and knew they would be hard to replace. We also lost defensive coordinator Larry Jones, who was named head coach at Florida State, and secondary coach Buddy Bennett, who was hired at the same position at Arkansas.

We signed Condredge Holloway, an outstanding three-sport athlete, in 1971. Ray Trail, offensive line coach, did the heavy lifting in our recruiting effort. Condredge was All-State in football, basketball and baseball, and as it turned out, professional baseball was who we were recruiting against. Condredge was drafted as a shortstop by Montreal in 1971 with the Expos' first pick, and fourth overall. He was offered a $100,000 signing bonus, which was big in those days. Deep down, Condredge probably wanted to play baseball. He was recruited by Auburn and Alabama. Coach Bryant told him they wanted him, but Alabama wasn't ready for a black quarterback, and Condredge appreciated his honesty. Condredge asked me if Tennessee would allow him to play quarterback. I honestly didn't know if he could be an SEC quarterback, but I told him if he was good enough, certainly he could play. When the freshman team reported, it didn't take us long to figure out he could definitely play quarterback in the SEC. If freshmen would have been eligible to play, he could have helped us in 1971 as we struggled with injuries at the quarterback position.

We played a freshman schedule that consisted of about three games. For the third one, we had Notre Dame and its highly recruited quarterback Tom Clements scheduled on the Saturday of our open-date week. Condredge had attracted a lot of attention by word of mouth, as well as some press coverage, with his play in our first two freshman games. About 31,000 fans showed up against the Irish, primarily to watch Condredge. He didn't disappoint, as he lit up the Notre Dame defense in a back-and-forth game that ended with a Tennessee victory. After that game, there was no doubt in anyone's mind that

Condredge was not destined to just play quarterback, but to be a very good one.

The varsity opened the 1971 season against the University of California, Santa Barbara. The defense played very well, and Bobby Majors contributed to the 48-6 victory with a 47-yard punt return for a score. Dennis Chadwick started the game at quarterback and threw a 45-yard touchdown pass to split end Joe Thompson. Curt Watson, Bill Rudder, George Silvey and Phil Pierce each scored touchdowns as we led 24-6 at halftime, and added another 24 points in the second half. Bill Rudder, the backup behind Watson, had a great day rushing for 143 yards in 14 carries.

The next week Auburn came to town with its deadly passing combination of Pat Sullivan and Terry Beasley. The first three quarters were a defensive struggle, with us leading 9-3 well into the fourth quarter after Hunt kicked field goals of 30, 45 and 50 yards. We had a time-consuming drive that reached the red zone, and it appeared we had the game well under control with a third and 2 from the Auburn 16-yard line. If we didn't make the first down, a high-percentage field goal would have put the game out of reach the way our defense was playing, especially linebacker Jackie Walker, who was named UPI Player of the Week in the South. We ran the option to our left and our quarterback kept the ball, made enough for the first down, but fumbled and Auburn recovered on their own 14 with 6 minutes to go. We had controlled the Auburn offense all day and I was confident we could keep them out of our end zone.

Sullivan, who ultimately won the Heisman Trophy, went to work. Passes to Beasley and Dick Schmaltz were key to making first downs on a 4-minute drive that ultimately was capped when Harry Unger ran for a 5-yard touchdown for a 10-9 Auburn lead. This isn't an excuse, as Sullivan and his receivers completed several highly contested passes to take the lead, but two 15-yard penalties were called away from the action when our corner did as he was coached and hit the receiver to his side as he released on his route. Those penalties, I believe, should not have been called, and those 30 yards were very helpful to the Tigers in their 86-yard drive. This game still haunts me almost 50 years later, as we had the game won and let it slip out of our hands. Our players played their hearts out, and the thing that still eats at me is they deserved to win.

Our team traveled to Gainesville the next week to face Florida, as Tennessee's legendary voice John Ward said, "At night, in white." The SEC implemented the "Tennessee rule" earlier in the year that required visiting teams to wear white. UT's jerseys were light orange, and for decades had been the only color worn by the Vols. The color contrasted very well against pretty much every SEC team's primary color, but there was no doubt the rule was implemented to force the Vols to wear white as the visiting team.

We scored first as Hunt kicked field goals of 33 and 34 yards, and Watson scored on a 8-yard run to take a 13-0 lead in the second quarter. UF's John Reaves answered with two second-quarter touchdown passes to Jackson and Foldberg to knot the score at 13 going into halftime. In the third quarter, the Gators punted deep in our territory. As the ball was rolling rapidly toward our goal, a Florida player dove on it as it was crossing the goal line and slid about halfway through the end zone. The official ruled the Gator had possession at the 1-yard line. Before I knew it, I was on the 15-yard line telling the official it was a touchback and to bring the ball out to the 20. He promptly threw his flag and told me to get back to my place in front of our bench. I couldn't believe the call. Obviously, he was closer than I was, but in my playing or coaching career, I had never seen a play that close, especially with the player recovering the ball going so far into the end zone, that it wasn't ruled a touchback. The penalty could have been the shortest in history, as he moved the ball from the half-yard line up against the goal line.

Phil Pierce was our third starting quarterback in three games. He was highly recruited, but had not played much, and here he was, in extremely hostile territory, at night, with the score tied, and 99 3/4 yards to go for a touchdown. Phil rose to the occasion. I think our players were mad that the ball didn't come out to the 20, because our first play, a quarterback sneak, got us out to the 5-yard line. Phil led us on a long drive, accounting for about 75 of the 100 yards with accurate passes and effective running. He hit Stan Trott for a 20-yard touchdown on what could have been the most important drive of the season. It was definitely the longest. Our defense continued to dominate the potent Gator offense, holding them scoreless in the second half. Hunt continued his perfect kicking record, making all eight extra points and all seven field goals. With a great defense and a great kicking game, a lot of games can be won. Our 20-13 victory on the road was a real confidence builder for our team.

Georgia Tech was our next opponent in Knoxville. Watson scored a 19-yard touchdown run on our first possession, but the game quickly became a defensive struggle. Injuries to quarterbacks kept us from building the consistency we needed. We had seven fumbles, and the offense definitely needed to settle down. Watson rushed for 76 yards, passing the famous Beattie Feathers' career running mark of 1,888 yards. The Vol defense continued to play great football, with linebackers Jamie Rotella, Ray Nettles and Jackie Walker leading the way. "Those Tennessee linebackers, they are the best," said Georgia Tech head coach Bud Carson after we overcame the turnovers for a 10-6 win.

We traveled to Birmingham to take on Alabama next. The Tide had secretly committed to the wishbone offense in the summer of 1971. After going 6-5-1 and losing by big margins to both Southern Cal and us in 1970, Alabama shocked the world in its opening game in 1971 by beating Southern Cal 17-10 in the Los Angeles Coliseum. Before our game, a member of the press reminded Coach Bryant that Tennessee had intercepted eight passes the previous year. He quickly responded, "Well they won't intercept eight this year. We won't throw eight." They threw five and caught three. We caught two, but lost the game 32-15.

The Tide's wishbone was effective, as they built a 22-7 fourth-quarter lead on Terry Davis throwing two touchdown passes to David Bailey and running one in from the 6. Bill Davis added a field goal. Midway through the fourth quarter our team engineered a beautiful 90-yard drive that made it 22-15, and we believed at that point we would win the game. A long kickoff return put Alabama in scoring position that led to a victory-clinching field goal. Alabama's Johnny Musso, Steve Bisceglia and Joe LaBue made a formidable group of running backs. Watson scored both Vol touchdowns and Dennis Chadwick ran for a two-point conversion. Ray Nettles had an outstanding game on defense being involved in 22 tackles. We suffered four fumbles and four interceptions.

Jim Maxwell was a fifth-year senior and primarily had made the traveling squad the previous three years as a holder for Hunt's field goals and extra points. He was a good passer and more of a pro-style quarterback than an option quarterback, which was the basis of our offense. He was a factor in spring practice to succeed Bobby Scott. When he reported for fall practice, he had mono and missed the first few weeks. I sort of wrote him off, as we had to try to get Chadwick, Pierce and Howard ready to play. It was unfortunate that injuries to all three kept that from happening.

As we were getting ready to play Mississippi State in Memphis, I was watching warmups and Jim Maxwell was out practicing. He definitely had the best arm of the four and he was humming it pretty well. So well in fact that we put in a special play for him in the game. He took a lot of snaps in practice all week and seemed ready to play.

In the first quarter Hunt kicked a 51-yard field goal that was his personal best. It wasn't so much the distance but how it happened that stunned Tennessee fans as well as State fans. George took his first step, but a bad snap took time to get on the tee. Without stepping back to get a full swing, he took a mini-step and punched the ball against the wind and through the uprights.

Early in the second quarter of a defensive struggle, we put Jim in the game and called "the play." The receiver ran a deep post route, Maxwell threw a

162

perfect strike that should have been caught for a touchdown but the receiver dropped the ball, stumbled and fell on his face, breaking his nose as his helmet slid down. That was indicative of how our offense faired in 1971. We had great coaches and they did a great job, but the inability to stabilize the quarterback position was costly. At least that part was about to change. Maxwell looked so good on that pass, we left him in the game.

In the third quarter Jackie Walker intercepted a pass and returned it 42 yards for a touchdown, but MSU responded with a 54-yard punt return for a TD. A scoreless fourth quarter allowed us to escape with a 10-7 victory.

In those days, cowbells in the stands were still legal, and the noise they made as our offense approached the ball was deafening. I think we had about 10 false-start penalties, as our linemen weren't used to Maxwell's cadence calling signals at the line, and they couldn't hear them anyway. That game made me change our early practice schedule every day to have a drill where all centers and quarterbacks were present. The quarterbacks rotated taking snaps from all centers and everyone got used to everyone else's cadence, hopefully causing them all to develop the same rhythm. Years later, the SEC finally outlawed the cowbells when the offensive team approached the ball.

The next week we played Tulsa in another game that gave breathing room to the 62,500 Vol fans in the stadium. Maxwell started, our fourth quarterback to do so in our seventh game of the season. Maxwell was not a particularly good runner, but he rose to the occasion by scoring our first touchdown on a 5-yard run, and gaining 45 yards for the day. Fullback Steve Chancey scored another first-quarter touchdown for a 14-0 lead. Watson scored in the second quarter after a Tulsa field goal to make it 21-3 by halftime. In the third quarter, Hunt kicked a 25-yard field goal, and Watson scored in the fourth for a comfortable 31-3 lead. Soon afterward, one of my favorite plays of the year took place.

Ernie Robertson and staff filmed all of our games and practices. They regularly stayed late in our University Photographic Center developing the 16mm film. It was very helpful for our coaches to find that film on our desks when we came in from supper in the athletic dining room. The film crew was very receptive to our coaching them, and we considered them a very valuable part of our team.

This Tennessee team, primarily led by linebacker Ray Nettles, celebrated scores, turnovers and all the good things more enthusiastically than any team I was ever around. Our defense scored a lot of points in 1971 on intercepted passes, punt returns, kickoff returns, fumble returns and safeties. Whenever one of our players took an interception or punt back for a touchdown, as they rounded the turn in the end zone, they were met with a full-speed tackle from

Nettles, knocking them on the ground. By that time, most if not all of the defense had sprinted to the end zone and piled on, and sometimes the extra-point team coming out to kick joined the pile. I feel pretty sure these celebrations were the genesis of the NCAA passing a rule against excessive happiness. I hated that, because what these guys did was so spontaneous and team oriented, not like the "bring attention to myself" antics seen today.

Anyway, deep in the fourth quarter, reserve safety Gordon Turnage intercepted a pass on our own 29-yard line. Gordon had not seen a lot of action up to this point and was not blessed with great speed, but he made one of the prettiest 71-yard returns I ever saw. I think everyone on the Tulsa team had a shot at him, and about half of them got two shots. He twisted, turned, broke tackles and survived the gauntlet, taking his interception to the house. Nettles hit him in the end zone and I think our whole bench got in on the action. When asked by the media why he made those end-zone tackles of his own teammates, Nettles responded, "I have never scored a touchdown, but if I did, I would be very excited. It excites me to see my teammates score and that's my way of congratulating them."

As I said, Ernie's group took coaching pretty well and we asked them to keep the cameras rolling if there were spontaneous instances of team spirit celebrations. The next day as we were grading the film and saw the team unpile off Gordon, we were interested to see that our team doctor, Bill Yeomans, got up from near the bottom of the pile. Enthusiasm is definitely contagious, and an organization with that as a part of its DNA is dangerous.

Watson scored twice and gained 72 yards on 21 carries while Chancey scored once and gained 53 yards on 12 rushes. The defense again played a critical role getting a 38-3 near shutout, with Gordon's interception as well as two more picks and a fumble recovery that led to a touchdown.

The next week saw Paul Dietzel return to Knoxville with his South Carolina team. It was another defensive struggle through the first quarter. The Gamecocks had kept our team backed up in a punting duel that gave us the ball around our own 5-yard line. Neither team had any success moving the ball, so on second down I called for a quick kick, the same kind Coach Bryant employed so successfully when I was a player at Alabama. We had been working on it all season, and Chancey, the fullback, was a natural. We would line up with quarterback under center, fullback in normal position behind the quarterback, and tailback in normal position to the fullback's left. Steve was a right-footed kicker so we always had a tight end to his side for protection. As our defense came off the field after forcing the punt, I ran over and grabbed them and told them to get ready to go back in the game. I would have called it on first down but didn't want our defensive players to be shocked, or get lost going for water. The ball was snapped between the center's legs, Chancey caught it, turned to his right and executed the kick perfectly. The ball sailed end-over-end and over the safety's head, hitting the ground and rolling for 66 yards. It changed our field position, and our defense forced a short punt to give us the ball on the Carolina 48. Our offense took it in from there, with Chancey blasting across from the 5 to take a 7-0 lead into halftime.

In the second half, two Majors' interceptions led to short drives, ending with Watson and Chadwick scoring touchdowns. The icing on the cake came from a 72-yard Eddie Brown interception return for a touchdown, only to be topped by Danny Jefferies' interception and an 83-yard score, both in the last three minutes, for a 35-6 final.

After an open date, we traveled to Lexington to take on Kentucky, coached by John Ray. It was another really hard-fought defensive struggle. Watson, a three-time All-SEC fullback, carried 30 times for 152 yards. It was his best game of the year and came at a great time. Watson's 26-yard second-quarter touchdown, along with Maxwell's 4-yard run, gave us 14-0 lead we would never relinquish in a 21-7 victory.

The Vanderbilt game was no longer the final regular-season contest, with the addition of the 11th game, and some bad things happened in the first half. Vandy scored a first-quarter touchdown on a play that surprised our defense, and the half ended with a sure touchdown pass that was dropped. George Hunt missed his first field goal after 10 straight scores, and Curt Watson was lost to a rib injury in the first quarter. Things did not look good as we trailed 7-0 at halftime. The third quarter was a 0-0 wash, but we caught fire in the fourth. The offense made up its mind that it was going to run at the Commodores, even without Watson. Maxwell engineered a brilliant 82-yard drive, passing to tight end Sonny Leach for a 7-yard touchdown, and another drive capped by a 7-yard run by Chancey. After Hunt kicked his 11th field goal of the year, defensive end Anthony Edwards sacked the Vandy quarterback for a safety to finish off a 19-point fourth quarter — probably our best fourth quarter of the season — and a 19-7 victory.

Our 11th game was Penn State. This was one of Coach Woodruff's best athletics director moves of his career, and maybe one of the best all time. He had the negotiating skill to schedule a home-and-home with Penn State in 1971 and 1972. Our home game was played in Knoxville in December 1971. Their home game was played in Memphis in September 1972. How about that for good athletic directing?

Penn State came into Knoxville undefeated and a 14-point favorite, and on their way to face Texas in the Cotton Bowl. They were loaded with giant offensive and defensive linemen, excellent linebackers and safeties, and

All-American running backs Lydell Mitchell and Franco Harris. Their quarterback and team leader, John Hufnagel, pulled the strings that made them go. But, in those days, nobody came into Knoxville as a 14-point favorite, and of course, we took offense (and defense, too) at that. And it was a special day in many ways.

First, Coach Woodruff had invited the entire Majors family to be honored in pre-game ceremonies for their contribution to intercollegiate football. Johnny Majors was an All-American tailback before my time. Billy Majors was a UT tailback in the 1960s that our Alabama team played against, and he coached on Coach Dickey's staff until his untimely death in 1965. Bobby Majors was an All-American safety on our team. Joe Majors played at FSU. Majors patriarch Shirley Majors was a legendary football coach for 21 years at the University of the South at Sewanee.

Second, the weather was horrible and snow was expected, but it ended up snowing all around Knoxville — except by the stadium, where it was sunny and delightful.

It started with us kicking off and Penn State pounding us with Harris inside and Mitchell outside. After they crossed midfield and made it to our 25, it looked like we couldn't stop them. About that time, Hufnagel faked to the fullback and reversed field on a counter option. As he came down the line to our left, Jackie Walker scraped off around the offensive tackle and hit Hufnagel just as he pitched. Cornerback Conrad Graham was screaming upfield playing the run and intercepted the bobbled pitch, turned and ran to his right down the line of scrimmage while dodging a couple of would-be tacklers, then turned upfield on our right sideline. A few Vols alertly turned upfield to block for Graham, and he ran 76 yards for a touchdown and a 7-0 lead. Bill Rudder finished off a UT drive with a 1-yard plunge and Bobby Majors returned a punt 44 yards for a touchdown that gave us a 21-3 lead at the half. The third quarter saw neither team score, but a 43-yard interception return by Walker and a George Hunt field goal in the fourth gave us a 31-3 cushion. Penn State scored late and went for two to make the final score 31-11.

It was a great team victory, but Majors added a huge exclamation point to his family's pre-game honor with two punt returns for 82 yards and the TD, and two kickoff returns for 113 yards. Bobby was named Offensive Player of the Week for his dominating performance returning kicks. He never played a down on offense, which made this honor extra special. Coach Paterno was very gracious after the game and complimented our team's performance, as well as our fans' enthusiasm. Penn State went on to crush Texas 30-6 in the Cotton Bowl, finishing with an 11-1 record.

We went to the Liberty Bowl to play Arkansas, which got a bid before we did. Even though we were the team from Tennessee and the Liberty Bowl was a Tennessee venue, Arkansas Coach Frank Broyles had maneuvered to get the home team dressing room and the right to wear their red jerseys. We were proud to be there, and were glad to take anything they would give us.

A week or 10 days before the game, SEC Commissioner Boyd McWhorter called me and told me we had a problem, and asked if I would consider helping. In those days, bowl games were officiated by split crews, three from each participating conference. McWhorter said Broyles, a Hall of Famer, wanted the three officials that included the umpire. I said the home team gets the three that gets the referee; the visiting team gets the umpire. I thought it a very brazen request by Coach Broyles. Then, in a show of stupidity, I said, "Give him the umpire, I don't think coaches should be involved with officiating decisions anyway." McWhorter was stunned and said "Do you really mean that?" I replied I did, and went back to preparing for the game.

A few days later when the bowl officials were announced, I had to pinch myself. I don't know if Dr. McWhorter was trying to help or not, but two of the three SEC officials were teammates of mine at Alabama. I thought, "If I ever had it made on the officiating front, this was it!" Unfortunately, if I had thought more about it, Bobby Boylston and Goobie Stapp had too much class to officiate any way from neutral, and I thought, like a man coaching his son, they would be harder on me than neutral — and they were.

As reported earlier, Coach Buddy Bennett, who did a fantastic job for us and our secondary, left after the 1970 season to head up Coach Broyle's defense. During the course of the bowl coverage, Buddy made a pretty derogatory comment about one of our players. There was definitely some personal heat between our two coaching staffs as we prepared to face the Razorbacks.

Game day came and unbeknownst to me, there were two Razorback fans, one wearing a red plastic hog hat, outside our third team bus. I always rode on the first bus and, apparently, Nettles always rode on the third. I think the two Hog fans may have done some friendly needling of our team, or maybe it was just their presence, but Nettles disembarked the bus, walked over to the two fans and snatched the hog hat off the one wearing it. As he walked back to the bus, the hat wearer's friend said to his buddy, "Don't let him get away with that!" The now-bareheaded one replied, "Are you crazy? I'm not about to get on that bus!"

When we got to the stadium, our team got off the bus in their orange blazers, brown trousers, white shirts and color-coordinated ties. One of our guys was wearing a hat — guess who?

We walked the field in customary fashion and then came in, finished getting taped, and got dressed for pre-game warmups. Our team was fired up and we were facing a very good Arkansas opponent. After warmups, we came back in the dressing room and, as always, we were notified how much time we had before coming out on the field for the game. We had plenty of time for players to make adjustments to equipment and meet with position coaches, and I would speak to the team before we went out. Timing was important, as it was optimal to talk to them to try to get their full attention zeroed in on the challenge we faced right before we went out to play. I had started a tradition of letting the seniors talk before bowl games, and then I would finish up. They would say what their four years meant to them and whatever else they had on their hearts.

Nettles was the last senior to speak with about six minutes to go before we were to go out. Ray finished up a great talk on how much this team meant to him and how much fun he had with his great teammates. All of a sudden he reached down beneath the bench he was standing on, picked up the hog hat, and said, "And I guarantee one thing, ain't nothing this ugly going to beat us!" With that, he slammed the hog hat down on the floor, his teammates exploded out of their chairs whooping and hollering, and all rushed to the door. The bad news was that we had five minutes to go. We had to get them back in their seats and calm them down a little, which was the last thing we wanted to do. You never want to peak too early!

We did go out and play pretty well in the first quarter, driving for a 7-0 lead on a 2-yard Bill Rudder blast. Arkansas responded with a 21-yard Joe Ferguson pass in the second quarter. It was another defensive struggle that took a 7-7 tie going into the fourth quarter, but the Razorbacks kicked two field goals for a 13-7 lead.

There were controversial calls after that point. My road-game roommate my sophomore year, Goobie Stapp, could have made the right call and helped me a lot before one of the Arkansas field goals. I thought there was an obvious third-down offensive interference call in the end zone, which if called, would give us possession on the 20. Goobie reached for his flag, thought about it, but left it in his pocket. Of course, that was a judgment call, and Goobie's and my judgment disagreed on that call. They made the field goal on fourth down.

Another controversy came on another long field-goal attempt that would have put the game out of reach. On the attempt, an offensive holding call was made by our third official that took the Hogs out of field-goal range.

The next controversial call came with time running out and us electing to punt on fourth down. We punted to the Hogs deep in their own territory. On first or second down they completed a screen pass to our side of the field but the back was hit with a bone-crushing tackle, separating him from the ball.

There was a massive pile-up, and the scrambling underneath the pile was ferocious. As the line judge was looking at the pile, trying to see who had the ball, I believe it was Anthony Edwards who stepped in front of the official and in a very enthusiastic manner gave the first-down signal our way. The official looked inside the pile, made his decision and gave the first-down signal our way.

That all took place around the Arkansas 36-yard line. We still had 36 tough yards to go with less than a minute to play. On the second play we ran the counter option to our right as our blockers knocked Coach Bennett's cornerback and safety to the ground as Curt Watson took it 17 yards for a touchdown to tie the score at 13. Hunt came in and confidently kicked the winning extra point for a great come-from-behind victory.

I went out after the game to shake hands with Coach Broyles. I extended my hand and he growled, "Blankety blank SEC officials!" I was stunned for a few seconds, but then responded, "Blank you!" and walked off.

I couldn't believe what was happening, but later thought, even if he did get a couple of bad calls, and I truly don't believe he did, he probably deserved it with the maneuvering that went on before the game.

The victory, our second straight bowl win, enabled this 10-2 Vol team to finish No. 9 in both the AP and UPI polls. The NFL drafted Bobby Majors (Eagles), George Hunt (Browns), Jackie Walker (49ers), Curt Watson (Saints), Gary Theiler (Colts), Joe Balthrop (Saints) and Ray Nettles by the Miami Dolphins, but Ray instead signed with the BC Lions in the Canadian Football League. Walker was the captain of the 1971 team, with Theiler and Phillip Fulmer serving as co-captains.

After the 1971 season, as I always did, time was spent taking stock of where we were and where we needed to go from there. We had gone 10-2, with losses to Auburn and Alabama. Even then, a 10-2 season with a strong finish against a great Penn State team bode well for the future, but it wasn't as much fun as it should have been. I had spent too much time in the 1970 off-season speaking at clinics, Alumni Association meetings, and doing things other than tending to my team. As a result, the group of seniors were out on the edge of leading the way I wanted them to lead. A big lesson I learned was, "Leaders in your organization are going to lead. If they didn't lead in the direction the coach/ manager wanted, he or she had failed to sell them on the mission."

We started a leadership council. It was important to me that more, rather than less, make up the council. All upcoming seniors were included, as well as three elected members from the upcoming sophomore and junior classes. We started meeting in January and met until spring practice when we could meet with the entire team. There were two primary things I wanted to accomplish:

(1) Listen to what they had to say; hopefully players from every class would communicate with one of the members of their class or the seniors, and all the questions would come out; (2) Lead the council to answer their questions, and of greater importance, determine what they wanted the 1972 team to look like, in every detail. We met regularly. Interestingly enough, one of the issues that came up was that the toilet paper in the dorm was too rough. That was an easy one to fix and when we got that done quickly, it sent the message we were listening and would take action. Other issues weren't that easy to resolve, but they did take their leadership role on the council seriously. It was pretty amazing that when we got right down to what we wanted people who watched us practice and play to see, our players wanted what we the staff wanted. The goal was to get everyone pulling in the same direction, and I think we were able to do that with the 1972 team.

1972

We opened the '72 season with Georgia Tech in Atlanta. The game drew national media attention and a TV audience on ABC, as it may have been the first game in the South featuring two starting African American quarterbacks, Condredge Holloway at Tennessee and Eddie McAshan at Tech. Condredge at quarterback gave us the ability to open up our offense.

Early in the game, we had driven into Tech's red zone. Condredge threw an out route behind the receiver. The cornerback picked off the pass and it looked like he would return it about 80 yards for a touchdown. Condredge, on one of his better plays of the game, chased him down and tackled him hard around our 10-yard line. My stock in Condredge went way up even though his pass left a lot to be desired. Our defense held and we ended the first quarter with a 3-0 lead.

Our great kicker George Hunt had graduated and next in line was Ricky Townsend, a barefooted soccer-style kicker. He kicked field goals of 28 and 30 yards to top Tech's 22-yard field goal that took us to halftime with a 6-3 lead.

We had a legendary former Tennessee tailback and punter coaching our kickers, and George Cafego was the best I ever saw. He made it through all Tennessee head football coaches, from General Neyland to Coach Phillip Fulmer. George worked with our scout squad and they loved him. Tennessee sent a lot of punters and kickers to the pros that learned under George's tutelage. He was probably the most loyal person to the University of Tennessee I ever knew. He would have done anything for that school. He definitely did a great job on our staff from 1970 to 1976 and meant the world to me.

The defense set up two touchdowns in the third quarter, led by captain Jamie Rotella, our only returning linebacker. Bill Rudder ran one in from the 7-yard line, and on a halfback pass, threw to Chip Howard from 21 yards out for the other. That gave us a commanding 20-3 lead going into the final quarter. A 20-yard touchdown pass from Gary Valbuena to Emmon Love, and a tailback Haskel Stanback TD run finished our scoring. Rotella, whose dad, Al, played at Tennessee, was named the AP National Lineman of the Week. The major takeaways from the Tech game to me were: (1) Condredge was introduced to the pressures of big-time college football before a national television audience and responded like an experienced, hardened veteran; and (2) the overdependence on defense that we experienced in 1971 was over, because now had an explosive offense.

Next came Penn State, back in Neyland Stadium for their part of a home-and-home contract. It was the first Tennessee game ever under the lights. The good guys jumped out to a 21-0 lead in the first half on a 41-yard run by Stanback, and a 3-yard run, in the first quarter. Steve Chancey scored from the 22-yard line in the second quarter. We went in at halftime thinking we would do to them what our last year's team did. Obviously, they weren't thinking that way. The Nittany Lions came out with an entirely different look in the second half and took the fight to us. They scored third-quarter touchdowns on a 69-yard pass and a 1-yard run. We went into the third quarter with a 21-14 lead but Penn State had the momentum. Condredge led us on a fourth-quarter drive that culminated with Stanback's third touchdown of the game, which, along with his 101-yard rushing performance, earned him the AP's Back of the Week honor. The Nittany Lions also scored a fourth quarter touchdown, making the final score 28-21, and they were driving in our territory as the game ended.

When Coach Paterno came out to shake hands, he said, "Congratulations on your win today. You guys play the game as it should be played. I'd like to get our fans at Penn State to be more like your fans. I'd also like to come over and talk to your team." I told him I'd love to have him talk to our team. I held out the press while he spoke with his team, then he walked into our dressing room. He congratulated our team and told them the same things he had told me. At the end, he said, "But I want to tell you the real reason I came over here to talk to you. I told my friends back in State College that I wasn't leaving Knoxville without being in the winning dressing room, I just didn't anticipate doing it this way!" We all broke out laughing and I thought that was one of the classiest things I had ever seen. From that point on I became a huge Joe Paterno fan and really hated to see the way he went out. I hope and pray that over time the great things he accomplished, both as a football coach and personal donor to the university, will be recognized, and his legacy will be greatness that I think he deserves.

Wake Forest came to Knoxville next as part of another home-and-home series negotiated by Coach Woodruff, with our home games in Knoxville and theirs in Memphis, where we played them in 1971. At the end of the first half, the score was 31-0 in our favor. Holloway threw a 69-yard touchdown pass to Chip Howard, UT's third-longest pass of all time. Holloway also scored on a 29-yard run. Gary Valbuena threw for three touchdowns, two to Stan Trott and a 52-yard strike to Neal Clabo, who also served as our punter. Conrad Graham scored on a 13-yard return of a blocked punt in the 45-6 win.

The next week we traveled to Birmingham to play Auburn. Our previous game with the Tigers was a 10-9 loss, and it gave me a lot of sleepless nights — and a start to my many gray hairs. Another defensive struggle ensued, as we had 189 yards of total offense to Auburn's 143. We also had four turnovers to their one, which cost us the game. After a scoreless first quarter, AU drove 81 yards for a touchdown in the second to take a 7-0 lead into halftime. The Tigers scored a third-quarter field goal, and Gary Valbuena completed a 3-yard TD pass late in the fourth for a 10-6 loss.

We traveled the next week to Memphis to play Memphis State, coached by Spook Murphy, an excellent coach and a real character. Our team bounced back and let their frustrations out on Memphis State. Stanback played a great game to lead the offense and Conrad Graham did the same to lead the defensive effort. Stanback scored three touchdowns, the longest on a 25-yard run on which he burst through a gang of tacklers at the line of scrimmage, popped out in the clear and eluded the would-be tackles in the secondary. Chancey scored on a pass from Condredge Holloway. Ricky Townsend kicked three field goals and three extra points, the latter being the 77th extra point without a miss, tying an NCAA record. On the defensive front, Art Reynolds, Jack's brother, came to Tennessee as a walk-on linebacker. Art didn't have Jack's ability, but he did have his tenacious drive to go full speed every play and in every drill, and he earned a scholarship after his freshman year. Art intercepted a pass and scored a touchdown. Conrad Graham had eight tackles, a fumble recovery and an interception, leading to a 38-7 victory.

Next came Alabama in Knoxville. Our defense played as well as it could play. The Tide led 3-0 at halftime, but Condredge led a drive in the third quarter and scampered in from the 2-yard line to take a 7-3 lead. Townsend kicked a field goal in the fourth to give us a 10-3 lead with minutes remaining. Alabama drove into our territory and scored on a Wilbur Jackson 2-yard plunge that tied it with less than two minutes to go. I knew Coach Bryant would not leave Knoxville without playing to win, so we called our regular defense and prepared for the two-point conversion, but Alabama kicked the extra point to tie it. I knew he would try an onside kick, so we lined up to prepare for that with our "Hands Team" — a mixture of offensive backs and receivers. We had a single receiver to field the kick if they kicked deep. Sure enough, they kicked it deep, but short and to our side of the field. Stanback was our deep receiver, because he was as sure-handed as we had on the team. The ball hit him in the chest and bounced out on the 16-yard line.

I told Condredge to sprint out to the left, but don't throw an interception. If no one was open, keep the ball and get what yardage he could. He kept for a couple of yards, and he did the same on second down, but this time to the right. Another couple of yards and the clock was under a minute. On third down we ran a quarterback draw designed to block the middle linebacker. Condredge and our line executed it well. Condredge popped into the secondary, I believe with enough yardage to get the first down, but he was hit from his left by Alabama's weakside linebacker. Condredge didn't go down, and the Tide's strong safety put his helmet on the ball, knocking it out of Condredge's hands. Alabama recovered. On first or second down, Terry Davis ran an option 22 yards for the winning touchdown with 34 seconds left. It was the most devastating loss I ever experienced, and to this day, I wake up reliving that loss in my dreams. About a minute before the final score, we led 10-3 and seemingly were headed for a monumental upset of the nation's No. 3 team. Indeed, the "winning edge" is a razor-thin margin.

I wondered for weeks why Coach Bryant would play for a tie in Knoxville. I finally found out that Alabama had scheduled an extra SEC opponent. In the event of a tie and the rest wins, he would win the SEC Championship over a one-loss team.

The following week the Rainbow Warriors from the University of Hawaii came to Knoxville. This was another great home-and-home series Coach Woodruff scheduled, especially because we would travel to Hawaii in a few years. Holloway and Stanback didn't play due to injuries suffered in the Alabama game. We were downbeat and we didn't play with much consistency, but we did put 14 points on the board in the first quarter and another 17 in the second. Conrad Graham intercepted a pass on Hawaii's first play and returned it 25 yards for a quick 7-0 lead. The defense held and Eddie Brown brought a punt back 30 yards. A few plays later, Paul Careathers scored from the 4-yard line. In the second quarter, Hawaii caught us in the end zone for a safety. Townsend, kicking from the 20, booted the ball 80 yards, all the way to the goal line. Careathers scored again on 1- yard plunge. David Allen intercepted a pass and returned it 57 yards for a touchdown. Townsend kicked a 34-yard field goal to get us into halftime up 31-2, and he added another later for a 34-2 final. Graham and tackle Robert Pulliam were standouts on defense.

We traveled to Athens to play Georgia next, and our team responded extremely well to the challenge the Bulldogs presented. Our offensive line played very well, clearing the way for Stanback to gain 96 yards and Rudder 78. In all, the offense put together five drives of 50 yards or more in the 14-0 win. Our defense handed Georgia's offense its first shutout since 1963. Interceptions by Conrad Graham and Art Reynolds stopped Bulldog drives. Rotella and sophomore Robert Pulliam also played outstanding games. Both of our touchdowns came in the second quarter after lengthy drives. Rudder caught a 7-yard pass for the first one, and tight end Sonny Leach caught the other. We rushed for 262 yards to Georgia's 185.

We then won three straight over Ole Miss, Kentucky and Vanderbilt — 17-0, 17-7 and 30-10, respectively.

The blanking of Ole Miss marked the first back-to-back shutouts for the Vols since 1963. Rotella was named UPI Lineman of the Week, while UPI singled out journeyman defensive tackle John Wagster for his outstanding play. Rudder ran 98 yards on 10 carries and Haskel contributed 96 more and two touchdowns.

Against Kentucky, Sonny Collins put the Wildcats on the board first with a 3-yard touchdown. That was soon matched by Rudder's 8-yard touchdown run. Townsend kicked a second-quarter field goal that held until the fourth. The Wildcats had played very conservatively up to this point, but behind 10-7, they started to put the ball in the air. Our defense rose to the occasion by intercepting two passes, of which one led to our first touchdown. Stanback took it 30 yards into the end zone to seal the 17-7 win.

Our 30-10 win over Vandy was a tougher fight than the score indicated, as we were only up 16-10 going into the fourth quarter. Our team then bowed its collective necks and shut out the Commodores while driving for two touchdowns of our own. Stanback ran for 143 yards and three touchdowns. In doing so, he ran for 890 yards in the regular season, breaking All-American tailback Hank Lauricella's record of 881 yards that had stood since the Vols captured a national title in 1951.

That ended our regular season at 9-2, with nightmare losses to Auburn and Alabama. We happily accepted the Astro-Bluebonnet Bowl invitation against LSU (9-1-1), led by Coach Charlie McClendon and quarterback Bert Jones, as we were eager to face another great team in Houston. Our team got off to a fast start, as our seniors did a good job on making a rodeo-damaged field a positive and not a negative. Condredge turned in an electrifying performance, completing 11 of 19 passes for 94 yards with a touchdown pass to Jimmy

Young. He also scrambled for 74 yards and two touchdowns, and was given the Offensive Player of the Game award. Our defense also played well against Jones and a very good offensive team. They surprised us with an unbalanced line and some other things we hadn't seen, but we adjusted. We were ahead 24-3 at the half, but LSU made a second-half comeback by scoring on a Jones 2-yard run in the third quarter, and another 1-yard run in the fourth. Conrad Graham, a veteran in a superb secondary, broke up a fourth-down pass at our 10-yard line to seal the 24-17 victory. Veteran defensive end Carl Johnson, who had given us outstanding play for three years, was named Defensive Player of the Game for his fierce pass rush.

When the NFL Draft came, Rotella was selected by the Colts, Graham by the Bears, Johnson by the Cowboys and Richard Earl by the Bills. Rotella served as our 1972 team captain, with Tim Townes and Bill Emendorfer as co-captains.

After his senior season in 1972, Townes began in earnest his desire to go to medical school and become an orthopedic surgeon. Tim played a lot in 1970, way more than enough to learn a letter, and earned a scholarship after that season. He was a starter in 1971 and 1972, and a major contributor to our success. Getting into the University of Tennessee Medical School in Memphis was not an easy task. When his Med Cat scores came back in spring 1973, they were not sufficient for Tim to be admitted. I learned about that and went over to console him. He was pretty cool about the whole thing and said, "I didn't do well enough in making grades my freshman year. That's OK, I'll go get my Master's degree and then they will have to take me."

The next spring, even with his Master's, he was not admitted to Med School. I went over to see our president and told him that if I ever need to get operated on, Tim Townes is the guy I want doing my surgery. "Isn't there any way we can help him get in?" Dr. Boling said Memphis didn't like us or anyone interfering with their admissions process, and there was nothing we could do.

I went back to console Tim and he said, "That's OK, I'll go get my Ph.D., and then they will have to take me."

Tim graduated from the University of Tennessee in 1973 with a B.S. degree in Biology. He completed a M.S. degree in Biology in 1976 and a Ph.D. in Microbiology in 1980 from Tennessee. After postdoctoral training in Biochemistry and Molecular Genetics at the University of Cincinnati School of Medicine, Tim accepted a faculty position in August 1984 at the UAB School of Medicine in the Department of Biochemistry and Molecular Genetics. He was promoted to full professor in 1992 and served as chairman of the Department of Biochemistry and Molecular Genetics from 2001-2016. He also founded the UAB Stem Cell Institute in 2010. The major research interest of Tim's laboratory was the development of genetic therapies for blood disorders such as sickle cell disease and severe combined immunodeficiency. He has published over 90 peer-reviewed papers and has several issued patents. His most recent work established a foundation for the safe and effective correction of inherited and acquired blood disorders with a modified version of the CRISPR/Cas system. Tim is a frequent speaker at international conferences on gene regulation and gene therapy. He has given invited lectures in Johannesburg, San Francisco, Washington, D.C., Boston and Seattle.

When I came back to Alabama in 2013 as athletics director, I was telling that story to John McMahon, a trustee at Alabama, but also himself involved with UAB. "It would have been a waste of talent for Tim to be operating on knees and shoulders," said John. "The work he's doing at UAB is Nobel Peace Prize possible."

After the season, I encouraged our staff to visit other programs that would give them access to stay up with current offensive and defensive trends. We also entertained college and high school coaches at our place. One day I received a voicemail from a man in broken English asking if he could send his football coach from Mexico Polytechnic Institute to spend a week during our spring practice. The caller's name was Angel Martinez and his coach's name was Jacinto Licea. Mexico Polytechnic Institute today has over 171,000 students at high school, undergraduate and postgraduate levels.

Of course I wanted to do my part for international college football discussions, so I gladly accepted his request and set up the date, time and agenda for what he wanted to accomplish. He was going to travel to the University of Oklahoma to learn the Wishbone Offense, and the University of Tennessee to learn the "Bubble Defense."

When the day arrived, I decided to go meet Jacinto at the Knoxville airport. Back then there was little security getting on and off planes. The plane landed and I walked out to the tarmac looking for a Mexican football coach. I didn't see one. I went back to the baggage claim area and as most passengers had picked up their bags and departed, I saw a man with a full beard and mustache speaking Spanish to a policeman. I knew that was my man.

I went over, introduced myself and we rode back to the dorm together. Dr. Jacinto Licea was an orthopedic surgeon and a teacher at the Institute. He coached one of 11 football teams there. He was from the College of Arts and Sciences. I thought it was a great combination that as a coach, he could work his teams hard, and if they did get hurt, he could operate on them and fix them.

He was obviously a brilliant man. He told me he learned to speak English as a boy listening to American football games with his Spanish-American dictionary guiding him. To me, it was very hard to understand and vice-versa, but we put him up in the players' dorm, and gave him access to all coaches' meetings and practices.

I thought the coaching staff meetings would be very helpful as we went over each day what we were trying to accomplish on the field that day. But the language barrier was probably too great for him to comprehend what we were talking about. Our coaches did spend some one-on-one time with him, and he spent a lot of time copying different information pieces to which he had access. That was prior to copiers being invented, so he did it the old-fashioned way, by hand.

We bonded over that week and we were sorry to see him leave. He told me he wanted badly to win his big game every year with Mexico City University. Mexico City University today has an enrollment of more than 300,000 students. I asked how many people attended that game. He told me the stadium seated about 100,000 people and they filled it up. I asked how much the tickets sold for and he told me 25 pesos, i.e., about $1.25 at today's exchange rate.

So, fast-forward to after the 1972 season. I attended the American Football Coaches Association annual conference in January 1973. I didn't know Jacinto was coming, but saw him across the room at one of the meetings. I went over and spoke to him, we hugged and talked a few minutes. I asked how his season went and his head drooped as he told me they went 3-6 and lost to Mexico City University by three touchdowns. But we had a great visit and he asked if I would bring my staff to Mexico City for his spring practice. I asked when it was scheduled and his answer was, "When can you come?" I told him we were very limited but might make a week in June work.

One summer our defensive staff went down to Mexico and worked with their players, and the following summer our offensive coaches went down. I'm sorry to say that I let something interfere both years with my going down, but if I had it to do over, I would definitely have made it work. Our coaches had a blast, and they too enjoyed being a part of teaching American football in a foreign country. We all pulled for the MPT Blanco A'guila's White Eagles!

The next January I saw Jacinto again at the AFCA meetings. He spied me, ran across the lobby, gave me a bear hug, and said his team went 7-2 and upset Mexico City University in the big game at the end of the season. It was a proud moment for both of us.

1973

The 1973 season started out with Duke in Knoxville. The Blue Devils jumped out to a 17-7 halftime lead after a Holloway to Emmon Love 27-yard pass got us on the board first. Duke surprised us with some offensive formations and plays in the first quarter, but our defense adjusted and shut them out in the second half. In the third quarter, Holloway broke free from a near-tackle and raced 49 yards for a touchdown to make the score 17-14. In the fourth, a drive ended with a Stanback run from the 1 for the decisive touchdown in a tough 21-17 win. Holloway was named AP's National Back of the Week while Stanback rushed for 104 yards on 25 carries.

Our second game was at West Point. It was sort of a homecoming for me as I had spent two years there on the staff and developed a love for the Academy, what it stood for, and the beauty of the countryside in which it was located. To give our team a special trip, we spent Thursday night in New York City, eating dinner at SpindleTop and getting a mini tour of the city. Among honking horns in heavy traffic and homeless people lying around the streets, our team — dressed in orange blazers, brown pants, white shirts and ties — walked in a group from the hotel to dinner. New York City may be the only place in America where a group of 60 to 70 larger-than-average-sized athletes, in orange blazers, could walk down the streets and no one would even turn their heads in wonder.

The next morning, we traveled by bus up the Palisades Interstate Parkway and stayed at the Bear Mountain Lodge, a short distance from the Academy. Palisades Parkway was financed years earlier by a family who stipulated with the gift that there would never be commercial advertising along the entire length of the parkway. It was a beautiful drive.

After we practiced in Michie Stadium, I had the privilege of speaking to all the West Point Cadets at lunch that day at noon. The food there was outstanding, and the organization and service was incredible. Time was such a valuable commodity there in all phases of Cadet life. Meals are served for some 1,800 Cadets at the same time, from start to finish in about 45 minutes.

The game started as a defensive struggle, but we had two Townsend field goals and a 1-yard Stanback touchdown run for a halftime lead. Freshman Stanley Morgan began to make his presence known as a receiver, grabbing long passes of 52 and 29 yards in the second half, the latter for a touchdown. Sophomore wide receiver John Yarbrough also got in the scoring column by catching a 37-yarder from Gary Valbuena in the fourth for a 37-18 final.

Auburn came to town the following week. Our team was 0-3 against the Tigers under my watch, even though two of the three were ultra-close losses. I think the Good Lord was looking after me that day, as we got out to a 13-0 lead in the second quarter, and maybe the hardest rain I ever saw came down the rest of the game.

As the deluge continued in the second half, both teams started kicking on third down, so that if the punter did bobble the soaking wet ball, he could have another down to get it off. It was raining so hard that it was nearly impossible to run a play effectively. With a 13-0 lead, I didn't want to risk a turnover in those conditions, and started punting on first downs until the rain slacked up. Auburn Coach Shug Jordan thought I was making fun of them, but that never crossed my mind. We had lost one game of the last three that we almost won, but a fumble changed the outcome, and I didn't want to risk another one slipping away. The rain finally subsided and we kept the Tigers out of our end zone, and added another score with a Holloway-to-Rudder pass and a two-point conversation to finally beat Auburn 21-0. Hank Walter, a junior linebacker from Knoxville, had a great game, making 12 tackles and eight assists. In addition, he recovered a fumble and intercepted a pass, running it back 38 yards for a touchdown. Hank, for his efforts, earned AP National Player of the Week honors.

The next week saw us return to our annual trek to Memphis to play Kansas. That year, the Jayhawks had a very good team with a terrific offense led by quarterback David Jaynes. Our pass defense was a few notches below our 1972 team, as we lost pretty much our entire secondary to graduation. We scored first on a 30-yard touchdown run by Rudder, but Jaynes came back with two touchdown passes and a 5-yard scoring run to take a 21-7 lead into halftime.

Jaynes was a talented and confident young man. As he was taking his team up and down the field, whenever he passed me on the sideline, he would smile and wink. I never had that happen before or after, but I thought, "We've got to put this guy in his place." At halftime we rallied our troops, and our coaches did a good job of figuring out what adjustments we needed to make.

In the third quarter, Rudder scored another touchdown on an 8-yard run. In the meantime, Eddie Brown, our outstanding free safety, turned the game around on his own. He blocked a Jayhawk field-goal attempt, losing three teeth in the process. He intercepted a pass and returned it 74 yards for a touchdown. He also recovered a fumble. Stanback scored two touchdowns in the fourth quarter to give us a 28-21 lead. When Kansas scored near the end of the game to make the score 28-27, their attempted two-point conversion to win was met by a large group of Vol defenders, and leading the charge was Eddie Brown. For his efforts, UPI named him Defensive Player of the Week in the Southeast, and *Sports Illustrated* named him National Back of the Week.

Georgia Tech came to Knoxville the following week. Condredge Holloway made two plays that could have been highlight reels by themselves. Tech scored first to take a 7-0 first quarter lead. On the first of his amazing plays, Condredge passed to Rudder for an 11-yard touchdown after eluding a cluster of five Yellow Jackets. The second came a few minutes later after Eddie Brown intercepted a Tech pass. Condredge, back to pass, was rushed but scrambled for a 20-yard touchdown as at least six Jackets touched him, and it looked like all 11. We were able to make that 14-7 halftime lead hold up, as Paul Careathers scored in the third quarter on a 40-yard run. The point-after kick was no good, the first miss after 105 successes. George Hunt had the first 60 PATs and Ricky Townsend the last 45. Tech scored late to make the final score 20-14, but the outcome was decided much earlier.

We traveled to Birmingham on the third Saturday in October to meet Alabama, a team that had established dominance in the SEC again under Coach Bryant. Both teams entered the game undefeated. We scored on a 20-yard pass from Holloway to Yarbrough in the first quarter, a Holloway 6-yard run in the second and a 64-yard pass to Mitch Gravitt in the third. The score was tied at 21-21 going into the fourth quarter, but Robin Cary returned a Vol punt 64 yards to open the floodgates for the Crimson Tide, as they scored two more touchdowns for a 42-21 win. Holloway was a hero in defeat, leading Coach Bryant to say, "He has more moves and is harder to get hold of than any back I ever saw."

Texas Christian University came to Knoxville the following week. Holloway threw touchdown passes to Tommy West (2 yards), Tim Fitchpatrick (18 yards) and Stanley Morgan (23 yards), and ran in a two-point conversion. Condredge brought his rushing and passing totals past the 1,000-yard marks, joining an elite group of Vol stars from over the years. Valbuena completed a 52-yard strike to Morgan, helping Morgan earn the UPI Offensive Player of the Week honors for the Southeast, as he caught eight passes for 201 yards in the 39-7 victory over the Horned Frogs.

In a wild game with Georgia the next week, it seemed like neither team could stop the other. The Bulldogs took a 21-14 lead into halftime, with our scores coming on a 7-yard Holloway run and a 6-yard Chancey reception from Holloway. We outscored Georgia 17-0 in the third quarter to take a 31-21 lead. Eddie Brown returned a punt 85 yards for a touchdown, Stanback took one in from the 1 and Townsend kicked a 48-yard field goal.

The Bulldogs drove for another touchdown to close the gap to 31-28. Less than 3:00 was on the clock when we took the kickoff, and we needed to run out the clock to preserve the win. On third and 2 from our own 28, we called a pass. Haskel Stanback, our best running back, flared out to our left. Condredge checked down from targets downfield to Haskel and got him the ball. It was one on one in the open field and the Georgia defensive back made a great open-field tackle for no gain. It was fourth and 2 with 2:27 on the clock. I didn't believe we could stop them, so I called for a fake punt. It didn't work.

Georgia drove down to the 2-yard line. Georgia quarterback Andy Johnson was handing off to his halfback when linebacker Andy Spiva collided with them at the junction. The ball bounced out, hit the ground and bounced right back up in the waiting arms of Johnson, who ran it in for the winning touchdown in the 35-31 victory.

When you make those calls, you're either a hero or a goat. I fully accepted the goat label and didn't sleep well for many nights after that fake punt call. After seeing the defensive alignment, there was a call that should have been made to get us out of the fake and back to kicking the ball. I coached the play and obviously didn't coach it well enough to get it executed.

We traveled to Jackson, Mississippi, the following week to play Ole Miss. Our team was still hungover from the Georgia loss, probably because I was so down. We didn't play well and got beat 28-18 by a team that probably wasn't as good as we were. We accepted a Gator Bowl bid after the loss, as we had a New Year's Day game pretty well locked up prior to the first back-to-back losses we had suffered during our tenure at Tennessee.

We did rebound to beat Kentucky and Vandy in tight wins. We played Kentucky in Lexington on a muddy, rain-drenched field and hung on to win 16-14. Stanback and Rudder scored touchdowns and Townsend kicked a field goal. Art Reynolds had 21 tackles and three assists. We played Vandy at home and led 14-0 on a Stanback 7-yard run and Eddie Brown 76-yard punt return in the first quarter. That lead held until the fourth when we let them back in the game. Holloway was hurt early, but came back in to lead us to two fourth-quarter field goals to preserve the 20-17 victory.

Our Gator Bowl appearance against Texas Tech was an exciting battle, and like most all of our games in 1973, went down to the wire. The Red Raiders jumped out to a 14-3 first-half lead, but we closed the gap to 21-19 in the fourth quarter. Townsend missed a 32-yard field-goal try, and soon after, Tech broke a long touchdown run to seal the 28-19 victory. Stanback, with 95 yards on 19 carries and two touchdowns, won the Outstanding Player Award for UT.

Our 8-4 record kept the streak of winning eight or more games since 1965 alive, still the longest in the nation. The captain of the 1973 Tennessee team was Eddie Brown, with co-captains Condredge Holloway and Art Reynolds. Bill Rudder was drafted by the Chargers, Haskel Stanback by the Bengals, Gary Valbuena by the Dolphins, Gene Killian by the Cowboys and Eddie Brown by the Cleveland Browns.

1974

We opened our 1974 campaign at home in an ABC televised game against the UCLA Bruins. In a series that started in 1965 in Memphis, the Tennessee-UCLA series had risen to rivalry status.

In analyzing our previous year, we decided Stanley Morgan was so talented, we needed him to touch the ball a lot more than we could get it to him as a wide receiver. So we moved him to running back, which would not be his position in the NFL. But like Richmond Flowers' move from wide receiver to running back in 1968, it was best for the team. Stanley had a long and illustrious career with the New England Patriots as a receiver after UT, and while he would have much preferred staying at wide receiver at Tennessee, I think if asked, he would tell you that playing running back toughened him up and helped his pro career.

We had also noticed in UCLA film study that on normal downs with the ball on the hashmark, and with formations to the field and a tight end lined up into the boundary, the safety would cheat to the middle of the field. The cornerback in the boundary would line up about 2 yards deep and 2 yards outside the tight end. So for this game, we had a two-play call in the huddle from the left hash. On the first play we handed the ball to the fullback up the middle to stay on the hash. Stanley lined up to the wide side on the play, flared to the tight end side and lined up at tight end for the second play.

As the first play ended and players were lining up, on command our guys got back in position and snapped the ball. Sure enough, the free safety lined up around the middle of the field and the cornerback lined up 2 and 2 off of Stanley. It was no contest. Condredge faked to the fullback to the strong side and dropped back to pass. The safety took the fake and stayed in the middle and Stanley had the corner beat by about 10 yards. Condredge made the easy throw for a 74-yard touchdown and we took a 7-0 lead. A short time later, Townsend kicked a 47-yard field goal.

Our defense played very well and sophomore Andy Spiva added toughness to our effort by keeping UCLA quarterback John Sciarra in check for most of the game in Coach Dick Vermeil's very offensive attack. In the second quarter, Condredge came off the field with a shoulder injury. Mickey O'Brien, our trainer, said he had a separated shoulder and was out for the game. Back then, that usually meant out for the season. As Mickey used to say, "When you go into combat, you suffer casualties; just close ranks and keep marching." That's what we did. Unfortunately, we weren't getting much done on offense and fell behind 17-10 midway through the fourth quarter.

After a play to my right that wasn't a particularly exciting play, our fans went wild, clapping and shouting as if something big had happened. I thought, "Alabama must have gotten beaten and they heard it on the radio." About that time, Condredge ran up to me and said, "I'm OK, I can play." I didn't know he had gone to the hospital for x-rays. I thought he had just gotten tired of seeing us fall behind. The crowd noise was from Condredge running into the stadium on my left. I didn't believe him, so I told him to get Mickey to tell me it's OK. I looked down where Mickey was standing and he gave me a thumbs up. I grabbed Condredge and said, "Well, get your butt out there."

When Condredge left, we were ahead 10-0. When he got back, we were behind 17-10. It didn't take him long to get us back in scoring position again. From the 12-yard line he rolled to his right on a run-pass option, pulled it down and headed for the end zone. Around the 5-yard line he was confronted by a UCLA linebacker who was coming at him full speed. He dove and the linebacker's shoulder clipped Condredge's knee in mid-air as he turned a flip, landing on his back in the end zone for a touchdown.

I wanted to go for two, but I saw the pain in Condredge's face and him holding his knee, so I decided to kick the extra point for the 17-17 tie. I thought we could get the ball back, but UCLA used up the remaining time. It was a heck of a game. Our defense looked a lot better and made two goal-line stands that kept the score tight until Condredge's return. Our biggest problem was that Condredge's shoulder was badly bruised, and on that last touchdown hit, he tore some cartilage in his knee.

Kansas came to Knoxville the following week. Thankfully, David Jaynes had been drafted by the NFL. Condredge didn't play against the Jayhawks, as we were trying to get him healthy for the next week's journey down to Auburn. We were eager to see how redshirt sophomore Randy Wallace, a highly recruited quarterback out of Jacksonville, would do. Randy was another multi-sport player who was also recruited by professional baseball teams. We thought Randy would be an exceptional quarterback for Tennessee. In the night game, Mike Gayles, a sophomore, rushed for 80 yards on 14 carries, while our defense gave up only a field goal. Wallace completed a 26-yard touchdown pass to Tim Fitchpatrick, Morgan scored from the 1 and Townsend kicked a 29 yard field goal for a 17-3 victory.

We traveled to Auburn the next week, the first time in the modern era that Tennessee didn't play the Tigers in Birmingham's Legion Field. It was not a pretty day for the Vols for several reasons.

Condredge was still not ready to play with his right shoulder and knee problems. The shoulder kept him from throwing effectively and the knee took at least a couple of steps off his quickness. But, if you are alive and breathing, a Tennessee player would play against Auburn, and vice-versa. Well, I thought that having Condredge in the game, even if he could just hand off, would inspire our team and might even affect the Tigers. Obviously, that didn't work, and Auburn shut us out 21-0 to match the same score we defeated them in the previous year's game. Even then, we had held them to 6-0 going into the final quarter.

The next week, Tulsa came to Knoxville. We opened with a 54-yard scoring drive and finished it with a 1-yard Careathers plunge. A Townsend field goal gave us a 10-0 halftime lead, but Tulsa countered in the third quarter with 10 points of its own. Then Stanley Morgan returned a punt 48 yards for the deciding touchdown. Senior punter Neal Clabo kept Tulsa backed up all day, and one of his two punts that were downed inside the 5-yard line preceded Stanley's punt return. Tennessee won 17-10.

We traveled to Baton Rouge the next week, my first trip to Death Valley, and it was all it was cracked up to be. The Bayou Bengal crowd was loud, the environment was hostile, and it was all it should be in an SEC stadium. The mascot in Baton Rouge was Mike The Tiger. His cage was positioned right outside the visitor's dressing room. When the visiting team was getting dressed, Mike's keepers would rake the bars on his cage with broomsticks or something that would cause Mike to roar. It was definitely an unsettling atmosphere.

Townsend kicked a 32-yard field goal to give us a 3-0 second-quarter lead. LSU countered with a touchdown, but we quickly followed with a 33-yard touchdown pass from Holloway to Larry Seivers, taking a 10-7 lead into the half. A fumble by us while nursing a 3-point lead turned the momentum, and LSU closed the game out in the fourth quarter with a 20-10 victory, avenging our 1972 Astro-Bluebonnet Bowl victory over them. Defensive end Ronnie McCartney and linebackers Steve Poole and Andy Spiva were defensive standouts.

Alabama came to Knoxville in its traditional October slot, but both teams had questions at quarterback. Richard Todd did not play for the Tide, and Holloway was still at less than 100 percent for us. We hung in there in the first half with an impressive goal-line stand. We pulled within a point when Morgan broke into the Tide secondary, was hit hard and stopped in his tracks by a defensive back, but then regained his footing and scampered 64 yards for a touchdown. Charlie Boswell, the beloved and famous former Alabama football player and blind golfer who was in the press box, told me years later, "That run by Stanley Morgan in the 1974 game is the best run I ever saw!" Alabama's wealth of backfield talent enabled them to overpower our defense in the second half for a 28-6 victory.

Vol fans saw one of the wildest games in history when Clemson came to Knoxville the following week. Holloway was returning to his early season form and started the game with a 65-yard touchdown pass to Morgan.

We had planned what we thought was a legal "hide out" play. My understanding of the rule was that if the player was within 17 yards of the ball, he didn't have to join the huddle. Our plan was to call the play when the ball was around midfield and on the hashmark to our side. In those days, the hashmarks divided the 53-yard field width in thirds. The distance from the hashmark to the sideline was 17.67 yards. There were two plays called in the huddle. With the ball on our left hashmark, we called a handoff to our fullback over left guard, which we thought would result in a 2- or 3-yard gain but would keep the ball on the left hashmark. Without lining up Morgan, who had lined up at tailback on the previous play, he flared to his left and ran to our sideline to line up at split end, a yard inside of the sideline, for the second play.

The second play was a half sprint right and throw back to Morgan, who we hoped would be wide open down the left side. As fate would have it, the fullback took the handoff to the left, broke a tackle and cut back to his right for an 8-yard gain and almost in the middle of the field. The team went ahead with the second play, lined up and snapped the ball quickly. Stanley was about a yard from our sideline, lost in all the orange jerseys there. The head linesman on that side lined up just outside our tackle and the defensive halfback was about the same place. The ball was snapped, Condredge half sprinted to his right and threw the ball to Morgan, who was so wide open it was unbelievable.

The officials gathered, scratched their heads, and eventually let the play stand, which put us ahead 7-0. My coach in the press box said, "Hey Coach, you're going to have trouble explaining that one." My response was, "Of all the bad calls that have gone against us over the years, I can live with a bad call in our favor." Actually, I didn't get much heat for that one the way the game turned out. Soon after that, Clemson responded with a touchdown to tie the game at 7-7.

Mike Gayles ran for a 35-yard touchdown in the second quarter, but the Tigers scored a TD for a 14-13 halftime lead. A scoreless third quarter set up the fourth-quarter fireworks. Clemson scored to take a 21-13 lead quickly, followed by a Morgan 33-yard touchdown. Holloway rolled out to his right and elected to run it in for the two-point conversion to tie it at 21-21. After the Tigers scored again to take a 28-21 lead, Morgan ran one in from the 8, making it 28-27.

I elected to go for the win and called the same two-point play that worked so well after the last touchdown. It had run-pass options that I thought we could execute. Charley Pell, one of my teammates at Alabama and Clemson's defensive coordinator, evidently figured I would do that and slanted everyone to our right. As Holloway started right, he was confronted by two defenders, so he turned and scampered back to his left. Larry Seivers, who was running a crossing route from left to right, saw Holloway turn back left and he too reversed field. As Holloway was being dragged down he saw Seivers running in the back of the end zone, raised up and threw the ball. Seivers, with his

6-foot-4 frame and rare leaping ability, used it all to haul in the pass for a 29-28 victory. Coaches frequently talk about players "rising above coaching." Holloway's plays on many previous occasions, but definitely on that second two-point conversion, rose above coaching.

We finished with 364 yards rushing and 187 passing. Morgan had 117 yards rushing in 19 carries. Holloway had 250 yards combined rushing and passing. Running backs Careathers, Gayles and Terry Moore enjoyed noteworthy performances. Holloway was named AP and UPI Southeastern Player of the Week.

We rolled over Memphis State 34-6 in Knoxville the next week. When Holloway ran a keeper for 9 yards with 2:22 left in the first half, he became Tennessee's all-time career yardage leader, breaking Bobby Scott's record of 3,580 yards from 1968-1970. Morgan scored two touchdowns while Gayles had one on the ground. John Yarbrough and Tommy West each caught touchdown passes from Holloway, and Townsend kicked two field goals. Randy Wallace, the talented quarterback being groomed as Holloway's replacement, directed an 85-yard drive that consumed a large chunk of the third and fourth quarters. The best part of the game to me was the play of our defense, almost getting the shut out, but intercepting four passes. That number equaled the number of interceptions we had made in the previous seven games.

We traveled to Memphis for our ninth game to play Ole Miss. Tennessee and Ole Miss were usually fighting for a spot at or near the top of the SEC, but this time we were both fighting for our first conference win. A defensive struggle in the first half ended with us taking a 7-3 lead on Morgan's 38-yard first-quarter touchdown. Early in the third quarter, Hank Walters intercepted a pass and returned it to the Rebels' 2-yard line, then Gayles took it in from there for a 13-3 lead. Holloway scored on a 6-yard run in the third. Seivers caught a 52-yard Holloway pass and Townsend kicked a field goal in the fourth quarter for a 29-17 victory. That raised our record to 5-3-1 with Kentucky and Vandy left in the regular season.

In our annual game with Kentucky to retain possession of the "Beer Barrel" that we had kept for longer than my time at Tennessee, we decided to go back to power football. We had run an unbalanced line a good deal during the season as we faced many five-man fronts. With Paul Johnson (Bob's brother), a small center, and Mickey Marvin, our best offensive lineman at strong guard, the unbalanced line forced the defense to move over a man, putting their nose guard over Mickey and leaving Paul uncovered. Sunday night we were drawing plays on the blackboard. Since it was homecoming, we thought about starting the game with a single-wing formation and running the old No. 10 play off tackle to honor the former players who ran the single-wing for years. As we were drawing up the play, we put it up with an unbalanced line. Then we put up our short-yardage formation, which featured all three backs in the backfield — the fullback and tailback in the "I" formation and the wingback behind the strong guard. Then somebody drew that up with unbalanced line, and moved the three backs over a man to the strong side. That looked pretty darned good on the blackboard, as we drew it up against Kentucky's defense. We ran it some the next day in practice and it looked really good on the field.

We came back Monday night and put in three plays. If the defense didn't move over a man, we ran the pitch sweep. If they did move over a man, we ran the power off tackle. And to break the pattern of running to our strong side, we faked to the fullback strong side and ran a swing pass with a pulling guard leading the quarterback on a run-pass option to the weak side. Our split end (lined up at weak tackle) ran a deep corner route and our tailback flared. It looked better and better on Tuesday and Wednesday, our two heavy-pads practice days. If we beat Kentucky and Vanderbilt, we had a good shot at returning to the Liberty Bowl, so we called that formation "Liberty."

On the first play, we ran the standard single-wing No. 10 play off tackle, with the quarterback taking a direct snap and running off tackle, with the blocking back and the fullback leading. We told our quarterback to call "check with me at the line." We were going to run either the off-tackle play if the defense moved over or the sweep if they didn't. On second down, they didn't, and we ran the sweep for a first down. We ran those plays pretty much the rest of the half, as we were controlling the ball and clock. Townsend kicked 25-yard field goals in the first and second quarters, and Morgan capped an 80-yard, 16-play touchdown drive with a 2-yard run before the half. In the third quarter, Townsend kicked his third field goal and Tommy West caught a 7-yard touchdown pass from Holloway. The Wildcats scored in the fourth, but the "Liberty" formation baffled them in the 24-7 win. Fran Curci, Kentucky's head coach and a friend of mine, told me after the game that they didn't even recognize we were in an unbalanced line until halftime. It was a good plan, because Morgan rushed for 94 yards and Gayles for 93.

In our final regular-season game in Nashville against Vanderbilt, we got off to a good start with two touchdowns in the first quarter by Morgan and Gayles after good drives. It was a rainy, ugly day, and from that point forward, Vandy's defense held our offense in check. After Commodore touchdowns in the first three quarters, we found ourselves behind 21-13 with almost no time remaining. We had punted them deep in their own territory and on fourth down we called for a punt rush. The Vandy punter bobbled the ball and our rush got him, giving us possession at the 12-yard line. Four straight Morgan rushes got us in for the touchdown. Our two-point conversion was good as Holloway hit

Seivers in the back of the end zone and we escaped with our second tie of the season.

While we weren't overly proud of a 6-3-2 regular season, I was proud we didn't fold after losing to Auburn, LSU and Alabama, and won five straight to get us a bid to the Liberty Bowl to face a good Maryland team coached by Jerry Claiborne.

On a personal note, my mother was diagnosed with cancer back in August. The doctor said, "good news and bad news." The bad news was it was terminal and there was nothing we could do to stop it. The good news was it was relatively painless and it wouldn't take too long. Eugenia was pregnant with our daughter Shannon and was due in early November. Shannon was born Nov. 12. My mom was hanging on so she could see and hold the baby. As soon as Eugenia and Shannon could travel, we flew to Birmingham to let Mom spend some time holding Shannon. My dad called on Monday, Nov. 25 to say Mom had passed away and we would have the funeral on Sunday. As the preacher said at her funeral describing her will to see the baby, "It was like one was on the way to heaven, while the other was coming into the world, and they passed along the way."

After the Vanderbilt game on Saturday, we flew to Birmingham to spend time with my dad and prepare for the funeral. That night, Coach and Mrs. Bryant stopped by the house to visit and pay their respects. I'm not sure how they found out, but I thought it was an amazing thing for them to do. It was very difficult burying my mother. She was the nicest, sweetest lady ever. She was only 64, and I was sad and mad that there was nothing we could do after her diagnosis.

I went back to work preparing for the Liberty Bowl with a heavy heart, but duty called. Maryland had won the Atlantic Coast Conference and had a great defense anchored by tackle Randy White. He was probably the best defensive lineman I had ever seen. He would make the play if you ran at him, he was a ferocious pass rusher, and if you ran away from him, he would run you down on the other side of the field. In Coach Claiborne's even defense, the tackles lined up inside the shoulder of our tight end. About the only thing we figured out to run against him was the option, and our quarterback optioned to keep or pitch depending on what he did. He was really hard to block. The game evolved as a classic defensive struggle, as our defense played very well and so did theirs. Maryland took a 3-0 lead going into the half and that score continued into the fourth quarter.

In the second half, we were attempting a field goal with Holloway holding. Randy White rushed in and drilled Holloway, which caused a miss. Worse, Condredge was out for the game, so Wallace came in at quarterback. Late in the fourth quarter, with the Terrapins backed up deep in their own territory, we called for a punt rush, and a bad snap followed, and gave us good field position. On third down from the 12-yard line, I called for a pass to Seivers running a cross route from left to right deep in the end zone. We had Morgan at tailback flaring wide to the left to hold the linebackers and safety. I told Wallace to half sprint to his right, look back at Morgan flaring and lay the ball up high for Seivers to go get. I told the line to do whatever it took to keep White out of the play. They executed it to perfection and Seivers leaped to take a 7-3 lead with only two minutes left. Maryland unleashed a passing attack that was moving the ball down the field, but time ran out. Gayles rushed for 106 yards on 17 carries and was named Tennessee's outstanding offensive player. Ron McCartney, junior end, was named outstanding defensive player.

Afterward, I shook Coach Claiborne's hand. He was definitely another mentor that I had the pleasure to coach against. He helped recruit me to Alabama, and was a great defensive coach for two years while I was there. He left before my junior year to take the head coaching job at Virginia Tech, and then a few years later, he moved on to Maryland.

After I accepted the winning Liberty Bowl trophy in a short TV presentation, a man rushed out to me and said, "Your dad has had a heart attack up in the stands." I threw down the trophy and game ball, and took off with him up the stands. When we got to Dad, there were four or five paramedics that had him stretched out on a bench. They had an IV in him to give him fluids, they were giving him air and pumping on his chest. Soon they transferred him to a gurney and took him to an ambulance and on to the hospital. They said he was still alive when they got to the hospital, but he never regained consciousness, and sometime later, they pronounced him dead.

We had talked Dad into coming to spend the week with us in Memphis. Pat was 11 and Mike was 7. Dad had a ball all week taking the boys around Memphis and to practice. It was a nice time of relief for him since my mom's passing a few weeks earlier. In the fourth quarter of the Liberty Bowl, Dad was sitting with Pat, Mike and Eugenia, and some of the official party were in the same area. After we scored to go ahead 7-3 and Maryland was driving, Pat told me that Dad was saying, "Run clock run" over and over. About that time, he slumped over in his seat. Fortunately, Breezy Yeomans, wife of team doctor Bill Yeomans, was sitting in the row behind Dad. She worked in the coronary care section of the hospital and knew exactly what to do. She cleared the bench, laid Dad down, called for someone to get the medical staff on call at the stadium up there, and began artificial respiration.

I was not able to talk to the team after the game, and I'm sorry because I was so proud of the difficulty that they overcame during the season and during the bowl, as we finished 7-3-2. While our streak of eight wins over the last 10 seasons was not continued, technically two ties equals one win, one loss — and so counted, our record would be 8-4.

When we got back to Birmingham for my dad's funeral, I was a wreck. Losing both parents in three weeks was a shock, as I had never really been around death very much up to this point. We were at my parents' house the night before the funeral and again Coach and Mrs. Bryant knocked on the door. I opened it and was so surprised to see them. Mrs. Bryant came in, hugged me and said how sorry she was at our loss. Feeling really sorry for myself, and halfway crying, I said, "But Dad was going with us to the Hula Bowl in Hawaii and would have had so much fun with us." Mrs. Bryant, with all her wisdom, said, "Now Billy, you know your dad would much rather be with your mom in heaven than with you in Hawaii." That brought a smile to my face and put everything in perspective.

We got through the funeral, and my sister and I stayed in Birmingham a few days going through our parents' house. It was a mixed experience, laughing at some things we found, and crying at others. Overall, it was tough.

Then it was back to recruiting, analyzing our 1974 team and preparing for the '75 team. I thought we had some really good young players that grew up in the '74 season, and was excited about the future.

Condredge Holloway and Robert Pulliam, an excellent defensive tackle, had been invited to play in the Hula Bowl in early January and I was invited to be the head coach of the South team. Dad was supposed to come with us.

The Hula Bowl experience was a lot of fun. As an all-star game, they allowed two hours of practice/meetings a day, and the rest of the time the team could enjoy Hawaii. My assistant coaches were Pete Elliott, head coach at the University of Miami, and Dee Andros, head coach at Oregon State University. With Condredge as our quarterback, it was pretty easy to put in an offense and construct a simple way to signal in plays. Both teams were supposed to play the same set defense. With all the extra time, we had fun on Waikiki Beach. The coolest thing we did was get Pat and Mike on surfboards. Before the week was up, both were able to go from a kneeling to a standing position and ride waves in toward the beach. It was a blast.

The game was also a blast. Our team had seven first-round draft choices. Bill Yeoman from the University of Houston was the head coach of the North squad and Barry Switzer was an assistant coach. Barry didn't get in until the day before the game because his Oklahoma team was playing in a New Year's Day bowl game. The Sooners went undefeated, 12-0, and when Alabama lost to Notre Dame in the Orange Bowl, they were named National Champions.

In the first half, Condredge was brilliant, and the running backs and wide receivers we had were terrific. We got out by a three touchdown lead early. In all-star games, if one team gets ahead by two touchdowns, the team that is behind gets to receive the kickoff, whoever scores. The North received the second-half kickoff and drove down to score. We had to kick it back to them. The second half went that way, and our defensive team, which didn't have many backups, was about worn out by the fourth quarter. But we kept scoring when we did get the ball and won the game. It was a bittersweet win, with the sweet part being around Pete and Dee all week on the staff, and a really talented but also good bunch of players to celebrate the victory. The bitter part was the memories of the last month's personal losses.

In the NFL Draft, Paul Careathers by selected by the Raiders, Ricky Townsend by the Giants and Neal Clabo by the Vikings. Team captain Condredge Holloway was selected by the Patriots, but he took his talents to Ottawa in the CFL. The co-captain was Jim Watts.

1975

There are three primary factors in building successful football programs: players, coaches and schedules. Coach Bryant believed the schedule — spacing tougher opponents out over the season — was critical to successful years. It is difficult to build the optimum schedule, because some are made 10 years in advance. In sports, strong teams can become weak over time, and vice versa. The respective conferences also play a role in lining up league games and determining dates in which scheduling non-conference games are to be played.

Our 1975 schedule shaped up to be the most difficult in my several years as head coach at Tennessee. It was front-loaded with really good teams, but was a challenge we were eager to accept. Our first two games were against Maryland, which went on to win the ACC title, and UCLA in Los Angeles, and the Bruins went on to win the Pac 8 Conference that season. The third game was against always difficult Auburn, followed by a tough LSU team, and then came Alabama, which went on to win the SEC.

Not that the last half of the season wasn't difficult, but we built our motivational message in spring practice, summer and fall camp around "MUALA 5-0." Having this schedule, we didn't need to worry too much about our players coming back out of shape, and they actually came back in excellent shape. We were all very excited about the challenge. We were playing without Condredge Holloway at quarterback for the first time in three years, but we were confident in Randy Wallace, Gary Roach and Joe Hough.

In our opening game with Maryland, we played about as well as we could play, especially on defense. It was a very physical game and our defensive team caused four fumbles and intercepted a pass. Mike Gayles scored our first touchdown on a 13-yard run. Stanley Morgan followed up with touchdowns on a 50-yard run, a 70-yard punt return and a 1-yard run, and was named AP and UPI Southeast Player of the Week. Our defensive effort won the ball game, although I was proud of the physicality displayed by both offensive and defensive units that resulted in a 26-8 victory over the Terrapins. Coach Jerry Claiborne said after the game, "We just took an old-fashioned country licking."

In Tennessee, country music is a big deal. Nashville is obviously the hub, but there was always a big concert and golf tournament every summer in Knoxville led by Chet Atkins, Boots Randolph and Floyd Cramer, i.e., Mr. Guitar, Mr. Saxophone and Mr. Piano, respectively. Atkins, at that time, had just about put everyone in country music, and they all owed him favors. So they all (or many) came back for that weekend. We got to know many of them and got invited to play in their summer golf tournaments, where we got to know them even better. My assistant, Wayne Stiles, had a meeting with Tom T. Hall, the famous bluegrass artist of "Old dogs and children and watermelon wine" and many other hits. Wayne talked Tom and his band into playing for our team after Monday's practice following the Maryland game, if we won. They were going to be in the area anyway, so they came over and set up while practice was going on. Tom came out on the practice field toward the end of practice and I showed him what we were trying to do, and we chatted about the game. He had a plastic cup full of something that looked like iced tea, but I don't think that's what it was.

Practice ended and the whistle blew, indicating for everyone to come up to me for a final message before going to shower. Our custom was whenever the whole group came together for someone to shout "Everybody ... Break Down!" With that, the whole team would jump into a football position and shout "HAAAH!" When that happened, it scared the bejeebers out of Tom, and his plastic cup spilled all over the place. I introduced him to the team and told them his band was set up to entertain them at dinner, and sent them on to the showers. I apologized for them scaring him, and we walked and talked going in. After a while, he said, "Can I ask you a question?" I said, "Sure." He said, "You've got that team of big, strong, athletic and highly motivated men you are involved with every day. Did you ever worry about them turning on you?" With that, I busted out laughing and told him I had never thought about that before, but I would add that to my list of things to worry about.

Tom and his band did a great job, as the team thoroughly enjoyed their performance. I appreciated so much Wayne Stiles inviting them, and even more their coming to be a part of a Big Orange celebration after a big win.

During my 11 years at Tennessee, I met several country and western stars, and everyone I met was nice, down to earth, and a pleasure to be around.

For our second game, we traveled to Los Angeles to play UCLA, coached by Dick Vermeil, who went on to coach the Philadelphia Eagles to a Super Bowl appearance, the St. Louis Rams, and the Kansas City Chiefs to a Super Bowl victory. Our defensive staff had come up with some schemes and reads that were very effective, and through the previous season, no one had really cracked those codes. Prior to the 1975 season, one of our graduate assistants who had worked with our defensive coaches was hired by UCLA for a similar position. In 1974, our defense played very well against UCLA, with the game ending in a 17-17 tie. When we played in 1975, their offensive scheme was designed to neutralize our reads, and in effect, much of the advantage we had built.

The game evolved into a shootout, with us losing 34-28, but losing the effectiveness of our reads not only affected the outcome of this game, but exposed us to all future opponents. It was difficult to change in the middle of the season with the intense competition that we faced. This game went down to the final play before it was settled. I thought we needed two quarterbacks to get through the season and was committed to getting both early experience. Wallace was our first-teamer but Roach was not far behind. Both led touchdown drives against the Bruins, but John Sciarra, their Heisman candidate at quarterback, won MVP honors, even though our defense held him to 70 yards rushing and 140 yards passing, well below his average.

Stanley Morgan scored on a 1-yard run, Wallace on a 23-yard run, and Roach threw touchdown passes to Tommy West for 36 yards, Larry Seivers for 2 yards, and a two-point conversion pass to Mike Gayles. It was a long ride home, but I was proud of the way our team had fought, and was encouraged by our offensive performance in a big road game. But we had to quickly go back to the drawing board to try to regroup from our defensive issues.

Fortunately, we played Auburn at home next. It was a classic Tennessee-Auburn game, going down to the final quarter. It was knotted at 14 each after the second quarter and 17-14 Auburn going into the fourth. Wallace played the entire game and did an excellent job, especially in directing the 80-yard go-ahead touchdown drive. Three big third-and-long situations arose, and three times he connected with Seivers to move the sticks. On one of the three, Seivers had to make an acrobatic catch. Wallace also hit Seivers with the 38-yard touchdown pass that capped the drive and put us up 21-17 to stay. The defense held the Tigers the rest of the way to preserve the victory. We continued to have problems with our run defense, but held them to 8 yards passing.

We had an open date before playing LSU, we were in pretty good shape healthwise and I felt good about where we were at "MUALA 2-1". But the LSU game was a slugfest. It was physical, and every inch had to be earned. We scored first on a Jimmy Gaylor field goal in the first quarter, but Morgan left with a bad ankle sprain that affected him for the next few games. West caught a Roach pass for a 2-yard touchdown and a 10-7 halftime lead, which carried into the fourth quarter until the Tigers kicked a field goal to tie it at 10-10. An 81-yard drive fueled by two Wallace-to-Seivers passes got us to the LSU 11 late in the fourth. A "Utah pass" to Gayles fooled the LSU rushers, and he was able to sneak through the defenders for the 11-yard score. Ernie Ward intercepted a desperation pass to set up another Gayles 1-yard run to finish the 24-10 victory. It was MUALA 3-1, but costly because in addition to Stanley being hurt, West, Seivers and Andy Spiva were all injured.

Nevertheless, the third week of October was upon us and everybody warm and breathing on either side suits up for Tennessee vs. Alabama. Unfortunately, even though all those injured guys played, we weren't playing with the same team we played with earlier. The minds and the effort were there, but the bodies couldn't deliver. We lost 30-7 in the only Alabama game in my time at Tennessee in which we weren't competitive.

Being at MUALA 3-2 wasn't the end of the world, but we had played two physical games in a row, and were pretty beaten up. Because of the Alabama defeat, we were also down mentally. I saw that the air was out of the balloon, and our staff tried to pump it back up, but we couldn't get it done.

We outgained North Texas State 469 yards to 220 the next week in Knoxville. We gave them turnovers to aid their two second-quarter scores, and we were in scoring position enough to have won big, but couldn't capitalize. Give credit to their defense. We tied the score at 14 in the fourth quarter. On the ensuing kickoff, our team covered hard, but ran by the ball carrier, who emerged from a bunch and broke into the clear. There was only one freshman safety to make the tackle and it wasn't a fair fight. He ran 98 yards for the 21-14 victory — a bad loss for our team and our program. Running past the ball carrier was a mistake, but the biggest mistake was me not having two safeties. We changed after that game.

We played Colorado State the next week and coasted to a 28-7 victory. Morgan and Seivers were out with injuries, but Gayles and John Yarbrough filled in nicely. Gayles carried 22 times for 105 yards and Yarbrough caught two Wallace touchdown passes of 29 and 33 yards. Eddy Powers also filled in superbly for injured free safety Mike Mauck by intercepting two passes. Wallace, improving every week at quarterback, gained 128 yards rushing, including a beautiful 43-yard touchdown run. He was named UPI Southeast Player of the Week.

Homecoming week in Knoxville brought in the Utah Utes. The 40-7 victory allowed us to again rest some injured players and give younger players a good opportunity to gain experience. Running backs Frank Foxx, Kelsey Finch and Bobby Emmons all showed abilities that caught the eyes of Vol fans as exciting players for the future. Gayles, who sat out most of the second half, scored two touchdowns and gained 87 yards. Foxx scored three touchdowns and gained 68 yards. Roach scored on a 7-yard run.

But then it was back to SEC action against Ole Miss in Memphis. We finished two promising first-quarter drives with Gaylor field goals. Ole Miss followed with a touchdown to go ahead 7-6, and it was downhill from there, as we floundered on both sides of the ball, ending with an embarrassing 23-6 loss.

A trip to Lexington to face Kentucky came next. We took a 17-7 halftime lead on an 80-yard Morgan run, a 1-yard Gayles run and a 32-yard Gaylor field goal. The Wildcats made a comeback with a long touchdown pass from Derek Ramsey, but we prevailed 17-10.

Vanderbilt came to Knoxville the following week. After two very close games in the previous two years, Vandy made this one stick with a 17-14 victory. After it was 7-7 at the half, we went 68 yards for a touchdown on a drive that ate up most of the third quarter and a 14-7 lead. The Commodores mounted a long fourth-quarter drive to tie it at 14-14, then intercepted a pass returned it to our 6. Our defense held and forced a field goal, but our offense couldn't respond and the game ended 17-14.

Coach Woodruff scheduled home-and-home games with the University of Hawaii, and our trip to Honolulu couldn't have come at a better time. It was welcome relief after a very trying season. The players very much enjoyed the beauty of Hawaii and the weather. Our fans traveled with us in large numbers and they too enjoyed the trip. Hawaii had a very good team and expected to win, but our offense scored in every quarter, and the defense held the Rainbow Warriors to two second-quarter field goals. Morgan's return to full strength from his ankle injury in the LSU game was a welcome relief to the team and Vol fans, as he broke Curt Watson's single-game rushing record with 201 yards in 10 carries. Morgan opened up our scoring with a 67-yard punt return, then added an 8-yard touchdown run in the second quarter, and a 68-yarder in the third. Yarbrough caught a 1-yard TD pass from tailback Frank Foxx to complete our 24-6 victory. Our defense successfully engineered three goal-line stands. Two resulted in field goals and the third stopped a fourth-down attempt at the 2-yard line.

Thus ended the 1975 season with a 7-5 overall record while going 3-3 in the SEC for a fifth-place finish. What started out as a season so full of optimism, ended up poorly. Looking back, we probably spent too much time stressing the first five games. We played well in the first three and went into the LSU game pretty much injury free. We had an open date to rest up and prepare for LSU and Alabama. The injuries we sustained against the Tigers were a big factor in our loss to Alabama, but I think the loss to the Tide broke the spirit of our team. Preparing differently might have made a difference, but we couldn't do anything about the past but learn from it.

The Hawaii trip, at least temporarily, put smiles on our faces and gave us renewed energy to work hard to prepare for the 1976 season.

The captain of the 1975 team was Ron McCartney, with co-captains Tommy West and Tim Fitchpatrick. Ron McCartney was drafted by the Rams and Tommy West by the Buccaneers.

1976

Going into the 1976 season, we had added 9,600 seats to Neyland Stadium, taking capacity to 85,000. We had a good enough first team to be competitive, but as the previous season so clearly indicated, we didn't have the depth to overcome injuries to really good players. The other thing that depth provides is competition for position. However, serious players are about being their best, so if they are not pushed by a player trying to beat them out, they typically do not achieve their maximum proficiency. That's not a knock on the players, it's human nature. It is rare to find players with that degree of mental toughness, to do their very best all the time. We had some over the years, but Jack Reynolds and his brother Art were two of the best I ever saw. Whether it was in a big game or a routine practice, they only knew one speed, and that was full speed. It made those around them better.

We knew we would have to fight for our lives every game in '76 and hope to be lucky with injuries. The one player I thought we really needed to stay healthy and couldn't afford to lose was safety Mike Mauck. As it turned out, Mike got a neck injury in the first quarter of the first game and was out for the season. We had an outstanding freshman, Roland James, to take Mike's place, but Roland was a freshman in a very key position that needed experience. He got plenty of "baptism by fire" and turned out over time to be a great player for UT.

Our 1976 schedule was better than in '75, so I thought we had a good chance to get back to the top of the SEC. We opened with Duke. It was a very tight game, ultimately decided by missed extra points and field goals. In those days, both were kicked off a hard rubber tee, which was flat on top but slanted at 45 degrees at the back. I guess that design was to avoid the kicker's foot from hitting a square edge. Regardless, after the first two touchdowns, and on what should have been the winning field goal, when the holder put the ball on the tee, the ball slipped off the back. Each time the kicker's foot hit the ball, it "thudded" against the tee and the ball hardly cleared the line of scrimmage. I never saw that happen in my life, in practice or otherwise, but what a way to lose a game. Tailback Frank Foxx scored in the first quarter on a 2-yard run, Randy Wallace scored in the second on a 1-yard run and sophomore tailback Kelsey Finch scored in the fourth of a tough 21-18 loss.

Despite TCU coming to Knoxville the following week with a sophisticated passing game and an All-American receiver, we routed the Horned Frogs 31-0. It is rare that a team gains 400 yards of offense and does not score a touchdown, but that's what happened, as Tennessee's Thomas Rowsey intercepted two passes and Russ Williams intercepted a third. The defense rose to the occasion time after time, keeping TCU out of our end zone. Wallace ran 17 yards for the first touchdown, and completed a 69-yard pass to Larry Seivers for our second. Bobby Emmons ran one in from the 11-yard line and Morgan ran in another from 29 yards out. We got our kicking game straightened out, with Jimmy Gaylor kicking all four extra points and a 49-yard field goal to boot. No pun intended.

The normal defensive struggle against Auburn in Birmingham turned into a shootout. We took a 7-3 first-quarter lead on a 1-yard touchdown run by Finch, who finished with 124 yards on 22 carries. A 73-yard touchdown pass from Wallace to Morgan and a 2-yard Morgan scoring run gave us a 21-17 lead going into halftime. The Tigers scored in the third quarter to take a 24-21 lead, and added two more TDs in the fourth for a 38-28 win.

Clemson came back to Knoxville the following week. After a scoreless first quarter, we scored second-quarter touchdowns on a 1-yard Wallace sneak, a 21-yard Finch run and a 4-yard pass from Wallace to Seivers. We took a 21-7 lead into the fourth quarter and held on to stave off a Tiger comeback, winning 21-19. We finished strong by driving to the Clemson 7 as the game ended. Larry Seivers joined Gary Kreis (1960) and Johnny Mills (1966) in the Vol record book with 11 passes caught in a single game.

A trip to Atlanta to face a Pepper Rogers' coached Georgia Tech team ended in a very sweet 42-7 win. Pepper, who was a great player at Tech, had come back to coach the Yellow Jackets after a successful stint coaching at UCLA. He evidently learned some California ways, as his antics made great fodder for the media. It was reported that he came out one game leading the team doing cartwheels. When asked later he said, "I always wanted to do that." Another game he left the sideline, went up and sat in the stands, and ordered a hot dog.

When the team ran a play that didn't work, he allegedly said to the fan he was sitting next to, "That was a terrible play, I wouldn't have called that."

The week before the game, Pepper called me and told me they did a pre-game interview with the visiting coach and was I OK with that? I told him, "Sure, I'd be glad to participate." I actually forgot about it, but in our pre-game warmup, someone came down and asked if I'd go to midfield for the interview. There was a cameraman present and Pepper was holding the microphone. He said, tongue in cheek, "This is a low-budget show and we can't afford celebrity hosts, so I'm doing this interview." He welcomed me to the show and then said, "When the opening whistle blows, coaches are as competitive against each other as can be, but after the final horn blows, coaches are very friendly with each other, don't you agree?" I said, "Yes." He then went on about how coaches pull together to get certain things done and finally ended with, "It's kind of like coaches against the world, don't you agree?" I said, "Yes, I guess so." He then thanked me for the interview and left. It was the fewest words I had ever spoken in an interview.

Morgan scored three touchdowns on two runs and a pass from Wallace, while Foxx and Finch each scored on the ground. After the game, Pepper referred to Larry Seivers, Stanley Morgan and Andy Spiva as three of the best players the Yellow Jackets had faced.

Alabama came to Knoxville on the third Saturday in October. It was a low-scoring, field-position battle like many in the past. Tony Nathan scored first to give Alabama a 6-0 lead, then Gaylor kicked two field goals for a 6-6 tie at the half. Each team scored in the third quarter to knot the score at 13-13 going into the fourth.

In order to add better tacklers to our punt coverage team, we had brought some defensive players over in practice to serve on our punt team. We put a strong safety back at the fullback position to protect the punter and serve as a safety in coverage on a fourth-quarter punt. Alabama didn't even have their "punt rush" on. A single player came in from our right to force the kick. Our punter, Craig Colquitt, was taking his time to let our coverage get down field, knowing his protector would block the single rusher. Our protector broke down as if he was going to block the rusher, and at the last minute, took off running downfield. The surprised rusher came in and blocked the punt. Colquitt was about the fastest I had ever seen in getting punts off, but in this case, he was doing what he was supposed to do. When the strong safety came off the field, I put my arm around him and said, "What were you thinking?" He said, "I was going downfield in coverage." That was obviously poor coaching on our part, switching players to try to get an edge, but not communicating well enough that everyone knew what to do. It seemed so simple! The blocked punt changed the momentum and the Tide came away with a 20-13 victory.

The next week, we got out to a 10-0 first-quarter lead on a Gaylor field goal and Morgan 10-yard run against Florida in Knoxville. The Gators answered in the second quarter to make it 10-10 at the half. Florida took a 17-10 lead in the third and added a field goal in the fourth. Wallace was injured and left the game early in the third. Backup Joe Hough engineered an 80-yard fourth-quarter touchdown drive capped by a 1-yard Morgan run, and Morgan also ran it in for the two-point conversion to make it 20-18, which would allow a field goal to win. Unfortunately, our onside kick failed and Florida won, making the victory very sweet for Coach Dickey after losing twice to the Vols in our two previous meetings.

The next week we traveled to Memphis to face Memphis State. The Tigers took advantage of a sluggish Vol team in the first half for a 14-7 lead. The second half ended their dream of their first-ever victory over Tennessee as Morgan exploded for 98 yards and two touchdowns, and Seivers became UT's all-time leading pass catcher. Hough, a tough quarterback recruited from Oklahoma, scored the winning touchdown on a 6-yard scamper that bore resemblance to quarterback Dewey Warren's famed TD run to beat UCLA in the same stadium 11 years earlier. The Vol defense rose to the occasion in the second half and kept the Tigers out of the end zone. Two interceptions and three fumble recoveries helped seal the 21-14 victory.

We returned home to face Ole Miss amid homecoming festivities. Our defense produced big plays, intercepting five Rebel passes and recovering five fumbles. Spiva led the charge with an interception, two sacks, caused a fumble and made 13 tackles. David Parsons, a cornerback converted to free safety out of necessity, played well at the new position and intercepted two passes. Morgan, Emmons, Foxx and Hubert Simpson all scored touchdowns on the ground, resulting in a 32-6 happy homecoming win for the Volunteer grads returning for the weekend.

Kentucky unveiled a trick play that caught our defense off guard and resulted in a 62-yard first-quarter touchdown the following week in Knoxville. The rest of the day was a defensive struggle in which neither team could score. The 7-0 defeat was the first loss to Kentucky and first shutout in my 11 years at Tennessee.

It was a really tough loss for me, and made me decide to resign with a year remaining on my contract. I announced my resignation the next day. Had we won and then beaten Vandy, we would have finished 7-4 and gone to a bowl. I would have fought to continue to work toward returning Tennessee to its rightful place at the top of the SEC. I thought we had some good recruits committed to playing for us. I knew Coach Woodruff was behind me, win or lose. But at 6-5, the negativity among the fan base was such that I didn't believe we could turn it around. I also thought that my resignation early would help Coach Woodruff and better allow for a smooth transition. Johnny Majors was winning big at Pitt, and he was already the favorite of fans as my logical replacement. But to go 6-5, we still had to beat Vanderbilt in Nashville.

It was an ugly, rainy day in Nashville when we faced off against the Commodores. I did a sorry job of coaching before the game, as I encouraged our team to play its most physical game of the season. Robert Shaw, a really good young player who ended up later playing for the Dallas Cowboys, probably took that message a little too far. In pre-game warmups, the Vandy team came on the field and ran through where Robert's group was practicing. Whether words were exchanged or not I don't know, but something provoked Robert, who rose up and hit a Commodore in the chest with a football. A brief skirmish ensued that was quickly broken up, but that set the tone for the day.

It was a sloppy game by both sides and not particularly aided by the weather. Vandy took a 10-7 lead into the half with a fumble recovery and subsequent touchdown pass with less than two minutes remaining. As I was jogging off the field with the team at the half, I heard a Vol fan say, "That's OK, Bill, you can get 'em next year." I broke out laughing and thought that was pretty clever.

We came out in the second half and seized the momentum and the lead on a drive capped by a Simpson touchdown run. Our defense shut out Vandy in the second half, aided by two fourth-quarter interceptions. Seivers nudged Johnny Mills down the record books, as Seivers finished with 51 receptions, a new UT single-season record. Larry actually broke several Tennessee receiving records during the season.

As a side note, there had been many instances of brothers playing at Tennessee over the years. During my time, there were the Majors (Johnny, Billy and Bobby) and the Johnsons (Bob, Tom and Paul), while Craig Colquitt was the first of many Colquitts to punt at UT and in the pros. Two other brothers, the Andersons (Charlie and Terry), also played for the Vols. Charlie Anderson played from 1971-1975 and lettered for three years at defensive end. He was a solid and consistent player all three years. Terry Anderson came in 1975 and was a sophomore in 1976, my last year. The Anderson family connection had an interesting twist that showed up later in my life. The Anderson family home was in Florence, Alabama. Charlie's and Terry's dad, Charles Sr., was one of the first businessmen to go to China and import products into the United States. He developed an incredible business that still thrives today. When I became Director of Athletics at The University of Alabama, Terry's son

Keaton was signed by Coach Saban as a linebacker/defensive back. Terry quickly became an Alabama fan and switched allegiances to follow his son. Keaton was a good position player, but really excelled on special teams. Of even greater importance, Keaton graduated with a 4.0 GPA.

So my career as a head coach ended with a 59-22-2 record, and wins in four of the five bowls we played in. Our first three teams finished in the top 10, the next two in the top 20, but the final two finished outside the rankings. Up to that point in time, our 1970-76 teams won more games and more bowl games than any other Tennessee coach except General Neyland. The 1976 team lost five games by 29 points — 3, 10, 7, 2 and 7 — and there were some goofy ways we lost some of those games. It was almost like the Good Lord was telling me, "Your time here is done!" But the bottom line was, we didn't win a championship, and our record against Alabama was 1-6. The Tide and Coach Bryant, from 1971 to 1979, won eight SEC Championships and three National Championships. I had been worried a lot over the years about going 1-6 against Alabama. In doing research for this book, I learned that Coach Bryant was at Maryland for one year before moving on to Kentucky, Texas A&M and then Alabama. Tennessee's General Neyland was Coach Bryant's biggest rival, and I think somewhat of a mentor. Coach Bryant went 0-6-1 against Tennessee in the seven seasons that he faced General Neyland. That made me feel a little better about my 1-6 record against Coach Bryant!

The captains of the 1976 Tennessee team were Larry Seivers and Andy Spiva. After the season, Stanley Morgan was drafted in the first round by the New England Patriots, while Seivers went to the Seahawks, Mickey Marvin to the Raiders and Spiva to the Cardinals.

1977

Before I announced my decision to resign, I called Eugenia, Pat, Mike and Shannon into the room, and told them that with all the negativity in the air, we wouldn't be able to recruit well enough to turn our team around and that I was resigning. I didn't know yet what I was going to do, but it was going to be bigger and better than what we were doing at Tennessee. I told them to be proud of what we accomplished here and don't take any guff off anyone as long as we stayed there. But actually, after I resigned, people were very gracious to me and wished us well in our next venture.

Tennessee honored the last year of my contract, so I had some time to look around. Every coach is physically worn down after working every day and night from late August to mid-December. I didn't realize how mentally drained I was. I decided to take several weeks or even months to look around, hunt, fish, play golf, and spend time with family in ways I had not been able to do in my life thus far. We had lived in our Fox Den house for seven years, and one day I came home and told Eugenia that from the road in front of our house I could see the mountains with snow on the tops. I asked if she had seen that before. She said of course she had. I guess during that time of year I was never home much during daylight hours.

Soon after I resigned, I was offered a job coaching at a Power Five school, making twice as much money as I was making at Tennessee. I was offered another job that I declined before salary was even discussed. I finally decided I was going to take some time off and see if I could make it in the business world.

It was interesting to me to see the opportunities that arose. Some were crazy and seemed like fly-by-night deals. Others appeared to be good businesses with strong potential, but none felt right, so I kept looking. There was even an approach about running for political office, but I definitely am not a politician!

Lake Loudon was about a 10- to 15-minute drive from my house. I bought a boat and spent a fair amount of time fishing, thinking, and dreaming about finding the right opportunity. I got Pat and Mike interested in fishing, and when the weather warmed up, I pulled them around the lake on skis. It was a ton of fun playing with them and watching them enjoy fishing, skiing and just being together.

I did spend time meeting with different groups of people and exploring opportunities. That time off was very important in my life. I am grateful to the University of Tennessee for many things, but making that time possible for me was a real blessing.

Coach Bryant was very good to me and invited me to speak at his spring coaching clinic. It was an honor for me to do that, and I know he was trying to help keep me in the conversation for future coaching jobs.

I took Pat and Mike over to Alabama's practice one day, as they had never been on the UA campus. In fact, they had never known anything but Tennessee in their young lives. A few years earlier I had came home one day and Eugenia told me Mike had gotten in a fight at school that day. I said, "Good. What was he fighting about?" She said, "One of his classmates told him his dad played for Coach Bryant at Alabama, and Mike punched him in the nose!" I said, "Wow, we need to talk to our kids."

Coach Bryant invited the boys to go up on his tower. He invited me, too, but I declined. He asked why, and I told him that someone would probably take a picture and make a big deal of it. He told me nobody covered Alabama practices anymore. I asked how the paper got the stories. He said after practice, he told Charley Thornton what to report and that's how it worked. I said, "Coach Bryant, you don't live like other coaches!" I had newspaper people at every practice, taking roll, and reporting on everything that went on. Later in

1981 when Coach Bryant was on the path to breaking Amos Alonzo Stagg's record of 315 wins, the national press began to converge on him and the Alabama team. He didn't like it.

After a few months of retirement in 1977, I had pretty much decided I was going to work for a large firm that had Alabama and Tennessee connections. Its No. 2 executive, soon to become president, was recruiting me. I really liked him, and thought I might be able to do pretty well there.

A short time later Coach Bryant called and asked if I knew Larry Striplin. I told him I knew Larry pretty well. Larry was my first little league football coach and I had watched him play basketball at Birmingham-Southern. During my head coaching tenure, Larry, as president of the Birmingham Quarterback Club, asked me to come speak. I flew to Birmingham, Larry met me and took me out to his Nel-Bran Glass Company operation before my presentation. Afterward, Larry asked if the Insurers of Tennessee were a major sponsor of my TV show, to which the reply was "yes." He then asked if I would go in with him to start a glass company in Tennessee. He said if we got the independent insurers to give us all their auto windshield replacement business, we would make a fortune. I told him I wasn't interested in being in the glass business. All I wanted to do was coach the Tennessee football team and have everybody leave me alone! But Larry was always selling!

Coach Bryant went on to tell me Larry had started a commercial window company in Selma, Alabama. He said Larry wanted to hire me and that he had made a lot of money with the company. He thought I could, too. My immediate thought was "I'm not going to Selma to work for a window company!" Obviously, I didn't tell Coach Bryant that.

Larry called soon after that conversation and asked me to come visit Selma. He wanted to show me what he was doing there. I told him I appreciated the offer, but I had decided what I was going to do. I didn't want to waste his time. He then said he would like to see me anyway and that he would send his plane. He told me to bring my golf clubs and we'd play. I had plenty of time on my hands, as I was retired at 35. I told him I'd come play golf with him, but I wasn't coming to work there.

My visit there was most interesting. Larry had purchased the rights to a high-performance commercial aluminum window from the Decatur Iron and Steel Company (DISCO) in Decatur, Alabama. The company was founded in 1887. DISCO was primarily a security detention (jail) window and door company, using iron and steel as its primary materials. The aluminum division was pretty much a stepchild that allowed them to respond to bids requiring aluminum security windows on certain projects. An engineer from Europe came to work for DISCO, and persuaded them to allow him to develop an operable aluminum window with very high-energy performance numbers that could save energy costs in buildings. Larry actually brokered those windows from DISCO earlier on a Nel-Bran bid for windows, doors and storefront on St. Vincent's Hospital in Birmingham. He was able to get those windows specified by the architect, which eliminated much of his current competition, and he got the job, which included windows, doors, storefronts and louvres.

A few years later, DISCO workers went on strike for about a year. Larry was able to purchase the rights to the aluminum window division and the name "DISCO — founded in 1887". He also hired key personnel in that division and made "DISCO Aluminum Products — 1887" the name of his company.

Larry grew up in Selma. He was friend and schoolmate with four-time Mayor Joe Smitherman. He also caddied for professional golfer Otey Crisman, about whom you will learn more later.

Larry negotiated a favorable bond issue and received help in acquiring land and building a manufacturing plant there. He was very proud of Selma and saw it continue to evolve past the infamous "March to Montgomery over the Edmund Pettus Bridge" setback to the community. He also knew that Craig Air Force Base would be closing in the next few years, which would cause a significant impact to the economy. Larry wanted to help Selma by bringing employment to town and hopefully being so successful, he could help in many other ways. He did exactly that in his time there.

Larry got his business at DISCO started around 1972. By 1977 he was doing about $5 million in annual sales. He began by going to architects and general contractors he knew, and had successfully done Nel-Bran business in the past. His biggest and best client in those early days became Hospital Corporation of America (HCA), run by the Frist family in Nashville.

Through membership in the Young Presidents Organization, Larry met and became friends with Joe Rodgers. Joe was an Alabama graduate whose claim to fame, he said, was playing quarterback behind Bart Starr at Lanier High School in Montgomery. Joe owned a successful construction company in Nashville that was a primary contractor in building new and renovated hospitals for Hospital Corporation of America. With HCA as a client, Joe built and renovated hospitals all over America and in several foreign countries, including Saudi Arabia. Later, Joe became the chief financial officer and fundraiser for Ronald Reagan's presidential campaign. After President Reagan's election, Joe was awarded an ambassadorship to France, a very plush job.

HCA, as an owner-operator of hospitals, was very interested in window systems that were energy efficient and saved money on HVAC equipment and operations. In addition, hospitals, by law, had to have operable windows. Larry and Joe were starting to do a lot of business together when I got there. Joe also helped get Larry's foot in the door on a small project in Saudi Arabia. Energy in 1977 was not a real problem in this country as it had been for decades in Europe. Energy was beginning to be perceived as a problem in the U.S. when long gas lines in service stations began forming. Demand exceeded supply, and gasoline shot up to an unbelievable $1.50 a gallon!

During that time, Larry was chasing a huge job in Saudi Arabia. He had sold one job in Saudi Arabia, somewhat by accident, but had begun to work hard at trying to get more work there. Part of the problem was that OPEC had begun to flex its muscles as a cartel of oil-producing countries and forced the price of oil from $12 a barrel to $34. That fact alone caused a huge problem in the U.S. and world economies, cost Jimmy Carter the U.S. presidency, caused inflation to skyrocket, and made U.S. citizens painfully aware of the need to conserve energy. Billions of dollars flowed into Saudi Arabia and other OPEC countries over the next few years.

Larry showed me his operation in Selma and introduced me to his key staff members. He believed that DISCO had great potential. He offered me a job and said he would give me an opportunity to buy stock. If I decided I wanted to sell it later, he would buy it back from me. He also told me about that really big job he was chasing in Saudi Arabia. We played some golf at the Selma Country Club, but I was very impressed with what Larry and his team were doing. I went back home thinking this was a pretty cool opportunity that would allow me to get in on the ground floor of something that had a chance to be big. As good as that appeared, I couldn't see our family living in Selma. But the more I talked about it with family and friends, the more positives I heard about Selma. It had a reputation for its racial divide in the past, but it actually had to face those problems and deal with them long before other cities and states. It was a fairly wealthy community, and life revolved around the home, the school, the church, and the Selma Country Club. It was an hour and a half from Birmingham and 45 minutes from Montgomery.

The "straw that broke the camel's back" on my decision was Larry telling me to get a passport. I was leaning in his direction anyway. He said he needed to go to Saudi Arabia to the place where he hoped to land "The Big Job" he had been chasing for a few years. He also wanted to go to Warsaw, Poland, to see windows in three sausage factories he supplied through an order he got from another vendor who bought and resold them. He had planned to go to Tehran, Iran, to call on a Blount Construction site there. Red Blount owned a Montgomery construction company that did business all over the world, and that was very exciting to me. I had never been out of the country, except a brief entry to Canada to see Niagara Falls when I was in Buffalo speaking at a coaching clinic. I decided to join a window company in Selma!

LESSONS LEARNED

- There is a big difference in sitting in the head coach's chair than the assistant coach's chair, however much you think you might know about the job.

- I was a lot better coach with more talented players than I was with less talented ones. The plays worked a lot better.

- Have a plan for everything that you anticipate might happen. When things go bad, if you believe in your plan, stick to it.

- Enthusiasm is contagious, and an organization with that as a part of its DNA is dangerous.

- You never want to peak too early.

- Leaders in your organization are going to lead. If they didn't lead in the way the coach/manager wanted, it was failure on his/her part to sell them on the mission.

- Most people in any organization don't have strong feelings about most anything. If leaders say the working conditions, or whatever else is good, the followers will follow. If they say it's bad, they will follow in that direction. Communicate frequently with your leaders, keep them focused on the mission.

- The Winning Edge is a razor-thin line. Focus on the "little things."

- Don't get fat-headed with success. Keep your nose to the grindstone and make your staff stay abreast of the changes in the industry. Stay up with, if not ahead of, your competitors. Keep learning!

- On game day, be organized, and use every resource available to watch every play. Understand if the opponent is doing what you thought they would do, great, but if not, figure out what is different and communicate that to the coaches on the field and to the players. If you can't make changes in the first half, make them at halftime. Be alert for opponents who save something new for the second half.

- It is the head coach's responsibility to recruit and develop players good enough to compete with your top opponent.

- Sometimes your best coaching job can result in a 6-5 season.

The 1981 class inducted into the Alabama Sports Hall of Fame was amazing. Pictured are, left to right: Tarzan White, Alabama; Gov. Fob James, Auburn; Pat Sullivan, Auburn; Fred Davis, Alabama; Monte Irvin, Major League Baseball; me; and Joe Namath, Alabama (not pictured).

CHAPTER 5

DOING DISCO IN SELMA

As a new member of the DISCO Aluminum Products Team, in August 1977, I left our home in Knoxville to fly to New York and then go on a two-week trip overseas. Meanwhile, Eugenia, Pat, Mike and Shannon oversaw the movers coming to our house. They got the van loaded and took off driving to Selma. We had rented a nice house to live in until we decided where we wanted to buy later. It was a herculean effort on Eugenia's part to have our new life organized by the time I got home.

My trip overseas was fantastic. We landed in Copenhagen, Denmark, and spent the night there. We didn't have much time for sightseeing, but did see the infamous Red Light District. We didn't participate, but we did see the sights. It was most interesting to see a whole block of houses located off the street about 30 to 40 yards. Ladies were either standing outside the doorways or behind picture windows inside the houses. It appeared "the world's oldest profession" was doing pretty well in Copenhagen.

From Copenhagen, we flew to Warsaw, Poland. In the "it's a small world" phenomenon, the deputy ambassador to Poland grew up in Selma and was a classmate of Larry's. He met us at the airport and facilitated our getting through customs. It was a little scary, because there were security people with AK-47s all over the place. Larry's friend made us feel safe and productive our entire trip.

The reason for the trip to Warsaw was that through the *Sweet's Catalog*, DISCO's Venetian-blinded, in-swinging casement windows were purchased by a builder, who sold them and had them installed in three sausage plants there. Larry had never seen them, and was both proud and curious about the job. When we went to the first plant, he was devastated. The building was only 3 years old, but looked like it was 50. The windows were propped open, most of them had the blinds laying down in the bottom, or otherwise in a state of disrepair.

Larry's face got red and he said, "It's obvious these people have no pride." This was my first look at a DISCO window job and I was wondering what I had gotten myself into. We went back and met with the powers-that-be, and discussed what we saw. Larry said he was embarrassed by the way the windows were installed and maintained. He offered to send a crew in to properly set them up at his cost, but was told it would take too much red tape and just to leave it alone.

The deputy ambassador explained to us that the Polish people did have pride, but their socialist system treated everyone as equals. There was no incentive to work harder, stay late, or go to work early. We saw long lines around the stores that sold meat, vegetables, bread, etc. Interestingly, there were vodka shops all over the place, but no lines waiting to be served there.

One night after work, we walked a few blocks from our hotel to a popular bar that had a band, and people were dancing and seeming to have fun. We ate dinner, enjoyed the music and the atmosphere, and headed back to our hotel. The streets were dark and there was little to no traffic. We crossed a street in the middle of a block (yes, we jaywalked), heard a whistle blowing, and saw a policeman running toward us. He was spouting out words, none of which we understood, until we heard "passport." We nervously pulled out our passports, thinking, "Here we are in a foreign country, about to be put in jail, and we may never be heard from again." Fortunately, he chastised us — at least that's what we thought he was doing — and let us go on our way. The atmosphere in the bar that night was far different from what we saw on the streets every day. I guess that is why so many vodka stores are available to the people.

The people on the street did not look happy. I didn't see smiling faces or hear laughter in conversation. The clothes, and especially the shoes, did not look like they were made with quality. The soldiers wore uniforms that looked worse than those we wore in ROTC at Alabama.

Larry had planned our trip from there to Geneva, Switzerland, for the weekend to relax and get over jet lag. Our hotel was located on Lake Geneva, and the town and countryside were beautiful. I could understand why world summit meetings were held there. There was some kind of holiday at the time and they put on a fireworks display one night that was absolutely amazing. There were barges staged in different places on the lake and each held fireworks that were orchestrated in their execution in a breathtaking performance.

From Geneva, we went to Tehran, Iran. Our trip in August 1977 was prior to the fall of the Shah, as he still was in power. He was overthrown in 1979 due to discontent over the oil crisis there. Ayatollah Khomeini was invited back by the government and returned to Tehran to a greeting by several million Iranians.

Blount Construction out of Montgomery had an operation in Tehran. I'll never forget our presentation of DISCO windows there. Larry had hired an interpreter. We had a fairly high-tech (for the era) self-contained video/audio machine that, using U.S. electrical currency, told a very impressive story. Unfortunately, using Iranian electrical currency produced a voice very much slower and deeper audio that was hard for us to understand, much less the interpreter. We quickly silenced the machine and Larry went into his sales pitch. Needless to say, we didn't get any orders there.

Tehran was a very busy city, alive and bustling. Traffic was heavy and drivers very aggressive. It seemed like at most every intersection, there was a game of "chicken" going on where drivers going in different directions would try to bluff each other with who got there first. There were a lot of dented cars and a lot of angry drivers shouting at each other. Our taxi driver was also very aggressive. It seemed to me like every time he passed a rider on a bicycle, he would come as close as possible without hitting him. He also was aggressive at intersections. I had to close my eyes, buckle my seat belt and pray.

From Tehran we departed for Riyadh, Saudi Arabia. When we were on final approach into the city, it was after dark and the city was lit up and looked beautiful. When we landed, I was ready to see this country I had heard and read about so much. When we disembarked through the airplane doors, the heat hit me in the face, almost like stepping into an oven. It was almost midnight and the temperature was still in the 90s.

Riyadh was a very interesting city. We spent a couple of days there. Joe Rodgers was building a hospital there for the Crown Prince. It was to have everything that was the latest and greatest in hospitals. The heating and air condition system could freeze or cook you. They had partnered with Dr. Michael E. DeBakey, a famous cardiovascular surgeon, to establish a heart surgery clinic there. Dr. DeBakey later became the chancellor emeritus of the Baylor College of Medicine in Houston, and director of the Methodist DeBakey Heart and Vascular Center there. They were also building a university in Riyadh, that when finished, would accommodate 25,000 students.

I thought about what it might be like coaching a football team at the University of Riyadh. Money would be no object, and you could recruit and schedule games all over the world. You wouldn't have to worry about the NCAA. And then it dawned on me. If you stole something, they would cut off your hand; if you killed someone, they would cut off your head. So, one could only imagine what they would do if you went 6-5!

While in Riyadh we went to a marketplace called the Gold Souk. There were dozens of vendors in an area about a U.S. city block in size. Each had a stand that displayed jewelry of all sorts made out of gold. The stands were made of wood, and not very elegant as one might expect considering the value of the jewelry on display. Looking online today I think it has taken on a nicer look. It didn't appear that security there was very tight. Most stands had one or two people behind them, and when they were busy talking to customers, it looked like the merchandise within easy reach of passersby might be vulnerable to theft. But the aforementioned punishment laws put a damper on stealing there. We found some really nice stuff at what seemed to be very fair prices. Each product was weighed, and the price was determined by the price of gold on that day. I was very pleased with the purchases I made for gifts for loved ones.

From Riyadh we were driven by one of DISCO's employees to Tabuk to see where the big job that Larry had been chasing was located. It was to be a military city and would be bid in four phases, each one expected to come in at several hundred million dollars. Larry had relentlessly worked with the architect in Athens, Greece, to get DISCO windows specified. On this trip he set more meetings with the owners' representatives to continue to push the value of DISCO windows in this development. He reiterated repeatedly to the energy-saving properties of his products, but also the tight seal that would effectively eliminate the dust penetrating the buildings through the windows from the dust storms that occurred frequently in the region.

When we left Saudi Arabia, our plan was to drive from Tabuk to Aqaba, Jordan. It was a two- to three-hour trip over the same route that Lawrence of Arabia crossed the desert in 1917 with his army to defeat the Ottomans and capture the Red Sea port of Aqaba. The defenders never expected to be attacked from the desert and had their big guns anchored in rocks facing the water where they expected any attacks to be initiated.

One of DISCO's employees was assigned the task of driving us to our destination. Once we left the city, there was nothing to see but desert. No gas stations, stores or any signs of civilization came into view over most of our trip. After an hour or so of driving, we had a flat tire. We all kind of thought that was funny, even the driver who had to change the tire. While we were on the side of the road, we saw two camels in the distance. They evidently saw us and walked toward us to see what we were doing. We took their picture, raved about the thought that they had come to see us, and continued on our journey.

About 45 minutes later, we had another flat tire. We didn't think this one was very funny. Traffic was very sparse during our entire trip, as we didn't pass many vehicles coming either way. After a while, a Toyota pickup stopped to see what was going on. The language barrier was difficult to overcome, but they obviously could see we had a flat tire. Through much conversation and hand signals, we evidently succeeded in communicating we had no spare and we needed to get to Aqaba. They hand signaled for us to get in the back of the truck. We grabbed our bags, threw them in the back, and climbed aboard. Now you might think we were really scared back in Warsaw, when late at night with no cars on the street, a policeman came running at us blowing his whistle when we were jaywalking, shouting, "passport, passport." But riding in the back of a pickup, in a desolate country, with people who didn't speak or understand our language, made me wonder if we would ever get back home.

As luck and fate would have it, they not only got us to Aqaba, but took us to our hotel there. Larry compensated them nicely. I do wonder what the bellman at our Intercontinental Hotel thought when we jumped out of the back of a truck covered with dust and checked into their hotel. That afternoon I went down to the water and swam in the Gulf of Aqaba, which is part of the Red Sea.

I don't recall much about our time in the Jordan other than seeing the interest the country had in World Cup soccer. There were huge headlines and articles on the front page of the papers proudly proclaiming a victory their team had achieved the previous day. Up to that point, I never realized how important that competition was to countries all over the world. Soccer in the USA in 1977 was not very high profile. Even today, when kids all over the country play soccer at early ages, the popularity of professional soccer trails football, basketball, baseball, hockey and racing by large margins. I have always thought they could increase the popularity in America if they could create scores that ended 29-24 instead of 2-1.

While we were in Saudi Arabia, we heard that Joe Rodgers had a heart attack on a flight to the Middle East a few days earlier. They had taken him to a hospital in Geneva, so we flew back to Geneva and spent another few days there to see and visit with him. It was nice to be back in Geneva after the harsh climates of Iran, Saudi Arabia and Jordan. Joe told us about his ordeal. He had the heart attack on the plane coming over but they had gone too far to turn back. The flight attendants and a doctor on board did the best they could to stabilize and comfort him, but he said it was definitely his worst flight ever. He had only been in the hospital in Geneva a few days, but he was not a proponent of the socialized medicine practiced there. Joe was accustomed to primo treatment whenever he went to doctors or had health issues. Here, he was just another guy, and they would see and treat him whenever they had time. He couldn't wait to get stabilized to the point he could get back to the good ol' USA.

We bid goodbye to Joe in Geneva and departed for London for a short stop there. We landed and took a cab to our hotel. It was very nice to hear the English language and especially the British accent. We got up the next morning planning to do a brief tour of London before catching our flight back home. We were surprised to read the British newspaper that morning in August 1977. In the largest headline print I've ever seen, maybe 6 inches on the front page, read, "THE KING IS DEAD". It didn't take long to see that the King they were talking about was Elvis Presley. The Brits worshiped Elvis.

We toured part of the city, saw two beautiful cathedrals, ate lunch and went to the airport. They say travel broadens ones horizons. This trip definitely made my interest in geography, foreign languages and foreign cultures rise several notches. It is much more interesting now to read about current events in Europe and the Middle East. I applaud universities offering trips abroad in many different subjects to students interested enough to take them. I would encourage all students to participate.

The best part of the trip was returning to America and Selma, my new "Home Sweet Home." Our rental house was terrific, and our landlords, Myrna and Stumpy Todd, were terrific. They were huge Auburn fans, but we became great friends over our six years in Selma. All the moving boxes were gone, and closets and drawers were full. My two weeks overseas had been far better than Eugenia's, Pat's, Mike's and Shannon's tasks. Thus began a new chapter in our lives. We were all excited about the opportunities and the challenges that a move to a new city presented. The six years we spent in Selma also led us into a life-changing adventure.

We enrolled the children in Morgan Academy, joined the Methodist Church and the Selma Country Club. I went to work while Eugenia looked for sections of town and houses we might want to live in somewhere in the near future. It was fall, and football season was heating up. Pat earned the starting quarterback job and we were able to attend all the games, home and away.

It was the first time since I started high school that I was not working on weekends, including Labor Day. This particular Labor Day weekend, I mowed the grass and cleaned out weeds in flowerbeds. I knew how to identify poison ivy, to which I am very allergic. Working in shorts with no shirt, there was some similar plant that I didn't recognize that attacked me with a vengeance. The next day, I had welts all over my body, including my face and around my eyes. I took that as a sign that I should never work in the yard again. I took that to heart and tried to hire someone else to do that chore for the rest of my life.

The greatest thing about the fall was being able to go watch football games in which Pat was playing. It was also nice to get to see some of Mike's practices and games, and Shannon's recitals. We drove to surrounding towns to see away games and got to see the Alabama countryside. I got to play golf in the fall, which I had never experienced before. These were some really neat things that were available to me after coaching.

Changing careers is both exciting and challenging on the business side of the change. It generally means taking a few steps backward, both in stature and pay. The learning curve required can take quite a while, depending on how different the new path is from the old. What I believe is that the future is built on these things: The knowledge and relationships that you have built, the credibility in each that you have attained, and how you use each to accomplish your goals.

From my coaching experience, I learned many valuable lessons in leadership:

- Team dynamics — pulling together, a team is greater than the sum of its parts.
- Preparation — mental and physical preparation is critical for every goal.
- Time management — better never than late! It shows lack of respect for others to be late.
- The "IT" factor — identify those who can rise to the occasion when the going gets tough to accomplish the goal, and better yet, have "IT" yourself.
- Salesmanship — the skill required to get the right people on the team, get them to buy into your vision, and get them to buy into their role.
- Leadership — create and sell the vision, surround yourself with people smarter than you, give them a job and let them do it. When times get tough, don't let 'em see you sweat.

I started out trying to learn everything I could about our company, our mission, our executive staff and employees, our customers, our potential customers and our products. I also tried to understand the process of how we engineered and manufactured products, how we estimated the costs of the jobs, and how we sold them in the marketplace.

Larry, the DISCO CEO, was a great salesman and the ultimate entrepreneur. He actually was a basketball coach prior to going into business. He was hired to start the basketball program at Belmont College in Nashville. He spent much of his time raising money to build the program. He got the program off the ground and had quite a bit of success. Belmont basketball today is a very strong program that frequently makes the NCAA tournament and competes well there.

While at Belmont, Larry was in his mid-20s and was invited to interview for the Alabama head basketball coaching position in 1956. Being the positive thinker that he was, he came back from his interview thinking he had the job. He spent the weekend plotting how he was now going to get to recruit and coach against Adolph Rupp at Kentucky and the other SEC basketball leaders. When he got the call on Monday and was told Alabama was going in a different direction, he was deflated.

Soon after that experience, he became frustrated with coaching at a place with no resources other than what he created. He decided to take advantage of some of the relationships he had built while raising money for Belmont and went to work for Pittsburgh Plate Glass Company. He quickly rose up in the sales ranks to the point he was training PPG sales groups around the country. One of his clients, the owner of Nelson-Brantley Glass Company out of Birmingham, invited him to buy their firm. Two older gentlemen ran the company and both wanted to retire. They made Larry an offer he couldn't refuse.

Larry took over that company and expanded it into 16 stores in four states. Nel-Bran specialized in installing storefront glass and glazing jobs. It also had a division that did auto windshield replacement work. Larry developed relationships with architects and general contractors in selling Nel-Bran's products and services. Those relationships proved beneficial when Larry bought out the aluminum window division of Decatur Iron and Steel Company (DISCO) and located DISCO Aluminum Products Company in Selma, where he grew up.

When I got to Selma in 1977, Nel-Bran was doing $7 million in annual sales and DISCO was doing $5 million, for a total of $12 million, but the growth potential was in DISCO. Larry had used his prior contacts well. He quickly began getting DISCO windows specified in architects' building plans, and getting general contractors on board with this new energy-saving product. His relationship with Joe Rodgers and Hospital Corporation of America became a major source of business to get the company off the ground.

The sales process in this business was typically long and arduous. It might take months or years to get the products specified. From there, it typically took at least a year before the job went out to bid, and another year or two before the general contractor was ready for the windows.

DISCO didn't make stock windows. All were custom built to the architect's specifications. I believe the least expensive window we sold during my six years there was $475. On the high end, the cost was around $1,000. It took strong selling, with backup data to convince architects and owners that these products would pay for themselves over a relatively short period of time. If energy costs continued to rise as expected, the payback time would be shortened even further.

My title at DISCO was assistant to the president. That meant I spent the first six months trying to learn the business and doing whatever Larry assigned me to do. In January 1978, I became vice president of Sales & Marketing. DISCO at the time was still a relatively new business. Our potential clients didn't know us, and selling a product ahead of its time was difficult.

What Larry and his team did in a few short years, with very few resources, was remarkable. He used his relationships from his days at Nel-Bran to get architects and contractors to listen to his energy-efficient window story. Even with our limited success up to 1977, our sales history and sales materials for staff were embryonic. On the domestic front, we needed more sales and longer backlogs for engineering and manufacturing to efficiently schedule work.

Our sales team was low in numbers and experience. Larry was "the world's greatest salesman" and was responsible for most of the sales. His righthand technical support man was Ken Jenks. Larry hired Ken from Decatur Iron and Steel Company when he bought the company. The combination of Larry and Ken was powerful. Those two had done most of the work in getting established with Rodgers/HCA, as well as "The Big Job" they were chasing in Tabuk, Saudi Arabia.

On the manufacturing side, Larry had hired Larry Jones, also from Decatur, to head up our manufacturing operation. He did a great job of getting the plant set up and operating. On the administrative side, Larry hired Ms. Arden McKenzie, who had been the administrative assistant to Gov. George Wallace. Arden was extremely well organized, efficient down to the smallest detail, and tough when the need arose. In our case, the need arose quite often. All three — Ken, Larry and Arden — were extremely valuable to the growth and success of the company. We were pretty well set up to estimate jobs, and engineer and manufacture them when we were successful in sales.

As VP of Sales & Marketing, I was responsible for building a sales team that could keep the plant going, whether or not we were able to get big, profitable international jobs or not. Due to the lack of sales support and technical support to staff on sales calls, there was a heavy burden on our sales staff. Other than two guys, most were inexperienced, including me. We had one salesman, Jim Frazier, who was an old hand at the business of selling windows. He knew how the game was played leading up to and making bids on projects. We made Jim our sales manager, and he did a great job of working with our guys, once they got our products specified in architects plans, to lead them to and through the bid process.

We also developed a sales compensation plan that placed a premium on getting DISCO specified and winning bids. There were strong financial incentives to sales staff who could get that done. Our sales force was highly motivated to go out and produce. The rest of our company was supportive as well, as they all knew we needed more work in the factory. We immediately focused on adding more resources to get more business from existing DISCO clients, especially HCA.

TABUK, SAUDI ARABIA

In 1979, phase one of the four-phase military city in Tabuk, Saudi Arabia, went out for bids. Larry and team had done a great job with the architect in Athens, Greece, and the project owner in Tabuk. Through Joe Rodgers, Larry had made a deal with an English general contractor, which our team thought would get the bid. If they were successful, we would get the business on which we had bid. It looked like everything was in place and our odds were good.

Unfortunately, a German general contractor won the bid, and it was as if World War III had begun.

They did everything in their power to get us kicked out so they could hire people with whom they had done business in the past. Our bid was loaded with profit and we had never done a job of that magnitude before. Right before we were about to give up, the German company gave up and DISCO was awarded the business. Larry's relentless courting of the architect and the owner finally paid off. A book should be written about this job.

Larry brought home a check in "front money" for the amount of $8 million, and a signed contract for $42.5 million. That made us responsible for producing about 25 percent of the job in DISCO windows, buying out the other 75 percent in glass, doors, vents and louvres, and installing everything on the job site. The gross sales of the window company the previous year was $5 million. We were all ecstatic, but recognized we had a tiger by the tail. Could we handle it?

Soon after that, Larry promoted me to president and chief operating officer of DISCO Aluminum Products. It was a fantastic learning opportunity for me, and definitely an incredible challenge. The Tabuk job took DISCO Aluminum Products from a small company to a mid-sized company overnight. The $8 million Larry brought home was quickly put to use in expansion. We bought the plant next door, and over the next several months, doubled the size of our operation from 90 to 180 employees. The new plant was set up to produce high-volume jobs, the first of which was the Tabuk job. Our current plant remained set up for smaller and more custom jobs. Staff was added in all departments.

I knew where to go to hire coaches, and had to immediately learn where to hire engineers, estimators and people who had knowledge and experience in making high-performance aluminum windows. That was a very limited market. If that was not challenging enough, Larry sent our plant manager, Larry Jones, to Saudi Arabia. He was charged with the responsibility to prepare to receive the windows and other products we bought, and install them when the time came. He knew more about building windows than anyone there, so replacing him was another challenge.

Our team rose to the occasion. We managed the growth of the company and the magnitude of the job very well. Our company did such a good job on phase one, in the next few years, DISCO was successful in getting three of the four construction phases in Tabuk for a total of about $90 million.

The size of the job and the backlog of work for the plant gave us time to expand our domestic sales staff. We were also able to significantly improve our sales materials and sales support, as discussed earlier. We created a compensation system that really incentivized our sales team to close sales. As success is a journey and not a destination, so are compensation systems. In early stages of manufacturing companies, or with new product lines, I believe the sales force needs to be incentivized to get business for the company. As the product line becomes more well known and sales support becomes more professional, more incentives should move toward manufacturing. From a morale standpoint, there is nothing more important than getting and keeping compensation systems right.

Word spread about DISCO's Saudi Arabia success, which also made architects, owners and contractors more open to listening to our proposals. We added more effort to continue to grow the Rodgers/HCA business and gained entry into doing business with Humana, another large hospital company.

In business, there is a push-pull among departments and even sister companies over priorities. In our company, the Sales Force pushed Estimating to get estimates done more quickly They pushed Engineering to get the orders to Manufacturing, and for Manufacturing to build the windows faster to meet delivery schedules. Estimating pushed back on Sales as to the growing number of estimates requested, and what they considered wasted time on the jobs we didn't close. Engineering and Manufacturing pushed Sales to sell what we made and reduce the number of custom jobs. Sales answered back that we needed to build what the customer wants to buy. Up to a point, that push-pull among departments is healthy. It keeps people on their toes. Leadership's challenge is to stimulate some conflict, but manage it to improve all areas of the company. Fortunately, everyone in all departments was so excited about landing the job in Saudi Arabia, and saw the growing orders from domestic sales as a positive. Everyone was fully committed to doing whatever it took to get the job done.

DISCO grew to $40 million in annual sales over the next two years as a result of the Tabuk sale. Success breeds success. Success helps everyone be motivated, have more fun, make more money, and live a better life. It also comes with a price. Staff members often had to work nights and weekends, and everyone was challenged to manage the increased workload more efficiently. The bar had risen dramatically. Now we had a monster to feed and before that job ran out, we had a lot of capacity to fill. We now had a more effective sales team in place and we were able to keep feeding the monster with both domestic and foreign sales.

Another critical area of need in all companies, but especially manufacturing companies, is cash flow. Materials must be acquired, and equipment and staff put in place to manufacture and deliver products before money can be collected. We had to establish a partner-type relationship with our banker. Larry had done that with bankers in Birmingham and Selma in expanding Nel-Bran's business and getting DISCO off and running. Even though there was front money to start the Tabuk job, and much projected profit at the end, it took a lot of cash to expand the company, acquire materials and get to the finish line. Larry was a master at building successful banking relationships and he needed to; as with Larry, there was always another reason to borrow money, or use up the liquidity we had on hand.

Great salesmen can really get fired up. They research and find every reason in the book that their product is the answer to the customer's needs. You can't ignore them and hope they go away. They are very, very resilient. They don't take "no" for "no." They usually take it as "not yet" and go back to the drawing board to find a better approach to meet the prospect's needs. If you ever need to sell someone something, go to a great salesman. Not only do they get fired up about what they are trying to sell you, if they are intrigued with what you are trying to sell them, they can get equally fired up and sometimes may not buy just your product, but maybe your whole company.

In the six years I was in Selma, we went from two companies (DISCO Aluminum Windows and Nel-Bran Glass & Glazing), doing $12 million in sales, to 10 companies doing $60 million. Larry formed Circle S Industries to serve as the holding company to manage its operating companies. Virtually none related to our core business. "The boss ain't always right, but he is always the boss!" We bought a helicopter leasing operation, a financial company that moved money internationally betting on the rise and fall of various currencies, and Otey Crisman Putters, to name a few. Buying the latter happened to provide a life-changing experience for me.

OTEY CRISMAN

Otey Crisman was a very interesting character. He was a professional golfer. He was also a strong Christian man who served as a circuit preacher around the Selma area. In addition, he had a temper that caused him to break many golf clubs after bad shots.

The one thing that held him back from beating the legends of that day was on the greens. Some of those legends were Ben Hogan, Doug Ford and Jimmy Demaret, and Otey had to find a way to compete.

At the 1946 U.S. Open qualifying in Birmingham, Otey showed up with a putter he had designed and built for himself. It was a mallet-head style putter with a hickory shaft. The putter head was also ahead of its time, as a soft brass insert was embedded in the aluminum head. Two lead weights on either side of the insert created a "center balance" to reduce torque and improve solid contact.

Otey finished with the fourth-lowest qualifying score in the country with his new putter. He told the story that one night during a tournament, he crawled in bed with his wife and started chuckling. She asked, "What are you laughing about?" Otey replied, "I have orders for six dozen putters and I'm not yet in the manufacturing business." As the season progressed, Otey's new putter got more attention than his play did.

Demaret won the 1947 and '50 Masters with an Otey putter. As Otey began to concentrate on his growing business, it can be documented that hundreds of PGA, LPGA and amateur players used Otey putters. Here is a partial list of some of the legends that used Otey putters: Bob Goalby, Cary Middlecoff, Doug Ford, Jack Burke (1956 Masters), Miller Barber, Arnold Palmer (1958 Masters), Paul Runyan, Rick Massengale, Ben Crenshaw, Tony Lema, Carol Mann, Mickey Wright, Nancy Lopez and Babe Didrikson Zaharias.

Otey had a nice career as a golfer, but his putters lived long after he retired from professional competition. By the time I got to Selma, he had turned the putter business over to his son, Bubba Crisman. Otey was running an organ and piano business in Selma, and preaching at two or three different churches. He was inducted into the Alabama Sports Hall of Fame in 1979.

I got to know Otey during my six years in Selma and found him to be an outstanding man in every aspect of his being. He was fun to be around, as he had many stories from his golf background. One of his most memorable quotes to me was, "It's a shame God wasted all the abilities of youth on young people!"

Larry caddied for Otey growing up in Selma and got to know him very well. When Larry returned to Selma and got DISCO Aluminum Products rocking and rolling, he acquired Otey's company. Larry believed that if he could sell expensive, high-quality windows all over the world, he could do the same with high-quality putters.

That proved to be a mistake. When Larry would ask the reps to sell more putters, the response was often, "Man, we can't even make gas money selling putters. You need to either get in or get out of the golf business." Larry was pretty stubborn, and was bound and determined to make Otey Crisman Putters a profitable operation. He set up a meeting with Jack Nicklaus' Golden Bear Licensing Group in Palm Beach, Florida, in late 1979, and he asked me to go with him. I was flattered and accepted, even though I was working like crazy as president of DISCO.

We met with Jack's licensing people. I soon learned that Nicklaus' heirs would earn royalties off the Golden Bear logo and Jack's signature long after Jack's life on earth had ended. This was the first time I had ever heard of

Trademark Licensing. He had licensees like Hathaway, Hart Schaffner Marx, and the like, who were selling his merchandise all over the U.S. and Japan.

By the end of the day, we had become exclusive licensees of Golden Bear golf gloves, socks and accessories sold to the Green Grass pro shops distribution channel. Before we left, we did get to meet with Jack. He was a very pleasant personality, so much so that he talked Larry into buying out his interest in Jack Nicklaus Eyewear, sold to the ophthalmic trade. Larry named this new venture Golden Eagle Enterprises (GEE), based on his new relationship with the Golden Bear, Jack Nicklaus, and the DISCO/Nel-Bran mascot, the eagle. He used a public relations guy from South Carolina to come up with that name. They didn't realize until later that Golden Eagle was a popular Alabama syrup brand, and definitely was not the best name we could have picked. But it was done and we lived with it. Every time I heard it, the jingle popped in my mind, "Golden Eagle table syrup, pride of Alabam...!"

Larry identified and hired a young man named Eddie Dobbs to move to Selma and run the newly acquired putter company with licenses to produce and sell Golden Bear golf accessories and Golden Bear glasses and sunglasses. Eddie didn't have a formal education. He told me he had to quit school before graduating to go out and make some money, but Eddie was one of the smartest people I had ever been around. He was street smart, inquisitive about everything, and had enough brass in his demeanor to not be afraid to ask anyone about anything. He knew a lot about licensing, manufacturing and sales from experience and research.

Eddie took the process of manufacturing putters to much higher standards. He designed and built bathroom accessories — towel racks and toilet tissue holders — out of Otey Crisman mallet heads and hickory shafts. He quickly acquired the licensing rights to Disney characters to develop a children's line of eyewear to go with our Golden Bear men's line. Interestingly, he got those rights for only $25,000. He went to International Management Group (IMG), which represented many athletes, and acquired the rights to Chris Evert Lloyd, one of the leading women's tennis players on the circuit. He got those rights for nothing, except agreed, "If we produce and sell them, we'll send you royalties."

I was fascinated with the concept of trademark licensing, and often met with Eddie after work to talk about how he was developing this business. After the first year, Golden Eagle paid Nicklaus $75,000 in royalties. I asked Eddie why in the world would we pay him that much? He explained that we paid 8 percent royalty on everything we sold that used the Golden Bear logo. He further explained that the people we were selling to didn't know us. They had vendors with whom they were accustomed to doing business, but they very much knew the Jack Nicklaus brand, and the consumers that bought from them knew it, too. His brand stood for quality. It was well worth what we were paying him to use his logo on our products, and his name, image and likeness in our advertising and printed materials. That made sense to me.

There were many advantages of our having licenses with Nicklaus, Disney and IMG. We learned a lot about licensing from those three licensors. They had approval rights for everything we did, but were very helpful to us as the more merchandise we sold, the more we paid them. In addition, the more we were able to sell high-quality products associated with their logos, the equity they had built in their brands continued to grow. It was definitely a win-win situation.

Nel-Bran (glass), DISCO (windows) and Circle S Industries (holding company) each held a board meeting in different months of every quarter. The Board Members were paid $500 each for Nel-Bran and DISCO meetings, and $1,000 for Circle S.

COACH BRYANT, THE BUSINESS MAN

In January 1981, we had a DISCO board meeting, which I ran as president. Larry had assembled a very impressive board comprised of general contractors and other successful people. Having no engineering (or even business) background, I had to work hard to prepare effective presentations about our business for the board. Coach Bryant was one of our board members. My job was to run the DISCO board meetings, but I also had to go pick Coach Bryant up at the hotel and bring him to the meetings. On the way to this particular board meeting, Coach Bryant was talking about his decision to change agents. I was surprised to learn he even had an agent, and was more surprised to find that Mark McCormack's company, IMG, was representing Coach Bryant. IMG was arguably the best sports marketing company in the world. During the board meeting I had a hard time focusing on DISCO business, as my mind was whirling with ideas that here was the best coach in America, who was within nine victories from becoming the all-time winningest college coach ever, and he was about to change agents.

I thought that with the right plan, we might be able to do for Coach Bryant what Golden Bear had done for Jack Nicklaus. That was pretty bold and not very well-educated thinking, but that was what was on my mind. Walking back down to the car after the meeting I told Coach Bryant that we had started a little sports marketing company, and that we would like an opportunity to represent him. I told him I didn't know anything about being an agent, but I knew about him and we would do it right and the way he wanted it done. His response was priceless: "I ain't got nothin' to sell. The best in the business have been trying to sell me for years. All I'm looking for is to find someone who will take my requests for speaking engagements and tell 'em I can't come!" I said, "Coach, we can handle that!"

We signed an exclusive agency agreement with Coach Bryant shortly thereafter. Coach Bryant told me he didn't want to deal with anybody in the company but me. Eddie drafted the agreement and I presented it to Coach Bryant. He didn't even read it, but told me to make sure it got done the way he would want it done. Eddie started out in the marketplace getting the word out that if anyone wanted to use Coach Bryant's likeness or name, they had to come through our company, Golden Eagle Enterprises.

The closer to the season we got, the more interest Eddie stirred up in the marketplace. Many people were willing to pay a fair amount of money in up-front fees and against substantial percentages of future sales to get the rights to Coach Bryant's name and likeness. I was still running the window company, but had to screen all deals and take the ones I thought he would like to Tuscaloosa to get his written approval. It got more and more hectic as the season kicked off, but we were beginning to make Coach Bryant and GEE a fair amount of money.

Our agency agreement with Coach Bryant gave us rights to use his name, image and likeness to attract licensees that would develop marketing plans to take his licensed products to the marketplace. We also had rights to attract companies to use him to advertise their products and services, as well as to have him for speaking engagements to employees, customers and potential customers. Coach Bryant certainly did his part, as he attracted major media attention in his pursuit of passing Amos Alonzo Stagg as college football's all-time winningest coach.

One of the most important contests of the season occurred in the ninth game when No. 8 Alabama faced No. 7 Mississippi State in Bryant-Denny Stadium in a fight for the SEC Championship. Emory Bellard was the MSU coach. His wishbone offense had taken him from the top of Texas state high school football to the University of Texas, where as offensive coordinator he installed it and helped turn around a struggling Longhorn program. Those successes led to his hire at MSU in 1979 as head coach. The Bulldogs had beaten Alabama 6-3 in 1980 in Jackson, and they were confident they could win again. Their 6-1 record coming into the game looked good against Alabama's 6-1-1 record, with a loss to Georgia Tech and a tie against Southern Miss early in the season.

This game may have been the hardest-hitting game I ever witnessed. Both sides were laying it all on the line. The hitting was so hard, there must have been a dozen fumbles. Players would get hurt, limp off the field, shake if off on the sidelines and charge back out again a few plays later. It was tied at 10 at the half, but a fourth-quarter field goal put Alabama up 13-10. In the final minute, MSU completed a 50-yard pass that almost won the game. The receiver caught the ball at about the Tide 20 and dragged a defender 10 yards until he was finally downed at the 10. On third and goal from the 10, a State pass was tipped at the line, and All-American safety Tommy Wilcox intercepted to save the game. That victory marked Coach Bryant's 313th win, one shy of Stagg's record of 314. Alabama had an open date before its next game in State College, Pennsylvania — known affectionately as Happy Valley — against Joe Paterno's Nittany Lions, and another open date before its final regular-season game against Auburn.

The stage was set to tie and break Stagg's record, and, if successful, the mark would be broken against archrival Auburn. Eddie Dobbs came up to me after the MSU game and asked, "Do you think Coach Bryant would agree to wear a wire and record everything all day the day of the next two games?" I shuddered about asking him, but said, "It could be pretty historic stuff if he would."

I was pretty nervous the next day when I approached Coach Bryant. I congratulated him on the great win and we replayed the game a little in his office, with him telling me how proud he was of his staff and team in one of his best victories. When I finally built up enough nerve, I said to Coach Bryant, "Hey Coach, if they had a recording of Knute Rockne's 'Win one for the Gipper speech,' it would be pretty valuable. What you are about to do these next two games might be every bit as valuable. Would you agree to wear a wire so we can record all day, the next two games, as you have your various staff and team meetings leading up to the game, and then the game itself?"

He took a big drag on that unfiltered Chesterfield, burning down about half of it, inhaled for what seemed a minute, blew it out, sending smoke all over the room, and the words," I think that's a great idea! I've been telling Charley Thornton I needed to be recording more stuff this season." He went on to say, "I'll take my little Lanier recorder that I dictate with and record all messages to the team over the next two weeks."

It was so good to hear him say he would wear a wire. I barely heard anything after that. He did record all messages to the team for the next two weeks. It was so fascinating. What he said getting his team off of the "big game high" of the Mississippi State victory, then getting through an open-date week, and finally getting them ready to play another big game was maybe as valuable in some ways than what he said on game day.

His first message was to praise the players and coaches for the great victory on Saturday. He was lavish in praise, and discussed player grades and big plays. At the end, he challenged them that they had two weeks to prepare for a game that would have national implications on the record. He closed with, "If you don't put everything you've got into these next two weeks, it would be a shame."

After a few practices and toward the end of the bye week, he got on them a little. Then early in game week, he got on them pretty hard, saying, "Everybody on this team hasn't given everything they have in preparing for Penn State. If we look back after the game and say 'I wish I had given more,' we'll regret it forever."

Then on Thursday he started to get back on their side, telling them the strategy they were going to use against the Nittany Lions. "We've studied our tendencies, as well as Penn State's. We have a really good game plan to stop their potent offense, and to move the ball against their defense." Coach Bryant continued, "We are going to play every play on offense like we are behind. We've been pretty conservative over the last few games on offense, and we think our passing game will hurt them, as they may not be ready for us to open things up." He did make the exception that when Penn State punted, they would not play like they were behind. That's because Coach Paterno had a punt formation that was spread across the field, and Coach Bryant wanted to make sure the Tide conservatively defended against a fake from that formation.

Coach Bryant told me that when he was talking about playing from behind, he was talking to his players, but he was really talking to his coaches. He said toward the end of the season, Mal Moore, the offensive coordinator, and Ken Donahue, the defensive coordinator, tightened up and went too conservative. I thought that was a hoot!

Game day came in Happy Valley, and sure enough, Coach Bryant wore the wire all day with no problems. The post-game headline in one paper read, "Most Embarrassing First Half in Joe Paterno's Career," as Penn State lost 31-16 on Nov. 14, 1981. Penn State planned to "break the bone and got burnt by the bomb" wrote *Patriot-News* sportswriter Ronnie Christ. Alabama opened up 24-3 lead and held off the No. 5 Nittany Lions 31-16 before a record 85,133 fans.

If there was an offensive hero for Bama, it had to be Walter Lewis, who completed 6 of 10 passes for 167 yards and two touchdowns. The game got away from the Nittany Lions early, as Alabama had 334 yards and 24 points in the first half against a team that for two weeks had been No. 1 earlier in the season. Those numbers being flashed to much of the nation on TV, and a record 460 media people and scouts from six bowls, was a very positive experience for the Tide.

My favorite series in the game, which we discovered as we replayed Coach Bryant's tapes on our flight home, came on the first series of the second half. Penn State established a drive and made it to the Alabama 4-yard line with a first down. Todd Blackledge was Penn State's quarterback and Curt Warner was their All-American running back. After two runs by Warner gained nothing, a third-down out route was thrown to PSU's left side. On the play, the receiver slipped down, with no contact from Alabama, the pass went incomplete, and the back judge threw a flag and called interference. The ball was placed at either the 1 or 2, with four more downs to go. Warner carried four straight times, getting stopped on all four.

Listening to the tapes, Coach Bryant was walking out on the field greeting his jubilant players who had held off the Lions for seven plays inside the 4-yard line. Coach Bryant kept saying, "I tip my hat to you, I tip my hat to you," which had to be the ultimate in praise. About that time, the ref who threw the flag must have run by, because Coach Bryant yelled, "And I tip my hat to you too, you blankety-blank, give 'em four more downs and they still won't score!"

It was a great win for Alabama and relieved a lot of pressure off Coach Bryant as Stagg's record was now officially tied at 314. I didn't realize how much the media's focus on the record had put pressure on Coach Bryant, but it really did. Now another open date allowed some breathing room, but in two weeks, Pat Dye, the Auburn Tigers and breaking the record were all on the line. It was only fitting that this record should be tied and broken by two top 10 teams, with the record game coming against Alabama's archrival.

A similar pattern was employed over the open-date week. Rest up, get healed, focus on the game plan, and get ready physically, mentally and spiritually to play the best game of your life. When game time came, Coach Bryant told the team they were going to use the same plan used against Penn State, to play every play like we were behind. He liked what throwing deep did in making big plays, but also making the running game more effective. Auburn also had a great defense, and it was going to be physical.

A record crowd was on hand to watch the Iron Bowl in Legion Field, half filled with Tide fans and half with Tiger fans. With both teams running the wishbone offense, the first half ended 7-7 in a defensive struggle, although Auburn missed two field goals. A Paul Ott Carruth touchdown gave Alabama a 14-7 lead in the third, and its defense was playing very well. But then the unexpected happened. Auburn punted to sure-handed Joey Jones, who fumbled when catching the punt, and it was scooped down the field inside the 10-yard line. Auburn tied the score at 14-14 a few plays later. Again, the Tigers punted and Jones bobbled the catch, giving Auburn the ball in Alabama territory again. Coach Dye chose to go for a field goal on fourth and short in the red zone.

After missing three on the afternoon, Al Del Greco nailed his fourth attempt to give the Tigers a 17-14 lead with 12 minutes to play in the fourth quarter. The Tide then pulled ahead 21-17 on a Walter Lewis pass to Jessie Bendross.

After an Auburn punt went out of bounds on the Alabama 5-yard line, Coach Moore went up to Coach Bryant and asked, "Do you still want to play like we're behind?" Coach Bryant screamed, "Hell no!" — so they went back to the conservative. They did get the ball off the goal line with a Lewis scramble. Later, a Tommy Wilcox interception, the Tide's third of the day, got the ball in Auburn territory. Lennie Patrick did the rest with two long runs, the last for a touchdown, icing the game 28-17.

Coach Bryant had broken Coach Stagg's record with 315 wins, against their archrival Auburn Tigers, coming from behind in the fourth quarter, in front of a packed Legion Field stadium and a national TV audience. At 6-0, Coach Bryant won his last SEC Championship, a co-championship with 6-0 Georgia. In the jubilant Alabama dressing room, Coach Bryant was interrupted as he was congratulating his team and coaches. Someone said, "President Reagan is holding on the phone." Coach Bryant ambled over to the phone and began with, "Hello Gipper." As a young actor, President Reagan had played George Gipp in the 1940 movie "Knute Rockne, All-American."

Following win No. 315, we were able to attract many licensees and signed some sponsorship agreements that were very lucrative. The most unusual licensing opportunity was with a company that bought basic vans and customized them. For Coach Bryant, they produced a crimson van with houndstooth seat covers and a gold commemorative coin featuring Coach Bryant's likeness mounted on the dashboard.

The best sponsorship opportunity came with a contract for TV commercials with South Central Bell. They brought a very professional crew from New York to film his commercials and would take a full four hours to shoot 30- and 60-second commercials. Ma Bell was about to break up into Baby Bells, and South Central Bell wanted to get ahead of that announcement and promote its primary services. He did several commercials for them, but the most noteworthy was his commercial promoting long-distance services.

I was present for all of the commercials. Coach Bryant was promoting long-distance services by explaining that every fall when his team came back to school for camp, he would remind them to call home and stay in touch with their Mamas and Papas. The commercial ended with the line, "Have you called your Mama today?" He had done it for more than three hours, but they wanted perfection and kept on. I was standing outside his office with the door cracked, and as he finished that take, he said, "Have you called your Mama today? I sure wish I could call mine." The producer went nuts and said, "That was great, let's do it again." So that went on for another hour!

When they left, they didn't know which version they would use. They went with the latter, and the results were phenomenal. They received more positive responses from this ad than any they had ever run. The highlight was an eight-page letter from a man who explained that he and his mother had not spoken in years. The commercial with Coach Bryant motivated him to reach out to his mom, they had a very pleasant conversation and talked for 45 minutes. As it turned out, soon after that call, the man's mother passed away. He was so grateful that he had heard the message from Coach Bryant.

Spending time with Coach Bryant was very interesting and very enjoyable for me. I knew Coach Bryant when I was a player, but players rarely talked to him unless they were in trouble. As a freshman and sophomore, I loved him and hated him on different occasions, but I always respected him, and our teams knew from the start that we were part of something special. As I became a junior and senior, my love and respect for him grew greater, and after graduation it continued to grow.

When I became coach at Tennessee, we couldn't talk very much. We chatted at SEC meetings, but always social talk and rarely about business. So working with him in this business venture allowed me to travel with him, and we talked about everything — players, coaches, Xs and Os, politics, and a lot about business. It was a thrill for me to know him on all three levels. The time he spent helping other peopled amazed me. He would make calls to Alabama fans who were ill. He helped a lot of former players, and many times, they didn't even know he had helped them. To me, that is the mark of a great man.

A funny thing happened at several board meetings when I would go pick him up. For some reason, he always seemed to talk about two things. His first question was, "Is this the $500 or $1,000 meeting?" Then he would often go into a diatribe about the Internal Revenue Service. He believed that all his issues with the IRS were due to them assigning an Auburn grad to his case. I didn't know if he had real problems or not, but I said, "Coach, you probably don't tell them enough and they are probably afraid to ask!"

One day when I was on the Alabama campus, I took him a manila envelope filled with license agreements I wanted him to approve. He was sitting at his desk. I handed him the envelope and asked if he could look it over and get it back to me when I came back next week. He said that would be no problem. The next week I called, told him I was coming the next day and needed to pick up those contracts. He said they were in his vault at the bank. I thought "Why in the world would he have put them in his vault?" I said OK, but I needed to pick them up. When I went to see him, he handed me a manila envelope and I stuck it in my briefcase. We talked for a while and I went back to Selma.

When I looked in the envelope, I was shocked. He had given me all his contracts with the University of Alabama, including back to January 1958, when his salary was $17,500. He didn't want to make more than the deans. He also received a $10,000 expense account and a home in Indian Hills. In early 1962, there was a letter to Coach Bryant from President Frank Rose after Alabama had won the 1961 National Championship that read something like this: "Dear Paul, you have brought fame and honor to the University of Alabama and have restored Alabama football to its rightful place. I appreciate you turning down a bonus, but we are giving you $5,000 anyway."

On another occasion, I asked him how much he was making on his radio and TV shows. He told me he was making $25,000. I said, "Coach, Fran Curci at Kentucky is making $50,000 on his Monday night call-in radio show." Coach Bryant replied, "Coke and Golden Flake have been with me from the start and I'm not asking them for more money." That was the end of that discussion, but it told a lot about Coach Bryant's loyalty and character.

As we got closer to the 1981 football season, the media interest in Coach Bryant's proximity to Coach Stagg's record began to explode. That helped fuel interest in more companies wanting to associate his name with their products. Many began to request permission to use Alabama's logos on Coach Bryant's merchandise. I went to the SEC and asked if we could acquire rights to all SEC universities. I was told that they could only grant rights to SEC logos, and I would have to go to each university to discuss their rights.

I went to Alabama and asked who I would need to talk to about licensing the university's marks. No one knew what I was talking about. After going to four different offices, I was about to go home. Instead I entered the assistant purchasing manager's office and met Finus Gaston. I remembered Finus from when I was a player. His dad was Alabama's sports information director and young Finus was a frequent visitor to our practices.

I asked Finus if Alabama had a trademark licensing program like the NFL. He said they did not, but they were thinking about starting one. I asked if anyone else in the country had a program and he said a few were thinking about it. I told him about our concept of putting together a Consortium of universities modeled after the NFL's centralized management of all teams. I also told him we were managing Coach Bryant's licensing efforts and it would be natural for The University of Alabama to join our program, which was already established. Finus acted as if he thought we would have a good chance of convincing UA's VP of Business & Finance of our concept.

It might help you if I describe a few types of intellectual property. A trademark includes any word, name, symbol, or device, or any combination, used, or intended to be used, in commerce to identify and distinguish the goods of one manufacturer or seller from goods manufactured or sold by others, and to indicate the source of the goods. In short, a trademark is a brand name. Trademark rights are granted by the U.S. Patent and Trademarks Office (USPTO). Common law rights are acknowledged by establishing proof of first use in commerce. Trademarks differ from other forms of intellectual property, including copyrights and patents.

A copyright is a form of protection provided by the laws of the United States (Title 17, U.S. Code) to the authors of "original works of authorship," including literary, dramatic, musical, artistic, and certain other intellectual works. This protection is available to both published and unpublished works.

A patent for an invention is the grant of a property right to the inventor, issued by the United States Patent and Trademark Office. Generally, the term of a new patent is 20 years from the date on which the application for the patent was filed in the United States. Patent grants are effective only within the U.S., U.S. territories and U.S. possessions. The right conferred by the patent grant is, in the language of the statute and of the grant itself, "the right to exclude others from making, using, offering for sale, or selling" the invention in the United States or "importing" the invention into the United States. What is granted is not the right to make, use, offer for sale, sell or import, but the right to exclude others from making, using, offering for sale, selling or importing the invention. Once a patent is issued, the patentee must enforce the patent without aid of the USPTO.

Here is a Licensed Products Sales Chain:
- Licensor = Trademark Owner (Alabama) → manages licensing program
- Licensee = Manufacturer (Nike) → sells licensed products at wholesale prices to retailer
- Retailer (Dick's Sporting Goods) → Buys from Licensees
- Consumer (You) → Buys from Retailers

And here is the monetary breakdown:
- Licensee Sells to Retailer for $10 – Retailer to Consumer for $20
- Licensor (Trademark Owner) Receives the Royalty on the $10 wholesale price
- Average Royalty Range is 6.5% to 15% ($.65 to $1.50 per unit)

COLLEGIATE LICENSING

I went back to Selma excited about the possibility of landing the University of Alabama as our first client. They would be the cornerstone of the Consortium we hoped to build. Their word-of-mouth approval to other universities, provided we did a good job for them, would be very valuable. We did land Alabama, and that initial thought proved to be true.

In discussing the concept with Larry Striplin, he was very enthusiastic, as we were starting to have some nice revenues coming in from Coach Bryant's program. I told him to get someone else to run DISCO and let me devote full time to building this business. I became president of Golden Eagle Enterprises, working closely with Eddie on building a collegiate licensing program to go with our putters and eyewear. I also became vice chairman of Circle S Industries, which added to my business education.

So how do you build a collegiate trademark licensing company from scratch when you are located in Selma, Alabama, and part of a construction materials/putter company? You do it with a vision, a plan, as much knowledge as you can muster, a lot of hard work, good timing in the marketplace, relentless focus on the mission, and a lot of luck.

The timing was perfect. To put things in perspective, the overall market for all licensed products in 1980 was $9.9 billion in retail sales according to *The Licensing Letter*. The market was projected to grow to $50 to $75 billion by 1990. In fact, the market grew to $66.5 billion. Collegiate sales in 1980, by my estimate, were about $250 million. Virtually all sales came from college bookstores located on and just off campus. I knew that the passion created by sports, mainly football and basketball, would extend the market for collegiate products far beyond college campus cities and towns.

While licensing was still embryonic in the overall marketplace, it was pretty much unknown on college campuses. We had learned a lot about licensing as a licensee with Golden Bear/Nicklaus, Disney and IMG. We had also learned about licensing from a licensor's perspective from managing Coach Bryant's licensing program. My visit with Frank Vuono, head of the NFL's licensing program, enabled me to clearly see how the NFL model, centralized management of its 28 teams at the time, would be a perfect fit for colleges and universities. Later I spent time and became friends with Rick White, president of MLB Properties. I learned a great deal from Rick as well.

I was confident that if we could get 50 of the right universities in a Consortium, all pulling in the same direction with regard to trademark licensing, that it could rival the professional leagues in licensed merchandise sold. I recognized that we couldn't use names and likenesses of players due to NCAA restrictions, but I believed that we could create a major new stream of revenues for universities, and at the same time, protect their intellectual property and build and expand their brand equity.

Do you understand the power of licensing? Think about this: The Coca-Cola Company has done a masterful job of licensing. It has very carefully managed its program to protect its already prominent brand, and in the process created a significant revenue stream for the company. It was able to attract very strong manufacturing companies in many different categories of products that sold to many different retail distribution channels. Then, Coke was able to convince those companies to use their own money to develop a marketing plan with products, designs and distribution, all approved by Coke. In most cases, Coke was able to negotiate an 8 to 15 percent royalty on all sales, often receiving a considerable upfront payment, and always a substantial financial guarantee.

Now let's take the apparel category for example. Can you imagine the Coca-Cola Company getting all of the above from another manufacturing company, and at the same time having that company put the Coca-Cola brands on quality merchandise, and selling into national and international markets? They were able to get people of all ages, races and religions to wear t-shirts, sweatshirts, jackets and caps with various Coca-Cola images. They literally created walking billboards to support the brands and the image of the company — and were paid a lot of money!

Centralized management of 50 universities described above would eliminate duplication of effort, minimize expenses, maximize revenues, and create a powerful marketing and enforcement force. It would also save licensees time, effort and money in not having to go to 50 different universities for license agreements, royalty reporting procedures, etc.

The only problem was that universities typically believe they can do anything better than anyone else, if they choose to take it on. So the big question was, "Can this company in Selma, Alabama, get universities to join our Consortium?"

The good news for us was that these university vice presidents of Business & Finance didn't believe there was a lot of money in licensing. In their view, the bookstores weren't making money and they were marking up products at 100 percent of the wholesale price, known as a keystone mark-up. How could anyone make money charging 6 1/2 percent of wholesale prices? I knew the answer to that one.

My contacts with universities at the time were primarily with athletics departments. I saw a major stumbling block: bookstore managers, as they enjoyed the exclusivity of being the only place university merchandise was sold. They also were concerned that someone other than them would be involved in the approval process, and they definitely didn't like a 6 1/2 percent royalty added to wholesale prices.

We decided we needed to convince VPs of Business & Finance that in our model, everyone in the chain would win, even the bookstores. We needed the bookstores, Athletics Departments and alumni associations to buy into the concept that every item with collegiate marks that was offered for re-sale or used in conjunction with a promotional offer would require being bought from licensees.

We spent a tremendous amount of time studying the licensing plans of the professional leagues, Jack Nicklaus/Golden Bear, Disney and IMG. We learned a lot about licensing by representing Coach Bryant.

I believed the greatest assets that I possessed in building the company was the knowledge, reputation and relationships that I had built growing up on a college campus and over my 14 years as a college football coach. I knew how college administrators thought, I had some relationships and credibility in the world of college athletics, and I believed the model we had created could be sold to university administrators if they were willing to listen.

The business education and experience I gained during my six years in Selma were extremely valuable. I took a half-day seminar put on by the Small Business Association (SBA) on "How to Develop a Business Plan." It was both timely and valuable as it laid out the questions I needed to answer to get the business off the ground.

Mission

Our Mission is to be the guiding force in collegiate trademark licensing and one of the top sports licensing firms in the country. As such, we dedicate ourselves to being a center of excellence in providing licensing services of the highest quality to our member institutions, our licensees, our retailers, and our consumers.

Strategic Plan

Our Strategic Plan in 1982-83 consisted of six basic elements:

1. To build a strong Consortium of colleges and universities.
2. To build a strong base of licensees that could cover all potential market segments with a wide variety of acceptable products.
3. To identify and work with retailers to encourage them to promote and sell Officially Licensed Collegiate Products (OLCP).
4. To identify and teach consumers the value of buying OLCP.
5. To establish an enforcement program to protect the rights of universities and create a level playing field for licensees.

6. To establish marketing programs to help develop 1-4 above and to take advantage of the synergy of the group.

In 1984 we added a seventh element:

7. To develop internal administrative systems and a database to provide critical management information to CLC staff and unparalleled services to colleges, universities and licensees.

We tried to work on all seven at the same time, but it was obvious we had to add universities before we could add licensees, etc. We did try to make progress every quarter in all seven goals.

To be successful, everyone in the chain needed to win. It was important that licensees and retailers needed to make money or they wouldn't manufacture and sell university merchandise. The ultimate judge was the consumer, who needed to be happy with the product, design and cost. If those things happened, the university would make money and so would our company. While the universities were our ultimate bosses, we had to make sure that licensees and retailers were treated fairly — in good times and bad. We were fortunate that we were able to create long-term successful partnerships with all four in the chain.

The pitch we made to universities was as follows: If 50 universities had an independent licensing program administered in-house, they would need at least two people running the program. Let's say the director made $25,000 and the administrative assistant made $15,000 (remember, this was 1981). That added up to $40,000, and multiplied by 50 universities, equaled $2 million. At each university, those two individuals would spend the bulk of their time signing license agreements, approving designs and products, and maybe doing a little local marketing and enforcement. If the universities bought into our system, they would spend the majority of their time utilizing our staff and resources. We told the schools our entire staff was at their disposal, and they didn't need to worry about adding office space or benefits.

That concept would create a nightmare for licensees, as every university attorney would require a different license agreement. Dealing with one entity for all 50 universities in one license agreement for product approval, royalty collection, etc., would enable the Consortium to attract and manage licensees much more efficiently. And with $2 million annually and 50 universities all pulling in the same direction, we could create a powerful force in the marketplace and provide broad services in administration, marketing, enforcement, auditing, legal and PR for all 50 universities. It actually made too much sense for most to resist.

We also agreed to keep each university in control by allowing them to approve all products, designs, licensees and significant actions by our company that related to their institution. On the financial side, I wasn't worried about making them enough money. I was more concerned about making them too much money. I was concerned if we paid them a lot of money, someone in the university that didn't understand the dynamics might think we were making more money than we deserved and decide to take the program in-house. To combat that, we presented them with contracts that had a sliding scale that grew in their favor as revenues rose.

As an example, our first contracts were for three-year terms and gave them 60 percent of all royalties collected on their behalf. Remember, our only source of revenue was a percentage of royalties, and we had the upfront costs in setting up the infrastructure to manage the program. Universities had no financial risk. By the time our initial contracts were in the third year, some schools were generating $100,000 to $150,000 a year. Our next contracts were for five years and offered, on an annual basis, 60 percent of the first $50,000, 67 percent of the next $50,000, and 75 percent of all over $100,000. As universities began to make the million dollar a year range, they averaged receiving 85 to 90 percent of their gross royalties.

We wanted them to: (1) be our partners in helping us grow their program; (2) encourage them not to keep "special projects" that came their way outside our program; and (3) fully understand that for our fee, they couldn't administer their program nearly as well as we could together. That concept was agreeable to universities and it allowed us to present the same contracts to all schools, big and small.

In serving our universities, I required two major services that many on our staff hated, but I believed were essential to providing great customer service:

We gave approval rights to the university on every product and design. I could see a university president or high-ranking official seeing something in the marketplace he or she didn't like. I wanted someone's name from the university on an approval form authorizing us to license and market that product and design. It created much more work for our staff, but was vital in making the universities happy and protecting their brands.

We provided each university with very detailed quarterly reports. We did this for two reasons. I wanted our University Service Representatives (our client account managers) to treat every client as if it were our most important. Therefore, each client deserved to know specifically what we were doing for them every quarter. Of greater importance, I wanted our staff thinking and planning ahead as to what we were going to do for them in future quarters. That also encouraged our staff to form great relationships with the bookstore manager, the university licensing director and, if possible, the athletics director, the alumni director, the general counsel, and anyone else in the chain involved in collegiate sales. The reports over time got pretty thick. Our staff complained that they were so big the university licensing directors didn't read them. My response was when a change in direction at a university occurs, someone above the licensing director comes in and asks why they are paying us that much money, and I wanted to be able to show them documented files on what we were doing for them.

The best time to send the reports was at the same time we sent their quarterly royalty checks. We thought the checks would get their attention, hopefully bring a smile to their faces, and encourage them to read about what we had done for them individually and as a Consortium. We encouraged them to send copies to their bosses, as well as everyone in the licensing chain at the university. A side benefit to those quarterly reports occurred when I found them recently in an old storage box. They added much more to the depth and accuracy of this section of the book than I could have ever called from memory.

My challenge to our staff was, "Our business is based on building long-term relationships with all clients. The first and most important part of that building process is understanding what our clients expect, and exceeding their expectations with a customer service mentality."

1981-1983

In 1981, we signed our first agency agreement with the University of Alabama. Dr. Finus Gaston was assigned to manage the licensing program for UA. Alabama had a national trademark law firm in Washington, D.C., named Baker and Hostetler. Dave Kera, a former judge, was the manager of the Alabama account. Between Dave, Finus and me, we developed an agency agreement between Alabama and Golden Eagle Enterprises, and a license agreement for manufacturers to become licensees. I was able to use those contracts as models to sign more universities and licensees.

I had reached out to all SEC and Atlantic Coast Conference universities. Dr. Mary Ann Connell, general counsel at Ole Miss, responded very quickly and the University of Mississippi came on board in early 1982. Bill McClellan, athletics director at Clemson, fully understood what we were trying to do and got me an appearance at an ACC athletics director's meeting. He introduced me and told them that if any of them were thinking about starting a licensing program, they should all do it together.

Also in 1981, Clemson won the National Championship in football. Danny Ford, an Alabama graduate, had become the Tigers' head football coach in

1978 when Charley Pell, a teammate on our 1959-62 teams at Alabama, left Clemson to take the Florida head coaching job. You may remember the Gator Bowl game that year between Clemson and Ohio State that clinched the title for the Tigers. Toward the end of the game, with victory out of reach for the Buckeyes, a Clemson player intercepted an Ohio State pass and was tackled in front of the OSU bench. OSU Head Coach Woody Hayes was outraged about the defeat, lost his temper, grabbed the Clemson player and punched him. The next day, Ohio State fired Hayes, which was a very sad way for the legendary coach to end a great career.

A few days after the game, McClellan called me and said, "We have Tiger paws coming out our ears over here on every kind of product you can think of. When can you come help us?" I replied, "Today" and sent a team over that day.

Our team in Selma from January 1981-83 consisted of Rita Smith, my administrative assistant; Barry White, a young marketing major fresh out of the University of Alabama-Birmingham (UAB); my son Pat; Henry Pitts, a local Selma attorney; my wife Eugenia; and me. Sometime in 1982 or early 1983, Pat was working for us at Golden Eagle Enterprises, while deciding where to go to college after an unsuccessful first year at Alabama. During that year, Alabama decided to replace its AstroTurf field. In taking off the turf, they rolled it in balls from one sideline to the other. It was cemented to asphalt, so in taking it up, there were big chunks of asphalt attached. When I saw what they were doing, I went to Finus and asked how much it would cost to buy all that AstroTurf. I thought about the number of All-American players and famous coaches that had performed there. It had a rich history, as Coach Bryant and his staff's record on that turf was incredible. I envisioned cutting it in pieces, mounting it on wood or something, and preparing a letter of authenticity that told the historical highlights.

The buying price was something like $2,500, but we had to haul it off. They really should have paid me $2,500 to haul it off and dispose of its remains! It probably cost us more than $2,500 to move it to Selma because it was rain-soaked, and the extra chunks of asphalt made it much heavier and more difficult to cut into pieces.

I gave Pat the responsibility of managing the move, storage, the resulting products, and the sale. He soon figured out that the process of cutting and mounting it would not only be expensive, but in Selma, in the peak of the summer heat, it wasn't a very pleasant task. He convinced me that we should sell the whole thing. I had imagined big dollars in cutting it up and selling it in pieces, but also realized it cost time and labor every time it was cut and mounted. I left town one week and when I returned, Mike met me and told me Pat had sold the turf and was scared to tell me the number. When I saw Pat, I made certain my body language would be positive whatever the price. When he told me he had sold it for $24,000, I congratulated him, hugged him and back-slapped him. It was actually a great price and one of the best sales jobs he ever made — other than selling Alice Ann on marrying him!

In 1981, Ronald Reagan was president of the United States and George H.W. Bush was vice president. The Dow ranged from 824-1,024, the minimum wage was $3.35, the average income was $21,073, a new car cost $7,718, a new house cost $78,220, a loaf of bread was 53 cents, a gallon of milk was $2.23, a gallon of gas was $1.31, and gold was $460 an ounce. Indiana, under Coach Bob Knight, won the NCAA Basketball Championship, Marcus Allen from USC won the Heisman Trophy, and Paul W. Bryant became the all-time winningest coach in college football history with a victory over the Auburn Tigers.

By 1983, colleges and universities were moving from "thinking about trademark licensing" to "getting started." The competition to our company at the time was Steve Crossland (ICE), who ran the Bookstore at the University of Southern California, as well as those universities that decided to keep licensing all in-house.

Steve actually started his licensing program before we did. He was running the USC Bookstore and had been getting letters from manufacturers wanting to get licensed to put USC logos on various products. He said he had been throwing them away, but started thinking about getting USC to start a program and wondered if he couldn't get other schools to do the same thing. Steve later told me that at a cocktail party one night he met a trademark lawyer and the attorney encouraged Steve to start a licensing program.

Steve went to his boss and asked if he could start a licensing program at USC, and also see if he could get other universities to join. Steve said his boss told him to go ahead and further said, "My boss felt if I made money outside the university that would mean less he would have to pay me." Steve learned the business about like I did, by trial and error. He formed a family corporation, International Collegiate Enterprises (ICE), and started going around the country to speak to universities about joining his team. I attended one of his speeches and thought his model was good, but I thought our model was better. Although Southern Cal elected to remain independent, Steve signed Michigan and Ohio State, which was huge. Don Canham, the athletics director at Michigan, was known as a marketing genius and introduced advanced marketing concepts to other collegiate ADs. His blessing of a Consortium approach to licensing was a great accomplishment on Steve's part.

When I was in college, most of my teammates were from small towns and grew up hunting with their dads or older siblings. I went fishing a lot with my dad, but he wasn't a big hunter and I only went with him a few times. At Alabama, I heard a lot about hunting doves, deer and turkeys. It was curious to me that people might enjoy turkey hunting, because it didn't sound all that much fun to get up at 4 in the morning, dress up like a bush, sit still for two hours and try to sound like a female turkey to attract a gobbler within shotgun shooting distance when the gobbler expected the hens to come to him. That sounded to me like it was reversing nature. I was told, "don't ever start, you can't quit!" I said, "Yeah, right!"

In Selma, one could go out early, try to call a gobbler off the roost, and be back in the office by 8:30 or 9 a.m. I got invited by two older gentlemen who were really good turkey hunters, Frank Wilson, the president of Peoples Bank, and Green Suttles, who owned the marina. On the first day, Frank called in a turkey gobbler, and after a long conversation of turkey talk, he came within range. The experience was so cool, it made my heart pound. I aimed and when Frank said "shoot," I pulled the trigger. The turkey was only about 30 steps away but had turned away from me and lowered his head. After I shot, he spread his wings and took off flying. I was too stunned to pull the trigger again and fire the other two shells in my automatic shotgun. I asked, "How could I miss a target so big and so close?" Frank said, "You have to shoot them in the head, because their feathers are so thick and skin so tough, they can withstand body shots much of the time." I said, "This is fun, how do I learn how to call?" Frank said, "Go down to Walter Craig Sporting Goods and buy a mouth call and a Ben Rodgers Lee tape." I did and started trying to make noises like I heard on the tape and like I heard Frank making on our hunt.

When I saw Frank a few weeks later I asked, "Who is the Ben Rodgers Lee guy? He's the funniest guy I ever heard. He reminds me of Jerry Clower." Frank said, "Ben's a janitor at the Ciba Geigy Chemical plant in Coffeeville, Alabama." Frank went on to tell me that Ben had won several national turkey calling championships over the years. He made his own turkey calls and started to sell them at trade shows where he participated in contests and spoke as a celebrity turkey hunter. After a while he started making more selling his calls than his salary as a janitor so he went full time into the call business.

I kept on practicing my calling and went a few more times with Frank and Green, and actually killed a couple of turkeys that spring that Frank called in. Wild turkeys aren't as good to eat as store-bought Butterball turkeys, but I thought they tasted pretty good when cooked in a smoker. Even if I'd never seen or heard a turkey on those trips, the stories to and from the hunts were well worth getting up so early in the morning. Frank and Green were long-time turkey hunters and pretty much went every day of the season, which lasted four to six weeks. They had a myriad of stories and never told the same one twice.

As fate would have it, one day, about five or six months later, my secretary buzzed me and said, "Ben Rodgers Lee is here to see you." I said, "Well, send him in." Ben entered the room, a larger-than-life man, literally weighing about 400 pounds. We chitchatted a bit and finally I asked, "What brings you to Selma?" Ben said, "I've been hearing about what you are doing for Coach Bryant and I need somebody to do something for me." I said, "I'll do something for you if you will teach me to call turkeys." Ben said, "If you've got me, you don't need to learn how to call turkeys."

We developed a business relationship and a friendship that lasted only a few short years before Ben tragically died in an automobile accident. There are a lot of great stories to be told about Ben's antics over the years. It was a sad day in my life when Ben passed away. I never did get to hunt with Ben, but in the process with Frank, Green and Ben, I did get addicted to turkey hunting.

The Pony shoe involvement came about with our Selma attorney, Henry Pitts, telling me that Pony was paying his client, Kenny Stabler, who was playing with the Oakland Raiders, a lot of money to wear their brand of shoes. He suggested we ask them what they might pay to Coach Bryant. We followed up and went to New York to meet with them. They said if Coach Bryant would put Pony shoes on his team, they would pay him $25,000 a year and give most of the team free shoes. I took the offer to Coach Bryant and he strongly considered it but decided not to accept. At the time, Alabama was wearing Nike shoes, and Nike was paying the trainer and equipment manager a few thousand a year. Coach Jim Goostree, who was our trainer when I was in school, got mad at me, but I think I got back in his good graces before he passed away. He is a legendary figure in Alabama Athletics history.

After that missed opportunity, Pony offered me a consulting position. I asked, "So you want me to go to college coaches and tell them we'll pay them money and give free shoes to their teams if they wear our shoes?" They said, "That's right." I said, "I can help you!" I did get several schools interested that probably helped make Nike step up their game, as they started paying coaches hundreds of thousands of dollars to wear Nike shoes. I was able to convince several coaches to get their teams to wear Pony shoes, and that generated income to me for as long as they wore them. The income was great, as it took three years for our licensing company to become profitable. Those dollars helped a lot.

By June 1983, we had signed Clemson, North Carolina, North Carolina State, Duke, Wake Forest, Georgia Tech and Maryland, in addition to

Alabama and Ole Miss. I bought out the rights to what we had started in Collegiate Licensing and Sports Management (Coach Bryant). I had also signed Ben Rodgers Lee to a management contract, and was representing Pony athletic shoes, helping them give away shoes and pay college coaches to put them on their players. Coach Bryant had passed away in early 1983, but there were still some of his contracts that were winding down. I formed Collegiate Concepts, Inc. (CCI) to handle collegiate business and Battle Enterprises, Inc. (BEI) to handle sports management and non-collegiate clients.

Later in 1983 I made contact with Steve Crossland, met his wife Jean, son Steven and daughter Tina. What I saw in the collegiate marketplace at the time was a very delicate balance in choices available to university administrators. They could choose to sign with Steve at ICE, with us at CCI, or run their programs in-house. I thought if Steve and I could get our acts together, that we could offer universities a company with significant infrastructure for a start-up. We would have offices on East Coast and West Coast time zones and a combined staff of 12 to 15 people that would grow as universities and licensees were added. Of greater importance, their number of choices would be reduced to either joining our fast-growing Consortium of universities or starting their program in-house.

Steve and I were very different in personality and philosophy, but we were both honorable people and both planned to make our families a significant part of our businesses. We believed correctly that we could go farther and faster together if we could agree on our mission and strategic plan. Every partnership of more than one person is a challenge, and ours was as well, but the opportunity ahead of us was so great that we were able to work together very effectively.

When we decided to merge our companies in June 1983, together we had about 25 universities. Our (CCI) lead universities were Alabama, North Carolina and Clemson. Steve (ICE) had signed Michigan, Ohio State, Illinois and Florida State. By the end of 1984, we had more than 50 universities between us. We called our new company CCI/ICE — The Collegiate Licensing Company.

In our merger arrangement we pooled all revenues, which we shared on a 50-50 basis. We were responsible for our own expenses. We had Price Waterhouse, a Big Eight accounting firm, auditing our respective books, and had close relationships with Baker and Hostetler, a national trademark licensing law firm in Washington, D.C. Our finances were very transparent to universities and we invited them to audit our books. The few that did were very impressed with our operation and went back home telling university leaders there was no way they could do what we were doing for the price we were charging.

Steve left USC in 1982 and took up offices in Woodland Hills, California. Our intention was to move to Atlanta in the summer of 1983, but with the merger and the growth of our business, we put off moving to Atlanta until January 1984, which allowed Mike and Shannon to start school there at mid-term. Pat was already there at Kennesaw State University just north of Atlanta.

Our offices in Atlanta were 1,900 square feet, and when we started, there was a lot of empty space. Our staff consisted of Barry White, Eugenia, Pat (on a part-time basis) and me. We quickly hired Lisa Kronovet, a recent Business Administration graduate from the University of Florida, and a secretary.

We attacked the collegiate marketplace from both offices, telling our story to whomever would listen. Trademark licensing was indeed in need of an education to universities, licensees, retailers and consumers since the licensed products industry was so new. Our first and most important needs were to get universities to sign with CCI/ICE — The Collegiate Licensing Company. It was extremely important that we do our best to get university administrators to understand what we were trying to do, and to get all parties within the universities to agree to purchases intended for resale only from official licensees.

The bookstores, where most of the collegiate merchandise was sold, were not very happy for the most part. That is actually an understatement, as some resisted vigorously. At this time, university bookstores were independently run by the schools. Depending on how strong the bookstores were, the managers were able to assert more influence, and many tried to get their administration to exempt royalties on all sales made directly by the university. The vendors who sold to the bookstores were also very resistant to licensing and fought us in the early years.

Our argument against exceptions was that licensees didn't particularly like to go through this licensing process anyway, including submitting products, designs and distribution channels for approval, and paying royalties on all sales. The more exceptions we gave them, we felt the more mistakes they would make, and we didn't believe they would be in our favor. I also believed there were potential anti-trust issues if the university bookstores were buying logoed merchandise at more favorable prices than other non-university affiliated bookstores in the same city or state. We were able to convince most to avoid making exceptions, and over the years, we were able to get most all universities on board. As Barnes & Noble and Follett began to consolidate management of most all university bookstores under outsourced partnerships, they were not interested in exemptions. Our argument to potential licensees was that licensing was coming, they wouldn't resist licensing with the NFL and they would be far better off working through our company than they would dealing with 50 different university attorneys. We further told them that in our licensing model, everyone in the chain would win. The losers would be those who declined to get licensed.

Dealing with universities wasn't "a piece of cake," to say the least. As mentioned earlier, universities were very reluctant to sign exclusive licenses and didn't want the "town and gown" issues of complaints from local manufacturers and retailers that CCI/ICE — CLC was charging too much money for a license, or wouldn't grant them a license. Someone from the NFL once said to me, "Most licensors start licensing programs to protect their marks and make money. It seems to me universities are starting their programs to protect their marks and not make waves!" That was a pretty good assessment. In the grand scheme of a university's budget, athletics was a very small piece and they didn't want a call to the VP of Business from a little old lady telling them she had been selling university logoed hot-pan holders for years and now we were telling her she had to pay to continue!

Making it easy and inexpensive to get licensed wasn't the normal way one would start a licensing program, but there were some very positive outcomes in that strategy. Since most universities had not registered their logos with the U.S. Patent and Trademark Office, getting licensees to sign an agreement acknowledging the university's ownership in all of its marks was very beneficial to the university as it formally began to protect and manage their use in commerce. Since the retail distribution channels were virtually empty of collegiate merchandise, getting more companies licensed and calling on retailers with a diverse mix of products and designs was very good — up to a point. Many manufacturers learned about licensing through our collegiate program, and went on to be major licensees with the professional leagues and other properties. Two notable examples are Nutmeg Mills and The Game Sports Novelties.

Marty Jacobson and his brother Dick had sold a family business unrelated to apparel or licensing in the Midwest a few years earlier. They retired at early ages to Tampa, Florida, to play golf and take it easy. They soon bought a company called Nutmeg Mills that manufactured apparel for young women. Marty was the marketing force in the new company and Dick was the financial/operations force. Being sports fans, they began to produce sports apparel and made a deal with the University of Florida Athletics Department to supply logoed caps, tees and fleece to their football stadium store. At the time, Florida ran its own licensing program, as the few suppliers to university bookstores produced merchandise with very bland designs and fashion looks. Nutmeg came up with fashion-forward designs and different logo applications. The merchandise at Florida sold very well, so they started to offer their products to other retailers in the area. They soon learned that licensing was a requirement to get rights to other properties. They went to the NFL, NBA and MLB, none of whom were interested in adding start-up companies to their apparel categories.

Marty called me, and after a short conversation, summed up the call and said, "You mean I can come to Atlanta and get the rights to your 50 universities and it only costs $1,500?" I said, "That's right." He said, "I'll be up there Thursday afternoon." Sure enough, he came up Thursday, laid out an array of beautifully made caps, tees and fleece. At the end of the day, he was licensed, and upon leaving he said, "What you are doing is great. The professional leagues won't give me the time of day. In five years we'll be your No. 1 licensee."

Marty made deals with J.C. Penney and Foot Locker, among others, and soon began to send in big royalty checks. He continued to sing our praises, as he in fact did become our No. 1 licensee by 1990. He was so successful, in fact, that he also became licensed with all four leagues and one of their top licensees. After that, Marty saw that the college marketplace was far more overlicensed than the professional leagues, and from then on every time he saw me he said, "You're screwing up the whole licensed market by licensing so many people!" My reply was, "You wouldn't be where you are today if we hadn't granted you a license!" That was all in fun of course, and Nutmeg remained a top collegiate licensee for years. In fact, today, the original warehouse and printing facilities that were set up as the foundation of Nutmeg Mills is still occupied by Fanatics Brands, the apparel manufacturing arm for Fanatics, which is now the world's largest retailer of sports licensed merchandise.

The other example was Neil Stillwell. After dropping out of college, he started Neil's Sports Shops, a sporting goods retailer in Columbus, Georgia. Neil was a great salesman and entrepreneur. He pretended to be an "ol' country boy" who wasn't very smart, but he was smart like a fox. He hustled around the community selling sports gear to Fort Benning, and got into Auburn University before licensing had started.

John Burgess was Auburn's chief financial officer and developed a liking to Neil. He gave him a contract to sell his merchandise at Auburn's football stadium. He was very successful there, and later got concession contracts at Alabama, Florida, Florida State, Clemson and Southern Mississippi. He paid those universities a 25 percent commission on retail prices of items sold in their stadiums.

Neil had to order caps from other manufacturers and soon became disenchanted with the long lead-time required, as well as the high prices. The entrepreneur in him came out and he researched the overseas market and took a trip to Taiwan. There he met with the company that manufactured for Nike, the New York Yankees and others. He bought some of the first embroidered caps in this country, but had to buy 500 dozen per style, per color. He bought at least four styles of caps for every school. On the plane ride home, he totaled up his orders and figured out he had ordered 2,000 dozen caps for each school, in addition to a lot of other stuff because it was so cheap. He thought, "Oh my God, Neil, you have gone absolutely crazy." When he got home he went to his banker and convinced him that he could manage the debt. Then he went to the football coaches at those schools, starting with Pat Dye at Auburn. He paid them to wear the style he was selling, and would change the style every few games.

Next he convinced his brother Phil to leave Nike and come to work for him. Neil was bringing in great-looking caps at $2 each and selling them in football stadiums and in his Sports Shops for $15. He started selling them wholesale to retailers for $5 and telling them he was retailing them for $15, which made the sales pretty easy.

Neil started selling to Auburn before licensing started, and his new friend, John Burgess, when licensing did start at Auburn, didn't require him to sign a license agreement in addition to his concession agreement. Finus Gaston, the licensing director at Alabama, did make him sign a license with us.

After the first season, although he was required by our agreement to report and pay royalties monthly on all sales, we had not heard from Neil. I called Neil and told him we needed to get his royalty reports ASAP as I knew he had sold a lot of merchandise at Alabama football games. Neil responded in his slow southern drawl, "Mistah Battle, I promise I ain't trying to cheat you, I just don't understand this s** t! You can send someone ovah heah and help me figure it out and I'll pay you?" Obviously, Neil hadn't thought about our agreement for a minute after he signed it. That wasn't unusual in the early days.

We sent Barry White, our new young marketing major grad from UAB to work with Neil, go over his invoices and calculate what he owed to our schools. Later, as our universities grew in numbers and licensing got a little more attention from licensees, Neil invited me over to speak to his staff and help educate them about the requirements. Neil grew rapidly and soon sold to the W.C. Bradley Company in Columbus, Georgia, and Chris Martin was assigned to oversee Neil's new company, The Game Sports Novelties. The Bradley Company had its act together and had built accounting systems to properly track the royalties. With Chris Martin's oversight and Neil's sales ability, The Game Sports Novelties, much like Nutmeg Mills, grew from knowing little about licensing to being our No. 1 licensee in a short period of time. They, too, became licensed with the four professional leagues, plus the Olympics, NASCAR and others. Neil and the Jacobson brothers are each inductees in the National Sporting Goods Association (NSGA) Hall of Fame.

LESSONS LEARNED

- Changing careers is both challenging and exciting. It generally means taking a few steps backward, both in stature and in pay.
- The future is built on the knowledge and relationships you have built, the credibility in each you have attained, and your ability to use each to accomplish your goals.
- Lessons learned growing up, playing and coaching football, all came into play when I entered the business world.
- Learn everything possible in the new career about the organization, the market, and what makes the new company tick.
- One of the great aspects of leadership is to identify those with the "IT" factor who can rise to the occasion when the going gets tough. It's even better to have "IT" yourself.
- As success is a journey and not a destination, so are employee compensation systems. From a morale standpoint, there is nothing more important than getting and keeping compensation systems right.
- There is push-pull in people and departments within organizations up to a point. Leadership's challenge is to stimulate some conflict, but manage it to improve all areas of the organization.
- Success breeds success, but it also creates a different set of issues that must be managed.
- If you ever need to sell something, take it to a good salesman. Not only do they get fired up when trying to sell you something, they also get fired up if they like your product, service or presentation, and if they like it enough, they may buy your whole company.
- The Boss ain't always right, but he's always the Boss! If you can't believe in his vision, you and the company are better off if you go elsewhere.
- How do you start a business? You do it with a vision, a plan, as much knowledge as you can muster, good timing in the marketplace, relentless focus on the mission, and a lot of good luck.

CONGRATULATIONS — Disco Chairman of the Board Larry Striplin, left, and Coach Paul "Bear" Bryant, right, congratulate Bill Battle, who today was named president and chief operations officer of Disco Aluminum Products Co. of Selma. (Photo by Jackie Walburn)

Battle is named Disco president, top officer

> *Coach Bryant shakes my hand after I was named President and Chief Operating Officer of Larry Striplin's DISCO Aluminum Products.*

Joining me for the dedication of the Bill Battle Academic Center were Dr. Finus Gaston, Mal Moore and Paul Bryant Jr.

CHAPTER 6

THE COLLEGIATE LICENSING COMPANY

This chapter is an overview of the decade following the CCI/ICE merger. From 1983 to 1992, there was tremendous growth. It started like a snowball rolling downhill, picking up speed and size as it went. By the time it reached the bottom of the hill, it was massive, but when it slowed down, it stopped growing in size.

1983-1984

In 1983, the *Pittsburgh v. Champion* case presented the first major legal challenge to collegiate trademark licensing. The University of Pittsburgh sued bookstore supplier Champion Products after the company refused to sign a license agreement. The court held that Pitt's 45-year delay in bringing a trademark infringement action did not prevent Pitt from protecting its marks going forward. The court found that Champion was "exploiting Pitt's popularity and consumer's desire to identify with the university by purchasing merchandise with Pittsburgh's marks." The parties settled out of court, but Champion did sign a license agreement with Pitt, and this case paved the way legally for collegiate licensing to take off.

On the licensing front, our staff worked hard in trying to get current suppliers to college bookstores of logoed products to sign license agreements. Those companies were Artex, Velva Sheen, Russell, Chalk Line, Angelus Pacific, Delong Sportswear and College House. Interestingly, Artex and Velva Sheen bought blank goods from Russell and, as screen printers, added designs and sold them to college stores under their respective brands. As a result, much of the apparel products in university bookstores was manufactured by Russell, but the Russell brand had only a small presence.

Manufacturers in general were balking at this new concept of licensing. We were called many things in those days. We heard that we couldn't do what we were trying to do at a public university and charge taxpayers. Our answer was always the same, "Licensing is coming. You wouldn't produce NFL or MLB products without a license, and you'd be much better off working with a company like ours dealing with one entity as opposed to 50 different university programs."

The North Carolina State University basketball team, coached by Jim Valvano, beat the heavily favored Houston Cougars to win the 1983 NCAA Men's Championship. Coupled with the Clemson's National Championship in football in 1981, we were forced to learn about "hot markets" and the challenge and opportunities that went with them. Not only did those two championships provide a significant boost to our royalties in those markets, they greatly enhanced our staff's learning curve in another facet of the collegiate licensing business. That knowledge would prove valuable to plan and manage hot markets in the future. Miami won the 1983 National Championship in football, with Nebraska, Auburn, Georgia and Texas finishing No. 2 through 5 in the AP Poll.

Before our merger with Steve's company, CCI signed Alabama, Ole Miss and seven of the eight Atlantic Coast Conference universities. It is interesting to note that Auburn and Virginia signed with ICE, out of California. I believe that Auburn did not want to go with the same company that managed Alabama. Virginia was a little different in that the bookstore manager asserted a very strong voice in the conduct of the UVA licensing program and I think he thought he could relate better to a former bookstore manager than a former football coach. After the merger, Steve and I decided to divide universities to be managed by our respective offices on an east/west basis, so Auburn and Virginia had to work with our offices anyway! It was no problem, as we worked very well with both universities. We were able to convince competitive universities like Alabama-Auburn and South Carolina-Clemson that we could really help both in getting their merchandise licensed by manufacturers and sold all over the state and region. We knew there were Alabama fans all around Opelika and Auburn fans all around Tuscaloosa. We encouraged licensees and retailers to put both in their stores — and it worked.

On the retail front, we continued to build relationships with bookstore managers and local retailers in the university communities. We published our first *Buyers Guide*, which was distributed widely to educate retailers that collegiate licensing was coming and to promote those licensees who were on board with getting licensed.

We developed the Officially Licensed Collegiate Products (OLCP) label to help consumers identify merchandise authorized by their favorite schools and represented the goodwill of those institutions. Manufacturers balked at this, too, as they complained that adding labels was an additional expense. Developing the label and forcing its use on all of our schools' products was one of the best things we ever did. Over the years, the OLCP Label became almost as valuable as some of the properties we represented as a symbol of quality and authenticity.

On the legal front, the Trademark Counterfeiting Act was passed in 1984. It provided an effective statutory framework for lawsuits involving counterfeit products. In addition, the TCA proved to be a valuable tool for trademark owners in light of the reluctance of federal law enforcement agencies to become active in cases in this new arena. The feds would get involved occasionally, if the counterfeiting operations were huge, but they were much more concerned with products that threatened public health and safety, or valuable U.S. technology. Over the years, we worked hard at encouraging state and federal agencies to consider that counterfeiting of trademarks was a major problem. We also worked to strengthen all anti-counterfeiting laws and develop new ones. Over time, we developed a growing relationship with the U.S. Customs Office to give us notice if identifiable counterfeit merchandise was coming in from overseas.

In the early years we asked licensing directors to help us with local enforcement and marketing efforts, and we would handle the rest. If there were major rivalry football games on campuses or other events, we would come in and lead the charge. Our biggest source of information on infringement was from our licensees. If they lost a bid or a job, they would call to make sure that company was licensed. We followed up on all leads and signed many companies in the process. Much of the game-day infringement was from small "mom and pop" companies, and even student entrepreneurs who hooked up with a local screen printer and sold game-day t-shirts. We saw it all.

CCI/ICE started with 25 universities in June 1983, but by the end of 1984, we had agency agreements with 51. Our top 10 selling universities in 1983-84 were Alabama, Michigan, North Carolina, Ohio State, Illinois, N.C. State, Clemson, Ole Miss, Auburn and Virginia. We were ecstatic that our top two universities each exceeded $100,000 in gross royalties. The retail sales in North America in 1983-84, according to *The Licensing Letter*, was $40.1 billion. Our estimate of collegiate retail sales was about $400 million.

1984-1985

In 1984-85 fiscal year, we signed 11 more universities, including Georgetown, Vanderbilt and Montana, bringing the total to 62. We had signed up more than 100 licensees. The market was starting to take off. It was interesting to see that manufacturers would usually try to sell to college bookstores first, because at the time, they bought and sold the most logoed merchandise. When they found out that they weren't needed there, they moved to retail stores outside the university community as far geographically as there appeared to be demand for a particular university's products. They developed products with university logos other than the popular tees, fleece, caps and jackets. It was living proof that if there is demand, the supply will come. Market forces do work.

Our goal was to get the top 50 universities with the market appeal to ultimately generate $1 million each in royalties annually. We did sign universities with much less market appeal, primarily because they wanted us to represent them, and we felt we could economically manage them if they were geographically close to those schools we considered more valuable. After we got to this point with university clients, we really didn't work too hard to get more unless they showed interest in us or we met them at trade shows, conventions or sporting events. We believed if we did a great job serving the ones we had signed, and continued to help expand the market nationally, that we would get our fair share of those top schools. By this time, most of the schools we didn't represent had started in-house programs run by university employees.

We did work hard at continuing to educate our own universities, licensees, retailers and consumers. We were learning as we went, but we started with more experience than most. Every day was a new licensing experience, and our collective base of experience grew. With universities, we tried to understand what protectable logos, slogans, symbols and other marks they did have, and show them how to better protect their marks for the future. Since universities really didn't understand licensing, they put their one or two people in charge that were located in one of several different departments. Most put them somewhere under the vice president for business, which was our preference. Some were housed in athletics, our second most preferential department. Others landed in the bookstores, patents and technology, the P.A. announcer at ballgames, and the cheerleader coach. One client even put the woman who ran the arcade game room in the student union in charge of licensing!

A big part of the education of universities was to advise them on what they should approve in products and designs. Logos that had been registered with the U.S. Patent and Trademark Office should carry "®" beside the licensed mark. If it was not registered and the university claimed ownership, a "™" should appear beside the mark. Our administrative staff worked closely with universities to help educate them, and we always gave them advice on what we thought was acceptable. Of course, the final decision was up to them.

Another big issue we had to address with universities as we signed them was "who gets the money?" Since we were primarily trying to work with the VP of Business at many universities, their feeling was that athletics already had too much power and money. We obviously would do whatever they pleased, but my feeling was that we would get better cooperation out of the athletics department, bookstore and alumni association if they were participants in the revenues. Since it was soon determined that successful athletics drove the sale of logoed products, most included them in the revenue. Some universities were concerned about criticism from faculty and students, so many allocated royalties to scholarships, athletics or otherwise. It was hard for anyone, particularly students or faculty, to complain about money going to scholarships.

One recently hired executive VP at a major university came to visit with me. He introduced himself as "The President's Spear Catcher," meaning he was assigned the tough jobs by the school president. When licensing started at his university, no one really cared about it, so athletics took it over. Athletics at this institution was set up as a separate corporation and thus received all the licensing revenue. Since it grew so fast and beyond everyone's expectations, more people at the university wanted some of the money. He asked me, "How much royalty income comes from university marks as opposed to athletic marks?" My answer was, "Look, we take the position that anything they do that relates to the university, they must get approval and pay a royalty. We have a hard enough time getting them to report on all royalties by university. If we asked them to report by each logo, I don't believe we would get accurate information. My suggestion is to sit down with the athletics department and negotiate a split of the university's share of the revenue; whether it is 50-50 or more or less would probably depend on what else you are doing for them or vice versa. But since we know that successful athletic programs drive revenues, I believe a 50-50 split is the right number." They did successfully negotiate that arrangement.

Our administrative staff had an even harder time with the signing of license agreements. In addition to acknowledging the university's ownership of all marks associated with the school, licensees also had to provide copies of product liability insurance, the amount depending on the product. In this litigious society, attorneys will follow the money, and if a product causes harm, they will likely sue the manufacturer who made it, the retailer who sold it, and the university who approved it. At this point in our lifespan, we didn't have attorneys on staff, so I had to get involved in a lot of this work. Many licensees didn't like this additional cost to their products, and didn't exactly put their best and brightest people in the licensing jobs. Over time, that improved dramatically as the market for collegiate goods took off and became very profitable.

We also had to deal with arguments from those who were anti-licensing that: (1) Michigan is a state name; (2) Clemson is a city name; and (3) universities are supported by taxes, and this is taxation without representation. We were able to answer those arguments as universities successfully registered state and city names with the U.S. Patent and Trade Office when those names were used in association with the university. To the taxation argument, we explained to consumers and licensees that royalties were not a "tax" but rather royalties were "cost of goods sold" just like there is cost in a shirt in cotton, buttons, logo application and royalties. You are paying for a manufacturer to sell and a consumer to buy a product with a protectable trademark. If you don't want to pay a royalty, sell the same shirt without the logo/trademark.

Brigham Young University won the 1984 AP No. 1 ranking in football, with Washington, Florida, Nebraska and Boston College rounding out the top five. Georgetown defeated Houston to win the 1984 NCAA Championship in basketball, with Kentucky and Virginia being the other semifinalists in the Final Four. Our top 10 selling universities in the 1984-85 fiscal year were Alabama, North Carolina, Michigan, Clemson, Ohio State, Illinois, Auburn, Hawaii, Nebraska and Indiana. Alabama brought in more than $150,000. Our company brought in $1.4 million and reached break-even in the third year following our 1981-82 start-up. It was nice to be able to tell family members we could now be assured of paychecks in the future, as there were months when cash flow didn't allow such funds the first two years.

The Licensing Letter reported retail sales of all licensed products were $50.1 billion. Sports licensed products were $5.5 billion (10.9 percent of the total), and we estimated collegiate licensing to be $500 million, still only 9.9 percent of all licensed sports products, and a tiny piece of the overall market. It was a hard, slow grind, but everything was in place for the licensed products market to explode.

1985-1986

In the 1985-86 fiscal year we started our licensee audit program. Tom Harrison of Barnes Wendling CPAs (1986 to 1997) had audited for Disney and was starting to audit for NFL Properties. We knew that with some of the licenses we signed, the owners were not very likely to be set up to properly track royalties. We agreed to a limited number of audits with Tom and gave him a list. I wanted to pay him a percentage of what he generated, but he insisted on a flat fee. His reasoning was correct, as he said he always told the company he was auditing that his fee would be the same whether he found anywhere from zero to a million dollars. In questioning Tom about the certain designs the company thought might not be royalty bearing, his answer was, "If it's gray, they pay!"

We learned a great deal from audits. We were right when we believed that when licensees made mistakes in reporting, they were rarely in our favor. But the most interesting thing we learned was how different licensees defined what 6 1/2 percent of the wholesale price meant. One licensee said if he sold a shirt for $10 and had to add 65 cents for royalty, he was going to sell it for $10.65, but report $10. Another said, because of the overhead in staff they were adding to handle the program, they were going to sell a $10 shirt for $13 and report $10. Thank goodness Tom had some experience with Disney and others, and he told them that the rule in trademark licensing was that adding university trademarks to a product should be treated as a "cost of goods sold" — royalties should be paid on the price sold to the customer. There was some wailing and gnashing of teeth over that one, but over time, it all worked out.

We hired Bruce Siegal, a recent University of Alabama Law School graduate, to come in as corporate counsel. Bruce helped work his way through school by working with a screen printing company. That was a very helpful background to have, as state-of-the-art screen printing had evolved to the point that for a few hundred dollars, one could set up shop in their garage and crank out logoed t-shirts that would often appear at college football games. Many times, the t-shirts would be of poor quality and the designs grew to be pretty aggressive, e.g. "Nothing Sucks Like the Big Orange" and worse. Many years later Bruce reminded me that when I hired him, I was choosing between two candidates who I ranked pretty close to neck-and-neck. He said I chose him because the other candidate was a good golfer and Bruce didn't play golf. I had forgotten about that, but it was true.

As stated earlier, VPs of business didn't think there was much money in charging only a 6 1/2 percent royalty on wholesale sales, but they did appreciate the fact that someone would be policing the marketplace to stop those who put out merchandise that was embarrassing to the university.

Bruce had only taken one course in trademark law during law school. As we had done hiring a Big 8 accounting firm to audit our books, I thought hiring a full-time attorney would make our university clients feel better about our evolution as a company and provide more "teeth" to our enforcement and compliance program. Bruce stayed with the company for more than 25 years, became a vice president and general counsel, and helped make an indelible impact on the growth of collegiate licensing.

Speaking of compliance, up to this point we worked hard at getting licensees to submit designs for approval, but were pretty lax in requiring them to submit product samples. I have to admit our process was pretty archaic, but it was all we had available at the time. Most designs were submitted via fax, often in black and white with arrows pointing to where different PMS colors were located. Each university had official PMS colors that were required to provide consistency in the marketplace. We had to crack down on making sure that happened, which meant market surveys provided by our university account managers and licensing directors. We also began to require submission of product samples for the first time. Licensees complained, and it was more work for our administrative staff, but it did dramatically improve our quality control of products and design when we could review a licensee's proposed products in person, rather than via fax.

Our education of licensees and retailers was in full swing by now. By this time we didn't find many companies in the marketplace that could honestly say, "I didn't know anything about having to get approval from the university to print this merchandise." Retailers were starting to carry collegiate merchandise in sporting goods stores around the states, and Nutmeg Mills had gotten collegiate products in J.C. Penney and Foot Locker. Licensees were getting creative with designs, fabric, fashion and marketing approaches. Success breeds success, and if manufacturers and retailers sense they can make money, they jump on board.

We signed eight more universities, including Tennessee and Kentucky, bringing our total to 70. The overall market for all licensed products sold at retail in North America grew to $54.3 billion. Sports licensed products grew to $6.5 billion, and we estimated that college grew to $600 million.

The University of Oklahoma finished No. 1 in the AP Poll in football and was awarded the mythical national title. Michigan, Penn State, Tennessee and Florida ranked 2 through 5. In hoops, Villanova shocked the world by defeating Georgetown to win the 1985 NCAA Championship. Memphis State and St. John's were Final Four semi-finalists. Our top 10 universities in 1985-86 were Alabama, North Carolina, Michigan, Ohio State, Georgetown, Indiana, Illinois, Florida State, Arizona State and Tennessee. Eight of our top 10 generated more than $100,000, while Arizona State and Tennessee were close. Alabama approached the $200,000 mark by itself.

1986-1987

In fiscal year 1986-87, the program grew dramatically. From the beginning, I saw our company as a marketing company, but our initial focus had to be signing university clients, signing license agreements with manufacturers, administrative efforts to manage the licensing process, and enforcement. It was more educational than true marketing.

We hired our first marketing director, Barb Botch (later to become Barb Bailey), into a role that was not yet well identified. That changed dramatically as she soon wore several hats. We started marketing programs aimed at retailers, licensees and consumers. We created some "Look for the label" ads to promote "Officially Licensed Collegiate Products" to consumers and tailored them to fit each university. With the licensing directors' assistance, we were able to get those ads published in athletic game programs, campus newspapers and other university publications. The message was for consumers to "Look for the Officially Licensed Collegiate Products label" to ensure that the product bearing that label was authorized by the university, and a portion of each sale went back to the school for scholarships. In getting many of our universities to join us in this program, we were able to reach millions of consumers around the country with our message.

We also began to develop Retail Recognition programs in which we would give certificates to retailers in specific university markets. We, and the universities, developed ads and promoted them through CCI/ICE-CLC and university publications. We would invite retailers to attend athletic events at the university and show our appreciation for their support. We also were able to gain valuable feedback as to how to improve our program from their perspective.

Promotional Licensing (as opposed to Retail Licensing) is when licensed products are used as "giveaways" (or self-liquidating premiums) in conjunction with the sale of other products. Examples might be a fast-food company giving away logoed plastic cups with a burger or chicken sandwich meal and a drink. One of the largest promotional licensing opportunities we developed was an Atlantic Coast Conference promotion with Hardee's. With the purchase of a meal, one could buy a basketball for $1.99, with the ACC and all eight (at the time) university logos printed on the ball. They went through thousands of basketballs that generated significant royalties to the conference and its member institutions. The $1.99 cost of the ball covered costs for Hardee's, so it was a great promotion for all concerned.

As universities got control of their existing logos, symbols, names and slogans, we encouraged them to think about freshening up some of their current ones with new accent colors. We also encouraged them to create new logos that might appeal to children or other target audiences. Georgia Tech, Kentucky and Louisville all created new mascot logos.

The demand for fleece began to soar. Demand actually exceeded supply, and licensees scrambled to produce greater quantities and improved products and designs. College shops began to appear within stores and as stand-alone stores.

There was a trend toward higher quality merchandise and upscale products. One retailer became licensed for Waterford Crystal miniature footballs that that sold for $150. They primarily commemorated national championships in football and basketball, but sold very well. As we represented more universities, we got better and better at managing championship "hot markets" in planning for them with the top universities in the running, and executing those plans with the champion. It was a rush that those with independent programs were ill-equipped to handle, as we were with our first one. We began to ask independents if we could help manage their championship events, and some contracted with us to do so. That led them to a better understanding of what we did, and led to more full-agency agreements over time.

We also signed an agency agreement with the Sugar Bowl. Mickey Holmes was the executive director and really helped us be successful in New Orleans. As our universities played in bowl games, we expected our royalties to rise. When they didn't, we researched the issue and found out that no one was paying attention. The bowls were having merchandise printed to be sold at the stadiums, but never thought about working with the universities. This was another gray area that we turned into black and white. We worked with the Sugar Bowl to put in their game contracts with the schools that any merchandise using school marks would be bought from licensees. If the bowls wanted to buy from a local screen printer, they would let us know, and with the school's approval, we would license them for the one game.

The screen printers favored by the Sugar Bowl was a company named Kelley & Abide. They did a great job and produced good products, and were very timely with deliveries. But they were screamers! Any little thing that they didn't like, from contract issues to other people selling in the New Orleans area, they yelled and screamed. After a while, they would settle down and we would smile and be friendly again. We developed a great relationship with them over time, but they never did quit screaming!

My favorite story about signing agency agreements with bowls came with the Cotton Bowl in Dallas, where Jim "Hoss" Brock was the executive director. He was a larger-than-life figure and always had a cigar in his mouth whenever I saw him. He never lit it — just chewed on it until it was gone. He called everybody "Hoss," at least all the men. We were talking and I asked the question, "Do you have a provision in your game contract with universities that spells out that any merchandise authorized by the Cotton Bowl, with university marks, will be bought from university licensees?" We were sitting with the president of the Cotton Bowl, a very well respected and successful businessman. Jim replied, "Hell Hoss, we don't even have a game contract. We don't even have a contract with CBS. If you can't do business on a handshake, to hell with you!" At that moment, his president appeared a little shaken and said, "Well, Jim, maybe we should have contracts in place." Jim said, "The only game contract we ever had was when Alabama played and 'Bear' wanted 200 tickets for friends and family." The Cotton Bowl soon provided game contracts with the participating universities that included the language we suggested.

Not only did getting the bowls in compliance add to our revenue streams, it gave us more opportunities to work with independent universities in "hot market" situations. We did a good job of policing the cities of the two participating teams, from the time the teams were named, until school was out for the holidays. We also did a good job preparing for and policing in the cities of the bowls. Our staff and our diligence usually impressed the independents with whom we worked.

On the enforcement front, we continued to aggressively pursue those who produced collegiate products without a license. We discovered a campus retailer in Chapel Hill, North Carolina, that printed its own UNC logoed products. The store was named Johnny T-Shirt and was operated by a UNC alumnus who felt that as a citizen of North Carolina and a former student, he had every right to use the university's marks. After several settlement offers failed, the University of North Carolina filed a lawsuit. The *Johnny T-Shirt* case, decided in 1989, resulted in UNC stopping the company from producing and selling unlicensed UNC products. The court held that the university did not legally "abandon" its marks, which remained strong despite years of use before UNC started its licensing program. Universities as a group were well on their way to validating trademark rights and establishing legal ownership in their intellectual properties.

We outgrew our space in our building, so we moved across Interstate 75 into a newer Atlanta building. We doubled in size to 3,800 square feet and thought that would hold us for the four-year term of our lease. It didn't, but we will talk more about that later.

We added 12 more universities to bring our total to 82. Retail sales of all licensed merchandise in 1986-87 was $55.9 billion. Sports licensed merchandise grew to $7.3 billion, and collegiate grew to $800 million. Gross revenues from our group of schools doubled from the previous year. From our sliding scale of revenues, our universities were getting higher percentages as their annual royalties increased. We were able to continue to grow our share with increased volume, and more university and bowl game clients.

Penn State was awarded the 1986 AP National Championship in football, followed by Miami, Oklahoma, Oregon State and Nebraska in the rankings. Louisville won the 1986 NCAA Championship in basketball by defeating Duke, while Kansas and LSU were the semi-finalists. Our top 10 universities in 1986-87 were Michigan, Alabama, North Carolina, Indiana, Kentucky, Arizona State, Tennessee, Ohio State, Louisville and Auburn. By this time, Michigan was pushing $400,000 in annual revenue, the next seven were well over $200,000, and Louisville and Auburn were close to $200,000.

1987-1988

In the 1987-88 fiscal year, Nutmeg Mills kept its promise and became CCI/ICE-CLC's No. 1 licensee. Other top licensees during this period were Champion, Artex, Chalk Line and Logo 7.

The SEC was the first conference to join our Consortium. We developed a program in which licensees could create designs using the conference logo with all SEC institutions, or in conjunction with one, two, or all 12. Most of this use came about in SEC championship events, but we were successful in getting some SEC shops within shops in department stores and airports. In joint-licensed designs, licensees would pay a higher royalty that was split between the licensors. For example, an SEC-Ole Miss design might require a 10 percent royalty, with 7 percent going to Ole Miss and 3 percent to the SEC. If all 12 schools were in the design, the universities' 10 percent would be split 12 ways.

We added 19 universities to bring our total to 99. The new universities included Georgia, Wisconsin and Purdue. Here are my two favorite "sidebars" about Georgia and Wisconsin.

When we moved to Atlanta in 1984, we represented Georgia Tech, but the University of Georgia program was run by associate athletics director Avery McLean, a great guy who had a ton of responsibilities other than licensing. One day when we were together at a convention, I was talking to him and said, "Avery, this is embarrassing to me to be in the state of Georgia and not represent your university." Avery replied, "Well, we're making a lot of money and not spending much time on it." I said, "I know you are, we're out hustling to sign up good licensees and every time we get one for Georgia Tech, they say they might as well get Georgia, too, and we send them to you. We are also out auditing licensees and we recover back royalties for our schools. In the process we see back royalties due Georgia and don't have the right to collect. We have a lot of people working from coast to coast to build this program and we can do a great job for you." It wasn't too long after that that Avery called and we went to work for him and UGA.

When Wisconsin joined the Consortium in 1983, Dr. Donna Shalala was chancellor at UW. There had been a turnover of a few presidents before her, and just as many general counsels. When licensing first started and requests came in to use the "Bucky Badger" logo, there were letters in the file on general counsel stationary saying that the university didn't own the Bucky Badger logo and it was in the public domain. I discussed with Dr. Shalala that I believed the university had common law ownership of Bucky Badger and we should aggressively take that approach until it was proven that we did not. If we ever reached that point, we would need to create a new mascot that the university owned. In the meantime, Wisconsin had a semblance of a licensing program, but felt they couldn't enforce the embarrassing use of vulgar Bucky designs saying and doing some really bad things. Bucky was the most abused mascot in history. Those particular designs were plentiful in the marketplace, and they commonly were referred to as "F!*k 'em Bucky" designs.

We went in, met with the screen printers who were producing them, and told them we had to stop them one way or the other. We encouraged them to get licensed, and get all designs approved, as we believed the program was undervalued and had a chance to be really big. One or two were leaning toward getting licensed, but didn't want to be the first in the group of four or five who were fighting Wisconsin's program.

An interesting thing happened. Barry Alvarez was hired as Wisconsin's head football coach in 1990. He inherited a program that had not had a winning season since 1984. In 1993, Wisconsin won 10 games, lost one, tied one, and got a bid to the Rose Bowl. We had made good progress with the Wisconsin program for five years, but still had not totally resolved the rogue companies' abuse of the Bucky Badger logo. When UW got the Rose Bowl bid, the whole fan base went ballistic. They had not been successful in so long that there arose a great demand for Wisconsin-Rose Bowl merchandise. We worked with the Tournament of Roses to develop a joint licensing program. All the "bad guys" didn't believe the university owned the rights to Bucky, but for some reason, they believed the Tournament of Roses owned "Rose Bowl" rights. They all signed license agreements acknowledging Wisconsin owned all of its marks, including Bucky Badger. The licensing program took off from there, and Wisconsin became a consistent top-selling university. Chancellor Shalala went on to become president at the University of Miami, and under her leadership, Miami signed with our company after being very independent for years. Whenever I see Donna, she always introduces me as the guy who saved Bucky Badger!

Both CCI/ICE-CLC offices continued to add staff and programs. We had 950 licensees and a 24-person staff. We were creating an infrastructure that could handle additional universities up to a point without hiring more people. We held firm to our principles of treating each and every university like they were our most important. Because our business was a fun one, we were able to attract the best and the brightest to our staff. Most were recent college graduates, and some had served as interns for us, which gave us an opportunity to get to know them, and vice-versa. The characteristics I looked for in new staff members were:

1. Character — One of my favorite quotes, attributed to Horace Greeley, is "Fame is a vapor, popularity an accident, riches take wings, those who cheer today will curse tomorrow, only one thing endures — character." I didn't want to worry about what one of our people might do either inside or outside of our business.

2. Work Ethic — We were a fast-growing operation and I wanted people who would do whatever needed to be done, whenever it needed to be done.

3. Team Spirit — Team dynamics are among the most important lessons one can learn through sports. People working together can create more accomplishments as a whole than the sum of their respective

parts. That's also called synergy.

4. Relentless Pursuit of Excellence in the Mission — The staff must buy into the vision. Every minute should be devoted to something that contributes to the overall mission — from the janitor to the CEO.

5. Service Mentality — We are a service organization. If we don't provide excellent service to our clients, we won't stay in business.

6. Intelligence — My old boss Larry Striplin had a saying, "Dumb is forever!" We couldn't find many people with experience, so I did want "smart."

7. Communication Skills — I was shocked at the poor writing skills of some very bright people. When I was in college, most every course conducted tests by passing out "Blue Books" that required written answers. In the 1980s, it seemed that most tests were either true or false, or multiple choice. Because they didn't have to write, they didn't learn how to write. Verbal skills are important, but the written word is very effective in any business.

8. Talent , The "It" factor — This characteristic was very hard to find in interviews. Often times it developed or surfaced later. But, like in athletics, certain players could make the play at the right time. So it is in business. That is a rare trait, but having a few in your organization makes a big difference.

We were growing so fast and working so hard that it was difficult to set up a proper training program, and I didn't really know how to do that anyway. Ours was "trial by fire" training. We would put new staff members with current ones and let them listen to phone conversations, travel with them, if the job required such, and otherwise learn from on-staff mentors. To accomplish that, you must have buy-in from senior leaders, who in turn live the vision and pass it along to junior members. If younger or newer staff members see that in those above them, they will quickly either buy-in or leave. And of greater importance, they will appreciate leadership skills being passed along to them, and will take pride in passing it along when their time comes.

While one of my biggest regrets in coaching was not recruiting and developing players well enough in our last few years, one of my proudest accomplishments was recruiting and developing staff members at CLC. We built a great culture there, making senior staff members feel like owners. They had a stake in seeing that culture permeate throughout the company. We did a lot of good things to get that done, and we had an outstanding staff.

There were so many things necessary to keep up with and improve as we grew. One was our phone system. We started out with a simple system. Over time we were about to drive our receptionist crazy and had to upgrade. I always believed that we should have a real person answering every call, but that eventually became impossible and I finally agreed to a system that directed callers to a directory. But, we did make sure that it was easy to get to an operator if that's what the caller needed.

The evolution of our system and technology was an interesting study. When we started, we didn't have computers. Steve sold us on the need to get a TelVideo system, which was an early entry into computerization, then followed copiers and faxes, and finally more advanced computer systems. The administrative side of the business always gave me heart palpitations, and fortunately we had a team in place that could manage that side of the business, getting me involved only when major decisions needed to be made.

On the legal front, on Oct. 20, 1988, the Trademark Law Revision Act of 1988 passed in Congress. This bill made for sweeping changes to U.S. Trademark Law. It was to go into effect one year later and was expected to substantially ease the burden on U.S. companies registering trademarks and their ability to sue competitors for false advertising claims. Further, it was expected to bring the U.S. Trademark system in line with those of most countries and substantially eliminate the disparate advantages granted foreign companies under the current act.

The Association of Collegiate Licensing Administrators (ACLA) was formed in 1988. Collegiate licensing was booming and there was a need to form an association that could provide dialogue to all who were interested. There was a bit of a feeling of competition between those members of our Consortium and those members who ran independent programs. There were also differences between the larger, more marketable schools than the smaller, less marketable ones. The association wisely chose Dr. Finus Gaston from The University of Alabama as its first president. Finus wrote his doctoral dissertation on "Collegiate Licensing" back in the early 1980s when we established Alabama's program.

Finus had been our primary contact at Alabama since the program started in 1981. He was always responsive, and in doing so was largely responsible for UA being the Consortium's top revenue producer for the first several years. The fact that ACLA, which was formed primarily by independent universities, chose Finus was a tribute to his openness and objectivity in working for the greater good of collegiate licensing. He was the perfect choice to lead the group. ACLA and its successor organizations — NCLA (National Collegiate Licensing Association and ICLA (International Collegiate Licensing Association) — played an important role in the evolution of collegiate licensing. It was a great honor to the University of Alabama that Finus and I were the first two members inducted into the NCLA Hall of Fame.

Leaders in ACLA in the early years were: Dickie Van Meter, University of Iowa; Anne Chasser, Ohio State; Cecil Phillips, Georgia Tech; Kim Allen, Michigan State; Danny Davis, Oklahoma; Liz Kennedy, Southern Cal; David van Der Hyde, University of Washington; and many others.

UCLA was one of the first to start a licensing program in the early 1980s under director Jack Revoyr. They learned that many Japanese tourists to Los Angeles adopted the UCLA brand as a souvenir marking their visit to America. UCLA started a domestic licensing program, but the success of licensing their marks in Japan became a major source of revenue.

Our audit of licensees' programs started to gain traction as we conducted 123 audits and collected $319,000 in back royalties. We actually were the leader in the industry in this program, but our need to do so was greater, as we were required by our universities to license so many companies.

Miami won the AP Poll in football in 1987, followed by Florida State, Oklahoma, Syracuse and LSU. Indiana defeated Syracuse to win the 1987 NCAA basketball Final Four, which included UNLV and Providence. Our top universities in 1987-88 were Michigan ($605K), Indiana ($518K), Alabama ($436K), North Carolina ($435K), Kentucky ($344K), Baylor ($311K), Tennessee ($281K), Ohio State ($269K), Florida State ($246K) and Auburn ($242K).

Retail sales of all licensed merchandise in North America grew to $59.8 billion. Sports licensing grew to $8 billion, of which we estimated collegiate sales to be $1 billion. The "B" word sure sounded nice, as six years earlier our estimate of collegiate sales was $250 million.

1988-1989

In the 1988-89 fiscal year, we finally dropped the CCI/ICE-CLC brand and became The Collegiate Licensing Company (CLC). That actually had already taken place gradually, but we finally pulled the plug on the alphabet name. CLC had contracts with more than 1,700 licensees, 107 universities, 10 bowl games and one athletic conference. We had 30 full-time employees and 10,000 feet of office space.

We worked with the NCAA in our first joint licensing venture with them and secured $32,000 for our schools. The NCAA had set up its own licensing and merchandising program to sell generic NCAA merchandise in their home offices and events. In order for them to use university marks, they had to secure rights from the universities — through CLC.

A marketing executive from Alpo, a manufacturer of dog food, got really interested in putting university logos on dog food bags. We worked with him as he really thought this was a big enough idea that they would pay us enough royalties to build buildings on campus. He said, "Just imagine a Cornhusker fan walking through a grocery store and seeing a red bag with the Nebraska logo on it, how could he resist?" We hoped he was right, but we didn't build any buildings from the royalties. We did get a few comments from friends reading about it and saying to us, "I see your business is going to the dogs."

Champion Products, which was sued by the University of Pittsburgh in 1983, had become licensed with virtually all universities. Champion owners were vehemently opposed to universities licensing their marks and didn't believe they had the rights. After the Pittsburgh lawsuit they finally recognized that if they were being sued by their customers, those customers probably wouldn't buy much from them in the future. The interesting part in Champion's about-face toward licensing was that they became the licensing agency for the University of Notre Dame. I called and asked them if they intended to go after other universities. They said they really didn't want to represent Notre Dame, but they felt they needed to protect their turf with the Notre Dame Bookstore. (Side note: If you haven't been to the Notre Dame campus, put it high on your bucket list and, if possible, attend a football game. Also go to the Notre Dame Bookstore, which sells an incredible amount of merchandise and has ample space allocated for customers to ship their merchandise home so they don't have to carry it around with them).

Our marketing staff put together our first national promotion with Procter & Gamble. It included more than 70 universities and gave us the opportunity to include independent universities for a percentage of their share.

In addition, we developed a trade advertising campaign to promote the power of the CLC Consortium and the growth opportunities in collegiate licensing to potential licensees and retailers.

After five years of being affiliated with them, CLC became a sponsor of the National Sporting Goods Association (NSGA). The NSGA held an annual trade show that included manufacturers and retailers of almost everything in the outdoor world. Many of our licensees showed there, and as a result, many of our university licensing directors attended. Because licensing was growing so fast, we encouraged the NSGA to consolidate a section for all sports licensing organizations to be able to set up booths in one section of the building. They liked the idea and agreed to do so. The Industry Breakfast was a big deal. They had General Norman Schwarzkopf as a speaker right after the Persian Gulf War. General Colin Powell spoke the following year. They were both incredible speakers.

Two of General Schwarzkopf's quotes that I love are: (1) "Leadership is a potent combination of strategy and character, but if you must be without one, be without the strategy"; and (2) "A dream doesn't become reality through magic, it takes sweat, determination, and hard work." I thought General Powell's speech was the best I had ever heard, and I believed he could one day be president of the United States.

CLC conducted its first annual Licensing Directors Seminar in conjunction with the Super Show in Atlanta. We believed it was a good idea to try to get as many licensing directors as we could together in an educational setting to bring them up to date on what we were doing and our future plans. It was also a chance for them to see our presence and many of their licensees at the sporting goods industry's fastest-growing trade show — the Super Show. And, an added bonus in Atlanta was they could stop by, see our offices and meet our administrative staff that many had conversed with often via telephone.

It was hard to get a booth at the Atlanta Super Show, but after a few years of trying, we were finally able to get a 10-foot by 10-foot space to put a booth. The cost of the booth, plus dealing with the union workers to install, run electricity, etc., was astronomical to me. I complained to our staff that this 10x10 booth cost more than my first house in 1966, and it didn't even have running water! My staff got on me for years about comparing costs to my first home.

On the legal front, the Trade Law Revision Act went into effect Nov. 16, 1989. The University of North Carolina prevailed in its lawsuit against Johnny T-Shirt, a local retailer who had printed and sold merchandise using UNC marks that were unlicensed.

An interesting sidebar to the UNC-Johnny T-Shirt litigation was that we agreed to participate with UNC in the costs, and possible recoveries, in the case. We had the opportunity to meet with UNC attorneys on several occasions. One day, the lead attorney called me aside and asked if I knew Bill France Jr. at NASCAR. I told him I was well aware of NASCAR, but had never met any of its people. He said they really needed somebody like us to represent them in trademark licensing. He evidently told Bill France the same thing, as not long after that, Jim Foster, VP for Marketing, and Mike Helton, manager of Bristol Speedway, set up a meeting.

My son Pat and I had been invited to the Talladega 500 a few years earlier, which was my first introduction to NASCAR. The guy who invited us had heard what we were doing with Coach Bryant and universities. We were amazed by all the activity, and particularly the sponsorships and merchandising opportunities. In the pits before the race, we met Richard Petty and several other drivers, all who appeared so nice and relaxed as if racing for 500 laps at about 200 miles per hour was no more dangerous than going to the store to pick up a loaf of bread.

The really amazing thing, though, were the number of sponsor decals on the cars and the sponsor patches on the uniforms. It seemed like there were about 75 on each. Some were NASCAR sponsors that appeared on the left-front fender. The major sponsor had the hood and trunk. Pretty much every spot on both the cars and the uniforms were sold to a sponsor. After the race, which Bobby Allison won, in Victory Lane, with all of the media asking him questions, there was a young man whose job it was to change Bobby's hat about every 30 to 45 seconds. A photographer was standing by to get a photo of Allison wearing every sponsors' hat in Victory Lane. It was amazing.

Our conversation with the gentleman who invited us had worked some with Petty and others. He explained all the sponsors and rights they got with sponsorship. He explained that most of the merchandise sold around the track was either the individual drivers or Winston (R.J. Reynolds Tobacco Company). NASCAR had basically acquiesced its merchandising rights to R.J. Reynolds for their Winston Cup Series sponsorship. Most of the drivers' trailers were staffed by family members who drove from track to track every week during the season. At that time, all the souvenir business went to the drivers. We asked, "So, what does NASCAR own?" He said, with a growl, "They don't own sh*t." The drivers and the cars are what people want to buy." So, with that, we left thinking NASCAR wasn't a great licensing opportunity unless you could work with the drivers.

That was my thinking when I met with Jim Foster and Mike Helton. They said they didn't know anything about licensing, and when people came to ask about it, they just threw out a number that they thought would send them away. Most did, but a few took them up on it. Even so, it never got to a place where they wanted to get serious about a program. After they left, I forgot about it. I thought we could get the rights, but didn't think it worthwhile.

Two years later I got a call from one of our collegiate t-shirt licensees. He asked if I represented NASCAR. I told him I did not. He said, "Jim Foster told me you were their agent." I said, "I haven't seen Jim in two years." After talking a while, I said, "Let me ask you a question. Can you take the NASCAR bar logo (which, by the way, was a great-looking logo) and use it with generic cars and make it work?" He replied, "We sold 10 million dollars worth of Harley Davidson t-shirts last year, we can make it work!" He sent me a proposal guaranteeing $50,000 for exclusive rights to NASCAR apparel. I thought, we have the infrastructure in place to handle another property, and with $50,000, we could hire one person to manage it and I could assist in communication with the NASCAR executives.

I called Jim Foster and asked if he still wanted to explore us starting their licensing program. He said he did, so we met and got a deal worked out. He asked what we thought we could do. I responded I didn't know, with not being able to use drivers and cars, but it wouldn't take long to find out, and we were willing to invest in seeing what we could do.

In 1989 we signed NASCAR in Battle Enterprises, Inc., and hired Charlie Cooper, the son of a former executive director of both Daytona Speedway and the Indianapolis Motor Speedway. Charlie grew up in racing and knew the ins and outs of the sport as well as anyone. He was very young, but extremely bright and did a good job for us. Jim Foster talked to me about NASCAR's loyalty to those who worked with them. He told me when Bill France Sr. was building the Daytona Speedway that he needed cash badly. At the time, the Daytona races were held on the beach, so there were a few races that had to be stopped when the tide came in. He sent telegrams to both Coke and Pepsi. His offer was for "$30,000 by next Monday and we'll give you 10-year sponsorships of our Speedway and pouring rights." He got a negative response from Coke and a $30,000 check from Pepsi. Jim said the France family owns five race tracks now and Pepsi is in every one. He said, "If you ever pay us $500,000 a year, you'll watch the Daytona 500 from the France suite."

We represented NASCAR and the five race tracks owned by the France Family — Daytona, Talladega, Bristol, Phoenix and Watkins Glen. The first event of the racing season was the Daytona 500. We worked really hard, got a list of all vendors around the previous years' race that had permits from city hall. We sent them letters telling them what we were doing, and that if they intended to use any Daytona 500 or NASCAR marks, we would be pleased to work with them. Some did, but many didn't. We got "John Doe" Cease and Desist orders from a local judge and an attorney to serve the papers. Not many vendors used the Daytona 500 mark itself, but featured a race car scene with generic cars. Above the cars was a big "DAYTONA" and under the cars was a little bitty "Beach Florida" so their obvious claim was that we didn't represent the city of Daytona Beach, thus their designs were legal. We took issue with that.

Again, it was an educational experience that took time to grow. With a small staff dedicated to NASCAR, and with our infrastructure, we were able to manage the business very well. In many ways it was synergistic to our business. We had collegiate licensees that wanted to get into NASCAR and vice versa. We signed NASCAR in 1989 and represented them for five years. We did in fact pay them $500,000, and did get to watch the Daytona 500 from the France suite. In fact, in 1994 we paid them $5.5 million, but then they fired us and took the program in-house. It was fun getting involved in the sport and helping get the NASCAR brand on a lot of the licensed merchandise sold. We also did a good job of getting track-related merchandise under control, and even were able to get some in markets outside the tracks. It was also interesting running into many of the vendors we had caught selling unlicensed collegiate merchandise, who had moved from college to selling NASCAR stuff. But, probably our most interesting experience was helping turn much "gray" as relates to rights into "black and white."

The drivers resisted licensing even though we tried to work with them. They believed that if Walmart or Sports Authority were selling their t-shirts, that people wouldn't pay the high prices their families were charging at the tracks. They didn't want to license apparel, but two different licensees came into the picture that helped change everything for NASCAR licensing. Maxx Trading Cards came out with a line of cards when trading cards in all sports were hot commodities. Racing Champions came out with a line of die-cast aluminum racecars with the exact markings as the actual cars. All drivers agreed to sign those licensees. Neither car owners nor car sponsors worried about the souvenir business at that time, so their approval wasn't a problem. We worked with both licensees to get the NASCAR bar logo on each product. Bob Dodds, president of Racing Champions, asked why I thought adding the NASCAR logo to their already successful program was worth the additional royalty. My answer was, "The NASCAR logo ties your collection together and adds authenticity. It may not seem valuable to you, but it will definitely add value to retailers and consumers. It would be like the NFL logo appearing on all NFL licensed merchandise." Bob bought into our concept and became a great licensee and friend. He ran his company as well as any licensee with which we ever dealt. We developed a friendship over the years. Because of the demand for his products, I wanted to see his factories in China. We took a trip to Hong Kong together and spent a day in China going to see his factories. It was a unique experience.

Both products took off like gangbusters. Before long, some of the drivers began to make as much from these two licenses as they were making as a driver. Over the next few years, as licensing revenues grew, the owners started to want a piece of the action, as they owned the cars. The sponsor also started to want a piece of the action, as they paid big dollars to decorate the cars. We talked to the Valvoline people who sponsored the No. 6 Mark Martin car. Their response to their rights in the sport was, "Mark Martin owns his naked body and his signature, but when he puts on that uniform, sits in or stands next to our car, he is ours!" Rights evolved based on the strength of the driver, owner and sponsor. Dale Earnhardt in the No. 3 GM Goodwrench Chevrolet was so strong that he controlled all licensing and merchandising around his program.

Our experience with NASCAR was great. Brian France came into power and wanted to get NASCAR recognized along with the four professional leagues. I believe we helped him get there from a licensing perspective. On the cover of the June 1994 *Sports Trend* magazine it showed NASCAR ranked up there with the four professional sports leagues and CLC. We were sorry to lose them, but they were fair to us all the way through, and I have nothing but respect and admiration for what the France family built as a sport. It is one of the great sports stories in this country.

The NASCAR experience proved that the infrastructure of CLC was powerful enough to successfully take on and manage major non-collegiate properties without interfering with our primary collegiate business. As stated before, it was really synergistic in that our licensees were selling shirts, caps, jackets, other clothing and other non-apparel items. Applying logos, whether it be different universities or other sports, was no big deal for them. It turned out to be an added benefit we offered to our licensees.

Notre Dame won the 1988 National Championship in football, followed by Miami, Florida State, Michigan and West Virginia. In basketball, Kansas defeated Oklahoma to claim the NCAA Championship in 1988. Arizona and Duke were Final Four semi-finalists. Our top-selling universities in 1988-89 were Michigan, North Carolina, Indiana, Alabama, Georgia, Kentucky, Georgetown, Florida State, Tennessee and Auburn. Michigan generated more than $900,000 during the year, which equaled to almost $28 million in retail sales. Retail sales of all licensed products grew to $64.6 billion, sports licensed sales grew to $9.3 billion, and collegiate sales reached an estimated $1.2 billion.

1989-1990

The retail market in general, as well as the economy, began to slow down in 1989-90. The Persian Gulf War, triggered by Iraq's invasion of Kuwait, led to U.S. involvement in a war that began in August 1990 and went through February 1991. The war effort caused some consternation among businesses and the economy. Licensees and retailers began to understand that carrying more universities in their lines was inefficient. They began to drop universities that didn't sell well, and double down on those that did.

The growth in overall collegiate sales at retail slowed down, but for CLC, we were able to maintain growth by adding additional universities and developing bigger programs with our top universities. Retail sales in all of North America were $66.5 billion, a 2 percent growth from the previous year. Sports licensed products grew to $10 billion and collegiate sales grew to $1.5 billion, 15 percent of sports licensed sales. Promotional licensing generated $750,000 in royalties toward our cause.

Miami won the 1989 football title, its third during the decade. Notre Dame, FSU, Colorado and Tennessee finished second through fifth in the final AP Poll. During the year, Notre Dame signed a six-year, $30 million deal with NBC, guaranteeing the network the exclusive rights to broadcast Fighting Irish football starting in 1991. Also, Barry Switzer resigned after 16 seasons and three national championships at Oklahoma, Michigan Coach Bo Schembechler retired following the season and Florida hired Steve Spurrier away from Duke.

Michigan defeated Seton Hall to win the 1989 NCAA Basketball Championship, with Illinois and Duke being the others in the Final Four. Starter and The Game were our top licensees. The Game headwear became famous for its "Bar" and "Circle" designs on Sports Novelties headgear. You've heard the story about Neil Stillwell and The Game.

The Starter story is equally compelling. Starter was founded in 1971 by David Beckerman in New Haven, Connecticut. He was a former basketball player who was passionate about the game. His company started out slowly, selling golf and other apparel to sporting goods stores. He quickly evolved into a licensed products business and tried hard for a few years to get a license with either of the professional leagues, to no avail.

The name "Starter" was chosen for its simplicity. He thought all great brands were one word, and he believed every athlete dreamed of being on a starting team. He began with salesmen working in three states: Ohio, Michigan and Indiana. He thought it was silly that a Chicago Cubs fan couldn't walk into a shop and buy a team jacket or hat.

By 1981, Starter was selling a nice satin jacket to bowling alleys and any sports-related retailer he could find. Sales reached $300,000. He finally convinced Licensing Corporation of America (LCA) — who represented Major League Baseball (MLB), National Basketball Association (NBA) and National Hockey League (NHL) — to grant him a license to produce and sell jackets with MLB logos. Sales quickly rose to $500,000 a year.

Beckerman didn't want to settle for officially licensed apparel; he wanted to be defined as "authentic" by having players and coaches wearing the same apparel on the field that a fan could buy from stores. Joe Torre, manager of the New York Yankees, was an early convert. He was friends with the Starter truck driver and began wearing the Starter brand regularly. Licensing for the NHL and NBA followed quickly. Around 1990, after years of rejection, the NFL granted him a license. By that time, Starter had every major professional sport in its lineup, along with hundreds of colleges. They were all gathering fans thanks to increased television exposure for all sports.

The company also went from selling jackets to teams and fans to consulting on clothes that could radically improve a team's bottom line. When the Chicago White Sox agreed to a Starter-branded color scheme, annual revenues on apparel sold at the stadium went from $100,000 to $4.5 million. Having the teams wear Starter products was only part of Beckerman's strategy, because he knew fans were loyal and would identify as closely as possible to the team and its players.

When the trend among young adults moved toward wearing caps backward, Beckerman applied a very visible and well-designed Starter star logo on the back of caps and the wrist of the jacket sleeves. That gave a huge lift to the popularity of the Starter brand, as did the dollars he spent on signage featuring the brands in professional league stadiums that partnered with him. In addition, his son Brad was plugged into the music industry and got Will Smith and others on board.

Starter was on fire in the sports licensed products space, carving a significant and unique niche in the industry. They entered the collegiate space, as Starter retail customers began asking them to produce collegiate merchandise. Although Starter never, to my knowledge, became an on-field supplier to any colleges, the Starter jacket and cap, and the Starter brand, caught on quickly among college fans.

On the enforcement front, CLC, NFL, MLB and NHL all combined in Operation Dizzy Fox, a criminal seizure of merchandise bearing sports team logos. It was the largest ever crackdown in the United States. Our respective compliance people identified the problem, quickly spread the word, and we all agreed to financially participate in the seizures. It was well planned, well executed, and sent a message to both good guys and bad guys that the licensors would fiercely defend their trademarks. There was real power in all five organizations coming together in a consolidated sting.

Our top 10 selling universities in 1989-90 were Michigan, Georgetown, North Carolina, Georgia, Alabama, Illinois, Florida State, Yale, Auburn and Tennessee. Michigan and Georgetown were our first two universities to each generate more than a million dollars in gross royalties, as Michigan reached $1.65 million and Georgetown $1.12 million. Interestingly, the Georgetown silver and blue Starter jacket and cap became popular nationwide in better department stores. Those high-end department stores jumped on the licensed products bandwagon where sales were hot, but later were quick to drop off when sales cooled. Georgetown had an Ivy League-type reputation in academics, which appealed to better department stores. But the Hoyas basketball program under Coach John Thompson also drove sales in traditional athletic-related stores. In a very interesting phenomenon, street gangs all over the country seemed to pick up Starter's Georgetown jacket and cap color and style combination, which drove sales even higher.

In October 1990, the Atlanta Organizing Committee was awarded the 1996 Olympic Games. It was a euphoric time for Atlanta. The story behind the successful bid, to me, is one of the great sports stories in American history. Billy Payne, an All-SEC defensive end for the Georgia Bulldogs in the late 1960s, entered the commercial real estate business after graduation. (As a side note, Billy played on Georgia's team in 1968 against Tennessee when I was an assistant. UT scored on the last play of the game, and a two-point conversion tied it at 18-18. To this day, Billy complains that our receiver dropped the ball on the touchdown). Billy made a lot of money and became very interested in sharing through philanthropy. He helped raise several million dollars for his church in a building program, but he was looking for another cause.

It is my understanding that Billy was in a meeting with someone in Nashville in the mid-1980s and was asked if Atlanta had placed a bid for the 1996 Summer Olympic Games. Billy came home and inquired about the bid, which he learned Atlanta had not even put in an offer. He became furious, and in a story that I hope will come out, if he ever writes a book, he single-handedly went into the community and pretty much forced nine highly respected businessmen and attorneys to be on the Atlanta Organizing Committee (AOC). I'm told he wouldn't take no for an answer. They put together an incredible bid, and it was determined in 1988 that if the 1996 Olympic Games came to North America, they would come to Atlanta.

In a recruiting job that would have made most coaches proud, Billy and his committee traveled around the world meeting with leaders and selling Atlanta. They invited them in to show all of the sites that would be made available if Atlanta was selected. They made the University of Georgia football field available for Olympic soccer matches. In doing so, they had to remove the beloved "hedges" for a year. (As a side note, they planted sprigs of the hedges on South Georgia fields, and not only replaced them in the stadium after the Olympics, but CLC developed a program to take the original pots with "Official Georgia Hedges" to the retail market the following year. It was a successful venture). The promises made to world leaders were very real and very effective.

The licensing and merchandising side of the Atlanta Olympics story was equally interesting and impressive. When it was determined in 1988 that Atlanta would be the host city if the 1996 Olympics came to North America, the AOC had the rights to develop a bid-city logo. They hired a local firm and came up with a beautiful logo. It was a five "A" star, which each "A" bearing one of the five colors of the Olympic rings. The design was made to look like it was done with crayons, which made for a fantastic look. Under the design was "ATLANTA 1996" — as they were not authorized to use the Olympic rings until after the 1992 Games in Barcelona, Spain.

I went down and met with Billy, who is not only brilliant and highly motivated, but a great guy as well. The AOC had contracted with four screen printers in the area to produce t-shirts with the Bid-City logo. It was a six-color design and the merchandise was very attractive. The AOC had the ability to license that mark, so I asked Billy if we could work with his staff to handle that for them. Billy's response was that he didn't want to get into licensing at that time, but if they were successful in getting the Olympics to Atlanta, we would talk.

As the 1990 award date neared, the impact of the AOC's recruiting efforts gained traction and Atlanta was being mentioned as one of the top choices. T-shirt sales picked up dramatically in the weeks before the bid was awarded. Everyone believed Athens, Greece, would get the bid, but Atlanta was feeling pretty good about getting the 2000 bid. In the few weeks before the award, the infrastructure and security required to host the games in Athens was coming into question by the International Organizing Committee (IOC). Billy and his team's hopes were growing about getting the 1996 Olympics. Sure enough, in a very dramatic announcement in October 1990, IOC President Juan Antonio Samaranch proclaimed, "The bid for the 1996 games goes to A-A-Atlanta!"

Euphoria swept the city. It was amazing. A few days later when I got to the office around 7:30, I checked the fax machine, and lo and behold there was a fax from Billy sent at 4:30 a.m. on Oct. 16. I called and told him I was impressed receiving a fax at 4:30. He said, "I was here two hours before I sent that fax. Let's meet tomorrow with our friends from King & Spalding (law firm) and John Krimsky, head of the United States Organizing Committee." We met and discussed what they wanted to do, which was primarily to raise money to fund the start of pre-Olympic Games preparation. The rules were very strict. They told me, "If anything went wrong they would blame us." I told them, "That was fine. Universities have been doing that for years."

The USOC said they were going to allow the AOC to use the Olympic Rings under the "ATLANTA 1996" Bid-City logo. The rings were not supposed to be used by the next host city until after the Barcelona 1992 Olympics, but with the IOC, forgiveness was easier to get than permission. Our company, Battle Enterprises, Inc. (BEI), was given three months for licensees to sell-in and three months to sell-out and deplete their inventories. We could not license anyone to sell t-shirts other than the four local companies they had been using. Three were minority-owned companies who had never been involved in licensing of any kind, and the fourth was Caucasian and had been licensed by CLC to do some local business. I thought, "Man, this is mid-October and we have until Christmas to get people licensed, product approved, and merchandise in stores, and this is our busiest time of the year with collegiate licensing. Could we get companies to respond?" Well, it was the "hottest market" in which we had ever been involved, and they got involved in a big way.

The four t-shirt companies were selling shirts in booths around town faster than they could print them. At the end of the day, they were carrying home suitcases full of cash. It was crazy. Since most had no experience in licensing, I sent in one of our auditors to lay down the law on reporting and paying royalties. They were to fax us a report every Friday for the past seven days of sales and pay royalties monthly. I didn't want to disrupt our staff who were all fully engaged with our collegiate business, so I went into operational mode. With my administrative assistant, and some involvement from Pat when we got overloaded, I was carrying boxes every day to AOC offices with products for approval.

The approval process was a little frustrating. They would want to see logo applications moved around, and had other suggestions that may have been OK if the time crunch wasn't so bad. I finally said, "Look, I see this product and design as OK. It doesn't conflict with our rules, and let's let the consumer be the judge. If we keep going back and forth with changes, the consumers will never see them!"

Dan Paradies, the owner of the main retailer in the Atlanta's Hartsfield-Jackson Airport, came to see us. They badly wanted to become a licensee and get ATLANTA 1996 products as quickly as possible. They were great retailers and had sources to get products manufactured quickly and of high quality. We normally prefer to license the manufacturer, but in this case, we did grant Paradies a license. They did a phenomenal job. Paradies and his president, Dick Dickson, and VP Rick Lillie became great partners and great friends, which lasted long after the Olympic run. They were able to sell to Atlanta travelers coming home from trips, and they sold a tremendous amount to passengers stopping by when changing planes or on layover. ATLANTA 1996 merchandise became one of the top Christmas gifts of the year.

Our next meeting with the AOC and USOC occurred after we had collected our first month's royalties. There was still merchandise in the process of approval and manufacturing, but the royalty check was for about $850,000. The USOC's Krimsky said, "Alright Mr. Battle, that's the power of the Olympic brand." I replied, "The Olympic brand is powerful, but this is a result of the euphoria in Atlanta about getting The Games to our city."

We were able to monitor and manage the process very well, without disturbing our staff's work on our collegiate program. At the end of the six months (collections went on until June 1991), we had generated $6 million in royalties. If the rules were not so restrictive, I believe we could have doubled that amount. It was a huge honor to be selected to develop Phase One of the AOC's licensing program and made all of us bigger fans of the Olympics movement than we already were. We were able to buy tickets to opening and closing ceremonies and most of the events we wanted to see. We also attended the 1992 Winter Olympics in Albertville, France, and the 1992 Summer Olympics in Barcelona, Spain, with Dr. Harvey Schiller and his wife, Marcia. I had gotten to know Harvey well when he was SEC Commissioner from 1986-1989. He became president of the USOC in 1990. We were able to stay in the IOC hotel and enjoy many behind-the-scenes activities. Harvey is an amazing man and we remain friends to this day.

The licensing program in Atlanta shut down after our six-month run, and waited until after the 1992 Olympics were held before they resumed the program. By that time, Billy wanted everything run in-house and had a volunteer with retail experience managing the licensing program.

It was a great feeling to know that we generated a significant amount of revenue in 1990 that gave the USOC and ACOG operating capital to build on in preparation for the 1996 Olympics. One of the best things to come out of our new relationship with Billy and his organization was a friendship between the Payne family and ours that remains strong to this day. From flyfishing trips out West and in the Bahamas, to golf outings at Augusta National and other great courses, the social side of our friendship was framed. We have also developed a strong business relationship with Billy and his son Porter over the years. All in all, the 1996 Atlanta Olympics was a life-changing experience in many different ways.

1990-1991

Fiscal year 1990-91 showed the first significant shifts in the buying habits of retailers, which dramatically

leveled off the double-digit growth that many universities enjoyed in previous years. Saturation (over-licensing) of collegiate products started to take its toll. Every licensor was guilty, but those in the collegiate space were the worst.

CLC continued to grow in spite of the negative headwinds we faced, as more universities continued to join. We represented 121 universities, seven bowls and three conferences. Several universities decided to increase their royalty rates from 6.5 percent to 7.5 percent, which was still well behind the professional leagues. The raise in royalty rates did not affect the number of licensees willing to produce and sell those university's products.

The CLC audit program recovered $1.2 million in back royalties. The audit program was designed to produce a level playing field for all universities. We had hoped that by publicizing the scope of our program that licensees would audit themselves and get their books and records in full compliance with our contracts. CLC led the country in the number of audits conducted annually.

Team Hanes by Champ Knit unveiled a revolutionary concept as it introduced an Electronic Data Interchange (EDI) that catered to the mass market. Team Hanes received daily reports of merchandise sold, so they could restock weekly. This was another step in the evolution of technology in retail sales.

In 1991 the Starter brand was doing $200 million in sales on pretty much all sports licensed properties. Demand was so intense, the company's "media mentions" began to frequently occur in police blotters, as Starter's appeal in the early 1990s was a major factor in a string of robberies. The jackets, priced at up to $300, were so coveted that some serious incidents occurred. That bad publicity, combined with a bizarre string of misfortunes to Starter, all resulted in major inventory losses (a warehouse fire, a hurricane, a tornado, a 250,000-piece shipment of jackets from overseas that arrived with a devastating lice infestation). Some thieves quit robbing people and started hijacking trucks carrying Starter merchandise. In spite of all of this, Starter kept rocking and rolling. In 1992, Phil Knight, CEO of Nike, offered to buy Starter. Beckerman declined, choosing to take Starter public the following year, in which Starter posted $350 million in sales.

CLC moved its annual Licensing Directors Seminar from Atlanta to Chicago in association with the National Sporting Goods Association Trade Show. Our annual seminar continued to grow in numbers, as we met to talk about what was happening in the industry. A good portion of the program was having individual licensing directors reporting on successful programs they had implemented at their universities. There was real benefit from the programs, but equally important were the peer-to-peer conversations held away from the meetings. Having the seminar in conjunction with a trade show gave them the opportunity to meet with licensees and retailers as well.

The Atlanta office held its first staff retreat at Stone Mountain outside Atlanta. It was nice for the team to get away for a few days and meet a few hours, and enjoy recreational activities together after the meetings.

Georgia Tech and Colorado shared the National Championship in football in 1990, as the Jackets were No. 1 in the Coaches' Poll and the Buffaloes No. 1 in the AP Poll. We implemented programs at both institutions and found the fan bases to buy National Championship merchandise equally as well when they were co-champions as they did when they were single champions. This split led to the creation of the Bowl Coalition, a precursor to the Bowl Alliance and the Bowl Championship Series (BCS).

In basketball, UNLV defeated Duke in the Final Four, while Arkansas and Georgia Tech were the other semi-finalists. Our top-selling universities in 1990-91 were Georgetown, Michigan, UNLV, North Carolina, Florida State, Illinois, Alabama, Georgia, Yale and Tennessee. Georgetown and Michigan topped $2 million in royalties while UNLV broke the $1 million barrier.

The UNLV basketball team, coached by Jerry Tarkanian, reached the NCAA Final Four four times, getting to the title game twice, and winning one in 1990. He was famous for his combative stance toward the NCAA. He complained for years about the unfairness of the NCAA being reluctant to punish the top basketball schools, but making examples of those in lesser conferences. His most famous quote was, "The NCAA is so mad at Kentucky, they gave Cleveland State two more years of probation." He filed a suit against the NCAA for harassment. The NCAA paid him $2.5 million, and then-NCAA President Cedric Dempsey released a statement that said, in part, "The NCAA regrets the 26-year ongoing dispute with Jerry Tarkanian and looks forward to putting this matter to rest." With UNLV's four Final Four appearances in the last five years, including a National Championship, "Tark" proved that national prominence in basketball can take a university to the top of the heap in the sale of licensed products.

1991-1992

In fiscal year 1991-92, CLC joined with the NFL, MLB, NBA, NHL and Starter in the formation of CAPS, Coalition to Advance the Participation of Sports Logos. As we had begun to work together to fight counterfeit operations like "Dizzy Fox" the previous year by accident, we decided to join forces on purpose and have a major impact on the problem. Bruce Siegal, our general counsel, was instrumental in getting CLC and Starter included. Starter seemed like a strange fit, but their brand — jackets and caps — were among the most counterfeited in the industry. We all supported an office and staff who tracked the bigger counterfeit operations. Much was coming from outside the country and being sold to the growing flea markets and other non-traditional retailers. CAPS proved to be an important weapon in the never-ending fight against counterfeiters.

Our company now had 50 staff members, 20,000 square feet of office space, and represented 124 universities, including newcomers LSU, Pitt, the U.S. Military Academy and Central Florida. We made my son Pat president and chief operating officer, and he led the charge to develop our marketing department to meet the changing needs of the collegiate market. Pat turned 28 years of age in 1991, but he was more prepared to take the reins of CLC at the time than I was to take the head coaching job at Tennessee at that age. He was ready, but I remained CEO and really enjoyed guiding our senior leadership team, even more than running the operations of the company. It was so neat to watch our young staff grow in confidence and assert their own leadership in the organization. I believe that was a primary reason the culture in our organization was so unique.

The marketing department launched *The Collegiate Retailer*, a publication designed to provide retailers with useful information on a monthly basis to expand shelf space for our university merchandise. We were competing with the four professional leagues for shelf space that retailers, in growing numbers, were trying to sell. The leagues had much larger budgets than CLC for those kinds of costs. We had to compete with "guerilla marketing" tactics that didn't cost much but had big impact. We provided some very creative tactics to help our cause, like cheerleaders and mascots at promotional programs, and tickets to big games to be used in other promotions.

In 1991-92, retail sales of all licensed products grew 4.3 percent to $66.2 billion. Sports licensed products grew to $12.1 billion and collegiate sales grew to $2.1 billion. Miami won the 1991 National Championship by finishing on top of the AP Poll in football, followed by Washington, Penn State, Florida State and Alabama. Duke won the 1991 NCAA Basketball Championship over Kansas. North Carolina and UNLV played in the semi-finals.

As a company, we tried to not only plan for and execute marketing and enforcement programs around those "hot market" opportunities, but we also diligently worked to expand the geographical boundaries for those teams in added merchandise sales in the following season.

Our top 10 universities were Georgetown, Michigan, UNLV, Florida State, Duke, North Carolina, Tennessee, Alabama, Illinois and Georgia. Georgetown was our first university to reach $2 million in royalties, and this year became our first to reach $3 million. The first six universities noted above generated more than $1 million in royalties, with Michigan again topping $2 million.

On the downside, we had lost a few major universities that decided to go independent. Ohio State and Stanford left in 1988, Indiana and Oregon State in 1990, Rutgers in 1991, Hawaii in 1992, Kansas and Virginia Tech in 1993, and Arizona State in 1994. Stanford returned to CLC in 2000 and Arizona State in 2011.

The story behind losing Indiana on a Friday the 13th in 1990 provided an experience that has affected my life to this day. Dr. Harvey Schiller, commissioner of the SEC and former executive director of the USOC, suggested I consider trying to work with the Olympic National Governing Bodies (NGBs) to see if we could create a new revenue stream for them, as we were doing for our collegiate clients. There was an NGB for all Olympic sports and most were located in either Indianapolis or Colorado Springs. I decided to arrange meetings with the Indianapolis NGBs (gymnastics, rowing, track and field, and synchronized swimming). On Thursday the 12th, I met with all four, had positive meetings, and had a nice dinner with some of them at the famous St. Elmo's in downtown Indianapolis. I had a 9 a.m. meeting the next day with a VP from Indiana University in Bloomington that had recently taken over responsibility for IU's licensing program.

Indiana won the NCAA basketball title in 1987, and I thought we had done a great job in preparing before and executing after the event to maximize "hot market" opportunities. IU's royalties had gone from $27,300 in 1984, to $46,700 in 1985, $112,000 in 1986, $265,400 in 1987, $518,600 in 1988 and $673,700 in 1989. I was very proud of the job we had done since inception in building Indiana's licensing program, and taking advantage of the size and prestige of the school, as well as its success in basketball. Working with Indiana also gave me an opportunity to renew an acquaintance with head basketball Coach Bob Knight from our time together at Army.

So, after dinner at St. Elmo's, I saw an empty parking space on the street near the entrance to my hotel and decided to park there since I would be leaving around 6:30 the next morning. At the time, there were several cars parked along that street. When I went out the next morning — Friday the 13th — there were no cars parked on the street, including mine! In those days, Budget Rent-a-Car offered a Lincoln Town Car for $39 a day, and that's what I rented.

Rushing back into the hotel, I asked, "What happened to my car?" I had failed to notice the sign that said, "NO PARKING AFTER 11:00 PM". They told me where to go to retrieve my car and pay the fine for parking illegally. I hailed a cab and rushed over to the site to retrieve my car. They were busy chatting and drinking coffee, and not too interested in helping with my emergency. After about an hour, I finally got my car freed from lockup and hit the road for my meeting, which by now I couldn't make on time. I had to call ahead and the VP was gracious enough to reschedule for an early afternoon meeting. I drove on to Bloomington, got there in plenty of time to park, walk around the campus, and then take my meeting. The parking deck where it was suggested that I park had a typical parking lot entry with a moving arm that lifted when a button was pushed and ticket taken from a meter. There was a scaffold above the entrance as I pulled up to the meter and stopped. Two men were working above, applying mortar to some bricks they were replacing. Before I

283

could remove the ticket to raise the arm, there was a big "SPLAT" that sounded as a pile of dark gray mortar landed in the middle of the hood of my clean white Lincoln Town Car. I shook my fist and yelled some words at the workers and entered the parking deck. I angrily searched for and found a parking attendant inside and yelled at him, "Somebody better clean the mortar off the hood of my car before I get back."

That was just the start of one of the worst days in my life. But I was on time for my rescheduled meeting, and I had charts, graphs and lists of all the things we had done to build the Indiana licensing program into one of our best. When I arrived at my meeting, the mood was "icy" to say the least. After apologizing for being late, we started to talk about the university and the basketball program. I think I started out the business discussion by saying something like, "Indiana has one of the fastest-growing licensing programs in the country." His opening line was, "We're paying you too damned much!" I said, "That's what I'm here for, to tell you what we're doing for you to earn our pay!" He responded, "I don't care about hearing that, we're paying you too much!" The conversation went on for about an hour. He finally lightened up a little, but his mind was made up.

I drove back to Indianapolis with my tail between my legs. It was a long trip back to Indianapolis to catch my plane, and a long plane flight home. About the only good thing that happened that day was the parking attendant had gotten someone to clean the mortar off the hood of my rental car. I vowed never to do business of any kind again on Friday the 13th, and I have lived up to that vow. I also vowed to do whatever it took to keep our base of clients updated with our services and the reasons for their growth or decline in royalties. There were a lot of changes that needed to be made.

1992-1993

The 1992-93 fiscal year was a most interesting year in the life of The Collegiate Licensing Company.

In January 1993, Richard D. Schultz, executive director of the NCAA, made a push to take over collegiate licensing and bring it under the NCAA's management. The NCAA had established a licensing program for NCAA marks after universities had already "plowed ground and planted seeds in trademark licensing that had sprouted." In an address to the organization, among many other agenda items, he was quoted in the Jan. 20, 1993, edition of the *NCAA News* with the following:

"So we look down the road the next few years to the challenging financial times. I want to point out to you that there are two areas that we have looked at that seem to be the best potential resources for new income. The first is licensing revenues. During

the past year there was about $60 million in licensing revenue from collegiate products. Unfortunately, only $10 million went back to colleges and universities. About $2 million went to companies that handle domestic licensing. The rest of that difference between $12 million and $60 million represents pirate and counterfeit licensing. While it may be impossible to capture all of that $60 million, a strong licensing program with good enforcement represents an excellent way to immediately increase revenue for many of our member institutions.

"We propose you consider an NCAA Properties concept that would have the potential to generate a higher percentage back to the individual institutions, but also a program that could vigorously enforce a licensing program and reduce dramatically the amount of counterfeit licensing. We'll provide you with more information on this in the very near future."

When I read that, I was so furious that smoke came out of my ears. It was not uncommon for agencies to start up licensing programs only to have the trademark owners take over when the program got up and running. It happened to Licensing Corporation of America when their clients — NBA, MLB and NHL — all took licensing in-house. It happened later with our BEI Company when NASCAR took their program in-house after we paid them $5.5 million in our fifth year. That was the owner's right and it was to be expected, but the NCAA didn't own the university trademarks. We thought they were very naïve about collegiate licensing and knew that Schultz was badly misinformed about the numbers he threw out in the article. But we knew this might happen, and were well prepared to address the situation if it ever came up.

We wrote a position paper to our university clients meeting this attack head-on. The following is an executive summary of that paper:

"As you no doubt are aware, the NCAA has become increasingly aggressive in recent months regarding its proposed plan to take over collegiate licensing. The Collegiate Licensing Company is very concerned with some of the statements being attributed to the NCAA and would like to take this opportunity to clarify our position on the matter.

"NCAA Executive Director Dick Schultz began to discuss the possibility of an NCAA Properties licensing concept with athletics directors over a year ago. In October 1992, Mr. Schultz made a speech to the Sporting Goods Management Association (SGMA) in which he discussed the NCAA Properties concept to the industry. Then at the convention in January 1993, Mr. Schultz discussed licensing as a major potential for new income in his state of the Association address. His other big idea for revenue was an NCAA Division I football championship game.

"We believe the points presented by Mr. Schultz concerning licensing are either false or misleading. Please find below our response to those major points.

1. *Revenue — This is his major point and it is just not true. CLC represents*

125 universities in its Consortium. During the 1991-1992 fiscal year CLC paid its member institutions alone almost $25 million. That does not include the 25-30 major independent licensing programs that probably generated another $20-$25 million. To state that the schools received only $10 million and to infer that only 20 percent of the products in the marketplace were actually licensed was absolutely false.

2. Non-exclusivity — The NCAA is correct in stating that there are too many licensees in the marketplace. The misleading part is the NCAA's inference that companies such as CLC have licensed as many companies as possible to generate more and more revenues. This is not the case. CLC believes very strongly that the market for collegiate merchandise would be stronger and overall revenue greater if the approximately 1,800 licensees across the country would be reduced. However, CLC has operated under a mandate from universities since the very inception of collegiate licensing to run a totally non-exclusive licensing program. This is due to the political sensitivity associated with exclusivity. Universities, unlike professional sports and entertainment licensors, have set objectives that include more than just generating dollars. CLC has worked for more than a decade to ensure that we ran Collegiate Licensing in a way that would meet revenue, trademark protection, and public relations objectives of each institution.

3. Enforcement — While the NCAA enforcement programs surrounding the Final Four is impressive, it covers one city for one week. Collegiate licensing is a nationwide, year-round business that requires an incredible network to control. CLC, since its inception, has been on the leading edge in ensuring that companies who use the universities names and marks are properly licensed. Most recently CLC has been instrumental in founding an organization named CAPS, the Coalition to Advance The Protection of Sports Logos. Its members are the National Football League, Major League Baseball, National Basketball League, National Hockey League, CLC and Starter Sports. CAPS is making a major impact in combatting counterfeit operations nationwide. Speaking of enforcement, dealing with infringers is only one aspect of a comprehensive enforcement program. CLC spends a great deal of time and money each year ensuring that licensees report proper royalties and are in full compliance with their contracts. CLC employs three full-time auditors who conduct more than 150 contract compliance reviews per year. This is the most comprehensive auditing program of any licensor anywhere in the country. During the past three years, CLC has recovered, on behalf of its member institutions, more than $3 million in unreported royalties for licensees.

4. Commission — That NCAA plans to distribute 100 percent of gross reve-

nues back to institutions is something that should be examined very closely. The collegiate market has not grown from a $250 million retail industry in 1981 to a $1.7 billion retail industry in 1992 by accident. It has taken a great deal of time, effort and money on the part of many people to make this happen. CLC employs a full-time staff of 50 professionals focused 100 percent on collegiate licensing. The CLC staff specializes in all areas important to a successful licensing program — marketing, enforcement, contract administration, P.R., accounting, legal and auditing. If similar levels are not maintained for the future, not only will the collegiate market fail to grow for the future, but the base that has been built will likely erode.

"One last point on the subject. Over the last decade, universities have protected and built great equity in their brands. As the market has grown, some universities are generating several million dollars a year. Many more are generating six-figure revenues annually. Your brands have become very valuable. We believe that joint licensing with other brands is a strategy that should be employed only when both brands add value and the results would be more royalties for each. The NCAA brand is of value around NCAA championships. I would argue that attaching your logos to the NCAA on all licensed merchandise would provide for more value to the NCAA than it would to your institution."

I arranged a meeting with Mr. Schultz and told him that he had been misinformed about the numbers he had spoken about at the recent NCAA convention. He was cordial, but not particularly responsive. Later, Jack Waters, who administered the NCAA licensing program, made a presentation to university licensing directors at an ACLA meeting. He got blistered, primarily by independent university licensing directors, about the idea that he could run university licensing programs better than they could. It wasn't long before the NCAA backed off of that idea and went on about their business. Actually, a few years later, they put out a bid for someone to manage the NCAA program. They awarded the bid to another company in the 1993-94 fiscal year.

In the 1997-1998 fiscal year the NCAA had a change in senior leadership, ultimately turning over control of licensing and marketing to the late Dave Cawood. Dave was a friend of CLC as he had seen the power of outsourcing to the right partner via Host Communications, which managed the launch of the NCAA Corporate Partner program.. They allowed their contract with the other licensing company to expire and asked us if we would take over the NCAA licensing program. We agreed to do so, as long as they understood what we were going to do and how we were going to do it. We carefully added NCAA marks on products and programs in which the NCAA marks added value to university joint-licensed marks. We fairly quickly were able to do that on two major programs already in place with a generic "College Football" themed program that raised the values across the board and added revenues to all parties. The NCAA remained a valuable client up to the time I left CLC in 2013, and still remain a client at the time of this writing.

Steve Crossland and I had talked extensively about the changing dynamics in the industry, and the need to transform ourselves into a more formidable marketing company. While offices on the East and West Coasts had staffs to service the rapid growth and had served us well for the past decade, we found that we had a great deal of duplication of effort. If we eliminated that, we would free up dollars to make the changes needed to continue to grow and flourish. We talked about the need for one of us to buy out the other. He indicated that at this stage he was not interested in buying, but would entertain an offer to sell. We put together an offer to which he and his family agreed, and in April 1993, acquired all interests in CLC's domestic licensing operation. *Sports Licensing International* wrote the following article:

College Licensing Industry Changes Shape as CLC Splits

"The face of the collegiate licensing business changed dramatically last week with the radical reorganization of The Collegiate Licensing Co. (CLC), the leading player in the market. Under the surprise reorganization, Bill Battle, president of the Atlanta office of CLC, has acquired all of the interests of CLC from former partner Steve Crossland; all CLC operations, which were previously split in an unusual joint venture between the Atlanta and Carpenteria, CA offices, will be consolidated in Battle's Atlanta headquarters.

"Meanwhile, Crossland will concentrate solely on the licensing of American collegiate merchandise in international markets through Crossland Enterprises, Inc. (CEI).

"Battle and Crossland formed the CLC into the leading consortium for collegiate licensing during their 10-year partnership. In 1983, the two men formed a joint venture that became CLC, which now has more than 130 colleges, universities, bowl games and athletic conferences under contract.

"Both parties have indicated that the decision was mutual. Crossland has been devoting more time to the international side of the business. By divesting the company of domestic responsibilities, CEI will focus exclusively on overseas collegiate licensing. CEI now represents 48 schools internationally, including Georgetown, Miami, Florida, Florida State, Michigan, Duke and University of Georgia.

"Tina Crossland, vice president-marketing, told SLI that while the international market is certainly not as broad based as the domestic collegiate licensing business, there remains the opportunity for a more focused company to take it to the next level. "We see great opportunity to create," she said. "The international market has grown tremendously in the last 18 months and will continue to do so."

"International licensees for CEI products are being given until next fall to change their labeling from CLC to CEI. CEI will make a major push at the next ISPO in September in Germany to make the European community aware of its new commitment and to clear up any confusion among the industry."

There is a back-story to our purchase of Steve's interest in CLC. Steve and I had actually talked about making that change a few years earlier. I made an offer that I thought was fair and told Steve I would buy at that price, or I would sell at 10 percent across the board higher. A few days later he sent me a Fed-Ex package saying he accepted my offer to sell my interest for my price plus 10 percent. I couldn't sleep! I thought I could walk away, but it was eating me up. I called Steve a few days later and asked if we could talk. Eugenia and I flew out and met with Steve and his wife Jean all day. We cleared up some areas of concern on both sides and they graciously agreed that we would continue as we were doing. I was, and still am, most appreciative of their generosity.

When we discussed it this time around, some things had changed and they were less interested in buying. I needed a good attorney and a good banker. I was raised to believe what my dad had taught, "If you can't pay cash, don't buy it!" I definitely couldn't pay cash, but had a great relationship with my banker, Rod Knowles. Rod was president of the Chattahoochee National Bank, a small bank in Marietta, not far from our Atlanta office. Rod and his wife Dixie had become great friends. He was ahead of his time as a banker. A few years later when banking laws changed so that banks could buy other banks beyond state lines, Rod had positioned his bank to be purchased, and did so in a very favorable deal. Rod put together a loan package that I could borrow what I deemed to be "a whole lot of money!" I was scared, but pretty confident that we could pay it off in three years.

We had used Maynard, Cooper & Gale in Birmingham to form my companies and later to advise on our merger with Steve and ICE in 1983. They did a great job, but this time around I wanted an Atlanta lawyer. The only one I knew was Horace Sibley, a senior partner at King & Spalding. Horace and King & Spalding were instrumental in helping Billy Payne with his legal needs in getting and running the Olympics. I had met Horace during the time we worked with the AOC and the USOC on Phase I of the AOC licensing program. I told Horace what I wanted to do and he came up with a young attorney named Russ Richards. Russ was working on big merger and acquisition clients, and when approached by Horace about helping us, his first response was, "Horace, I'm really busy." Horace told him who was involved and he said, "OK, I'd like to do this."

Back in spring 1970, shortly after I had been named head coach at Tennessee, I decided to get out and meet with UT students to see what they were thinking. When I was at Alabama, fraternities were sort of on the liberal side of campus thinking. In the late 1960s and early '70s, they seemed to be more on the conservative side. I scheduled lunch or dinner meetings with just about every fraternity on campus. After I met Russ and we chatted about what we were trying to do to buy out Steve and Jean's interest in CLC, he remembered my visit to his fraternity house at Tennessee, when he asked, "I asked you why we were scheduling weaker teams and not more like Notre Dame?" My response was, "We can't win the national championship playing in the SEC and scheduling all non-conference games with the Notre Dames of the world." Russ proved to be an incredible help in making a deal to complete the buyout with everyone feeling good.

As we went into the final meeting, we had "the number" in mind. We started with our "best offer," and it was a good one. We also had an investment banker working with us. His thought was, "You won't be able to buy at that number." I believed we could, but I told both that if we get it for this number, we would celebrate with our wives in a warm climate, and there would be a substantial bonus (which I named) for each of them.

We got it for the number, although we sweetened the deal with an all-cash payment instead of our three-year payment offer. We did enjoy a nice vacation with our wives in Aruba. When I went to pay Russ his bonus, he said, "Put that money in your pocket." How many lawyers have you known to ever do that? Russ and his wife Melanie became great friends with both Pat and me. He was a rock star in our negotiations and closing documents 14 years later when we sold our licensing business to IMG. And he's been helpful in pretty much every business deal that Pat and I have had ever since. It was a blessing in my life when Russ Richards entered. I am thankful that I had an answer to his question back in 1970 that impressed him. We never know when the people we meet will have a significant impact on our lives.

The reception from the industry was positive. The reception from most of our CLC clients was also positive, although there were some questions from some universities that had most of their contact from Steve and his staff. We hired two of Steve's people and brought in Tad Schroeder, the former recruiting coordinator at Army. Tad was great. He had been working with many of our university clients in the Midwest when he lived in Cincinnati. Tad went on from West Point to be the head football coach at the Coast Guard Academy. After that, he returned to Cincinnati to manage his family assets. He returned to athletics as an assistant AD at SMU when the stock market went down. Licensing was under his area of responsibility, so we worked with him there, too. Later when he returned to Cincinnati, Steve and I hired him to work on Midwestern universities. With his pleasant but business-like manner, we assigned Tad to some of our most high-maintenance licensing directors.

Including the three above, we hired 15 new people as we consolidated all operations in Atlanta. We changed the look of our offices and also changed our look to the industry. At the 1993 NSGA Trade Show in Chicago, CLC unveiled its new booth, which cost way more than my first house! We also unveiled the CLC VISION 2000 concept. It laid out our plans to move the collegiate market to $4 billion in retail sales by the year 2000, a bold goal for growth over the next seven years..

Holding our fifth-annual Licensing Directors Seminar in conjunction with the NSGA Show, we were able to explain in detail our vision for the remaining seven years in the 20th century. We had some great programs with outside speakers, many of whom were CLC clients. But some of our most valuable programs were deep discussions with clients about the components of our plans. The feedback was great and we learned a lot about proceeding with our reinvented marketing plan. The entire effort in Chicago received very positive responses from universities, licensees and retailers.

The bulk of our new hires were assigned to marketing and administrative functions. We expanded our number of personnel devoted to calling on retailers to get more shelf space for our clients, teaming up with licensees to put together more and better retail promotions, and working to bring more well-known brands into the collegiate space. Our university services staff also focused on working more with athletics departments and their media rights holders to get more and better promotions featuring licensed products going out on their radio networks, delayed telecasts, coaches' shows and print media distribution.

As mentioned earlier, in 1984 we signed a four-year lease in Atlanta for 1,900 square feet. By 1988 we needed to expand, so we moved across I-75 to another office complex. We doubled in size to 3,800 square feet and thought that would last for the four-year term of that lease. By the time that lease was up, the Atlanta office had expanded seven times and the staff had grown from five to 30 associates. In addition, we had three outside auditors who spent most of their time auditing CLC licensees. We also had consulting agreements with firms who assisted us in developing marketing programs with licensees and retailers. We had agreements with computer hardware and software analysts, and of course, attorneys for advice and counsel on enforcement methods, and auditors of our own books and records.

Like any company, our staff changed from time to time. Some people outgrow companies and some companies outgrow people. Our goal was to replace people who left with well-trained candidates who would carry on the business relationships with the same service-first attitude. One of our greatest compliments regarding staff turnover came from LSU's licensing director at the time, Ralph Gossard. After a couple of staff replacements over a period of years, Ralph said to me, "You must have a farm team out there somewhere because everyone you send in is as effective as the last." That was definitely music to my ears and a credit to our senior staff for helping us either in hiring new replacements or rewarding current staff members with promotions. I very much preferred the latter, especially in critical situations that dealt directly with clients.

Alabama won the 1992 National Championship by defeating Miami in the Sugar Bowl. Florida State, Miami, Notre Dame and Michigan rounded out the top five in the AP Poll. Duke completed back-to-back national titles in basketball, defeating Michigan's Fab Five to win the 1992 NCAA tourney, with Indiana and Cincinnati also making the semi-finals.

Our top universities in the 1992-93 fiscal year were Michigan, Georgetown, Duke, Florida State, North Carolina, Alabama, Tennessee, UNLV, Kentucky and Georgia. Michigan and Georgetown each reached $4 million, Duke passed $2 million, Florida State, North Carolina and Alabama were over $1 million, while UNLV, Tennessee, Kentucky and Georgia were close.

1993-1994

The next fiscal year saw a great deal of change in how we approached our business. As we did every year, we looked back at our strategic plan to determine where we were in each of the seven categories, and set forth goals in each area. As time went by, our needs changed and this exercise helped us get on point to achieve our overall goal — to help the market for collegiate sales to grow to $4 billion by 2000. The base from which we started 1993 at $2.5 billion in collegiate retail sales was miles higher than at the time of our 1983 merger at $400 million. Having everything consolidated into the Atlanta office was very exciting. Our current staff, as well as our new hires, were highly energized.

Penn State joined the CLC Consortium, and this was the first major independent university to come on board since our Atlanta office consolidation in 1993. This was a big deal, both for Penn State and for CLC. There is truly strength in numbers, and the addition of Penn State sent another message to the industry that the heretofore fragmentation of the collegiate market was dwindling rapidly. There were still 15 to 20 major independents that we needed to get on board to further strengthen the collegiate impact on the marketplace.

Nike decided to become a collegiate licensee and bring a new dimension to the cause. They created a line of on-field merchandise worn by coaches and players. This line was offered at retail, which created excitement in the industry. At the time though, Nike was more interested in the brand awareness it achieved by getting the Nike logo on collegiate football and basketball players than it was in selling licensed merchandise. They took a very conservative approach by selling only to certain retailers. Since their products were manufactured overseas, they advised retailers to place big orders, as there would be no products available after those sold out. Nike became one of our leading licensees over time, but there were some problems along the way. They produced a line of non-logoed products in the colors of the respective teams in the markets in which they sold. They claimed they were generic and we couldn't enforce team colors. When retailers started tagging the items by the collegiate name, like "Carolina Blue," we convinced them this was not a good idea as a partner with the universities. Another problem we had was the size, position and number of their Nike logos on licensed products. As had previously occurred with The Game and Starter, the manufacturer's label became popular on the outside of the product, as opposed to the inside as had been the norm in the past.

It was obvious they were using the popularity of the collegiate products to further build their brands. That was OK to a point, but became problematic when people started to say that their logo doesn't just talk, it screams! As an example, Nike caps for Florida State University were very popular with the FSU fanbase. We saw the Nike FSU design go from a big FSU design on the front of the cap with a small Nike "swoosh" on the back, to a big Nike swoosh on the front of the cap with a small FSU logo on the sides or the back. On apparel products, we saw Nike's name or marks begin to appear multiple times on individual products. We got with our schools and came up with some recommended guidelines. They agreed and we negotiated some mutually approved guidelines. Regardless of the issues, Nike produced great products and helped the collegiate market grow by elevating the brand perception of licensed merchandise and introducing innovative new products each year.

Nike wisely saw that the advertising and public relations value they could receive through media coverage of college and professional athletes who were wearing the Nike "Swoosh" on shoes, socks, pants, jerseys and t-shirts was worth far more than the amounts of money and free products they were providing. Nike has been a great partner with many universities, including The University of Alabama, with on-field uniforms and shoes for many sports, and a robust licensed product offering at retail.

In 1994, Starter was CLC's top apparel licensee, but bad news was in store for sports licensed products in general. Major League Baseball players went on strike and the league canceled its post-season play. Traditionally the hottest time of year for apparel sales occurred in the fall. Back-to-school, the start of high school, college and professional football, the MLB pennant races and the World Series all drove sales of sports licensed products. But the lack of televised baseball games hit Starter hard.

The National Hockey League lockout followed shortly thereafter. Starter was suddenly without two sports that drove its business. Nothing could be "authentic" when the players, coaches and trainers weren't working. After treading water for a few years, Starter declared bankruptcy in 1999, citing over $120 million in debt to the professional league creditors. The company changed hands several times before landing at Nike in 2004. By 2007, Starter was acquired by Iconia, a brand management company, which currently issues licenses to apparel licensees for distribution at Walmart, Amazon and others. More on that subject later.

Electronic Arts produced a college football video game in 1994 entitled, "Bill Walsh College Football." It was carefully constructed to try to avoid lawsuits from colleges and universities. All team names were either state names or city names, for example, Clemson, South Carolina, Auburn, Alabama, etc. Two names that were included were South Bend, Indiana, in place of Notre Dame, and Tallahassee, Florida, in place of FSU. All team uniforms were at least three PMS colors away from the official color. Our general counsel, Bruce Siegal, started writing mild cease and desist letters when we heard what they were doing. The C&D letters got more aggressive as time passed with no response. One day when I was out of town, I made my normal call to the office and spoke with various departments to see what was going on. When I got to Bruce, he told me that Electronic Arts had filed a lawsuit against us. I was stunned and blurted out, "They are suing us?!" I couldn't believe it. The president of EA called and said he and his attorney would like to meet with us. At the meeting, we all sat down around our conference table and introductions were made, but there was little conversation as the atmosphere was cold.

A quiet came over the room and I finally said, "OK, you asked for the meeting. What do you want to talk about?" He said, "This is a friendly lawsuit," to which I interrupted and said, "You may have friendly lawsuits out in California, but we don't have them here." He went on to say that they would love to get the rights to official college teams, including cheerleaders and mascots. They weren't sure if we had the rights to deliver that to them. He went on to say, "Our lawsuit was filed in California in a circuit friendly to our side, but primarily to determine rights. We were afraid you or a university might file suit in a small town in the South."

We continued the discussion and saw that he was sincere about wanting to work with us. We went to lunch and talked about our position that before we could move forward, we needed to collect back royalties for their infringement in the "Bill Walsh College Football" games. We agreed on a small amount as he convinced us that they would spend a lot of money developing a great game and a lot more marketing dollars taking it to the market.

We went to the universities for approval. Most already contained a provision in their scholarships spelling out the universities' rights to use player names and likenesses in promoting games on radio, television and print advertising. Language was later modified to include their numbers on things like video games, jerseys, etc. This put them in sync with NCAA regulations.

Electronic Arts, over the years, did a remarkable job. Their marketing slogan was "If it's in the game, it's in the game." Each year they improved the look and feel of the game to put numbers on jerseys that coincided with players' positions, size and color. No names on jerseys were authorized, but they did a great job of duplicating the look of actual players, mascots and cheerleaders. We had approval rights of all of the content, but got copies with a very short time to get approval. We never did anything without approval of our licensing directors at client universities. Actually, on products like this, as well as in bowl games and promotions, manufacturers didn't want to fool with clearing rights to multiple universities, so we were able to include independent schools. We always looked hard at every product and design, and pretty much knew what our universities wanted, therefore we wouldn't send it to them unless we thought they would approve. There was very little that universities changed in the EA video games. One independent university, however, objected to the size of the busts on their cheerleaders and made them change. EA evolved to be CLC's No. 1 non-apparel licensee. The royalties were nice, but we were more interested in reaching the video-game-playing consumers in order to educate them on the positive attributes of college — intense rivalries, cool and unique stadiums, passionate fans, marching bands, cheerleaders and mascots. EA eventually added a dorm room and a classroom element in the game to highlight the uniqueness of college as opposed to professional leagues. All of this was done in incredible detail by EA, as they became one of our key business partners for the next two decades.

A funny story about video games occurred in the mid to late '90s. Tennessee Coach Phillip Fulmer was the speaker at an Atlanta Touchdown Club meeting. Since I was a member of the club, and Phillip was a co-captain of our 1971 Tennessee team, they asked if I would introduce him. I was pleased to do so and came early to visit with him. He asked how the video games were doing. I told him they were doing great, and paying the schools a lot of money. Then he went into a diatribe about how he was frustrated with them. "How in the world could they bother you?" I asked. Phillip responded, "Ol' Johnny, who was a good player for us, seemed to be in a funk and wasn't playing well. I called him into my office and asked what in the world was his problem. Johnny bowed his head, looked embarrassed, and finally blurted out, 'Why am I not on the first team on the EA video game?'" Phillip said he laughed and told the player, "Son, there are a few things I can control around here, but that's not one of them."

I was sad to see the litigation involving "Name, Image, and Likeness" rights as pertaining to collegiate video games. It is my strong belief that, at that time, had players had their choice about being in a video game without payment, 98 percent would have elected to be in the game. What a cool thing it was to be able to play a game with your buddies against SEC opponents or other teams with your own number and body characteristics in the game. It could happen again in line with EA's agreement with the NFL Players Association if colleges can figure out how to get there. As of this writing, the NCAA, universities and student-athletes are in deep dialog around both the legal and legislative solutions to open up a student-athlete's name, image and likeness rights across college athletics.

The biggest loss in the ending of collegiate video games was not the dollars involved. Our number one goal of licensing EA to do collegiate video games was another step in our ultimate desire to "make college cool!" We were able to reach hundreds, if not thousands, of young people in a way that led them to learn college teams, mascots, fight songs, cheerleaders and stadia. They could play on the Oregon team, even if they lived in Florida, and become more interested in Pac-10 football.

From a marketing standpoint, CLC upped the time and energy devoted to creative ways to expand collegiate brand equity and generate more royalties. We encouraged and led major promotions around Centennial events in university and athletic programs. We aligned with Sean Michael Edwards Design firm to encourage universities to update logos, add accent colors, and create new logos directed at women, children and other sectors.

We held our seventh-annual Licensing Directors Seminar at Callaway Gardens, Georgia. Callaway is a lovely 6,500-acre resort, which was a nice break from previous seminars in Atlanta and Chicago. At those previous seminars, breaks and down times were mostly occupied with walking the trade show floors and meeting with licensees. At Callaway Gardens, our clients could swim, boat, fish, ride bikes and tour the beautiful gardens.

The title of our seminar was, "Vision 2000, One Year Later." We were able to bring our members up to date on the new staff we had hired and our stepped-up marketing efforts. Because of the proximity to our offices in

Atlanta, we invited most of our staff to spend some time there to meet the licensing directors they had dealt with by phone but never in face-to-face meetings. It was good for both sides to have this opportunity in a relaxed setting.

Our message to our clients, in a nutshell, was: "Consolidation in the Atlanta office is now complete, with 15 new staff members brought on board last year; Although overall retail sales of licensed products were down in 1991 and flat in 1993, and some universities saw a decline in revenues, Consortium revenues continued to grow at a 20 percent rate; Our belief since we started has been when revenues grow, we invest in staff and services to keep the Consortium growing; We have 42 CLC staff members, 16 who have been there more than five years, and four who have been there more than 10 years; Our philosophy has always been to take advantage of the power of the group of universities (macro), while providing excellent services to each institution (micro), so to keep the group strong, we must satisfy the needs of each institution; We want you to especially be aware of the importance of "macro" or big-picture programs, therefore, as a group, we must aggressively increase national marketing and enforcement programs to compete with the growing number of licensors in the marketplace; You are the boss, you can run your program by yourself, or we can run your program by ourselves — but together we are much more effective; We are proud that in the last 10 years (1983-1993) we have generated more than $100 million in royalties for our member institutions, and with your help, we will generate the next $100 million in three years (1996), and reach our objective of $4 billion in collegiate retail sales by 2000; Overall retail sales of licensed products rose to $70.1 billion, sports licensed products rose to $13.8 billion, and collegiate sales remained at $2.5 billion."

Sports Trend put both the CLC and NASCAR logos and estimated market share — along with NFL, MLB, NBA and NHL — on the cover of its *1994 Licensed Product Guide*. It was gratifying to see that our company had grown to the point where we were now positioned with the best licensors in the industry. As can be seen, we were able to get NASCAR's growth in licensed products sales in with the professional leagues. Brian France always wanted to build NASCAR to the point it was recognized as a major professional league, and we were glad we were a part of helping NASCAR achieve that recognition. As a side note, Battle Enterprises, Inc. signed a letter of intent in a joint venture with the Paradies Shops to manage the licensing for the PGA Tour, located in Ponte Vedra, Florida. More to come in a later chapter.

Florida State won the 1993 National Championship in football, with Notre Dame, Nebraska, Auburn and Florida next in the final AP Poll. Arkansas won the 1993-94 NCAA Basketball Championship, defeating Duke, while Arizona and Florida also made the Final Four. Our top universities in 1993-1994 fiscal year were Michigan ($6.2 million), Florida State ($3.0 million), Georgetown ($2.9 million), North Carolina ($2.5 million), Alabama ($2.1 million), Kentucky ($1.629 million), Duke ($1.623 million), Tennessee ($1.3 million), Wisconsin ($1.25 million) and Georgia ($739,000). Michigan crossed the $6 million mark in annual royalties, Florida State $3 million, Georgetown $2.9 million, and nine of the 10 earned more than $1 million.

LESSONS LEARNED, FROM 1983 MERGER WITH ICE TO 1993 ACQUISITION OF ICE:

- Consolidation in ownership can produce efficiencies that in partnerships are more difficult to achieve. Timing is the key to everything.
- There are no such things as friendly lawsuits.
- Sometimes coaches do their best job to get their team to 6-5. The team and the plan might be good, but market forces create headwinds that will eventually go away. Organizations that can stay the course can come out stronger. Obviously that doesn't apply to coaching.
- This is a repeat, but it is important to keep working to improve all facets of the organization in both good times and bad.
- One can achieve tremendous growth in the pursuit of the mission by gaining five years of cumulative experience, as opposed to getting one year's experience five times.
- You never know when you will meet someone who can change your life. Pay attention. I call them "Angels" and as can be seen in this book, I have been lifted up by many.
- Data is a blessing and a curse. Technology can provide a plethora of data, but it is only effective if one can harness and understand the meaning. "I.T." people love to churn out data, but someone in the organization may need to "dumb it down" to let the CEO or department head understand how it can help the organization.
- Making staff members feel like owners can make a huge difference in the operation of the organization. Phantom stock is a proven method, especially if real stock is not a viable option in a privately held company.
- If you are selling your organization to one with high-powered attorney negotiations, you had better match them. The price will be well worth the investment.
- It is good to celebrate milestones. Your staff and your clients appreciate reminders of the never-ending chase to accomplish the mission.
- There are silver linings in every cloud. Sometimes you need to look hard to find them, but they are there. It is better to find hope in them than to wallow in the pity created by the cloud.
- Morale is helped if you can promote from within. Sometimes it is necessary to bring hires in from the outside, but bringing them in over other people tends to hurt morale unless handled properly, but like anything else, it can be managed.

1994-1995

The 1994-95 fiscal year saw another previously independent major university, the University of Florida, join the CLC Consortium. Jeremy Foley, the athletics director at Florida, had begun his tenure as an intern in the UF ticket office in 1976. He served in just about every position in the department until named AD in 1992. He was one of the best in the business at that time, and was still there when I returned to the University of Alabama as AD in 2013. Adding Florida as a client was a major accomplishment, sending another message to the industry that CLC was indeed the guiding force in collegiate licensing, and one of the top trademark licensing firms in the country.

The overall retail market for licensed products in North America declined in 1995 from $70.1 billion to $69.9 billion. Sports licensed products declined from $13.7 billion to $13.4 billion, and college licensing remained flat at $2.5 billion. CLC's gross revenues grew 7.2 percent in 1995, its lowest percentage of growth since inception. The previous year's growth rate was 18.2 percent, which at that time was its lowest percentage growth rate since inception. The message was clear, as industry headlines began to pop up saying, "The Bloom is off the Licensing Rose." That was the bad news. The good news was the licensed products market was huge compared to where it was in 1981, and by now, our strategic and tactical directives were to fight for a bigger piece of the retail space devoted to licensed products.

The fact that major independents continued to join our cause gave added strength to our efforts. My son Pat played a major role in the development and execution of our marketing strategies. My focus from start to finish was making sure we were doing the best we possibly could to provide excellent service to our university clients and to keep them signing long-term contract extensions with CLC. I believed that was the best possible way to get the remaining major independents to join in our collective fight for more retail shelf space.

We made some great hires back in 1992, 1993 and 1994 when we acquired all U.S. collegiate licensing rights from ICE. Kit Walsh in 1992 and Derek Eiler in 1993 were two of our best. Both started out in University Services and did a great job working with university clients, which was a great way for them to learn our business. Pat recruited Kit to move to a position as full-time marketing director, while Derek moved to director of University Services and was helpful in making sure we were providing excellent services to our collegiate clients.

Over the next few years, we made a major push into developing relationships with top retailers around the country. While the professional leagues had money to spend to put together major promotions with specific licensees in specific retail chains, we still had to use smoke, mirrors, collegiate cheerleaders and mascots, tickets to big games, and a lot of "elbow grease." To young readers, "elbow grease" can also be defined as "sweat equity" or "hard work" or "anything we could think of other than hard cash." Over time, retailers began to expect cash, and we figured that one out as well.

In the retail market place, when Major League Baseball cancelled its post-season playoffs and soon afterward the NHL had a lockout, my initial thought was that retailers would have more "open to buy" money that would go to NFL and collegiate merchandise. That didn't happen. Many retailers that jumped on the licensed products bandwagon as it was going up, jumped off entirely when it started going down. They marked down the merchandise and began to replace their "licensed" shelf space with other categories. That was a serious problem for all licensors.

In athletics, sometimes coaches do their best coaching jobs to get their teams to 6-5 seasons. We clearly saw the next two to five years would be very challenging. Not only did we need to compete with the other sports and entertainment marketers for retail shelf space, we also had to convince universities that they needed to strengthen their overblown number of licensees, but they also needed to reinvest some of "their share" of royalties generated. Due to possible anti-trust issues, we had to do that one university at a time, rather than as a collective force. It was a challenge, but our whole career in dealing with universities was a challenge. We had built trust over the years, and it never wavered in good times or bad.

We liked to create task forces among our licensing directors, selecting a few to come to Atlanta for a several days to focus on specific issues. It helped us with the issues, but it also gave us the opportunity to introduce them to our staff and show them how many different people touched their programs every day. We always tried to treat our universities as partners, and made sure we listened to their ideas and, as best we could, solve their problem and address their opportunities.

It took years to address the market saturation problem created by over-licensing, but most universities worked diligently with our staff to put more product categories out for bid, and grant exclusive and semi-exclusive licenses in certain product categories. This not only allowed us to give licensees better protection, but to also significantly increase royalty rates and guarantees.

Our marketing efforts increased across the board. Our Public Relations and Publications staffs bombarded licensees, retailers and media with CLC activities, accomplishments and programs. Retail Services staff communicated regularly with licensees and retail buys, developing relationships of trust, much like what we had done over the years with universities. This was done with different staff members assigned to both apparel and non-apparel categories.

Promotional licensing staff developed impressive collateral materials to attract more companies into collegiate promotions. Our alignment with Sean Michael Edwards Design greatly improved graphics, new logos and colors at a growing number of institutions.

On the enforcement side of the company, we added staff and programs that truly formed a national network through which we could aggressively deal with infringers. Our affiliation with CAPS had a major impact in the marketplace. Only two years old, CAPS had seized tens of millions of dollars' worth of counterfeit merchandise. As reported earlier, CAPS was funded by NFL, MLB, NBA, NHL, CLC and Starter Sportswear. On the preventive enforcement side we all worked together to strengthen anti-counterfeiting laws, and worked diligently with our universities to advise and assist in their registration of university trademarks. On the contract compliance front, CLC continued to audit more licensees than any other licensor in the industry. Licensing administration had made considerable progress since consolidation in 1993 by adding staff and the company's commitment to improving our data management systems.

Arkansas won the 1994 NCAA basketball tourney over Duke, with Arizona and Florida also in the Final Four. Nebraska won the 1994 college football National Championship, Penn State, Colorado, Florida State and Alabama filling out the top five. Our top universities in fiscal year 1994-1995 were Michigan, Florida State, North Carolina, Nebraska, Kentucky, Alabama, Georgetown, Tennessee, Arkansas, Wisconsin and Duke. Actually that is 11 universities, but they all generated over a million dollars each. Michigan led with $5.9 million, while FSU, UNC and Nebraska each generated more than $2 million.

1995-1996

The 1995-1996 fiscal year was probably the most painful in the 15 years of the licensed products explosion.

At our ninth-annual Licensing Directors Seminar in Atlanta, Craig Koenig, CEO of Koenig Sporting Goods, said, "The 1980s were just too easy in which to do business. Now there is a lot of pain. The trick is to be left standing when the pain stops."

Tracy Benson of *Sports Style* magazine said, "It was 12 months the sports licensing business would like to forget. Labor strife in the pro leagues and a fashion turn away from the 'licensed look' combined to make sales increases the exception rather than the rule."

There were four key negative trends that we believed licensors, such as ourselves, needed to figure out how to overcome:

The retail market was still saturated with licensed products. Apparel led the way during the high-growth years. Too many apparel licensees and imports resulted in discounted prices. More supply than demand resulted in a very soft market for apparel.

Competition for retail shelf space was at an all-time high. Shelf space for licensed products was shrinking. Every day, new licensors entered the marketplace. Professional leagues had more resources than most to "buy retail shelf space." "Character and entertainment" had become the most popular property type. "Trademarks and Brands" passed "Sports Licensed" in 1995, in most industry rankings.

Industry consolidation changed the mindset of licensees and retailers. In the 1980s, Starter, Nutmeg, The Game Sports Novelties, Chalkline, and even Champion, all got started in the collegiate licensed products business. Today, conglomerates own them all. Big corporate thinking was very different from entrepreneurial thinking. Retail consolidation had also occurred. Big corporations focused on global issues and the profit picture made decisions to cut losses and move on, where entrepreneurial thinking might have tended to fight through current problems and come out stronger on the other end.

There was a definite shift away from licensed sports products by consumers. It seemed that back around the early 1990s, walking downtown in New York City, or in most any city, that about one in 10 people were wearing clothing with professional, collegiate or entertainment logos. Licensed apparel was definitely in as a fashion statement. As fashion goes, things change rapidly and dramatically and move on to the next fad.

CLC introduced a new corporate identity. Up to now, the only logo associated with CLC had been the Officially Licensed Products red, white and blue circular mark. Now the blue label "Collegiate Licensing Company — CLC" added a new corporate identity to the industry, in CLC's 25th year of doing business. At the same time, we modernized our Officially Licensed Collegiate Products label.

The annual Licensing Directors Seminar was held in Atlanta in May, three months before the 1996 Atlanta Olympics. Georgia Tech served as our host, and Tech's licensing director, Tammy Tuley, did a great job in opening the Institute's doors to our group.

We treated our guests with an Olympic experience, as we were able to enjoy the Atlanta Olympic Stadium Opening Ceremony. Ambassador Andrew Young, Major Bill Campbell, Governor Zell Miller, International Olympic Committee President Juan Antonio Samaranch and the man responsible for bringing the Olympics to Atlanta, Billy Payne, all spoke, officially cut the ribbons and opened Atlanta Olympic Stadium. After the ceremonies, we were able to watch the Atlanta Grand Prix, where premier track and field athletes competed to qualify for the Olympic Games. Later we toured the Georgia Tech campus to view the Olympic facilities there. They included dormitories built to house Olympic athletes, and were later turned over to Georgia Tech and Georgia State University to house students. The swimming and diving competition also took place on the Georgia Tech campus in the heart of Atlanta.

Holding the Olympics in Atlanta and its suburbs left many legacy facilities. Two of the best in my opinion included Atlanta Centennial Park and the Atlanta Olympic Stadium. The Centennial Park areas tore down a blighted section in the city and converted it into a vibrant area that attracts millions of visitors each year. The stadium was designed to house the Olympics, but further designed to undergo immediate renovation to house the Atlanta Braves baseball facilities, until just recently when the Braves moved north outside the city.

In spite of the difficulties over the last 18 months in Team Sports Licensing, overall retail sales of licensed merchandise rose from $69.9 billion to $72.3 billion. Sports Licensed edged back up to $13.8 billion, and collegiate remained flat at $2.5 billion. CLC added nine more universities to the Consortium, bringing the total to 147. We represented the Sugar, Orange, Cotton, Aloha and Copper bowls, as well as the Southeastern, Atlantic Coast, Big East and Western Athletic conferences. We also added three other Collegiate Properties: the Kick-off Classic, the Pigskin Classic and College Football USA.

Our top-selling universities in 1995-1996 were Michigan, Nebraska, North Carolina, Kentucky, Penn State, Florida State, Alabama, Florida, Tennessee, Georgetown and Wisconsin. Michigan generated $4.8 million, Nebraska $2.9 million, UNC $2.9 million, Penn State $2.3 million and the others more than a million each.

Consolidation of Sports Licensed Products manufacturers and retailers would continue for five more years until the shakeout was completed and the market turned around to double-digit gains. Those who survived were indeed stronger for the experience, and the market worked for those who listened and responded. CLC was one of those who emerged far stronger than before.

1996-1997

The NCAA asked CLC if it would manage the NCAA Licensing Program in fiscal year 1996-1997. You may recall that in 1992, the NCAA made a push to take over collegiate licensing, but it was met with such a negative response from its members that it backed off that effort, made peace with university licensing directors, and soon after that signed an Agency Agreement with a company that started in 1991 as a competitor to CLC. That relationship lasted a few years.

The NCAA recognized the huge difference in infrastructure and manpower in our two organizations, and asked us if we would take on assisting the NCAA in managing its programs. We were pleased to do so. CLC was fortunate that the only major competition it had up until 1991 were those universities who elected to handle their own programs. The startup company in 1991 really never bothered us from our focus on representing major universities. It did affect our margins some, as after its entry we had to go through more bids, but the way our financial offers to universities were structured, the effect was minimized.

We decided to have our 10th-annual Licensing Directors Seminar out west since all previous ones had been held in the eastern part of the country. This one was held in Las Vegas, and UNLV served as our host institution. The agenda was primarily to accomplish "the integration of athletic marketing and trademark licensing." Southeastern Conference Commissioner Roy Kramer, one of the great orators of our time, gave the keynote address. Kramer led the evolution, or maybe revolution, of not only the first conference championship game as an extra game to the season. He was also a big player in the evolution of the college football National Championship from the Bowl Coalition to the Bowl Alliance to the Bowl Championship Series (BCS), and ultimately, to the College Football Playoff, with the conferences rather than the NCAA in control of college football.

We made a presentation entitled, "The Power of One" that included NCAA Licensing Director Angie Lovett, Mark Kidd from Host Communications, and CLC's Pat Battle, Bruce Siegal and Kit Walsh. Host Communications managed the Corporate Sponsorship program for the NCAA. Jim Host, founder and CEO, became a great friend and colleague. He used his marketing experience with the NCAA to pioneer in taking those same services to many universities around the country. Our companies ran in parallel paths, and corporate sponsorships interfaced with licensing only in promotional licenses where licensed products were used as premiums in the promotion. We stayed out of each other's businesses and worked together very well when there were conflicts. Not only did we work well together, we became great friends for life. I always admired Jim's leading efforts in collegiate media rights. His business acumen was only exceeded by the great person that he was. This presentation was about how powerful collegiate media rights and licensing could be if harnessed and properly directed.

We knew that athletics departments had an abundance of promotional resources through their advertising and marketing programs, e.g., radio networks for major sports, print advertising in game programs and other publications, and mailings to donors and ticket holders. Host Communications held the key to several universities' media rights programs. We could promote their services to our universities, showing how using athletics department resources could help enhance each individual licensing program with minimal charges to licensing. Host, in turn, could promote our services to properties they managed. Jim Host's support had a lot to do with CLC getting NCAA licensing rights.

The direction we were taking to expand the market for collegiate products was clear. The changes we had made since consolidation in 1993 were very dramatic and very successful.

Retail sales of all licensed products increased slightly 1.2 percent to $73.2 billion. Sports licensed products decreased slightly 0.7 percent to $13.7 billion, and collegiate licensed products increased to $2.6 billion.

Florida won the 1996 National Championship in football, followed by Ohio State, Florida State, Arizona State and Brigham Young in the AP Poll. It was the second year of the Football Bowl Alliance, and it ended in controversy. Florida defeated Florida State in the Sugar Bowl to capture the national title, but FSU beat the Gators earlier in the season. Were it not for Texas beating No. 3 Nebraska in the first-ever Big 12 Championship Game, Florida wouldn't have even been in the Sugar Bowl, and once it was there, it wasn't certain that even if UF won they would be awarded the championship. Arizona State was ranked No. 2 and faced No. 4 Ohio State in the Rose Bowl. Even though the Rose Bowl, Pac-10 and Big Ten weren't a part of the Football Bowl Alliance, an Arizona State victory over Ohio State might have gotten them to the top spot. ASU took a 17-14 lead with 1:40 left to play, but the Buckeyes marched down the field to take a heart-stopping 20-17 win. That series of events showed the Pac-10 and Big Ten that the rest of the country wanted a clear National Championship, and they could no longer hold on to tradition.

The 1996 college football season was also notable as it marked the end of tie games. An overtime system was put in place across all Division I teams. The 1995 season had overtime rules, but only for post-season games.

Kentucky defeated Syracuse 76-67 to win the 1996 NCAA Championship in hoops, with UMass and Mississippi State also making the Final Four. It was the last Final Four played in a traditional arena, as the NCAA moved exclusively to domed stadiums thereafter so they could expand attendance to 60,000 or more fans.

Our top universities in 1996-1997 were Michigan ($4.7 million), North Carolina ($3.1 million), Kentucky ($2.8 million), Florida ($2.7 million), Penn State ($2.4 million), Nebraska ($2.2 million), Tennessee ($1.8 million), Florida State ($1.7 million), Georgetown ($1.7 million), Alabama ($1.5 million) and Wisconsin ($1.2 million).

As I mentioned earlier in the book, in January 1997, Eugenia and I agreed to divorce after a year-long separation in 1996. It was a very difficult decision and one I never thought would happen, but we developed problems we couldn't resolve and decided this was the best course to take.

* * * * *

At this point, I think it's important to give you a history on how National Championships in football have been decided for about the past 120 years.

The concept of a National Championship dates back to the early years of the sport in the late 19th century. The earliest contemporary polls can be traced back to *The Sun* in 1901 by Casper Whitney and Charles Patterson. A mathematical system developed by Frank Dickinson named undefeated Stanford the national champion of 1926 prior to its tie with Alabama in the 1927 Rose Bowl. Knute Rockne, the Notre Dame coach, asked Dickinson to backdate the two previous seasons, which then named Notre Dame as the 1924 champion and Dartmouth the 1925 title winner.

A number of other mathematical systems of selecting national champions were created in the 1920s and 1930s. Then the Associated Press began polling sportswriters in 1936 to obtain rankings, which resulted in a National Championship for Minnesota. The AP's main competition, United Press International (UPI), created its first Coaches' Poll in 1950. For that year and the next three, the AP and UPI agreed on the national champion. The first "split" national title occurred in 1954 when the AP chose Ohio State and UPI chose UCLA. The two polls also disagreed in 1957, 1965, 1970, 1973, 1974, 1978, 1990, 1991, 1997 and 2003.

The split national championships did not affect licensing. Fans from both schools took great pride in the success of their teams and bought licensed merchandise to display that pride. There was very little championship merchandise to buy until the late 1980s as collegiate licensing got going.

As the popularity of college football continued to grow throughout the 1960s, '70s, '80s and '90s, bowls aligned with television networks and conferences aligned with bowls. It was very difficult to ever get matchups between the two top-ranked teams in the country. It only happened if a major independent was ranked No. 1 or No. 2 and was invited to play in a major bowl against a conference champion ranked No. 1 or No. 2. Prior to 1992, the AP Poll had only seen its No. 1 and No. 2 teams meet in bowls eight times in the previous 56 years.

To address that problem, a group of major conferences, bowls and independent Notre Dame got together and formed the Bowl Coalition from

1992-1994, and the Bowl Alliance from 1995-1997. Both concepts were positive in moving the needle to finally be able to match No. 1 vs. No. 2, but were flawed, because the Rose Bowl, Big Ten and Pac-10 refused to participate. During that period from 1992-1997, there was much conversation between the conferences, the bowls and the networks.

In the 1992, '93 and '94 seasons, the Bowl Coalition was set up to force a "de facto" National Championship Game between the two top teams in the nation. It entirely excluded the Big 10 and Pac-10, as the Rose Bowl refused to cooperate in giving up contractual rights to its conference champion and its exclusive window of time on Jan. 1 with ABC. As a side note, NBC began broadcasting the Rose Bowl Game on radio in 1927. In 1957 it began televising both the Rose Bowl Game and the Rose Parade. In 1988, NBC gave up its TV rights to ABC with two years left on its contract, and the ABC contract then ran through 1997.

The Bowl Coalition's six bowls all had contractual tie-ins with various conferences, but agreed to release those teams in order to achieve a No. 1 vs. No. 2 matchup. The National Championship Game was to be played in either the Orange, Fiesta, Cotton or Sugar bowls. For the first two years (1992 and 1993) of the Coalition, there were no issues, as the Sugar and Orange (on Jan. 1, 1993 and Jan. 1, 1994, respectively) featured No. 1 vs No. 2 matchups.

The problem came after the 1994 season when Penn State and Nebraska finished the season ranked No. 1 and No. 2. Since Penn State was a member of the Big Ten, and the Big Ten, Pac-10 and Rose Bowl were not a part of the Bowl Coalition, the top two teams could not meet in a bowl. Nebraska , with a contract to go to the Orange Bowl, faced off against No. 3 Miami. On Jan. 1, 1995, Nebraska defeated Miami 24-17 in the Orange Bowl to clinch the championship. The next day, Penn State defeated Oregon 38-20 in the Rose Bowl to secure the No. 2 spot in the polls.

In the off-season that followed, the Bowl Coalition was replaced by the Bowl Alliance, which attempted to accomplish the same thing by rotating a National Championship Game between the Sugar, Fiesta and Orange. Like the Bowl Coalition, the new Bowl Alliance did not include the Rose Bowl, so two of the next three National Championships — in 1995 and 1996 — did not feature No. 1 vs No. 2 teams. The 1997 season saw another split national championship.

In 1998, the Bowl Championship Series (BCS) was formed with six conferences (Atlantic Coast, Big East, Big Ten, Big 12, Pac-10 and SEC, plus three major independents. Getting the Rose Bowl, Pac-10 and Big Ten in the group pretty much assured that finally the top two teams would be matched in a designated championship bowl. SEC Commissioner Roy Kramer played a lead role in getting all parties together and agreeing on the process. He is considered the "Father of the BCS." The six commissioners were successful in structuring the BCS under their control instead of the NCAA. The selection process featured the Coaches' and AP polls, combined with six computers in a mathematical formula to rank the top two teams in a championship bowl game that rotated annually from 1998 to 2005 between the Sugar, Fiesta, Rose and Orange.

From 2006 to 2013, a stand-alone game was created, entitled the BCS National Championship Game. The winner of that game was automatically awarded the National Championship of the Coaches' Poll and the American Football Coaches Association's trophy, along with the MacArthur Bowl from the National Football Foundation. Neither the AP Poll, nor the other selectors, had contractual obligations to select the BCS champion.

The BCS had several controversial moments, including the 2003 season when the BCS Championship Game did not include the eventual AP Poll No. 1, Southern Cal. That was the only time the two systems disagreed during the 16-year BCS tenure. The other situation came after the 2011 season when two members of the SEC West Division played in a rematch in the BCS Championship Game in New Orleans. LSU had defeated Alabama 9-6 in overtime in November, but the Crimson Tide shut out the Tigers 21-0 in the championship rematch. The BCS formula ranked them in the top two despite the late loss in the regular season by Alabama, which won the title.

The College Football Playoff (CFP) replaced the BCS in 2014 with a four-team playoff. Six bowls were involved on a rotating basis: the Rose, Cotton, Sugar, Orange, Peach and Fiesta. Each year, two bowls hosted semi-final games around Jan. 1, and the winners played in the CFP National Championship Game within a couple of weeks.

The conference commissioners are to be commended for dealing with the problem directly and forming the Bowl Alliance in 1992. They improved the system some in the Bowl Coalition, but the model was in place for the next Bowl Championship Series in 1998 that captured all major bowls and conferences, and enabled the top two ranked teams to play for the national title. To me, each were great moves that created a championship atmosphere in every college football game from the first week until the last. No other regular season in college or professional sports has such a meaningful regular season.

1997-1998

In fiscal year 1997-1998, Oklahoma and Texas joined the Consortium. This was a very big deal for us as the University of Texas was supported by oil money, among other things, and had always been very independent in everything they did. Several years earlier, I called to ask if Texas would like to go in with us as we conducted audits, or "contract licensing reviews" as we preferred to call them. I was told, in no uncertain terms, "If the University of Texas desires to conduct audits of licensees, we'll send in our own auditors!" Times change and needs change. UT decided to put its program out for bid a year earlier to explore joining the power of a group.

Texas Athletics Director DeLoss Dodds, one of the best in the business, led the effort, along with Chris Plonsky. Pat and I got to know DeLoss and Chris very well over the years and felt like we had a solid relationship. A few years earlier, DeLoss and I were having coffee around the annual National Football Foundation Hall of Fame meetings in New York. He told me the story of Coach Bryant trying to hire him when he was head track and field coach at Kansas. It was a great story, and he told me that Alabama had decided to be competitive nationally in the sport so they were building a state-of-the-art new track. He ultimately told me he decided to remain at Kansas. I then told him the back-story. In 1965, Richmond Flowers was one of the nation's top high school high hurdlers. Richmond was also an outstanding football player and was being recruited in both sports, and he was the son of the current Alabama attorney general, who was a graduate of the University of Alabama. Chuck Rohe at Tennessee had one of the best track and field programs in America. He was also the football recruiting coordinator under Coach Doug Dickey. Tennessee convinced Richmond that he could go to UT to play football and run track. He could go through one football spring practice and from then on could run track in the spring. He would also be groomed to participate in the 1968 Olympics, and if he was competitive, could redshirt his senior season, participate in the Olympics and play his senior year in football in 1969. Much to Coach Bryant's chagrin, Richmond went to Tennessee. Coach Bryant decided that Alabama would never lose another good football player because its track program wasn't competitive.

We all went all out to convince Texas that CLC was their best option. We told them we would pay their way to have their group visit our competitor if they would visit our offices. They declined our offer to fund their trips, but did visit both offices on their own dime. Our staff was prepared. We changed every computer screen and mouse pad in the office to a Texas-theme and had the staff wear the famous Texas burnt orange. They were impressed with our commitment and passion among our team. After some discussions, they asked, "When can you come to Austin and get to work on our program?" I said, "We'll buy seats on the plane you fly back on if they are available." It was a great addition to our program. The entire Texas system of universities joined our Consortium.

Oklahoma Athletics Director Joe Castiglione was also one of the best in the business. We had met Joe when he was AD at Missouri, and also had a good relationship there. Oklahoma ran its program in-house, but we believed there was a good deal of growth at both Oklahoma and Texas. Fortunately for us all, both athletics programs went from "not so good" to "good," which propelled them much higher in our rankings from the time they signed contracts with CLC. Maybe we brought them good luck!

We were also very pleased that Northwestern, Syracuse, Coppin State, New Hampshire and Towson joined the CLC Consortium of universities. The Alamo, Fiesta and Holiday bowls also joined our group.

We held the 11th-annual Licensing Directors Seminar at Marco Island, Florida, in conjunction with the National Association of Collegiate Directors of Athletics (NACDA) and its associated member organizations. Among them was the newly formed National Association of Collegiate Marketing Administrators (NACMA), which was an important group for us to cultivate. There were other association meetings as well for sports information directors and other athletic-related disciplines.

Leading up to the 1997-1998 year, the leadership in the Association of Collegiate Licensing Administrators (ACLA) appeared to be taking the association in a direction that alienated a growing number of members. That ultimately led to the formation of the National Collegiate Licensing Association (NCLA), which was organized by Bob Vecchione. He set it up so those meetings took place at the same time as the NACDA, NACMA and other athletic-related organizations met each June. It offered a new approach to licensing directors that seemed to appeal to many who were attracted to its mainstream approach.

Mike Cleary and Bob Vecchione ran the organizations. My son Pat did a great job of working with them to get access to these meetings in years leading up to us bringing in licensing directors. Because CLC was one of NACMA's first sponsors, and because many people in athletics spoke highly of us, we gained Mike's and Bob's favor. We were able to set up some joint sessions in which we could attend meetings with NACDA and NACMA. It enabled our licensing directors, who were not directly associated with athletics, to better understand that world from a business perspective. It gave them ideas of how to work better with their athletics departments, and our joint sessions continued to present successful working models of athletics and licensing working together.

We began managing the NCAA's licensing program in February 1997. We were very pleased with the results after our first full year. Before we took on the management of NCAA marks we were criticized because we blocked some of its initial approaches. We did so because we believed those approaches to joint-licensing NCAA marks with university marks added far more value to the NCAA than it did to the universities. We always believed joint licensing was worth considering, if both licensors brought value, and one did not poach from the other. Our concept was that national programs could be tied together with NCAA marks that would add great value to universities, but wouldn't keep them from running regional programs with conferences and bowls, nor would it keep them from running local programs.

We worked on and made progress on the following fronts:

NCAA Football (to be followed by NCAA Basketball, Women's Sports and Olympic Sports) was an initiative that the NCAA agreed to put its share of revenues back into the promotion of college football.

Premiums and promotions were stimulated by the inclusion of CLC staff members on teams that advised and worked with all NCAA Corporate Partners. We were able to place heavy emphasis on the value to corporate partners to activate their NCAA national promotions using premiums bearing individual, group and collective university logos.

Retail sales were stimulated through aggressively seeking national Final Four promotions. Major efforts were undertaken to set up NCAA concept shops in national chains.

The approval process, enforcement and compliance around NCAA championships were dramatically improved.

The 1998 Super Show in Atlanta was extremely successful. The NCAA and CLC combined spaces into a very impressive 20-foot by 60-foot new booth. Twenty-foot towers bearing NCAA and CLC logos allowed traffic through the show to easily locate our booth. In addition, we also had another 10-foot by 30-foot booth solely devoted to NCAA Football. Our goal was to provide collegiate licensors with a presence at the Super Show on par with the NFL and other top licensors. Word from the show was that we attained our goal.

The National Sporting Goods (NSGA) Show was held at the newly renovated McCormick Place in Chicago. CLC introduced the NCAA program as an addition to its 40-foot by 40-foot booth there to further promote the relationship to licensees, retailers, and the media.

Retail sales of all licensed merchandise in North America in 1998 dropped 2.7 percent to $71.2 billion. Sports Licensed product sales dropped 8 percent to $12.6 billion, but collegiate retail sales grew 3.8 percent to $2.7 billion. Collegiate sales had also grown from 12.5 percent of all Sports Licensed sales in 1989 to 21.4 percent in 1998. We were slowly but surely taking retail shelf space from other sports properties. That was good news, but there was bad news on several fronts in 1997-98. "Entertainment/Character" and Trademark/

Brands" surpassed "Sports" in overall sales of licensed products. There was continued consolidation or bankruptcies among both licensees and retailers during the year.

Starter, amidst published financial losses, made key staff changes. Starter dropped from CLC's No. 2 apparel licensee to No. 6, and represented the Consortium's third-largest decrease for the year. Starter was expected to continue its internal reorganizations over the next several quarters to combat the negative forces it was experiencing in the marketplace.

Nike was also experiencing difficult times as its products were losing the "cool factor" it had enjoyed for years among consumers. Part of the problem was that kids brought up on Nike products were new parents and were still wearing them. That made their kids not want to wear what their parents were wearing. Saturation of licensed products added to the problem, and Nike projected up to 20 percent decreases for the upcoming quarters.

On the worldwide scene, the economic crisis in Asia was expected to result in reduced prices to consumers. More than 40 percent of U.S. apparel imports came from Asia (China, Hong Kong, Indonesia and South Korea). The decline of Asian currencies over the previous several months had caused even lower prices. In the meantime, the dollar had soared, giving retailers even more purchasing power. While lower prices are good for consumers, they reduce royalties to licensors.

In the continuum of "Every action leads to an equal and opposite reaction," the greater the number of manufacturers that moved to foreign countries to seek lower costs, the greater was the possibility that factories would be used that abused the rights of workers. The challenges to universities from students and faculty (fomented to some extent by American labor unions) continued to grow. Not since the student and faculty sit-ins in university president's offices during the Vietnam War in the 1960s had student and faculty emotions been as stirred up as their interests in ensuring that collegiate licensed products were made under labor code protections. There was serious unrest, some involving sit-ins, on several university campuses. Bruce Siegal and our legal staff continued to work hard trying to seek university's consensus in developing reasonable labor codes of conduct to require licensees to follow. Our staff also had to work with licensees to get their feedback on what was reasonable. Then we had to work together to come up with workable solutions.

Twenty-six CLC universities played in post-season bowl games, while the 1997 National Championship was split for the third time in the 1990s. Michigan finished atop the AP Poll with a 12-0 record and a Rose Bowl victory over Washington State. Nebraska finished 13-0 and No. 1 in the Coaches' Poll and the Bowl Alliance. Both teams were deserving of their National Championship rankings, and both received substantial benefits from their title merchandise. The Bowl Championship Series (BCS) was instituted the following year, which included the Big Ten, Pac-12 and the Rose Bowl. Arizona earned its first NCAA Basketball Championship in 1997 over Kentucky 84-79 in overtime. North Carolina and Minnesota were also in the Final Four.

It is interesting to note that CLC had managed the last six national football champions and 12 of the last 13 national basketball champions. That experience proved invaluable in helping leverage opportunities in the marketplace for not only the champion, but for all CLC schools.

Our top ranking universities in 1997-1998 were Michigan ($5.8 million), Kentucky ($2.99 million), North Carolina ($2.95 million), Penn State ($2.45 million), Nebraska ($2.27 million), Florida ($2.4 million), Tennessee ($2.1 million), Florida State ($1.8 million), Georgetown ($1.67) and Alabama ($1.3 million). It was another year of slugging it out in the marketplace, but the future looked encouraging as independent universities continued to join CLC. We were up to 154 schools, six conferences, seven bowls, the NCAA, the NACDA Kickoff and the Pigskin Classic.

1998-1999

Three more major independents joined CLC in fiscal year 1998-1999 — Miami, Missouri and Baylor. All three added greatly to the growing marketing and enforcement clout of the Consortium. We were especially pleased to work with Baylor again. They were a CLC university member from 1983-1991, managed their own program from 1992-1998, and joined six other Big 12 universities by returning to the Consortium in 1999. The Heisman Trophy Trust also became a prestigious member.

Pat was named to the inaugural *Sports Business Journal* "40 under 40" list honoring influential people in the sports marketing business. Our staff had grown to 60 full-time members, six interns and several consultants. We represented 169 universities, seven conferences, seven bowls, the NCAA, NACDA, Kickoff and Pigskin Classics, and the Heisman Trust.

Soon after we arrived in Atlanta in 1994, Pat and I joined an "early birds" racquetball group that met in a nearby sports club at 6 a.m. every morning. A group of guys would start their days with an early workout. To me, playing racquetball felt like cheating, because it was too much fun to be called a workout. In our first few years, I was better than Pat, and showed him little mercy while I was teaching him the finer points. As time passed, his skills improved to the point that equaled or exceeded mine, but I could still beat him most days. Then the time came when "the worm turned." Not only did he beat me regularly, but also he paid me back in full with the "no mercy to an old man" treatment.

One day I was playing with a young man I had played with some, but really didn't know him. His name was Paul Eurek. Our typical matches were the best two out of three sets in which the first to 15 points won, but you had to win by two points if the score got to 15-14. We would rest a few minutes between sets. This particular day we were resting and got to talking about what we each did for a living. Paul told me he had developed a software company that worked with National Cash Register and McDonald's to solve their order entry — inventory control problems. The system allowed the person taking the order at the cash register to electronically send the message to the kitchen, and at the same time, send a message to inventory control personnel. It became so effective, they bought Paul's company. He worked for them for about six months and decided that wasn't much fun, so he retired for a while. I caught him as he was figuring out how to build his next company.

I told him about the growth we had experienced and the labor-intensive processes we were using to get products and designs sent to us by licensees, approved by universities, and then getting those responses back to licensees. We were literally burning up fax machines and killing forests with the amount of paper we were going through. Paul said he had plenty of time on his hands and thought he could help. He knew I had a strict dress code — ties for men and dress/skirts for women. He asked if he could wear jeans. I told him if he could help us, he could wear whatever he wanted.

I went to the office that day and got Derek Eiler and Catherine Singer together and told them I was bringing in one of my racquetball buddies that I thought could help with our product approval issues. Derek was a VP in charge of our University Services department, but a very savvy computer guy with great interest in systems. Catherine was our director of Apparel Licensing at the time and was a Georgia Tech Industrial Engineering graduate. She was way overqualified when we hired her, but we were finally evolving to what she was trained to do. At the time, I didn't have a computer in my office and saw no need to have one, as my administrative assistant, Linda Jordan, took great care of my communication needs.

A few years earlier, Linda was the administrative assistant to my banker, Rod Knowles. Whenever I needed banking assistance, I called Linda, who always got my problem solved. After Rod sold the bank, Linda tried working for another bank but wasn't happy. I developed a need for an assistant and caught up with Linda, and she came to work for us. She was the ultimate in keeping calm and focusing on her work when chaos was boiling all around her, and there was chaos boiling much of the time! Linda made a great impact on our company.

When I told Derek and Catherine I had Paul coming in later that morning and wanted them to meet with him, they both rolled their eyes thinking, but not saying, "Right, his racquetball buddy is coming in to solve all of our technical problems!" Paul did come in wearing jeans and met with them for over two hours. After the meeting, I asked Derek and Catherine how it went. They both responded, "This guy knows what he's doing!"

Over the period of about 24 months, we went from being one of the most inefficient agencies in terms of product and design approval to one of the most efficient in the industry. We devised a system called *i*CLC, which, when completed, became the industry's first-ever online design approval system. The approval process went from three to four weeks in some cases down to three or four minutes. Most of our designs were approved the same day they were submitted. Our phone calls from licensees calling to inquire about the status went away. We provided robust transparency right inside the system so every party — the licensee, CLC and the university — could all see where the design was in the approval process. If it was being delayed, it was easy for the other parties to determine who was responsible for the hold up. Not only was the speed of the process improved dramatically, but the quality of the designs was equally dramatic. Compliance with standards and speed to market resulted in more sales and royalties.

Over time, Paul started another software company and we continued to work with his company first in design approvals, then with contract management, and later in royalty reporting. We ended up being able to process upwards of 50,000 products/designs annually on average for our top 10 universities. It was a powerful tool that revolutionized our business, saved the fax machine and forests worth of paper, and gave us a leadership edge as an innovative agency to service our clients.

Paul's new company hired dozens of engineers from India among his other employees. Over the next few years, our IT staff held regular conference calls with his Indian employees and talked about a foreign exchange program, among other things. We remain friends today as Paul and his wife Deb have retired to their home in Nebraska.

With an increased reliance on the Internet as a go-between platform for licensees and our university partners, we continued to add technological additions and refinements to improve the speed at which products reached the market. Two other elements that became leading-edge programs in the licensing industry were Logos on Demand and Stitches on Demand. We invested in a full-time staff and a significant amount of dollars in developing this service for licensees. As a brand advisor to our university partners, we felt compelled to ensure we were holding up our end of the bargain in delivering 100 percent accurate logos to all licensees, sending them clean and consistent brand presentations on finished products produced by licensees. Rather than continuing to rely on licensees to scan printed logo slicks with color separations, we began the process of digitizing all school logos on our own, resulting in more than 3,000 college logos being cleaned and packaged for our licensees to access through the *i*CLC system. In parallel, we did the same process with logos for embroidered apparel, which required a unique digitizing format that only worked on large sewing machines. We built a library of more than 1,000 of the most popular logos from our college clients and licensees producing embroidered logos so they could now access the pre-approved versions — complete with proper thread colors as chosen by our universities. These two programs ended up becoming a revenue stream for the company, offsetting the initial expense of properly producing all of the materials required to get the program up and running. Catherine and Derek, along with many others, deserve credit for the transformative changes in our administrative systems. We decided to partner with J. Patton Sports Marketing to take advantage of their expertise in handling the many challenges that come with using digital art files across a variety of computer platforms and software programs.

Again, I call attention to our contractual model with universities. They received an agreed upon percentage of the gross royalties that we received, from whatever source. As their individual royalties grew, their dollars and percentages grew. As long as collective gross royalties grew, we reinvested our share of those dollars into getting better in each of the seven elements of our Strategic Plan. To keep growing, we needed to aggressively develop new programs, even going so far in 1993 to redefine ourselves and chart a different course. I think that was the secret in successfully signing and renewing exclusive agency agreements with universities and other collegiate properties, and keeping new schools joining our program.

One area of service to our clients with no sign of remuneration was in the area of labor code issues. In late 1997, we began to see signs of activism on college campuses among students and faculty members over what they believed were unfair labor practices in the manufacturing of products sold into this country. For whatever reason, concern became focused on unfair labor practices in factories producing collegiate licensed products.

As always, when problems or opportunities arose at our universities, we wanted to be on the leading edge of bringing about solutions. We organized a task force that collaborated on drafting a model "labor code of conduct" that could be made available to our university clients that wanted to add that to our license agreement for their member institutions. We invited any universities that were interested and began a very laborious process. Getting 10 to 15 universities together by conference call and trying to get them to agree on the same contract was difficult. Bruce Siegal and I spent hundreds of hours working to get a code of conduct to which 10 to 15 university attorneys and other executives could agree. After it got close, my heart was palpitating every time we met, and I turned it fully over to Bruce who, along with his staff, did a great job of shepherding it to conclusion. Even more important, he continued to oversee the program and work with other university clients whose needs involved other parts of the code.

By 1999, the task force completed a draft of code standards and recommended that other CLC universities join together to require uniform standards and monitoring procedures that would be credible, practical and enforceable. During that time period, CLC and its member institutions were approached by the Fair Labor Association (FLA) and offered the opportunity to participate in the FLA monitoring program. More than 180 schools joined the FLA.

Monitoring labor code violations in foreign countries is a complex and detailed process, and requires cooperation and coordination between licensors, licensees, factory management and monitoring agents. There was resistance from licensees that had to be worked through. Change came slowly when dealing with so many parties. Student and faculty sit-ins outside the president's office usually led to resolutions, because no president wants people outside his or her office. It was our task to handle that anxiety.

The Workers' Rights Consortium (WRC) entered the marketplace as a competing organization to the FLA. The WRC called on universities with another model for monitoring and another financial charge for membership. Our role was to provide universities with a contractual mechanism to formalize labor code standards and to pass on their contractual decision to licensees. CLC also took the lead in gathering and organizing factory site organizations, making them available to our university clients.

Changing the worldwide problems dealing with workers' rights is a multi-faceted challenge. It can't be done with one category of products, i.e., collegiate licensed products. The work done in this area, however, did move the needle toward improved working conditions in many factories and in many countries during our time at CLC. It was definitely a difference-making effort.

The 1998-99 fiscal year was a very difficult one for licensees and retailers. In the year-to-date top 10 decreases of CLC licensees, four declared bankruptcy: Starter, Brazos/C.S. Cable, P.M. Enterprises and Imprinted Products. In addition, Hutch & DeLong Sportswear also declared. All owed CLC universities significant amounts of back royalties, which our legal staff closely monitored and successfully recovered most of it.

Starter was an incredibly successful company. It was a leader in getting its brands on many professional teams, and offering them as licensed products to consumers throughout the country. Starter had a successful IPO launch in 1996-97, in which it raised almost $100 million. Its demise came quickly after the Major League Baseball and National Hockey League strikes, and agreeing to ever increasing guarantees to licensors. David Beckerman's innovative programs were missed in the industry, and the $100 to $300 jackets went away, significantly reducing the average sale of outerwear, and as a result reduced royalties.

Mattel launched a Collegiate Barbie program in 1997 with about 20 universities, in which Barbie wore a collegiate cheerleader's uniform. I spoke with CEO Jill Barad who said Mattel had engaged in a few joint-licensed programs, but this was the first in which Barbie had multiple brands under one program. We did negotiate a deal with Mattel to produce NASCAR Barbie with only the NASCAR logo on her uniform. The Collegiate Barbie hit the market around holiday 1997. We received reports they were so popular that people were fighting for them in the stores. As a result, Mattel added universities in 1998 and produced larger numbers of each. Unfortunately, Mattel distribution centers had a difficult time getting the different Barbies in the right retail locations. Having Wisconsin Barbies offered in Atlanta, and Georgia Barbies offered in Milwaukee, didn't work. That and the fact that they overproduced led to having excessive inventories left in 1999. They said they were going to take a year off and re-enter the market again in 2000. As big companies do, they decided to drop the price and sell them off to Kay-Bee Toys, a retailer who sold them at greatly reduced prices. We met with Mattel, told them what they did was unacceptable, and received full royalties on all sales at our original agreed upon prices. It was a shame that such a popular program couldn't have been managed and continued, as Mattel actually had plans to introduce Collegiate Ken in its next line-up. However, that was the new world in which we lived. Big companies, licensees and retailers tend to pull the plug quickly when problems arise, take a quick loss and move on to the next program.

On the other hand, Nike was a big company that, because of its overall commitment to collegiate and professional sports, took a longer-term view of the ups and downs of the marketplace. Even though it suffered declining sales of licensed products in 1998 and 1999, it reorganized its Nike Teams Sports (NTS) division and came out stronger on the other end.

The University of Michigan, under the direction of associate AD Will Perry and Licensing Director Kristen Ablauf, created a private-label program called

"Big House" to capitalize on its famous 110,000-seat football stadium. CLC and Michigan partnered with three apparel companies selling to varying levels of retailers to carry a line of Big House branded apparel. All products in the line featured special Big House sewn-in neck labels and Big House hang tags. Designs on the outside of the garments carried popular Michigan logos and slogans around football-themed designs.

The University of Montana created a "Griz Gear" logo, which would serve as a label on apparel products. Bob Frazier, executive vice president and No. 2 man at Montana, had a dramatic impact on promoting the image of the university. The "Bucking Horse and Rider" logo very much added to the cool factor that was attractive to visitors to the state. Those visitors would go back home, wear their UofM cowboy gear, and create interest in the school from many who saw how cool it looked. Hang tags on the Griz Gear merchandise actively promoted the university, including driving them to the school's website. Bob believed getting Montana-licensed products in general and Griz Gear in particular distributed in surrounding states would enhance the university's ability to attract students.

Brian White, the CLC MVP for 1999, was the University Services Representative who worked with Bob and Montana. When we started back in 1981, we asked universities for three-year contracts, and later as we were successful, we asked for five. Brian came in one day and told me Bob had said he would sign a 10-year contract with CLC, but wanted me to come visit. Of course my response was, "When can I come?"

It was autumn, so I went out on a football weekend. When I arrived I met with Bob and Licensing Director Denise Lamb, who was also the assistant bookstore manager, so she was very familiar with licensed merchandise. She took me on a tour of the bookstore, then around campus, then to the stadium a few hours before the game. I got to know Bob very well and we signed the 10-year contract. Montana won a few Division 1AA National Championships and its licensing program took off. With Bob's oversight and ideas, and Denise's management, Montana became one of my very favorite universities. The football stadium seated 20,000 and it was full every week. The crowd really got into the games and fans were very proud of their team's success. We later hired Denise at CLC and she became a fantastic representative of western universities in helping solve their problems and maximizing their opportunities. We all remain friends today.

Our 12th-annual Licensing Directors Seminar was held in Reno, Nevada, June 9-10, 1999. One of the areas of focus of the seminar was protecting university brands, managing those brands, and investing in those brands. Back in 1981, we didn't really think of collegiate logos as brands, but as licensing evolved, we all recognized what they were and how valuable they had become.

Our dinner on the final night was held on Lake Tahoe on the *M.S. Dixie II*, an old-fashioned paddlewheel boat complete with open bar, spectacular views and a sit-down dinner. The bus drive to Zephyr Cove on Lake Tahoe featured a beautiful 60-minute drive through the Sierra Nevada Mountains. It was a great event.

The recently formed National Collegiate Licensing Association (NCLA) held its inaugural workshop on the following day and ran through Sunday. Most of our seminar attendees signed up, attended the workshop and joined the new association, which considerably weakened the ACLA. Our position, however, was to recommend to CLC universities to join both associations. Eventually the two merged into the International Collegiate Licensing Association (ICLA).

In 1998, overall licensed merchandise sales in North America declined 2.7 percent to $71.2 billion. Sports licensed merchandise declined 8 percent to $12.6 billion. Collegiate licensed merchandise rose 3.8 percent to $2.7 billion. The percentage of collegiate share of sports licensed products in 1998 rose to 21.4 percent, which was up from 12.5 percent in 1998.

In the inaugural BCS National Championship Game, the University of Tennessee Volunteers defeated the Florida State University Seminoles 23-16 in the Fiesta Bowl in Tempe, Arizona, to win the 1998 National Championship. Of the 44 teams participating in 1998 post-season bowl games, 33 were CLC members. Ohio State, FSU, Arizona and Florida finished behind the Vols in the final BCS rankings.

College football attendance in 1998 increased by more than 633,000 fans and surpassed the 37 million mark for the first time in history. Michigan ranked first with average home attendance of 110,965 per game. Other CLC member universities in the Top 20 were Tennessee (106,914), Penn State (96,532), Georgia (85,618), Florida (85,299), Alabama (82,670), Auburn (81,110), Florida State (80,490), LSU (80,280), Texas (77,440), Wisconsin (77,428), Nebraska (76,186), South Carolina (74,794), Oklahoma (70,777) and Clemson (68,829).

The 1998 NCAA Basketball Final Four was held at the Alamodome in San Antonio, Texas. Kentucky defeated Utah 78-69 for its seventh title. North Carolina and Stanford also reached the Final Four semi-finals.

Our top universities in 1998-1999 were Tennessee ($4.5 million), Michigan ($3.8 million), North Carolina ($3.2 million), Kentucky ($2.6 million), Penn State ($2.1 million), Nebraska ($1.97 million), Florida ($1.8 million), Georgetown ($1.7 million), Florida State ($1.4 million), Alabama ($1.26 million) and

Wisconsin ($1.23 million). Eleven CLC universities crossed the million-dollar mark in annual royalties.

1999-2000

CLC passed two significant milestones in 1999-2000. First, we entered the 21st century amidst "Y2K" — Year 2000 — the fear that every computer on this planet would crash at midnight Dec. 31, 1999. Second, we passed the milestone of $300 million in payments to CLC universities since our inception in 1981.

*i*CLC was fully introduced to licensees and universities for online approval over the Internet. The system was well thought through, developed and made it through the dreaded Y2K fear just fine. It was an immediate hit, but did take some time teaching everyone exactly how to make it work. The Collegiate Exchange — an online resource for retailers to search for products by university, licensee or product category — was also launched. Technology was not only allowing us to make our licensing process much easier for licensees and universities to navigate, but was also enhancing our marketing department's ability to reach out to retailers to provide them with reasons for them to carry collegiate products in their stores.

On the client front, Stanford rejoined CLC after dropping out in 1988, and Kansas, who had dropped out in 1993, also came back. This was another sign that the power of the Consortium was working. Gonzaga University was another school that signed up. We didn't know much about Gonzaga, but soon learned a lot as their basketball team was becoming a regular in making the NCAA Men's Basketball Tournament and knocking off much higher-ranked schools. Its reputation was rising, which enabled our company to help Gonzaga not only in the Spokane area, but also throughout the state of Washington and surrounding states. They never reached the Final Four during our time at CLC, but over the last few years have made it or come close many times. Gonzaga's staff did a great job in its own bookstore and in the Spokane area, and during our time at CLC, regularly generated more than $200,000 in royalties, and reached the $300,000 mark twice.

In what we deemed as a major coup, the Tournament of Roses joined the CLC Consortium in the 1999-2000 fiscal year. This addition completed CLC having licensing rights to all four Bowl Championship Series games — the Rose, Orange, Sugar and Cotton.

The Rose Bowl is truly "The Granddaddy of Them All." It started 50 years before the next bowl, and has a remarkable history. It is a part of the Pasadena Tournament of Roses Association, which also includes the historic Rose Parade. The first Tournament of Roses was held in 1890 with a parade in which entrants would decorate carriages with hundreds of colorful blooms. In 1902, the Valley Hunt Club decided to add a football game between a powerful West Coast team and a team from the East, so it invited Michigan to play Stanford. The game was such a rout in Michigan's favor that the Tournament of Roses dropped football games until 1916. In the meantime, they hosted other competitions, including ostrich and chariot races. Football was re-introduced in 1916, and the Rose Bowl Stadium opened in 1922, in time for the 1923 game.

Originally, the championship team of the Pacific Coast Intercollegiate Athletic Conference (now the Pac-12) simply invited a winning team from anywhere in the eastern United States to be its opponent. Football was gaining popularity even though it was a violent game with its share of critics. Alabama President George "Mike" Denny believed that a winning football team could bring national media coverage that would attract students from all over the country, build excitement and esprit de corps among students and fans, and improve contributions to the university. In 1923, he hired Coach Wallace Wade, who was coaching at Vanderbilt, the most powerful team in the South. In 1925, Coach Wade led Alabama to an undefeated 10-0 record, outscoring its opponents 277-7. The Crimson Tide was selected to play in the 1926 Rose Bowl, the first Southern team ever invited to Pasadena. Interestingly enough, the Rose Bowl Committee did not think much of Southern football, and sent invitations to Dartmouth, Yale and Colgate before reluctantly inviting Alabama. The committee, and most national sports writers, did not believe Alabama could stand up to the mighty Washington Huskies.

The Alabama team took a four-day train ride to get to Pasadena. Coach Wade stopped periodically along the way to let the players work out. As with most football coaches, Coach Wade was paranoid about many things, so he brought 55-gallon drums of Tuscaloosa water, fearing that drinking water along the way might cause sickness to his players.

In Pasadena, the team found themselves among movie stars and Hollywood big-money people. Coach Wade finally sequestered them in a hotel and closed it to the public. Alabama shocked the world and catapulted into the national spotlight with a 20-19 victory over Washington in front of 50,000 fans. Johnny Mack Brown, an outstanding Alabama running back, through contacts made on this trip, went on to become a Hollywood star and even acted in some John Wayne movies.

That was Alabama's first Rose Bowl and first National Championship, but not its last. Coach Wade took Alabama back to the Rose Bowl in 1927 to play a Stanford team coached by Pop Warner to a 7-7 tie. In 1930, Coach Wade went undefeated again, outscoring opponents 271-13. Alabama played in the 1931 Rose Bowl and beat Washington State 24-0. Coach Wade left after that season and was replaced by Coach Frank Thomas. Coach Thomas led Alabama back to the Rose bowl after the 1934 season and beat Stanford 29-13 before 84,000 fans. Johnny Mack Brown by then was a Hollywood movie star and provided a solid scouting report on Stanford. Stars on that Rose Bowl team were fullback Joe Domnanovich, halfback Dixie Howell, quarterback Riley Smith, and ends Don Hutson and Paul "Bear" Bryant. In attendance that day was a young sportscaster and future Hollywood star, who happened to be a friend of Coach Thomas. Five years later, that actor would portray Coach Thomas's former roommate at Notre Dame, George "The Gipper" Gipp in the motion picture "Knute Rockne — All American." That actor was Ronald Reagan, future President of the United States.

As a side note, when I was in Selma, I was invited to attend a reunion of the 1934 Rose Bowl and National Championship team. One of the players, Bob Ed Morrow, hosted the reunion. I can't remember the year, but it was between 1977 and 1983. A large number of players attended and they were mostly in very good health. They had a ball telling stories and catching up with what was going on in their lives. It was a great place to be a "fly on the wall" and take in all of this conversation and history. The highlight to me was when they showed the film of the game on black-and-white 16-millimeter film with a projector capable of stopping and running back plays to be seen again. It was amazing to watch and listen as they individually spoke out in anticipation of a play that was upcoming. The best of all was Coach Bryant speaking out, "Oh no, don't watch the next play, I'm about to get knocked on my back!" It was one of the highlights of my life to be present at that event.

Coach Thomas led the 1937 team to an undefeated 9-0 season. The team was invited to the relatively new Sugar Bowl, but opted to go to the more popular Rose Bowl. Alabama lost to the University of California 13-0, and, according to the media, suffered embarrassment and a public slap in the face. Expectations were high for the Alabama football team going back in the 1930s. In 1945, Coach Thomas' last year at Alabama, he took the Tide back to the Rose Bowl to beat Southern Cal 34-14 for another National Championship. It was Alabama's sixth and final trip to the Rose Bowl. Beginning in 1947, the Tournament of Roses committed contractually to pairing the champion from the Big Ten and Pacific Coast conferences, which eliminated all others — at the time.

So we were delighted to get on board with the Pasadena Tournament of Roses. We became great friends, as they were terrific partners in sharing their storied history and working with us to take their licensing program into the future with the upcoming BCS National Championship on the horizon. As we met with the staff and officers, I met an upcoming president of the Pasadena

Tournament of Roses, who would see the first BCS National Championship Game played after the 2001 season under her watch. Libby Wright grew up in Birmingham, Alabama, and went to Woodlawn High School. Woodlawn was a big rival of West End. They beat us most of the time, but I did go across town and date a few of their majorettes. Libby was to become the first female Tournament of Roses president, and I thought it was quite a feat for a young lady from Birmingham to make it to the top of the prestigious Tournament of Roses. We became great friends, and I think we did a very good job of managing their trademark licensing program.

The Rose Bowl (Big Ten and Pac-12) agreed to join the Bowl Championship Series on a rotating basis with three other bowls beginning with the 1998 season. The goal was to match the two best teams in the BCS National Championship Game, with the first scheduled for the Fiesta Bowl in 1998, followed by the Sugar Bowl in 1999, the Orange Bowl in 2000 and the Rose Bowl in 2001.

Alabama returned to play in the BCS Championship Game in Rose Bowl Stadium on Jan. 7, 2010, defeating Texas 37-21. When I came back to Alabama as AD from 2013-2017, we had a good shot at making it back to the Rose Bowl for the 2013 National Championship, but didn't quite get there.

The licensed products market at retail in 1999 continued in the doldrums. Overall retail sales in North America improved slightly to $74.2 billion. Sports licensed products declined 4.0 percent to $12.1 billion, and collegiate products remained flat at $2.7 billion. The fiscal year 2000 was the first and only time in our time at CLC (1981-2011) that its gross revenues declined. It was only 2.4 percent, but there was a good reason for the decline. The 1999 champs in football, Florida State University, had a significant increase in its royalties, but its totals were far less than the 1998 Tennessee national title royalty increases. UConn won the 1999 NCAA Final Four, and although its royalties more than doubled, the increase was far less than that of 1998 winner Kentucky. Those two events more than accounted for the decrease in overall royalties. Approximately 61.4 percent of CLC universities experienced an increase in royalties over the previous year.

During the year, CLC conducted 142 licensee compliance reviews and collected $305,000 in unpaid royalties. This revenue number was down 43 percent from the previous year. Hopefully, licensees were educated to the point that they were paying more accurately and on time. Promotional licensing revenues were up 12 percent over the previous year. A record 138 universities shared in more than $1.4 million in promotional licensing revenue. Promotional licensing revenues were up 12 percent. More than $1.4 million in promotional licensing revenues were distributed to 138 universities.

In our VISION 2000 we launched in 1993, we believed we needed to make changes to ultimately get to $4 billion in collegiate licensed product sales by the year 2000. We made significant changes in our staff, programs and operations. The overall licensed product market had changed dramatically over the last few years, which prevented us from reaching our goal.

The March 6, 2000, edition of *The Licensing Letter* painted a true and accurate picture of the market for licensed products in the current business environment. There was no debating the precipitous drop of the apparel sports licensing market over the previous two or three years. The question was what to do about it. "There's no question this is an industry problem that needs to be addressed from a total industry standpoint," said Ed Doran, president of VF Corp's Licensed Knitwear Division.

It was a theme that ran through many conversations. It wasn't just a single league or licensing entity that was at issue, but rather an entire business sector that was going through a necessary, if painful, period of self-correction. On the manufacturer's side, casualties of the first few years included Apex, Starter, and later, Pro Player. The faltering Logo Athletic had renegotiated down with at least two leagues, according to published reports.

The toll had been nearly as heavy on the retail side, with the demise of Just for Feet and major closings by Venator (the owner of Foot Locker and Champs), and the Sports Authority. Meanwhile, though there were no absolute numbers available, there was no doubt the amount of floor space devoted to team licensed apparel had dropped steadily.

While market forces had a downward effect on sports licensed products, CLC remained fully confident that we would reach that goal of $4 billion in collegiate sales in the next few years. We were well positioned to come out stronger. Collegiate sports continued to grow in popularity and media coverage. Independent universities continued to join our Consortium. Collegiate sales continued to rise as a percentage of sports licensed products. The present in 1999-2000 was dim, but the future never looked brighter.

Our marketing staff compiled a comprehensive survey of the market for collegiate apparel in 1999-2000 that provided a good overview of the marketplace. Two points of concern were quickly identified. While retailers were generally saying good things about their college business and its future, there were fewer retailers carrying licensed products, and price points for collegiate products had declined drastically over the previous seven years. The increasing quality of merchandise offered by discount stores without increasing prices forced mid-level retailers out of the licensed products business altogether, or forced them into price competition. The number of units sold each year increased, but the price points on tees, fleece, women shirts and headwear dropped over the years. As overseas manufacturers improved production and the U.S. government lowered taxes and tariffs on imports, the result was better quality apparel at lower costs. The demand for licensed outerwear and expensive fleece, prevalent in Starter and Galt Sand's heyday, was no longer there. The authentic and replica jersey business was not strong enough to offset that decline. The lack of cold winters over the previous few years further contributed to the decline of outerwear and fleece sales.

Our top universities in 1999-2000 were Michigan ($3.05 million), North Carolina ($3.01 million), Tennessee ($2.8 million), Florida State ($2.2 million), Florida ($1.93 million), Penn State ($1.888 million), Kentucky ($1.882 million), Nebraska ($1.766 million), Wisconsin ($1.6 million), Alabama ($1.3 million) and Texas ($1 million).

2000-2001

During the 2000-2001 fiscal year, CLC celebrated its 20th year of doing business in the collegiate licensing industry it helped create. To better support the infrastructure we had built up over that period, we moved our offices to a larger space in a separate building within the same office complex. The move enabled us to occupy an entire floor with 20,000 square feet of space. As I like to say, "Our offices were located in the 'Penthouse Floor' of a two-story building." Our previous floor move was in 1987. Since that time, we had nine lease amendments and were scattered all over the building. With time to plan the move, we were able to locate departments, equipment, and meeting and storage rooms in a much more efficient setting for our staff.

The April issue of *License Magazine* featured its "Nifty Fifty" — a power block of 50 global licensors that drove hundreds of brands to the total tune of $83.5 billion in retail sales of licensed goods in 2000. CLC appeared ninth on the list, directly behind NFL Properties and MLB Properties. The April issue of *Sporting Goods Business* devoted its "Eye on Licensing" feature to CLC. The article discussed the 2002 Rose Bowl game, which would determine the next year's national champ; *i*CLC, our Internet-based artwork approval system; the Collegiate Exchange, an internet marketplace powered by iCongo for licensed products; and a write up of the strength of headwear in the collegiate marketplace. It was really great to see our company mentioned among not only top national licensors, but top global licensors as well.

We also faced some challenges, the biggest being the decline of apparel royalties because price points of units sold had dropped significantly over the past few years. There were multiple causes, some of which were warmer weather during previous fall and winter seasons, bankruptcies of apparel licensees and retailers, and over-licensing of their apparel product category.

Nike geared up its efforts to dramatically grow its collegiate lines. Nike Team Sports finished the year up 40 percent over the previous fiscal year. It expanded its offering of collegiate merchandise, as well as the marketing resources put behind the program, so further growth was expected.

Internet licensing continued to grow rapidly, not only with online retailers, but with licensees as well. This caused our staff to stay abreast of the learning curve, as the business of the Internet would precede the law by several years.

Headwear companies were dominating the top apparel companies, as Zephyr Graf-X finished the year as CLC's No. 2 apparel company, with Top of the World and Twins Enterprises in the top seven.

After declaring bankruptcy in 1999, Starter Sportswear's brand was acquired by an LLC. The Starter brand resonated well with sports fans, and the LLC continued to conduct national advertising of Starter in sports venues. It licensed some of CLC's licensees to sell the Starter-branded merchandise primarily to Walmart and Kmart. I was advised by some of our marketing staff, who had heard from other retailers, licensors and licensees, to NOT license the Starter brand to go to mass merchants. Since revenues had been flat to declining over the past few years, I was looking for "someone to do something" to stop the decline and get apparel sales growing. I made the decision to license them, and it was almost a disaster. You will hear more about this later, and we did get it fixed, but this one could have been a problem.

Non-apparel sales were beginning to grow as video games, trading cards, collectibles, sporting goods (balls and helmets), snacks and outdoor grills were getting in the pipeline. Our non-apparel marketing staff made positive strides in getting licensees bunched together in sections at places like the Merchandise Mart in Atlanta. Non-apparel royalties grew to 33.3 percent of all CLC royalties for the year.

Other highlights included: CLC auditors conducting 128 contract compliance reviews, resulting in more than $304,500 being recovered in back royalties from 96 licensees; promotional licensing revenues totaled $1.35 million, with 151 universities receiving those revenues; retail sales of licensed products in North America in calendar year 2000 were down 0.6 percent for a total of $73.75 billion, but Sports Licensed merchandise sales were up 2.9 percent for a total of $12.45 billion; CLC finished the 2000-2001 fiscal year up 4.9 percent; 30 universities enjoyed the best year in their history.

With the work we were doing in the apparel and non-apparel sectors with licensees and retailers, we believed that positive growth was on the horizon. I felt that we would see double-digit growth again in the near future.

Oklahoma defeated Florida State in the Orange Bowl to win the BCS National Championship. Thirty-four CLC universities participated in post-season bowl games.

Michigan State defeated Florida 89-76 to capture the 2000 NCAA Basketball Championship, while North Carolina and Wisconsin were Final Four semi-finalists.

Our top-selling universities for 2000-2001 were North Carolina ($3.6 million), Michigan ($3 million), Florida State ($2.7 million), Tennessee ($2.5 million), Nebraska ($1.9 million), Florida ($1.89 million), Oklahoma ($1.8 million), Penn State ($1.7 million), Kentucky ($1.5 million), Alabama ($1.307 million), Texas ($1.304 million), Wisconsin ($1.1 million) and Georgia ($1.0 million).

2001-2002

We were all saddened and angered by the tragic acts that took place in our country on Sept. 11, 2001. It was a day we will all remember the rest of our lives.

The 2001-2002 fiscal year was a very good year for collegiate licensing in general and CLC in particular. In our annual Consortium overview for 2Q 2002, I sent CLC's Licensing Directors a letter announcing the promotion of Derek Eiler to chief operating officer, my son Pat to chief executive officer, and me to chairman of the board. "It has been delightful for me to watch Pat, Derek, Bruce Seigal, Kit Walsh, Catherine Singer and Cory Moss each use their special skills to expand our comprehensive base of licensing services and accomplish our mission to be the guiding force in collegiate licensing and one of the top sports licensing companies in the U.S.," I added. "We have strong depth and breadth of staff throughout the entire organization. I am especially pleased with our corporate culture, which is based upon customer service and teamwork. My goal as a manger has been to attract brighter, more energetic, harder-working people than me, who believe in CLC's philosophy and goals. I believe that I have been successful in this regard."

I continued, "My role will remain what it has evolved into over the last few years, to guide and direct the company strategically, to address major opportunities, and to help solve major problems. I enjoy working with our staff and clients too much to get too far removed — and besides, I'm still pretty young! I look forward to our two new partnerships with Bob Bernard (Strategic Marketing Affiliates) and with Mark Geddis (Collegiate Images). These are two companies that we believe can generate significant dollars for colleges and universities that are in separate but related areas to our role in collegiate licensing.

"You, as a CLC client, should not see anything but continued progress in all areas of our service to you and your institution. If that ever changes, I hope that you will call me personally."

It was a good time for promotions, as CLC Consortium gross royalties were up 21 percent over the previous year. We were also pleased that 79.67 percent of all CLC universities enjoyed increased royalties over the previous year, and 85 CLC members enjoyed their best year ever. It was the largest percentage increase in Consortium royalties since 1993.

Miami was the undisputed champion of college football in 2001 after its 37-14 victory over Nebraska in the Rose Bowl, played Jan. 3, 2002. Oregon, Texas, Florida and Tennessee all had chances to make it to Pasadena to face the Hurricanes, but there is no doubt the legitimate champion was crowned.

Duke defeated Arizona 82-72 to win the 2001 NCAA Basketball Championship. Also making the Final Four were Michigan State and Maryland.

Top licensees for the fiscal year were Nike in apparel and EA Sports in non-apparel products. Nike continued to improve its internal organization and focus on growing its licensed products division. Sales were up 37 percent for the 2001-2002 fiscal year. They reported that it had already almost matched this year's sales numbers with next year's bookings. They expanded their licensed product line from apparel to also include inflatables (footballs and basketballs) and footwear. They were looking to expand into collegiate golf apparel and equipment, which they were successful in doing.

Electronic Arts' 2002 NCAA Football game sold in excess of 700,000 units, the most successful collegiate video game in history. The 2003 game was promoted more than any previous EA Collegiate game. In addition to video games, five companies were licensed to do collegiate trading cards and paid nearly $400,000 in the fiscal year.

Promotional licensing generated $1.7 million going to 157 CLC institutions. The largest promotion was a Mountain Dew "Don't Miss the Madness" concept around the NCAA Tournament that generated $500,000. The newly structured NCAA program with CBS, Host and CLC was expected to produce more collegiate programs as NCAA Corporate Partners were encouraged to use premiums in activating their respective sponsorships.

In one of the neatest retail promotions of the year, our staff teamed up with FANSonly.com to create a huge retail promotion through its network of official athletic sites. The program was called "The Road to the Races" and was promoted on more than 50 athletics department sites, including FANSonly. com Internet broadcasts of regular-season games. The program culminated with Miami's National Champions program that saw more than $500,000 worth of Rose Bowl and National Champions products sold through

HurricaneSports.com. Products for more than 70 Consortium members were offered through this promotion.

Staff wise, we created NCAA and Bowl Properties (NBP) within CLC to manage all collegiate properties that were not universities. Cory Moss led that initiative to make sure CLC was managing them in all areas of our strategic plan. During the 2001-2002 fiscal year, total bowl revenues increased 24 percent compared to 2000-2001. NCAA revenues increased 47 percent and NCAA Football revenues increased 67 percent. CLC signed long-term renewal agreements with the Sugar and Cotton bowls, while new agreements were signed with the Sun Belt Conference, the Seattle Bowl and the Silicon Valley Football Classic.

As consolidation had occurred among both licensees and retailers, the challenges to both increased. Retailers began requiring better products, shorter lead times, quicker replenishment of fast-selling products, and even in some cases, requiring the licensee to manage the space its products occupied. Many began to require promotional dollars to advertise. The game was definitely changing. Licensed products were moving to more embroidery and other methods of logo application than printing. Consolidation allowed licensees more resources to accommodate those needs, which was a great thing for consumers.

And getting back to game changers, you might recall Starter's bankruptcy and subsequent purchase of the brand by a company that licensed the Starter brand to companies strategically designed to go to Walmart, Kmart and mass merchants. I was advised not to grant them a collegiate license, but I was looking for somebody to do something to ramp up collegiate licensed sales after a few years of single-digit growth. What I did almost cost us the mid-tier retail market.

The Starter licensees came up with great-looking products with outstanding logo applications and were meeting the price points that the mass merchants required. One of the top sporting goods companies came to me with the jacket he was trying to sell at $60 and brought along a jacket Walmart was selling for $29.95 — and the Walmart jacket looked better.

Our entire life in the company was a learning curve, but I quickly learned that if we wanted to sell collegiate products in mass, mid-tier and better department stores, we had better control the products' quality and logo application to provide differentiation for consumers to purchase in each. There are not many licensors that can sell in all three tiers. Typically, if a licensed product or any brand is sold at mass, it can never get back up the retail ladder. Fortunately, since collegiate and professional sports are in the news year-round and its consumers are passionate about their teams, they can accomplish that feat, but only if they approach it properly. We had to restrict the product quality and logo applications that were sold in the mass distribution channel, add more bells and whistles to products sold at mid-tier, and even more that went to better department stores. There were some licensees that were able to sell at mass and mid-tier, but they had to use different brand names and "good, better, best" strategies in the products and price points they offered. In essence, we had to create perceived value to consumers in all those tiers. We did correct that problem and lived to tell about it, but it was a pretty scary time for me.

Consolidation forced CLC to add staff and services to keep up with the trends and manage the business. Fortunately, we worked with so many licensees, retailers and universities, we had the infrastructure to support them. We were on the leading edge of pretty much everything that was going on in our marketplace, and we were fortunate that we had no outside competition for several years. When it did come, we were far enough ahead in contracts, relationships with universities, and infrastructure that included manpower and programs devoted to every facet of the business. If we performed up to our ability, they could never catch us. I always thought that our biggest competition were those major universities that managed their programs in-house. I spent most of my time making sure our universities didn't drop out to run their own programs. If we could do that, I believed that those major independents would come to us eventually.

Our legal staff worked with J. Patton Sports Marketing to develop and implement the new "Officially Licensed Collegiate Products" numbered hologram label and accompanying policy regarding its use by licensees. This was a significant upgrade in our label system, which put CLC up to speed with professional sports licensors. The numbering system was closely monitored so that our staff, universities, and all our family and friends could be on the lookout for merchandise that wasn't of good quality and call in the number. Our staff could see exactly who owned the labels and could respond accordingly. It was equally easy to see who produced the merchandise because it looked so good, people might want to buy from that supplier. The main purpose of the label system was to communicate to consumers the authenticity of the products to which the label was attached.

Bruce Siegal and our legal staff also got involved in helping block a proposed "IP Protection Restoration Act," which could have had a negative impact on the ability of public institutions to enforce their trademarks and intellectual property rights. Fortunately, due to pressure from public universities and related associations, the proposed legislation was tabled.

The previously mentioned Stitches on Demand (SOD) program was fully up and running with more than 100 universities represented. SOD was a web-based program that made pre-approved embroidery files available for purchase by licensees. Those files were digitized for use in a wide variety of applications with approval thread colors and sequence sheets containing sew-out information. CLC worked with our hologram and digital logo provider, J. Patton Sports Marketing, to develop this program.

Our 15th-annual Licensing Directors Seminar was held in Dallas, with 100 Consortium member attendees joining in meetings and fun. We had our basic training sessions, including presentations by CLC members who were doing leading-edge programs on their campuses. As always, we carved out plenty of time for enjoyment, this time visiting the Southfork Ranch, home of the popular television series "Dallas." Activities included, but were not limited to, riding a mechanical bull, country line dancing, a prize-filled auction and armadillo races. It was a great occasion.

We had 16 universities exceeding the million-dollar mark in gross licensing revenues: North Carolina ($4.2 million), Michigan ($3.4 million), Tennessee ($2.4 million), Nebraska ($2.35 million), Florida ($2.2 million), Penn State ($1.7 million), Florida State ($1.67 million), Texas ($1.65 million), Kentucky ($1.57 million), Oklahoma ($1.51 million), Georgia ($1.38 million), Alabama ($1.36 million), Miami ($1.28 million), Auburn ($1.1 million), Wisconsin ($1.08 million) and Maryland ($1.05 million). That's over $30 million for those 16 universities. It took us six and a half years from 1983-84 to halfway into 1990 for our entire Consortium to generate $30 million collectively. But the snowball was rolling, gathering size and speed, and the best was yet to come.

2002-2003

The 2002-2003 fiscal year was the best one ever for the CLC Consortium. We celebrated our 22nd anniversary in the collegiate licensing business by enjoying a record year in payment of royalties to our university partners. Overall, university royalties increased 9.8 percent, which was a good follow-up to the previous year's 22.1 percent increase. During the year, 73.4 percent of Consortium universities experienced gains over the previous year. Promotional licensing generated more than $2 million, surpassing the previous high in 2001-02 by 21 percent. In addition, we made great strides in expanded services in several major areas.

The Officially Licensed Collegiate Products hologram-labeling program was fully operational after its launch the previous year. It was vastly superior to previous labeling in that each label was numbered to enable our staff and university administration to know who was producing every product. The hologram was also much more difficult for infringers to produce a counterfeit label. This put us on par with and better than most licensors in terms of protecting our clients.

A well-thought-through Product Category Management (PCM) was launched with Michigan, North Carolina, Arizona and Penn State. We created a framework and procedure from which individual universities could implement their own PCM strategies. Each of the four universities elected to start with the headwear category, and the results were very positive. With this experience, we could expand the process to other universities and other product categories.

A new Licensing Administration Database was launched to assist licensing directors in managing their licensees. This three-year initiative gave us industry-leading technology to provide clients with broader and deeper data on their licensee base, and much more useful reports for program analysis. Reports were provided over the Internet, and the first ones were to serve as a foundation from which we could build. This included all licensee lists and other pertinent licensing information through a secure interface on iCLC. The system also provided improved services to licensees, which also included the announcement that online royalty reporting was slated to launch in 2004-2005.

We upgraded and enhanced the CLC License Agreement during the first quarter of 2003. This was necessary to keep up with the changing dynamics of the industry and provide more flexibility to individual university clients. Specific additions/improvements were made in the areas of dealing with audits, importing goods from overseas, contract compliance and breach of contract.

The video game category set a record during the year. Our marketing staff had spent a remarkable amount of time working with Electronic Arts and others. For the first time, EA treated "NCAA Football" as a first-tier title and allocated significant financial and human resources to the marketing and development of "NCAA Football 2003." EA produced 10 30-second television commercials focused on great college football rivalries and ran spots during ESPN and Fox college football telecasts. They featured the game on three platforms, which helped sell more than 1.2 million units of "NCAA Football." It was the second-leading title (behind EA's "Madden") in the marketplace. It outsold Microsoft and Sega's NFL titles. EA expected the 2003-2004 games to be much better.

The Consortium was greatly strengthened by the addition of Notre Dame, Washington State and South Florida. After successfully managing its program over the previous decade, Notre Dame performed the most extensive due-diligence process that we had ever experienced. In the end, they recognized that its best opportunity for licensing growth would be through CLC. They were right. Together we were able to accomplish growth for Notre Dame and for the Consortium.

We also finalized an agency agreement to represent the NCAA and its portfolio of trademarks, such as Final Four, College World Series, Frozen Four, etc. We were confident we could position the NCAA as an effective national umbrella brand for the collegiate market. Our position on the NCAA all along was that it could and should be used in conjunction with university marks in programs that would provide incremental revenues to both brands. That was the route we took, and it did prove beneficial to both the NCAA and the university brands with which it was associated.

At the request of several universities, we developed and launched a new restricted license during the 2002 2003 year. This allowed universities to gain better control over their internal campus suppliers, especially as it related to labor code requirements. In conjunction with this change, we added a staff member to oversee the servicing of local and restricted licensees, which typically applied to the most sensitive personalities around the university.

Several universities also requested we formally launch CLC International. Our 10-year non-compete agreement had expired while the Crosslands had pretty much lost interest and moved on to other things. The focus of CLCI was to provide additional service to our clients to manage their trademarks outside the United States. We did make a significant investment in staff and infrastructure, and promised we would provide clients with the same professional service they received domestically. But we wanted to manage their expectations, because we were treading in unknown waters. We brought in former Nike college sports marketing executive Chris Prindiville to run CLCI for us. Chris was a client of CLC at Miami after leaving Nike and learned the licensing ropes as a client and was there for the launch of CLCI.

The number of audits were increased, and the quality of audits and auditors were improved during the year. We scheduled 140 audits in the next year and received $732,691 in lost royalties.

We added another staff member to our Retail Marketing Division, which enabled us to implement a record number of retail promotions for clients. There were now four full-time staff members focused on retail marketing initiatives, and we planned to keep ramping up programs in the future.

Our Information Technology staff continued to add upgrades to *i*CLC to improve speed and efficiency of the system. The primary change impacted the database structure, which resulted in licensing directors being able to access archived designs much faster.

Retail sales of all licensed merchandise in North America in 2002 calendar year increased slightly to $71.5 billion. Sports licensing sales improved 7.6

percent to $11.3 billion and Collegiate licensed sales rebounded 4.2 percent to $2.5 billion.

Team sports licensing was on the rise again in fashion circles after six years of flat to declining sales. In the October 21-22 issue of *Street & Smith's Sports Business Journal*, the NBA's Sal Rocca wrote that for their fiscal year that ended in September, retail sales of NBA-licensed products were up 35 percent, with the league's apparel business doubling from the previous year. "Those of us who were around for the last licensing boom (early to mid 1990s) think we've got the right formula this time with fewer licenses and a better handle on building a sustainable business," said Rocca. "Much of the league's successes are being fueled by well-orchestrated 'retro' or 'throwback jersey' programs."

In the 2003 BCS National Championship Game after the 2002 season, Ohio State defeated Miami 31-24 in double overtime. Maryland won the NCAA Basketball Championship, defeating Indiana 64-52. With two straight Final Four appearances and a BCS bowl game, it was no surprise that Maryland's royalties climbed dramatically in 18 months.

CLC made an investment to help launch Collegiate Images (CI), which now has formal agency agreements in place with more than 40 universities across the U.S., including Michigan, Ohio State, Kentucky, Tennessee, USC, Florida, Missouri, Wisconsin, Syracuse, Clemson, Georgia Tech and others. Mark Gaddis, CEO of CI, did a great job of positioning his company for growth. With a 35 percent ownership stake, we believed we could help them with marketing and enforcement initiatives in the still and moving image space — combining our expertise in trademarks with CI's vision for copyrighted college content licensing.. The goal of CI was to create a significant revenue stream through the centralized management and marketing of archival athletic video footage. In addition to the development of new revenues for collegiate copyright owners, CI was also responsible for enforcement and prevention of misuse of copyrighted or trademarked moving images. Our staff worked closely with CI and its partner institutions to collect royalties from moving images on broadcast, cable and satellite channels. Another major benefit of partnering with CI was their efforts to clear up ambiguous and/or unknown ownership of rights in collegiate moving images.

CLC also invested in Strategic Marketing Associates (SMA) managed by Bob Bernard. CMA was a trademark licensing firm that focused on providing services primarily to universities with market potential below what we were looking for at CLC. Bob's model was a good one and he was doing an excellent job of serving his clients. We believed that as partners, CLC could provide knowledge and infrastructure to SMA. We also had some universities in our

Consortium that Bob's model for managing them would work better than ours. We split profits on a 50/50 basis, and CLC owned 51 percent of SMA.

In the 2002-2003 fiscal year, 18 universities crossed the million-dollar mark in gross royalties: North Carolina ($4.1 million), Michigan ($3.15 million), Tennessee ($2.38 million), Texas ($2.35 million), Florida ($2.2 million), Oklahoma ($2 million), Penn State ($1.95 million), Georgia ($1.93 million), Nebraska ($1.8 million), Kentucky ($1.7 million), Florida State ($1.6 million), Alabama ($1.5 million), Miami ($1.2 million), Wisconsin ($1.16 million), Auburn ($1.11 million), Maryland ($1.048 million), Arizona ($1.041 million) and Duke ($1.040 million).

2003-2004

We had another great year in 2003-2004, breaking records on royalty collection, and making dramatic improvements in administrative, marketing and legal services to our base of licensor and licensee clients. We also crossed the threshold of paying our clients more than a half-billion dollars, which sounds better to me than $500 million. But it wouldn't be long before we crossed the billion-dollar mark.

One area of improvement that deserves mentioning is in our contract compliance review program, better known as audits. Even though we had been doing reasonably well, our performance had slipped below our standard of excellence over the previous few years. So we put our controller, Rick Waugaman, in charge. We identified and hired new auditors, and intensified our internal focus on better preparation for — and better follow up — after all audits. The results were outstanding. We conducted a record 175 audits and collected almost $1.5 million from 136 licensees. Staff members in addition to Rick who deserve recognition for bringing our audit program back to new levels of excellence were associate general counsel Michael Drucker and VP of Systems Administration, Catherine Singer.

The Promotional Licensing Division of CLC generated $1,685,000 in promotional royalties for the year. Royalties were distributed to 156 members that included CLC and independent universities, the NCAA, bowls, athletic conferences and the Heisman Trust.

With the growing strength of the Consortium, we were focused on aggressively improving our impact in the marketplace. Our company had reached the goal set forth in our Mission Statement, "To be the guiding force in collegiate licensing and one of the top trademark licensing companies in the nation." It takes great people to make a great organization, and I could not have been prouder of our staff from top to bottom. We were poised to continue to grow the collegiate licensing business both in increased revenues to our clients and even greater value in the protection of their intellectual property. As a result, there was an increase in universities' brand expansion geographically and brand equity.

In the early years, apparel was the fuel that drove the royalty engine. Non-apparel products finally reached a 75/25 percent ratio with apparel. As creativity from manufacturers and popularity of collegiate sports and licensed apparel began to rise, interest in putting college logos on many different products grew. Our non-apparel staff, headed by Dave Kirkpatrick and Tammy Donnan, did a great job of fanning those flames and encouraging manufacturers to get in the licensing game. The EA video game success took non-apparel licensed sales to new levels.

Nike continued to dominate as the Consortium's No. 1 overall licensee. In the 2003-2004 fiscal year, Nike ranked No. 1 in six different apparel categories (t-shirts, replica team apparel, fleece, authentic sideline apparel, miscellaneous apparel and clothing accessories). Nike ranked No. 2 in outerwear and No. 3 in headwear. They had identified fashion apparel and women's apparel as areas of future growth.

Overall, the fleece category was the highest increasing apparel category by dollar volume, followed closely by women's apparel. In the early days, licensees did not cater to the women's segment of the market. They assumed that small and medium men's sizes would fill that need. Red Oak Sportswear, which primarily sold to Walmart, ended up being the top women's apparel licensee, with a 90 percent increase in sales over the previous year. Most of the other women's apparel was sold in the campus channel by Champion, Gear, Russell and U-Trace. We believed that the mid-tier retailers could become a significant channel for growth in the women's category and worked hard to make that happen. Antiqua, College Concepts, and 5th & Ocean all made inroads. Headwear continued to be strong, and the youth category held good growth potential.

On the non-apparel side of the business, EA continued to dominate the video game category. Our staff, led by Dave Kirkpatrick, worked hard to get collegiate products in the Gift Marts in Atlanta, Dallas and New York. The Atlanta Gift Mart held the largest gift show in the country, and in 2000, five licensees rented space and showed merchandise at that event. At the 2003-04 show, more than 50 vendors of collegiate licensed non-apparel products rented space and showed their wares to retailers from all over the country. They had the ability to occupy an entire section of the show for collegiate vendors. The show promoted their presence and this proved to be a significant milestone for growth.

The overall market for retail sales of licensed merchandise in 2003 was down 0.1 percent to $71.4 billion. Sports licensed merchandise was up 1.8 percent to $11.5 billion, and collegiate was up 14 percent to $2.85 billion. CLC's gross royalties in 2003-04 were up 24.2 percent over the previous year. Compared to the same period the previous year, 74.2 percent of CLC universities experienced increases for the fiscal year, and 86 Consortium members enjoyed their best year ever. This was the third straight year of significant growth in the Consortium. University royalties had grown 65.45 percent since the end of the 2000-2001 fiscal year.

There were 23 universities in the CLC Consortium that generated more than $1 million each: North Carolina ($4.1 million), Michigan ($3.9 million), Texas ($3.15 million), Notre Dame ($2.985 million), Louisiana State ($2.965 million), Oklahoma ($2.92 million), Georgia ($2.7 million), Tennessee ($2.5 million), Florida ($2.3 million), Penn State ($2.1 million), Kentucky ($2.09 million), Alabama ($1.8 million), Florida State ($1.7 million), Nebraska ($1.6 million), Auburn ($1.5 million), Miami ($1.34 million), Wisconsin ($1.3 million), Arkansas ($1.22 million), Oklahoma State ($1.1 million), Kansas ($1.08 million), Connecticut ($1.06 million), Arizona ($1.018 million) and Illinois ($1.015 million).

The 2003 NCAA Basketball Championship was played at the Superdome in New Orleans, where Syracuse held off Kansas, coached by Roy Williams, 81-78. Texas and Marquette also reached the Final Four semi-finals.

LSU defeated Oklahoma in the 2004 Sugar Bowl in New Orleans to win the BCS National Championship. During the season, Southern Cal lost one game in triple overtime at Cal on Sept. 27. LSU lost at home to Florida on Oct. 11. Oklahoma — which had been No. 1 in every BCS rating, and the AP and Coaches' polls — lost 35-7 to Kansas State in the Big 12 Championship Game on Dec. 6. Although USC, then 11-1, finished No. 1 in both the AP and Coaches' polls, with LSU (12-1) ranked No. 2 and Oklahoma (12-1) No. 3, Oklahoma surpassed both USC and LSU on several BCS computers. OU's strength of schedule was ranked 11th to LSU's 29th and USC's 37th. Despite the timing of Oklahoma's loss affecting the human voters, the computers left the Sooners No. 1 in the BCS rankings. LSU was ranked No. 2 by the BCS, in AP and Coaches' polls. LSU was also ranked No. 2 in six of seven computer rankings, and No. 1 in the other. USC's No. 3 BCS ranking resulted in No. 1 rankings in both AP and Coaches' polls, but No. 3 in five of seven computer rankings (with other two coming in at No. 1 and No. 4). Therefore, Oklahoma and LSU met in the Orange Bowl, where the Tigers beat the Sooners 21-14, while Southern Cal defeated Michigan 28-14 in the Rose Bowl. The Coaches' Poll was contractually committed to ranking the BCS National Champion as

No. 1. The AP Poll had no such arrangement and left Southern Cal at its No. 1 ranking.

While having two national champs was confusing to the public and controversial to BCS critics, it was stimulating to CLC. Having two national champions in different sections of the country made for tremendous sales of licensed merchandise for both USC and LSU. There was such excitement from LSU fans that 2003-04 royalties tripled as compared to the previous year.

2004-2005

In fiscal year 2004-2005, we enjoyed another record year of royalties paid to CLC clients. From 2001-2005, royalties increased 55.66 percent. The previous five years, 1995-2000, were relatively flat, showing only a 9 percent increase. Collegiate royalties for the year increased 8.6 percent. Sales of licensed products in North America in 2004 were down 1.3 percent to $70.50 billion. Sports licensed product sales were up 9.6 percent to $13.4 billion, and collegiate sales were up 1.8 percent to $2.9 billion in sales. We were definitely feeling better about the market and were well positioned for the future. Our fourth quarter (April 1-June 30) in the 2004-2005 fiscal year showed a 13.2 percent increase in CLC royalties, bringing the overall increase for the year to 8.6 percent. We were pleased to note that 74.5 percent of our Consortium members enjoyed increased royalties over the previous year's totals.

The 2004 BCS National Championship Game was fraught with controversy. The season ended with five teams ending their regular seasons undefeated — Southern Cal (Pac-10), Oklahoma (Big 12), Auburn (SEC), Utah (Mountain West) and Boise State (Western Atlantic). USC, the dominant team in 2004, and Oklahoma were ranked No. 1 and No. 2, respectively, in the AP and Coaches pre-season polls, but the other three were ranked outside the top 15. USC stayed undefeated and never went below the top ranking. The other four each had arguments for a No. 2 spot, but the human and computer elements picked Oklahoma. The three undefeated teams had to go to other bowls. Auburn beat Virginia Tech (the ACC Champion) in the Sugar Bowl, and Utah became the first "BCS buster" and beat Pittsburgh, the Big East champion. Southern Cal beat Oklahoma 55-19, proving without a doubt they were college football's No. 1 team. Unfortunately, USC's National Championship in 2004 was vacated following an NCAA investigation into Heisman Trophy winner Reggie Bush. USC appealed the decision, but was denied by the NCAA, and the 2004 BCS title was officially vacated June 6, 2011.

The 2004 Final Four was held at the Alamodome in San Antonio, where UConn defeated Georgia Tech 82-73. Duke and Oklahoma State also reached the Final Four.

In the 2003-2004 annual year-end report to universities, I praised our internal staff assigned to our auditing committee for a dramatic turnaround in both the quality and quantity of our contract compliance reviewed of licensees. Our staff of auditors conducted 208 reviews (compared to 175 the previous year) and collected $2,074,186 (compared to $1,465,079). We hired an additional auditor and planned to conduct nearly 300 audits in the coming year.

On the administrative side, we crossed the 200,000 mark in designs processed through CLC. Our system showed transparency on every design as submitted by the licensee, review and response by the CLC staff back to the licensee or forwarded to university, then university's approval, disapproval or comments from university to CLC, then back to licensee. It was easy to track any holdup along the way. This greatly added to the efficiency of the process.

Our Systems and I.T. staff worked hard over nine months to engage in a project that ultimately impacted all CLC member institutions. The project was titled "CLC One" and its goal was to merge as many systems and operational functions as possible into one unified process. The essence of CLC One was for our entire organization to focus on licensing processes and policies. More than 1,600 licensees were surveyed on all aspects of our licensing services. Valuable feedback was gathered in areas needed to improve: speed, efficiency and effectiveness. Much feedback was positive, some was neutral, and some was negative. We listened! Our focus was to resolve the negative and improve the neutral so that all would be positive in the future. Brian White, one of our longtime senior directors, headed up the project — including actually setting up a secret company to obtain a CLC license and report back on his findings along the way. His base of services was a University Representative, and his tech-savvy abilities suited him perfectly for the role.

During the 2004-2005 fiscal year, the growth of *"performance apparel"* necessitated that it became its own product category, thus all licensees were notified. The manufacturing of performance apparel required technical capabilities and investment in research/development, in addition to the ability to manufacture the goods, which were made popular by the sudden rise of Under Armour and its compression and moisture-wicking fabrics. If this category was properly managed, it could result in solid growth for many years to come. If universities were pressured politically into licensing companies with only the ability to manufacture, without being committed to investing in the category, it would greatly reduce the long-term stability.

Non-apparel royalties were up 8.04 percent compared to 2003-04. Domestics were up 65 percent, office products up 190 percent, and furniture/home furnishing up 33 percent. This was a result of new retailers such as Bed Bath

& Beyond, Home Depot and Staples making significant commitments to collegiate vendors. Licensees continued to develop items that consumers would be proud to put in their bedroom, kitchen, office and game room. Previously, most items were sold around the Christmas season. Our staff worked hard to encourage licenses and retailers to carry collegiate products year-round. There had been a push to encourage licensees to create college Halloween kits with costumes, resin ghost and goblins and mascot pumpkin carving kits. We also saw interest in Father's Day, Easter and Thanksgiving for those seasonal licenses.

The CLC Consortium finished the most successful five-year growth period in its history. During that time, most institutions achieved record royalty totals, significant increases and a positive diversification of their license base. Much progress was made during this time to add staff, improve and refine systems, enhance retail relationships, and evolve collegiate licensing into a much more sophisticated enterprise than it was during the pre-2000 era. The challenges we faced were much different from those we faced five years earlier.

Our top selling universities in the 2004-05 fiscal year were: North Carolina ($4.24 million), Michigan ($4.22 million), Texas ($4.07 million), Georgia ($3.5 million), Oklahoma ($3.16 million), Notre Dame ($2.95 million), Tennessee ($2.75 million), Florida ($2.48 million), LSU ($2.26 million), Alabama ($2.25 million), Auburn ($2.11 million), Kentucky ($2.02 million), Florida State ($2 million), Penn State ($1.98 million), Illinois ($1.6 million), Wisconsin ($1.599 million), Nebraska ($1.593 million), Miami ($1.47 million), Arkansas ($1.36 million), Oklahoma State ($1.3 million), South Carolina ($1.18 million), Maryland ($1.17 million), Kansas ($1.13 million) and Clemson ($1.03 million). Twenty-four universities surpassed the million-dollar mark.

Because of our success, we created a way to reward our employees, in addition to the above-average benefits at CLC. We had an excellent insurance plan and also a generous defined contribution profit-sharing plan. The latter provided staff members with the ability to contribute tax-deferred amounts to the plan, through salary deductions, up to a maximum of $14,000 in 2005. CLC agreed to match up to 8 percent of staff compensation. I believed in providing incentives for employees to think long term and this was a means of rewarding their loyalty in the company over a long period of time. We also had a generous annual bonus program based on the performance of the company and the staff member.

We were very protective of CLC stock, as I had observed how a minority shareholder in my former company in Selma created nightmares for Larry Striplin and his companies. We wanted our staff to feel like owners beyond the benefits described above. So we came up with a Phantom Stock Program that was designed to accomplish the following objectives, and we wanted key staff members to: (1) Think like owners and have a defined stake in the growth and profitability of the company — to maximize revenues and minimize expenses; and (2) To stay at the company.

We instituted a five-year plan from 2001-2005. There was a formula that created a pool of revenues based on the difference in gross profits at year-end 1999-2000 and 2004-05. They were given units based on salary at year-end 2000. The payout, at CLC's option, could be distributed over five years. If they left the company during that period, their share would go back into the pool and be divided among remaining staff members based on their number of units.

Phantom Stock Plan I went from 2001 to 2005 and was extremely successful. Our senior leadership team was highly motivated before the plan, but they indeed acted like owners in everything they did. We accrued Phantom stock expenses each year, so there was not a huge hit to the CLC financials in any one year. The amount to be distributed in 2005 was about $2.5 million among four senior staff members. At the beginning of the 2005-06 fiscal year, we started Phantom Stock Plan II. It was tweaked with minor changes to Phantom Stock Plan I, and we also added a several senior leaders who had distinguished themselves during the five-year period.

When we sold the company to IMG in 2007, the strike price was set by the purchase price and we paid about 15 people about $5 million. The amounts were tiered, with senior VPs, VPs, senior directors and directors getting different amounts based on their respective salaries.

2005-2006

The 2005-2006 fiscal year marked our 25th of doing business in the collegiate licensing industry. Our annual Licensing Directors Seminar in Atlanta in mid-May served as the focal point of our Silver Anniversary celebration. It was fun to reflect heavily on the past, as well as to look at the future. We had come a long way from the days when we had to explain what licensing was, that it was not taxation without representation, and that acquiring a collegiate license was a privilege and not a right.

To jog your memory about what happened back in 1980-81, the top television programs were, according to the Nielsen ratings, were "Dallas," "The Dukes of Hazard," "The Love Boat," "The Jeffersons," "Three's Company" and "Magnum P.I." Only one sports program was in the top 20 — "NFL Monday Night Football" with Howard Cosell and "Dandy" Don Meredith. Prince Charles and Lady Diana were married, NASA launched the first U.S. Space

Shuttle mission and President Ronald Reagan was shot in an assassination attempt. We also had new inventions named cable TV, VCR and Sony Walkman. "Donkey Kong" was the first major arcade video game, and the Rubik's Cube captured our attention. Basketball players wore short pants, long socks and tight jerseys. The average new car price was $7,718, home price $78,220, loaf of bread 53 cents, gallon of gas $1.31, Dow Jones Industrial Average 932, and U.S. debt $1 trillion.

We were pleased to report that the upward trend we enjoyed over the previous five years continued in the 2005-06 fiscal year. The CLC Consortium enjoyed another double-digit increase, as well as another record-breaking year in royalty collections. Royalties increased 14.7 percent compared to 2004-05 royalties. Excluding universities that entered or exited the Consortium, the increase was 12.8 percent.

The CLC One corporate improvement program conceived two years earlier had begun to produce major accomplishments. Some included the re-launch of *CLC.com*, the introduction of *MyiCLC* web portal for licensing directors, the development of more streamlined applications and insurance processes, and the initial phases of developing a comprehensive online royalty reporting system for licensees.

We were excited to announce the launch of the *MyiCLC* portal for licensees in fall 2006, which was followed by the launch of the industry's first-ever online royalty reporting system. The combination of these two services further enhanced the efficiency and effectiveness of our overall program to licensees.

College Colors Day, which was conceived a few years earlier by Tim Hawks in our Retail Marketing Department, occurred on Friday, Sept. 1, 2006, to help kickoff the "back to school" season on campuses nationwide. College Colors Day also ushered in a new season of college football. The Labor Day holiday was beginning to gain traction among consumers, retailers, licensees and corporations nationwide. The goal of the holiday was to promote the tradition and spirit that drove collegiate athletics by encouraging fans, alumni and students to wear apparel of their favorite university throughout the day of Sept. 1. When we started this program to take place the day before the first college football game was played, Tim Hawks told us, "College Colors Day will one day be more famous than Cinco de Mayo." We were trying to make the entire Labor Day weekend, from Thursday night's ESPN college game through its Monday night game, "College Colors Week" owned by collegiate properties.

Apparel royalties were up 16.83 percent from the previous year's totals. This was good news as the majority of the growth came from the "mid-tier/better" channel of distribution. The previous year's growth came from increases in the "mass" channel, and that also performed well again with a 10 percent increase. The "campus" channel increased 7 percent. Our estimate was that of all apparel royalties collected in 2005-06, "mid-tier/better" comprised 44 percent, "mass" 30 percent, and "campus" 25 percent. Looking back to 1981, "campus" was responsible for about 85 to 90 percent of all collegiate logos sold.

Texas defeated USC in the 2006 BCS National Championship Game in the Rose Bowl, taking a 41-38 victory that was in doubt to the very end. The 2005 Final Four was held at the Edward Jones Dome in St. Louis, where North Carolina beat Illinois 75-70. It was Coach Roy Williams' first NCAA basketball title. Louisville and Michigan State reached the semi-finals.

In 2005, overall licensed products in North America increased 1.0 percent to $71.21 billion. Sports licensed products increased 6.3 percent to $13.4 billion, and collegiate increased 3.4 percent to $3.0 billion, 22.4 percent of Sports Licensed royalties.

Top-selling universities in 2005-06 were Texas ($8.28 million), Michigan ($5.04 million), Notre Dame ($4.05 million), Georgia ($3.94 million), North Carolina ($3.55 million), Florida ($3.21 million), Oklahoma ($2.8 million), Tennessee ($2.72 million), Alabama ($2.53 million), Penn State ($2.4 million), Florida State ($2.38 million), LSU ($2.21 million), Auburn ($2.12 million), Kentucky ($1.97 million), Wisconsin ($1.92 million), Miami ($1.85 million), Illinois ($1.8 million), Nebraska ($1.76 million), Arkansas ($1.46 million), South Carolina ($1.3 million), Oklahoma State ($1.29 million), Kansas ($1.18 million), Duke ($1.17 million), Clemson ($1.16 million), Maryland ($1.14 million) and Arizona ($1.01 million). Twenty-six universities generated more than a million dollars. In the five years from fiscal year 2001 to 2006, the number of universities generating more than $1 million doubled from 13 to 26.

LESSONS LEARNED

- Sometimes a person or organization can go farther, faster by joining forces with the competition "IF": (1) Mission and strategic plan are bought into by both parties; and (2) no anti-trust issues are created.

- If you are going to be in the service business, you had better listen to your customers and provide the kind of service they want.

- Under-promise and over-deliver. You read that earlier and you will read it again later. Anticipate your customers' problems and solve them quickly and thoroughly. The same goes with opportunities.

- Success breeds success. It creates a different set of problems, but those are good problems to have.

- To build the culture in your organization that you want, your senior leaders all need to buy in. If they all reflect what you want, it will flow to the next levels, and then to the next, freely. Everyone in the organization should answer the "what does your company do?" question the same way.
- If you can make your senior leaders feel like owners in the company, adapting to your culture goals will come more naturally.
- Character should be the No. 1 characteristic in hiring staff, but always be on the lookout for those with the "IT" factor.
- People outgrow organizations, and organizations outgrow people. Change in personnel is not necessarily bad.
- It's not so much what you do, it's how you do it that counts. I've fired people and had them thank me as it helped them realize they were in the wrong place. I've also given people promotions and raises who were mad at me for not giving them more.
- Partnerships are hard whether it's a two-person marriage or a 2,000-employee public company. Much work must occur on a regular basis to keep partners on the same page. When a partnership ends, the results are best long term when both sides can claim victory. That actually applies to any negotiation.

BATTLE ENTERPRISES, INC. — NON-COLLEGIATE LICENSING

As explained earlier, when I formed Collegiate Concepts, Inc. in June 1983 to manage collegiate intellectual properties, I also set up Battle Enterprises, Inc. to work with non-collegiate personalities. My primary motive for the latter was that we were working with Ben Rodgers Lee, a celebrity outdoorsman and world champion turkey caller. I didn't think news of that relationship under the umbrella with a prestigious university would sit well with the president or trustees. In the end, it worked out very well as a "sister company" to CLC. With the ever-growing infrastructure we were building to accommodate the growth of collegiate licensing, taking on another client or two, university or otherwise, was not a big deal. We could service them immediately with very little increase in cost.

The first opportunity came from Southeastern Conference Commissioner Harvey Schiller. Harvey was a general in the Air Force with 25 years of service, a former jet fighter pilot with hundreds of combat hours flown during the Korean War, and a former instructor at the Air Force Academy. He had a Ph.D. in chemistry from the University of Michigan. His tenure at the SEC was from 1986-1990. When we met, I asked if he wanted to be called Doctor, General or Commissioner. He replied in a General's tone of voice, "Commissioner." We convinced Harvey and the SEC to sign an agency agreement with our company. We formed a terrific business relationship and friendship during his time there. He elevated the marketing interests of the SEC exponentially during his term. For example, when he got there, the SEC Basketball Tournament was costing the conference about $100,000 to put on every year. By the time he left, the conference was making at least that much. It is my understanding that the ideas and initial efforts to expand the number of teams in the conference and to create the SEC Football Championship as an additional game belonged to Harvey.

In one of our many marketing and licensing discussions, Harvey suggested that the Olympic National Governing Bodies (NGB) needed help with licensing. The NGBs were primarily headquartered in two locations, Indianapolis and Colorado Springs. I went to both cities and met with the various organizations. The idea was that maybe we could get several sports under contract, form Olympic shops at retail, and sell merchandise from U.S. Boxing, Swimming and Diving, Gymnastics, Rowing and others. We did sign them to agency agreements but were not successful in helping them move forward with a successful licensing program. There were many reasons why this did not work, but I did gain great respect for what the NGBs and USOC were trying to do.

We got involved with NASCAR in 1989 and did what we believed to be a great job in launching and building its program into professional-league status before they took it in-house. We developed a detailed business plan for NASCAR under the same framework as for CLC, and one of our goals was to get NASCAR Licensing recognized along with the four professional leagues and CLC within five years. We helped make it happen.

In 1990 we successfully led Phase One of the Atlanta 1996 Olympic licensing effort by raising $6 million in royalties in a six-month period. It was a euphoric time in Atlanta, and it was euphoric to me and our entire staff. The experience made me a bigger fan of the Olympic movement. From a business perspective, successfully managing the startup of NASCAR's program and the 1996 Atlanta Olympic program proved that we could take on big opportunities outside of our core business of collegiate licensing in ways that didn't hurt that business, but actually helped.

The relationship we developed with the Paradies Company during the Phase One Atlanta 1996 Olympic program led us to the PGA TOUR. Paradies had developed PGA TOUR Shops in a number of airports under the close supervision of the PGA. The stores were elegant! They were built out beautifully to look like what a member might walk into somewhere like the Augusta National Golf Club. They purchased golf apparel from major golf brands and their presentation was exquisite.

The Tour marketing staff had discussed licensing the PGA TOUR brand with Paradies owners and decided that since they understood the quality expected by the Tour, they should become the licensing agency to represent taking the PGA TOUR brand to the marketplace. Paradies didn't understand being a licensing agent any more than we didn't know about being a retailer. They asked if we wanted to partner up with them. We responded we would be delighted to do so.

We signed an agency agreement in 1994 to represent the PGA Tour in a 50-50 partnership with Paradies. The Tour was very restrictive on what we could and couldn't do (as they should have been) and wanted their brand to appear only in major department stores. Their view was, "We can always come down to mid-tier or the mass." It was a difficult challenge. After a while we signed an exclusive apparel deal with Russell Athletic, who we deemed an excellent manufacturer of sports-related uniforms and apparel. Wesley Haynes was the VP from Russell charged with putting the program together. We had some limited successes, but couldn't achieve the growth that the Tour and we wanted. We worked hard, had a huge opportunity at J.C. Penney for a significant commitment, but the Tour wasn't ready to go to mid-tier.

After our first term we were negotiating a five-year extension and had verbally agreed on a deal. In the meantime, the PGA Tour director of Licensing sold the TOUR on the idea that as things had transpired, they should bring their program in-house. They advised us of their decision, but because of the respect they had for Paradies, and to an extent our company, they asked us to make them a proposal to buy out our verbally agreed upon deal. We went to them with the number that we thought would be our profits over five years. They told us if they could pay it over five years, they would accept. We agreed. So every year, for five years, we got paid a significant amount. The most interesting part was a few months after our last payment was received, I got a call from Rick Lillie, vice president at Paradies, saying the PGA Tour wanted us to take back over their licensing program. That was great news, and in our new deal, we would take PGA Tour-licensed products to sporting goods and mid-tier, as well as upper department stores. It was a win-win situation.

We took on the Paralympics program in 1996. The athletes competing in that program are to me, the most amazing in the world. The marketing program was not near what was done for the Olympics, but very effective. My favorite ad from which posters were made was of an athlete with only one leg, the other was a prosthesis. It showed him in a full-speed action shot with the verbiage above saying, "I only have one leg," and the verbiage below saying, "I use it to kick butts!" With the primary help of W.C. Bradley's Chris Martin and Neil Stillwell, we had a very nice presentation of licensed products for sale at Paralympic events.

In 2002 we signed the Canadian Football League and hired Fred Sclera and Jim Neish to run it. We successfully developed a licensing program from scratch for the CFL.

In 2004 we started and developed a program for Churchill Downs, the Kentucky Derby and the Sport of Kings — horse racing. That was managed by Wesley Haynes, who had come on board to manage our PGA Tour business as well.

The bottom line on BEI was that it was an excellent vehicle to take on non-collegiate properties and, if managed properly, wouldn't affect our core business. If the need was too great for our staff to handle internally at CLC, we partnered up with or hired others to handle the heavy lifting, while we actively managed the program. When we sold, our BEI assets added significantly to our buyout price.

LESSONS LEARNED — BEI

- We fully understood that our core business was collegiate licensing. With infrastructure in place, we had opportunities to start and develop non-collegiate properties. DO NOT MIX BUSINESSES THAT WILL DISTRACT FROM YOUR CORE BUSINESS. With Ben Rodgers Lee and Pony Shoes in the beginning, and later NASCAR, we proved we could take on non-collegiate clients without affecting our core business.

- In the licensing business, adding new properties, even though they were not collegiate, presented opportunities for our licensees and retailers, which often actually accrued to the benefit of our collegiate clients.

- Adding non-collegiate clients added to our reputation as an industry-leading licensing agency, as well as adding a significant boost to our sales price when we sold the companies.

2006-2007

The 2006-2007 fiscal year was another year of double-digit growth in CLC revenues. In addition to revenue growth, great progress was made in virtually every area of our operation. Revenues were up 14.9 percent, and the graphic below illustrates how revenues for Consortium members doubled over six years. It was our goal to double again by the 2013 fiscal year. Product category management was the most critical element in our strategy to achieve the optimum number of licensees in each product category and distribution channel. Accomplishing this one university at a time proved to be slow and arduous, but the results were very positive.

Fiscal Year	Gross Royalty Increase	Universities With Increase Over Previous Year
2001-2002	22.1 percent	79.7 percent
2002-2003	9.8 percent	73.4 percent
2003-2004	24.4 percent	78.3 percent
2004-2005	13.2 percent	74.5 percent
2005-2006	14.7 percent	78.6 percent
2006-2007	14.9 percent	76.1 percent

The most earth-shaking news in the year was that we agreed to sell the company to the International Management Group (IMG). You may recall that earlier in the start of our business that Coach Bryant terminated, or let expire, his contract with IMG. At that time in 1981, IMG was run by Mark McCormack, an American lawyer, sports agent and writer. Even then it was a worldwide sports marketing and media company with offices around the world. IMG managed sports, fashion figures and events. McCormack, in his 43 years running the company, was recognized as the man who created sports marketing.

His first client was Arnold Palmer, who signed in 1960. Palmer's annual income skyrocketed from $50,000 a year to $500,000, and ultimately $10 million. His next two clients were Jack Nicklaus and Gary Player. In the words of *Business Age*, "McCormack was the first who realized that, within the golden triangle of sport, sponsorship and television, lay vast wealth, just waiting to be tapped. Without his ruthlessness and marketing skills, his clients would be a great deal poorer."

IMG went on to handle licensing, merchandising and television contracts with organizations such as Wimbledon, the Grammy Awards, the U.S. Olympic Committee, the Smithsonian Institute, the U.S. Golf Association and The Nobel Foundation. By 1990, IMG was the world's largest sports management company, and so all-encompassing that it promoted Pope John Paul II's 1982 tour of Britain. In 1986, McCormack published a book that is still popular today, *What They Don't Teach You at Harvard Business School: Notes from a Street-smart Executive.*

In 2003, McCormack died of cardiac arrest. Mark was the sole owner, and only chairman and chief executive officer the company had ever had. Controlling interest was transferred to his widow, Betsy Nagelsen. She was a retired tennis player turned sportscaster with no management experience. The estate tax liability was predicted to be in the hundreds of millions, but in addition, the company was faced with significant debt. By the end of 2002, IMG had financed an enormous expansion with loans from 12 different banks. *The Wall*

Street Journal reported it as over $200 million. After a difficult period of deciding whether to keep the business going, selling it to her three stepchildren, who were all IMG executives, or selling to all employees, the decision was finally made to sell the company to Ted Forstmann.

Forstmann & Little was a leveraged buyout firm that throughout the 1980s and '90s had bought struggling firms like Dr. Pepper and Gulfstream Aerospace, and later flipped them for huge profits. Ted Forstmann was such an icon of Wall Street greed that the 1980s book, *Barbarians at the Gate*, featured him as a central figure. McCormack was a business builder; Forstmann was a business trader.

In 2006, George Pyne was brought on as president of IMG Sports & Entertainment, and a board member. We knew George back when he worked in Atlanta for the Portman Companies and later when he became chief operating officer at NASCAR. He became familiar with our company when we were working with NASCAR's licensing program. When he got to IMG he began talking to my son Pat about IMG buying our companies.

We talked in late 2006, and Pat and I had long discussions about what to do. I told him I was comfortable keeping the company going, as it was very strong at the time. I would be happy seeing my grandchildren come into the business if they were interested, but if he and Derek Eiler, our chief operating officer, were interested in selling, I would be happy moving in that direction as well. Pat said, "If we can get enough money to satisfy you, and if we are convinced that we can go further, faster with IMG resources, then we would be interested in selling."

I began to get very comfortable with the numbers, as the offer was about 90 percent cash and 10 percent equity in IMG. Pat began to get comfortable with the opportunities to use IMG resources to begin to consolidate collegiate licensing and media rights, which up to that point in time had remained totally separated. CLC held the large majority of collegiate licensing rights while Host Communications (Jim Host), Learfield Sports (Clyde Lear, Roger Gardner and Greg Brown) and ISP Sports (Ben Sutton) owned most collegiate media rights. We each purposefully stayed out of the other's businesses, but it was inevitable that they would and should merge. Pat wanted to lead that charge.

When we sold to IMG they insisted on buying all of our licensing interests. At the time, CLC and CLC International were our primary businesses, but we also had Battle Enterprises Inc. (BEI) properties that were contracted with the PGA Tour, Churchill Downs, the Kentucky Derby and the Canadian Football League. We had some partners in the non-collegiate business that had to go along with the sale. IMG told us they loved our collegiate business and wanted to keep it running with the same name, the same staff and the same strategic plan. They bought into Pat's vision to consolidate licensing with media rights. We went out to Host, Brown and Sutton to see if there was interest in selling to IMG. Host Communications was the first to agree, and IMG brought the media rights that Host owned under the IMG College umbrella with CLC.

We did our best to communicate to our company the upcoming sale to IMG. Our senior staff members spread out to meet with as many of our top universities as possible. The rest we did through phone calls and email. IMG allowed us to use its plane to travel and help spread the message. I flew out to the University of Texas to meet with Athletics Director DeLoss Dodds, General Counsel Patti Ohlendorf and Licensing Director, Craig Westemeier. When I arrived, DeLoss and Craig were there, but Patti was in a meeting and would join us as soon as she could.

We chatted for a while about news, sports and weather, then DeLoss asked, "What time did you fly into the airport?" I responded, "About 10:30." He said, "What airline did you use?" I said, "I flew in private." He turned to Craig and said, "Oh, you flew in private. Craig, go get our contract." We laughed and I said, "We'll talk more about that when Patti gets here." Patti arrived a few minutes later. I said, "I've got good news and bad news. The good news is that we have brought IMG into the collegiate licensing space, and with their resources we can take our business to higher levels. The bad news is that you will still have to deal with us, as they intend to leave the CLC brand and staff and strategic plan in place. One of those resources enabled me to use their plane to get out to meet with you." Their response was very positive and showed how much we valued the partnership with the University of Texas and all CLC clients. DeLoss would later go on to report back to our senior staff how much it meant to him that we flew in to share news of the IMG acquisition personally and face to face. Texas remained a great client of CLC and IMG for many years after.

LSU defeated Ohio State 38-24 on Jan. 7, 2008, to win the 2007 National Championship in the Louisiana Superdome. Georgia, Southern Cal, Missouri and Ohio State finished No. 2-5 in the final AP Poll.

The 2006 NCAA Final Four was held in the RCA Dome in Indianapolis, where Florida defeated UCLA 73-57 to win the title. LSU and George Mason also reached the Final Four.

Top-selling universities in the 2006-07 fiscal year were Texas ($7.58 million), Notre Dame ($6.09 million), Florida ($5.98 million), Michigan ($4.59 million), Georgia ($4.35 million), North Carolina ($3.71 million), Alabama ($3.3 million), Oklahoma ($3.13 million), Tennessee ($3.13 million), Penn State ($3.1 million), LSU ($3.01 million), Florida State ($2.67 million), Auburn ($2.58 million), Nebraska ($2.14 million), Wisconsin ($2.13 million), Kentucky

($2 million), Illinois ($1.93 million), Arkansas ($1.83 million), Miami ($1.75 million), South Carolina ($1.52 million), Clemson ($1.52 million), Kansas ($1.21 million), Duke ($1.2 million), Oklahoma State ($1.12 million), Minnesota ($1.067 million), Arizona ($1.066 million), Louisville ($1.0357 million), Maryland ($1.0354 million), Texas Tech ($1.02 million) and Purdue ($1 million). Thirty CLC universities reached or exceeded the million-dollar mark.

2007-2008

The completion of the 27th year in the business of collegiate licensing brought both good news and bad news. On the good news side of the ledger, we completed our first full year as an IMG company and made a great deal of progress in identifying and applying IMG resources to the collegiate marketplace. The acquisition and integration of Host Communications into IMG College was a positive step in the consolidation of the collegiate sports marketplace. We believed further consolidation would create many benefits to IMG College clients.

We finished the 2007-2008 fiscal year with an 11 percent increase in royalties over the previous year, marking the fifth straight year of double-digit increases for CLC's overall client base. Eighty-two universities enjoyed their largest royalty total in history.

Our audit, infringement and compliance programs brought in $2,725,581, and over a five-year period, collected $11,727,366.

On the bad news side of the ledger, the economy was in tough shape. The high cost of gas and oil, the mortgage and credit crisis, the decline of the dollar, and other factors caused great concern to consumers and retailers alike. Personal and corporate bankruptcies rose, companies downsized, the stock market fell and inflation concerns were significant.

Even though we finished the year with an 11 percent increase, the quarterly trend was downward. The first fiscal quarter produced a 28.8 percent increase, but declines were experienced in each succeeding quarter. There was a (1.8 percent) decline in the second quarter (fourth fiscal quarter). Only 64.3 percent of universities ended the year with increases over the previous year, our worst total in many quarters.

Our sale to IMG was met with tremendous approval from the industry. Universities were a little nervous at first, but they appeared to be pleased there was a seamless transition with the name and staff remaining in place. Universities continued to join the CLC Consortium, and each year most signed long-term renewals. As our infrastructure and staff continued to grow, our ability to service all facets of the program improved.

Florida defeated Ohio State 84-75 for back-to-back NCAA Basketball Championships, the first school to repeat since Duke's 1991-1992 titles. UCLA and Georgetown were also semi-finalists at the Georgia Dome in Atlanta.

In looking at data from the licensed merchandise market, most industry publications indicated that $4 billion in retail sales of collegiate licensed products were sold for the first time in the 2007 calendar year. Sales faded some in the first two quarters of 2008, but the distribution of sales across multiple product categories in multiple channels of distribution was a positive sign for its long-term health. The unknown factor in predicting the future was how deep and how long the economic downturn would affect consumer spending.

The issue of pressure on collegiate licensees that manufactured abroad continued to rise. Bruce Siegal, CLC general counsel, led that discussion with CLC universities that had a labor code in their license agreements, as well as working with the Fair Labor Association and Workers Rights Consortium in the oversight of factories abroad. At the end of the second quarter, Bruce, Kit Walsh, Chris Prendiville and Derek Eiler traveled to Asia to participate in FLA's annual meeting and to visit factories in the region, which included stops in Shanghai, Hanoi and Hong Kong. In each region they were able to get a good feel for the market potential of producing collegiate merchandise. They were able to meet with suppliers for several top licensees.

The highlight of the trip was a two-day visit to Hanoi, where they met with PNG Headwear, the primary supplier to Top of the World, the collegiate market's leading headwear licensee. Harold Koh, PNG Headwear's owner, was a long-time industry veteran and the epitome of what all universities should be seeking in a factory owner. He ran an impeccable factory with policies and systems in place that focused on transparency and workers' rights. North Carolina Licensing Director Derek Lochbaum and Stanford's Susan Weinstein accompanied our staff on this tour. The success of this trip encouraged our staff to make annual trips with university licensing directors to broaden our horizons and validate the complexities faced in meeting the challenges of labor rights, contract compliance, and other issues.

Back to U.S. markets, apparel-marketing notes of interest included the fact that the NCAA "Blue Disk" was replacing the Starter program at Walmart in fall 2008. Another significant development was the launch of the PINK Collection through Victoria Secret/Limited Brands. This collection co-branded the popular PINK line with college logos through Victoria Secret's website, catalog and stores in late June 2008. The launch was with 27 CLC institutions, but CLC marketing staff was working closely with the PINK executive team to develop plans to roll out additional universities in upcoming seasons. The initial weeks of the selling met with tremendous success. There was great value in this program to the collegiate market as it targeted a customer not easily reached by current programs, and it also helped promote college as a fashion brand.

On the non-apparel side of the business, royalties were up for the 12th consecutive year. Video games continued to be the market leader, but our staff was bullish on growth opportunities in tailgating, home décor and footwear. Walmart committed to a significant collegiate domestic program in 1,104 stores that was to begin August 2008. If successful, this program could take domestics to unprecedented levels.

College Colors Day kept growing by leaps and bounds. CLC staff coordinated a satellite media tour featuring ESPN college football analyst Lee Corso as a spokesperson for the event. On Friday, Aug. 22, television stations around the country conducted interviews with Corso via satellite as he discussed the upcoming football season and College Colors Day. Millions of viewers were exposed to the event on their local networks.

CLC shipped standup Toby Keith signs promoting College Colors Day to college bookstores across the country. Of course, the bookstores had a wide variety of college licensed products to sell. CLC produced a 30-second TV commercial, which ran nationally on sports and news networks leading up to College Colors Day. All ESPN networks, CNN, CNBC, Fox News, MSNBC and others carried the spot. CLC staff also worked with J.C. Penney to secure 30-second radio spots utilizing existing J.C. Penney ad inventory. Those spots ran nationally on talk radio the week leading up to College Colors Day on such shows at Mike and Mike in the Morning, The Herd with Colin Cowherd, The Jim Rome Show, Tirico & Van Pelt, and others.

Two College Colors Day games kicked off on Thursday, Aug. 27 for the 2007 football season. North Carolina at South Carolina and Oregon State at Stanford played with the College Colors Day logos on the fields. The games were televised on ESPN and ESPN2, respectively. The third College Colors Day Classic game took place on Friday, Aug. 28 with SMU playing at Rice.

Twenty-five governors issued proclamations declaring it College Colors Day in their respective states. Postcards were mailed to more than 100,000 organizations across America encouraging them to allow their employees to wear college apparel on Aug. 28. This program served as an example of the expansion of our overall marketing philosophy and proof that if we utilized our significant collective resources to promote college products directly to consumers, retail buyers would respond through more aggressive promotions and stocking of collegiate products. This program definitely moved the needle in helping grow the college business.

354

Thirty-two universities surpassed the million-dollar mark in the 2006-07 fiscal year. Top-selling universities were Texas ($8.2 million), Michigan ($5.58 million), Florida ($5.311 million), LSU ($5.3 million), Notre Dame ($5.1 million), North Carolina ($4.5 million), Georgia ($4.4 million), Alabama ($3.73 million), Penn State ($3.72 million), Tennessee ($3.3 million), Oklahoma ($3.2 million), Auburn ($2.9 million), Wisconsin ($2.8 million), Kansas ($2.5 million), Kentucky ($2.94 million), Florida State ($2.43 million), Nebraska ($2.2 million), Illinois ($2.1 million), Arkansas ($2 million), South Carolina ($1.7 million), Clemson ($1.5 million), Miami ($1.3 million), Cal-Berkeley ($1.27 million), Missouri ($1.2 million), Duke ($1.19 million), Arizona ($1.17 million), Syracuse ($1.15 million), Purdue ($1.1 million), Oklahoma State ($1.06 million), Texas Tech ($1.055 million), Louisville ($1.053 million and Maryland ($1.01 million).

2008-2009

We were proud to announce that during the 2008-09 fiscal year, CLC passed the ONE-BILLION DOLLAR mark in gross royalties collected on behalf of its university clients since inception in 1983. It was quite a ride. In our 28 years of serving our collegiate partners, we had never seen quite as rocky a road as we experienced during the latest fiscal year. Despite all the retail malaise and the daily drumbeat of doom and gloom from the media, we amazingly navigated through the situation quite well, registering a 3.6 percent increase in university royalty collections as compared to the prior fiscal year. It was the ninth consecutive year of annual comparative royalty increases, but the lowest annual percentage increase since 2000-01.

The National Retail Federation projected a 7.7 percent decline in overall shopping in back-to-school for the 2008 season. This was a very important season for collegiate licensed products. This same survey projected that American consumers would trade down in spending, and that discount retail channels would enjoy the bulk of that business. As the cost per unit went down at retail, wholesale prices went down, which lowered the royalties per unit. As happened in the economic downturn in the early 2000s, it appeared there would be a shakeout of both licensees and retailers, either getting out of the business altogether or consolidating with other companies. This cleansing process was painful and not much fun, but it did make for a healthier environment when the market turned back up.

The licensed products business, particularly sports licensing, proved to be resilient in tough economic times. People tended to put off buying larger items, but spending on items that make them feel good. Premium ice cream, better foods, and products that keep them in touch with their favorite teams were somewhat resilient to recession.

Universities also felt the need for help in tough economic times. We were very pleased Texas A&M and UCLA, two long-time very independent universities, joined the CLC Consortium. Cal Poly, Missouri State, the PapaJohns. com Bowl and the New Mexico Bowl all decided CLC was their best alternative in 2008 to stabilize and grow their licensing programs. In turn, they added great strength to the Consortium.

I haven't spent much time talking about our Legal Department, but they were quite efficient in enforcement on local, regional and national levels, guidance to universities on trademark registrations, active engagement in anti-counterfeiting legislation, managing licensee bankruptcies to get in line to collect unpaid royalties, and litigation. There were two lawsuits that were filed during the year that should be mentioned. Both involved the use of player likenesses in collegiate video games and other commercial products in an attempt to challenge the NCAA's rules and procedures related to compensation for their name, image and likeness. In *Keller v EA Sports*, the lawsuit was filed against EA Sports, the NCAA and CLC, by Sam Keller, a former Division I quarterback at Arizona State. It was filed as a class-action lawsuit in the federal district court in California and contended that EA's sale of a series of college football and basketball video games violated the personal rights of college athletes by using their images in games. Unlike the various licensed professional league sports games, the EA collegiate games did not designate individual players' names, which would violate NCAA bylaws that prohibited the commercial use of any student-athlete's name, image or likeness. The second lawsuit, also a class action, was filed by Ed O'Bannon, a former basketball player for UCLA seeking similar rulings on anti-trust grounds.

The Victoria's Secret PINK Collegiate Collection was one of the most significant accomplishments in women's apparel for the collegiate market in 2008-09. The program started in June 2008 with 33 universities and grew to 58 universities, with prospects to add more in the future. With the high-profile success of their PINK University program, CLC was contacted by other brands in pursuing other collegiate programs. The interest ranged from character and entertainment brands to other fashion brands to household product brands. Success does breed success.

On the non-apparel front, Walmart's fall collegiate program contributed to a staggering 50 percent increase in royalty revenue in the third quarter of 2008. EA Sports, North Pole, Northwest and Whitman Publishing — with its *College Football Vault* series of history books containing replicas of memorabilia — kept the overall non-apparel royalties at double-digit growth for the year.

In our 2008-2009 annual report, our mission to university clients was straightforward. The road ahead was clear. We lived in a reset world, and the assumptions that once drove our business had been challenged. The recession and associated retail meltdowns gave us good reason to pause and re-assess where we were at this point in our life cycle, and more importantly, where we wanted to go from here. The next several years were marked with an even more strategic approach to licensing:

Fewer licensees with far deeper partnerships;

A more critical assessment of licensees abilities in areas like corporate responsibility and sustainability;

Targeted program analysis and execution of specific programs by category, distribution, channel and even by specific consumer segments;

Aggressive macro and micro marketing efforts to fend off competition fighting for our retail shelf space.

To accomplish these goals, our staff was committed to continuing our evolution as an organization in terms of systems, personnel and services. We re-invented ourselves in 1993-94, and again in 2001-03. Changing times causes changing behaviors. I have always believed that "there are no good times or bad times, just changing times." When times change, there are those who understand and manage both the problems and opportunities associated with the change. Those people prosper, those that don't, fail. We were well prepared and committed to being in the former category.

Florida won its second BCS National Championship in three years with a victory over Oklahoma in Miami Gardens, Florida, on Jan. 8, 2009.

Kansas won the 2008 NCAA Men's Basketball Championship in memorable fashion over the Memphis Tigers. The semi-finalists were North Carolina and UCLA. The Final Four was held in the Alamodome, one of my favorite venues, in San Antonio. The history of the San Antonio Riverwalk development is worth checking out. Some great decisions were made even back before the territory belonged to Texas and the United States.

A record 33 universities generated more than a million dollars in the 2008-09 fiscal year, including Texas ($8.87 million), Florida ($5.89 million), Georgia ($5.63 million), LSU ($5.12 million), Alabama ($4.85 million), North Carolina ($4.82 million), Michigan ($4.27 million), Arkansas ($2.23 million), FSU ($2.22 million), Kansas ($2.2 million), West Virginia ($2.19 million), Illinois ($2.167 million), Nebraska ($2.165 million), Missouri ($1.82 million), South Carolina ($1.58 million), Clemson ($1.49 million), Cal-Berkley ($1.37 million), Purdue ($1.32 million), Texas Tech ($1.25 million), Miami ($1.23 million), Oklahoma State ($1.13 million), Arizona ($1.11 million), Minnesota ($1.06 million), Washington ($1.04 million), Louisville ($1.019 million) and Duke ($1.018

million). As a Consortium, we were still in a great place and positioned very well for the future.

From the beginning of CLC, I had written the introduction and conclusion to our quarterly reports, while many staff members contributed to make up "the meat" of the reports. Beginning with the April-June introduction and conclusion, the baton was passed to Chief Operating Officer Derek Eiler. Derek was one of our very best since joining our company in 1993, and like everything else he did, I expected him to improve on all of the aspects of the reports.

2009-2010

The 2009-2010 fiscal year saw collegiate licensing regain momentum in the marketplace following two very challenging years. The last half of the year produced increased royalties and optimism by licensees and retailers that the future looked positive.

The CLC Auditing Program generated a record collection of lost royalties for the year — topping the $2,000,000 mark for the second time in history and posting an 18 percent jump over the previous year's total collections. The continued complexity of PCM contracts and global sourcing arrangements by licensees created challenges in reporting royalties. The experienced CLC audit team continued to provide a great value to our clients.

The 2010 BCS National Championship Game was played after the '09 season in the Rose Bowl, where Alabama beat Texas 37-21 for Coach Nick Saban's first national title at Alabama. It was quite a trip for Crimson Tide fans to return to the Rose Bowl for the first time since Alabama's successful run in the 1920s, '30s and '40s.

North Carolina won the 2009 NCAA National Basketball Championship by defeating Michigan State 89-72 at Ford Field in Detroit, where UConn and Villanova were the other semi-finalists.

In the 2009-10 fiscal year, 35 universities generated more than a million dollars in royalties. Leading the way was Texas ($10.15 million), followed by Alabama ($8.04 million), Florida ($5.75 million), LSU ($4.97 million), North Carolina ($4.77 million), Georgia ($4.75 million), Michigan ($4.43 million), Kentucky ($4.2 million), Penn State ($3.97 million), Oklahoma ($3.56 million), Notre Dame ($3.52 million), Tennessee ($3 million), West Virginia ($2.65 million), Nebraska ($2.56 million), Auburn ($2.52 million), Wisconsin ($2.43 million), Kansas ($2.28 million), Missouri ($2.25 million), FSU ($2.08 million), Arkansas ($2.03 million), Texas A&M ($1.93 million), Illinois ($1.85 million), South Carolina ($1.77 million), Texas Tech ($1.58 million), Clemson ($1.39 million), Oklahoma State ($1.34 million), Miami ($1.29 million), Purdue ($1.22 million), Minnesota ($1.17 million), Duke ($1.13 million), Louisville ($1.12

million), Arizona ($1.07 million), Cal-Berkeley ($1.07 million), Washington ($1.04 million) and UCLA ($1.03 million). This was another record year, and during the year, CLC crossed the one-billion-dollar milestone of royalties paid to universities since 1983. You may recall that in fiscal year 2009, we crossed the one-billion-dollar mark in gross royalties, which included CLC's share plus NCAA and other non-university payments.

2010-2011

After the sale in 2007, Pat had been going to New York every month to meet with the worldwide leaders of all of IMG's enterprises. He did a great job meeting and getting to know the IMG leaders, and learned a lot about running a really big business. His view of that was "it's the same principles as running our business, the numbers are just bigger." From 2007 to 2011, CLC was one of, if not the, fastest growing and most profitable divisions of IMG. Host Communications also enjoyed positive growth. IMG in fact did leave us alone, and also provided assistance from its vast resources to help. Pat had promised four years and then he wanted to move on to other things.

In 2011, Ben Sutton's International Sports Properties (ISP) believed he was close to merging with or acquiring Learfield. At the 11th hour, Learfield backed out and Ben decided it was time to talk to IMG. He wanted to talk directly to Ted Forstmann, so Pat encouraged him to do so. About the time Ben was making a deal with Ted, Pat had decided he was ready to move on.

I hated to see Pat leave, but knew he had bigger and better things he wanted to accomplish. When Pat left, some key senior leaders at CLC also decided they wanted to start their own company. Derek Eiler, Kit Walsh, Chris Prindiville and Scott Bouyack all moved on. Each had contributed greatly to the success of CLC. I was grateful for their service and knew they would be successful, and they have been.

This CLC chapter of the book obviously holds a special significance for me and my family, primarily because of the amazing colleagues, partners and characters we encountered along the way. One of the things that makes me most proud is to have started something in 1981 that continues to have a significant impact on collegiate revenues nearly four decades later. Cory Moss, who we hired in 1995, is leading CLC at the time of this writing, along with many of the great teammates who were instrumental in building the business over the past 10, 20 and even 30 years. CLC is now part of Learfield-IMG College, and Pat, who was instrumental in working with the owners of both Learfield and IMG College to merge the two companies, currently serves on the Board of Directors.

We still had a talented and deep staff that was important for me to protect. Wake Forest's Ben Sutton was one of the first universities I called on back in 1981-82. He was an associate athletics director at the time, and one of his many responsibilities was trademark licensing. We had remained friendly throughout the years and Ben asked me to stay on as chairman. He agreed to pay me very well and not ask too much of me. I enjoyed coming to the office every day that Mary and I were in town.

Being around our young and energetic staff made me feel good and kept me young. Since we sold, I had a lot more assets that needed managing, so I had plenty to keep me occupied at the office. I think my presence made our staff feel comfortable, and I also think our clients felt more comfortable that there was ample gray hair still in the office!

From 2011 to 2013, my routine was to be in the office Tuesday, Wednesday and Thursday. Friday through Monday was usually spent with Mary and me going up to our ranch in Ellijay, Georgia, which is about an hour and 15-minute drive, depending on traffic. We discovered our place in Ellijay, and fell in love with the property and the town. Ellijay calls itself the "Apple Capital of Georgia" and hosts a fall Apple Festival that attracts people from all over the South. Our ranch is a beautiful property in and surrounded by mountains looking into a valley with an eight-acre lake, and about seven miles of white vinyl fencing throughout the property to separate pasture lots for horses. It has a beautiful log home, a 16-stall barn, a nice guesthouse, and a nice pool located a few hundred yards from the house. The property is bordered by National Forest land on the north side and half of the west side. There are trails all over the property leading well up into the National Forest. A couple of different trails join together north of our property that lead all the way up into Tennessee.

Mary grew up with horses, so we soon got in the horse business. After a few years, I was asked if there was a lot of money in the horse business. My response was, "There's a lot of money in the horse business, but I've never found any that came in!" Mary is at peace with the world in the barn or out working with horses. My love got to be using a chain saw and lopping shears from a 4-wheeler while discovering old logging trails on and off the property and cleaning them so the horses, 4-wheelers and hikers could use them. We really enjoy spending time there.

In March 2013, the call came from Paul Bryant Jr., and the rest is history. I had not told anyone in Atlanta about my decision to take the athletics director position at Alabama. George Pyne from IMG and Ben Sutton from IMG College had asked me to join them for lunch. We had a nice lunch and as we were wrapping up, I said, "I have a bombshell to throw on you." They looked surprised and probably thought I had some bad news about the company, but

I said, "When we came to this lunch, you were my two bosses. As we leave this table, I am now your boss, as I have accepted the position of Director of Athletics at The University of Alabama and I expect extraordinary service out of CLC and IMG." We all laughed, but they were definitely committed to keeping Alabama happy. I was very pleased to see that Alabama's gross royalties in 2012-13 were just under $10 million. I am very pleased with the revenue stream we helped create back in 1981.

LESSONS LEARNED

- "Make hay while the sun shines" is an old quote that references life on the farm. It applies to business as well. When times are tough, it requires much time and effort to maintain growth or even the status quo. When times are good, work extra hard to move the organization as far as possible. That is no time to relax.

- If you sell your organization to a larger one, make sure your attorneys match theirs. This is the time that little wins may make a big difference.

- Make up your mind about whether you want to sell or not. "Seller's remorse" is a pitiful disease to catch. Your attitude after the sale should comfortably be, "I hope they make a skillion dollars."

- If you sell, be sure to alert your best customers so they are not shocked at the news.

- If you stay on with the new company after the sale, work like you did prior to the sale, unless you have an agreement with the new owner to do otherwise.

- You are actually in a good place as you, better than anyone, know how resources from the new company can be used to expand your sales, brand awareness and other goals.

- Timing is the key to most everything, but as said before, there are no good times or bad times, just changing times. Pay attention.

- Data is critical to future success. Unchecked, you can get swamped with so much data it overwhelms you. Manage closely data output and make sure it is valid and useful.

- Typically "less is more." It may be better to have fewer but bigger and better customers. Same might apply to staff, systems and others.

- If things don't work out well for you under the new company ownership, work out your departure. If there is a non-compete clause, live that out honorably. If you have the energy and desire, after that, get the band back together and go for it when the time is right.

My first press conference as Director of Athletics at The University of Alabama.

CHAPTER 7

DIRECTOR OF ATHLETICS AT THE UNIVERSITY OF ALABAMA

I'm not sure why I got the call from Paul Bryant Jr. to be The University of Alabama's Director of Athletics when Mal Moore decided to retire.

My belief is that the conversation got started a few years earlier when Lee Roy and Biddie Jordan invited Mary and me to go to an Alabama game in Tuscaloosa, and also to spend the weekend at their farm west of town. Teammates Benny Nelson, and wife Shelby, and Richard Williamson, and wife Norma, were there, along with classmate and current Trustee Angus Cooper and his fiancé. We had a great time replaying old games and bragging on Lee Roy's career.

I had known Angus back in school during the 1960s and had met up with him a time or two over the years at Young Presidents' Organization meetings. It was fun reminiscing with Angus, and learning how he and his brother David had taken their small family business and turned it into a major industrial enterprise.

A few months later Angus invited me to hunt ducks at his place in Lake Charles, Louisiana, on opening day of the second season in December. It was me, Lee Roy Jordan, Mal Moore, Paul Bryant Jr. (UA Trustee and president *pro tem*), John McMahon (UA Trustee), Edgar Weldon, Angus and Angus' longtime buddy Gin Taylor. It became an annual event, and Jerry Duncan started coming in later years. Angus had converted a barge into a Hyatt Regency-type lodging facility with about 10 upstairs bedrooms, a great room that included a kitchen, a dining room, and a den with a bar, TVs, sofas and lounge chairs. It was a great place for Alabama people to gather.

The hunting was great, but when duck hunting at a place like this, the hunt is over by 9 a.m. or so because you have your bag limit. That leaves a lot of time for visiting, storytelling, second-guessing coaches, and watching December bowl games and basketball on TV.

These hunts went on for three or four years, and in December 2012, one of our football conversations discussed the strategy behind when to go for two points after a touchdown. It was caused by a tight game we were watching on TV in which a team went for two late in the fourth quarter. Paul has a photographic memory, and not only can he recite every game I ever played in at Alabama, but also the score and the plays leading up to the final score. He also is extremely knowledgeable about the rules and strategy. We talked about when the two-point option after a touchdown came in back in the '60s, coaches prepared charts that indicated when to call for two after a touchdown. Depending on the score, it could have been early in the game. The strategy was sound in that defenses prevailed in those days and scoring was typically low. Today, with scoring typically high, it has proven better to wait until the end of the game to employ the two-pointer. It was a very interesting discussion that got every-one in the group engaged.

A few days after I got back home, I found my game-day reminder chart that listed all the scores that would suggest a two-point play was needed. I mailed it to Paul. It was a laminated 8x10 piece of cardboard with some orange color and some Tennessee logos. After Paul had time to read and review the chart, he called and asked if he could pass it along to some people. I certainly had no objections, and forgot about it.

In March 2013, Mary and I were at our ranch one weekend. Paul sent me a text and asked when might be a convenient time to talk about some serious Athletics Department business. I thought that very strange, as Paul and I had never really talked about serious Athletics Department business. I replied that Sunday early evening would be a good time as Mary and I had separate cars and I would be driving home alone. We normally would spend Sunday night at the ranch and come back mid-morning on Monday, but we each had things to do that Monday. A tornado had come through Ellijay and knocked down about a hundred trees on the property. Fortunately, most of them were up in the woods and not a problem, but I spent most of the weekend with my chain-saw, cutting and moving trees. Mary, as usual, spent her time with the horses.

When I left Sunday and called Paul, he asked if I had heard that Mal Moore had been admitted to the hospital, and it was serious. Mal was a former team-mate and friend, and he coached at Alabama for years. Mal did an absolute great job as an offensive coordinator for Coach Bryant and Coach Gene Stall-ings. But Mal's wife, Charlotte, had become ill with Alzheimer's, so in 1994 he moved into an associate AD position to avoid the amount of time and travel required as a coach. Then in 1999, Mal became Director of Athletics at Ala-bama, at which he did a great job.

I responded to Paul that I had not heard about Mal. We talked a while and he said, "We want you to come help us." I said, "What does that mean?" He said, "Come take the job." Being stunned, I said, "Noooo! I can't do that." We talked awhile and Paul finally said, "Am I being too blunt?" I said, "Paul, this is the most flattering thing I have ever heard, but you are talking about an in-terim term until you can find the right person, aren't you?" He said, "No, that won't work. We need you to come in and do the job." I said, "Hey, I'm 71 years old." He said, "But you're a young 71."

Dr. Judy Bonner, previous provost at the university, had recently been named president. I had planned to attend the President's Cabinet meeting, which numbered about 300, as I wanted to meet her. I said, "Paul, I'm coming to Tuscaloosa Friday to go to the President's Cabinet meeting. Let's go to the meeting, then drive down to Demopolis to hunt turkeys on my friend Alex Jones' place. We'll drive back after the hunt as I have to be in Birmingham Saturday night to attend a wedding shower for our daughter Kayla." He bluntly said, "How about tomorrow?" I said, "Man, I don't even know what's on my calendar for tomorrow, but I know I can't come to Tuscaloosa."

I got home, walked in the house and Mary was sitting on the couch in the den. As I walked by, she said, "What's wrong? You look like something is going on." I replied, "My whole world has been shaken up in the last 45 minutes." She said, "Go put your stuff up and let's talk." I did and came back in the den, sat down and explained what had transpired on the call. After hearing the story, she said, "Now my whole world is shaken up."

We were living a great life at the time. We had a great house in a neighborhood with the best neighbors either of us had ever had. Our lifestyle was great in that we could travel and do pretty much what we wanted, and I had a good place to go every day when we were in town. We thought we would live the rest of our lives there. All three of my children lived within 10 minutes, and Mary's daughter lived in Birmingham.

I got in the office Monday, checked my calendar and told Paul I would come over the next day. My head was spinning. I had told Mary earlier that we were enjoying our life, but probably needed to do something a little more substantive. It never occurred to me, however, to go back to work full-time in an "all day, every day" job.

Just thinking about the athletics director job at Alabama made me flash back to my experience with Coach Bob Woodruff at Tennessee. He was a great mentor and helped me in many ways. He was responsible for helping turn around a struggling program when he got there and getting it back to the top of the SEC with good hires. His most magical moment to me was making the home-and-home football series with Penn State, with our home game in Knoxville and theirs the following year in Memphis. And then magically he got the Memphis game moved to Knoxville and back-to-back home games with Penn State, which also paid to light Neyland Stadium.

The most interesting athletics director decision that came to mind was made by Coach Frank Howard. I wrote earlier about Coach Howard's unique personality and his role as both head football coach and athletics director at Clemson University. On one particular occasion, a group of young men had gotten together and developed a proposal to present to AD Howard in hopes that they could get the sport of rowing added to Clemson's list of NCAA sports. They had put a great deal of thought into their proposal, including budgets and reasons the addition would be important to the university.

Coach Howard listened attentively to the boys as they one-by-one choreo-graphed their presentation. At the end, Coach Howard had not asked any questions, but the boys were pretty proud of their presentation they had made. At the end, there was an uneasy silence. The leader of the group broke the silence by saying, "Well, Coach Howard, what do you think about adding rowing as a sport at Clemson?" Coach Howard cleared his throat and calmly said, "Boys that was a nice presentation, but as long as I am AD at Clemson University, we will not add any sport whose primary goal is to sit on your butt and go backward!" It was a mental image that was hard to shake.

My trip to Tuscaloosa on that Tuesday was very interesting and certainly very flattering. I met with Dr. Bob Witt, who had transformed the university, almost doubling the enrollment and creating infrastructure to accommodate that growth in beautiful architecture and landscaping. Dr. Witt was now the System Chancellor, but thankfully still actively involved in Athletics. Also in the meeting was Finis (Fess) St. John, chair of the Athletic Committee of the Board of Trustees, and Paul, president *pro tem* of the Board. They told me it was very important to have as seamless a transition as possible, as the department was in great shape. They further told me that Mal was planning to retire and enjoy the fruits of his labor at Alabama and write a book. They said they had been thinking, not about people, but about the background, they wanted for the next AD. The main traits were having a business background and coaching at the college level, if possible. They were telling me all the things that were going well in both athletics and the university. At one point, I said, "I never thought being an athletics director would be a fun job." Fess said, "We didn't say it was a fun job," and everyone got a good laugh. I had already met with Finus Gaston and got his perspective on the state of the department. Finus had served as interim AD in 1999 before Mal was named AD. At the time, he was CFO and one of the top three in the department. I asked them to set up a meeting with Coach Nick Saban on Friday morning, then I would attend the President's Cabinet meeting that afternoon and then meet with Dr. Bonner.

From Tuesday through Thursday night I would go from feeling like I should, to feeling like I didn't want to disrupt our lifestyle. Every time I would get down, Mary would say, "Now think about this or that" and try to pick me back up. When Friday came, I drove over there not knowing what I was going to do.

I had a very positive meeting with Coach Saban. We talked a lot about the state of the department and the football program. After winning an unprece-dented three of the previous four National Championships, I told him as an alumnus and former player how proud I and all our teammates were of the amazing job he was doing. All I wanted to do, if I took the job, was to help in any way I could. Knowing that he didn't like meetings, I tried to leave after about 30 minutes but he said, "No, this is important to me." And we kept talking. I thought it was a very positive meeting and he said at the end, "Well, I hope you take the job, if you want it." I thanked him and went to the President's Cabinet meeting.

The President's Cabinet meeting was great, however, I really don't like long meetings. This one went from after lunch to about 5 p.m. There were great presentations by students and faculty, and Dr. Bonner made a very impressive presentation. But sitting through one session after another made my heart palpitate. I thought, "Man, if I take this job, this is what my life is going to be for the next four years — meetings about so many things." By the time the meeting ended, and during cocktail hour, I had decided to turn the job down. I was comfortable with that decision, but decided to go ahead and have dinner, which was being served on the lawn of the President's Mansion. Bud Moore, my high school and Alabama teammate, said, "I'll save you a seat, come sit at my table."

I was headed to Bud's table when Karen Brooks, a Trustee, came up to me and introduced herself. She said, "I've been praying about what I was going to say to you." I thought, "Uh-oh." She said something to the effect that, "The university is in a unique position and needs what you can bring to a potentially serious situation. You are also in a unique position in your life in that you don't need to take this job, but you can." That hit me like a ton of bricks. I thought, "How can I say no to that?" After that it came to me that if I didn't do this, I would regret it for the rest of my life. I went on to have a nice dinner with Bud and other cabinet members, and then had a very nice conversation with Dr. Bonner.

I left without telling anybody anything, but I had made up my mind. Now all I had to do was convince Mary that this was going to be a great four-year adventure for us. When I got back to Atlanta, I told her I had decided to take the job, and I thought it would be an exciting adventure from what had been a pretty docile, but enjoyable, lifestyle. I told her that this was a team effort; she would have to be all in or it wouldn't work. We discussed the turmoil that would come with making the move, selling the house, packing and moving, finding a new house and so on. I told her if she wasn't 100 percent sure this was the right thing for us as a couple, that I would turn it down. She told me that she was all in, but this time I had to do the occasional lifting of her spirits as the process evolved.

I called Paul on Sunday and told him we would accept the offer. That Tuesday, we flew to Durham, North Carolina, to meet with Mal, who had been transferred from Brookwood Medical Center to Duke University Hospital in their lung center. Mal was in good spirits. He told me what I needed to do, then he told Paul what he needed to do. I thought that was a really good sign.

On Friday, we held the press conference announcing my hiring and it was "game on!" This was the press release:

Bill Battle Introduced as Athletics Director at The University of Alabama

Bill Battle was introduced as The University of Alabama's Director of Athletics by UA President Dr. Judy Bonner at a press conference in the Mal M. Moore Athletics Building on Friday morning. The announcement and introduction of Battle came shortly after the former Crimson Tide football letterman and business leader was approved by the University of Alabama System's Board of Trustees in a conference call.

"Coach Battle has a strong record as the founder and CEO of a highly successful corporation," Bonner said. "These skills, as well as his background as a student-athlete, a winning coach and a very intimate understanding of what the Crimson Tide tradition represents affords him the expertise he needs to successfully lead every facet of the University of Alabama Athletics Department."

Battle was joined on the dais by his family, led by his wife, Mary, his sons Pat and Mike, his daughter Shannon Tanner and son-in-law Chad Tanner, his step-daughter Kayla Kitchens and her fiancé Frankie Smeraglia. Battle succeeds Mal Moore, who stepped down Wednesday after 14 years as Director of Athletics. Moore has been named as Athletics Director Emeritus, as well as Special Assistant to the President.

"The direction from the University's leadership is clear about what is expected of athletics, as well as the entire university," Battle said. "My goal is to work with these great coaches and the great staff that Mal has assembled. I want to know what is working, and make sure we support those efforts. Those areas that aren't working as well may need tweaking or overhauling. It's important that we keep working hard and keep moving forward. Athletics is a special challenge. Getting to work with student-athletes and preparing them to compete at the highest level is fun and challenging. Getting them to do all of that with honor and integrity is another challenge and those are the things that we hope to do."

"When it became apparent that I was no longer going to be able to direct the Athletics Department," Moore said, "I felt that Bill Battle was the one person who could sustain all the good things that have happened the past few years, while also moving us forward with planned improvements. Certainly, his background at the University as a student-athlete, coupled with a career as a coach and his creativity and unparalleled success at Collegiate Licensing, gives him an extensive background to lead the Crimson Tide Athletics Department.

"Bill is a man of unimpeachable integrity who understands the heritage and tradition of The University of Alabama. He has been a friend of mine since we were teammates, and an individual who has always gone beyond the call of duty in helping the Athletics Department during my tenure as its director. I personally recommended

369

Bill to Dr. Bonner for this job knowing he will appropriately support our coaches in their efforts to bring championship teams home to Tuscaloosa and ensure that our student-athletes earn their degrees and represent the Crimson Tide in the same manner that Bill did as a player and as an alumnus."

At the press conference I told the media I would much rather be in the audience with them listening to Mal give his insight into next season. I told them that I had never wanted to be an athletics director, but this was an opportunity I couldn't turn down. I was reminded of the old story that everyone had heard about a chicken and a pig walking down a rural Alabama road one morning just as the day was breaking. Up ahead they saw a restaurant with neon signs flashing. As they got closer, they could read the sign that read, "Ham and eggs $2.50." The chicken turned to the pig and said, "My, my, my, how lightly they take our services." The pig looked at the chicken and said, "My friend, to you it's a service, to me it's total commitment." I told the media I recognized the seriousness of this challenge I was about to undertake and didn't know how well I would do, but I promised the university my total commitment.

When I was offered the job and we talked about terms, everything was great. Money was not why I took the job and I was pleased with the offer. Dr. Witt proposed a four-year term. I agreed to sign a four-year contract, but promised Dr. Witt I would stay for at least two years. I was committed to filling the gap created by Mal's retirement, and doing the best I could to keep the department unified and motivated. I was also committed to trying to make us "uncomfortable" in resting on our laurels, and working to improve in every area possible.

When my contract came, I passed it along to my attorney Russ Richards of King & Spalding in Atlanta. I knew Russ was busy working with big clients on major mergers and acquisitions but hoped he could squeeze in time to review my contract. His response was, "I always wanted to handle an athletic director's contract and the first one is free!" After a day, Russ called and said, "Everything in that contract spells out what you said and you and Dr. Witt had agreed upon." He went on to say, "Much of this contract spells out the many reasons they can fire you. If we take all that out, and replace it with 'you serve at the pleasure of the President,' we can cut out about half of the contract." I said, "Let's do it." Russ worked with university counsel to get all changes approved. It was very easy.

The next day our basketball team, under Coach Anthony Grant, defeated Stanford 62-58 in the second NIT game in Coleman Coliseum, after beating Northwestern 62-43 a few days earlier. Men's basketball went 23-13 overall, 12-6 in the SEC, which was tied for second. Trevor Releford earned numerous honors for his play during the season, including 1,299 career points, which ranked at the top of several categories among SEC active leaders going into the 2013-14 season. Guard Levi Randolph was named to the Capital One Academic All-District 4 Final Team as selected by the College Sports Information Directors of America (COSIDA). Coach Grant continued to rank among the best defensive coaches in America, with the 2012-13 Tide high in the SEC and the nation in defensive stats.

I stayed in one of the two luxury suites in the Bryant Hall Academic Center and Dormitory Complex for the first week or so. Dr. Bonner said the university owned the Senior Living Center, and they had some nice garden apartments where we could stay. We were very impressed with them, as they were two-bedroom units with a garage. But after thinking about it for a while, I went back and said, "Dr. Bonner, we loved those garden apartments, but I'm 71 years old and if the media finds out you've already put me in the Senior Living Center, neither of us would live that one down."

I moved into the Bryant Hall suites for about three months until Mary, with her mom's great help, got us moved to Tuscaloosa. They told me to stay away from the packing at our old house and the moving into our new house. That proved to be a blessing for me, and I'm certain they felt it a blessing for them, too.

Bryant Hall has an interesting history. It was originally dedicated on May 8, 1965, and served as the home for Crimson Tide football and men's basketball players for over three decades. Construction on the original building was completed in 1963 at a cost of $1 million and it was equipped with rooms for 136 athletes and a dining hall to feed 150 people. As mentioned earlier, our class graduated and moved on in spring 1963, and the incoming class moved in that August. We never got to live there.

Over the past 55 years, Bryant Hall has been part of many historic events in the life of University of Alabama Athletics. On April 22, 2005, a massive renovation began on the venerable old building that has allowed it to keep making history for years to come. Buildings don't win championships, people do, but great buildings help attract good people. The Academic Center was set up and run first by Kevin Almond. Later, he and Mal hired Jon Dever. The Alabama Academic facilities went from very bad to very, very good as the building was completed. Mal had totally supported it, bragging that this was the "Crown Jewel" of the buildings he had built. I was impressed with Mal's plan and contributed to the cause.

Before I reported for duty, I had breakfast with Mike Slive in Birmingham. Mike was a great SEC commissioner and led the conference to a most successful run in athletic and academic success. His fingerprints were all over the Power Five commissioner's running of college football championships and the evolution from the BCS to the College Football Playoff systems. Mike's fingerprints were also all over the negotiation with ESPN for the SEC Network. He provided insight into a lot of things, from a conference perspective, that were valuable for me to know.

Soon after I reported for duty and set up the Listen and Learn tour, it became evident the women's basketball team was struggling. I decided a change was needed, and after the season I called in Wendell Hudson for an evaluation. Wendell was three years away from retirement. I told him we needed to make a change in coaches of our women's basketball team but I wanted him to be a special assistant to the Director of Athletics and serve as an ambassador to the program, making speeches, meeting with donors and fans, and assisting wherever it made sense.

Like all competitors, he wasn't pleased with the news, but he had always been a team player and accepted the re-assignment. Everyone who met Wendell loved him and definitely appreciated his great performance as a player. On my first real day in the office, we called an all-staff meeting. We had about 300 staff members, and all who were in town showed up. It was very impressive to me. The energy in the room was electric. I could tell the staff was ready, willing and able to do what was necessary to keep Alabama at the top. I told them this meeting was going to be about me, where I'd been, what I'd done, and what led up to this occasion. I further told them I was going on a "Listening and Learning Tour" and the next meetings we had were going to be about them. I told them I didn't like long meetings and we weren't going to be in there long. I appreciated Coach Saban and his staff being in attendance and certainly didn't want to waste his time.

I began by telling everyone that the department was in good shape. Alabama had won five National Championships in multiple sports, and I knew it was a great place. All I wanted to do was carry on what Mal had started. I told them I wanted to improve in every area and I wanted to know what we needed to work on to make those improvements. I tried to quickly tell them about my journey from Birmingham, 60 miles away, to this day.

I closed by saying, "Respect, trust and love are three characteristics that can't be given, they have to be earned. I know that Mal earned all three from you, as he did from me and I hope that as I stand before you, I have your respect. If that grows, hopefully I will earn your trust and hopefully for some of you that may turn into love."

As time went on, people asked me what I wanted my legacy to be. I told them I didn't worry about my legacy. I wanted to win championships in all sports, make sure the department was financially solvent, and graduate our student-athletes. I wanted to make sure we carried out our mission, which was,

"To recruit and develop student-athletes to compete at the highest level in college athletics, to educate and prepare those student-athletes for life after graduation, and to do both with honor and integrity." If we accomplished that, that's all I cared about.

I was obviously interested in academics. Years earlier, I had heard people at Tennessee telling recruits to be sure to go through Alabama's academic center before they chose to go there. I never saw it, but I'm told, at that time, it wasn't up to Alabama's standards. Mal was really smart in making Bryant Hall the focal point of his facility improvement projects. It showed the university that the Athletics Department was interested in academics. Bryant Hall was the "Taj Mahal" of athletic dormitories when it was originally built and Mal made it the "Taj Mahal" of academic centers in college athletics. I was proud Mal made it a priority that this would be the first in his improvements and building program.

When I became AD, I realized Alabama was doing a great job graduating players. They did an amazing job of convincing the faculty of the dynamic academics programs that were in place. In the licensing business I got to know a lot of universities from the top on down. I can tell you, there aren't many with the great relationships Kevin Almond, Jon Dever and their staff made with the university faculty. I would say in the majority of universities I saw, athletics was at least somewhat crossways with faculty.

We had heard about a few universities that were doing a good job in the area of teaching life skills. While we were graduating players and they learned many life lessons from their coaches and teammates, there was not an organized approach to trying to teach, or at least reinforce, those lessons that would prepare them for life after graduation. Kevin and Jon brought in some candidates, but when Jessie Gardner came in from the University of Nebraska, we knew she was the one to lead us into this venture and keep Alabama ahead of the pack. Dr. Gaylon McCollough and his wife Susan, along with the A-Club Alumni Association, made nice gifts and together they helped us create the Gaylon and Susan McCollough A-Club Career and Leadership Development Center.

The goal was to better prepare student-athletes for life after graduation, and ultimately track their successes and create a network of University of Alabama letterwinners throughout the world. Can you imagine the power that group could wield? It might range from directions to nice hotels, restaurants and things to see in their area, to really serious stuff like helping down-and-out members, or taking applications for good jobs. The A-Club established a website that all former letterwinners can visit to keep up with what is happening on campus, and to communicate with teammates.

I first met with our Executive Staff, which at the time consisted of: Deputy Athletics Director/COO Shane Lyons, Executive Associate Athletics Director/CFO Finus Gaston, Senior Associate AD-Support Services Kevin Almond, Senior Associate AD-Technology Advancement Milton Overton, Senior Associate AD-Development Ronny Robertson, Associate AD-Compliance Jonathan Bowling, Associate AD-Student Services Jon Dever, Associate AD-Business Carol Park, Associate AD-Football Communications Jeff Purinton, Associate AD-Senior Woman Administrator Marie Robbins and Associate AD-Communications Doug Walker.

They were all outstanding. I asked them three questions and told them to think hard about how to answer them, but to do so in writing and turn them in to me. The questions were:

- What do you think are the five most important things that need to be done in the department?
- What are the five most important things you need to do in your area of responsibility this year?
- If you were the AD, what five things would you focus on first?

Athletics at the Power-Five level is a pretty amazing operation. As I occupied Mal's office, it looked out over the football practice field from one view, and the entrance to the Strength & Conditioning Complex and Coleman Coliseum from another view. One could look out almost 24/7/365 and see people running around like ants. Players were coming and going to lift weights or practice, managers were loading equipment for road trips, and coaches and administrators were looking after their flocks. On game days, fans were everywhere, looking at facilities and hoping to see players or coaches. In the summer, there were camps in all sports and cheerleaders from all over the country that swarmed the place. It was quite invigorating.

The first month, while getting oriented to the university and our staff, was very trying from my personal point of view. During the first week, Mal took a turn for the worse and passed away. The second week, our youngest daughter Kayla got married, which was most enjoyable but stressful as well with planning and executing the events leading up to, during and after the wedding ceremony. The third week, our ranch manager in Ellijay, Larry Dalrymple, had triple-bypass surgery. The fourth week, on the day the football team went to the White House to celebrate the 2012 National Championship, my son Mike had quadruple-bypass surgery. Fortunately, Mike was in about as good physical shape as our Alabama athletes. Mike handled the surgery extremely well, and he was back exercising and riding mountain bikes in about six weeks. But all that didn't help my stress levels very much!

I met with every department head and head coach in their offices. It was important to me for them to see me on their turf with genuine interest in their responsibilities, and their assessment of their staffing and infrastructure needs. Whenever it worked, I tried to meet their staff members as well. Time spent in that endeavor was very helpful to me and I believe sent a message to the department that my goal was to build on what Mal and they had built. The other message I wanted to send was to give them my version of our Mission: Recruit and develop student-athletes to compete at the highest levels in inter-collegiate athletics, educate and prepare our student-athletes to compete at the highest levels in life after graduation, and accomplish both with honor and integrity. I told them that everything they did should contribute to our accomplishment of that Mission. If it didn't, they didn't need to waste the time or money.

I determined a lot of things from my "Listening and Learning" tour, but four things stood out most to me.

We were in the event management business. Alabama participated in almost 400 events annually from 2013-2017. We hosted almost half of these events. With 21 teams in 17 sports, you could easily see how these numbers added up. The events ranged from track-and-field and swimming events that probably had as many participants as fans, to football games with over 101,000 fans in the stands and sometimes 30,000 to 40,000 tailgating on the campus. We were blessed with an outstanding event management team, headed up by Red Leonard. His area of responsibility was the heart and soul of the business of Alabama Athletics. Some say the job of an AD is akin to being a hospital administrator. They have to deal with and please the public; then have to raise money to keep ahead of the game in building and equipment needs; and then have to deal with high-priced and celebrity doctors.

If one were running a business with 17 divisions and two of them were profitable, it wouldn't take long to reduce the number of divisions significantly. The business of college athletics was not so much to make a profit, but to be fiscally responsible in managing the business and reinvesting revenue generated in facilities, coaches and administrative staff. The goal was to compete for and win championships, and teach all team players to become champions in life. There was no other country with sports programs like ours in the U.S. Out of our 500-plus student-athletes, about 80 percent played on teams that were not close to breaking even financially. Football contributed the most, with men's basketball contributing a little. If true "pay for play" were to come into being, many sports would be dropped back to club sports. It was my hope that smart people would figure out a solution to the "Name, Image and Likeness" litigation and legislation coming to colleges and universities.

The business of our enterprise only generated about 80 percent of what we needed to operate the way we liked to run our business. Steve Sloan, during his time as AD at Alabama, implemented the Tide Pride program, which charged extra dollars for the right to buy better seating in the venue. We can all thank Steve because Tide Pride contributions made up for the 20 percent deficit. If we wanted to build more buildings or carry out major renovations to existing buildings, that had to come from donations and contributions.

I determined that the area of greatest need for improvement was our Development Department. At that time (2013), Ronny Robertson was the director while Aaron Vold and Chris Darling were assistants. Ronny played for Alabama in the 1970s. Mal would set up the donors for a contribution and Ronny would come behind him to close the deal. Everybody loved Ronny, as his personality was magnetic. Aaron was the only one of the three with fundraising experience, and he did a good job of cultivating and closing. Chris had executive experience as director of Special Programs in providing strategic and analytical support for the president of Georgetown University for eight years. He had Undergraduate and Master's degrees from Alabama, and another from Georgetown.

What I found was that they were able to raise money fairly handily selling north and south end zone suites over the previous few years. For many years, athletics had no development staff and someone in the University Advancement office sort of looked after and helped them, so when Mal started his major fundraising effort in 2000, it was just him. Later, Pam Parker in University Development provided assistance. At some point later, he hired Ronny, and later still, Aaron and Chris were hired.

When I came on the scene, we were nearly out of skyboxes to sell and virtually no premium seating in Bryant-Denny Stadium. We had to find other things we owned to sell, and begin to try to raise money from philanthropic, rather than transactional, means. We did a search of every room in every building owned by the Athletics Department that we thought someone might want to name. Then we applied the formula the university required for minimum naming-rights contributions. After that was put together, it was submitted to the Board of Trustees for approval. Obviously, that process took time.

The previous goal for asking donors for scholarship or philanthropic gifts was $250,000. We had never really asked for million-dollar gifts. There was in place a Bryant Society honor for donors who had contributed a million dollars to the Crimson Tide Foundation over time. When they reached that level, they were rewarded with a large portrait, which was hung in the entrance of south end zone development offices. It was a great idea, but not very many people knew about it. I was shocked to learn that there were only nine one-million-dollar donors, and Paul and I were two of them.

After thinking hard about alternative fundraising strategies and tactics, I came to the conclusion that we could sell the Bryant Society concept and ask people for million-dollar contributions. There was no name better we could come up with than Bryant. We started pitching that concept to donors and it began to get traction. Our goal was to get 50 Bryant Society members.

We planned a formal induction of all who were already members, plus those new ones we could attract. Our development team, primarily Katie King and Lindsey Blumenthal, planned an exquisite black-tie event in the south end zone. It was spectacular. Our team did know how to entertain. We invited donors who we hoped would see that this was an honor, or milestone, or whatever incentive it might be to step up their cumulative gifts to a million dollars. We started the induction ceremony with Joe Namath thanking them for their contributions. They received a small bronze statue of Coach Bryant, a 24-carat gold Bryant Society ring for the men and a pendant for the women. They were introduced on field at halftime of the Alabama-Tennessee football game the next day. We inducted 16 (nine original and seven new members) at our first induction ceremony. By the time I left the job in March 2017, we had 26 Bryant Society members.

We could show donors how the infusion of capital in 2003-2008 that Mal, Ronny and Pam raised, plus the bond issue money that Dr. Witt contributed, had a direct effect on our success. We were able to build or renovate buildings that attracted coaches and student-athletes, and won championships again. My pitch to them was, we are in pretty good shape now, but we don't want someone 10 years from now looking back and saying, "Why didn't they keep improving facilities and attracting the best coaches?"

If there was ever a good time in the year to take the AD job, March was as good as any. Football was over and Alabama had won its 15th National Championship with a 42-14 victory over Notre Dame in Miami Gardens, Florida, on Jan. 7, 2013. The Tide finished 13-1, also winning Alabama's 23rd SEC Championship along the way. It was Coach Saban's third national title at UA, and the fourth of his coaching career.

Looking back at 2013 calendar year, Alabama excelled on the playing fields and courts, and in the classroom as well. One of our primary goals was to have every team make it to post-season play and competing for championships. In 2013, 14 of our 17 teams met that standard, while all of our teams had individual student-athletes earn recognition of some sort for their performance.

We enjoyed a stellar fall semester in the classroom. A total of 545 student-athletes posted a total combined grade-point average of 3.196 for the semester — the highest GPA for a semester in school history. Fifteen of our 17 teams posted GPAs above 3.0, and two teams (women's soccer and women's tennis) had GPAs above 3.8.

Basketball, gymnastics and soccer were also over or winding down around that time. The "Listening and Learning" tour was very beneficial. I listened intently and tried to learn as many "new tricks" as an old dog could handle. It was most enlightening.

The men's golf team, under Coach Jay Seawell, won the SEC title and the NCAA Baton Rouge Regional. They set a school record for team victories with eight in 12 events. They reached the pinnacle of college golf by winning their first NCAA Championship in Atlanta. I was able to attend and enjoy great golf among a dominant home crowd that gave a boost to our team. Four All-Americans included first-team honorees Bobby Wyatt, Cory Whitsett and Justin Thomas. Trey Mullinax made honorable mention.

Coach Seawell was invited to coach in the prestigious Palmer Cup in Delaware against a top collection of European collegiate players. Jay took his All-Americans with him and they made Jay and all Alabama fans proud by taking Team USA to a convincing 20 1/2 to 9 1/2 victory.

Coach Mic Potter led the women's golf team to its second SEC Championship in history. The 2013 squad pulled away from the competition in the second and third rounds on the way to a 14-shot win on the par-72, 6,401-yard Greystone Golf & Country Club to win the league title. The Crimson Tide shot 14-over 302, which was within one shot of the low round of the day in windy conditions for a 54-hole total of 35-over-par 899. Georgia finished second at 49-over 913. Stephanie Meadow lapped the field for medalist honors with an even-par 216 for a nine-shot win. She was the first Alabama women's golfer to capture medalist honors at the SEC Championship. The team went on to compete in the NCAA Tournament and finished seventh.

The Alabama baseball team, under Coach Mitch Gaspard, went 35-28 overall and 14-15 in the SEC, and then defeated Auburn and Mississippi in the SEC Tournament. They suffered Wednesday and Friday losses to No. 2 LSU 3-0 and 3-2, respectively, to end their tourney run. The NCAA Regional in Tallahassee began with an opening 5-2 loss to Troy on May 31, a 3-2 win over Savannah State on June 1, and a 9-8 loss to Troy on June 2, closing out the season for the Tide.

Dan Waters' track and field team went from 23rd to 11th place overall at the end of day three of the NCAA Championships with a high relay finish and a sixth-place Imani Brown finish in the triple jump. It was Alabama's first top-15 finish since 2002, and it marked great progress in Coach Waters' tenure in his drive to compete for championships.

The gymnastics team finished second in the SEC Championships, were NCAA Regional Champions and finished third in the NCAA Championships. Alabama now had 22 top-three finishes in the NCAA Championships, more than any program in the country. Consistency had been a key characteristic in Sarah Patterson's tenure at Alabama. Kim Jacobs won the Elite 89 Award to give Alabama a winner of the honor every year since its inception in 2010. Kassi Price won the inaugural award in 2010, and Rachel Terry in 2011-12. The award goes to the student-athlete in each of the NCAA's 89 championships with the highest cumulative grade-point average. Kim's 4.0 GPA led the pack.

Since I didn't want to appear as a "short timer," I was committed to buying a house and tried to get involved in the community as much as my job would allow. My mindset regarding the job was to treat it as a business that was built to last. In the first 100 days, I attended more meetings than I had attended in the previous 10 years, maybe 20. Most were meetings with staff, getting to know who did what and how well they were performing. It was also important to hear from them if they needed additional resources to be successful.

Other meetings were about building. When I arrived in March 2013, there was some significant construction that had been or was recently being completed. The Sam Bailey Track and Field stadium had undergone a rebuild from the ground up, giving Alabama athletes everything they needed to be successful at the highest level. The $4.5 million project had transformed the facility into a viable venue for hosting meets from the high school level to international events. It gave Coach Waters much ammunition to recruit elite athletes. The facility was dedicated March 22, 2013.

The Strength & Conditioning Complex was also being finished. The 34,000-square-foot facility was designed to help all Crimson Tide teams in training and nutrition.

The three buildings I got involved with from the start were the Sarah Patterson Champions Plaza, the Boathouse for the rowing team, and the Sewell-Thomas Baseball Stadium renovations. The Sarah Patterson Champions Plaza was on green space outside the right-field section of the Sewell-Thomas Baseball Stadium. It was designed to honor Coach Sarah Patterson and represent all Olympic sports with marble plaques on the outfield wall for each team to display SEC and National Championships. It included space to honor individual sport All-Americans. A pergola was reserved to honor National Championship coaches. The plaza was finished and dedicated in October 2013.

We started a tradition of having an "unveiling ceremony" in the fall after all students had returned to campus. In the inaugural ceremony for the Sarah Patterson Champions Plaza in October, we honored SEC and National

Champions from the 2012-13 fiscal year in gymnastics, men's and women's golf, and softball. Also unveiled were the bronze plaques of Sarah Patterson, Mic Potter, Jay Seawell and Patrick Murphy. It was a special occasion and has grown to be even more special. If you haven't seen it, on your next trip to campus, make it a point to stop by and check out the honorees.

Shortly after my arrival on campus and involvement in the "Listening and Learning" experience, I went to tour our rowing teams' facilities. They were located near downtown on the north side of the river. When I got there, what I saw reminded me of what I thought a prisoner of war camp looked like. It had barbwire running all around the trailers that the rowing coaches used as offices, and also around a couple of areas that housed the team's equipment — boats, paddles, etc. The facilities were quite spartan, but help was on the way.

During my time in business, I never built a building. We were a service company and our biggest expense was people. We owned furniture, fixtures, computers and the like, but rented office space. Going through the design and budget for the rowing facility (The Boathouse) was quite educational. I will never forget one particular meeting. I had been in meetings all morning and this one started right after lunch. We were $2 million over budget and talking about what to do. I was about half-asleep when I heard that number and woke up pretty quickly.

They told me that they had to dredge part of the river at a cost of $750,000 to build a road down to the river to get jon boats down to the water. I asked, "What is a jon boat?" Finus Gaston said, "That's the first boat in which you ever went fishing…the jon boats are what the rowing coaches go around in during practice." I asked, "Why don't we leave them down in the water, locked to the dock?" Someone said, "People might steal them." I said, "For $750,000 we can buy a lot of jon boats!" I then asked, "What does Coach Davis say?" Finus said, "Mal never talked to the coaches before he had everything done."

I called a meeting with Coach Larry Davis, who started the rowing team as an intramural sport on campus. He was named the head coach in 2006 when rowing became a full Athletics Department sport. He was overjoyed we were building a boathouse on the university side of the river. It was close to the Presidential dorms that would house his athletes. And there was no barbwire in the plans! He could do without the "Jon Boat Road," and we saved $750,000. He worked with us and we were able to get the project in on budget.

The grand opening of Alabama rowing's the Boathouse at Manderson Landing was held on Oct. 23 on the banks of the Black Warrior River. It included a floating dock and storage space for up to 54 shells of varying length. Across the street, the Student Activity Center had a 2,200-square-foot ergometer room, a 1,700-square-foot training space, locker rooms, athletic training room, meeting room and coaches offices.

It is a really neat facility. It is located adjacent to Manderson Landing on Jack Warner Parkway, close to the Bi-Centennial statue of Minerva, Goddess of Wisdom, War, Art, Schools and Commerce. When we cut the ribbon to open the building, the entire rowing team was present. I don't believe any facilities that we ever built improved the life and training of student-athletes more than taking our rowing program from a POW camp to a competitive SEC venue. The rowing team helped in seeking compliance with Title IX regulations, and athletes put in the time, at the hours they operated, and were as dedicated as any team on campus. Some of the best resumes I saw, and personalities I met during my tenure, came from the rowing team.

The spring sports were ongoing and our softball team really captured my heart. I had watched them on TV when Alabama won its National Championship. In my mind, I thought, "That's one tough bunch of girls!" I went to some games and some practices. Head Coach Patrick Murphy and Assistant Coach Aly Habetz and their staff do an amazing job, not just teaching them how to compete for championships at the highest level, but they also teach them how to embrace their fans and everybody that comes to see them play. Early on, Pat invited me to come on the field and meet the team. They lined up single file and came up to me with a gleam in their eye, a smile on their face, and gave me a big hug. They welcomed me to Alabama and thanked me for coming to see them practice and play. When they finished, I was blown away. The first thing that popped in my mind was "These ladies look and act like angels, but play like the devil!"

Having similar experiences at gymnastics with Coach Sarah Patterson and her gymnastics team, and Coach Jenny Mainz and her tennis team, my whole perception of women's athletics went from neutral to off-the-charts high. When I took the job, I thought I would leave most of the Olympic sports to staff members, and we did have one senior staff member assigned as oversight to every sport. I felt the coaches and teams deserved the director's attention and I tried to give it to them.

After the women's basketball season, I told Wendell we had decided to make a change. No one likes to exit any position unless on his or her own terms, and Wendell was no exception. While I believe he was relieved to get out from under that responsibility, he was hurt being asked to step down. He responded well to his new position and remained a great ambassador for the university until his retirement.

So I went about hiring my first coach at Alabama, before I even got settled in Tuscaloosa. Shane Lyons had developed a list of candidates that I started to research and learn about. Shane was a great help in the process. We studied the list and interviewed a few candidates. Kristy Curry was high on our list. She had a marvelous run at Purdue, but then followed a legend at Texas Tech and was struggling, and we didn't think she was in our price range. We went about interviewing candidates. We had some early conversations with Kristy and we were encouraged that she was interested in taking a visit. When she and Kelly, her husband (who was her assistant coach), came in, we were very impressed. Kristy indicated that money wasn't the most important factor in their decision. She moved quickly to my top choice if we could make it work. We went to work trying to talk her into coming to Alabama.

In the meantime, our shopping for houses in Tuscaloosa came down to making an offer on the home we ended up buying and still living in today. The house was owned by LeeAnn Livingston, who had passed away several months earlier. LeeAnn, like her sister, Judy Livingston, was a builder and they said she was building and improving the house up until the week she passed. Judy took over the house after LeeAnn passed and put a halt to any further construction. The house had been on the market for over a year when we began to show interest.

Judy Livingston was a member of a family of longtime supporters of Alabama Athletics. Judy and LeeAnn were actively engaged in the family's successful roofing business with their father. They were among the first to buy a North End Zone Skybox in Bryant-Denny Stadium. Judy and LeeAnn were partial to women's athletics.

It may have been a coincidence, but when Mary looked online and saw the price of the house, we didn't have it on our list. The day we started looking, our real estate agent said they had dropped the price on that house. It had building materials all along the righthand side of the yard as one entered the driveway. It had an estimated $10,000 worth of outdoor lighting in the downstairs garage. It looked like an unfinished house. But when we went inside, it was spectacular. What LeeAnn had done in improving the house was pretty amazing. She actually bought the lot next door and expanded the driveway onto that property, expanded the upstairs deck and downstairs kitchen, and made it a "smart house."

The week after announcing the change in women's basketball, I got a text from Judy in pretty direct language telling me I needed to hire Kristy Curry. I sent Judy a letter, as I did everyone who contacted me about recommendations, saying that Kristy was on our list and would get our consideration. At this stage in our coaching search, and unbeknownst to Judy, we had negotiated with Kristy and pretty much made a deal. There was a $300,000 buyout that Texas Tech was asking, to which we had not yet agreed.

We made an offer on the house and came to agreement with Judy. At the closing, when all paperwork was signed, Judy asked everyone to leave so that she and I could talk. She told me that LeeAnn would be so happy that an Athletics Department official had bought her house and she knew that we would bring joy and happiness to the home. She further told me that she had recently learned that LeeAnn had made a significant pledge to Alabama women's athletics. Then she lit into telling me other things I needed to do. I said, "Hold it a minute, back up, how much did LeeAnn pledge?" She said, "$500,000." I said, "Do you think she would have been supportive of spending $300,000 to handle Kristy Curry's buyout to Texas Tech?" She replied, "I think she would be very pleased." At that point we started to talk about Divine Intervention, and how I thought it had occurred in my hiring and in some early activities in the department. After a few minutes, she said, "Do you want to see Divine Intervention?" I said, "Yes." She turned over the check she had received as her portion of the payment on the house. The check was for $309,000!

We actually negotiated the payment to Texas Tech to about half their asking and the rest went to Alabama's women's basketball. Two years later, Judy paid for the women's basketball team to go to Italy to play some pre-season games and enjoy the education and bonding that comes with international travel. Judy and I remain friends today. She's still bossy, but we understand each other! And her mom, Ms. Ethel, keeps us all down to earth and smiling.

Football season was approaching and it was fun watching outside my office window as the players worked on their own during the summer, and even more fun when the coaching staff conducted full-team practice. Coach Saban's practices are legendary in their sophisticated teaching of techniques and organization.

2013-2014

The following statement was my message to our alumni and fan base after the 2013-14 fiscal year:

Welcome to the 2013-14 University of Alabama Athletics Annual Report! What an amazing year The University of Alabama Crimson Tide enjoyed in 2013-14. From the classroom to competition and everywhere in between, we experienced one of the best all-around years in our storied history.

Athletically, we won our second consecutive NCAA Championship in men's golf, as well as earning four Southeastern Conference Championships, tying our record for the most in a single academic year. In addition to our men's golf team winning their third SEC title in a row and fifth overall, women's gymnastics won its eighth, softball won its fifth, and women's tennis won its first regular-season title in program history.

Nationally, we enjoyed success at the highest level. A total of seven of our teams finished in the top 10 nationally, including men's golf (1st), softball (2nd), gymnastics (4th), women's tennis (5th), men's indoor track and field (6th), football (7th), and women's golf (9th). We also had four other teams — men's swimming and diving (12th), men's outdoor track and field (15th), women's outdoor track and field (18th), and women's indoor track and field (19th) — finish in the top 20 nationally.

Individually, seven athletes brought home eight NCAA Championships over the past year. Both totals were bests in Alabama history.

As good a year as we had athletically, the Crimson Tide was even better in the classroom. Alabama led the nation in Capital One Academic All-Americans with a school-record 13 over the past year. The Crimson Tide also saw three student-athletes earn the prestigious NCAA Elite 89 Award, as well as a nation's-best seven NCAA Postgraduate Scholarship winners.

Our women's swimming and diving team had the highest team grade-point average in the nation within the sport. Our men's track and field team was named the 2014 Indoor Scholar Team of the Year by the U.S. Track & Field and Cross Country Coaches Association. Hayden Reed was also honored by that organization as the men's outdoor field events NCAA Division I Scholar Athlete of the Year.

Gymnast Kim Jacob and golfer Cory Whitsett led the way in the classroom. Both earned Academic All-American honors, NCAA Postgraduate Scholarships and were named the SEC Scholar-Athlete of the Year for their respective sports. In addition, Kim was named the Capital One Academic All-American of the Year, which goes to the nation's top student-athlete regardless of sport or gender. Cory led the way on the conference level, earning the men's SEC H. Boyd McWhorter Scholar-Athlete of the Year honor. In total, over 100 Alabama athletes graduated while our 550 student-athletes carried a 3.2 cumulative GPA for the 2013-14 academic year.

With Kim's honor, Alabama is now the only school in the award's history to have student-athletes named the Academic All-American of the Year for three years in a row — an astonishing feat when you consider the fierce level of competition for this honor.

While this past year stands among the best in school history, in looking at the larger picture, this season confirmed that we were witnessing a golden age of Alabama Athletics. Last year we had five national championship head coaches on our staff at the same time, which is simply phenomenal. As a department, Crimson Tide teams have won nine national championships in five sports and 16 SEC Championships in seven different sports since 2009.

In the classroom, Alabama tied with Stanford for the most NCAA Elite 89 Awards in the honor's five-year history with 13. The Tide also leads the SEC and is second only to Stanford in NCAA Postgraduate Scholarships over the past four years with

20. *The Tide is fourth nationally since 2000 in Academic All-American honors and first in the SEC with 91.*

All this success has been built on the foundation of our tradition of excellence and our legacy of champions while following the tenets of our ongoing mission:

We will recruit and develop student-athletes to compete at the highest levels in intercollegiate athletics;

We will educate and prepare our student-athletes to compete at the highest levels in life after graduation;

We will accomplish all this with honor and integrity.

While our student-athletes, coaches and support staff are the engine that makes our success go, our fans are the ones that provide the fuel for that engine. There is no describing what the roar of the crowd means to our student-athletes when any of our teams take the field, the court or the floor. I want to encourage our fans to become an even more integral part of our success — supporting the Alabama nation in every way — in the stands, on the streets and online. We need loud and proud fan support, but always in a sportsmanlike manner.

We also need the support of our fans financially as we continue to build championship-level facilities for our teams. The capital campaign from 2002-2007 paved the way in facility improvements that has been a key factor in our latest run of championships. While we are proud of everything we have accomplished, we are always mindful that our competition is fighting hard to duplicate our success. Getting athletic and academic facilities to championship levels is one thing, keeping them there is another. If we are not moving forward, we are falling behind. Our goal is to provide our coaches and student-athletes with the resources they need to compete for championships and build champions on and off the field for life.

It is a privilege to lead the Crimson Tide during this time of historic success. I am proud of the outstanding quality of our entire athletics department staff. They are as dedicated a group as I have ever been around. The leadership at the top of the university is terrific. And our fans are the best in the country. As the saying goes, "A rising tide lifts all boats," and it takes all of us pulling together to Keep the Tide Rising!

After the first year, it became pretty obvious that filling 101,000 seats at Bryant-Denny Stadium was becoming harder to sell out, but at Alabama from 2013-2017, we were enjoying the best of times. High-definition TV and expanded coverage gave people a good reason to stay home with easy access to food, beverages and restrooms, all enjoyed in air conditioned or heated comfort. We set about listening to fans and trying to make the stadium experience something they couldn't get at home.

The Million Dollar Band, Big Al, Cheerleaders, Crimsonettes and the Dance Team all added to the game-day experience. We worked hard to provide better food and better service. We placed more TV screens throughout the concourse so fans going to buy food or to the bathrooms could keep up with the game. We strived to reduce long lines for food and drink, and keep bathrooms clean and stocked with toilet paper and paper towels. We tried to have good music, but found it very difficult to please ages from the teens to the over-60 crowd. In all honesty, a good bit of our music selection went to what our players and recruits wanted to hear.

We made improvements every year, and fortunately, the performance by Coach Saban and his teams enabled us to pretty much sell out every game. Selling 101,000 tickets to every game was an important part of the athletic budget. We also worked hard at trying to make football games for students a positive experience. There was a small charge for football tickets, but all other sports were free to students.

I set out to find answers to two important questions that were on my mind. First, what was the true value of a full athletic scholarship? Second, what was the value of a skybox in Bryant-Denny Stadium? The first answer was fairly easy to determine. The second took me about three years to fully understand.

The value of a full scholarship started with tuition, fees, room and board. In 2013-14 that cost the Athletics Department about $60,000 for out-of-state students and about $35,000 for in-state students. Assuming four years to get a degree, total cost to the Athletics Department for tuition, fees, room and board ranged from $140,000-$240,000. In 2014-15, a ruling came down that a full scholarship could include an annual "cost of attendance" provision that took into consideration a trip or two home and back, cell phone, computer and other miscellaneous expenses. At Alabama, that number amounted to a little over $5,000 a year, which raised the four-year total to from $160,000 for in-state to $260,000 for out-of-state athletes.

In addition, Pell Grants up to $5,600 a year could go to student-athletes who met certain need requirements. A majority of football and men's and women's basketball teams met those requirements. Rules also came down to be able to have almost all-day long feeding options. We established fueling stations in several locations for athletes to have seated meals or grab-and-go breakfast wraps, sandwiches, bagels, smoothies, and about 30 different kinds of drinks from Gatorade to Muscle Milk to all kinds of healthy beverages.

Then think about the fact that most regular students leave college with student loans ranging from a few thousand up to $100,000. Student-athletes leave with zero student debt. Plus, you can't put a price on the following benefits to scholarship and walk-on players with access to: best-in-class coaches, academic counseling, tutors, computer labs, books, etc.; strength and conditioning programs tailored to one's team, position and body type; nutrition advice and counseling tailored to team, position and body type; life skills, career and leadership development programs; medical care from top-rated doctors and athletic trainers; competition against the best teams, played in prestigious athletic venues; media coverage providing student-athletes with a platform to showcase their skills at the highest level, with most games televised regionally, if not nationally; best-in-class facilities to live, work and play.

While it is difficult to place a value on the nine factors listed above, there is no doubt that there is significant value there. It also reinforces the Athletics Department's commitment to accomplishing our mission. Some of our student-athletes go on to very successful careers in professional sports, but the vast majority leave Alabama and become professionals in careers other than sports. Having played a sport and graduated from Alabama serves as an impressive entrée into most job interviews.

The answer to the skybox question got complicated by the fact that in different times over the years, there were different members of the Athletics Department doing the selling. When times were tough, prices often dropped. When the east side skyboxes were built, it wasn't a known fact that people would buy them. They were charged the fee for the box and cost of tickets. By the time the north end zone boxes went up for sale, there was a one-time commitment of $300,000, but that rose to $500,000 due to the overwhelming demand from prospective buyers. That was in addition to the Tide Pride fee and cost of tickets. The same was required on the south end zone boxes built a few years later.

After the south zone boxes were filled, the Development Staff went to the east side box holders and asked for a one-time gift of $300,000. This upset many box holders who had been supporters through good times and bad. But in the end, because the money went toward keeping Alabama ahead of the pack in coaches and facilities, everyone came into compliance.

As skyboxes were made available through death or the unwillingness to continue, we offered to lease the boxes at whatever we felt justified to ask, and which soon rose to $1 million or more, plus annual Tide Pride fees and cost of tickets.

Fall sports at Alabama include football, soccer, cross country and volleyball. Obviously, football is the sport that attracts over 100,000 people at most home games. As an alumnus, fan, and north end zone skybox holder, all I had to worry about was traffic getting to and from the stadium parking area, and whether my halftime stadium dogs were hot. As athletics director, obviously, I had to worry about everyone in the stadium, parking, food and beverage, restrooms, traffic, safety, behavior, and everything else involving the game. It was an ominous responsibility.

The stadium contained a "War Room" with TV monitors showing traffic coming in and out from all directions. There were monitors reporting the weather, while others showed crowd behavior inside and outside the stadium. There were representatives from campus police, Tuscaloosa police, Alabama State Troopers and FBI.

We also had to hire and train personnel to perform scanning tickets, going through security checks, monitoring bag or purse sizes and making sure unapproved items were not allowed stadium entry. There were those who monitored getting people in their proper seats and dealing with those sitting in seats that didn't match up with their tickets. And all this had to be done with a smile and customer-service attitude that didn't upset fans. Our Event Management team handled these difficult challenges very well.

The 2013 football season looked favorable as we played home games against Ole Miss, Arkansas, Tennessee and LSU, with road trips to Texas A&M, Kentucky, Mississippi State and Auburn. We opened in a neutral-site game in Atlanta against Virginia Tech. We had a very good team and were set to go for a third straight National Championship. The Tide opened with 11 straight wins, including 35-10 over Virginia Tech. The trip to College Station to face Johnny Manziel and No. 6 Texas A&M turned out to be hotter in more ways than just the heat in the stadium, which was brutal.

A funny thing happened before the game. A&M Athletics Director Eric Hyman had graciously allowed our party to sit in his box, as it was larger than the visiting AD box and he knew we had a large crowd. He welcomed us to the stadium and we thanked him for his generosity. In a few minutes his wife, Pauline, came in and also welcomed us, and said, "We can't control the temperature in this box and if it gets too cold we have blankets for the ladies." We all laughed as it was heat-stroke weather outside and we thought it was a joke. By midway through the first quarter, goose bumps were rising on Mary's arms, and the other ladies were shivering. We got up and got those blankets! We didn't tell many people that story, because with the heat they endured, they wouldn't think that story to be too funny.

A&M jumped out to a 14-0 lead. At the end of the first quarter, Terry asked me what I thought. I told her I felt great. This time the previous year we were down 21-0 in the first quarter but came back with a chance to win at the end with the ball in the red zone. An interception stopped the drive and the Aggies held on for the upset, however.

Sure enough, the Tide responded with 28 consecutive points, taking a 28-14 lead at the half. The second half produced an offensive frenzy that wasn't settled until the last play as AJ McCarron led a clock-ending drive to preserve the 49-42 victory.

McCarron threw for a career-high 334 yards and four touchdowns. Alabama rolled for 570 total yards, with running back T.J. Yeldon rushing for 149 yards. Linebacker C.J. Mosley led the team with 12 tackles. The teams combined for 1,196 yards of offense, with A&M gaining 628 yards, the most ever given up by an Alabama team. It was great to get out alive. The Aggie fans were more than gracious in defeat. One of our great friends of the university, after witnessing so many congratulatory comments from Aggie fans, said, "They haven't been in the league long enough, that attitude will change!"

Alabama cruised the next few weeks, beating Colorado State 31-6, Ole Miss 25-0, Georgia State 45-3, Kentucky 48-7, Arkansas 52-0 and Tennessee 45-10.

After an open date, the LSU Tigers, ranked No. 10, came to Bryant-Denny Stadium to take on the Tide. It was a perfect fall day with blue skies, sunshine and nice cool weather. The 101,000 seats were filled, and there were probably 40,000 to 50,000 fans tailgating on campus.

Phil Knight, Nike's founder and CEO, his wife and son, along with his college roommate and his wife, were our guests for the weekend. We had taken the group to dinner the night before at NorthRiver Yacht Club. I found Phil Knight to be one of the most down to earth and interesting people I had ever met. The next day he was dressed to the hilt with Nike-made Alabama apparel. As an Oregon grad and huge donor to the university, I thought that to be a very generous gesture. I was well aware of the amount of Alabama merchandise Nike sold, so it really was a pretty good move for him as well.

The game was a hard-fought defensive struggle for three quarters, as Alabama scored a first-quarter field goal and took a 17-14 lead into halftime. It was 17-17 late in the third quarter, but a well-designed and executed fake punt changed the Tide's field position and seemed to break LSU's back. A Yeldon 1-yard touchdown plunge and a 3-yard pass from McCarron to Jalston Fowler gave the Tide a 38-17 victory. Yeldon led a physical Alabama offense with 25 carries for 133 yards and two touchdowns. Mosley led all defenders with a game-high 12 tackles, 1.5 tackles for loss, and two pass breakups. It was a huge victory for the Tide, and Knight said the atmosphere at the game was the best he had ever seen. It was definitely the epitome of big-time college football.

Alabama went on to defeat Mississippi State 20-7 and Chattanooga 49-0. Things were set up perfectly for another SEC title and National Championship run, we just needed to get through Auburn in Jordan-Hare Stadium.

Alabama fell behind 7-0 in the first quarter but scored 21 in the second to take a 21-14 lead into halftime. Auburn tied it up in the third, but a 98-yard McCarron to Amari Cooper pass gave the Tide a 28-21 lead with 10 minutes remaining. A 39-yard pass off a run-pass option saw the quarterback take it way outside, looking like he was going to run. An offensive tackle was 5 yards downfield blocking a linebacker and our corner came up to tackle the quarterback. There was definitely an illegal receiver downfield that wasn't called. The quarterback pitched it over the corner's head to a wide-open receiver who scored untouched to tie it at 28-28 with 32 seconds on the clock. Alabama returned the kickoff and completed a first-down pass, and the receiver went out of bounds as the clock ran down to zero. But replay showed one second left on the clock. A 60-yard field-goal attempt was short, and with a return setup, Auburn's Chris Davis returned the kick 100 yards (plus 9 yards deep in the end zone) for a 34-28 victory.

In most close games, there are three or four plays that make the difference. In that game, there were at least 15 that would have resulted in a double-digit Alabama win. We missed three very makeable field goals, missed a fourth-and-1 in the red zone to give Auburn the ball, and there were several other plays that would have put the game out of reach. It was a devastating loss that knocked us out of the SEC and National Championship pictures. It did get us a bid to the Sugar Bowl to play Oklahoma, which in most any other year would have been a blessing.

The Sugar Bowl was very exciting to me. It was sort of like winning a trifecta. As a player, I played in the January 1962 Sugar Bowl and our team beat Arkansas for the 1961 National Championship. As a head coach at Tennessee, we handily beat the Air Force Academy, and as athletics director, I got to participate at another level thanks to Coach Saban and our great Alabama team.

Since the team went to New Orleans for about a week, I never realized how much difference there was in coaches' needs in the 2010s compared to the 1970s. Recruiting and other priority work had to go on without missing a beat. The managers packed up the equipment needed to play the game, but they literally set up a command center for coaches and players to meet, recruit and get things done. Obviously they required an advance team to go ahead, review and pick a hotel, and work with that hotel to provide for team meetings, individual group meetings, recruiting needs, meals and snacks, and security. As stated earlier, nobody manages athletic events better than Alabama.

The game didn't go as well as we had hoped and expected. Alabama scored first but Oklahoma answered and went on to take a 31-17 lead into halftime. Derrick Henry came to life in the second half, scoring on a 43-yard run in the third quarter and a 61-yard screen pass to get us within a touchdown at 38-31 with 6:22 to go in the fourth quarter. With 47 seconds on the clock, Oklahoma recovered a fumble and scored again for a 45-31 win.

While the last two games left a bitter taste, the 2013 team did win 11 games and a No. 7 ranking in the final polls. Coach Saban and his staff went hard on the recruiting trail and came up with another No. 1 recruiting class, which helped ensure the future of Crimson Tide football.

I had decided early in my tenure as Alabama's AD that I wanted to treat this job like I treated my grandchildren. Parents naturally have high expectations for their children and pay attention to every little thing. They want them to make better grades, play better in sports or other extracurricular activities, use better grammar and behave better in church. Grandparents don't see their grandchildren's "warts" — they only see the good things — and thus their relationship is usually pretty good. I had decided I was going to try to overlook all "warts" that didn't affect the pursuit to accomplish our mission.

At CLC I wanted to communicate frequently with our staff, even though after we grew in staff size I didn't see them all every day. I enjoyed learning about great leaders and collecting quotes on their style and accomplishments. I started sending out quotes that I thought relevant to our company at that time. In addition, I wrote a piece below the quote about what that quote meant to me and our organization. In June 2013, I started to put out a "quote for the day" to our staff at Alabama. I thought it might mean something to someone on our staff, and it also gave the staff insight as to those things important to me and the way I thought.

By December 2013, I was so impressed with the things our people were doing that I decided to start a blog that went out to staff and various mailing lists of donors, season-ticket holders, A-Club members and others. I wanted them to see what I was seeing as the great work our coaches, players and administrators were doing. It was also important to me that it become a source of information to our fans on timing of upcoming sporting events — radio stations, TV games and replays, and other Athletics Department events. It was published every week or two, depending on the season. We called the blog, "The Battle Plan." Not only was it a good way to showcase the good things going on in the department, but I thought my grandchildren would think their granddad was cool and high tech. In writing this book, it has also been very helpful in providing detailed information on Athletics Department activities and accomplishments.

An example of "The Battle Plan" is found below. It was posted on January 24, 2014 (not included is the television events schedule):

The Battle Plan

We're in the midst of a very busy time in the Athletics Department right now. The basketball seasons are at their midway point and several other sports are shifting into high gear. Meanwhile, the baseball and softball seasons are on the horizon, hopefully bringing some warm weather with them!

Our gymnastics team hosts the annual Power of Pink meet tonight against Arkansas at Coleman Coliseum. We expect another sellout crowd for the event, which Coach Sarah Patterson has made through her efforts into one of the most memorable athletics events of the entire year. Meanwhile, all of our teams need your support. We need you to show up early, be loud and stay late. It makes a tremendous difference to our student-athletes.

Developing Leaders and Ambassadors

One of the Athletics Department's initiatives of which I am proudest is our Emerging Tide Leaders program. This is meaningful to me primarily because it is a visible example of one of my primary objectives as Director of Athletics — to help our student-athletes develop into leaders and ambassadors for our department, our University and our state. Comprised of sophomore, junior and senior student-athletes, the Emerging Tide Leaders program involves athletes from every sport that we sponsor. They are hand-picked by their coaches as emerging leaders on their respective teams. They range from team captains to others that simply have shown the ability to be influential in a positive way on their team.

Kevin Almond (our Senior Associate Athletics *Director for Support Services)* works with *Jon Dever* (our Associate Athletics Director for Student Services) to organize the program, but the student-athletes guide the leadership initiatives. Under the guidance of Kevin and Jon, Emerging Tide Leaders works to create and nurture a culture that understands that ultimate team success actually is derived from the attitude and outlook of influential people on the team. The program embodies a commitment to building leaders who not only win on the field, but cultivate leadership qualities in their teammates that will benefit society after they graduate.

Dr. Tim Elmore of Growing Leaders, Inc., presented to our Emerging Tide Leaders on Sunday, Jan. 12. He spoke to the group about "The Primary Colors of a Leader." The presentation was coupled with engaging hands-on activities that not only focused on techniques, skills or mechanics of how to be a leader, but challenged them to look at the inward qualities that make effective leaders. The student-athletes came away with a formula that they could apply to Healthy Effective Leadership: Character + Perspective +Courage + Favor = Healthy Effective Leadership, what Dr. Elmore describes as the primary colors of a leader.

Character enables the leader to do what is right even when it is difficult. Perspective enables the leader to see and understand what must happen to reach the target. Courage enables the leader to initiate and take the risk to step out toward a goal. Trust enables the leader to attract and empower others to join them in the cause.

On Monday, Jan. 13, Dr. Elmore met with coaches and staff on "Marching off the Map: Charting a New Course for Student-Athlete Development." Dr. Elmore described how students differ today than from years past, and he told the coaches and staff that, by considering that students have grown up with various technologies, that they must be approached differently when it comes to drawing on their skills, creativity and leadership qualities.

We seldom hear about our student-athletes outside of their efforts in competition, or when they slip and get into some trouble. The overwhelming majority of our student-athletes at Alabama (and nationally) are intelligent, thoughtful, hard-working young people that represent the best of what our society has to offer. They are about so much more than the games that they play. The University of Alabama is about winning championships and building champions. Our Emerging Tide Leaders program provides a leading edge opportunity for our best and brightest.

A Special Visit with an Old Friend

I had an opportunity to spend about an hour on Thursday prior to the men's basketball game with Bob Knight, who was in town to do the color commentary on the ESPN telecast with broadcaster Rece Davis. Bob was a young head coach at Army back in the mid 60's when I spent two years as a football coach at the U.S. Military Academy. We had fun reminiscing about the old days and talking about how much collegiate athletics has changed over the years. Bob is very bright and definitely a colorful character, who does an excellent job of analyzing modern basketball. It was a special treat getting to spend some time with him.

A Milestone Victory

Hearty congratulations to our women's basketball team and their staff, led by head coach Kristy Curry. The Tide upset eighth-ranked Kentucky in Lexington on Thursday night on a last-second shot by senior Daisha Simmons. It gave our women's program its first road victory over a top 10 opponent since 1998 and is an impressive milestone for Coach Curry in her first year leading the team.

This Weekend on Campus

As we kick off all our spring sports, I hope that our students and fans will find a team to adopt, get to know, and show up often to support throughout the season. There are exciting events that will take place on many different fronts. Competing in the SEC gives us all a chance to see the finest that college athletics has to offer in virtually every sport. That will be particularly evident in the coming weeks as our outdoor sports begin their seasons. This weekend our women's tennis team hosts William & Mary on Saturday at 10 a.m., then plays another match on Sunday afternoon (check rolltide. com for details). Our men's basketball team hosts LSU on Saturday night at 7 p.m. at Coleman Coliseum. On Sunday at 2 p.m., come out to Foster Auditorium to see our women's basketball team take on Georgia.

Let's keep the Tide rising!

* * *

There is another season outside those of our 21 teams that may be as prominent as any of those. In February each year, football recruiting classes report on their signees. The signing class of 2014 exceeded expectations of Alabama fans, even though every class signed by Coach Saban and his staff were at or close to the top. Having had experienced recruiting in my past coaching career, it was amazing to me to see the dedication, perseverance, ability to close and get 4- and 5-star athletes on campus.

Our fans often make the difference in Alabama teams emerging victorious in close contests. Coach Saban speaks to that fan support before most every game and gives credit to fans when they do provide "the winning edge." A mid-February weekend showed how fans affected several teams' victories. Our No. 16 women's tennis team took an impressive, hard-fought victory over No. 10 Virginia at the beautiful Roberta Alison Baumgardner Tennis Facility. Coach Jenny Mainz's squad withstood a late rally, winning the match 4-3 after it looked as if the Cavs had come back to steal a victory. As impressed as I was by the grit and determination of our ladies on the court, something I heard about after the match made an even greater impression.

One of Virginia's top players remarked afterward that our Crimson Tide crowd that day was "the best crowd that I've ever played in front of." What she was describing was an intense, boisterous near-capacity crowd that, while being supportive of the Tide, did not conduct itself in unsportsmanlike fashion. As one who was there, I can tell you that the atmosphere at that match was electric. Not only did it reinforce my belief that we have the classiest and most supportive fan base in America, but it also affirmed my belief that our fans can make the difference for every sport in which we compete.

My experience at the tennis event wasn't the only one that weekend that pumped me up! Our crowds at women's basketball and baseball also were excellent. The Alabama fans at these venues were tuned in and supportive of two of our programs.

This support makes a difference, whether at home or away. We worked hard at trying to get fan support from students and fans at events other than football, which didn't need much help. We encouraged them to "Adopt a Team" to learn about the coaches and players and show up for events. It does make a difference, and Alabama fans are the best.

May 20, 2014 was one of the saddest days of my tenure with the untimely death of one of our best student-athletes, a swimmer named John Servati. A storm passed through Tuscaloosa and flash flooding was taking place. John and his girlfriend sought shelter in the basement of his house near campus in Tuscaloosa. A retaining wall began to collapse on top of them and John jumped into action, holding it up long enough for his girlfriend to get out. Unfortunately, John wasn't able to make it out.

John's coaches and teammates painted a picture of him as the model student-athlete — very bright, highly motivated, talented, unselfish and uplifting to those around him. One message in this tragic event was very clear: Life is precious and we never know what tomorrow will bring. We should enjoy the journey, do the best we can every day, and don't put off telling those we love how much we care about them. We created the John Servati Courage Award to be given to a student-athlete at the annual Student-Athlete Awards Banquet, if during the year someone exhibited above and beyond the call of duty in a courageous act. Hopefully John's spirit will live on through this award and future athletes will remember his name and deeds.

One of my favorite events of the year was our Student-Athlete Awards Banquet. This impressive event was planned and run entirely by our Student-Athletes Advisory Committee (overseen by Kevin Almond and Jon Dever). Its purpose was to recognize and honor student-athletes and their teams primarily in areas outside of sport, e.g. academics, community service and spirit. To me this was one of the coolest events of the year, as it spoke volumes about the well-rounded quality of Alabama student-athletes, and provided an up-close view of the contributions these young men and women were making, and would continue to make in society when they graduated and entered the work force.

At this banquet, our student-athletes came dressed in their finest attire. Well, at least our women did, as our men still needed a little coaching in that area! As competitors, they had a strong desire to excel in everything they did. They worked hard to win these awards. It was neat to see how teams erupted with pride when their teams or teammates won accolades. But it was even neater to see the camaraderie between our teams when major awards were announced and everyone loudly voiced their approval and congratulations. There was no better example of our Mission in action than what I saw that Monday evening. It was truly inspiring and uplifting.

The highlight of the program was the presentation of the Paul W. Bryant Student-Athlete Award, the highest honor given to an Alabama student-athlete. It was presented by the Tuscaloosa Chapter of the University of Alabama Alumni Association. The honor recognized one male and one female student-athlete who had achieved excellence in all facets of the college experience: athletics, academics and community service. The Bryant Award winners — men's golfer Cory Whitsett and women's golfer Stephanie Meadow — were terrific representatives of their teams and our university. Both were great examples of what a student-athlete should be.

One of my most memorable experiences in the 2013-14 year was going to Athens, Georgia, in May 2014 to watch our talented women's tennis doubles team of Erin Routliffe and Maya Jansen win the NCAA title. Playing on Georgia's court, Erin and Maya administered the most brutal beatdown I ever saw, winning in straight sets of 6-0, 6-1. It was fun taking pictures of Erin and Maya holding the championship trophy. Jenny Mainz won her third Coach of the Year award after leading her team to a 25-5 overall record and 12-1 in the SEC, thus earning a No. 6 ITA ranking. Emily Zabor captured her second straight Elite 89 Award and the third in a row for the Crimson Tide.

The women's and men's tennis teams were honored as the squads with the highest grade-point averages during the 2013 calendar year. The women's team posted a 3.74 team GPA, while the men's team had a 3.34.

We currently sponsor 21 teams in 17 sports programs. Overall, 13 of our 17 programs had GPAs of 3.00 or better. Nine of our 10 women's programs had GPAs of 3.00 or better and 10 of our 17 programs had GPAs of 3.30 or better.

2014-2015

In the football off-season, Doug Nussmeier resigned as offensive coordinator to take the same position at the University of Michigan. He was replaced by Lane Kiffin, who had been recently fired by USC.

Jake Coker, who had two years of eligibility remaining, transferred from FSU. Jake was a tall, pro-style quarterback with a strong arm. Three-year starter McCarron had graduated, after breaking most of Alabama's passing records in 2013. Blake Sims, a converted running back, went into spring training as the No. 1 quarterback after serving as backup to McCarron the previous year. Many expected Jake to be the guy, but a quarterback having to learn a new system with completely different terminology is akin to learning a foreign language in a few months. Not only do you need to understand and speak the language, you must learn how to think quickly in that language in the few seconds you have before the ball is snapped.

We also had Yeldon, who rushed for 974 yards in 2013, Derrick Henry, who rushed for 990, and Kenyan Drake, who rushed for 112. Also in the backfield was true fullback and great blocker Jalston Fowler. We also had a slew of good receivers led by Cooper, who as a sophomore the previous year caught passes totaling 1,727 yards. DeAndrew White, Ardarius Stewart and O.J. Howard added to the pass catching coop.

As I watched pre-season practice, I was concerned about the quarterback position. We opened the 2014 season in Atlanta at the Chick-fil-A Pigskin Classic against West Virginia. They were coached by offensive-minded Dana

Holgorsen and were a tough team to prepare for, especially in the first game. Neutral-site games had been good for Alabama since Coach Saban arrived at the Capstone. Playing a highly ranked non-conference team in the first game of the year at a neutral site had many advantages. Not too many coaches were willing to risk losing an opening game on national TV. Coach Saban believed that a tough opening opponent helped get his team more motivated to come back from summer break in better shape and mentally ready to prepare for the game. With the payouts that the neutral sites were offering, it made very good financial sense.

Sims was named the starter. Not only did Sims manage the 33-23 victory, he actually made several big-time third-down conversions and completed 24 of 33 passes for 250 yards with one interception. He looked like he had eyes in the back of his head as he dodged oncoming rushers who had him dead to rights. Yeldon rushed for 126 yards, Henry 113, and Sims six times for 42 yards. After the win, I congratulated Coach Saban and on the plane ride back to Tuscaloosa, and I saw that Kiffin and Sims were sitting together. I went up to them and congratulated both on the win, and told Lane, "That's one of the best coaching jobs I've ever seen."

We beat Florida Atlantic 41-0 and Southern Miss 52-12 before facing Florida in our first SEC game in Tuscaloosa. Sims threw for 445 yards and four touchdowns, including 10 passes to Cooper for 201 yards and two scores, beating Florida 42-21. Sims' 23 of 33 performance for 445 yards ranked second in single-game Alabama history, only behind Scott Hunter's 484-yard performance against Auburn in 1969.

The following week we traveled to Oxford to face No. 11 Ole Miss in Vaught-Hemingway Stadium. We led 14-3 at halftime and 17-10 going into the fourth quarter, but the Rebels outscored us 13-0 for a 23-17 upset. A fumbled kickoff inside our territory led to the decisive Ole Miss score.

We played at Arkansas next on a cool, rainy, ugly day — and the quality of play on both sides matched the weather. The Razorbacks went into the fourth quarter leading 13-7, but a turnover put the Tide in position for Sims to complete a 6-yard pass to DeAndrew White for the tying score, and Adam Griffith kicked the extra point for a 14-13 Tide victory. Sims threw two touchdown passes while the defense created two fumble recoveries, one interception and a blocked extra point. It was ugly, but it was a transformational game for this team. They refused to lose in a game in which they didn't play their best in front of a very hostile and vocal crowd.

The Texas A&M Aggies came to town the next week, and fortunately, Johnny Manziel had moved on to the pros. I had a friend of the university and generous donor sitting in our box. With about six minutes before the half, I asked if he wanted to watch the last few minutes and halftime show from the field. When we left the box and got down to the field, we were escorted by Tommy Horton, my assigned State Trooper and my friend to this day, the score was 24-0. In the next few minutes, Henry scored on a 8-yard run, Sims threw a 24-yard touchdown pass to Cooper and a 41-yard screen pass for another touchdown to Henry for a 45-0 halftime lead. Coker completed a 14-yard touchdown pass to close out the scoring at 59-0. We scored 21 points in the five minutes we were on the field. My friend was impressed. I don't care who you are, shutting out any team is difficult, but especially one coached by offensive-minded Coach Kevin Sumlin.

The next week, we traveled to Knoxville and beat Tennessee 34-20. Cooper had a career night, tallying a school-record 224 yards on nine catches

After an open date, the Tide recorded one of the most impressive wins in my four years as AD in front of LSU's hostile crowd. It was a typical defensive, physical, tough, heavyweight fight.

LSU opened by taking a 7-0 first-quarter lead, but Sims connected with Cooper for a 23-yard TD, and Griffith kicked a 39-yard field goal for a 10-7 lead by halftime. The third quarter ended 10-10. Late in the fourth quarter with a little more than a minute go to, it appeared to be lost when Alabama fumbled inside its own 10-yard line. After every LSU offensive play, Coach Saban called a timeout. The defense held and LSU kicked a field goal to take a 13-10 lead with 50 seconds on the clock. LSU kicked the ensuing kickoff out of bounds, giving the Tide the ball on its 35-yard line. A few completions got the ball inside the 20, where Griffith kicked the game-tying field goal with three seconds left on the clock. Coach Saban's clock management, Lane Kiffin's offensive play calling, and Blake Sims' "cool under fire" execution sent the game into overtime.

On Coach Saban's checklist of things to do before the game, he had already had in the game plan that if we went to overtime and had the option, we would take the end zone in front of where a large number of Alabama fans were sitting. We got that decision, and the noise made by our fans almost sounded like Bryant-Denny Stadium, at least to the players on the field. Sims threw a 6-yard touchdown pass to White as we escaped with a beautiful come-from-behind 20-13 victory. Of all Coach Saban's victories, I'll bet this one ranks up there among the best. I thought it was brilliant.

A tired and physically bruised team took on top-ranked Mississippi State the next week. But the Tide opened up with a safety followed by a Griffith field goal, a 4-yard scoring pass from Sims to Cooper, and a Henry 1-yard TD, and it a quick 19-0. We went into the fourth quarter with a 19-6 lead, but State narrowed the gap to 19-13 with 14 minutes remaining. Yeldon scored on a

6-yard run with eight minutes remaining and the two-point conversion failed, making it 25-13. State added a TD with three seconds left, and the Tide had a 25-20 victory over the No. 1 team in the country.

After beating Western Carolina 48-14, we prepared to meet Auburn at home in the Iron Bowl.

The 2014 Iron Bowl was a wild game in many ways. Auburn's 90 plays for 630 yards of total offense topped Alabama's 61 plays for 539 yards. At the end of the first quarter, we led 14-9. At halftime, Auburn led 26-21. In the third quarter Auburn scored to take a 33-21 lead, but we scored to make it 33-27. Auburn then kicked a field goal to make it 36-27 in AU's favor.

Then the Tide turned. Our defense started getting stops, and we scored touchdowns on the next four possessions — a 75-yard Sims-to-Cooper pass, an 11-yard Sims scamper, a 6-yard Sims completion to DeAndrew White, and a 25-yard run by Henry — for a 55-44 victory.

After beating Missouri 42-13 in the SEC Championship Game, we were first in the initial College Football Playoff rankings. Ohio State had lost two quarterbacks but beat a Wisconsin team 59-0 that was favored by 4.5 points in the Big Ten Championship Game. That put the Buckeyes at No. 4 in the CFP, and a matchup with Alabama in New Orleans Jan. 1.

We took a 14-6 first-quarter lead and led 21-20 at the half. But it was hard to overcome OSU's Ezekiel Elliott, who rushed for 230 yards, and third-team quarterback Cardale Jones, who threw for 243 yards. Alabama fought hard and had a chance to regain the lead late in the game when the Tide intercepted a pass at Ohio State's 25-yard line with the score at 34-28. But a first-down interception turned the ball over to the Buckeyes, and Elliott broke a 75-yard scoring run. Cooper caught a 6-yard TD pass with 1:59 to go, but time ran out in the 42-35 loss.

During the season, the Tide offense gained over 600 yards in four games and over 500 yards in eight games. If someone had placed a bet in Las Vegas that Blake Sims would break most of AJ McCarron's passing records, they would have won a lot of money. Five players received first-team All-America honors: wide receiver Amari Cooper, safety Landon Collins, punter JK Scott, linebacker Trey DePriest and offensive guard Arie Kouandjio.

I would especially like to congratulate and thank four players who were chosen by their teammates and coaches as the captains of the 2014 team. Collins, Cooper, Sims and Jalston Fowler each made plays throughout the season, and provided extraordinary leadership on and off the field. They had much to do with the "Refuse to Lose" spirit that became a trademark of this team. They earned the honor of "captain," which at Alabama puts your name, handprint and footprint in concrete to be recognized forever.

On Dec. 17, 2014, Dr. Judy Bonner announced her plans to step down as University of Alabama President by September 2015. It had been a genuine pleasure to serve under Dr. Bonner during my first two years as Director of Athletics at Alabama. She is a rare person, a strong leader with the heart of a servant. She commands respect, not by the mere force of her personality, but the class, dignity and thoughtfulness that she brings to any conversation. Her advice, counsel and support was been vital to the success of our department in fulfilling our mission.

Rookie gymnastics coach Dana Duckworth led her team to its ninth SEC Championship, a NCAA Regional Championship, and a No. 4 final ranking in the country. Sophomore Lauren Beers was announced the Elite 89 Award winner for the sport of gymnastics. Beers had a perfect 4.0 GPA in Exercise Science. She is a six-time All-American who won the all-around, balance beam and floor exercise in the 2015 NCAA Regional Championship.

The Alabama softball team had a 48-15 overall record, 17-7 in the SEC and No. 5 in the nation. It won a Super Regional Championship, and made its 10th appearance in the Women's College World Series, its 17th straight NCAA appearance. Junior outfielder Haylie McCleney was named the 2015 Capital One Academic All-American Team Member of the Year for Division I. That was the first ever for Alabama softball, and the seventh overall for any Alabama student-athlete. Haylie was also named SEC Scholar Athlete of the Year.

John Servati, who died in April 2014 while saving the life of another Alabama student during a severe storm that swept through Tuscaloosa, was honored with the NCAA Award of Valor. His parents, Janet Gaston and Al Servati, accepted the award from President Bonner, with head coach Dennis Pursley looking on.

Probably the biggest news of the year came when we replaced Anthony Grant as men's basketball coach with Avery Johnson.

I loved Anthony Grant and his family, and believed he could turn the Alabama program around. His strengths to me were his commitment to playing great defense and, after that, as good of an offense as he could build. He ran a clean program, recruited good student-athletes and was competitive in most games. He came close, but couldn't get over the hump of getting to the NCAA Tournament, as injuries were a factor in both 2013 and 2014. His detractors had been on me since the day I took the job, but I believed in him and supported him every way possible. In the 2014-15 basketball season we were struggling coming down the stretch. The "fire Anthony Grant" calls on social media were cranking up. I went to Anthony and told him I would draw a line in the sand and tell the world he would be our coach in the future. He responded that he needed to win and thought we could, adding, "Let's see how it plays out." As fate would have it, it didn't play out well. In our 18 regular-season SEC games, we were 8-10. We lost our first game in the SEC Tournament 69-61 against a mediocre Florida team, and didn't play with much energy. Of greater importance to me, we didn't play like there was much hope for the future. The winning edge is a very fine line. In Anthony's final season, several games went down to the last possession, and we went 2-5 in those games. Had we gone 5-2, our conference record would have been 11-7 and we would have likely not made a change.

We had put in a bid to host an NIT round of post-season play if we were invited to play in that tournament. C.M. Newton was no longer on the NIT Committee, but was close to the group. He told me we were definitely not going to get an invitation to the NIT. I called Anthony and we met at my house on the Sunday afternoon before the NIT teams were announced. As we talked about how the season played out, it could not have been much worse. After a while I told him I thought we needed to make a change. In some ways, I think Anthony was relieved. He wanted to tell his players, but it was one of the hardest things I ever had to do.

We called a meeting and Anthony told the players he was being relieved of his duties as a coach. It was very difficult to follow Anthony and meet with the team. They were obviously very somber and disappointed. I told them we would hire the best coach available and we would get Alabama basketball back to its rightful place in the SEC. But to make matters even worse, not long after meeting with the team, word came down that we had been invited to play in the NIT. It was a pretty embarrassing moment from a timing perspective, but we got through it. Assistant Head Coach John Brannen, with Anthony's blessing, accepted the interim head coaching position and led the team into the NIT. We defeated Illinois in the first game at home, then lost to Miami away. Brannen was later named head basketball coach at Northern Kentucky, where he enjoyed success, and then became the head coach at Cincinnati in 2019.

I took Fess St. John, our chairman of the Athletic Committee of the Board of Trustees, with me on all interviews for Anthony's replacement. It wasn't that I thought I needed help making a deal. But I was 73 years old at the time and wanted the new coach to establish a relationship with someone high in Alabama Athletics who would be there when I retired. Fess was very helpful in the effort.

After I struck out trying to hire Gregg Marshall from Wichita State, we interviewed four candidates. While I had Avery Johnson in my file, my first thought was he had no college experience and the learning curve would be too steep. As Fess and I were driving back in separate cars from stealth hotel meetings with two different candidates in Nashville (they both drove in from different cities), Fess called me and told me he had received a call from Avery and was impressed. I called Avery and learned he had a lot of college experience as his son, A.J. Jr., had grown up in the AAU ranks and Avery gained valuable knowledge about the AAU while getting close to several coaches and teams. Avery also got a heavy dose of learning collegiate recruiting rules from his son's recruitment. Avery added that he had a lot to do with Texas A&M landing such a highly ranked recruiting class in the 2014-15 year.

Fess and I were meeting with another coach down in Florida on the Saturday before Easter. The coach was on vacation from another state, so nobody figured out who we were meeting with, but even though the tail number on our plane had been blocked, I got an email about where we were about the time we landed. When I left home that day I told Mary I had the one trip scheduled and would be home for dinner. We had been invited to dinner with a neighbor.

I was scheduled to meet with Avery the next day on Easter Sunday. I asked our pilots if we could leave after my meeting and fly to Dallas. They said we could, but they needed to know ASAP to handle fuel needs and file a flight plan. I called Avery and asked if we could meet with him later that afternoon. He said he could and told me which airport to use and he would have someone there to pick us up and take us back.

The meeting in Florida went well. We left Florida and headed to Dallas. Avery was very well prepared and knew a lot about our players and our recruiting. After meeting a couple of hours, I saw Avery as a very pleasant and articulate young man with a wealth of NBA experience, both as a player and a coach. I became confident that Avery could sit down with prospective student-athletes and sell them on how to get to the NBA. And I was very confident he could sell mamas and papas. His knowledge of AAU basketball was very valuable, and he knew enough about the collegiate game that with the right assistant coaches, I thought he could definitely improve our talent levels and do very well.

I called Mary and told her I would be late for dinner, but to go ahead and go over to our neighbor's and I might get there for dessert. Mary was a great AD's wife, but she didn't pay too much attention to my schedule. She called our neighbor and said, "I don't know where Bill is, but he will be late." Our neighbor replied, "We've been watching on TV for hours and he's in Dallas meeting with Avery Johnson!" It seemed there was no way to conduct a job search in a high-profile sport in any sort of private talks. (At Avery's press conference, I talked about this observation and said, "I'm not hiring the next Alabama football coach." Everyone laughed as if that was a joke, but it wouldn't have been fair to the coach, the next AD, or the University President to hire that position at Alabama with the short time remaining on my contract).

I called two of my friends who were college basketball "lifers" and asked what they thought about Avery. Both thought it would be an exceptional hire, so he moved to the top of the list. We had four really good coaches who wanted the job. They were all mid-major coaches, and I thought we needed an out-of-the-box hire to ignite the media hype around Alabama basketball and see if we couldn't improve our talent levels.

We made the deal with Avery, but before I would hire him, I said, "I need to know the answer to two questions. Is your wife ready to move to Tuscaloosa over the next few weeks, and are you expecting an NBA salary?" Avery replied, "Good question coach. I'll talk to Ms. Cassandra tonight and you talk to my agent tomorrow." I spoke with Avery's agent and he told me his firm represented about 40 college coaches, and money would not be a problem. I called Avery later and he told me, "Ms. Cassandra said she is dying to come to Tuscaloosa."

A few weeks later Avery was on board and in Tuscaloosa. Cassandra stayed behind, working on making the transition, but she came in for a weekend, and she and Avery joined Mary and me for brunch at the NorthRiver Yacht Club. As anyone who knows Cassandra knows, she is not bashful. She opened up with, "I told Avery, 'Tuscaloosa, Tuscaloosa, who would want to go to Tuscaloosa?'" It was a light-hearted jab, but I turned to Avery and said, "Avery, I have a bone to pick with you. You told me Cassandra was dying to come to Tuscaloosa." Avery replied, "She was, coach, she just didn't know it yet!"

In a near simultaneous move, Kevin Almond had been leading our search for a new soccer coach, as Todd Bramble resigned to take another job. We interviewed a few candidates and ended up hiring Wes Hart, who was being groomed as the future head coach at Florida State University. FSU had an outstanding soccer program and had developed a strong reputation in attracting top international players, and Wes worked on those recruiting efforts. We believed Wes could build a program at Alabama that could be competitive.

During the 2014-15 year, ESPN published a story about a new way to evaluate college football polls. This report determined a top-25 football program by combining its rankings in the AP Poll and Coaches' Poll, then equating its position in football graduation rates. As the story started, if a university is No. 5 in one poll and No. 6 in another, and 10th in graduation rates, its "ESPN Grade" would be 5+6+10=21. Only teams receiving a vote in either the AP or Coaches' polls were ranked in the ESPN Grade. It was an academic-adjusted ranking of the power teams, not of all teams in college football. Alabama ranked No. 1 in that assessment. It was yet another testament to the incredible job that Coach Saban, his staff and our Academic Services staff were doing in fulfilling our Mission.

In another example of Alabama's depth and breadth of leading-edge programs beyond the playing fields and courts, NCAA Chief Medical Officer Dr. Brian Hainline selected our department's Behavioral Medicine/Mental Health program as one of three model programs in the nation to be used as an example and standard for best practices in these areas. After visiting with universities across the nation, Dr. Hainline deemed our department to have "exceptional mental health programs for student-athletes." The subject of student-athlete wellness had been a hot-button issue in all levels of athletics. Behavioral Medicine had been one of the chief areas of care in which Alabama had devoted staffing and emphasis over the previous few years. In our department, this encompassed areas of student-athlete mental health, substance abuse, crisis intervention, domestic violence and other behaviors potentially harmful to self or others.

On a personal note, Shane Lyons became the new athletics director at West Virginia University. I was proud for Shane in getting the job and thankful for our time together. He and Emily were great assets to Mary and me personally, and I wished him well in his new venture. I knew he would do a great job. We didn't replace Shane, as I believed that change was good and promotion from within, if possible, was the best way to go. Giving staff members additional responsibilities was a great motivator as we successfully divided up his responsibilities.

The NCAA Convention in January 2015 provided a historic moment. Several pieces of legislation were passed that would forever change the landscape of collegiate athletics.

First the "Power Five" conferences (SEC, Big Ten, Big 12, Pac-12 and ACC) were given "autonomy." In other words, the 65 member institutions of those conferences were now able to vote their own legislation to determine policies that govern them. That move enabled those conferences to pass legislation to improve the student-athletes' financial, educational and cultural realities. In the past, most of these actions were blocked by smaller institutions with lesser needs in those policies. The Power Five university presidents, athletics directors, faculty representatives and 15 student-athlete representatives voted on eight proposals with primary focus on establishing full cost of attendance, new concussion protocols, extending scholarship guarantees beyond a one-year commitment, and increasing options to buy insurance to mitigate potential financial hardships caused by career-ending injuries.

In another move with long-term positive impact on the SEC, Greg Sankey was named our new commissioner, replacing the retiring Mike Slive. After a national search was conducted, our presidents made the hiring a reality. Every AD had strongly favored the move and knew Greg was the best man for the job. Greg was Mike's right-hand man and was involved in all of the SEC's business at a high level. Greg was absolutely well-trained to take over as commissioner without missing a beat. He is a brilliant man, and a good communicator with University Presidents, ADs, coaches and administrators. He knew how to build consensus among disparate factions.

I would be remiss if I didn't take another opportunity to praise Mike Slive. Mike took over a conference that had become colossally powerful and used that power, not just for the SEC and its member institutions, but for college athletics in general, and especially for our student-athletes. His successes were about much more than revenues and the bottom line. About every piece of legislation in college athletics from 2002-2015 involved his influence. He did it all with what one media member described as a "velvet hammer." Mike was the type of leader people wanted to follow, a rare combination of toughness, empathy and intelligence. He groomed his successor to be well prepared to take his place.

While I don't like meetings that much, I really did enjoy our SEC AD meetings. They were very well run, didn't waste time, and zeroed in on the topics of the day. I was very impressed with the collegiality of the group. While very competitive on the fields and courts, and many with very different needs and agendas, everyone was very interested in doing what was best for the conference. There was healthy debate and many votes went close in either being passed or defeated, but everyone moved on in lock-step whichever way the vote went, all for the good of the conference.

It was amazing to witness what the SEC Network had accomplished only nine months into its fiscal year of operations. The programming had been excellent. Coverage had been national in scope. Financially, it was very successful. And of great importance, it had showcased virtually every sport, providing a national platform for our outstanding young men and women in the SEC. It had been viewed by some as the most successful cable television launch in history. The SEC Network gave Alabama a tremendous opportunity to continue to build the Alabama brand. It was a "game changer" that allowed the opportunity to stay at the forefront of providing the best resources for the benefit of our student-athletes.

As had been discussed previously, facilities alone don't win championships, but if done properly, they allow an institution to attract the best and brightest of coaches, students, faculty and administrators. Over the previous 12 years, Alabama spent over $2 billion for on-campus buildings and infrastructure. Enrollment during that time went from 19,000 students to 36,500.

2015-2016

In our 2015-16 Annual Report, my opening letter provided a snapshot view of the year:

To All Who Follow and Cheer on the Alabama Crimson Tide,

What an absolutely spectacular year for the University of Alabama Crimson Tide! Throughout the 2015-16 academic year, our student-athletes, coaches and staff strived for greatness each and every day, which led to championships, both team and individual, and inspired performance in all areas of the collegiate experience.

It all started in the fall as our football team battled their way into the second College Football Playoff, becoming the only team to play in both years of the new system, and winning our 25th Southeastern Conference football title along the way. Our men followed their SEC title with a dominating win in the CFP semifinals over Michigan State and finished things off with an instant classic against Clemson, closing out the Tigers 45-40, to earn our fourth national football championship in the past seven seasons. It was also our 10th national title in five different sports since the fall of 2009.

We went on to earn a trio of top-10 NCAA finishes over the winter and spring, including men's swimming and diving, gymnastics and softball. Our women's golf team also won their third SEC championship since 2010. In all, four of our programs finished in the top 10 — football (1st, our 16th national football title), gymnastics (3rd, marking an NCAA-best 23rd top-3 finish), men's swimming and diving (6th, our highest NCAA finish since 1983), and softball (6th, after earning our 11th Women's College World Series berth). We had three additional teams earn top-25 finishes, with women's golf finishing 12th and men's golf taking 23rd, while women's track and field finished 17th at the NCAA Indoor Championships.

Individually, our student-athletes continue to rank among the nation's very best. Derrick Henry became our second Heisman Trophy winner in addition to earning a slew of national and conference honors. Quanesha Burks won her second NCAA long jump title while Connor Oslin, Pavel Romanov, Luke Kaliszak and Kristian Gkolomeev combined to win the NCAA 200 medley relay, the first swimming relay title in school history. Katie Bailey finished off her junior season by winning our 26th individual NCAA gymnastics title, taking top honors on the vault.

Our men and women also shone brightly in the classroom. We became the first school in the history of the award to earn Academic All-American of the Year honors in three different sports, with Haylie McCleney (softball) earning her second such honor, and Lauren Beers (gymnastics) and Anton McKee (swimming and diving) earning the honor for the women's and men's at-large teams. Those three were joined by several additional Crimson Tide Academic All-Americans in 2015-16, giving us double-digit honorees in back-to-back years, as well as the best three-year total among all Division I programs!

Haylie was also the SEC Female Scholar-Athlete of the Year and the Senior CLASS Award winner for softball while Lauren was the SEC Community Service Leader of the Year and earned her third consecutive NCAA Elite 90 Award.

Our student-athletes are able to reach the heights they do because they are not only supported by the best coaches and staff in the nation, but also by our legendary fans. I can't overstate the importance that our fan support makes in what we do. — Roll Tide, Bill

On July 8, 2015, Alabama lost a legend when Kenny Stabler died of colon cancer. One of his many shining moments came in the 1967 Iron Bowl. In a torrential rainstorm, and trailing Auburn 3-0, Kenny somehow managed to scramble through the mud, driving rain and standing water 53 yards for the game-winning touchdown. Kenny was later drafted by the Oakland Raiders and he went on to lead the Raiders to the Super Bowl title after the 1976 season.

The No. 13-ranked football team opened in Dallas at the "Jerry Dome" against Big Ten power Wisconsin. Senior Jake Coker made his debut as the starting quarterback and was an efficient 15 of 21 for 213 yards and one touchdown, with no turnovers. Derrick Henry rushed 13 times for 147 yards and three touchdowns. The Tide defense dominated the No. 20 Badgers, holding them to 40 rushing yards on 21 attempts in the 35-17 victory.

After defeating Middle Tennessee 37-10, we hosted the Ole Miss Rebels in one of the strangest games I have ever seen. We fumbled the opening kickoff, but held Ole Miss to a field goal. They took a 17-10 lead into halftime. Cooper Bateman started the game at quarterback, but was replaced by Coker in the second quarter, and he led us to a touchdown with 1:05 left in the half.

Ole Miss led 30-17 going into the fourth quarter. I was thinking, "we could get beat by three touchdowns in our home stadium." I had never witnessed a Nick Saban-coached team not having a chance to win in the fourth quarter, and it didn't happen that day, as Coker completed an 8-yard pass to Ardarius Stewart to make the score 30-24.

Now a side note: I had not selected "Dixieland Delight" to be played up to this point. Our fans loved to sing it and I loved to hear them sing it, but the ad lib between the pauses had gotten vulgar. Before we improved the sound system in the stadium, it wasn't easy to understand unless you were in the middle of the stands. We had worked with the president of the SGA, presidents of fraternities, and generally tried to educate our fan base that if we didn't clean up the language, the song wasn't coming back. We had decided to test it out in this game.

Back on the field, it looked to me like we were wearing Ole Miss down with 12:30 to go in the fourth. As fate would have it, during a timeout when Ole Miss had the ball, we struck up "Dixieland Delight." Our crowd loved it, but our efforts to get them to leave out the ad lib didn't work. On the very next play, a run-pass option ensued that took the quarterback all the way outside. A tackle was 5 yards downfield blocking a linebacker and our corner came up to tackle the quarterback. The QB flipped the ball over the cornerback's head to a wide-open receiver who ran untouched for 73 yards and a two-touchdown lead. An official threw the flag and I was relieved the play would come back and a penalty would be assessed for an illegal receiver downfield. But the ruling was that it was an illegal forward pass, thinking the quarterback had crossed the line of scrimmage. Replay showed that the QB had not crossed the line and an illegal receiver downfield was not allowed to be called, so the touchdown counted. We closed the score to 43-37, but two touchdowns at that point proved too hard to overcome. I decided to not play "Dixieland Delight" during the rest of my tenure, as I told everyone who asked that playing that song at a fourth-quarter timeout was directly involved in the touchdown that caused us to lose to Ole Miss.

While I admit that I am strongly biased, it is very satisfying to know that others who have no ties to our university feel the same. I read an article online via *The Huffington Post* written by Dr. Aristotle Tziampiris, an Associate Professor of International Relations at the University of Piraeus in Greece who also is Standing Fellow at New York University's Remarque Institute. Dr. Tziampiris attended our game against Ole Miss and wasted no time getting to the point of his article as he opened with: "There is football, college football, and then there is University of Alabama football. A visit to Tuscaloosa for the night game against Ole Miss was an eye opener, dispelled many stereotypes and provided me with a renewed appreciation for SEC football."

I was blown away to see that he encapsulated a key part of our Mission that doesn't get nearly enough attention:

"What caught my attention was a huge billboard with a high definition photograph of three players, designated as the student-athletes of the week, having achieved the greatest academic improvement over the previous seven days," wrote Dr. Tziampiris. "The stereotype is of course that academics don't matter, that college football players are mere human fodder for a huge cash-making machine. But right in front of my eyes was palpable encouragement, acknowledgement and recognition of the importance of studying and learning and not just dominating opponents. Problem is, unless you have access to the inner sanctum of the training facility (and almost no one does), this positive emphasis remains unknown and unacknowledged. In fact, I would go even further and argue that the vibe that I got from the facility was that of one large classroom, the emphasis being on teaching. I understand that this sounds almost counterintuitive, but as a University Professor, I would like to think that I have a certain feel for such things; and if Coach Nick Saban is running first and foremost a teaching program, that may well be the source of his phenomenal success."

I couldn't have said it better. He closed by writing, "I left Tuscaloosa late that night with a sense of wonder and deep satisfaction, perhaps now a true concert to the mystique of Southern football. University of Alabama football is simply unique!"

I was tremendously gratified that a person from outside our state and our country had such a positive, memorable experience. I was particularly moved at his observations about our campus, our people and our culture. That's a tremendous compliment to all of you — our fans, our student-athletes and all those involved in the game-day experience throughout the campus and the city of Tuscaloosa.

Alabama went on to beat Louisiana Monroe 34-0, Georgia in Athens in the rain 38-10, and Arkansas 27-14 at homecoming, with Coker fully dialed in to the quarterback position.

The next week we traveled to Kyle Field to face the No. 9 Texas A&M Aggies in their newly renovated $450 million stadium. After Minkah Fitzpatrick took an interception 33 yards for the opening score, Henry scored on a 55-yard run. A&M kicked a field goal to make it 14-3. Henry added a 6-yard score for a 21-3 lead. After another A&M field goal, cornerback Eddie Jackson scored on a brilliant 93-yard interception return. We took a 28-13 lead into halftime. Late in the fourth quarter, with the score 34-23, Fitzpatrick ran back an interception 55 yards to close out the 41-23 victory. The defense was directly responsible for 21 of our 41 points.

We received quite a scare the next week when we hosted Tennessee. It was a hard-fought, physical game that was much like the "old days." After halftime, we kicked two field goals to go ahead 13-7, but early in the fourth quarter, the Vols mounted a TD drive to take a 14-13 lead. We responded with a drive that ended with a 14-yard Henry touchdown run. The defense took over, caused a fumble and we hung on to a 19-14 victory.

We rolled over LSU 30-16 at home, Mississippi State 31-6 in Starkville, and Charleston Southern 56-6 at home leading up to the Iron Bowl in Auburn's Jordan-Hare Stadium.

It was a typically tight Iron Bowl, as we led 19-13 going into the fourth quarter, but then we dominated Auburn for a sweet 29-13 win. Henry finished with 271 rushing yards and a touchdown, including 19 times for 114 yards with the game on the line in the final period. Our defense held Auburn's potent offense to 169 passing yards and 91 rushing.

That same week our men's basketball team played three ranked teams in a span of four days. We won two of those games, against No. 20 Wichita State 64-60, coached by Gregg Marshall, and No. 17 Notre Dame 74-73. Those two victories were the first since 2006 that the Tide had consecutive wins over ranked teams. Coach Johnson quickly reminded me when we got home that I made the right decision in hiring him instead of Coach Marshall.

The following week we met the Florida Gators, coached by former Saban assistant coach Jim McElwain, in the Georgia Dome for the SEC Championship. Henry rushed 44 times for 189 yards, breaking the SEC single-season rushing yards record previously held by Georgia's Herschel Walker. Coker had another good game, completing 18 of 26 passes for 204 yards and no interceptions. The dominant Tide defense registered five quarterback sacks and nine tackles for loss in the 29-15 victory, which marked the 25th Crimson Tide SEC Championship, and the first back-to-back SEC titles since Tennessee accomplished the feat in 1997 and '98.

A return to the College Football Playoff semi-final saw the Tide roll to a 38-0 rout of Big Ten champion Michigan State in Dallas, setting up the CFP National Championship Game against Clemson in Glendale, Arizona.

It was a back-and-forth fight between two heavyweight teams, as Clemson led 14-7 in the first quarter, it was tied 14-14 at halftime, and the Tigers led 24-21 going into the fourth quarter. In the fourth, a Griffith field goal tied it at 24-24, and then Coach Saban shocked the football world.

The scouting report on Clemson showed that their kickoff receiving team lined up inside the hash mark. So, Coach Saban called for an onside kick, a pooch kick up in the air that needed to land past the 10 yards required before it could be touched by the kicking team. Marlon Humphrey, on the kickoff coverage team, caught the ball before it hit the ground. Clemson Coach Dabo Swinney went ballistic on the sideline. It was a perfectly legal play and Alabama retained possession inside Clemson territory. By that time in the game, neither defense could stop the other, so that strategic move allowed the Tide to get ahead in the scoring race. O.J. Howard scored on a 51-yard pass from Coker to go up 31-24. The Tigers responded with a field goal to close the gap to 31-27. Kenyan Drake (who had broken both bones in his arm making a tackle on the shin of a ball carrier on a kickoff return in the Ole Miss game) took the ensuing kickoff and returned it 95 yards for a 38-27 Alabama lead. Clemson quarterback Deshaun Watson responded with a drive capped by a 15-yard touchdown pass to close the gap again, 38-33. With 1:07 remaining, Henry scored on a 1-yard run for a 45-33 lead. Watson answered again with a 24-yard touchdown pass with 12 seconds on the clock, but the Tide had a 45-40 victory, and Alabama's 16th National Championship. It was a great game to watch and was good to see how close the top two teams were to each other. The onside kick was the play that changed the tempo and helped win the game.

Between the SEC Championship Game and the CFP National Championship Game, Derrick Henry won the Heisman Trophy. Derrick's acceptance speech was remarkable. He thanked God for his abilities, his family for their support through good and bad times, and all his teammates and coaches for the support and opportunities they provided. He then looked to the future and challenged young people to follow their dreams and find positive role models to follow. I couldn't think of a better role model for young people to follow than Derrick Henry. (After that, I jokingly told friends that our Heisman Trophy winners at Alabama doubled under my watch. That was true in that Mark Ingram, who had won it in 2009, was Alabama's only previous Heisman winner).

In February 2016, Alabama baseball held its first official event in the newly renovated Sewell-Thomas Stadium. It was a roaring success, as Coach Gaspard invited all former baseball players to come back. Those who wanted could take batting practice and even play in an alumni game against the varsity. More than 200 former players came back and were blown away by the new stadium.

The baseball stadium plans had been on the shelf for a few years when we decided to dust them off and see if we couldn't get it built. Paul Bryant Jr. was the driving force around the design, and especially the sight lines. Paul had built stadiums in para-mutual racing and knew how to build stadiums. Trustee Karen Brooks also got involved in approving the "look and feel" of the stadium. A team went to college and professional stadiums around the country, taking ideas from each one. They came up with a brilliant design. The stadium has 5,400 fixed seats, with 1,300 standing-room-only spots in the right field area dedicated primarily for students. They can bring stools, chairs and coolers to sit on. There are three levels, each about 10 yards deep with grassy areas held by concrete retaining walls. It is dog friendly and one of the coolest places in the stadium. The students love and appreciate the special place. There is also a nice section in left field that can be leased by private companies, and a terrific playground close by for kids. It turned out to be a remarkable stadium.

At April's Crimson Choice Awards Banquet, the winner of the prestigious Paul W. Bryant Awards went to senior softball All-American Haylie McCleney and senior basketball All-SEC and Scholar Athlete-of-the-Year Retin Obasohan. Other prestigious awards included: Teams of the Year — football and softball; Coach of the Year — Patrick Murphy, softball, and Nick Saban, football; Comeback Athlete of the Year — Kenyan Drake, football; Athletes of the Year — Derrick Henry, football, and Emma Talley, women's golf; Highest Team GPA — gymnastics with a 3.74, and men's swimming and diving with a 3.25. Crimson Tide Athletics gave more than 3,000 hours of community service during the year. Our SEC Champion women's golf team joined our men's basketball team to capture top honors in community service.

After the 2016 baseball season, Coach Gaspard resigned. I offered him two more years to give him a chance to recruit to the new stadium, but he wanted a change of scenery. We narrowed our choice for Mitch's replacement down to four successful head coaches, and selected Greg Goff from Louisiana Tech.

On a personal note, I was diagnosed in spring 2014 with a solitary plasmacytoma, a soft-tissue tumor. More detail will be provided in the next chapter, but I underwent radiation therapy, which took care of that. In spring 2015, I was diagnosed with multiple myeloma, a fairly rare type of blood cancer. There is no cure at the present time, but it is very treatable. In the summer of 2016 it was determined I needed a stem cell transplant, which was a pretty invasive procedure. From the time I was diagnosed in 2014 until I went in for the transplant, only about five people knew about my condition. I never missed a day's work, and I could have been away for four weeks during the summer of 2016 for the transplant without much attention, but I knew that when I came back with no hair, the "cat would be out of the bag!"

Of course, Dr. Stuart Bell, University President, knew about everything. I told him the prognosis was good and that I fully expected to serve out my fourth and last year as AD, but he needed to find a replacement after the 2016-17 fiscal year.

When Mal Moore went into the hospital in 2013, he never came back. I wasn't in the same situation, but I wanted our staff to know that I was OK, and I was back in the office as soon as possible. My immune system (white blood count) had been reduced to near zero, which meant I was like a newborn baby as far as vulnerability to disease was concerned. I wasn't to be around many people and could not fly on commercial airlines. I was supposed to wear a mask when I went out, not shake hands, and not get hugs. I didn't shake hands, but it's hard to be around our women's teams and not get hugs!

2016-2017

Starting a new school year in the fall is like starting with a clean slate. It really doesn't matter what you did last year, good or bad. It was important that we pay attention to the Mission, and have that front and center in our minds as we took on the challenges ahead.

The football team opened against USC in AT&T Stadium in Dallas. Playing on the largest stage in the opening week of college football was both an honor and a privilege in which our players coaches, and staff all took pride. True freshman quarterback Jalen Hurts entered the game in the second quarter. On his first play, he fumbled an option play and lost the ball. Coach Saban put Hurts back in for the next series and he led a drive ending with a 39-yard touchdown pass to ArDarius Stewart. After a 29-yard field goal, Marlon Humphrey returned an interception for an 18-yard touchdown for a 17-3 Alabama halftime lead. In the third quarter, Hurts completed a 71-yard scoring pass to Stewart, and had 7- and 6-yard scoring runs to put the Tide up 38-6. In the fourth quarter, Bo Scarbrough scored from the 2-yard line and Blake Barnett completed a 45-yard touchdown pass to Gehrig Dieter for a big 52-6 victory over the Trojans.

Alabama defeated Western Kentucky 38-10 before playing another wild game against Ole Miss in Vaught-Hemingway Stadium in Oxford. Ole Miss took a 24-3 lead early in the second quarter, but we rallied to score 24 unanswered points for a 27-24 lead — a Calvin Ridley 6-yard run, an 85-yard Eddie Jackson punt return, a Da'Ron Payne scoop-and-score fumble recovery from the 3-yard line, and a Griffith field goal. After that, Scarbrough and Damien Harris scored on 1-yard runs, and Jonathan Allen scored on a 75-yard touchdown run after a fumble recovery. The defense scored three touchdowns and all were sorely needed. We stretched the lead to 48-30 with 5:28 left and hung on to win 48-43, with the game in doubt until the final play.

In dominating fashion, the Tide beat Kent State 48-0, Kentucky 34-6, Arkansas 49-30, Tennessee 49-10 and Texas A&M 33-14. No. 1 Alabama took on No. 15 LSU in Tiger Stadium and took a 10-0 shutout of the Tigers back home to Tuscaloosa. The game was tied at 0-0 going into the fourth quarter, but Hurts scored his 10th rushing touchdown of the year. Hurts led the team in rushing with 114 yards on 20 attempts and completed 10 of 19 passes for 107 yards with one interception. Linebacker Reuben Foster had 11 tackles. After rushing for a school-record 284 yards in his previous outing, LSU's Leonard Fournette was held to just 35 yards on 17 attempts.

Alabama beat Mississippi State 51-3, Chattanooga 31-3 and Auburn 30-12. We defeated No. 15 Florida 54-16 to win our 26th SEC Championship. On Dec. 31 in the Georgia Dome, we beat No. 4 Washington 24-7 in the College Football Playoff semi-finals. The next week took us to Tampa for the CFP National Championship Game in a rematch with Clemson.

The title game played out like the previous year, with high-scoring offenses setting the tone. Deshaun Watson proved to be almost unstoppable again, as the score seesawed back and forth all the way to the end. Scarbrough scored on 25- and 37-yard touchdown runs to take an early 14-0 lead. In the third quarter, Griffith kicked a 27-yard field goal and O.J. Howard scored on a 68-yard pass from Hurts for a 24-14 lead going into the fourth quarter. Clemson responded and took a 28-24 lead with 4:38 left on the clock. Hurts then scored on a 30-yard run to retake the lead at 31-28 with 2:07 left. The Tigers rallied to make some great plays, with a few controversial calls, on an 80-yard march to score the winning touchdown with one second left on the clock. It was a difficult pill to swallow, but the Tide team left it all on the field and came within one play of winning back-to-back national titles.

During the year, Linda Bonnin, Alabama VP of Strategic Communications, came up with and trademarked the slogan, "Where Legends are Made." She started a marketing campaign beginning with the USC game. The goals were to: (1) speak to the heart of who we were as a university; and (2) tout our academic and athletic successes together on a national stage. I thought it was a brilliant idea. It caught on and is still an effective slogan that recognizes successful individuals in all facets of university life.

Along those lines, one day I read an article about another team at the University of Alabama that had won three national titles since the inception of the program in 2010. Since the inaugural season, Alabama posted finishes of sixth in 2010, fourth in 2011, first in 2012, third in 2013, second in 2014, first in 2015 and first again in 2016. It was the Alabama Astrobotics Team, comprised of undergraduate and graduate students from the University of Alabama and Shelton State Community College. Team member academic disciplines included aerospace engineering, computer science, computer engineering, electrical engineering, mechanical engineering, metallurgical engineering, math, physics, marketing, business, geology, chemical engineering and elementary education. The competition was sponsored by NASA and consisted of two separate challenges/events. The first was the Robotic Mining Competition (RMC) in which the challenge was to build a robot that was capable of digging and collecting dirt from the Moon, Mars or other planetary surfaces and depositing it into a processing bin. The robot was to be a size and weight that could fit in a spacecraft without weighing it down. Upon landing, the robot would be deployed from the spacecraft to go out, dig up and collect surface material, then bring back the materials to the spacecraft to be converted into water, fuels and other useful products for use by astronauts. Each team got two chances to complete the challenge.

The second challenge event was the Sample Return Centennial Challenge (SRCC). The challenge in this event was similar to the RMC, but the robot in the event was required to use full, intelligent autonomy (the ability to complete the full challenge with only the press of the start button and no remote-control assistance to pick up samples, usually rocks of various colors and nonferrous metal objects). Alabama participated in this SRCC in 2016 and placed third out of 20 teams. Alabama was one of seven institutions to pass Level 1 and move on to Level 2. Level 1 required retrieving two samples within 30 minutes, and returning and dumping them in the lander. Level 2 required retrieving and returning 10 samples within two hours over a much larger territory.

Approximately 50 schools competed in the RMC each year, including Wisconsin, Virginia Tech, Virginia, Purdue, Florida, Michigan and Colorado School of Mines. I am told by our Dean of Engineering, Chuck Karr, that if this were a football schedule, it would compare to the SEC Western Division!

Each year, the team at Alabama was required to design and build a totally new model. In the seven-year history of the RMC competition, The University of Alabama was the only team to win the title more than once. It is also the only team in the history of the competition to complete the test using full, intelligent autonomy. To laymen, that meant a team member pressed the start button and the robot went out in a given period of time, found the proper place to gather soil, dug it up, brought it back and deposited it in a bin. The robot did that as many times as necessary to collect the desired amount of soil. If it ran into trouble, each team could finish the test with remote control of the robot, but only Alabama had completed the test in two different years without the use of remote control.

The professor leading our team was Dr. Kenneth Ricks, an associate professor in Electrical and Computer Engineering. He was definitely a hands-on leader, and he indicated to me he followed many of Coach Saban's principles in his process. He had a leadership group that he met each week to discuss progress made, needs for reallocation of manpower, technological needs and whatever issues arose from beginning to end.

As I had the great fortune to meet with this team, the pride they displayed was evident in everything they did. It was an impressive group of young men and women who guided me through examples of two different robots doing their respective tasks. Each year the robot was given a name, and among them were Jimmy, LeBron and Dale Jr. Congratulations were in order to these fine representatives of The University of Alabama who are aiding our country's space program and building equity in the Crimson Tide brand. There are so many stories like this around the university, and many are worthy of the "Where Legends are Made" label.

Soon after the National Championship Game, I announced I was retiring, effective March 1. I had told Dr. Bell before my bone marrow transplant that

I was planning to retire after this, my fourth year as athletics director. Let me say that working under Dr. Bell's leadership was a great honor. I very much enjoyed being a member of his executive staff and meeting every two weeks to discuss the state of the university and where we were going from here. He was a perfect fit to lead Alabama into the future. The 16 years he spent in Alabama's Engineering Department made him an "insider" in the unique culture of The University of Alabama. His experience at Kansas and especially LSU provided him with the knowledge needed to run Alabama. Dr. Bell and his wife, Susan, are great assets to the university.

Dr. Bell did his due diligence for my replacement, and after interviewing several sitting athletic directors, he landed on what we thought was the best fit for the position. Greg Byrne had worked in development at Kentucky and Mississippi State, and became AD at MSU before becoming the AD at the University of Arizona. I got to know Greg pretty well in the previous few years and was very impressed with his background, his reputation, and especially the way he went about hiring coaches.

I was very grateful for the opportunity to lead the department for four years. Being an athletics director is an all-day, every day job. The pressure from competition in the SEC is one thing, but outside pressure from lawsuits make it all the more difficult. Being the AD was much like I described my time playing for Coach Bryant — the farther I got away from it, the better it got. I can honestly say that some days in both positions were not very pleasant, but looking back, I loved every minute. The opportunity to be a part of turning boys and girls into men and women was an incredible experience. Being around our players and seeing their accomplishments in athletics and academics gave great hope that our future in their hands is safe. And being around our coaches provided great examples every day of leadership that built character along with sports competiveness.

In speaking with Dr. Bell earlier in the year, I told him the best of both worlds for me would be to stay connected with the university if I could help advise Greg if he needed help in the transition, and help Athletics and the university in fundraising. I didn't want to be a "hanger on" and if I couldn't earn my keep, I didn't want to stay. He graciously took me in as Special Assistant to the President, I was able to keep Judy Tanner, my assistant for four years, and we moved our offices into the Academic Center that bears my name.

Mary and I agreed to co-chair the $15 million Performing Arts Academic Center (PAAC), which will be built on the opposite side of the "Old Bryce Main" hospital building. That building will become the Welcome Center to The University of Alabama. It is a beautiful and historic building that will be the first place that future students, their families and friends will see as they visit our campus. The PAAC will be a separate building but connected to the Welcome Center in three corridors with green space in between. The architect described his design as "two buildings that act and flow like a couple slow dancing." The architecture is spectacular, and these buildings will transform the campus. They sit on 30 acres of green space that will stay that way in perpetuity, as proclaimed by the Board of Trustees.

It has been Mary's and my pleasure to work on special projects, have time to write this book, and be able to spend more time at our ranch in north Georgia and at our house in Jackson Hole, Wyoming.

Judy Tanner has been a blessing to both Mary and me. She was fantastic during my tenure as AD, even better keeping up with the university business, and even more so dealing with the mounds of paper generated in the writing of this book. I have written it out in longhand and literally cut with scissors and pasted with scotch tape. Edits, additions, deletions and moving sections around created a map-reading course for Judy, to which she passed with an A+ rating.

What follows is the University of Alabama's press release announcing my retirement, and a collection of quotes from head coaches at Alabama reflecting on my career.

Press Release from January 15, 2017:
Bill Battle to Retire as Director of Athletics
Bill Battle, Director of Athletics at The University of Alabama, announced Sunday evening that he is going to retire from his post to assume a new role as Special Assistant to the President.

Battle, currently in his fourth year as Director of Athletics, had led the Crimson Tide Athletics Department since March 2013, when he succeeded the late Mal Moore. University of Alabama President Stuart R. Bell said Battle will continue to lead the department until a successor transitions into the Director of Athletics role.

"Bill has done a tremendous job as Director of Athletics, and has accomplished so much during his career," said Bell. "His business expertise, coupled with his coaching experience and his strong understanding of the role an Athletics Department has in the daily fabric of a university, has allowed us to achieve the great successes we have enjoyed during his tenure. We are blessed to have the continued benefit of his counsel."

Alabama head coaches quotes (Jan. 19, 2017)
Nick Saban, head football coach:
"Bill Battle has done an outstanding job leading our Athletics Department over the last four years. I think we can all appreciate the way he has

represented Alabama in a first-class manner while setting the table for all of our sports to be successful. From a football standpoint, we've been able to compete at a championship level while also graduating our student-athletes, and that is all made possible by the foundation set by Bill and our administration. I know he will continue to be a great asset to our university in his new role as Special Assistant to the President, and we wish Bill and Mary all the best."

Kristy Curry, head women's basketball coach:

"Coach Battle will always hold a special place in my heart. I am honored to be his first hire at The University of Alabama and cannot thank him enough for giving me this opportunity. His love and passion for the Crimson Tide is contagious, and he genuinely and sincerely cares so much about the coaches, the staff and, most importantly, the student-athletes. It's all about people with him and how he can assist in putting them in a position to be successful in life after sport. Coach Battle is a man of great integrity, and his word is gold. He and Mary will certainly be missed, but we wish them both the best."

Patrick Murphy, head softball coach:

"All of us associated with the softball program absolutely loved having Mr. Battle as our leader the past four years. Our players and staff knew it was going to be a great day when we saw Mr. Battle in the bullpen prior to a game or practice. He was the ultimate southern gentleman and a great role model for me."

Dana Duckworth, head gymnastics coach:

"I will forever be grateful for the opportunity Bill Battle gave me to be the head coach of my alma mater. He's been a mentor, he's been a friend and he's been an inspiration. An incredible businessman, he has been approachable, wise and you can't help but see the love he has for The University of Alabama."

Jay Seawell, head men's golf coach:

"I would like to thank Coach Battle for his support of me, my family and our golf program. I am very proud that we gave him his first SEC and NCAA titles as Athletics Director. His leadership and passion for the Crimson Tide will be missed."

Below is the Jan. 23, 2017 edition of The Battle Plan:

Passing the Torch

Last week was a great week in the life of the University of Alabama Department of Athletics. Greg Byrne was introduced as the next Director of Athletics last Thursday, Jan. 19. He will officially report for duty March 1. Greg introduced his beautiful wife, Regina, his handsome sons, Nick and Davis, and his mom and dad, Marilyn and

Bill Byrne. Greg has had a very successful career and has been at the top of virtually every AD search over the last two years.

I have known his father, Bill, for several years. Our company worked with Bill when he was AD at Nebraska and Texas A&M. Bill was a great partner and director. Greg was raised on college campuses and pretty much knows all there is to know about the business of running an Athletics Department. Alabama is very fortunate to get him, and he is very fortunate to get the Alabama job at this time.

Greg has impressed me with the meticulous way he goes about hiring coaches. I have spoken with him over the last two years about our searches for coaches. He is highly respected in the industry by the leaders of the universities and conferences he has served. He is also much respected by those who work for him.

I hope you will join me in embracing Greg as he comes to Alabama. It is my hope that you will make him feel as welcome as you made me when I came back. Greg recognizes what a great place Alabama is and what a great time it is to be here. I will do everything in my power to make his transition as smooth as it can be.

I want to thank you, our staff, student-athletes, coaches, faculty, students and fans for the trust and support you have given me over these last four years. While I never wanted to be a Director of Athletics, you have made this an incredibly valuable and enjoyable experience in my life. I can't say that every day was enjoyable, but then I can't say that playing here for Coach Bryant was enjoyable every day, either! Looking back, both have been very educational and life-changing experiences. I am honored and feel very privileged to have been selected to lead our department these last four years. Thanks, again, for the opportunity.

Our plan all along was to stay four years, but I told Dr. Bell last summer, before my transplant procedure, that I planned to finish out this year through June. My doctors and I thought I could get through the transplant OK and could be back in action before the football season started, but I told him he needed to begin to identify my replacement, whenever that might be. As the end of the football season came around, I felt the department was in very good shape with staff, coaches, facilities and financially, and this year was a good time to pass the torch. The search process identified Greg early, so there was plenty of time to vet him. When the story broke, it broke before we planned but, at the end of the day, the best outcome was achieved. My only regret was not being able to work with Greg Goff, the baseball coach I hired, through his first season.

Mary and I have enjoyed our experience here so much, and we have chosen to stay in Tuscaloosa. Dr. Bell has agreed to allow me to serve as a Special Assistant to the President, to work on strategic initiatives to help him carry out his Mission. If I can make a significant contribution in that role I will enjoy staying involved.

Finally, and most importantly, I am thankful to my wife, Mary, for picking up from our comfortable lives in Atlanta with a week's notice, and getting us moved, settled into a new house, and embarking on a new career. She has been a champion in every respect, and has been a great asset both to me, the university, and the community. I am most proud of her and love her dearly.

In retrospect, having spent four years at Alabama playing for Coach Bryant, and being a part of an SEC Championship and his first National Championship team at Alabama was special. To spend my next four years at Alabama, 50 years later, working with Coach Saban, and being a part of three SEC Championships and his fifth National Championship was even more special. All Alabama people should be very proud and even more thankful that the two greatest college football coaches in history walked the sidelines of Bryant-Denny Stadium, led Alabama teams to championships, and made men out of boys at our great university.

One of my last acts as AD was one in which I took great pride. Mal envisioned "Tuska" — the big bronze elephant statute that resides outside the Golf Club at the NorthRiver Yacht Club — as being a great addition to the Alabama campus. He wanted to see it on the corner of University and Wallace Wade. That would be the first thing people coming from downtown to campus would see as they entered campus. I had talked to Mike Case at the Yacht Club about acquiring Tuska. In February 2017, the timing was right, as Troon was acquiring ownership of the Yacht Club from the Westervelt Company. We made a deal that Westervelt would receive Tide Pride credit for the value of a donation of Tuska to the university. We agreed to bear the moving expenses and any remedial site repairs required by the Yacht Club. A recognition plaque would be applied to the statute acknowledging the donation from the Westervelt Company. We all thought that spot would become one of the most popular spots for photos and selfies. And we all wanted to watch — and maybe even have a parade — as the truck carrying Tuska crosses the dam. It is up to the university and the Athletics Department when, or if, to move the elephant, but I hope to see that done sooner rather than later.

The University of Alabama honored me at graduation ceremonies on May 6, 2017, with an Honorary Doctor of Humane Letters degree. Coach Bryant said when he received an Honorary Doctorate, it was one of his proudest honors. He definitely earned his with 25 years of extraordinary service to the university. With the education I received during the four years I spent there from age 71 through age 75, I thought I earned mine too! It was definitely a proud moment in my life.

LESSONS LEARNED

- Taking over an organization is a challenge. Unless the company is in serious trouble and needs an immediate change of direction, it pays to take time to understand the dynamics of the organization prior to making changes.
- Identify leadership early. Be especially observant in finding leadership qualities in those below those already determined to be leaders.
- If there is not one to your satisfaction already in place, develop a strong Mission Statement to clearly state your vision for the organization. The Mission Statement should answer both the "What" and "Why" questions, and in our case, the "How" question. Every goal should answer the what, why, when, where and how questions.
- A Strategic Plan is essential. It should list in a page or two the essential elements needed to move the organization toward accomplishing the Mission. This should answer the "How" question in more detail.
- Tactics can change every year, or they can stay the same, but they need to move the needle farther in each element of the Strategic Plan. These tend to answer the "When" and "Where" questions.
- The written word is cold and hard. Face-to-face meetings to solve problems, address opportunities, reward good behavior, and hand down consequences associated with bad behavior are far more effective than letter or emails. The written word may well work with letters being physically passed along at the same time.
- Pressure turns iron into steel and coal into diamonds. It either polishes you up or grinds you down. It's all up to how you take it on.
- To change behavior, incentives need to be put in place that move people to earn them. If they are left to chance or applied without thoroughly thinking them through, the results will be less than desired.
- My experience has shown negotiations that end with both sides being able to declare victory usually result in long-term positive relationships. When one side can claim a big victory and the other side is openly defeated, it is much more difficult to establish a good long-term relationship.
- Humility is a wonderful trait that gets far better results than overconfident arrogance. The art of listening is also a wonderful trait. God gave us two ears and only one mouth, which should send a clear message to us all.

PAUL W. B

Your family should be the most important
thing in your life, as it is mine.

CHAPTER 8

NAVIGATING THE WORLD OF HEALTH CARE

Health care in this country is very complicated. People without good insurance and a good advocate to help navigate the system are in deep trouble. Fortunately for me, The University of Alabama has an outstanding insurance program. Even more fortunately, I am married to Mary, an oncology nurse who understands to the Nth degree how to navigate the system.

In spring 2014, soon after my first full year at Alabama, doctors discovered a plasmacytoma tumor on one of my vertebrae. Mary and I had decided to do the half-day physical at St. Vincent's One Nineteen program. We had completed the physical, which I was quite proud of, as I felt really good when most everyone at every station bragged about how fit I looked. But then the nurse-navigator came into the room in which we were eating and announced, "Bad news, they found a tumor on one of your vertebrae, and you need to go back for a couple of scans."

When you hear "tumor" you probably think the worst that it is "cancer" and not a happy ending. Actually, the only time I experienced fear was laying in the machine that engulfed my entire body and would slide back and forth to get the right pictures. I said, "Lord, if it's my time to go, I've lived a blessed life, don't have many regrets, and I am ready when you are."

The best oncologists and neurosurgeons at the University of Alabama-Birmingham looked at my pictures and their diagnosis was that I had a single plasmacytoma in my thoracic (T-12) vertebrae. At that time there was no evidence of disease elsewhere, which if found, would have resulted in a diagnosis of multiple myeloma. The interesting part is that it was discovered in a routine chest x-ray.

The treatment called for radiation therapy, five days a week for five weeks. If I started the next day, my treatment would end the day before our SEC meetings in Destin, Florida, which I didn't want to miss. The same radiation treatment could have been offered in Tuscaloosa, but it would have taken about three days to get it set up there. It would have been much more convenient than driving to Birmingham every day, but it would make me miss a few days of the SEC meetings, so I chose to be treated at UAB.

Treatments were scheduled at 7:30 a.m. I could be there, get treated in about 15 minutes, and be back in my office by 9 a.m. The treatments were non-invasive, and probably over the five weeks added to a feeling of fatigue, but the drive back and forth may have contributed more to fatigue than the treatments. I made the SEC meetings, the tumor was blown away, and all was good by Summer 2014.

Another year passed and in spring of 2015, Mary insisted I go back in for a PET scan that shows lesions in bones and soft tissue. I felt fine and didn't see the need, but she finally prevailed, and I signed up. The PET scan showed a few other lesions and confirmed the diagnosis of multiple myeloma. The on-cologist at UAB suggested chemotherapy. I didn't like that suggestion and sought a second opinion.

We looked at M.D. Anderson in Houston, the University of Arkansas and Emory Hospital in Atlanta as places that treated the disease. We decided on M.D. Anderson, as Mary had researched all three and saw that Dr. Robert Orlowski was the multiple myeloma guru there. In the meantime, we were getting bloodwork and other tests done at the Manderson Cancer Center at DCH in Tuscaloosa. Dr. David Hinton told us we would likely not see Dr. Orlowski, as he spent a lot of his time in research, but anyone we saw out there would be good. But he didn't know how Mary worked, as she got us an ap-pointment at M.D. Anderson within a few weeks, and with none other than the famous Dr. Orlowski.

After checking me out and understanding where I was, he confirmed UAB's suggestions of a chemo treatment that went in cycles of three weeks on, one week off. The chemo treatment was Velcade (two shots a week in the stomach at DCH), Revlimid and Dexamethasone pills. This plan was set forth about the first of June 2015. I told Dr. Orlowski that since the progression of the disease was relatively slow over the year, I would like to move forward with our planned trip to Europe for two weeks, followed by two weeks in Jackson Hole. We had not taken a vacation during my first two summers and I really needed a break. I asked if I could start treatment in August. Dr. Orlowski and Mary both thought I was crazy and irresponsible for delaying treatment for two months, but I was tired and had really looked forward to those trips. After much persistence, I finally got them to give the OK.

We had a great time in England and France. We watched Wimbledon and had strawberries and cream on July 4. We saw Serena Williams win a very close match for another championship. Before those finals, we watched wheel-chair tennis competition and practice, which was amazing. We were so im-pressed with those handicapped athletes who performed as if they weren't handicapped — and had made it to Wimbledon! We saw Paris and all of its beauty up close and personal.

When we returned, we spent two weeks in Jackson Hole, walked a lot, climbed a few hills, and generally tried to use the cool weather to get in better shape for the chemo treatment that was to come on Aug. 15. In three cycles — three weeks on the drugs and one week off — I was back in remission. In the meantime, I had lost 20 pounds, had fairly significant neuropathy in my feet, and was extremely fatigued. Still, no one knew about my disease. When a few asked about the weight loss, I told them I had been working out really hard. They were used to seeing me over in Coleman Coliseum on the elliptical and other machines, so I guess they believed the story.

Dr. Orlowski spent some time with us on the phone as we had questions. We were most appreciative of his time and advice. His strong advice was to get a stem cell transplant using my own stem cells, which could be harvested and frozen for future use. I liked the harvesting idea as it could be done in three hours a day over a two- to three-day period. The transplant was a very invasive procedure and I was hopeful I could delay that part until they came up with a less invasive solution.

Over the holiday period in 2015, Mary's research turned up evidence that Emory Hospital in Atlanta (Winship Cancer Institute) was doing about as many transplants as M.D. Anderson. They also had a leading-edge research doctor who saw patients a day or two a week. Mary made an appointment with Dr Sagar Lonial and we decided Atlanta was a lot more convenient than Houston. The transplant program called for two to three weeks in the hospital, then about two weeks of outpatient follow-up. Our sons, Pat and Mike, lived in Atlanta and would take care of the outpatient treatment time.

In early February, I went to Emory for harvesting of my stem cells. As I sat on a hospital bed with an IV in my arm, I was hooked up to a machine that ran my blood through another machine that spun out the stem cells and deposited them in a bag at the top. I expected the stem cells to be red, but they were actually yellow. We weren't able to harvest enough for two transplant procedures, but had plenty enough for one. The procedure was not at all uncomfortable, as I spent most of the time making phone calls, responding to texts and emails, and taking an occasional nap.

From the time of the harvest until late spring I tried to find someone to advise me that it was OK to put off the stem cell transplant for a year or two. I couldn't find anyone, so I agreed to undergo the treatment in late June. After I made the announcement, I was amazed at the number of multiple myeloma patients and alumni who reached out to me in support. Tom Brokaw and Pat Williams both called on the phone and later sent a copy of their books on the disease. It was very interesting to read about how my treatment differed from theirs.

One gentleman came to my room after we checked in for the transplant. Of course, Mary knew hospital rooms by heart and brought all kinds of things to make my stay more comfortable, including bedding and pillows. The gentleman was very thoughtful and offered much advice, most of which had already been done. The one piece of advice that got my attention, however, was his comment, "Bring soft toilet tissue, cause your *ss will get red!"

Dr. Lonial's advice was: (1) walk as much as you can before, during and after; (2) drink as many fluids as you can; and (3) eat what you can, but don't worry too much about that. We took his advice and walked a lot. Our hospital floor had rooms around a circle with nurses' stations and administrative offices in the middle. We measured it to be 21 laps to the mile. Being in the hospital all day with nothing else to do, we walked several times a day and averaged about five miles a day walking. We encouraged others on the floor to join us and some did. To help pass the time while walking we played a word game — all the letters we could think of starting with A, and on through Z. As we walked laps around the floor, nurses at their stations started to engage in our game and added words to the letter we were discussing. We definitely livened up the place.

The routine consisted of checking into a hotel two days before admission for pre-treatment. That consisted of a shot each day, which provided a coating (almost like swallowing Pepto Bismol) over mouth, tongue and digestive tract. The pre-treatment prevented sores in the mouth and digestive tract from the chemo, which we were told would be very painful.

The first day after admission, I got a central line sewn into my chest with three lumens that each could be hooked up to various fluids and medications. Then I got a shot of chemo. I thought the dose of chemo would really knock me for a loop. The doctor told me that wasn't the case, but it was like being on a table. The first four or five days would be pretty boring — meaning I would feel fine. Days six through eight were usually falling off the table and into the basement — meaning I would likely start to feel worse. Days nine and 10, I would be in the basement where my white blood count would go to zero and near zero — meaning I would feel pretty bad. On the day I went in the basement, my temperature shot up and they saw that I had a staph infection in the area of my central line. I was furious. They apologized and said they had a history of only between 1 and 2 percent of getting an infection. I said, "Well it is 100 percent with me." My belief about a staph infection was that it could be very serious. My doctor told me that this particular strain could easily be controlled by antibiotics. When Mary concurred with that diagnosis, I felt better.

Days 10 and 11 were pretty rough. There was a number that my white blood count was supposed to reach before I could get out of the hospital. When it didn't rise any on days 10 or 11, I got worried that maybe my stem cells didn't do their job, which was to attach to bones and start reproducing into marrow. I asked the doctor, "What if my stem cells aren't doing their job?" He paused and then said, "That would be very bad." Another pause, "But in my 15 years of medicine, I've never seen an autologous (using your own stem cells) transplant not work." On day 12, my white blood count passed the mark and they booted me out of the hospital two days early.

We went to son Mike's house for the outpatient portion of the treatment. Mike had a great basement with a bedroom, an exercise room with a treadmill, pool table and putting green. It was great. They set up an IV stand and Mary gave me two antibiotic infusions a day for about 10 days. I got through the transplant amazingly well. I didn't get nauseated, I didn't get diarrhea (my *ss didn't get red), and I didn't start losing hair until my last day in the hospital. The first thing we did when I got to Mike's was shave off the rest of my hair. People who saw my son Pat and I together would often say we looked alike. We took a picture of Mike and me both totally bald that showed we looked a lot alike, too.

I went back to the office for a week, then spent two weeks at our place in Jackson Hole where I walked every day before going back to the office for good in mid-August. I had built up stamina enough to walk more than five miles. The cool weather offset the high altitude and made walking pleasant. It was four miles from our house to the paved road in town, and I decided I was going to do the eight-mile trek. After four miles out and about two miles back, my cell phone rang. It was SEC Commissioner Greg Sankey. We chatted a while and he asked what I was doing. I told him. He said, "I hope you have someone with you." I replied, "Greg, this is a busy road, if I faint, somebody will drag me back home." He later told me that he signed up and went through the St. Vincent's One Nineteen physical evaluation program as well.

I had never missed a day at work since my diagnosis in 2014 and didn't miss another after returning from Jackson Hole. I was asked by a reporter if I felt bad about being bald. My response was, "Heck no, it saves me about 15 minutes a day not having to fool with hair!" I did embrace baldness and had pictures taken with everyone in the Athletics Department who was bald.

On some scans taken before the transplant, they showed plaque buildup in arteries around my heart and some spinal stenosis, which is calcium build-up in the canal in which the spinal cord passes through the vertebrae. It was determined I needed to take care of the transplant first and deal with the other issue later should I become symptomatic in either.

I was able to get through the 2016 football season without any problems. Dr. Lonial recommended I get on a maintenance program of chemo immediately after the transplant. I declined, as I had read that at least some people had reached remission through the transplant and never had to deal with it again, and I hoped I would fall in that category. But after the first of the year, my numbers went up and I went on a maintenance program in early 2017. It was necessary to change chemo regimens a few times as my numbers would go up from time to time, but they have always been able to keep me in near remission and a good quality of life thus far.

In the meantime, Mary was convinced I needed open-heart surgery. We met with Dr. Mark Sasse, who would perform surgery to insert stents if necessary, and Dr. Jamie Davies, who would do open-heart surgery if needed. At the time, I had about 90 percent blockage in my right coronary artery; however, my body had performed its own bypass and there was collateral circulation that was sending blood past the blockage. It was reaching my extremities and I had no symptoms of heart problems.

The human body is pretty amazing. Several years earlier I tore my rotator cuff. It bothered me, but not badly enough to go through the surgery. In about 2014 or 2015, I finished it off, if it wasn't already atrophied. Dr. Lyle Cain looked at my x-rays and said, "There's nothing left to repair." Rodney Brown, former athletic trainer who was our rehabilitation trainer at the time, saw that I could lift my arm and do things with it that one without a rotator cuff shouldn't be able to do. My body had replaced that function with other ligaments and muscles that has given me good use of my left shoulder. Rodney asked if he could show my x-rays and discuss my case with his classes. I was happy to oblige.

Back to the heart. In 2018 I went in for my six-month checkup and the tests showed I had blockage. My answer was, "Of course I have blockage. We've talked about that for two years." They thought there was blockage in another artery and Dr. Sasse told me I needed a "heart cath" procedure to determine for sure. In that procedure they give you a mild anesthesia so that you are half-awake and can see and hear what's going on. He told me he could give me a stress test on that artery after he got into the procedure.

My set up in the bed blocked me from seeing the monitor of my heart as they were going through the procedure, but Dr. Sasse had an assistant and was talking out loud about everything he was doing. I was about half asleep when Dr. Sasse said to me, "OK, we're going to do the stress test, are you OK?" I answered, "Well, I'm wide awake now." After a few minutes he asked, "Did you feel anything?" I responded, "No." He said, "You have plaque buildup but the blood is circulating fine." I thought that meant we were going to close up shop and go home.

All of a sudden I heard him giving commands that I had not heard before. It was soon obvious that he was putting a stent into the original blocked artery. In fact, he put in three. When it was over and he said we were done, I asked how it went. "Better than I anticipated," he responded. He later showed me a still picture of blood flow before and after the insert of stents, and the difference was pretty dramatic. My dad died of a heart attack at age 66 and this procedure would probably have added several years to his life, as his seven siblings all lived into or close to their 90s.

In spring 2019 I had been walking a lot. I felt so good, one day when I was in our indoor football facility walking laps, I started to do some 10-yard side-to-side touches for agility. That led to 10-yard run forward, touch the line and run backward 10 yards. The next day I felt like I had pulled something in my back. Four weeks later I couldn't walk. Being immobile was one thing, but it was accompanied by some pretty serious pain. I had Mary get me a wheelchair and a cane, and we went to see Dr. Cain in Birmingham. They diagnosed it as severe spinal stenosis in two lower vertebrae (calcification of the canal, which causes nerve on bone), and gave me a steroid shot. It did away with the pain, and that was great, but I knew I had to have the operation called decompressive laminectomy, which cleans out the calcium buildup in the canal. Dr. Swaid Swaid at Grandview Hospital in Birmingham had looked at my earlier scans and told me this day might be coming. He performed the procedure successfully, but it took six months to a year to regain most of the mobility I had lost from nerve damage. But it did come back.

After thinking I was done with different medical conditions, along came the COVID-19 global pandemic in 2020. Mary and I were very careful to avoid the virus all spring, and with The University of Alabama closed, we spent about seven weeks at our ranch in Ellijay. We were very safe there. We had planned a family get together in Colorado and decided to take the trip. There were more than family members there, and during the week, we tried to use masks and social distance, but we let our guard down and picked up the virus.

It affected Mary and me in very different ways. She immediately went into a fever of 102-103 degrees, with coughing and migraine headaches. I was asymptomatic for a little over a week and thought I could skate through, pick up antibodies and come out great. After about a week, the COVID-19 virus went to my lungs. Soon after in early July, I knew it was time to go to the hospital. The day I arrived at UAB Hospital in Birmingham, it was the busiest day in the history of the hospital. I checked in about 1:00 in the afternoon, and was put in a triage room that was not really a bedroom, although it did have a bed, but also had two motors that were functioning at full speed. Doctors did begin treatment, but it was 10:30 p.m. before I got in a real hospital bedroom. I was there three days and was getting good attention. On the fourth day, early in the morning, I had a situation in which I couldn't get my oxygen saturation number in the 90s. Doctors, nurses and the emergency team came in. They couldn't figure how to resolve the problem. At that time we briefly discussed intubation and ventilator, but not for long. Fortunately, an ICU bedroom opened up and I was sent there. They were truly outstanding. ICU had resources to handle most problems, and they promptly handled mine.

I was there a week and when I left, I was walking laps around my small room — which was the first time I had gotten out of bed since I arrived there. After a week, I went back to a regular room for two more days (two weeks total), and then progressed to the point where I got to go home. Getting home was great, as there was a time in the hospital I wasn't sure I would ever leave. The bad part was that Mary couldn't come see me or be with me because no one was allowed in the COVID rooms. I had lost 15 pounds and most of my muscle mass. It is frightening what two weeks of total inactivity can do to your body.

As fate, luck, whatever you may call it happened after I got home. I was able to increase walking, exercising, physical therapy and eating to improve breathing, gain weight, gain strength and feel better. COVID-19 is not something a 78-year old guy needs to catch. At the time of this writing in early 2021, I'm still fighting to get back to the "normal" breathing and walking I was able to do before COVID, but I have tested positive for antibodies.

So far, I have tested the medical practices of oncologists, cardiologists, neurosurgeons and now COVID-19 doctors. They have all passed with flying colors. I hope there are not more to be tested in the future, and so do the doctors. I'm living proof of the power of modern medicine combined with the power of prayer. Many people during my various medical challenges have reached out to tell me they had put me on their prayer lists. I respond to all to keep me there, because those prayers are working. At 78 in 2020, my quality of life is still good. I walk regularly, stretch, do cardio, go fishing and otherwise enjoy life. There are still aches and pains, but heck — I'm an old man!

The thought of going through all of the above without Mary, or someone to guide me through the health care maze, is frightening. The cost is off the charts, but getting to the right doctors and monitoring the right treatments is near impossible if you don't know what you are doing.

LESSONS LEARNED

- Early detection is very important in getting ahead of the curve in any disease. Get regular checkups, and I know you don't want to, but get colonoscopies anyway. After a certain age, get annual heavy-duty physicals.
- Pay attention to health insurance and make sure you have the major medical coverage you need to prevent possible financial disaster.
- At the first sign of disease — any kind — research and learn as much as possible. There are support groups for most everyone. Even better, find someone who understands the system and get them to help you navigate it.

- Beating any disease requires the positive attitude that "I may go down, but I'll go down kicking and screaming all the way and I'll do everything in my power to defeat this disease."
- If you haven't been infected by COVID-19 yet, don't get careless. Wear a mask, wash your hands, and practice social distancing until vaccines become available.
- Much of what happens to a body is genetic, but proper diet and exercise can prevent or solve many health-related problems.

CONCLUSION

Ihave lived a blessed life. If it could be done over, there are a few things I would change, but not many. Looking back, I can honestly say I'm thankful for every minute. The good things were enjoyed and appreciated. The difficult things made me stronger.

I truly believe there has been a *Master's Plan* throughout my life. Success is definitely a journey and not a destination. My journey has been circuitous, and I don't believe it occurred by accident. When we reach certain goals we define as "success," we either plow ahead and get better, or we rest on our laurels and get worse. Opportunities come and go, and those who are motivated and perceptive can reach out and grab them.

We are all a product of our experiences. My experiences growing up in Birmingham, my time as a player and coach, and my knowledge in business hopefully enabled me to bring value to the University of Alabama Athletics Department late in my career. I know the four years I spent in undergraduate school at Alabama in the 1960s made a positive difference in my life. It is my fervent hope that in all my dealings in athletics and in business, I helped make a difference in the lives of young people, staff members, and others in the marketplace. Any differences made, however, would not have been possible without other people's influences on me.

Because I so much enjoy collecting quotes from leaders in most every discipline, I will close with some of my favorites:

- "Fame is a vapor, riches take wings, those who cheer today curse tomorrow. The only thing that endures is Character."
- "Character is who you are and what you do when no one is watching."
- "We are products of those with whom we associate. It's hard to stay up with the owls at night and soar with the eagles the next day."
- "We don't own success, we rent it and the rent is due every day."
- "It is not so much what you do that counts, it's how you do it."
- "To every complex question, there is a simple answer and it is usually wrong."
- "There is no shortcut to success."
- "Your actions speak so loud I can't hear a word you are saying."

And the most meaningful quotation to me of all time comes from the book of John 3:16-17:

"For God so loved the world, He gave his only begotten Son, so that he who believeth in Him shall not perish, but have eternal life. God sent His Son into the world, not to condemn the world, but that the world through Him might be saved."

ABOUT THE AUTHOR

Growing up in Birmingham, Alabama, and playing on a high school football team that won six games in four years, Bill Battle received a scholarship offer from University of Alabama Coach Paul "Bear" Bryant and went on to start three years from 1960 through '62. Those Crimson Tide teams posted a 29-2-2 record, and won a Southeastern Conference title and a National Championship.

From there Battle was an assistant coach at Oklahoma under Coach Bud Wilkinson, at West Point under Coach Paul Dietzel and at Tennessee under Coach Doug Dickey. Battle became head coach at Tennessee in 1970 and posted a 59-22-2 record through 1976, and won four out of five bowl games.

Battle left coaching in 1977 to pursue business interests. He joined his first youth football coach, Larry Striplin, in a commercial window manufacturing company for six years. In that time he received valuable lessons in business and ultimately started The Collegiate Licensing Company in 1981. Under Battle's leadership, CLC grew to be one of the largest trademark licensing companies in the United States.

After selling CLC in 2007, and continuing to oversee the company through 2011, he remained as chairman in semi-retirement. In 2013, his alma mater called and he went back to serve as Director of Athletics at Alabama from 2013-2017, succeeding former teammate Mal Moore. Battle made a seamless transition, and Alabama continued its winning ways on and off the fields and courts.